W9-BDH-206

FIFTH EDITION

Literacy for the 21st Century

A Balanced Approach

Gail E. Tompkins

California State University, Fresno

Allyn & Bacon

Boston | New York | San Francisco
Mexico City | Montreal | Toronto | London | Madrid | Munich | Paris
Hong Kong | Singapore | Tokyo | Cape Town | Sydney

Executive Editor: Linda Ashe Bishop
Editorial Assistant: Demetrius Hall
Senior Development Editor: Hope Madden
Executive Marketing Manager: Krista Clark
Production Editor: Janet Domingo
Editorial Production Service: Nesbitt Graphics, Inc.
Composition/Prepress Buyer: Linda Cox

Manufacturing Manager: Megan Cochran
Electronic Composition: Nesbitt Graphics, Inc.
Interior Designer: Carol Somberg
Cover Administrator: Linda Knowles
Cover Designer: Susan Swan

For related titles and support materials, visit our online catalog at www.pearsonhighered.com

Copyright © 2010, 2006, 2003, 2001, 1997 Pearson Education, Inc.

All rights reserved. No part of the material protected by this copyright notice may be reproduced or utilized in any form or by any means, electronic or mechanical, including photocopying, recording, or by any information storage and retrieval system, without written permission of the copyright owner.

To obtain permission(s) to use material from this work, please submit a written request to Allyn and Bacon, Permissions Department, 501 Boylston Street, Suite 900, Boston, MA 02116 or fax your request to 617-671-2290.

Between the time website information is gathered and then published, it is not unusual for some sites to have closed. Also, the transcription of URLs can result in typographical errors. The publisher would appreciate notification where these errors occur so that they may be corrected in subsequent editions.

ISBN-13: 978-0-13-502892-6
ISBN-10: 0-13-502892-2

Printed in the United States of America
10 9 8 7 6 5 4 3 2   WEB   13 12 11 10

Photos by Gail E. Tompkins.

Allyn & Bacon
is an imprint of

www.pearsonhighered.com

ISBN-13: 978-0-13-502892-6
ISBN-10: 0-13-502892-2

About the Author

Gail E. Tompkins is Professor *Emerita* at California State University, Fresno. She regularly works with teachers in their kindergarten through eighth-grade classrooms and leads staff-development programs on reading and writing. Dr. Tompkins was inducted into the California Reading Association's Reading Hall of Fame in recognition of her publications and other accomplishments in the field of reading, and she has received the prestigious Provost's Award for Excellence in Teaching at California State University, Fresno. Previously, Dr. Tompkins taught at the University of Oklahoma in Norman, where she received the Regents' Award for Superior Teaching, and at Miami University in Ohio, where she taught at the McGuffey Laboratory School and worked with preservice teachers. She was also an elementary teacher in Virginia for eight years.

Dr. Tompkins is the author of six other books published by Merrill and Allyn & Bacon, imprints of Pearson Education: *Language Arts: Patterns of Practice*, 7th ed. (2009), *Language Arts Essentials* (2006), *Teaching Writing: Balancing Process and Product*, 5th ed. (2008), *50 Literacy Strategies*, 3rd ed. (2009), and two grade-level-specific versions of this text: *Literacy for the 21st Century: Teaching Reading and Writing in Pre-Kindergarten Through Grade 4*, 2nd ed. (2007), and *Literacy for the 21st Century: Teaching Reading and Writing in Grades 4 Through 8* (2004).

During the last three decades, Dr. Tompkins has also worked with kindergarten through college-level writing teachers at two National Writing Project sites. She directed the Oklahoma Writing Project when she taught at the University of Oklahoma, and more recently she was the director of the San Joaquin Valley Writing Project in California, where she initiated a program to encourage teachers to write for publication. Merrill and Allyn & Bacon, imprints of Pearson Education, have published three collections of classroom-tested teaching strategies and lessons written by teachers in the San Joaquin Valley Writing Project: *Teaching Vocabulary: 50 Creative Strategies, Grades 6-12*, 2nd ed. (2008), edited by Gail E. Tompkins and Cathy L. Blanchfield; *50 Ways to Develop Strategic Writers* (2005), also edited by Gail E. Tompkins and Cathy L. Blanchfield; and *Sharing the Pen: Interactive Writing With Young Children* (2004), edited by Gail E. Tompkins and Stephanie Collom.

Brief CONTENTS

CONTENTS

Part 1

Literacy in the 21st Century   1

Chapter 2

Teaching the Reading and Writing Processes   38

Part 2

Components of Literacy Development   103

Chapter 5

Cracking the Alphabetic Code   142

Chapter 6

Developing Fluent Readers and Writers   184

Chapter 7

Expanding Students' Knowledge of Words   220

Part 3

Organizing for Literacy Instruction   317

Chapter 10

Organizing for Instruction   320

Part 4

Compendium of Instructional Procedures   426

SPECIAL FEATURES

Assessment Tools

Literacy Portraits: VIEWING GUIDE

MiniLesson

New Literacies

Be Strategic!

Teaching Struggling Readers and Writers

PREFACE

Welcome to *Literacy for the 21st Century: A Balanced Approach*! I invite you to step into my vision for reading and writing instruction in kindergarten through eighth-grade classrooms. In this model school, diverse groups of students meet grade-level standards while becoming confident and thoughtful readers and writers. New technologies are certainly changing what it means to read and write. And today, effective literacy instruction is based on scientific research and classroom-tested approaches. It must also include a focus on developing strategic readers and writers, an increased understanding of how to scaffold English learners, and attention to new literacies that support students' use of technology. Teachers create a classroom climate where literacy flourishes, and differentiate instruction by adjusting their lessons and providing multiple options for learning so that every student can be successful.

My Goals

First and foremost, I've written this text for you. *Literacy for the 21st Century* is meant to serve as a valuable resource that you can take into the classroom with you. As I address the topic of each chapter, I've linked theory and research with classroom practice so that you'll understand what's important to teach, why it's important, and how to teach it effectively. I've featured real teachers throughout the text so you can envision yourself using the classroom practices I recommend. Also, I've compiled step-by-step directions for 40 of the best instructional and assessment activities—including guided reading, K-W-L charts, and running records—in the Compendium of Instructional Procedures, placed at the end of the text for easy access.

With this new edition, I've tried to answer all the questions you might have about teaching reading and writing—about instructional approaches, about English learners, about students who struggle, about using technology to teach reading and writing—and in doing that, to create the most relevant and valuable teacher resource possible. The text continues to balance this presentation of information with authentic classroom vignettes, student artifacts, and new video footage that shows students learning phonics, fluency, vocabulary, comprehension, and writing to help you understand what effective literacy learning in the 21st century really looks like.

Strategic Readers and Writers. You'll notice an increased emphasis on developing strategic readers and writers in this edition. I highlight research findings that can really improve the quality of literacy instruction because I believe that teaching students about reading and writing strategies is that important.

The word *strategies* has two meanings. First, teachers develop a repertoire of instructional procedures called *teaching strategies* that guide students to decode and comprehend what they're reading and to draft and refine their writing; many of them appear in the Compendium of Instructional Procedures at the end of this text. Teachers also teach their students to use *learning strategies* to actively direct their thinking. So, in this edition, I present the strategies that capable readers and writers use to identify unfamiliar words, learn the meanings of vocabulary words, comprehend what they're reading, write compositions, and prepare for high-stakes standardized tests, for example. With this information, you'll be prepared to help your students become capable readers and writers.

Look for features that emphasize and strengthen my goals for developing readers and writers.

New! ◆ **Be Strategic!** This feature helps you identify and teach the cognitive and metacognitive strategies that successful readers and writers use.

New! ◆ **Nurturing English Learners.** Expanded chapter sections focus on ways to scaffold students who are learning to read and write at the same time they're learning to speak English.

New! ◆ **Teaching Struggling Readers and Writers.** Using recommendations drawn from research, this expanded feature explains how to assist students who don't meet grade-level standards.

New! ◆ **Chapter 11, Differentiating Instruction.** A new chapter helps you understand how to vary instruction without sacrificing grade-level expectations and provide interventions so that all students can be successful.

> **Be Strategic!**
>
> **Phonemic Awareness Strategies**
>
> As students manipulate sounds orally, they learn to use these two strategies:
>
> ► Blend
> ► Segment
>
> Students apply these oral strategies to written language for decoding and spelling words.

Balance

Balance is the key to teaching reading and writing: balancing reading and writing, balancing explicit instruction with genuine application, and balancing assessment and instruction.

Balancing Reading and Writing. This text is unique because it links reading with writing in every chapter. You'll learn that reading and writing are related processes of constructing meaning, and that writing has a dynamic impact on students' reading achievement. These text features highlight this balance:

◆ **Chapter-Opening Vignettes.** As the signature feature of this text, these classroom stories illustrate how effective teachers integrate reading and writing to maximize students' literacy learning.

◆ **Book Lists.** These recommendations simplify your job of locating books to use when teaching about genre, as mentor texts, and as models for writing activities.

◆ **Teaching Struggling Readers and Writers.** This expanded feature provides pivotal information on topics such as fluency, revising, the difficulty of vowels, vocabulary in content-area texts, and comprehension to help students who struggle make real progress in developing literacy competency.

New! ◆ **New Literacies.** This new feature describes ways to prepare students for the reading and writing demands of the 21st century's digital information and communication technologies.

New Literacies
Online Games

Students practice phonics and spelling concepts they're learning as they play online games. These interactive games provide opportunities for students to match letters to pictures of objects illustrating their sounds, identify rhymes, sort words according to vowel pattern, and spell words, for example. They provide engaging practice opportunities because the colorful screen displays, sound effects, fast-paced action, and feedback about game performance grab students' attention, maintain their enthusiasm, and scaffold their learning (Chamberlain, 2005; Kinzer, 2005).

Teachers choose games based on concepts they're teaching and students' achievement levels. Teachers preview the games and bookmark those they want to use, and then students use the bookmarks to quickly access the game they'll play at the computer center. They play the games individually or with partners. Because most young children are experienced gameplayers and because many games have tutorial features, teachers don't have to spend much time introducing them, but it's helpful to have a parent-volunteer or older student available to assist when there are problems.

Here are some suggested websites with phonics and spelling games:

Game Goo: Learning That Sticks
www.earobics.com/gamegoo
Visit the Game Goo website to play gam
recognition, phonics an

PBS Kid
www.pbsk
Play games
"Between
"Word Worl
bet, rhyming

RIF's Readi
www.rif.org/re
Join the Readi
website to play
games at the Ga
Zone and Expres
books and learn

Scholastic Kids
www.scholastic.co
Check Scholastic's
a word, word scrab
the Big Red Do
Homework
usi

Balancing Explicit Instruction With Authentic Application. The m tive literacy instruction involves a combination of explicit instruction with opportuni apply what students are learning in genuine reading and writing activities. These text fea tures highlight this balance:

- ◆ **Minilessons.** This popular feature presents clear, concise strategy and skill instruction, ready for you to take right into your classroom.

- ◆ **Compendium of Instructional Procedures.** This valuable resource at the end of the text provides a bank of step-by-step, evidence-based teaching procedures. Look for orange terms in the chapter text that point you to procedures described step-by-step in the Compendium.

- *New!* ◆ **Chapter 10, Organizing for Instruction.** This new chapter condenses the information on basal reader programs, literature focus units, literature circles, and reading and writing workshop that appeared in separate chapters in previous editions. This arrangement makes it easier for you to compare and contrast the four most popular instructional approaches.

- ◆ **Overview of Instructional Approaches.** A special feature in Chapter 10, Organizing for Instruction, highlights the characteristics of basal reader programs, literature focus units, literature circles, and reading and writing workshop.

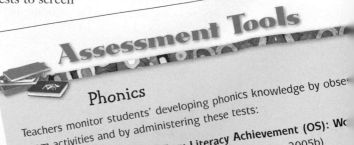

Balancing Assessment and Instruction. Assessment must drive instruction, a principle I examine in depth in this new edition. You'll learn how to determine students' reading levels and use informal assessment tools and classroom tests to screen students at the beginning of the school year, monitor their progress, diagnose reading difficulties, and document students' learning. These text features highlight this balance:

- *New!* ◆ **Chapter 3, Assessing Students' Literacy Development.** This chapter, placed early in the text, lays the groundwork for assessing students' achievement and for using the results to inform instruction. This chapter also provides critical information about preparing students' for high-stakes achievement tests.

- ◆ **Assessment Tools.** This feature found throughout the text recommends informal classroom tools and specific tests to screen, diagnose, monitor, and document students' progress in reading and writing.

Students' Literacy Development

E~~is~~ text to provide you with authentic experiences, grounded in today's multiethnic and mul-
~~guai~~ classrooms. I've always incorporated what I've learned throughout the text—in vignettes,
~~rudent~~ samples, book lists, minilessons, and other features—but for this edition, I've added something special. :You'll see what a year of literacy teaching and learning looks like in a second-grade
classroom through features in the text and online. Check these features to learn more about this
yearlong documentation of students' literacy learning, and watch the footage on MyEducationLab:

New! ◆ **Part 1 Opener.** In the Part 1 opening photo spread on pages 1–3, you'll meet Ms. Janusz, a
remarkable second-grade teacher at Worthington Estates Elementary School, outside
Columbus, OH, and see how she implements a balanced approach to literacy instruction.

New! ◆ **Part 2 Opener.** In the Part 2 opening photo
spread on pages, 103–105, you'll meet five students
from Ms. Janusz's class—Rhiannon, Rakie,
Michael, Curt'Lynn, and Jimmy—who are featured in the online Literacy Portraits that track
their reading and writing achievement through
their second-grade year.

New! ◆ **Literacy Portraits.** The five Literacy Portraits
are video case studies with footage showing
each student involved in reading and writing
activities along with teacher commentary and
related work samples. They're available online at MyEducationLab.

New! ◆ **Literacy Portraits:** Viewing Guide. You'll
find this feature in the text to draw your attention to specific video clips that best illustrate what I'm presenting in a chapter—
phonics, fluency, comprehension, and
more—as Ms. Janusz nurtures her students' reading and writing development.

PaRT 1
Literacy in t~~he~~
21st Century

*C*lassrooms are different
today; they've become
communities of learners
where students assume more
responsibility for learning. You often hear a hum in these classrooms as students ta~~lk~~
books they're reading, share their writing, and work together in small groups. The ~~~~
are more culturally and linguistically diverse, and many are English learners. The r~~ole~~
teacher has changed, too: They guide and nurture students' learning through the ins~~~~
tional programs they create. Here's what teachers do:

▶ **Balance explicit instruction with authentic application**
▶ **Integrate reading and writing**
▶ **Teach with trade books as well as textbooks**
▶ **Combine instructional approaches**
▶ **Incorporate new technologies into literacy instruction**
▶ **Differentiate instruction so every student can succeed**
▶ **Link assessment and instruction**

In this part opener, you meet Ms. Janusz and her second-grade class.
She and her students exemplify this 21st-century view of literacy
instruction, and students from this class are featured in the
Literacy Portraits section on the MyEducationLab website
at www.myeducationlab.com.

Literacy Portraits: VIEWING GUIDE

Ms. Janusz's classroom is filled with stories and informational books. She uses these books for instructional purposes, and plenty of books are available for
students to read independently. These second graders
know about genres. They can identify books representing each genre and talk about the differences between them. Ms. Janusz teaches minilessons on genres and points out the genre of books she's reading
aloud. She doesn't call all books "stories." Go to the
Literacy Profiles section of the MyEducationLab website and click on Rhiannon's Student Interview to
watch her compare fiction and nonfiction. As you listen to Rhiannon, think about the information provided
in this chapter. What conclusions can you draw about
what Ms. Janusz has taught about text factors? Also,
look at other video clips of Rhiannon to see how she
applies her knowledge about genres in both reading
and writing.

myeducationlab

Ms. Janusz works to develop her students' abilities to read a~~nd~~
~~w~~*rite fluently. She's teaching them to decode and spell word*~~s~~
~~~~ *strategies, and focus on meaning when they're read*~~ing~~

YOUR Learning Network

The fifth edition of *Literacy for the 21st Century* is more than a textbook; it's one part of a learning network that's been carefully developed to enhance your learning experience. In each chapter, you'll find the theory, research, and classroom practice to prepare you for a lifetime of teaching students to read and write, and you'll also learn the tools to equip you for the job, plus ideas, examples, and mentoring to inspire your own teaching. The second part is MyEducationLab, which provides online resources to further your learning.

Visit MyEducationLab. MyEducationLab, at **www.myeducationlab.com**, is the online part of the learning network designed specifically for this text. This robust website contains video footage, homework and activities, modules for building teaching skills, the Literacy Portraits, and much more! Look for these reminders in each chapter to help you make the most of this valuable online resource:

◆ **Literacy Portraits: Viewing Guide.** This feature throughout the text directs you to video footage on the five students that demonstrates how they're growing as readers and writers.

◆ **Margin Notes.** This reminder directs you to Building Teaching Skills and Dispositions activities that help you refine your knowledge and prepare to assess students' reading and writing development.

◆ **End-of-Chapter Element.** This feature outlines all the resources on MyEducationLab for you to explore to deepen your understanding of the topics you've been reading about.

Literacy Portraits: VIEWING GUIDE

Ms. Janusz uses flexible groups—whole class, small groups, buddies, and individuals—for instruction. Go to the Literacy Profiles section of MyEducationLab and watch these four video clips: Click on Michael's November button to see him reading a poem to the class; Rakie's December button to watch her participate in a guided reading group; Rhiannon's December button to view her reading individually with the teacher; and Curt'Lynn's March button to watch her read with a classmate. As you view these video segments, think about why Ms. Janusz grouped the students as she did. It's not enough to use varied grouping patterns; what matters most is that when students participate in a group, their learning is enhanced. When they set up groups, teachers consider their instructional goal, the activitiy, and group membership. How do you think Ms. Janusz's grouping patterns benefited these students' learning?

myeducationlab

Instructor Resource Center. The Instructor Resource Center at www.pearsonhighered.com has a variety of print and media resources available in downloadable, digital format—all in one location. As a registered faculty member, you can access and download pass code-protected resource files, course-management content, and other premium online content directly to your computer.

...rces available for *Literacy for the 21st Century: A Balanced Approach, 5e* include ...ing:

A test bank of multiple choice and essay tests.

◆ PowerPoint presentations specifically designed for each chapter.

◆ Chapter-by-chapter materials, including objectives, suggested readings, discussion questions, and in-class activities, and guidance on how to use the vignettes meaningfully in your instruction.

◆ A MyEducationLab guide to help you make the best use of MyEducationLab in your classes.

To access these items online, go to **www.pearsonhighered.com** and click on the Instructor option. You'll find an Instructor Resource Center option in the top navigation bar. There you will be able to log in or complete a one-time registration for a user name and password. If you have any questions regarding this process or the materials available online, please contact your local Pearson sales representative.

TestGen. A completely revised test bank also accompanies the text. These multiple-choice and essay questions can be used to assess students' understanding of chapter concepts and their ability to apply what they've read. A computerized version of the test bank (TestGen) is available, along with assessment software, allowing instructors to create and customize exams and track student progress.

Acknowledgments

Many people helped and encouraged me as I developed and revised this text. My heartfelt thanks go to each of them. First, I want to thank my students over the years at California State University, Fresno, the University of Oklahoma, and Miami University, who taught me while I taught them, and the teacher-consultants in the San Joaquin Valley Writing Project and the Oklahoma Writing Project, who shared their expertise with me. Their insightful questions challenged and broadened my thinking. Thanks, too, go to the teachers who welcomed me into their classrooms, showed me how they created a balanced literacy program, and allowed me to learn from them and their students. In particular, I want to express my appreciation to the teachers and students who appear in the part openers, vignettes, and video clips on MyEducationLab: Rich Abrams, Washington Intermediate School; Eileen Boland, Tenaya Middle School; Whitney Donnelly, Williams Ranch School; Stacy Firpo, Aynesworth Elementary School; Laurie Goodman, Pioneer Middle School; Susanne Hagen, Phoenix Learning Center; Sally Mast, Thomas Elementary School; Susan McCloskey, Greenberg Elementary School; Kristi McNeal, Copper Hills Elementary School; Nicki Paniccia McNeal, Century Elementary School; Jennifer Miller-McColm, Roosevelt Elementary School; Gay Ockey, Hildago Elementary School; Kacey Sanom, John Muir Elementary School; Leah Scheitrum, Jackson Elementary School; Stacy Shasky, Fairmead School; Darcy Williams, Aynesworth Elementary School; and Susan Zumwalt, Jackson Elementary School.

In addition, special thanks to Lisa Janusz, who welcomed us into her second-grade classroom every month while we videotaped her literacy instruction, collected writing samples, and interviewed students. She's a remarkable teacher who uses her knowledge of how children learn to propel her second graders toward high levels of achievement.

I also want to thank the professors and teaching professionals who reviewed my text for their insightful comments that informed my development of this text and this revision: Bonnie Armbruster, University of Illinois at Urbana; Jean Casey, California State University, Long Beach; Beth Cavanaugh, McGraw IB World School; Rosemary Fessinger, University of New Mexico; Kristen Gehsman, St. Michael's College; Amanda Grotting, Sun Valley Elementary; Helen Hoffner, Holy Family University; Leslie Hopping, Columbus Academy; Carolyn Jaynes, California State University, Sacramento; Laura Pardo, Hope College; Kimberly Penn, Dos Rios Elementary School; Molly Sperling, Devonshire Alternative; Dr. Preston Van Loon, Iowa Wesleyan College; and Janet Wicker, McKendree College.

Finally, I want to recognize Jeff Johnston and his remarkable team at Merrill in Columbus, Ohio who have produced so many high-quality publications. I've been honored to be a Merrill author for more than 20 years. Now that Merrill and Allyn and Bacon have been reorganized, I've become an Allyn and Bacon author, and I look forward to many years of working with Paul Smith and his team. Linda Bishop continues to be the guiding force behind my work, and Hope Madden is my cheerleader, encouraging me every step of the way and spurring me toward impossible deadlines. A special thank you to Linda for her inspired idea that led to the Literacy Profiles project in Lisa Janusz's classroom and to Hope for her yearlong supervision of the project and expert editing of the video clips. I know it will be an important resource for students and professors at the MyEducationLab website. I want to express my sincere appreciation to Janet Domingo, my most accommodating production editor who has skillfully supervised the production of this book and deftly juggled the last-minute details, and to Melissa Gruzs, who expertly copy-edited my manuscript, addressed my memory lapses and inconsistencies, and proofread my pages. It's because of the entire team's dedication that the text is so good. Thank you!

PaRT 1

Literacy in the 21st Century

Classrooms are different today; they've become communities of learners where students assume more responsibility for learning. You often hear a hum in these classrooms as students talk about books they're reading, share their writing, and work together in small groups. The students are more culturally and linguistically diverse, and many are English learners. The role of teachers has changed, too: They guide and nurture students' learning through the instructional programs they create. Here's what teachers do:

- ▶ **Balance explicit instruction with authentic application**
- ▶ **Integrate reading and writing**
- ▶ **Teach with trade books as well as textbooks**
- ▶ **Combine instructional approaches**
- ▶ **Incorporate new technologies into literacy instruction**
- ▶ **Differentiate instruction so every student can succeed**
- ▶ **Link assessment and instruction**

In this part opener, you meet Ms. Janusz and her second-grade class. She and her students exemplify this 21st-century view of literacy instruction, and students from this class are featured in the Literacy Portraits section on the MyEducationLab website at **www.myeducationlab.com.**

Ms. Janusz works to develop her students' abilities to read and write fluently. She's teaching them to decode and spell words, use literacy strategies, and focus on meaning when they're reading and writing.

Students read leveled books with Ms. Janusz in guided reading groups, and she assesses their progress by listening to them read aloud.

The second graders practice the phonics skills that Ms. Janusz is teaching as they do word sorts.

After she shares a trade book, Ms. Janusz often uses it to teach a mini-lesson on a reading or writing strategy or skill.

Visualizing

WIZ GROS

I make pictures in my mind when I read.

Because the students' reading levels range from first- to fourth-grade, and some students are English learners, Ms. Janusz differentiates instruction. She varies grouping patterns and instructional materials.

During reading workshop, students read "just right" books independently and with buddies.

Ms. Janusz balances explicit instruction with authentic reading and writing in her literacy program. Guided reading is the teaching component and reading and writing workshop are the application activities.

During writing workshop, the second graders draft, conference with Ms. Janusz, and revise and edit their writing with classmates. Later, they publish their books, sometimes using word processing so their writing will look professional.

CHAPTER 1

Becoming an Effective Teacher of Reading

Literacy is the ability to use reading and writing for a variety of tasks at school and outside of school. Let's begin with two definitions. *Reading* is a complex process of understanding written text. Readers interpret meaning in a way that's appropriate to the type of text they're reading and their purpose. Similarly, *writing* is a complex process of producing text. Writers create meaning in a way that's appropriate to the type of text and their purpose. Peter Afflerbach (2007) describes reading as a dynamic, strategic, and goal-oriented process. The same is true of writing. *Dynamic* means that readers and writers are actively involved in reading and writing. *Strategic* means that readers and writers consciously monitor their learning. *Goal-oriented* means that reading and writing are purposeful; readers and writers have a plan in mind.

Our concept of what it means to be literate is changing. Traditional definitions of literacy focused on the ability to read words, but now literacy is considered a tool, a means to participate more fully in the technological society of the 21st century. In addition, Kress (2003) and Kist (2005) talk about *new literacies*—sophisticated technological ways to read and write multimodal texts incorporating words, images, and sounds—which provide opportunities for students to create innovative spaces for making meaning, exploring their world, and voicing their lives. These texts often combine varied forms of representation, including computer graphics, video clips, and digital photos.

Students read and write them differently than they do traditional books (Karchmer, Mallette, Kara-Soteriou, & Leu, 2005).

Gambrell, Malloy, and Mazzoni (2007) recommend that teachers develop a vision of what they hope to achieve with the students they teach and then work to accomplish their plans. The goal of literacy instruction is to ensure that all students achieve their full literacy potential, and in that light, this chapter introduces eight principles of balanced literacy instruction. These principles are stated in terms of what effective teachers do, and they provide the foundation for the chapters that follow.

PRINCIPLE 1: EFFECTIVE TEACHERS UNDERSTAND HOW STUDENTS LEARN

Understanding how students learn, and particularly how they learn to read and write, influences the instructional approaches that teachers use. Until the 1960s, behaviorism, a teacher-centered theory, was the dominant view of learning; since then, student-centered theories have become more influential, and literacy instruction has changed to reflect these theories. In the last few years, however, behaviorism has begun a resurgence as evidenced by the federal No Child Left Behind Act, renewed popularity of basal reading programs, current emphasis on curriculum standards, and mandated high-stakes testing. Tracey and Morrow (2006) argue that multiple theoretical perspectives improve the quality of literacy instruction, and the stance presented in this text is that instruction should represent a balance between teacher-centered and student-centered theories. Figure 1–1 presents an overview of the learning theories.

Behaviorism

Behaviorists focus on the observable and measurable aspects of students' behavior. They believe that behavior can be learned or unlearned, and that learning is the result of stimulus-and-response actions (O'Donohue & Kitchener, 1998). Reading is viewed as a conditioned response. This theory is described as teacher centered because it focuses on the teacher's active role as a dispenser of knowledge. Skinner (1974) explained that students learn to read by learning a series of discrete skills and subskills. Teachers use explicit instruction to teach skills in a planned, sequential order. Information is presented in small steps and reinforced through practice activities until students master it because each step is built on the previous one. Students practice skills they're learning by completing fill-in-the-blank worksheets. They usually work individually, not in small groups or with partners. Behavior modification is another key feature: Behaviorists believe that teachers control and motivate students through a combination of rewards and punishments.

Constructivism

The constructivist theory describes students as active and engaged learners who construct their own knowledge. Learning isn't observable because it involves mental

Figure 1–1 ◆ Overview of the Learning Theories			
Orientation	Theory	Characteristics	Applications
Teacher-Centered	Behaviorism Skinner	• Focuses on observable changes in behavior • Views the teacher's role as providing information and supervising practice • Describes learning as the result of stimulus-response actions • Uses incentives and rewards for motivation	• Basal readers • Minilessons • Repeated readings
Student-Centered	Constructivism Piaget	• Describes learning as the active construction of knowledge • Recognizes the importance of background knowledge • Views learners as innately curious • Advocates collaboration, not competition • Suggests ways to engage students so they can be successful	• Literature focus units • K-W-L charts • Reading logs • Thematic units • Word sorts
	Sociolinguistics Vygotsky	• Emphasizes the importance of language and social interaction on learning • Views reading and writing as social and cultural activities • Explains that students learn best through authentic activities • Describes the teacher's role as scaffolding students' learning • Advocates culturally responsive teaching • Challenges students to confront injustices and inequities in society	• Literature circles • Shared reading • Buddy reading • Reading and writing workshop • Author's chair
	Cognitive/Information Processing	• Compares the mind to a computer • Recommends integrating reading and writing • Views reading and writing as meaning-making processes • Explains that readers' interpretations are individualized • Describes students as strategic readers and writers	• Guided reading • Graphic organizers • Grand conversations • Interactive writing • Reciprocal questioning

processes. It occurs when students integrate new knowledge with their existing knowledge. Constructivists believe that learning is what the brain does naturally (Smith, 1971). This theory is student centered. It differs substantially from the behaviorist theory and requires a reexamination of the teacher's role: Instead of being dispensers of knowledge, teachers engage students with experiences so that they construct their own knowledge. This theory has been widely applied to literacy instruction; here are the applications for teaching students to read and write:

◆ Students relate what they know to what they're learning.
◆ Students create their own knowledge.
◆ Motivated students are more successful.

New Literacies
The Internet

The Internet is rapidly changing what it means to be literate. Students are increasingly becoming involved in on-line activities such as these:

- Reading electronic storybooks
- Playing interactive phonics and spelling games
- Crafting multimodal stories
- Posting book reviews
- E-mailing messages
- Researching informational topics
- Exploring the websites of favorite authors
- Participating in virtual book clubs
- Collaborating with students in other schools on projects

These students are excited about literacy because the World Wide Web fosters their motivation and engagement with reading and writing.

Some students learn to surf the Web, locate and read information, and communicate using e-mail and instant messaging outside of school. Others, however, haven't had as many experiences or aren't as successful when they experiment with new technologies. Teaching students how to read and write online has become a priority so that they can become fully literate in today's digital world (Henry, 2006).

Internet texts are different than books (Castek, Bevans-Mangelson, & Goldstone, 2006). Whereas print materials are linear and sequential, online texts are a unique genre with these characteristics:

Nonlinearity. Hypertext lacks the familiar linear organization of books; instead, it's dynamic and can be used in a variety of ways. Readers impose a structure that fits their needs and reconfigure the organization, when necessary.

Multiple Modalities. Online texts are multimodal, integrating words, images, and sound to create meaning. Readers need to know how to interpret each mode and how it contributes to the overall meaning.

Intertextuality. Many related texts are available on the Internet, and they influence and shape each other. As students read these texts, they prioritize, evaluate, and synthesize the information being presented.

Interactivity. Webpages often include interactive features that engage readers and allow them to customize their searches, link to other websites, play games, listen to video clips, and send e-mails.

Because of these features, reading and writing on the Internet require students to become proficient in new ways of accessing, comprehending, and communicating information, which are referred to as *new literacies*. Four Internet reading strategies are navigating, coauthoring, evaluating, and synthesizing: Students navigate the Internet to search for and locate information; coauthor online texts as they impose an organization on the information they're reading; evaluate the accuracy, relevance, and quality of information on webpages; and synthesize information from multiple texts (Castek, Bevans-Mangelson, & Goldstone, 2006; Leu, Kinzer, Coiro, & Cammack, 2004).

Writing online differs from using paper and pencil, too. It's more informal, although messages should be grammatically acceptable and use conventional spelling like other types of writing. Immediacy is another difference: Within seconds, writers post their writing or send brief messages back and forth. Third, writers create multimodal messages by adding photos, video clips, and website links. The fourth difference is audience: Writers send e-mail messages to people in distant locations, including military parents serving in Iraq, and their postings can be read by people worldwide.

The Internet requires students to develop new ways of reading and writing. Literacy in the 21st century involves more than teaching students to read books and write using paper and pencil; it's essential that teachers prepare their students to use the Internet and other information communication technologies successfully (Karchmer, Mallette, Kara-Soteriou, & Leu, 2005).

Students Relate What They Know to What They're Learning. Students' knowledge is organized into cognitive structures called *schemas*, and schema theory describes the processes students use to learn. Jean Piaget (1969) explained that learning is the modification of students' schemas as they actively interact with their environment. Imagine that the brain is a mental filing cabinet, and that new information is organized with existing knowledge in the filing system. When students already know something about a topic, the new information is added to that mental file, or schema, in a revision process Piaget called *assimilation*, and when students begin learning about a completely new topic, they create a mental file and place the new information in it. Piaget called this more difficult construction process *accommodation*. Everyone's cognitive structure is different, reflecting existing knowledge and prior experiences, so when students read a novel set in India or revise a rough draft, some students are likely to be more successful than others. The more students already know about a topic, the easier it is for them to assimilate new information.

Students Create Their Own Knowledge. John Dewey, one of the first American constructivists, advocated an inquiry approach to develop citizens who could participate fully in our democracy (Tracey & Morrow, 2006). He believed that students are innately curious and actively create their own knowledge. Collaboration, not competition, is more conducive to learning, according to Dewey. Through the inquiry process, students collaborate to conduct investigations in which they ask questions, seek information, create new knowledge to solve problems, and reflect on their learning.

Motivated Students Are More Successful. Engagement theory examines students' motivation and interest in reading and writing to suggest ways to nurture students' engagement, because students who are engaged are intrinsically motivated, do more reading and writing, enjoy these activities, and have higher achievement (Guthrie & Wigfield, 2000). Engaged students have self-efficacy, the belief in their capability to succeed and reach their goals (Bandura, 1997). They have high aspirations and are more likely to be successful, and each success builds their feelings of self-efficacy. Students with high self-efficacy are resilient and persistent, despite obstacles and challenges that get in the way of success. These theorists report that students are more engaged when they participate in authentic reading and writing activities and when they collaborate with classmates in a nurturing community of learners.

Sociolinguistics

As the theory's name suggests, sociolinguists recognize the importance of language and social interaction in learning. They believe that oral language provides the foundation for learning to read and write (Snow, Burns, & Griffin, 1998). Probably the best-known sociolinguist is Lev Vygotsky (1978, 1986), who theorized that language helps to organize thought and that students use language to learn as well as to communicate and share experiences with others. Understanding that students use language for social purposes allows teachers to plan instructional activities that incorporate a social component, such as having students work in small groups, talk about books they're reading, and share their writing with classmates.

Social interaction enhances learning in two other ways: scaffolding and the zone of proximal development (Dixon-Krauss, 1996). Scaffolding is a support mechanism that teachers use as they teach. Vygotsky suggested that students can accomplish more difficult tasks in collaboration with adults than on their own. For example, when teachers assist students in reading a book they couldn't read independently or help students revise a piece of writing, they are scaffolding. Vygotsky also suggested that students learn very little when they perform tasks that they can already do independently; he recommended the zone of proximal development, the range of tasks between students' actual developmental level and their potential development. More-challenging tasks done with the teacher's scaffolding are more conducive to learning. As students learn, teachers gradually withdraw their support so that students eventually perform the task independently. Then the cycle begins again. Sociolinguistic theory is applied in these ways for reading and writing instruction:

◆ Culturally responsive teaching empowers students.
◆ Students learn through authentic literacy activities.
◆ Students use literacy to challenge injustices and inequities.

Culturally Responsive Teaching Empowers Students. The sociocultural theory adds a cultural dimension to our understanding of how students learn: These theorists view reading and writing as social activities that reflect the culture and community in which students live, and they explain that students from different cultures have different expectations about literacy learning and preferred ways of learning (Heath, 1983; Moll & Gonzales, 2004). Teachers apply the sociocultural theory as they create culturally responsive classrooms that empower all students, including those from marginalized groups, to become more successful readers and writers (Gay, 2000). Teachers are respectful of all students and confident in their ability to learn to read and write. Culturally responsive teaching acknowledges the legitimacy of all students' cultures and social customs and teaches students to appreciate their classmates' cultural heritages. Teachers often use books of multicultural literature to develop students' cross-cultural awareness, including *Goin' Somewhere Special* (McKissack, 2001) and *Feathers* (Woodson, 2007), stories describing the African American experience; *Esperanza Rising* (Ryan, 2002) and *The Circuit* (Jiménez, 1999), stories about the Mexican American experience; and *Happy Birthday Mr. Kang* (Roth, 2001) and *Project Mulberry* (Park, 2007), stories portraying the Korean American experience.

In addition, teachers who appreciate the contribution of culture and community to learning are often much more successful in building bridges between home and school. Becoming culturally responsive involves teachers' willingness to examine their instructional practices if they aren't working and to make changes so that all students can be successful (Banks, Cochran-Smith, Moll, Richert, Zeichner, LePage, Darling-Hammond, & Duffy, 2005).

Students Learn Through Authentic Literacy Activities. Situated learning explains that learning is a function of the activity, context, and culture in which it occurs or is situated; it's an extension of the sociocultural theory. Lave and Wenger (1991) contend that learning is contextual, or embedded in the social and physical environment. Two important tenets are that knowledge must be presented in an authentic way and that learning requires social interaction and collaboration. This theory rejects the notion of separating learning to do something and actually doing it and emphasizes the idea of apprenticeship (Brown, Collins, & Duguid, 1989). In an apprenticeship, beginners move from the edge of a learning community to its center as they learn and become more involved within the culture. Eventually the learners reach the center of the community as they become experts. For example, if you want to become a cook, you could go to a cooking school or learn as you work in a restaurant; situated learning suggests that working in a restaurant is more effective.

When applied to literacy, situated learning theory emphasizes that students learn to read and write through authentic reading and writing activities. They join a community of learners in the classroom and become readers and writers through social interaction with classmates. The teacher serves as an expert model, much like a chef does in a restaurant.

Students Use Literacy to Challenge Injustices and Inequities. Pablo Freire (2000) called for a sweeping transformation in education so that students ask fundamental questions about justice and equity. Critical literacy theorists believe that language is a means for social action and advocate that teachers do more than teach students to read and write; students should become agents of social change (McDaniel, 2004; Wink, 2005). This application of sociolinguistics has a political agenda: The increasing social and cultural diversity in American society adds urgency to resolving inequities and injustices.

Luke and Freebody's (1997) model of reading includes critical literacy as the fourth and highest level. I've adapted their model to incorporate both reading and writing:

Code Breakers. Students become code breakers as they learn phonics, word-identification strategies, and high-frequency words that help them learn to read and write fluently.

Text Participants. Students become text participants as they learn about text structures and genres in order to comprehend what they read and as they learn to develop coherent ideas in the texts they write.

Text Users. Students become text users as they read and write multigenre texts and compare the effect of genre and purpose on texts.

Text Critics. Students become text critics as they examine the issues raised in books and other texts they read and write.

One way that teachers help students examine social justice issues is to read and discuss books such as *The Breadwinner* (Ellis, 2000), the story of a girl in Taliban-controlled Afghanistan who pretends to be a boy to support her family; *Pink and Say* (Polacco, 1994), a story about two Civil War soldiers, one white and the other African American, and the heart-wrenching indignities that the African American soldier and his family suffer; and *Homeless Bird* (Whelan, 2000), the story of an Indian girl who has no future when she is widowed. These stories and others listed in Figure 1–2 describe injustices that students can understand and discuss (Lewison, Leland, & Harste, 2008; McLaughlin & De Voogd, 2004). In fact, teachers report that their students are often more engaged in reading about social issues than other books and that their interaction patterns change after reading these stories.

Critical literacy emphasizes students' potential to become thoughtful, active citizens. The reason injustice persists in society, Shannon (1995) hypothesizes, is

Figure 1–2 ◆ Books That Foster Critical Literacy

Avi. (1993). *Nothing but the truth*. New York: Avon. (U)

Bunting, E. (1997). *A day's work*. New York: Clarion Books. (P)

Bunting, E. (1999). *Smoky night*. San Diego: Voyager. (P–M)

Curtis, C. P. (2000). *The Watsons go to Birmingham—1963*. New York: Laurel Leaf. (M–U)

Fleischman, P. (2004). *Seedfolks*. New York: Harper-Trophy. (M)

Golenbock, P. (1992). *Teammates*. San Diego: Voyager. (M)

Hesse, K. (2001). *Witness*. New York: Scholastic. (U)

Hiaasen, C. (2006). *Hoot*. New York: Yearling. (M–U)

Hiaasen, C. (2007). *Flush*. New York: Knopf. (M–U)

Lowry, L. (2006). *The giver*. New York: Delacorte. (U)

Ringgold, F. (2003). *If a bus could talk: The story of Rosa Parks*. New York: Aladdin Books. (P–M)

Ryan, P. M. (2002). *Esperanza rising*. New York: Blue Sky Press. (M)

Uchida, Y. (1996). *The bracelet*. New York: Putnam. (P)

Winter, J. (2008). *Wangari's trees of peace: A true story from Africa*. San Diego: Harcourt. (P–M)

Woodson, J. (2001). *The other side*. New York: Putnam. (P)

P = primary grades (K–2); M = middle grades (3–5); U = upper grades (6–8) because people don't "ask why things are the way they are, who benefits from these conditions, and how can we make them more equitable" (p. 123). Through critical literacy, students become empowered to transform their world (Bomer & Bomer, 2001). They learn social justice concepts, read literature that reflects diverse voices, notice injustices in the world, and use writing to take action for social change.

Cognitive/Information Processing

Two closely aligned theories of learning are cognitive processing and information processing: These theories attempt to explain unobservable mental processes, including reading and writing (Tracey & Morrow, 2006). Readers and writers are described as active learners who use knowledge and strategies to solve problems. These theorists believe that the mind functions like a computer, and they hypothesize that information moves through a series of processing units—sensory register, short-term memory, and long-term memory—as it's processed and stored (Flavell, 1979). There's a control mechanism, too, that oversees learning.

Cognitive/information processing theorists create models of the reading and writing processes, often relying on flow charts to describe the complicated and interactive workings of the mind (Hayes, 2004; Kintsch, 2004; Rumelhart, 2004). They believe in an integrated approach to reading and writing, and their models describe a two-way flow of information between what readers and writers know and the letters and words written on the page. Here are other ways these theories guide literacy instruction:

◆ Reading and writing are meaning-making processes.
◆ Readers' interpretations are individualized.
◆ Readers and writers are strategic.

Reading and Writing Are Meaning-Making Processes. Models of the reading process describe what readers do as they read, and they emphasize that readers focus on comprehension as they read (Ruddell & Unrau, 2004; Rumelhart, 2004; Stanovich, 2000). Readers construct meaning using a combination of text-based information (information from the text) and reader-based information (information from students' background knowledge). In the past, theorists argued over whether students' attention during reading moves from noticing the letters on the page and grouping them into words to making meaning in the brain, or the other way around, from activating background knowledge in the brain to examining letters and words on the page, but they now agree that the two processes take place interactively and simultaneously. The interactive model of reading includes an executive monitor that manages the construction of meaning (Ruddell & Unrau, 2004). This control mechanism monitors students' attention, determines whether what they are reading makes sense, and takes action when problems arise.

Hayes's (2004) model of writing describes what writers do as they write. It emphasizes that writing is a meaning-making process. Students don't write one-shot compositions; instead, they move through a series of stages as they plan, draft, revise, and edit their writing to ensure that readers will understand what they've written. Writers use the same control mechanism that readers do to make plans, select strategies, and solve problems. Writing is a social activity, too, and students turn to classmates and the teacher to share their writing and to get feedback on how well they're communicating.

Readers' Interpretations Are Individualized. Louise Rosenblatt's transactive theory (2004) explains how students create meaning as they read. She describes comprehension, which she calls *interpretation*, as the result of a two-way transaction between readers and the text. Students don't try to figure out the author's meaning as

they read; instead, they negotiate an interpretation that makes sense to them based on the text they're reading and their knowledge about literature and the world. Their interpretations are individualized because students bring different background knowledge and experiences to the reading event. Even though interpretations vary, they can always be substantiated by the text.

There are two overarching purposes for reading: When readers read for enjoyment or pleasure, they assume an aesthetic stance, and when they read to locate and remember information, they use an efferent stance (Rosenblatt, 2005). This doesn't mean that students read stories and poems aesthetically and informational books and content-area textbooks efferently. Instead, these stances represent the ends of a continuum, and readers often use a combination of the two stances when they read, whether they're reading stories, informational books, or poems. But, when teachers emphasize that students should read to remember specific information from the story they're reading, they're forcing students to read efferently. Teachers need to consider the purposes they set for students because when students read stories efferently rather than aesthetically, they don't develop a love of reading and are less likely to become lifelong readers.

Readers and Writers Are Strategic. Students use both cognitive and metacognitive strategies to direct their thinking. Cognitive strategies are goal-directed mental operations that students use to manage their reading and writing and solve problems that arise (Dean, 2006; Pressley, 2002). Visualizing, drawing inferences, and evaluating are cognitive strategies that readers use to construct meaning, and organizing, revising, and proofreading are cognitive strategies that writers use to compose meaning in texts they're writing.

Metacognitive strategies, such as monitoring, repairing, and evaluating, regulate students' thinking and their use of cognitive strategies. The word *metacognition* is often defined as "thinking about your own thinking," but more accurately, it refers to a sophisticated level of thinking that students use to actively control their thinking (Baker, 2002; Flavell, 1979). Metacognition is a control mechanism; it involves both students' awareness about their thinking and their active control of thinking.

You've read about behaviorism, constructivism, sociolinguistics, and cognitive/information processing, and as you continue reading, you'll see each of these theories of learning reflected in the balanced approach to literacy instruction presented in this textbook.

RINCIPLE 2: EFFECTIVE TEACHERS SUPPORT STUDENTS' USE OF THE CUEING SYSTEMS

Language is a complex system for creating meaning through socially shared conventions (Halliday, 1978). English, like other languages, involves four cueing systems:

◆ The phonological, or sound, system
◆ The syntactic, or structural, system
◆ The semantic, or meaning, system
◆ The pragmatic, or social and cultural use, system

Together, these systems make communication possible; children and adults use all four systems simultaneously as they read, write, listen, and talk. The priority people place on various cueing systems can vary; however, the phonological system is especially important for beginning readers and writers as they apply phonics skills to decode and spell words. Information about the four cueing systems is summarized in Figure 1–3.

Figure 1–3 ◆ Relationships Among the Four Cueing Systems

System	Terms	Applications
Phonological System The sound system of English with approximately 44 sounds and more than 500 ways to spell them	• Phoneme (the smallest unit of sound) • Grapheme (the written representation of a phoneme using one or more letters) • Phonological awareness (knowledge about the sound structure of words, at the phoneme, onset-rime, and syllable levels) • Phonemic awareness (the ability to orally manipulate phonemes in words) • Phonics (instruction about phoneme-grapheme correspondences and spelling rules)	• Pronouncing words • Detecting regional and other dialects • Decoding words when reading • Using invented spelling • Reading and writing alliterations and onomatopoeia • Noticing rhyming words • Dividing words into syllables
Syntactic System The structural system of English that governs how words are combined into sentences.	• Syntax (the structure or grammar of a sentence) • Morpheme (the smallest meaningful unit of language) • Free morpheme (a morpheme that can stand alone as a word) • Bound morpheme (a morpheme that must be attached to a free morpheme)	• Adding inflectional endings to words • Combining words to form compound words • Adding prefixes and suffixes to root words • Using capitalization and punctuation to indicate beginnings and ends of sentences • Writing simple, compound, and complex sentences • Combining sentences
Semantic System The meaning system of English that focuses on vocabulary	• Semantics (meaning) • Synonyms (words that mean the same or nearly the same thing) • Antonyms (opposites) • Homonyms (words that sound alike but are spelled differently)	• Learning the meanings of words • Discovering that many words have multiple meanings • Using context clues to figure out an unfamiliar word • Studying synonyms, antonyms, and homonyms • Using a dictionary and a thesaurus
Pragmatic System The system of English that varies language according to social and cultural uses	• Function (the purpose for which a person uses language) • Standard English (the form of English used in textbooks and by television newscasters) • Nonstandard English (other forms of English)	• Varying language to fit specific purposes • Reading and writing dialogue in dialects • Comparing standard and nonstandard forms of English

The Phonological System

There are approximately 44 speech sounds in English. Students learn to pronounce these sounds as they learn to talk, and they learn to associate the sounds with letters as they learn to read and write. Sounds are called *phonemes*, and they are represented in print with diagonal lines to differentiate them from graphemes (letters or letter combinations). Thus, the first grapheme in *mother* is *m*, and the phoneme is /m/. The phoneme in *soap* that is represented by the grapheme *oa* is called "long o" and is written /ō/.

The phonological system is important for both oral and written language. Regional differences exist in the way people pronounce phonemes; for example, New Yorkers pronounce sounds differently from Georgians. Students learning English as a second language learn to pronounce the sounds in English, and not surprisingly, they have more difficulty learning sounds that are different from those in their native language. For example, because Spanish doesn't have /th/, native Spanish speakers have difficulty pronouncing this sound, often substituting /d/ for /th/ because the sounds are articulated in similar ways. Younger children usually learn to pronounce the difficult sounds more easily than older children and adults.

This system plays a crucial role in reading instruction during the primary grades. In a purely phonetic language, there would be a one-to-one correspondence between letters and sounds, and teaching students to decode words would be simple. But English is not a purely phonetic language because there are 26 letters and 44 sounds and many ways to combine the letters to spell some of the sounds, especially vowels. Consider these ways to spell long *e: sea, green, Pete, me,* and *people*. And the patterns used to spell long *e* don't always work—*head* and *great* are exceptions. Phonics, which describes the phoneme-grapheme correspondences and related spelling rules, is an important component of reading instruction. Students use phonics to decode words, but it isn't a complete reading program because many common words can't be decoded easily and because reading involves more than just decoding.

The Syntactic System

The syntactic system is the structural organization of English. This system is the grammar that regulates how words are combined into sentences; the word *grammar* here means the rules governing how words are combined in sentences, not parts of speech. Students use the syntactic system as they combine words to form sentences. Word order is important in English, and English speakers must arrange words into a sequence that makes sense. Young Spanish speakers who are learning English, for example, learn to say "This is my red sweater," not "This is my sweater red," the literal translation from Spanish.

Students use their knowledge of the syntactic system as they read: They expect that the words they're reading have been strung together into sentences. When they come to an unfamiliar word, they recognize its role in the sentence even if they don't know the terms for parts of speech. In the sentence "The horses galloped through the gate and out into the field," students may not know the word *through*, but they can easily substitute a reasonable word or phrase, such as *out of* or *past*.

Another component of syntax is word forms. Words such as *dog* and *play* are morphemes, the smallest meaningful units in language. Word parts that change the meaning of a word are also morphemes; when the plural marker *-s* is added to *dog* to make *dogs*, for instance, or the past-tense marker *-ed* is added to *play* to make *played*, these words now have two morphemes because the inflectional endings change the meaning of the words. The words *dog* and *play* are free morphemes because they convey meaning while standing alone; the endings *-s* and *-ed* are bound morphemes because they must be attached to free morphemes to convey meaning. Compound words are two or more morphemes combined to create a new word: *Birthday*, for example, is a compound word made up of two free morphemes.

The Semantic System

The semantic system focuses on meaning. Vocabulary is the key component of this system: Researchers estimate that children have a vocabulary of 5,000 words by the time they enter school, and they continue to acquire 3,000 to 4,000 words each year; by the time they graduate from high school, their vocabularies reach 50,000 words (Stahl & Nagy, 2005)! Students learn some words through instruction, but they learn many more words informally through reading and through social studies and science units. Students' depth of knowledge about words increases, too, from knowing one meaning for a word to knowing how to use it in many different ways. Think about the word *fire*, which has more than a dozen meanings; the most common are related to combustion, but others deal with an intense feeling, discharging a gun, or dismissing someone. To *light a fire under* someone and being *under fire* are idiomatic expressions, and compound words using *fire* include *firearm*, *fire extinguisher*, *firefly*, *fireproof*, and *fireworks*.

The Pragmatic System

Pragmatics deals with the social aspects of language use. People use language for many purposes; how they talk and write varies according to their purpose and audience. Language use also varies among social classes, ethnic groups, and geographic regions; these varieties are known as *dialects*. School is one cultural community, and the language of school is Standard English. This dialect is formal—the one used in textbooks, newspapers, and magazines and by television newscasters. Other forms, including those spoken in urban ghettos or in Appalachia, are generally classified as nonstandard English. These nonstandard forms of English are alternatives in which the phonology, syntax, and semantics differ from those of Standard English. They're neither inferior nor substandard; instead, they reflect the communities of the speakers, and the speakers communicate as effectively as those who use Standard English. The goal is for students to add Standard English to their repertoire of language registers, not to replace their home dialect with Standard English.

Teachers understand that students use all four cueing systems as they read and write. For example, when students read the sentence "Jimmy is playing ball with his father" correctly, they are probably using information from all four systems. When a child substitutes *dad* for *father* and reads "Jimmy is playing ball with his dad," he might be focusing on the semantic or pragmatic system rather than on the phonological system. When a child substitutes *basketball* for *ball* and reads "Jimmy is playing basketball with his father," he might be relying on an illustration or his own experience playing basketball. Or, because both *basketball* and *ball* begin with *b*, he might have used the beginning sound as an aid in decoding, but he apparently didn't consider how long the word *basketball* is compared with the word *ball*. When the child changes the syntax, as in "Jimmy, he play ball with his father," he may speak a nonstandard dialect. Sometimes a child reads the sentence as "Jump is play boat with his father," so that it doesn't make sense: The child chooses words with the correct beginning sound and uses appropriate parts of speech for at least some of the words, but there's no comprehension. This is a serious problem because the child doesn't seem to understand that what he reads must make sense.

PRINCIPLE 3: EFFECTIVE TEACHERS CREATE A COMMUNITY OF LEARNERS

Classrooms are social settings. Together, students and their teacher create their classroom community, and the type of community they create strongly influences the learning that takes place (Angelillo, 2008). The classroom community should feel safe and respectful so students are motivated to learn and actively involved in reading and writing activities. Perhaps the most striking quality is the partnership that the teacher and students create: They become a "family" in which all the members respect one another and support each other's learning. Students value culturally and linguistically diverse classmates and recognize that all students make important contributions to the classroom (Wells & Chang-Wells, 1992).

The teacher and the students work together for their common good. Consider the differences between renting and owning a home. In a classroom community, students and the teacher are joint "owners" of the classroom. Students assume responsibility for their own behavior and learning, work collaboratively with classmates, complete assignments, and care for the classroom. In traditional classrooms, in contrast, the classroom belongs to the teacher, and students are "renters" for the school year. This doesn't mean that in a classroom community, teachers abdicate their leadership responsibilities; on the contrary, teachers retain all of their roles as guide, instructor, monitor, coach, mentor, and grader. Sometimes these roles are shared with students, but the ultimate responsibility remains with the teacher.

Literacy Portraits:VIEWING GUIDE

Ms. Janusz spent the first month of the school year creating a community of learners in her classroom. She taught the second graders how to participate in reading and writing workshop, including procedures for choosing books, reading with a buddy, and keeping a writer's notebook. They learned to work cooperatively, take responsibility for their work and behavior, and show respect to their classmates. Ms. Janusz continues to build on this foundation that she laid in September so that the classroom functions effectively, and everyone is a contributing member of the class. View Curt'Lynn's March video clip in the Literacy Portraits section of MyEducationLab to see her buddy read with a classmate, and Jimmy's October video clip to watch him participate in a writing conference with Michael. Which of the characteristics of a community of learners described in Figure 1–4 do you notice in the video clips?

myeducationlab

Characteristics of a Classroom Community

A classroom community has specific, identifiable characteristics that are conducive to learning:

Responsibility. Students are valued members of the classroom community who are responsible for their learning, their behavior, and the contributions they make.

Opportunities. Students have opportunities to read authentic texts and write for real audiences—their classmates, their parents, and community members.

Engagement. Students are motivated to learn and actively involved in reading and writing activities, often choosing the books they'll read and their topics for writing.

Demonstration. Teachers provide demonstrations of literacy strategies and skills using **think-alouds**, and they encourage children also to demonstrate how they use strategies and skills.

Risk Taking. Students are encouraged to explore topics, make guesses, and take risks.

Instruction. Teachers provide instruction through **minilessons** and guided practice.

Check the Compendium of Instructional Procedures, which follows Chapter 12, for more information on the highlighted terms.

Response. Students share responses after reading and get feedback from classmates about their writing.

Choice. Students often make choices about the books they read and the writing they do within the parameters set by the teacher.

Time. Students need large chunks of time to pursue reading and writing activities; 2 to 3 hours of uninterrupted time each day for literacy instruction is recommended.

Assessment. Teachers and students work together to establish guidelines for assessment so that they can monitor their own work and participate in evaluating its quality. (Cambourne & Turbill, 1987)

Figure 1–4 lays out the teacher's and students' roles in a classroom community.

Figure 1–4 ◆ Characteristics of a Community of Learners

Characteristic	Teacher's Role	Students' Role
Responsibility	Teachers set guidelines and expect students to be responsible. They also model responsible behavior.	Students assume responsibility for their learning and behavior in the classroom.
Opportunities	Teachers provide opportunities for students to read and write in genuine and meaningful activities.	Students actively participate in activities, for example, reading independently and sharing their writing with classmates.
Engagement	Teachers nurture students' engagement through authentic activities and opportunities to work with classmates.	Students become more engaged in literacy activities and spend more time reading and writing.
Demonstration	Teachers model what good readers and writers do using think-alouds to explain their thinking.	Students carefully observe teachers' demonstrations and then practice by modeling their thinking for classmates.
Risk Taking	Teachers encourage students to take risks while exploring a new idea and de-emphasize the need to always get things "right."	Students understand that learning is a process of taking risks and exploring ideas.
Instruction	Teachers provide explicit instruction through minilessons and provide opportunities for guided practice.	Students participate in minilessons and apply what they're learning in literacy activities.
Response	Teachers provide opportunities for students to respond to books they're reading and to classmates' writing.	Students respond to books in reading logs and grand conversations and listen attentively to classmates share their writing.
Choice	Teachers offer choices because they understand that students are more motivated when they can make choices.	Students make choices about some books they read, projects they create, and compositions they write.
Time	Teachers organize the schedule with large chunks of time for reading and writing.	Students understand the classroom schedule and complete assignments when they're due.
Assessment	Teachers monitor students' learning and set guidelines about how students will be graded.	Students understand how they will be assessed and often participate in self-assessment.

How to Create a Classroom Community

Teachers are more successful when they take the first 2 weeks of the school year to establish the classroom environment; it's unrealistic to assume that students will instinctively be cooperative, responsible, and respectful of classmates. Teachers explicitly explain classroom routines, such as how to get supplies out and put them away and how to work with classmates in a cooperative group, and they set the expectation that students will adhere to the routines. They demonstrate literacy procedures, including how to choose a book, how to provide feedback about a class-mate's writing, and how to participate in a **grand conversation**. Third, teachers model ways of interacting with students, respecting classmates, and assisting them with reading and writing projects.

Teachers are the classroom managers: They set expectations and clearly explain to students what's expected of them and what's valued in the classroom. The class-room rules are specific and consistent, and teachers also set limits. Students might be allowed to talk quietly with classmates when they're working, for example, but they're not allowed to shout across the classroom or talk when the teacher's talking or when classmates are presenting to the class. Teachers also model classroom rules themselves as they interact with students. This process of socialization at the beginning of the school year is crucial to the success of the literacy program.

Not everything can be accomplished during the first 2 weeks, however; teachers continue to reinforce classroom routines and literacy procedures. One way is to have student leaders model the desired routines and behaviors; this way, other students are likely to follow the lead. Teachers also continue to teach additional literacy procedures as students become involved in new types of activities. The classroom community evolves during the school year, but the foundation is laid during the first 2 weeks.

The classroom environment is predictable with familiar routines and literacy procedures. Students feel comfortable, safe, and more willing to take risks in a predictable classroom environment. This is especially true for students from varied cultures, English learners, and students who struggle (Fay & Whaley, 2004).

The classroom community also extends beyond the walls of the classroom to include the entire school and the wider community. Within the school, students become "buddies" with students in other classes and get together to read and write in pairs (Friedland & Truesdell, 2004). When parents and other community members come into the school, they demonstrate the value they place on education by working as tutors and aides, sharing their cultures, and demonstrating other types of expertise.

PRINCIPLE 4: EFFECTIVE TEACHERS ADOPT A BALANCED APPROACH TO INSTRUCTION

The balanced approach to instruction is based on a comprehensive view of literacy that combines explicit instruction, guided practice, collaborative learning, and independent reading and writing. It's grown out of the so-called "reading wars" of the late 20th century in which teachers and researchers argued for either teacher-centered or student-centered instruction. Cunningham and Allington (2007) compare the balanced approach to a multivitamin, suggesting that it brings together the best of teacher- and student-centered learning theories. Even though balanced programs vary, they usually embody these characteristics:

◆ Literacy involves both reading and writing.
◆ Oral language is integrated with reading and writing.
◆ Reading instruction includes phonemic awareness, phonics, fluency, vocabulary, and comprehension.
◆ Writing instruction includes the writing process, the qualities of good writing to communicate ideas effectively, and conventional spelling, grammar, and punctuation to make those ideas more readable.
◆ Reading and writing are used as tools for content-area learning.
◆ Strategies and skills are taught explicitly, with a gradual release of responsibility to students.
◆ Students often work collaboratively and talk with classmates.
◆ Students are more motivated and engaged when they participate in authentic literacy activities.

Pearson, Raphael, Benson, and Madda (2007) explain that "achieving balance is a complex process that requires flexibility and artful orchestration of literacy's various contextual and conceptual aspects" (p. 33).

The characteristics of the balanced approach are embodied in an instructional program that includes these components:

◆ Reading
◆ Phonics and other literacy skills
◆ Reading and writing strategies
◆ Vocabulary
◆ Comprehension
◆ Literature
◆ Content-area study
◆ Oral language
◆ Writing
◆ Spelling

Each component is described in Figure 1–5, and as you continue reading this textbook, you'll understand what an instructional program that incorporates these components looks like. Creating a balance is important, according to Juel, Biancarosa, Coker, and Deffes (2003), because when one component is over- or underemphasized, the development of the others suffers.

A balanced literacy program integrating these components is recommended for all students, including students in high-poverty urban schools, struggling readers, and English learners (Braunger & Lewis, 2006; Duffy-Hester, 1999). What matters most is that teachers know their students well so they can adapt the components in their instructional program to ensure that all students succeed.

More Reading and Writing

Struggling students need to spend more time reading and writing.

Struggling students need to increase their volume of reading and writing. Allington (2006) recommends that teachers dramatically increase the amount of time struggling readers spend reading each day so that they can become more capable and confident readers and develop greater interest in reading. Reading volume matters; better readers typically read three times as much as struggling readers do. This recommendation for increased volume is for writing, too: Struggling writers need to spend more time writing.

In addition to explicit instruction and guided practice, students need large blocks of uninterrupted time for authentic reading and writing, and reading and writing workshop is one of the best ways to provide this opportunity. During reading workshop, students read self-selected books at their own reading level, and during writing workshop, they draft and refine compositions on self-selected topics. Practice is just as important for reading and writing as it is when you're learning to ride a bike or play the piano.

How much classroom time should students spend reading and writing? Although there's no hard-and-fast rule, Allington (2006) recommends that each day students spend at least 90 minutes reading and 45 minutes writing. Researchers have found that the most effective teachers provide more time for reading and writing than less effective teachers do (Allington & Johnston, 2002). It's often difficult for struggling students to sustain reading and writing activities for as long as their classmates do, but with teacher support, they can increase the time they spend reading and writing.

Figure 1–5 ◆ Components of the Balanced Literacy Approach	
Component	**Description**
Reading	Students participate in modeled, shared, interactive, guided, and independent reading experiences using picture-book stories and novels, informational books, books of poetry, basal textbooks, content-area reading textbooks, and Internet materials.
Phonics and Other Literacy Skills	Students learn to use automatic actions called *skills* in reading and writing, including phonics to decode and spell words.
Reading and Writing Strategies	Students learn to use problem-solving and monitoring behaviors called *strategies* as they read and write, including predicting, drawing inferences, revising, and repairing.
Vocabulary	Students learn the meaning of words through wide reading, listening to books read aloud, and content-area study, and they apply word-learning strategies, including using context clues, to figure out the meaning of unfamiliar words.
Comprehension	Students learn to use reader factors, including comprehension strategies, and text factors, including text structures, to understand what they're reading.
Literature	Students become engaged readers who enjoy literature through reading and responding to books and learning about genres, text structures, and literary features.
Content-Area Study	Students use reading and writing as tools to learn about social studies and science topics in thematic units.
Oral Language	Students use talk and listening as they work with classmates, participate in grand conversations, give oral presentations, and listen to the teacher read aloud.
Writing	Students learn to use the writing process to draft and refine stories, poems, reports, essays, and other compositions.
Spelling	Students apply what they're learning about English orthography to spell words, and their spellings gradually become conventional.

RINCIPLE 5: EFFECTIVE TEACHERS SCAFFOLD STUDENTS' READING AND WRITING

Teachers scaffold students' reading and writing as they demonstrate, guide, and teach, and they vary the amount of support they provide according to the instructional purpose and students' needs. Sometimes teachers model how experienced readers read or record children's dictation when the writing's too difficult for them to do on their own. At other times, they guide students as they read a leveled book or proofread their writing. Teachers use five levels of support, moving from more to less as students assume responsibility (Fountas & Pinnell, 1996). Figure 1–6 summarizes these five levels of support—modeled, shared, interactive, guided, and independent—for reading and writing activities.

Teachers working with kindergartners through eighth graders use all five levels. When teachers introduce a reading strategy, for instance, they model how to use it. And,

Figure 1–6 ◆ A Continuum of Literacy Instruction

Level of Support		Reading	Writing
High	**Modeled**	Teacher reads aloud, modeling how good readers read fluently and with expression. Books too difficult for students to read themselves are used. Examples: interactive read-alouds and listening centers.	Teacher writes in front of students, creating the text, doing the writing, and thinking aloud about writing strategies and skills. Example: demonstrations.
	Shared	Teacher and students read books together, with students following as the teacher reads and then repeating familiar refrains. Books students can't read by themselves are used. Examples: big books, buddy reading.	Teacher and students create the text together; then the teacher does the actual writing. Students may assist by spelling familiar or high-frequency words. Example: Language Experience Approach.
	Interactive	Teacher and students read together and take turns doing the reading. The teacher helps students read fluently and with expression. Instructional-level books are used. Examples: choral reading and readers theatre.	Teacher and students create the text and share the pen to do the writing. Teacher and students talk about writing conventions. Example: interactive writing.
	Guided	Teacher plans and teaches reading lessons to small, homogeneous groups using instructional-level books. Focus is on supporting and observing students' use of strategies. Example: guided reading lessons.	Teacher plans and teaches lesson on a writing procedure, strategy, or skill, and students participate in supervised practice activities. Example: class collaborations.
Low	**Independent**	Students choose and read self-selected books independently. Teacher conferences with students to monitor their progress. Examples: reading workshop and reading centers.	Students use the writing process to write stories, informational books, and other compositions. Teacher monitors students' progress. Examples: writing workshop and writing centers.

when teachers want students to practice a strategy they've already introduced, they guide students through a reading activity, slowly releasing more responsibility to them. Once students can apply the strategy easily, they're encouraged to use it independently. The purpose of the activity, not the activity itself, determines the level of support. Teachers are less actively involved during independent reading and writing, but the quality of instruction that students have received is clearest because they're applying what they've learned.

Modeled Reading and Writing

Teachers provide the greatest amount of support when they model how expert readers read and expert writers write. When teachers read aloud, they're modeling: They read fluently and with expression, and they talk about their thoughts and the strategies they're using. When they model writing, teachers write a composition on chart paper or an interactive white board so that everyone can see what the teacher does and how it's being written. Teachers use this support level to demonstrate procedures, such as choosing a book to read or doing a **word sort**, and to introduce new writing genres, such as writing a poem. Teachers often do a **think-aloud** to share what they're thinking as they read or write and the decisions they make and the strategies they use. Teachers use modeling for these purposes:

◆ Demonstrate fluent reading and writing
◆ Explain how to use reading and writing strategies, such as predicting, using context clues, and revising
◆ Teach the procedure for a literacy activity
◆ Show how reading and writing conventions and other skills work

Shared Reading and Writing

Teachers "share" reading and writing tasks with students at this level. Probably the best-known shared activity is **shared reading**, which teachers use to read big books with young children. The teacher does most of the reading, but children join in to read familiar and predictable words and phrases. Teachers who work with older students can also use shared reading (Allen, 2002). When a novel is too difficult for students to read independently, for example, teachers often read it aloud while students follow along, reading silently when they can.

Teachers use shared writing in a variety of ways. Primary-grade teachers often use the **Language Experience Approach** to write children's dictation on paintings and brainstorm lists of words on the chalkboard, for example, and teachers of older students use shared writing when they make **K-W-L charts**, draw graphic organizers, and write **collaborative books**.

Sharing differs from modeling in that students actually participate in the activity rather than simply observing the teacher. In shared reading, students follow along as the teacher reads, and in shared writing, they suggest the words and sentences that the teacher writes. Teachers use shared reading and writing for these purposes:

◆ Involve students in literacy activities they can't do independently
◆ Create opportunities for students to experience success in reading and writing
◆ Provide practice before students read and write independently

Interactive Reading and Writing

Students assume an increasingly important role in interactive reading and writing. They no longer observe the teacher reading or writing, repeat familiar words, or suggest words that the teacher writes; instead, they're more actively involved in reading and writing. They support their classmates by sharing the reading and writing responsibilities, and their teacher provides assistance when needed. **Choral reading** and **readers theatre** are two examples of interactive reading. In choral reading, students take turns reading lines of a poem, and in readers theatre, they assume the roles of characters and read lines in a script. In these activities, the students support each other by actively participating and sharing the work.

In **interactive writing**, students and the teacher create a text and write a message (Button, Johnson, & Furgerson, 1996; Tompkins & Collom, 2004). The text is composed by the group, and the teacher assists as students write the text word by word on chart paper. Students take turns writing known letters and familiar words, adding punctuation marks, and marking spaces between words. The teacher helps them to spell all words correctly and use written language conventions so that the text can be read easily. Everyone participates in creating and writing the text on chart paper, and they also write the text on small dry-erase boards. After writing, students read and reread the text using shared and independent reading. Teachers use interactive reading and writing for these purposes:

◆ Practice reading and writing high-frequency words
◆ Apply phonics and spelling skills
◆ Read and write texts that students can't do independently
◆ Have students share their literacy expertise with classmates

Guided Reading and Writing

Teachers continue to support students during guided reading and writing, but at this level, students do the actual reading and writing themselves. In **guided reading**, small, homogeneous groups of students meet with the teacher to read a book at their instructional level. The teacher introduces the book and guides students as they begin reading. Then students continue reading on their own while the teacher supervises. Afterward, they discuss the book, review vocabulary words, and practice skills. Later, students reread the book independently.

Minilessons are another type of guided reading and writing. As teachers teach about strategies, skills, and genres and other text factors, they support students as they learn. They also provide practice activities and supervise as students apply what they're learning.

In guided writing, teachers plan structured writing activities and then supervise students as they write. For example, when students make pages for a **collaborative book**, it's guided writing because the teacher organizes the activity and supervises students as they work. Teachers also provide guidance as they conference with students about their writing.

Teachers use guided reading and writing to provide instruction and assistance as students are actually reading and writing. Teachers use guided reading and writing for these purposes:

◆ Support students' reading in appropriate instructional-level materials
◆ Teach literacy strategies and skills
◆ Involve students in collaborative writing projects
◆ Teach students to use the writing process—in particular, how to revise and edit

Independent Reading and Writing

Students do the reading and writing themselves at the independent level. They apply the strategies and skills they've learned in authentic literacy activities. During independent reading, students usually choose their own books and work at their own pace as they read and respond to books. Similarly, during independent writing, students usually choose their own topics and move at their own pace as they develop and refine their writing. It would be wrong to suggest, however, that teachers play no role in independent-level activities. They continue to monitor students, but they provide much less guidance at this level.

Through independent reading, students learn how pleasurable reading is and, teachers hope, become lifelong readers. In addition, as they write, students come to view themselves as authors. Teachers use independent reading and writing for these purposes:

◆ Create opportunities for students to practice the reading and writing strategies and skills they've learned
◆ Provide authentic literacy experiences in which students choose their own topics, purposes, and materials
◆ Develop lifelong readers and writers

PRINCIPLE 6: EFFECTIVE TEACHERS ORGANIZE FOR LITERACY INSTRUCTION

There's no one instructional program that best represents the balanced approach to literacy; instead, teachers organize for instruction by creating their own program that fits their students' needs and their school's standards and curricular guidelines. Instructional programs should reflect these principles:

◆ Teachers create a community of learners in their classroom.
◆ Teachers implement the components of the balanced approach.
◆ Teachers scaffold students' reading and writing experiences.

Teachers choose among a variety of instructional programs, combine parts of two or more programs, alternate programs, or add other components to meet their students' needs. Four of the most popular programs are basal reading programs, literature focus units, literature circles, and reading and writing workshop. Figure 1–7 presents a comparison of these four instructional programs.

Figure 1–7 ◆ Instructional Programs

	Basal Reading Programs	Literature Focus Units
Description	Students read textbooks containing stories, informational articles, and poems that are sequenced according to grade level. Teachers follow directions in the teacher's guide to teach word identification, vocabulary, comprehension, grammar, and writing lessons. Directions are also provided for working with English learners and struggling students.	Teachers and students read and respond to a book together as a class. They choose high-quality literature that is appropriate for the grade level and students' interests. The book may be too difficult for some students to read on their own, so teachers read it aloud or use shared reading. After reading, students usually create projects.
Strengths	• Textbooks are aligned with grade-level standards. • Students read selections at their grade level. • Teachers teach strategies and skills and provide structured practice opportunities. • Teachers are available to reteach strategies and skills as needed. • The teacher's guide provides detailed instructions. • Assessment materials are included in the program.	• Teachers choose picture-book stories, novels, or informational books for units. • Teachers scaffold reading instruction as they read with the whole class or small groups. • Teachers teach minilessons on reading strategies and skills. • Students study vocabulary. • Students develop projects to extend their reading.
Limitations	• Selections may be too difficult for some students. • Selections may lack the authenticity of good literature. • Programs include many worksheets. • Most of the instruction is presented to the whole class.	• Students all read the same book whether or not they like it and whether or not it's at their reading level. • Many of the activities are teacher directed.

Basal Reading Programs

Commercially produced reading programs are known as *basal readers*. These programs feature a textbook containing reading selections with accompanying workbooks, supplemental books, and related instructional materials at each grade level. Phonics, vocabulary, comprehension, grammar, and spelling instruction is coordinated with the reading selections and aligned with grade-level standards. The teacher's guide provides detailed procedures for teaching the selections and related skills and strategies. Instruction is typically presented to the whole class, with reteaching to small groups of struggling students. Testing materials are also included so that teachers can monitor students' progress. Publishers tout basal readers as a complete literacy program, but effective teachers realize that they aren't.

Literature Focus Units

Teachers create literature focus units featuring high-quality picture-book stories and novels. The books are usually included in a district- or state-approved list of award-winning books that all students are expected to read at a particular grade level. These

Literature Circles	Reading and Writing Workshop
Teachers choose five or six books and collect multiple copies of each one. Students each choose the book they want to read and form circles or "book clubs" to read and respond to the book. They develop a reading and discussion schedule and assume roles for the discussion. Teachers sometimes participate in the discussions.	Students choose books and read and respond to them independently during reading workshop and write books on self-selected topics during writing workshop. Teachers monitor students' work through conferences. During a sharing period, students share with classmates the books they read and the books they write. Teachers also teach minilessons on reading and writing strategies and skills.
• Teachers differentiate instruction by providing books at varied reading levels. • Students are more strongly motivated because they choose the books they read. • Students work with their classmates. • Students participate in authentic literacy experiences using trade books. • Activities are student directed. • Teachers may participate in discussions to help students think more deeply about the book.	• Students read books appropriate for their reading levels. • Students are more engaged because they choose the books they read. • Students work through the stages of the writing process during writing workshop. • Activities are student directed, and students work at their own pace. • Teachers have opportunities to work individually with students during conferences.
• Teachers often feel a loss of control because students are reading different books. • To be successful, students must learn to be task oriented and to use time wisely. • Sometimes students choose books that are too difficult or too easy for them.	• Teachers often feel a loss of control because students are reading different books and working at different stages of the writing process. • To be successful, students must learn to be task oriented and to use time wisely.

books include classics such as *The Very Hungry Caterpillar* (Carle, 1994) and *Charlotte's Web* (White, 2006) and award winners such as *Officer Buckle and Gloria* (Rathmann, 1995) and *Holes* (Sachar, 2003). Everyone in the class reads and responds to the same book, and the teacher supports students' learning through a combination of explicit instruction and reading and writing activities. Through these units, teachers teach students about literary genres and authors, and they develop students' interest in literature.

Literature Circles

Small groups of students get together in literature circles or book clubs to read a story or other book. To begin, teachers select five or six books at varying reading levels to meet the needs of all students in the class. Often, the books are related in some way— representing the same theme or written by the same author, for instance. They collect multiple copies of each book and give a book talk to introduce them. Then students choose a book to read and form a group to read and respond to the book. They set a reading and discussion schedule and work independently, although teachers sometimes sit in on the discussions. Through the experience of reading and discussing a book together, students develop responsibility for completing assignments and learn more about how to respond to books.

Reading and Writing Workshop

In reading workshop, students select books, read independently at their own pace, and conference with the teacher about their reading. Similarly, in writing workshop, students write books on topics that they choose and the teacher conferences with them about their writing. Teachers set aside a time for reading and writing workshop, and all students read and write while the teacher conferences with small groups. Teachers also teach minilessons on reading and writing strategies and skills and read books aloud to the whole class. In a workshop program, students read and write more like adults do, making choices, working independently, and developing responsibility. Many teachers report that reading and writing workshop are more motivational than other literacy programs and that fourth through eighth graders particularly value the opportunity to make choices and work independently.

These approaches are used at all grade levels, and teachers generally combine them because students learn best through a variety of reading and writing experiences. Sometimes the books that students read are more difficult or teachers are introducing a new writing genre that requires more teacher support and guidance. Some teachers alternate literature focus units or literature circles with reading and writing workshop and basal readers, whereas others use some components from each approach throughout the school year.

Nurturing English Learners

Go to the Building Teaching Skills and Dispositions section of Chapter 1 on **MyEducationLab.com** to learn how Ms. Janusz supports Rakie, an English learner.

English learners (ELs) benefit from participating in the same instructional programs that mainstream students do, but teachers adapt these programs to create classroom learning contexts that respect minority students and meet their needs (Brock & Raphael, 2005; Peregoy & Boyle, 2009; Shanahan & Beck, 2006). Learning to read and write is more challenging for English learners because they're learning to speak English at the same time they're developing literacy. Here are some ways that teachers scaffold English learners' oral language acquisition and literacy development:

Literature Circles
These eighth graders are participating in a discussion during a literature circle featuring Rodman Philbrick's *Freak the Mighty* (1993), the memorable story of two unlikely friends. The students talk about events in the story, returning to the book to read sentences aloud. They also check the meaning of several words in a dictionary that one student keeps on his desk. They've read half of the book so far, and their conversation focuses on the friendship Max and Kevin have formed. They talk about their own friends and what it means to be a friend, and they make predictions about how the story will end.

Explicit Instruction. Teachers present additional instruction on literacy strategies and skills because ELs are more at-risk than other students (Genesee & Riches, 2006). They also spend more time teaching unfamiliar academic vocabulary related to reading and writing (e.g., *vowel, homonym, paragraph, index, quotation marks, predict, revise, summarize*).

Oral Language. Teachers provide many opportunities each day for students to practice speaking English comfortably and informally with partners and in small groups. Through these conversations, ELs develop both conversational and academic language, which supports their reading and writing development (Rothenberg & Fisher, 2007).

Small-Group Work. Teachers provide opportunities for students to work in small groups because classmates' social interaction supports their learning (Genesee & Riches, 2006). English learners talk with classmates as they read and write, and at the same time, they're learning the culture of literacy.

Reading Aloud to Students. Teachers read aloud a variety of stories, informational books, and books of poetry, including some that represent students' home cultures (Rothenberg & Fisher, 2007). As they read, teachers model fluent reading, and students become more familiar with English sounds, vocabulary, and written language structures.

Background Knowledge. Teachers organize instruction into themes to build students' world knowledge about grade-level-appropriate concepts, and they develop ELs' literary knowledge through minilessons and a variety of reading and writing activities (Braunger & Lewis, 2006).

Authentic Literacy Activities. Teachers provide daily opportunities for students to apply the strategies and skills they're learning as they read and write for authentic, real-life purposes (Akhavan, 2006). English learners participate in meaningful literacy activities through literature circles and reading and writing workshop.

These recommendations promote English learners' academic success.

Teachers' attitudes about minority students and knowledge about how they learn a second language play a critical role in the effectiveness of instruction (Gay, 2000). It's important that teachers understand that English learners have different cultural and linguistic backgrounds and plan instructional programs accordingly. Most classrooms reflect the European American middle-class culture, which differs significantly from minority students' backgrounds. Brock and Raphael (2005) point out that "mismatches between teachers' and students' cultural and linguistic backgrounds matter because such mismatches can impact negatively on students' opportunities for academic success" (p. 5). Teachers and students use language in different ways. For example, some students are reluctant to volunteer answers to teachers' questions, and others may not answer if the questions are different than those their parents ask (Peregoy & Boyle, 2009). Teachers who learn about their students' home language and culture and embed them into their instruction are likely to be more successful.

PRINCIPLE 7: EFFECTIVE TEACHERS LINK INSTRUCTION AND ASSESSMENT

Assessment is an integral and ongoing part of both learning and teaching (Mariotti & Homan, 2005). Sometimes teachers equate standardized high-stakes achievement tests with assessment, but classroom assessment is much more than a once-a-year test. It's a daily part of classroom life: Teachers use a variety of informal procedures and commercial tests to monitor students' reading and writing progress and ensure that they're meeting district and state standards. Cunningham and Allington (2007) describe assessment as "collecting and analyzing data to make decisions about how children are performing and growing" (p. 202).

Purposes of Classroom Assessment

Teachers assess students' learning for these purposes:

Determining Students' Reading Levels. Because students within a classroom normally read at a wide range of levels, it's essential that teachers determine students' reading levels so that they can plan appropriate instruction.

Monitoring Students' Progress. Teachers regularly assess students to ensure that they're making expected progress in reading and writing, and when they're not progressing, teachers take action to get students back on track.

Diagnosing Students' Strengths and Weaknesses. Teachers examine students' progress in specific literacy components, including phonics, fluency, comprehension, writing, and spelling, to identify their strengths and weaknesses. Diagnosis is especially important when students are struggling or aren't making expected progress.

Documenting Students' Learning. Teachers use test results and collections of students' work to provide evidence of their accomplishments. Students' work samples are often collected in portfolios.

Assessment is linked to instruction; teachers use assessment results to inform their teaching (Snow, Griffin, & Burns, 2005). As they plan, teachers use their knowledge about students' reading levels, their background knowledge, and their strategy and skill competencies to plan appropriate instruction that's neither too easy nor too difficult. Teachers monitor instruction that's in progress as they observe students, conference with them, and check their work to ensure that their instruction is effective, and they make modifications, including reteaching when necessary, to improve the quality of their instruction and meet students' needs. Teachers also judge the effectiveness of their instruction after it's completed. It's easy to blame students when learning isn't occurring, but teachers need to consider how they can improve their teaching so that their students will be more successful.

Classroom Assessment Tools

Teachers use a variety of informal assessment tools that they create themselves and classroom tests that are commercially available. Informal assessment tools include the following:

- ◆ Observation of students as they participate in instructional activities
- ◆ **Running records** of students' oral reading to analyze their ability to solve reading problems
- ◆ Examination of students' work
- ◆ Conferences to talk with students about their reading and writing
- ◆ Checklists to monitor students' learning
- ◆ **Rubrics** to assess students' writing and other activities

These assessment tools support instruction, and teachers choose which tool to use according to the kind of information they need. Teachers administer commercial tests to individual students or the entire class to determine their overall reading achievement or their proficiency in a particular component—phonics, spelling, fluency, or comprehension, for example. In upcoming chapters, you'll learn how to assess students' reading and writing and which assessment tools to use.

The results of yearly, high-stakes standardized tests also provide evidence of students' literacy achievement. The usefulness of these data is limited, however, because the tests are usually administered in the spring and the results aren't released until after the school year ends. At the beginning of the next school year, teachers do examine the data and use what they learn in planning for their new class, but the impact isn't as great as it would be for the teachers who worked with those students during the previous year. Another way the results are used is in measuring the effectiveness of teachers' instruction by examining how much students grew since the previous year's test and whether students met grade-level standards.

 RINCIPLE 8: EFFECTIVE TEACHERS BECOME PARTNERS WITH PARENTS

Parents play a crucial role in helping children become successful readers and writers. They support their children's learning by actively participating in literacy activities, such as reading aloud and modeling literate behaviors. Researchers have concluded again and again that home-literacy activities profoundly influence children's academic success (Bus, van Ijzendoorn, & Pellegrini, 1995): They score higher on standardized achievement tests, have better school attendance, and exhibit higher-level thinking when parents are involved in their education.

Most teachers recognize the importance of home-literacy activities and want to become partners with their students' parents. In some communities, parents respond enthusiastically when teachers ask them to listen to their children read aloud or monitor their independent reading, or when teachers invite them to participate in a home–school writing event, for example, but in other communities, there's little or no response. When partnership attempts are unsuccessful, teachers feel frustrated and conclude that they can't expect much support from their students' parents.

Teachers' expectations of parent involvement have been based on middle-class parents who typically see themselves as partners with teachers, reading to and with their children, playing educational games, going to the public library to check out books, and helping with homework. Other parents view their role in educating their school-age children differently (Edwards, 2004). Some are willing to attend teacher–parent conferences and support school projects such as bake sales and carnivals, but they expect teachers to do the teaching. Others feel inadequate when it comes to helping their children. Their own unsuccessful school experiences, cultural differences, or limited ability to read and write in English contribute to these feelings.

Lareau (2000) explained that parents' viewpoints reflect their culture and socio-economic status: Middle-class parents usually work with teachers to support their children's literacy development; working-class parents believe that teachers are better qualified to teach their children; and poor, minority, and immigrant parents often feel powerless to help their children learn to read and write. Parents' involvement is also related to educational level: Parents who didn't graduate from high school are less likely to get involved in their children's literacy learning (Paratore, 2001). Educational level also correlates with parents' personal and parental reading habits: Parents who are high school graduates are more likely to read newspapers and books, read to their children, and take them to the public library.

Ways to Work With Parents

Not all parents understand the crucial role they play in their children's literacy development and academic success. It's up to teachers to establish collaborative relationships with parents so that they can work together and meet children's needs more effectively. Edwards (2004) explains that parent–teacher collaborations "involve rethinking the relationship between home and school such that students' opportunities to learn are expanded" (p. xvii). Teachers begin by accepting that parents view their role in different ways and by becoming more knowledgeable about cultural diversity and how it affects parent–teacher relationships.

Respect the Literacy Activities of Families. Nearly all families incorporate reading and writing activities into their daily routines, but these activities may differ from school-based literacy activities that teachers value. In middle-class families, for example, parents read the newspaper, write messages using magnetic letters on the refrigerator, search for information on the Internet, and read bedtime stories to children, and in other families, they read the Bible and magazines, write letters, pay bills, and do crossword puzzles. Teachers often overlook the importance of literacy activities that differ from those they value. Because culture and learning are closely linked, some children are at risk of failing because they aren't familiar with the literacy activities and language patterns that teachers use (Gay, 2000; Purcell-Gates, 2000). Nieto (2002) urges teachers to recognize the value of parents' literacy activities, even though they may not match teachers' expectations, and use them in developing a literacy program that's culturally responsive.

Reach Out to Families in New Ways. Because their attempts to form partnerships with parents haven't been successful, teachers are striving to find better ways to foster parent–teacher communication and involvement. Based on her work in establishing effective partnerships, Edwards (2004) recommends that teachers work together to create schoolwide programs that begin in September with a yearlong schedule of activities that address particular literacy goals at each grade level. Effective communication is essential: When teachers demonstrate that they want to listen to parents, giving them opportunities to share insights about their children and to ask questions about how children learn to read and write, parents become more willing to give of their time to work with teachers and support their children's learning.

Build Parents' Knowledge of Literacy Procedures. Too often, teachers assume that parents know how to support their children's literacy learning, but many parents don't know how to read aloud, respond to their children's writing, or use other literacy procedures. Researchers have found that when teachers offer specific suggestions and provide clear directions, parents are more likely to be successful (Edwards, 2004).

Because today's classrooms are culturally diverse, it's essential that teachers examine their personal biases and critique the effectiveness of their instructional practices. Once they understand the role of culture in learning, teachers can create an empowering classroom culture and improve communication with parents. When teachers have faith in their students' ability to learn and commit themselves to ensuring that their students are successful, their efforts to involve parents will be more successful.

Home-Literacy Activities

Many parent-involvement programs focus on preschoolers, but parents continue to play an important role in supporting their children's reading and writing development through elementary and high school. Parents implement home-literacy activities as well as support their children's in-school literacy development through activities such as these:

- ◆ Reading aloud to children
- ◆ Listening to children read aloud and reading along with them
- ◆ Making time for children to read books independently a priority
- ◆ Providing books and other reading materials in the home
- ◆ Talking with children about books they're reading
- ◆ Asking children what they're learning at school
- ◆ Providing the materials and opportunities for children to write at home
- ◆ Taking children to the library to check out books and multimedia materials
- ◆ Giving books and magazine subscriptions as gifts
- ◆ Monitoring children as they complete homework assignments
- ◆ Emphasizing the value of literacy and the importance of school success

Teachers who work with older students expand parent–teacher partnerships by showing parents how to talk with their children about books they're reading, respond to their writing, and monitor their completion of homework assignments.

Teachers have developed a variety of innovative home-literacy activities for K–8 students that involve opportunities for parents and their children to read and write together. Here's a list of seven recommended activities:

Interactive Read-Alouds. Teachers not only encourage parents to read aloud to their children every day, but they also demonstrate how to read aloud effectively using **interactive read-alouds** (Enz, 2003). They teach parents how to choose appropriate books and use techniques to boost their children's engagement with the book, such as making predictions, asking questions, and talking about illustrations. Teachers also explain the benefit of rereading books and suggest that parents promote children's response after reading through role-playing, using puppets to retell the story, drawing pictures, and other activities.

Traveling Book Bags. Teachers put together traveling bags of books that beginning readers take home to read with their parents (Vukelich, Christie, & Enz, 2001). For each bag, they collect three or four books, usually on a single topic; a stuffed animal, puppet, or artifact; and a response journal. If parents have low-level literacy or don't speak English, teachers also include cassette-tape recordings of the books and a small tape player so that the whole family can enjoy the books. Children take the book bags home and spend a week reading and talking about the books and writing responses in the journal. Then they exchange the book bags for new ones. Teachers who work with older students make more sophisticated book bags, loaded with maps, brochures, charts and diagrams, magazines, lists of related website addresses, and books related to a thematic unit, for students to take home and explore.

Family Book Clubs. Parents and their children read and discuss books together, and sometimes they invite other families to join the book club. Parents and children choose a book that interests them (and is appropriate for the children's age and reading level) that everyone will read and discuss. After parents and children finish reading, everyone gets together to talk about the book. This activity, based on the book club popularized in *The Mother-Daughter Book Club: How Ten Busy Mothers and Daughters Came Together to Talk, Laugh, and Learn Through Their Love of Reading* (Dodson, 2007), is a great way for parents to foster their children's love of reading.

Online Reading and Writing. Computers are rapidly becoming part of everyday life, and parents and children can use computers together to search the Internet for information, read articles posted on websites, play literacy games, and use e-mail and instant messaging to stay in touch with relatives and friends (Rasinski & Padak, 2008).

Family Journals. Children and their parents write back and forth in special family journals (Wollman-Bonilla, 2000). At school, children write entries, explaining what's going on in their classroom and what they're learning, and then they take their journals home to share with their parents. Next, parents write back, commenting on children's entries, asking questions, and offering praise and encouragement.

Family Reading/Writing Nights. Parents and their children come to school for a special evening of reading or writing books together (Hutchins, Greenfeld, & Epstein, 2008). Individual teachers, a grade-level group of teachers, or an entire school can organize these programs. At a family reading night, children and parents read books together and participate in reading-related presentations and activities. Sometimes children dress up as book characters, perform a **readers theatre** script, or give **book talks** about favorite books. Teachers also give away books that children add to their home library. At a family writing night, children and parents write books together, usually about family events. Teachers also have opportunities at these events to share tips with parents about ways to support their children's literacy development.

Family Literacy Portfolios. Parents save samples of their children's reading and writing and collect them in large folders or portfolios, and then they share the portfolios with teachers during parent–teacher conferences (Krol-Sinclair, Hindin, Emig, & McClure, 2003). Samples of children's reading and writing can include drawings with captions, notes, stories and poems, handmade birthday cards, craft projects, lists of books read, and photocopies of the covers of favorite books. Parents also include observation notes about the ways their children use literacy. When parents bring portfolios to parent–teacher conferences, they assume a more active role in talking about their children's literacy development, and teachers gain valuable insights about their students' home-literacy activities.

These home-literacy activities are effective because teachers set specific goals, provide clear directions, and value parents' collaboration.

Working With Non-English-Speaking and Low-Literacy Parents

Many parents can't actively support their children's literacy through reading and writing because they don't read or write well themselves, or can't read or write in the same language their children do. However, all parents can support their children's literacy by telling stories, discussing current events, sharing cultural information and practices, and encouraging children to talk about what they're learning at school. In addition, there's a way that non-English-speaking and low-literacy parents can share a literacy activity with their children: They can "read" wordless picture books where the story is told entirely through illustrations. A list of recommended wordless picture books, including some that appeal to older students, is presented in Figure 1–8. One of the

---

Figure 1–8 ◆ Wordless Picture Books

Banyai, I. (1998). *Zoom.* New York: Puffin Books. (U)

Banyai, I. (2005). *The other side.* San Francisco: Chronicle Books. (U)

Faller, R. (2006). *The adventures of Polo.* New York: Roaring Brook Press. (P)

Faller, R. (2007). *Polo: The runaway book.* New York: Roaring Brook Press. (P)

Franson, S. E. (2007). *Un-brella.* New York: Roaring Brook Press. (P)

Geisert, A. (2006). *Oops.* Boston: Houghton Mifflin. (P–M)

Heuer, C. (2006). *Lola & Fred.* New York: 4N Publishing. (M)

Heuer, C. (2007). *Lola & Fred & Tom.* New York: 4N Publishing. (P–M)

Jenkins, S. (2003). *Looking down.* Boston: Houghton Mifflin. (P)

Khing, T. T. (2007) *Where is the cake?* New York: Abrams. (P)

Lehman, B. (2004). *The red book.* Boston: Houghton Mifflin. (P–M)

Lehman B. (2006). *Museum trip.* Boston: Houghton Mifflin. (P–M)

Lehman B. (2007). *Rainstorm.* Boston: Houghton Mifflin. (P)

Lehman, B. (2008). *Trainstop.* Boston: Houghton Mifflin. (P)

Mayer, M. (2003). *Frog, where are you?* New York: Dial Books. (M)

Newgarden, M., & Cash, M. M. (2007). *Bow-wow bugs a bug.* San Diego: Harcourt. (p)

Rogers, G. (2007). *Midsummer knight.* New York: Roaring Brook Press. (P–M)

Schories, J. (2006). *Jack and the night visitors.* Honesdale, PA: Front Street. (P)

Tan, S. (2007). *The arrival.* New York: Scholastic. (U)

Turkle, B. (1992). *Deep in the forest.* New York: Puffin Books. (P)

Van Ommen, S. (2007). *The surprise.* Honesdale, PA: Front Street. (P)

Varon, S. (2006). *Chicken and cat.* New York: Scholastic. (P)

Wiesner, D. (1995). *June 29, 1999.* New York: Clarion Books. (M–U)

Wiesner, D. (1997). *Tuesday.* New York: Clarion Books. (M–U)

Wiesner, D. (2006). *Flotsam.* New York: Clarion Books. (M–U)

most sophisticated books on the list is Shaun Tan's *The Arrival* (2007), which depicts the journey of an immigrant who leaves his family and comes to a bizarre new world. The book illustrates the displacement and awe with which immigrants respond to their new surroundings. Parents and children read these books by examining the illustrations and creating a story based on them. It's not as easy as it sounds; usually parents and children read a wordless book several times to thoroughly comprehend it. In the first reading, the focus is on grasping the story line, and then with successive readings, they notice new details in the illustrations, make inferences, and elaborate the story.

Teachers must establish two-way communication with parents and learn from parents about their children's strengths and needs and home-literacy practices. Creating a partnership means more than turning parents into homework monitors; instead, teachers can help parents develop the tools to support their children's literacy learning, and teachers can build on the knowledge and experiences that families bring to their children's education.

Chapter 1 Review

How Effective Teachers Teach Reading and Writing

▶ Teachers apply learning theories as they teach reading and writing.

▶ Teachers create a community of learners in their classrooms.

▶ Teachers adopt the balanced approach to literacy instruction that reflects teacher-centered and student-centered learning theories.

▶ Teachers scaffold students' reading and writing and then gradually withdraw their support as students become proficient.

▶ Teachers link instruction and assessment.

Go to MyEducationLab at www.myeducationlab.com to deepen your understanding of the concepts presented in this chapter:

▶ Judge the importance of community in Ms. Janusz's second-grade classroom by viewing video segments in the Literacy Portraits.

▶ Check your understanding of chapter concepts with the multiple-choice and essay quizzes in the Study Plan.

▶ Apply some of the main ideas discussed in the chapter in the Activities and Applications section of the website.

▶ Practice what you've learned in this chapter in Building Teaching Skills and Dispositions before applying the ideas in your own classroom.

PROFESSIONAL REFERENCES

Afflerbach, P. (2007). *Understanding and using reading assessment, K–12*. Newark, DE: International Reading Association.

Akhavan, N. (2006). *Help! My kids don't all speak English: How to set up a language workshop in your linguistically diverse classroom*. Portsmouth, NH: Heinemann.

Allen, J. (2002). *On the same page: Shared reading beyond the primary grades*. Portland, ME: Stenhouse.

Allington, R. L. (2006). *What really matters for struggling readers: Designing research-based programs* (2nd ed.). Boston: Allyn & Bacon/Pearson.

Allington, R. L., & Johnston, P. H. (Eds.). (2002). *Reading to learn: Lessons from exemplary fourth-grade classrooms*. New York: Guilford Press.

Angelillo, J. (2008). *Whole-class teaching*. Portsmouth, NH: Heinemann.

Baker, L. (2002). Metacognition in comprehension instruction. In C. C. Block & M. Pressley (Eds.), *Comprehension instruction: Research-based best practices* (pp. 77–95). New York: Guilford Press.

Bandura, A. (1997). *Self-efficacy: The exercise of control*. New York: W. H. Freeman.

Banks, J., Cochran-Smith, M., Moll, L., Richert, A., Zeichner, K., LePage, P., Darling-Hammond, L., & Duffy, H. (2005). Teaching diverse learners. In L. Darling-Hammond & J. Bransford (Eds.), *Preparing teachers for a changing world* (pp. 232–274). San Francisco: Jossey-Bass.

Bomer, R., & Bomer, K. (2001). *For a better world: Reading and writing for social action*. Portsmouth, NH: Heinemann.

Braunger, J., & Lewis, J. P. (2006). *Building a knowledge base in reading* (2nd ed.). Newark, DE: International Reading Association/National Council of Teachers of English.

Brock, C. H., & Raphael, T. E. (2005). *Windows to language, literacy, and culture: Insights from an English-language learner*. Newark, DE: International Reading Association.

Brown, J. S., Collins, A., & Duguid, S. (1989). Situated cognition and the culture of learning. *Educational Researcher, 18*(1), 32–42.

Bus, A. G., van Ijzendoorn, M. H., & Pellegrini, A. D. (1995). Joint book reading makes for success in learning to read: A meta-analysis on intergenerational transmission of literacy. *Review of Educational Research, 65*, 1–21.

Button, K., Johnson, M. J., & Furgerson, P. (1996). Interactive writing in a primary classroom. *The Reading Teacher, 49*, 446–454.

Cambourne, B., & Turbill, J. (1987). *Coping with chaos*. Rozelle, New South Wales, Australia: Primary English Teaching Association.

Castek, J., Bevans-Mangelson, J., & Goldstone, B. (2006). Reading adventures online: Five ways to introduce the new literacies of the Internet through children's literature. *The Reading Teacher, 59*, 714–728.

Cunningham, P. M., & Allington, R. L. (2007). *Classrooms that work: They can all read and write*. Boston: Allyn & Bacon.

Dean, D. (2005). *Strategic writing: The writing process and beyond in the secondary English classroom*. Urbana, IL: National Council of Teachers of English.

Dixon-Krauss, L. (1996). *Vygotsky in the classroom*. White Plains, NY: Longman.

Dodson, S. (2007). *The mother-daughter book club: How ten busy mothers and daughters came together to talk, laugh, and learn through their love of reading* (rev. ed.). New York: HarperCollins.

Duffy-Hester, A. (1999). Teaching struggling readers in elementary school classrooms: A review of classroom reading programs and principles for instruction. *The Reading Teacher, 52*, 480–495.

Edwards, P. A. (2004). *Children's literacy development: Making it happen through school, family, and community involvement*. Boston: Allyn & Bacon/Pearson.

Enz, B. J. (2003). The ABCs of family literacy. In A. DeBruin-Parecki & B. Krol-Sinclair (Eds.), *Family literacy: From theory to practice* (pp. 50–67). Newark, DE: International Reading Association.

Fay, K., & Whaley, S. (2004). *Becoming one community: Reading and writing with English language learners*. Portland, ME: Stenhouse.

Flavell, J. H. (1979). Metacognition and cognitive monitoring: A new area of cognitive-developmental inquiry. *American Psychologist, 34*, 906–911.

Fountas, I. C., & Pinnell, G. S. (1996). *Guided reading: Good first teaching for all children*. Portsmouth, NH: Heinemann.

Freire, P. (2000). *Pedagogy of the oppressed* (30th anniversary ed.). New York: Continuum.

Friedland, E. S., & Truesdell, K. S. (2004). Kids reading together: Ensuring the success of a buddy reading program. *The Reading Teacher, 58*, 76–83.

Gambrell, L. B., Malloy, J. A., & Mazzoni, S. A. (2007). Evidence-based best practices for comprehensive literacy instruction. In L. B. Gambrell, L. M. Morrow, & M. Pressley (Eds.), *Best practices in literacy instruction* (3rd ed., pp. 11–29). New York: Guilford Press.

Gay, G. (2000). *Culturally responsive teaching: Theory, research, and practice*. New York: Teachers College Press.

Genesee, F., & Riches, C. (2006). Literacy: Instructional issues. In F. Genesee, K. Lindholm-Leary, W. M. Saunders, & D. Christian (Eds.), *Educating English language learners: A synthesis of research evidence* (pp. 109–175). New York: Cambridge University Press.

Guthrie, J. T., & Wigfield, A. (2000). Engagement and motivation in reading. In M. L. Kamil, P. B. Mosenthal, P. D. Pearson, & R. Barr (Eds.), *Handbook of reading research* (Vol. 3, pp. 403–422). New York: Erlbaum.

Halliday, M. A. K. (1978). *Language as social semiotic: The social interpretation of language and meaning*. Baltimore: University Park Press.

Hayes, J. R. (2004). A new framework for understanding cognition and affect in writing. In R. B. Ruddell & N. J. Unrau (Eds.), *Theoretical models and processes of reading* (5th ed., pp. 1399–1430). Newark, DE: International Reading Association.

Heath, S. B. (1983). Research currents: A lot of talk about nothing. *Language Arts, 60*, 999–1007.

Henry, L. A. (2006). SEARCHing for an answer: The critical role of new literacies while reading on the Internet. *The Reading Teacher, 59*, 614–627.

Hutchins, D., Greenfeld, M., & Epstein, J. (2008). *Family reading night*. Larchmont, NY: Eye on Education.

Juel, C., Biancarosa, G., Coker, D., & Deffes, R. (2003). Walking with Rosie: A cautionary tale of early reading instruction. *Educational Leadership, 60*, 12–18.

Karchmer, R. A., Mallette, M. H., Kara-Soteriou, J., & Leu, D. (Eds.). (2005). *Innovative approaches to literacy education: Using the Internet to support new literacies*. Newark, DE: International Reading Association.

Kintsch, W. (2004). The construction-integration model and its implications for instruction. In R. B. Ruddell & N. J. Unrau (Eds.), *Theoretical models and processes of reading* (5th ed., pp. 1270–1328). Newark, DE: International Reading Association.

Kist, W. (2005). *New literacies in action: Teaching and learning in multiple media*. New York: Teachers College Press.

Kress, G. (2003). *Literacy in the new media age*. London: Routledge.

Krol-Sinclair, B., Hindin, A., Emig, J. M., & McClure, K. A. (2003). Using family literacy portfolios as context for parent-teacher communication. In A. DeBruin-Parecki & B. Krol-Sinclair (Eds.), *Family literacy: From theory to practice* (pp. 266–281). Newark, DE: International Reading Association.

Lareau, A. (2000). *Home advantage: Social class and parental intervention in elementary education* (2nd ed.). Lanham, MD: Rowman & Littlefield.

Lave, J., & Wenger, E. (1991). *Situated learning: Legitimate peripheral participation*. Cambridge, UK: Cambridge University Press.

Leu, D. J., Jr., Kinzer, C. K., Coiro, J., & Cammack, D. W. (2004). Toward a theory of new literacies emerging from the Internet and other communication technologies. In R. B. Ruddell & N. J. Unrau (Eds.), *Theoretical models and processes of reading* (5th ed., pp. 1570–1613). Newark, DE: International Reading Association.

Lewison, M., Leland, C., & Harste, J. C. (2008). *Creating critical classrooms: K–8 reading and writing with an edge*. New York: Erlbaum.

Luke, A., & Freebody, P. (1997). Shaping the social practices of reading. In S. Muspratt, A. Luke, & P. Freebody (Eds.), *Constructing critical literacies* (pp. 185–225). Cresskill, NJ: Hampton.

Mariotti, A. S., & Homan, S. P. (2005). *Linking reading assessment to instruction*. London: Routledge.

McDaniel, C. (2004). Critical literacy: A questioning stance and the possibility for change. *The Reading Teacher, 57*, 472–481.

McLaughlin, M., & De Voogd, G. L. (2004). *Critical literacy: Enhancing students' comprehension of text*. New York: Scholastic.

Moll, L. C., & Gonzales, N. (2004). Engaging life: A funds of knowledge approach to multicultural education. In J. A. Banks & C. A. M. Banks (Eds.), *Handbook of research on multicultural education* (2nd ed., pp. 699–715). San Francisco: Jossey-Bass.

Nieto, S. (2002). *Language, culture, and teaching: Critical perspectives for a new century*. Mahwah, NJ: Erlbaum.

O'Donohue, W., & Kitchener, R. F. (Eds.). (1998). *Handbook of behaviorism*. New York: Academic Press.

Paratore, J. R. (2001). *Opening doors, opening opportunities: Family literacy in an urban community*. Boston: Allyn & Bacon.

Pearson, P. D., Raphael, T. E., Benson, V. L., & Madda, C. L. (2007). Balance in comprehensive literacy instruction: Then and now. In L. B. Gambrell, L. M. Morrow, & M. Pressley (Eds.), *Best practices in literacy instruction* (3rd ed., pp. 31–54). New York: Guilford Press.

Peregoy, S. F., & Boyle, O. F. (2009). *Reading, writing, and learning in ESL: A resource book for teaching K–12 English learners* (5th ed.). Boston: Allyn & Bacon/ Pearson.

Piaget, J. (1969). *The psychology of intelligence*. Paterson, NJ: Littlefield, Adams.

Pressley, M. (2002). Comprehension strategies instruction. In C. C. Block & M. Pressley (Eds.), *Comprehension instruction: Research-based best practices* (pp. 11–27). New York: Guilford Press.

Purcell-Gates, V. (2000). Family literacy. In M. L. Kamil, P. B. Mosenthal, P. D. Pearson, & R. Barr (Eds.), *Handbook of reading research* (Vol. 3, pp. 853–870). Mahwah, NJ: Erlbaum.

Rasinski, T., & Padak, N. (2008). Beyond stories. *The Reading Teacher, 61*, 582–584.

Rosenblatt, L. M. (2004). The transactional theory of reading and writing. In R. B. Ruddell & N. J. Unrau (Eds.), *Theoretical models and processes of reading* (5th ed., pp. 1363–1398). Newark, DE: International Reading Association.

Rosenblatt, L. (2005). *Making meaning with text: Selected essays*. Portsmouth, NH: Heinemann.

Rothenberg, C., & Fisher, D. (2007). *Teaching English language learners: A differentiated approach*. Upper Saddle River, NJ: Merrill/Prentice Hall.

Ruddell, R. B., & Unrau, N. J. (2004). Reading as a meaning-construction process: The reader, the text, and the teacher.

In R. B. Ruddell & N. J. Unrau (Eds.), *Theoretical models and processes of reading* (5th ed., pp. 1462–1521). Newark, DE: International Reading Association.

Rumelhart, D. E. (2004). Toward an interactive model of reading. In R. B. Ruddell & N. J. Unrau (Eds.), *Theoretical models and processes of reading* (5th ed., pp. 1149–1179). Newark, DE: International Reading Association.

Shanahan, T., & Beck, I. (2006). Effective literacy teaching for English-language learners. In D. August & T. Shanahan (Eds.), *Developing literacy in second-language learners: Report of the National Literacy Panel on Language-Minority Children and Youth* (pp. 415–488). Mahwah, NJ: Erlbaum.

Shannon, P. (1995). *Text, lies, & videotape: Stories about life, literacy, & learning*. Portsmouth, NH: Heinemann.

Skinner, B. F. (1974). *About behaviorism*. New York: Random House.

Smith, F. (1971). *Understanding reading: A psycholinguistic analysis of reading and learning to read*. New York: Holt, Rinehart and Winston.

Snow, C., Burns, M. S., & Griffin, P. (1998). *Preventing reading difficulties in young children*. Washington, DC: National Academy Press.

Snow, C. E., Griffin, P., & Burns, M. S. (Eds.). (2005). *Knowledge to support the teaching of reading: Preparing teachers for a changing world*. San Francisco: Jossey-Bass.

Stahl, S. A., & Nagy, W. E. (2005). *Teaching word meanings*. Mahwah, NJ: Erlbaum.

Stanovich, K. E. (2000). *Progress in understanding reading: Scientific foundations and new frontiers*. New York: Guilford Press.

Tompkins, G. E., & Collom, S. (Eds.). (2004). *Sharing the pen: Interactive writing with young children*. Upper Saddle River, NJ: Merrill/Prentice Hall.

Tracey, D. H., & Morrow, L. M. (2006). *Lenses on reading: An introduction to theories and models*. New York: Guilford Press.

Vukelich, C., Christie, J., & Enz, B. (2001). *Helping young children learn language and literacy*. Boston: Allyn & Bacon.

Vygotsky, L. S. (1978). *Mind in society*. Cambridge, MA: Harvard University Press.

Vygotsky, L. S. (1986). *Thought and language*. Cambridge, MA: MIT Press.

Wells, G., & Chang-Wells, G. L. (1992). *Constructing knowledge together: Classrooms as centers of inquiry and literacy*. Portsmouth, NH: Heinemann.

Wink, J. (2005). *Critical pedagogy: Notes from the real world* (3rd ed.). Boston: Allyn & Bacon/Pearson.

Wollman-Bonilla, J. (2000). *Family message journals: Teaching writing through family involvement*. Urbana, IL: National Council of Teachers of English.

CHILDREN'S BOOK REFERENCES

Carle, E. (1994). *The very hungry caterpillar*. New York: Scholastic.

Ellis, D. (2000). *The breadwinner*. Toronto: Groundwood Books.

Jiménez, F. (1999). *The circuit*. Boston: Houghton Mifflin.

McKissack, P. (2001). *Goin' somewhere special*. New York: Atheneum.

Park, L. S. (2007). *Project mulberry*. New York: Yearling.

Philbrick, R. (1993). *Freak the mighty*. New York: Blue Sky Press.

Polacco, P. (1994). *Pink and Say*. New York: Philomel.

Rathmann, P. (1995). *Officer Buckle and Gloria*. New York: Putnam.

Roth, S. (2001). *Happy birthday Mr. Kang*. Washington, DC: National Geographic Children's Books.

Ryan, P. M. (2002). *Esperanza rising*. New York: Scholastic/Blue Sky Press.

Sachar, L. (2003). *Holes*. New York: Yearling.

Tan, S. (2007). *The arrival*. New York: Scholastic.

Whelan, G. (2000). *Homeless bird*. New York: Scholastic.

White, E. B. (2006). *Charlotte's web*. New York: HarperCollins.

Woodson, J. (2007). *Feathers*. New York: Putnam.

Chapter 2

Teaching the Reading and Writing Processes

Mrs. Goodman's Seventh Graders Read The Giver

The seventh graders in Mrs. Goodman's class are reading the Newbery Medal winner *The Giver* (Lowry, 2006b). In this futuristic story, 12-year-old Jonas is selected to become the next Keeper of the Memories, and he discovers the terrible truth about his community. Mrs. Goodman has a class set of paperback copies of the book, and her students use the reading process as they read and explore it.

To introduce the book, Mrs. Goodman asks her students to get into small groups to brainstorm lists of all the things they would change about life if they could. Their lists, written on butcher paper, include no more homework, no AIDS, no crime, no gangs, no parents, no taking out the garbage, and being allowed to drive cars at age 10. The groups hang their lists on the chalkboard and share them. Mrs. Goodman puts checkmarks by many of the items, seeming to agree with the points. Next she explains that the class is going to read a story about life in the future. She explains that *The Giver* takes place in a planned utopian, or "perfect," society with the qualities that she checked on students' lists.

She passes out copies of the book and uses shared reading to read the first chapter aloud as students follow along in their books. Then the class talks about the first chapter in a grand conversation, asking a lot of questions: Why were there so many rules? Doesn't anyone drive a car? What does *released* mean? Why are children called a "Seven" or a "Four"? What does it mean that people are "given" spouses—don't they fall in love and get married? Why does Jonas have to tell his feelings? Classmates share their ideas and are eager to continue reading. Mrs. Goodman's reading aloud of the first chapter and the questions that the students raised generate interest in the story. The power of this story grabs them all.

They set a schedule for reading and discussion. Every 3 days, they'll come together to talk about the chapters they've read, and over 2 weeks, the class will complete the book. They'll also write in reading logs after reading the first chapter and then five more times as they're reading. In these logs, students write reactions to the story. Maria wrote this journal entry after finishing the book:

> Jonas had to do it. He had to save Gabriel's life because the next day Jonas's father was going to release (kill) him. He had it all planned out. That was important. He was very brave to leave his parents and his home. But I guess they weren't his parents really and his home wasn't all that good. I don't know if I could have done it but he did the right thing. He had to get out. He saved himself and he saved little Gabe. I'm glad he took Gabriel. That community was supposed to be safe but it really was dangerous. It was weird to not have colors. I guess that things that at first seem to be good are really bad.

Ron explored some of the themes of the story:

> Starving. He has memories of food. He's still hungry. But he's free. Food is safe. Freedom is surprises. Never saw a bird before. Same-same-same. Before he was starved for colors, memories and choice. Choice. To do what you want. To be who you can be. He won't starve.

Alicia thought about a lesson her mother taught her as she wrote:

> As Jonas fled from the community he lost his memories so that they would go back to the people there. Would they learn from them? Would they remember them? Or would life go on just the same? I think you have to do it yourself if you are going to learn. That's what my mom says. Somebody else can't do it for you. But Jonas did it. He got out with Gabe.

Tomas wrote about the Christmas connection at the end of the story:

> Jonas and Gabe came to the town at Christmas. Why did Lois Lowry do that? Gabe is like the baby Jesus, I think. It is like a rebirth—being born again. Jonas and his old community didn't go to church. Maybe they didn't believe in God. Now Jonas will be a Christian and the people in the church will welcome them. Gabe won't be released. I think Gabe is like Jesus because people tried to release Jesus.

During their grand conversations, students talk about many of the same points they raise in their journal entries. The story fascinates them—at first they think about how simple and safe life would be, but then they think about all the things they take for granted that they'd have to give up to live in Jonas's ordered society. They talk

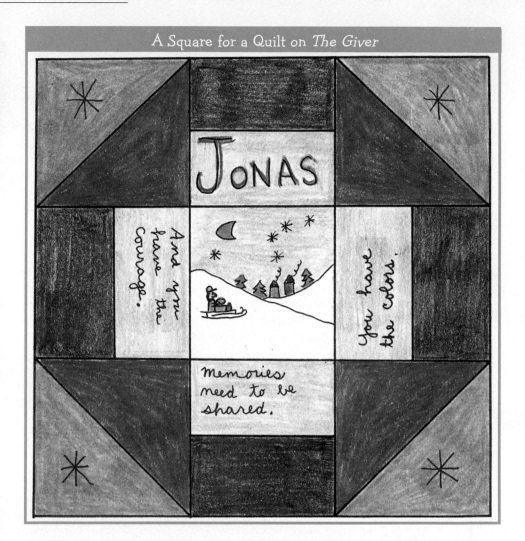

A Square for a Quilt on *The Giver*

JONAS

And you have the courage.

You have the colors.

memories need to be shared.

about bravery and making choices, and they applaud Jonas's decision to flee with Gabriel. They also wonder if Jonas and Gabe survive.

The students collect "important" words from the story for the **word wall**. After reading Chapters 4, 5, and 6, they add these words to the word wall posted in the classroom:

relinquish	bikeports	regulated	infraction
invariably	gravitating	rehabilitation	stirrings
serene	chastisement	assignment	reprieve

Sometimes students choose unfamiliar or long words, but they also choose words such as *assignment* that are important to the story. Students refer to the word wall for words and their spellings when they're writing. Later during the unit, Mrs. Goodman teaches a minilesson about root words using some of these words.

As students read the book, Mrs. Goodman teaches a series of **minilessons** about reading strategies. After students read about colors in the story, for example, she teaches a minilesson on visualizing. She begins by rereading excerpts about Jonas being selected to be the next Receiver and asks students to draw a picture of the scene in their minds. She asks them to focus on the sights, sounds, smells, and feelings, and she talks about how important it is for readers to bring a story to life in their minds. Then students draw pictures of their visualizations and share them in small groups.

Another minilesson is about literary opposites. Mrs. Goodman explains that authors often introduce conflict and develop themes using contrasts or opposites. She asks students to think of opposites in *The Giver*; one example she suggests is *safe* and *free*. Other opposites that the students suggest include the following:

alive—released	families—family units
choice—no choice	memories—no memories
color—black and white	rules—anarchy
conform—do your own thing	stirrings—the pill

Mrs. Goodman asks students to think about how the opposites relate to the story and how Lois Lowry made them explicit in *The Giver*. Students talk about how the community seemed safe at the beginning of the story, but chapter by chapter, Lowry uncovered the community's shortcomings. They also talk about themes of the story reflected in these opposites.

After they finish reading the book, the students have a read-around in which they select and read aloud favorite passages to the class. Then students make a quilt to probe the themes in the story: Each student prepares a paper quilt square with an illustration and several sentences of text. One quilt square is shown on the preceding page. The students decide to use white, gray, and black to represent the sameness of Jonas's community, red for the first color Jonas saw, and colors in the center to represent Elsewhere.

Students also choose projects to work on individually or in small groups. One student makes a book box with objects related to the story, and two others read *Hailstones and Halibut Bones* (O'Neill, 1990), a collection of color poetry, and write their own color poems. One student makes an **open-mind portrait** of Jonas to show his thoughts the night he decided to escape with Gabe. Some students form literature circles to read *Gathering Blue* (2006a) and *The Messenger* (2006c), two related books by Lois Lowry. Others write about their own memories. They use the writing process to draft, refine, and publish their writing, and they share their published pieces as a culminating activity at the end of the unit.

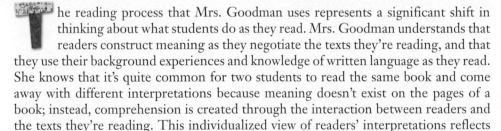

The reading process that Mrs. Goodman uses represents a significant shift in thinking about what students do as they read. Mrs. Goodman understands that readers construct meaning as they negotiate the texts they're reading, and that they use their background experiences and knowledge of written language as they read. She knows that it's quite common for two students to read the same book and come away with different interpretations because meaning doesn't exist on the pages of a book; instead, comprehension is created through the interaction between readers and the texts they're reading. This individualized view of readers' interpretations reflects Rosenblatt's transactive theory (2004).

The reading process involves a series of stages during which readers comprehend the text. The term *text* refers to all reading materials—stories, maps, newspapers, cereal boxes, textbooks, e-mail, and so on; it's not limited to basal reading textbooks. The writing process is a similar recursive process involving a variety of activities as students gather and organize ideas, draft their compositions, revise and edit the drafts, and, finally, publish their writings. Students learn to use the writing process to craft and refine their compositions—autobiographies, stories, reports, poems, and essays.

THE READING PROCESS

Reading is a constructive process of creating meaning that involves the reader, the text, and the purpose within social and cultural contexts. The goal is comprehension, understanding the text and being able to use it for the intended purpose. Readers don't simply look at the words on a page and grasp the meaning; rather, it's a complex process involving these essential components:

Phonemic Awareness and Phonics. Students use their knowledge about the phonological system, including how to manipulate sounds in spoken words and apply phoneme-grapheme correspondences and phonics rules, as they read. They develop these abilities through phonemic awareness and phonics instruction in the primary grades.

Word Identification. Students recognize common or high-frequency words automatically and use their knowledge of phonics and word parts to decode unfamiliar words. Until students can recognize most of the words they're reading, they're slow, word-by-word readers.

Fluency. Students become fluent readers once they recognize most words automatically and read quickly and with expression. This is a milestone because students have limited cognitive resources to devote to reading, and beginning readers use most of this energy to decode words. Fluent readers, in contrast, devote most of their cognitive resources to comprehension.

Vocabulary. Students think about the meaning of words they're reading, choosing appropriate meanings, recognizing figurative uses, and relating them to their background knowledge. Knowing the meaning of words influences comprehension because it's difficult to understand when the words being read don't make sense.

Comprehension. Students use a combination of reader and text factors to understand what they're reading. They predict, connect, monitor, repair, and use other comprehension strategies as well as their knowledge of genres, organizational patterns, and literary devices to create meaning.

These components are supported by scientifically based reading research (National Reading Panel, 2000). As you continue reading this text, you'll learn how teachers teach and assess each of these components.

Teachers use the reading process to involve students in activities to teach, practice, and apply these components. The reading process is organized into five stages: prereading, reading, responding, exploring, and applying. This process is used, no matter which instructional program teachers have chosen, even though some of the activities at each stage differ. Figure 2–1 presents an overview of the reading process.

Stage 1: Prereading

The reading process begins before readers open a book. The first stage, prereading, occurs as readers prepare to read. In the vignette, Mrs. Goodman built her students' background knowledge and stimulated their interest in *The Giver* as they talked about how wonderful life would be in a "perfect" world. As readers get ready to read, they activate background knowledge, set purposes, and make plans for reading.

Activating Background Knowledge. Students have both general and specific background knowledge (Braunger & Lewis, 2006). General knowledge is world knowledge, what students have acquired through life experiences and learning in their home

Figure 2–1 ◆ Key Features of the Reading Process

Stage 1: Prereading
- Activate or build background knowledge and related vocabulary.
- Set purposes.
- Introduce key vocabulary words.
- Make predictions.
- Preview the text.

Stage 2: Reading
- Read independently, with a buddy, or using shared or guided reading, or listen to the text read aloud.
- Apply reading strategies and skills.
- Examine illustrations, charts, and diagrams.
- Read the text from beginning to end.
- Read one or more sections of text to learn specific information.
- Take notes.

Stage 3: Responding
- Write in reading logs.
- Participate in grand conversations or other discussions.

Stage 4: Exploring
- Reread all or part of the text.
- Learn new vocabulary words.
- Participate in minilessons on reading strategies and skills.
- Examine the author's craft.
- Identify memorable quotes.

Stage 5: Applying
- Construct projects.
- Read related books.
- Use information in thematic units.
- Evaluate the reading experience.

communities and at school, and specific knowledge is literary knowledge, what students need to read and comprehend a text. Literary knowledge includes information about reading, genres, and text structures. Students activate their world and literary background knowledge in this stage. They think about the title of a book, look at the book cover and inside illustrations, and read the first paragraph to trigger this activation.

When students don't have enough background knowledge to read a text, teachers build their knowledge base. They build knowledge about reading by teaching reading strategies and skills, knowledge about genres by examining the structure of the genre and explaining how reading varies according to genre, knowledge about a topic by providing a text set of books for students to read, engaging students in discussions, sharing artifacts, and introducing key vocabulary words. It's not enough just to build students' knowledge about the topic; literary knowledge is also essential!

Setting Purposes. The purpose guides students' reading. It provides motivation and direction for reading, as well as a mechanism for students to monitor their reading to see if they're fulfilling their purpose. Sustaining a single purpose while students read the text is more effective than presenting students with a series of purposes (Blanton, Wood, & Moorman, 1990). Sometimes teachers set purposes for reading, and sometimes students set their own purposes. In literature focus units and basal reading textbooks, teachers usually explain how students are expected to read and what they'll do after reading. In contrast, students set their own purposes for reading during literature circles and reading workshop; they choose texts that are intrinsically interesting or that explain something they want to learn more about. As students develop as readers, they become more effective at choosing books and setting their own purposes.

Planning for Reading. Once students activate their background knowledge and identify their purpose for reading, they take their first look at the text and plan for reading. Students vary how they make plans according to the type of selection they're preparing to read. For stories, they make predictions about the characters and events in the story. They often base their predictions on the book's title or the cover illustration. If they've read other stories by the same author or in the same genre, students also use this information in making their predictions. Sometimes students share their predictions orally, and at other times, they write predictions in their reading logs.

Check the Compendium of Instructional Procedures, which follows Chapter 12, for more information on the highlighted terms.

When students are preparing to read informational books and content-area textbook chapters, they preview the selection by flipping through the pages and noting section headings, illustrations, and diagrams. Sometimes they examine the table of contents to see how the book is organized, or they consult the index to locate specific information they want to read. They also notice highlighted terminology that's unfamiliar to them. To help students plan, teachers often use **anticipation guides** and **prereading plans**.

Stage 2: Reading

Students read the book or other selection in the reading stage. Outside of school, most people usually read silently and independently, but in the classroom, teachers and students use five types of reading:

◆ Independent reading
◆ Buddy reading
◆ Guided reading
◆ Shared reading
◆ Reading aloud to students

These types of reading vary in the amount of teacher scaffolding: Teachers provide very little support during independent reading, and the most support as they read aloud to students. As they decide which type of reading to use, teachers consider the purpose for reading, students' reading levels, and the number of available copies of the text.

Independent Reading. When students read independently, they read silently by themselves, for their own purposes, and at their own pace. It's essential that the books students select are at their reading level. Primary-grade students often read the featured selection independently during literature focus units, but this is often after they've already read the selection once or twice with the teacher's assistance. In the upper grades, many students read chapter books independently, but less capable readers may not be able to read the featured book independently. Students also independently read related books from the text set as part of these units.

During reading workshop, students read independently; even first graders can participate by rereading familiar books as well as new books at their reading level. Because students choose the books they want to read, they need to learn how to choose books at an appropriate level of difficulty.

Independent reading is an important part of a balanced reading program because it's the most authentic type of reading. It's the way students develop a love of reading and come to think of themselves as readers. The reading selection, however, must be at an appropriate level of difficulty so that students can read it independently. Otherwise, teachers use another type of reading to scaffold students and make it possible for them to be successful.

Buddy Reading. Students read or reread a selection with a classmate or sometimes with an older student (Friedland & Truesdell, 2004). Buddy reading is an enjoyable social activity, and students can often read selections together that neither one could read individually. Buddy reading is a good alternative to independent reading, and by working together, students are often able to figure out unfamiliar words and talk out comprehension problems.

As teachers introduce buddy reading, they show students how to read with buddies and how to support each other as they read. Students take turns reading aloud to each other or read in unison. They often stop and help each other identify an unfamiliar word or take a minute or two at the end of each page to talk about what they've read. Buddy reading is a valuable way of providing the practice that beginning readers need

Go to the Building Teaching Skills and Dispositions section of Chapter 2 on **MyEducationLab.com** to watch second graders Rakie and Audri participate in buddy reading.

to become fluent; it's also an effective way to work with students with special learning needs and students who are learning English. However, unless the teacher has explained the technique and taught students how to work collaboratively, buddy reading often deteriorates into the stronger of the two buddies reading aloud to the other student, but that isn't the intention of the technique.

Guided Reading. Teachers use **guided reading** to work with groups of four or five students who are reading at the same level. They select a book that students can read at their instructional level, with approximately 90–94% accuracy. Teachers support students' reading and their use of reading strategies during guided reading (Fountas & Pinnell, 1996). Students do the actual reading themselves, although the teacher may read aloud to get them started on the first page or two. Young children often murmur the words softly as they read, which helps the teacher keep track of students' reading and the strategies they're using. Older, more fluent readers usually read silently during guided reading.

Guided reading lessons usually last 25 to 30 minutes. When the students arrive for the small-group lesson, they often reread, either individually or with a buddy, familiar books used in previous lessons. For the new guided reading lesson, students read books that they haven't read before. Beginning readers usually read small picture books at one sitting, but older students who are reading longer chapter books take several days to a week or two to read their books (Allen, 2000).

Teachers observe students as they read during guided reading lessons. They spend a few minutes observing each reader, sitting either in front of or beside the student. They watch for evidence of strategy use and confirm the student's attempts to identify words and solve reading problems. Teachers take notes about their observations and use the information to decide which **minilessons** to teach and which books to choose for students to read.

Shared Reading. Teachers use **shared reading** to read aloud books and other texts that children can't read independently (Holdaway, 1979). Often primary-grade teachers use big books so that both small groups and whole-class groups can see the text and read along. Teachers model what fluent readers do as they involve students in enjoyable reading activities (Fountas & Pinnell, 1996). After reading the text several times, teachers use it to teach phonics concepts and high-frequency words. Students can also read small versions of the book independently or with buddies and use the text's pattern or structure for writing activities.

Shared reading is best known as part of a balanced literacy program in the primary grades. Teachers read aloud books that are appropriate for children's interest level but too difficult for them to read themselves. As an instructional procedure, shared reading differs from reading aloud because children see the text as the teacher reads. Children often join in the reading of predictable refrains and rhyming words, and after listening to the text read several times, they often remember enough of it to read along with the teacher.

Shared reading is also used to read novels with older students when the books are too difficult for them to read independently (Allen, 2002). Teachers distribute copies of the book to all students, and students follow along as the teacher reads aloud. Sometimes students take turns reading sections aloud, but the goal is not for everyone to have a turn reading. Students who want to read and are fluent enough to keep the reading meaningful volunteer to read. Often the teacher begins reading, and when a student wants to take over the reading, he or she begins reading aloud with the teacher; then the teacher drops off and the student continues reading. After a paragraph or a page, another student joins in and the first student drops off. Many teachers call this technique "popcorn reading."

Reading Aloud to Students. Teachers use the interactive read-aloud procedure as they read aloud books that are developmentally appropriate but written above students' reading levels (Fisher, Flood, Lapp, & Frey, 2004). As they read, teachers engage students in activities rather than postponing student involvement until after reading. Students become active participants, for example, as they make predictions, repeat refrains, ask questions, identify big ideas, and make connections. In addition, when teachers read aloud, they model what good readers do and how good readers use reading strategies (Cappellini, 2005). Reading aloud also provides an opportunity for teachers to think aloud about their use of reading strategies.

Read-alouds are an important component of literacy instruction at all grade levels, not just for young children who can't read many books on their own (Allen, 2000). Teachers read books aloud during literature focus units, reading and writing workshop, and thematic units. There are many benefits of reading aloud: introducing vocabulary, modeling comprehension strategies, and increasing students' motivation (Rasinski, 2003).

The types of reading are compared in Figure 2–2. In the vignette at the beginning of this chapter, Mrs. Goodman used a combination of these approaches. She used shared reading as she read the first chapter aloud, with students following in their own copies of *The Giver*. Later, students read together in small groups, with a buddy, or

Figure 2–2 ◆ Types of Reading

Type	Strengths	Limitations
Independent Reading Students read a text on their own without teacher scaffolding.	• Students develop responsibility. • Students learn to select texts. • Experience is authentic.	• Students may not choose texts that they can read independently. • Teacher has little involvement or control.
Buddy Reading Two students take turns as they read a text together.	• Students collaborate and assist each other. • Students become more fluent readers. • Students talk to develop comprehension.	• One student may simply read to the other. • Teacher has little involvement or control.
Guided Reading Teacher supports students as they apply reading strategies and skills to read a text.	• Teacher teaches reading strategies and skills. • Teacher provides scaffolding. • Teacher monitors students' reading.	• Multiple copies of texts at the appropriate reading level are needed. • Teacher controls the reading experience.
Shared Reading Teacher reads aloud while students follow along using a big book or individual copies.	• Teacher teaches concepts about print. • Teacher models fluent reading and reading strategies. • Students become a community of readers.	• Big books or a class set of books are needed. • Text may not be appropriate for all students.
Reading Aloud to Students Teacher reads aloud and provides opportunities for students to be actively involved in the experience.	• Students have access to books they can't read themselves. • Teacher models fluent reading and reading strategies. • Students build background knowledge and vocabulary.	• Students have no opportunity to read. • Students may not be interested in the text.

independently. As teachers plan their instructional programs, they include reading aloud to students, teacher-led student reading, and independent reading each day.

Stage 3: Responding

Students respond to what they've read and continue to negotiate the meaning after reading. This stage reflects Rosenblatt's (2005) transactive theory. Two ways that students make tentative and exploratory comments immediately after reading are by writing in reading logs and participating in grand conversations or other discussions.

Writing in Reading Logs. Students write and draw their thoughts and feelings about what they have read in reading logs. As students write about what they have read, they unravel their thinking and, at the same time, elaborate on and clarify their responses. Students usually write in reading logs when they're reading stories and poems; sometimes they also write in reading logs when they're reading informational books, but during thematic units, they make notes of important information or draw charts and diagrams in learning logs.

Students usually make reading logs by stapling together 10 to 12 sheets of paper. They decorate the covers, keeping with the theme of the book, and write entries after reading. Sometimes students choose topics for their entries, and sometimes teachers pose questions to guide students' thinking about their reading. Teachers monitor students' entries, reading and often responding to them. Because these journals are learning tools, teachers rarely correct students' spellings; they focus their responses on the ideas, but they expect students to spell the title of the book, the names of characters, and high-frequency words accurately. At the end of the unit, teachers review students' work and often grade the reading logs based on whether students completed all the entries and on the quality of the ideas expressed in their entries.

Participating in Discussions. Students also talk about the text with classmates in grand conversations about stories and poems and discussions about informational books and chapters in content-area textbooks. Peterson and Eeds (2007) explain that in grand conversations, students share their personal responses and tell what they liked about the text. After sharing personal reactions, they shift the focus to "puzzle over what the author has written and . . . share what it is they find revealed" (p. 61). Often students make connections between the text and their own lives or between the text and other literature they have read. If they're reading a chapter book, they also make predictions about what might happen in the next chapter.

Teachers often share their ideas in grand conversations, but they act as interested participants, not leaders. The talk is primarily among the students, but teachers ask questions regarding things they are genuinely interested in learning more about and share information in response to questions that students ask. In the past, many discussions have been "gentle inquisitions" during which students recited answers to factual questions that teachers asked to determine whether students read and understood an assignment. Although teachers can still judge whether students have read the assignment, the focus in grand conversations is on clarifying and deepening students' understanding of the story they've read.

Teachers and students also have discussions after reading informational books and chapters in content-area textbooks. Students talk about what interested them and what they learned about the topic, but teachers also focus students' attention on the big ideas, ask clarifying questions, share information, and reread brief excerpts to explore an idea.

These discussions can be held with the whole class or with small groups. Young children usually meet as a class, whereas older students often prefer to talk in small groups. When students meet as a class, there's a feeling of community, and the teacher can be part of the group. When students meet in small groups, they have more opportunities to share their interpretations, but fewer viewpoints are expressed in each group and teachers must move around, spending only a few minutes with each group. Teachers often compromise by having students begin their discussions in small groups and then come together as a class so that the groups can share what they discussed.

Stage 4: Exploring

Students go back into the text to examine it more analytically. This stage is more teacher directed than the others; it reflects the teacher-centered theory. Students reread the selection or excerpts from it, examine the author's craft, and focus on words and sentences from the selection. Teachers also teach minilessons on strategies and skills.

Rereading the Selection. As students reread the selection or excerpts from it, they think again about what they've read. Each time they reread a selection, students benefit in specific ways (Yaden, 1988): They deepen their comprehension as they move beyond their initial focus on the events of a story or the big ideas in an informational book to understanding the theme of the story or the relationships among the big ideas in a nonfiction text.

Examining the Author's Craft. Teachers plan exploring activities to focus students' attention on the genres, text structures, and literary devices that authors use. Students use **story boards** to sequence the events in the story, and make graphic organizers to highlight the plot, characters, and other elements of story structure. Another way students learn about the structure of stories is by writing books based on the selection they have read. In sequels, students tell what happens to the characters after the story ends.

Teachers share information about the author of the featured selection and introduce other books by the same author. Sometimes students read several books by the same author and make comparisons among them. To focus on literary devices, students often reread excerpts to locate examples of onomatopoeia, similes and metaphors, and other types of figurative language and wordplay.

Focusing on Words and Sentences. Teachers and students add "important" words to the **word wall** posted in the classroom. Students refer to it when they write and use the words for word-study activities, including drawing word clusters and posters to highlight particular words, doing **word sorts** to categorize words, and completing **semantic feature analysis** charts.

Students also locate "important" sentences in books they read; these sentences are worthy of examination because they contain figurative language, employ an interesting sentence structure, express a theme, or illustrate a character trait. Students often copy the sentences onto sentence strips to display in the classroom. Sometimes students copy the sentences in their **reading logs** and use them to begin their entries.

Teaching Minilessons. Teachers present **minilessons** on procedures, concepts, strategies, and skills (Angelillo, 2008). They introduce the topic and make connections between the topic and examples in the featured selection students have read. In the vignette, Mrs. Goodman presented minilessons on visualizing and root words and affixes using examples from *The Giver*.

Stage 5: Applying

Readers extend their comprehension, reflect on their understanding, and value the reading experience in this final stage. Often they create projects to apply what they've learned, and these projects take many forms, including **open-mind portraits**, essays, **readers theatre** performances, and PowerPoint presentations. A list of projects is presented in Figure 2–3. Usually students choose which project they want to do and work independently, with a classmate, or in a small group, but sometimes the class decides to work together on a project. In Mrs. Goodman's class, for example, some students wrote color poems while classmates read other books by Lois Lowry or wrote about memories.

Figure 2–3 ◆ Application Projects

Visual Projects
- Design a graphic organizer or model about a book.
- Create a collage to represent the theme or big ideas in a book.
- Prepare illustrations of a story's events to make clothesline props to use in retelling the story.
- Make a book box and fill it with objects and pictures representing the book.
- Construct a paper quilt about a book.
- Create an open-mind portrait to probe the thoughts of one character.

Writing Projects
- Rewrite a story from a different point of view.
- Write another episode or a sequel for a book.
- Write simulated letters from one character to another.
- Create a found poem using words and phrases from a book.
- Write a poem on a topic related to a book.
- Keep a simulated journal from one character's viewpoint.
- Write an essay to examine the book's theme or a controversial issue.
- Create a multigenre project about a book.

Reading Projects
- Read other books from the text set.
- Read another book by the same author.
- Collect several poems that complement the book.

Talk and Drama Projects
- Give a readers theatre presentation of an excerpt from a book.
- Create a choral reading using an excerpt from a book and have classmates read it.
- Write a script and present a play based on a book.
- Dress as a book character and sit on the "hot seat" to answer classmates' questions.
- Present a rap, song, or poem about a book.

Internet Projects
- Write a book review and post it online.
- Investigate an author's website and share information from it with classmates.
- Create a multimodal project about the book using text, images, and sounds.
- Search the Web for information on a topic related to the book and share the results with classmates.
- Create a PowerPoint presentation about the book.

Social Action Projects
- Write a letter to the editor of the local newspaper on a topic related to a book.
- Get involved in a community project related to a book.

Reading Strategies and Skills

Reading is a complex process involving both strategies and skills. Strategies represent the thinking that readers do as they read, whereas skills are quick, automatic behaviors that don't require any thought. For example, readers use the connecting strategy to compare the story they're reading to their own lives, the world around them, and other books they've read. They're actively thinking as they make connections. In contrast, noticing quotation marks that signal a character's dialogue is a skill; students don't have to think about what these punctuation marks are signaling because they recognize their meaning automatically. The terms *strategy* and *skill* can be confusing; sometimes they're considered synonyms, but they're not. It's important to clarify the distinctions between the two.

Strategies are deliberate, goal-directed actions (Afflerbach, Pearson, & Paris, 2008). Readers exercise control in choosing appropriate strategies, using them flexibly, and monitoring their effectiveness. Strategies are linked with motivation. Afflerbach and his colleagues explain that "strategic readers feel confident that they can monitor and improve their own reading so they have both knowledge and motivation to succeed" (p. 370). Strategies reflect the cognitive/information processing theory. In contrast, skills are automatic actions that occur without deliberate control or conscious awareness. The emphasis is on their effortless and accurate use. Skills reflect the behavioral theory, and they're used in the same way, no matter the reading situation. It's crucial that students become both strategic and skilled readers.

Types of Strategies and Skills. Comprehension strategies are probably the best-known type, but readers use strategies throughout the reading process:

Decoding Strategies. Students use strategies, such as using phonic and morphemic analysis, to identify unfamiliar words.

Word-Learning Strategies. Students apply strategies, such as analyzing word parts, to figure out the meaning of unfamiliar words.

Comprehension Strategies. Students use strategies, such as predicting, drawing inferences, and visualizing, to understand what they're reading.

Study Strategies. Students apply strategies, such as taking notes and questioning, to learn information when they're reading content-area textbooks.

You'll learn more about these types of strategies in upcoming chapters.

Students also learn skills that they use when they're reading. Phonics skills are probably the best known, but, like strategies, they're used throughout the reading process. They can be grouped into the same categories as reading strategies:

Decoding Skills. Students use their knowledge of sound-symbol correspondences and phonics rules to decode words.

Word-Learning Skills. Students identify synonyms, recognize metaphors, notice capital letters signaling proper nouns and adjectives, and use other word-learning skills.

Comprehension Skills. Students recognize details and connect them to main ideas, separate fact and opinion, and use other comprehension skills.

Study Skills. Students use skills, including consulting an index and noticing boldface terms in the text, to help them locate and remember information.

Students often use these skills in connection with strategies; the big difference is that strategies are used thoughtfully and skills are automatic.

Guidelines
for Strategy Instruction

▶ Teach strategies in minilessons using explanations, demonstrations, think-alouds, and practice activities.

▶ Provide step-by-step explanations and modeling so that students understand what the strategy does, and how and when to use it.

▶ Provide both guided and independent practice opportunities so that students can apply the strategy in new situations.

▶ Have students apply the strategy in content-area activities as well as in literacy activities.

▶ Teach groups of strategies in routines so that students learn to orchestrate the use of multiple strategies.

▶ Ask students to reflect on their use of single strategies and strategy routines.

▶ Hang charts of strategies and strategy routines students are learning in the classroom, and encourage students to refer to them when reading and writing.

▶ Differentiate between strategies and skills so that students understand that strategies are problem-solving tactics and skills are automatic behaviors.

Minilessons. Students need explicit instruction about reading strategies because they don't acquire the knowledge through reading (Dowhower, 1999; Pressley, 2000). Teachers need to provide three types of information about a strategy for students to learn to use it:

◆ Declarative knowledge—what the strategy does
◆ Procedural knowledge—how to use the strategy
◆ Conditional knowledge—when to use the strategy (Baker & Brown, 1984)

Let's examine the declarative, procedural, and conditional knowledge for the questioning strategy, which is a comprehension strategy that students use to ask themselves questions while they're reading. They use it direct their reading, monitor whether they're understanding, and construct meaning (declarative knowledge). They ask themselves questions such as "What's going to happen next?" "How does this relate to what I know about _____?" and "Does this make sense?" (procedural knowledge). Students use this strategy again and again while they're reading (conditional knowledge).

Teachers use **minilessons** to teach students about strategies. They explain the strategy and model its use, and then students practice using it with teacher guidance and supervision before using it independently. Through this instruction, students develop metacognitive awareness, their ability to think about their strategy use (Paris, Wasik, & Turner, 1991). The feature on this page presents a list of guidelines for strategy instruction.

Teachers demonstrate the thought processes readers use as they read by using **think-alouds** (Wilhelm, 2001). Teachers think aloud or explain what they're thinking while they're reading so that students become more aware of how capable readers think; in the process, students also learn to think aloud about their use of strategies. They set a purpose for reading, predict what will happen next, make connections, ask questions, summarize what's happened so far, draw inferences, evaluate the text, and make other comments that reflect their thinking. Think-alouds are valuable both when teachers model them for students and when students engage in them themselves. When students use think-alouds, they become more thoughtful, strategic readers and improve their ability to monitor their comprehension.

Students can record their strategy use with small self-stick notes. Teachers distribute pads of notes and explain how to use them. Students can focus on their use of a single strategy or a group of strategies. They write comments about the strategies on the self-stick notes while they're reading and place them in the margin of the pages so they can locate them when the book is closed. Afterward, students share their notes and talk about the strategies they used in a discussion with classmates or in a conference with the teacher.

THE WRITING PROCESS

The writing process is a series of five stages that describe what students think and do as they write; the stages are prewriting, drafting, revising, editing, and publishing. The labeling of the stages doesn't mean that the writing process is a linear series of neatly packaged categories; rather, research has shown that the process involves recurring cycles, and labeling is simply an aid to identifying writing activities. In the classroom, the stages merge and recur as students write. The key features of each stage are shown in Figure 2–4.

Stage 1: Prewriting

Prewriting is the "getting ready to write" stage. The traditional notion that writers have a topic completely thought out and ready to flow onto the page is ridiculous: If writers wait for ideas to fully develop, they may wait forever. Instead, writers begin tentatively—talking, reading, brainstorming—to see what they know and in what direction they want to go. Prewriting has probably been the most neglected stage in the writing process; however, it's as crucial to writers as a warm-up is to athletes. Murray (1982) believes that at least 70% of writing time should be spent in prewriting. During prewriting, students choose a topic, consider purpose and form, and gather and organize ideas for writing.

Figure 2–4 ◆ Key Features of the Writing Process

Stage 1: Prewriting

- Choose a topic.
- Consider the purpose for writing.
- Identify the genre the writing will take.
- Engage in rehearsal activities to gather ideas.
- Use a graphic organizer to organize ideas.

Stage 2: Drafting

- Write a rough draft.
- Emphasize ideas rather than mechanical correctness.

Stage 3: Revising

- Reread the rough draft.
- Share writing in writing groups.

- Make substantive changes that reflect classmates' comments.
- Conference with the teacher.

Stage 4: Editing

- Proofread the revised rough draft.
- Identify and correct spelling, capitalization, punctuation, and grammar errors.
- Conference with the teacher.

Stage 5: Publishing

- Make the final copy.
- Share the finished writing with an appropriate audience.

Choosing a Topic. Students should choose their own topics for writing—topics that they're interested in and know about—so that they'll be more engaged, but that isn't always possible. Sometimes teachers provide the topics, especially in connection with literature focus units and content-area units. It's best when teacher-selected topics are broad so students can narrow them in the way that's best for them.

Considering Purpose and Form. As students prepare to write, they need to think about the purpose of their writing: Are they writing to entertain? to inform? to persuade? Setting the purpose for writing is just as important as setting the purpose for reading, because purpose influences decisions students make about form.

One of the most important considerations is the genre or form the writing will take: a story? a letter? a poem? an essay? A writing activity could be handled in any one of these ways. Students learn to use a variety of writing genres; six are described in Figure 2–5. Through reading and writing, students become knowledgeable about these genres and how they're structured (Donovan & Smolkin, 2002). Langer (1985) found that by third grade, students respond in distinctly different ways to story- and report-writing assignments; they organize the writing differently and include varied kinds of information and elaboration. Because students are learning the distinctions between various genres, it's important that teachers use the correct terminology and not label all writing as "stories."

Gathering and Organizing Ideas. Students engage in activities to gather and organize ideas for writing during the prewriting stage. Graves (1983) calls what writers do to prepare for writing "rehearsal" activities. To gather ideas, they draw pictures, brainstorm lists of words, read books, do Internet research, and talk about ideas with classmates. Students make graphic organizers to visually display the arrangement of their ideas. Their choice of graphic organizer varies with the writing genre: For stories, they often use a three-part diagram to emphasize the beginning-middle-end structure of stories, and to write persuasive essays, they use a cluster with one ray to develop the ideas for each argument.

Stage 2: Drafting

Students get their ideas down on paper and write a first draft of their compositions in this stage. Because they don't begin writing with their pieces already composed in their minds, students begin tentatively with the ideas they've developed through prewriting activities. Their drafts are usually messy, reflecting the outpouring of ideas with cross-outs, lines, and arrows as they think of

Teaching Struggling Readers and Writers

The Writing Process

Struggling writers need to use the writing process.

Many struggling writers don't like to write, and they avoid writing whenever possible because they don't know what to do (Christenson, 2002). One of the best ways to review the writing process with struggling writers is to use interactive writing, a procedure normally used with young children, to demonstrate the writing process and the strategies writers use, including organizing and revising. Because it's a group activity, students are more willing to participate.

Once they're familiar with the stages in the writing process, students apply what they've learned to write collaborative compositions. Each student drafts a paragraph or short section and then moves through the writing process; this way, the workload is manageable for both students and their teachers. Once students have learned to use the writing process and have developed a repertoire of writing strategies, they're better prepared to write independently.

Struggling writers who don't understand the writing process often break the process as soon as they write a first draft, thinking their work is finished; they don't realize that they need to revise and edit their writing to communicate more effectively. The key to enticing struggling writers to revise and edit is to help them develop a sense of audience. Many novice writers write primarily for themselves, but when they want their classmates or another audience to understand their message, they begin to recognize the importance of refining their writing. Teachers emphasize audience by encouraging students to share their writing from the author's chair. Lots of writing and sharing are necessary before students learn to appreciate the writing process.

Figure 2–5 ◆ Writing Genres

Genre	Purpose	Activities
Descriptive Writing	Students observe carefully and choose precise language. They take notice of sensory details and create comparisons (metaphors and similes) to make their writing more powerful.	Character sketches Comparisons Descriptive essays Descriptive sentences Found poems
Expository Writing	Students collect and synthesize information. This writing is objective; reports are the most common type. Students use expository writing to give directions, sequence steps, compare one thing to another, explain causes and effects, or describe problems and solutions.	Alphabet books Autobiographies Directions Essays Posters Reports Summaries
Journals and Letters	Students write to themselves and to specific, known audiences. Their writing is personal and often less formal than other genres. They share news, explore new ideas, and record notes. Students learn the special formatting that letters and envelopes require.	Business letters Courtesy letters Double-entry journals E-mail messages Friendly letters Learning logs Personal journals
Narrative Writing	Students retell familiar stories, develop sequels for stories they have read, write stories about events in their own lives, and create original stories. They include a beginning, middle, and end in the narratives to develop the plot and characters.	Original short stories Personal narratives Retellings of stories Sequels to stories Story scripts
Persuasive Writing	Persuasion is winning someone to your viewpoint or cause using appeals to logic, moral character, and emotion. Students present their position clearly and support it with examples and evidence.	Advertisements Book and movie reviews Letters to the editor Persuasive essays Persuasive letters
Poetry Writing	Students create word pictures and play with rhyme and other stylistic devices as they create poems. Through their wordplay, students learn that poetic language is vivid and powerful but concise and that poems can be arranged in different ways on a page.	Acrostic poems Color poems Free verse Haiku "I Am" poems Poems for two voices

better ways to express ideas. Students write quickly, with little concern about legible handwriting, spelling correctness, and careful use of capitalization and punctuation.

When they write rough drafts, students skip every other line to leave space for revisions. They use arrows to move sections of text, cross-outs to delete sections, and scissors and tape to cut apart and rearrange text, just as adult writers do. They write only on one side of a sheet of paper so it can be cut apart or rearranged. Wide spacing between lines is crucial. At first, teachers make small x's on every other line of students' papers as a reminder to skip lines during drafting, but once they understand the importance of leaving space, students skip lines automatically.

Students label their drafts by writing *rough draft* in ink at the top or by using a ROUGH DRAFT stamp. This label indicates to the writer, other students, parents, and administrators that the composition is a draft in which the emphasis is on content, not mechanics; it also explains why the teacher hasn't graded the paper.

Instead of writing drafts by hand, many students, even those in kindergarten through third grade, use computers to compose rough drafts, polish their writing, and print out final copies. There are many benefits of using computers for word processing. Students are often more motivated to write, and they tend to write longer pieces. Their writing looks neater, and they use spell-check programs to identify and correct misspelled words.

Stage 3: Revising

During the revising stage, writers refine ideas in their compositions. Students often break the writing process cycle as soon as they complete a rough draft, believing that once they have jotted down their ideas, the writing task is complete. Experienced writers, however, know they must turn to others for reactions and revise on the basis of these comments. Revision is not just polishing; it is meeting the needs of readers by adding, substituting, deleting, and rearranging material. *Revision* means "seeing again," and in this stage, writers see their compositions again with the help of classmates and the teacher. Revising consists of three activities: rereading the rough draft, sharing the rough draft in a writing group, and revising on the basis of feedback.

Rereading the Rough Draft. After finishing the rough draft, writers need to distance themselves from it for a day or two, then reread it from a fresh perspective, as a reader might. As they reread, students make changes—adding, substituting, deleting, and moving—and place question marks by sections that need work; it is these trouble spots that students ask for help with in their writing groups.

Sharing in Writing Groups. Students meet in **writing groups** to share their compositions with classmates. They respond to the writer's rough draft and suggest possible revisions. Writing groups provide a scaffold in which teachers and classmates talk about plans and strategies for writing and revising (Applebee & Langer, 1983; Calkins, 1983).

Writing **groups** can form spontaneously when several students have completed drafts and are ready to share their compositions, or they can be formal groupings with identified leaders. In some classrooms, writing groups form when four or five students finish writing their rough drafts; students gather around a conference table or in a corner of the classroom and take turns reading their rough drafts aloud. Classmates in the group listen and respond, offering compliments and suggestions for revision. Sometimes the teacher joins the writing group, but if the teacher is involved in something else, students work independently.

In other classrooms, the writing groups are assigned; students get together when all students in the group have completed their rough drafts and are ready to share their writing. Sometimes the teacher participates in these groups, providing feedback along with the students. Or, the writing groups can function independently: Each is made up of four or five students, and a list of groups and their members is posted in the classroom. The teacher puts a star

Literacy Portraits: VIEWING GUIDE

Michael and his classmates are confident writers who willingly share their rough drafts and revise their writing. Watch Michael share his rough draft with Ben in his May video clip. Next, view Michael's February video clip where Ms. Janusz teaches a minilesson on writing effective endings and then conferences with Michael about how he plans to end the story he's writing. You might also check Rhiannon's April video clip of her writing conference with Ms. Janusz. Because Rhiannon's writing is a challenge to read, Ms. Janusz usually combines revising and editing when she works with her. Ideas are born so quickly in Rhiannon's imagination that she forgets about inserting punctuation when she writes, and her abbreviated phonetic spellings are difficult to decipher. Getting students to revise isn't easy. What do you notice in these video clips to suggest why these second graders are so successful?

myeducationlab

by one student's name, and that student serves as a group leader. The leader changes every quarter.

Making Revisions. Students make four types of changes to their rough drafts: additions, substitutions, deletions, and moves (Faigley & Witte, 1981). As they revise, students might add words, substitute sentences, delete paragraphs, and move phrases. Students often use a blue or red pen to cross out, draw arrows, and write in the space left between the double-spaced lines of their rough drafts so that revisions will show clearly; that way, teachers can see the types of revisions students make by examining their revised rough drafts. Revisions are another gauge of students' growth as writers.

Revising Centers. Many teachers set up revising centers to give students revision options: They can talk about the ideas in their rough draft with a classmate, examine the organization of their writing, consider their word choice, or check that they have included all required components in the composition. A list of revising centers is shown in Figure 2–6. Teachers introduce these centers as they teach their students

Figure 2–6 ◆ Revising and Editing Centers

Type	Center	Activities
Revising	Rereading	Students reread their rough drafts with a partner and the partner offers compliments and asks questions.
	Word Choice	Students choose 5–10 words in their rough drafts and look for more specific or more powerful synonyms using a thesaurus, word walls in the classroom, or suggestions from classmates.
	Graphic Organizer	Students draw a chart or diagram to illustrate the organization of their compositions, and they revise their rough drafts if the organization isn't effective or the writing isn't complete.
	Highlighting	Students use highlighter pens to mark their rough drafts according to the teacher's direction. Depending on the skills being taught, students may mark topic sentences, descriptive language, or sensory details.
	Sentence Combining	Students choose a section of their rough drafts with too many short sentences (often signaled by overuse of *and*) and use sentence combining to improve the flow of the writing.
Editing	Spelling	Students work with a partner to proofread their writing. They locate misspelled words and use a dictionary to correct them. Students may also check for specific errors in their use of recently taught skills.
	Homophones	Students check their rough drafts for homophone errors (e.g., *there–their–they're*), and consulting a chart posted in the center, they correct the errors.
	Punctuation	Students proofread their writing to check for punctuation marks. They make corrections as needed, and then highlight the punctuation marks in their compositions.
	Capitalization	Students check that each sentence begins with a capital letter, the word *I* is capitalized, and proper nouns and adjectives are capitalized. After the errors are corrected, students highlight all capitalized letters in the compositions.
	Sentences	Students analyze the sentences in their rough drafts and categorize them as simple, compound, complex, or fragment on a chart. Then they make any necessary changes.

about the writing process and the qualities of good writing, and then students work at these centers before or after participating in a writing group. Teachers usually provide a checklist of center options that students put in their writing folders, and then they check off the centers that they complete. Through these center activities, students develop a repertoire of revising strategies and personalize their writing process.

Stage 4: Editing

Editing is putting the piece of writing into its final form. Until this stage, the focus has been primarily on the content of students' writing. Once the focus changes to mechanics, students polish their writing by correcting spelling mistakes and other mechanical errors. Mechanics are the commonly accepted conventions of written Standard English; they consist of capitalization, punctuation, spelling, sentence structure, usage, and formatting considerations specific to poems, scripts, letters, and other writing genres. The use of these commonly accepted conventions is a courtesy to those who will read the composition.

Students are more efficient editors if they set the composition aside for a few days before beginning to edit. After working so closely with a piece of writing during drafting and revising, they're too familiar with it to notice many mechanical errors. With the distance gained by waiting a few days, students are better able to approach editing with a fresh perspective and gather the enthusiasm necessary to finish the writing process. Then students move through two activities in the editing stage: proofreading to locate errors and correcting the ones they find.

Proofreading. Students proofread their compositions to locate and mark possible errors. Proofreading is a unique type of reading in which students read word by word, hunting for errors rather than reading for meaning. Concentrating on mechanics is difficult because of our natural inclination to read for meaning; even experienced proofreaders often find themselves focusing on comprehension and thus overlooking errors that don't inhibit meaning. It's important, therefore, to take time to explain proofreading to students and to demonstrate how it differs from regular reading.

To demonstrate proofreading, teachers copy a piece of writing on the chalkboard or display it on an overhead projector. The teacher reads it several times, each time hunting for a particular type of error. During each reading, the teacher reads the composition slowly, softly pronouncing each word and touching it with a pencil or pen to focus attention on it. The teacher marks possible errors as they are located.

Editing checklists help students focus on particular types of errors. Teachers can develop checklists with two to six items appropriate for the grade level. A first-grade checklist, for example, might have only two items—perhaps one about capital letters at the beginning of sentences and a second about periods at the end of sentences. In contrast, a middle-grade checklist might contain items such as using commas in a series, indenting paragraphs, capitalizing proper nouns and adjectives, and spelling homonyms correctly. Teachers revise the checklist during the school year to focus attention on skills that have recently been taught.

A third-grade editing checklist is presented in the Assessment Tools feature on page 58. The writer and a classmate work as partners to edit their compositions. First, students proofread their own compositions, searching for errors in each category on the checklist, and, after proofreading, check off each item. After completing the checklist, students sign their names and trade checklists and compositions: Now they become editors and complete each other's checklist. Having both writer and editor sign the checklist helps them to take the activity seriously.

Assessment Tools

A Third-Grade Editing Checklist

Author	Editor	
☐	☐	1. I have circled the words that might be misspelled.
☐	☐	2. I have checked that all sentences begin with capital letters.
☐	☐	3. I have checked that all sentences end with punctuation marks.
☐	☐	4. I have checked that all proper nouns begin with a capital letter.

Signatures:

Author: _____ Editor: _____

Correcting Errors. After students proofread their compositions and locate as many errors as they can, they use red pens to correct the errors independently or with an editor's assistance. Some errors are easy to correct, some require use of a dictionary, and others involve instruction from the teacher. It is unrealistic to expect students to locate and correct every mechanical error in their compositions; not even published books are always error-free! Once in a while, students may change a correct spelling or punctuation mark and make it incorrect, but they correct far more errors than they create.

Students also work at editing centers to check for and correct specific types of errors. A list of editing centers is also shown in Figure 2–6. Teachers often vary the activities at the center to reflect the types of errors students are making. Students who continue to misspell common words can check for these words on a chart posted in the center. Or, after a series of lessons on contractions or punctuation marks, for example, one or more centers will focus on applying the newly taught skill.

Editing can end after students and their editors correct as many mechanical errors as possible, or after students meet with the teacher for a final editing conference. When mechanical correctness is crucial, this conference is important. Teachers proofread the composition with the student, and they identify and make the remaining corrections together, or the teacher makes checkmarks in the margin to note errors for the student to correct independently.

Stage 5: Publishing

In this stage, students bring their compositions to life by writing final copies and by sharing them orally with an appropriate audience. When they share their writing with real audiences of classmates, other students, parents, and the community, students come to think of themselves as authors. Publication is powerful: Students are motivated not only to continue writing but also to improve the quality of their writing through revising and editing (Weber, 2002).

Making Books. One of the most popular ways for students to publish their writing is by making books. Simple booklets can be made by folding a sheet of paper into quarters, like a greeting card. Students write the title on the front and use the three remaining sides for their composition. They can also construct booklets by stapling sheets of writing paper together and adding covers made out of construction paper. Sheets of wallpaper cut from old sample books also make sturdy covers. These stapled booklets can be cut into various shapes, too. Students can make more sophisticated books by covering cardboard covers with contact paper, wallpaper samples, or cloth. Pages are sewn or stapled together, and the first and last pages (endpapers) are glued to the cardboard covers to hold the book together.

Sharing Writing. One of the best ways for students to share their writing is to sit in a special chair in the classroom called the *author's chair* and read their writing aloud to classmates. Afterward, classmates ask questions, offer compliments, and celebrate the completion of the writing project. Sharing writing is a social activity that helps writers develop sensitivity to audiences and confidence in themselves as authors. Beyond just providing the opportunity for students to share writing, teachers need to teach students how to make appropriate comments as they respond to their classmates' writing. Teachers also serve as a model for responding to students' writing without dominating the sharing.

Here are some other ways for students to share their writing:

◆ Read it to parents and siblings
◆ Share it at a back-to-school event
◆ Place it in the class or school library
◆ Read it to students in other classes
◆ Display it as a mobile or on a poster
◆ Contribute it to a class anthology
◆ Post it on the class website
◆ Submit it to the school's literary magazine
◆ Display it at a school or community event
◆ Send it to a children's literary magazine
◆ Submit it to an e-zine (online literary magazine)

The best literary magazines for students are *Stone Soup* and *Skipping Stones*. *Stone Soup* is a magazine of children's writing and artwork for children ages 8–13. This prestigious magazine seeks children's stories and poems. At its website (www.stonesoup. com), students can download a sample issue and listen to authors reading their own writing. Subscription information is available there as well as directions for submitting students' writing. *Skipping Stones* is an international magazine for children ages 8–16 that accepts stories, articles, photos, cartoons, letters, and drawings. This award-winning publication focuses on global interdependence, celebrates cultural and environmental richness, and provides a forum for children from around the world to share ideas and experiences. To read excerpts from the current issue and to get information about subscribing and submitting writing to *Skipping Stones*, go to the magazine's

Author's Chair
These fifth graders take turns sitting in the special author's chair to read their published writings aloud to classmates. It's a celebratory activity, and after reading, students take turns asking questions and offering compliments. These students have learned to show interest in their classmates' writing and to think about the writing so that they can participate in the discussion that follows the reading. Afterward, another student is cho-sen to share, and the pro-cess is repeated. As students sharing their writing from the author's chair, they learn to think of themselves as authors and consider their audience more carefully when they write.

website at www.skippingstones.org. Many teachers subscribe to these magazines and use the writings as models when they're teaching writing. Other literary magazines worth considering are *Magic Dragon* (www.magicdragonmagazine.com) and *New Moon: The Magazine for Girls and Their Dreams* (www.newmoon.org). Too often, literary magazines are labors of love rather than viable financial ventures, so even highly esteemed and popular magazines go out of business. Students should always check that a literary magazine is still accepting submissions before sending their writing.

Writing Strategies and Skills

Writing strategies are like reading strategies; they're tools students use deliberately to craft effective compositions. Students apply many of the same strategies for both reading and writing, such as activating background knowledge, questioning, repairing, and evaluating, and they also use some specific writing strategies. Dean (2006) explains that using the writing process makes writers more strategic, and writers use a variety of strategies at each stage:

Prewriting Strategies. Students use prewriting strategies, including organizing, to develop ideas before beginning to write. Examples: generating ideas and organizing ideas.

Drafting Strategies. Students apply drafting strategies to focus on ideas while writing the first draft. Examples: narrowing the topic and providing examples.

Revising Strategies. Students use revising strategies to communicate their ideas more effectively. Examples: rereading, detecting problems, elaborating ideas, combining sentences, and choosing precise words.

New Literacies
Online Publication Sites

The Internet offers unlimited opportunities for students to display their writing online, share it with a global audience, and receive authentic feedback from readers (McNabb, 2006). When students create multimodal projects that incorporate audio, video, animation, or graphics into their writing, electronic publication is essential so that readers can fully experience what students are communicating. Students are learning to use new literacies when they express their ideas with multimodal features and engage in online communication (Labbo, 2005).

Here's a list of five of the best online publication sites for students:

Cyber Kids

www.cyberkids.com
This site publishes original writing, mostly stories and poetry, written by 7- to 16-year-olds. The multimodal stories are especially interesting.

Kids' Space

www.kids-space.org
This website posts children's art, writing, and music pieces from around the world. In the writing category, stories, play scripts, and poems written by 5- to 16-year-olds are invited.

KidsWWwrite

www.kalwriters.com/kidswwwrite
Students' stories and poems are published in this e-zine that's divided into areas for 5- to 8-year-olds, 9- to 12-year-olds, and 13- to 16-year-olds.

Poetry Zone

www.poetryzone.ndirect.co.uk
This British website posts students' poetry in the Poetry Gallery and provides other poetry resources for teachers.

Stories From the Web

www.storiesfromtheweb.org
This website, divided into preschool–grade 1, grades 2–5, and grades 6–8 areas, accepts submissions of students' stories, play scripts, poems, raps, and songs.

Students can also use Internet search engines to locate new e-zines. It's inevitable that some online publication websites will shut down, but others will spring up to take their place.

Each electronic magazine posts its own guidelines for contributors and submission information that students should read and follow. Most e-zines specify that students' submissions must be original, and that writing that deals with violent or offensive topics or that employs inappropriate language won't be published. Students usually aren't paid for their writing. Submissions must be ready for posting; it's naïve to assume that an editor will format students' writing or correct misspellings and other mechanical errors. Students usually complete an online information sheet and e-mail their writing to the e-zine's website, and parents are required to submit a statement giving permission for their child's writing to be posted online.

Students can also display their writing on the class website for others to read and respond to in guest books, blogs, and e-mail messages (Weber, 2002). Even first graders can access and read the writing posted on their class website (McGowan, 2005)! If the teacher doesn't have a class website, students can work with their teacher to create one and post their writing there.

Editing Strategies. Students apply strategies to identify and correct spelling and other mechanical errors. Example: proofreading.

Publishing Strategies. Students use strategies to prepare the final drafts of their compositions and share them with classmates and other authentic audiences. Examples: designing the layout and reading expressively.

Students use these writing strategies purposefully as they draft and refine their writing.

Writing skills are knowledge-based, automatic actions that students learn to apply during the writing process. Here are five types of skills that writers use:

Content Skills. Students apply skills, including topic sentences, to arrange information into paragraphs. These skills are most important during the drafting and revising stages.

Word Skills. Students use skills, including synonyms and metaphors, during drafting and revising to make their writing clearer.

Sentence Skills. Students apply skills, including types of sentences, to make their writing more interesting to read. They use these skills during drafting and revising.

Grammar Skills. Students use skills, including verb tenses and subject-verb agreement, to correct any nonstandard English errors during editing.

Mechanical Skills. Students apply spelling, capitalization, and punctuation skills to make their compositions more readable, especially during the editing stage.

Teachers use minilessons with demonstrations and **think-alouds** to teach writing strategies and skills, and then students apply what they're learning during guided practice and independent writing projects. These strategies and skills are often reflected in **rubrics** that teachers and students use to assess students' writing.

Qualities of Good Writing

Students learn about the qualities of good writing through **minilessons** and apply what they're learning as they use the writing process. Spandel (2005) has identified these six qualities, which she calls *traits*:

Ideas. The ideas are the essence of a composition. Students choose an interesting idea and then narrow and develop it using main ideas and details. They choose an idea during prewriting and develop it as they draft and revise their writing.

Organization. The organization is the skeleton of the composition. Students hook the reader in the beginning, identify the purpose, present ideas logically, provide transitions between ideas, and end with a satisfying conclusion so that the important questions are answered. Students organize their writing during prewriting and follow their plans as they draft.

Voice. The writer's distinctive style is voice; it's what breathes life into a piece of writing. Culham (2003) calls voice "the writer's music coming out through the words" (p. 102). During the drafting and revising stages, students create voice in their writing through the words they use, the sentences they craft, and the tone they adopt.

Word Choice. Careful word choice makes the meaning clear and the composition more interesting to read. Students learn to choose lively verbs and specific nouns, adjectives, and adverbs; create word pictures; and use idiomatic expressions as they craft their pieces. They focus on word choice as they draft and revise their writing.

Sentence Fluency. Sentence fluency is the rhythm and flow of language. Students vary the length and structure of their writing so that it has a natural cadence and is easy to read aloud. They develop sentence fluency as they draft, revise, and edit their writing.

Mechanics. The mechanics are spelling, capitalization, punctuation, and grammar. In the editing stage, students proofread their compositions and correct spelling and grammar errors to make the writing easier to read.

Teachers teach series of lessons about each quality. They explain the quality, show examples from children's literature and students' own writing, involve students in activities to investigate and experiment with the quality, and encourage students to apply what they've learned in their own writing as they move through the writing process. Figure 2–7 presents a list of books and activities that teachers can use in teaching the qualities of good writing.

Figure 2–7 ◆ Teaching the Qualities of Good Writing

Quality	Books	Ways to Teach
Ideas	Baylor, B. (1995). *I'm in charge of celebrations*. New York: Aladdin Books. (P–M–U) Moss, T. (1998). *I want to be*. New York: Puffin Books. (P–M) Van Allsburg, C. (1996). *The mysteries of Harris Burdick*. Boston: Houghton Mifflin. (M–U) Wyeth, S. D. (2002). *Something beautiful*. New York: Dragonfly. (P–M–U)	• Read aloud books with well-developed ideas. • Choose photos, pictures, or objects to write about. • Quickwrite to narrow and develop an idea. • Make graphic organizers to develop an idea.
Organization	Brown, M. W. (2006). *Another important book*. New York: HarperTrophy. (P–M) Fanelli, S. (2007). *My map book*. New York: Walker. (P–M) Fleischman, P. (2004). *Seedfolks*. New York: HarperTrophy. (M–U) Ryan, P. M. (2001). *Mice and beans*. New York: Scholastic. (P–M)	• Analyze the structure of a book using a graphic organizer. • Collect effective leads from books. • Find examples of effective transitions in books. • Collect effective endings from books.
Voice	Browne, A. (2001). *Voices in the park*. New York: Dorling Kindersley. (P–M) Hesse, K. (2001). *Witness*. New York: Scholastic. (U) Ives, D. (2005). *Scrib*. New York: HarperCollins. (M–U) Raschka, C. (2007). *Yo! Yes?* New York: Scholastic. (P)	• Read aloud books with strong voices. • Have students describe the voice in a text. • Personalize a story by telling it from one character's viewpoint. • Add emotion to a voiceless piece of writing.
Word Choice	Barrett, J. (2001). *Things that are the most in the world*. New York: Aladdin Books. (P–M) Leedy, L., & Street, P. (2003). *There's a frog in my throat! 440 animal sayings a little bird told me*. New York: Holiday House. (P–M–U) Scieszka, J. (2001). *Baloney (Henry P.)* New York: Viking. (M) Shannon, G. (1999). *Tomorrow's alphabet*. New York: HarperTrophy. (P–M)	• Read aloud books with good word choice. • Collect lively and precise words. • Learn to use a thesaurus. • Craft metaphors and similes.
Sentence Fluency	Aylesworth, J. (1995). *Old black fly*. New York: Henry Holt. (P) Grimes, N. (2002). *My man blue*. New York: Puffin Books. (M) Grossman, B. (1998). *My little sister ate one hare*. New York: Dragonfly. (P–M) Locker, T. (2003). *Cloud dance*. San Diego: Voyager. (M)	• Do choral readings of books with sentence fluency. • Collect favorite sentences on sentence strips. • Practice writing alliterative sentences. • Reread favorite books.
Mechanics	Holm, J. L. (2007). *Middle school is worse than meatloaf: A year told through stuff*. New York: Atheneum. (U) Pattison, D. (2003). *The journey of Oliver K. Woodman*. San Diego: Harcourt Brace. (M) Pulver, R. (2003). *Punctuation takes a vacation*. New York: Holiday House. (P–M–U) Truss, L. (2006). *Eats, shoots & leaves: Why commas really do make a difference!* New York: Putnam. (M)	• Proofread excerpts from books to find mechanical errors that have been added. • Add capital letters to excerpts that have had them removed. • Add punctuation marks to excerpts that have had them removed. • Correct grammar errors that have been added to excerpts from books.

Adapted from Culham (2003); Spandel (2001, 2005).
P = primary grades (K–2); M = middle grades (3–5); U = upper grades (6–8)

As students study the six qualities, they internalize what good writers do. They learn to recognize good writing, develop a vocabulary for talking about writing, become better able to evaluate their own writing, and acquire strategies for improving the quality of their writing.

Assessment Tools

Writing

Teachers use rubrics to assess the quality of students' compositions. Some rubrics are general and can be used for almost any writing assignment, whereas others are designed for a specific writing assignment. Sometimes teachers use rubrics developed by school districts; at other times, they develop their own rubrics to assess the specific components and qualities they have stressed. Rubrics should have 4 to 6 achievement levels and address ideas, organization, language, and mechanics. Teachers often search the Internet for writing rubrics they can adapt and use. Many rubrics are available that have been developed by teachers, school districts, state departments of education, and publishers of educational materials.

Second-Grade Rubric for Stories	
5	Writing has an original title. Story shows originality, sense of humor, or cleverness. Writer uses paragraphs to organize ideas. Writing contains few spelling, capitalization, or punctuation errors. Writer varies sentence structure and word choice. Writer shows a sense of audience.
4	Writing has an appropriate title. Beginning, middle, and end of the story are well developed. A problem or goal is identified in the story. Writing includes details that support plot, characters, and setting. Writing is organized into paragraphs. Writing contains few capitalization and punctuation errors. Writer spells most high-frequency words correctly.
3	Writing may have a title. Writing has at least two of the three parts of a story (beginning-middle-end). Writing shows a sequence of events. Writing is not organized into paragraphs. Spelling, grammar, capitalization, or punctuation errors may interfere with meaning.
2	Writing has at least one of the three parts of a story (beginning-middle-end). Writing shows a partial sequence of events. Writing is brief and underdeveloped. Spelling, grammar, capitalization, and punctuation errors interfere with meaning.
1	Writing lacks a sense of story. Illustrations suggest a story. Writing is brief. Some words are recognizable, but the writing is difficult to read.

Assessing Students' Writing

Teachers assess both the process students use as they write and the quality of their compositions. They observe as students use the writing process to develop their compositions and conference with students as they revise and edit their writing. Teachers notice, for example, whether students use writing strategies to organize ideas for writing and whether they take into account feedback from classmates when they revise. So that students can document their writing process activities, teachers also have them keep all drafts of their compositions in writing folders.

Teachers develop **rubrics**, or scoring guides, to assess the quality of students' writing (Farr & Tone, 1994). Rubrics make the analysis of writing simpler and the assessment process more reliable and consistent. They may have 4, 5, or 6 levels, with descriptors related to ideas, organization, language, and mechanics at each level. Some rubrics are general and are appropriate for almost any writing assignment, whereas others are designed for a specific writing assignment. The Assessment Tools feature on the preceding page presents a second-grade rubric.

Teachers use rubrics to assess writing. They read the composition and highlight words and phrases in the rubric that best describe it. Usually sentences in more than one level are marked, so the score is determined by examining the highlighted sentences and noting which level is marked most often.

Students, too, can learn to create rubrics to assess the quality of their writing. To be successful, they need to analyze examples of other students' writing and determine the qualities that demonstrate strong, average, and weak papers; teachers need to model how to address the qualities at each level in the rubric. Skillings and Ferrell (2000) taught second and third graders to develop the criteria for evaluating their writing, and the students moved from using the rubrics their teachers prepared to creating their own 3-point rubrics, which they labeled as the "very best" level, the "okay" level, and the "not so good" level. Perhaps the most important outcome of teaching students to create rubrics, according to Skillings and Ferrell, is that students develop metacognitive strategies and the ability to think about themselves as writers.

READING AND WRITING ARE RECIPROCAL PROCESSES

Reading and writing are reciprocal; they're both constructive, meaning-making processes. Researchers have found that reading leads to better writing, and writing has the same effect on reading (Spivey, 1997). Not surprisingly, they've also learned that integrating instruction improves both reading and writing (Tierney & Shanahan, 1991). It's possible that students use the same type of thinking for both reading and writing (Braunger & Lewis, 2006).

Comparing the Two Processes

The reading and writing processes have comparable activities at each stage (Butler & Turbill, 1984). A comparison of the two processes is shown in Figure 2–8. For example, notice the similarities between the activities in the third stage of reading and writing—responding and revising, respectively. Fitzgerald (1989) analyzed these two activities and concluded that they draw on similar author-reader-text interactions. Similar analyses can be made for other stages as well.

Figure 2–8 ◆ A Comparison of the Reading and Writing Processes

	What Readers Do	What Writers Do
Stage 1	**Prereading** Readers use knowledge about • the topic • reading • genres • cueing systems	**Prewriting** Writers use knowledge about • the topic • writing • genres • cueing systems
Stage 2	**Reading** Readers • use word-identification strategies • use comprehension strategies • monitor reading • create meaning	**Drafting** Writers • use transcription strategies • use meaning-making strategies • monitor writing • create meaning
Stage 3	**Responding** Readers • respond to the text • deepen meaning • clarify misunderstandings • expand ideas	**Revising** Writers • respond to the text • deepen meaning • clarify misunderstandings • expand ideas
Stage 4	**Exploring** Readers • examine the impact of words and literary language • explore structural elements • compare the text to others	**Editing** Writers • identify and correct mechanical errors • review paragraph and sentence structure
Stage 5	**Applying** Readers • create projects • share projects with classmates • reflect on the reading process • feel success • want to read again	**Publishing** Writers • make the final copy of their compositions • share their compositions with genuine audiences • reflect on the writing process • feel success • want to write again

Tierney (1983) explains that reading and writing involve concurrent, complex transactions between writers as readers and readers as writers. It seems natural that writers read other authors' books for ideas and to learn about organizing their writing, and they also read and reread their own writing as they revise to communicate more effectively. The quality of these reading experiences seems closely tied to success in writing. Thinking of readers as writers may be more difficult, but readers participate in many of the same activities that writers use—activating background knowledge, setting purposes, determining importance, monitoring, repairing, and evaluating.

Classroom Connections

Many classroom activities involve both reading and writing. Making connections between reading and writing is a natural part of classroom life. Students read and then write or write and then read: They write reading log entries after reading to deepen their understanding of what they've read, for example, or they make graphic organizers to organize the information they're reading in a content-area textbook or informational book. Similarly, they read rough drafts aloud to make sure they flow and then read them to classmates to get feedback on how well they're communicating, or they use a structural pattern from a poem they've read in one they're writing. Shanahan (1988) outlined these guidelines for connecting reading and writing so that students develop a clearer understanding of literacy:

◆ Involve students in daily reading and writing experiences.
◆ Introduce the reading and writing processes in kindergarten.
◆ Plan instruction that reflects the developmental nature of reading and writing.
◆ Make the reading-writing connection explicit to students.
◆ Emphasize both the processes and the products of reading and writing.
◆ Set clear purposes for reading and writing.
◆ Teach reading and writing through authentic literacy experiences.

It's not enough, however, for students to see themselves as readers and writers; they need to grasp the relationships between the two roles and move flexibly between them. Readers think like writers to understand the author's purpose and viewpoint, for instance, and writers assume alternative viewpoints as potential readers.

Chapter 2 Review

How Effective Teachers Teach the Reading and Writing Processes

▶ Teachers use the reading process—prereading, reading, responding, exploring, and applying—to ensure that students comprehend books they read.

▶ Teachers use independent reading, buddy reading, guided reading, shared reading, and interactive read-alouds to share books with students.

▶ Teachers teach students how to use the writing process—prewriting, drafting, revising, editing, and publishing—to write and refine their compositions.

▶ Teachers teach students about the qualities of good writing—ideas, organization, voice, word choice, sentence fluency, and conventions.

▶ Teachers understand that reading and writing are reciprocal meaning-making processes.

PEARSON
myeducationlab
Where the Classroom Comes to Life

Go to MyEducationLab at www.myeducationlab.com to deepen your understanding of the concepts presented in this chapter:

▶ Examine how the second graders in Ms. Janusz's classroom revise their writing by viewing video segments in the Literacy Portraits.
▶ Check your understanding of chapter concepts with the multiple-choice and essay quizzes in the Study Plan.
▶ Apply some of the main ideas discussed in the chapter in the Activities and Applications section of the website.
▶ Practice what you've learned in this chapter in Building Teaching Skills and Dispositions before applying the ideas in your own classroom.

PROFESSIONAL REFERENCES

Afflerbach, P., Pearson, P. D., & Paris, S. G. (2008). Clarifying differences between reading skills and reading strategies. *The Reading Teacher, 61,* 364–373.

Allen, J. (2000). *Yellow brick road: Shared and guided paths to independent reading, 4–12.* Portland, ME: Stenhouse.

Allen, J. (2002). *On the same page: Shared reading beyond the primary grades.* Portland, ME: Stenhouse.

Angelillo, J. (2008). *Whole-class teaching: Minilessons and more.* Portsmouth, NH: Heinemann.

Applebee, A. N., & Langer, J. A. (1983). Instructional scaffolding: Reading and writing and natural language activities. *Language Arts, 60,* 168–175.

Baker, L., & Brown, A. (1984). Metacognitive skills of reading. In P. D. Pearson, M. Kamil, P. Mosenthal, & R. Barr (Eds.), *Handbook of reading research* (pp. 353–394). New York: Longman.

Blanton, W. E., Wood, K. D., & Moorman, G. B. (1990). The role of purpose in reading instruction. *The Reading Teacher, 43,* 486–493.

Braunger, J., & Lewis, J. P. (2006). *Building a knowledge base in reading* (2nd ed.). Newark, DE: International Reading Association/National Council of Teachers of English.

Butler, A., & Turbill, J. (1984). *Towards a reading-writing classroom.* Portsmouth, NH: Heinemann.

Calkins, L. M. (1983). *Lessons from a child: On the teaching and learning of writing.* Portsmouth, NH: Heinemann.

Cappellini, M. (2005). *Balancing reading and language learning: A resource for teaching English language learners, K–5.* York, ME: Stenhouse.

Christenson, T. A. (2002). *Supporting struggling writers in the elementary classroom.* Newark, DE: International Reading Association.

Culham, R. (2003). *6 + 1 traits of writing.* New York: Scholastic.

Dean, D. (2006). *Strategic writing.* Urbana, IL: National Council of Teachers of English.

Donovan, C. A., & Smolkin, L. B. (2002). Children's genre knowledge: An examination of K–5 students' performance on multiple tasks providing differing levels of scaffolding. *Reading Research Quarterly, 37,* 428–465.

Dowhower, S. L. (1999). Supporting a strategic stance in the classroom: A comprehension framework for helping teachers help students to be strategic. *The Reading Teacher, 52,* 672–688.

Faigley, L., & Witte, S. (1981). Analyzing revision. *College Composition and Communication, 32,* 400–410.

Farr, R., & Tone, B. (1994). *Portfolio and performance assessment.* Orlando: Harcourt Brace.

Fisher, D., Flood, J., Lapp, D., & Frey, N. (2004). Interactive read-alouds: Is there a common set of implementation practices? *The Reading Teacher, 58,* 8–17.

Fitzgerald, J. (1989). Enhancing two related thought processes: Revision in writing and critical thinking. *The Reading Teacher, 43,* 42–48.

Fountas, I. C., & Pinnell, G. S. (1996). *Guided reading: Good first teaching for all children.* Portsmouth, NH: Heinemann.

Friedland, E. S., & Truesdell, K. S. (2004). Kids reading together. *The Reading Teacher, 58,* 76–83.

Graves, D. H. (1983). *Writing: Teachers and children at work.* Exeter, NH: Heinemann.

Holdaway, D. (1979). *The foundations of literacy.* Portsmouth, NH: Heinemann.

Labbo, L. D. (2005). Fundamental qualities of effective Internet literacy instruction: An exploration of worthwhile classroom practices. In R. A. Karchmer, M. H. Mallette, J. Kara-Soteriou, & D. J. Leu, Jr. (Eds.), *Innovative approaches to literacy education: Using the Internet to support new literacies* (pp. 165–179). Newark, DE: International Reading Association.

Langer, J. A. (1985). Children's sense of genre. *Written Communication, 2,* 157–187.

McGowan, M. (2005). My Internet projects and other online resources for the literacy classroom. In R. A. Karchmer, M. H. Mallette, J. Kara-Soteriou, & D. J. Leu, Jr. (Eds.), *Innovative approaches to literacy education: Using the Internet to support new literacies* (pp. 85–102). Newark, DE: International Reading Association.

McNabb, M. L. (2006). *Literacy learning in networked classrooms: Using the Internet with middle-level students.* Newark, DE: International Reading Association.

Murray, D. H. (1982). *Learning by teaching.* Montclair, NJ: Boynton/Cook.

National Reading Panel. (2000). *Teaching children to read: An evidence-based assessment of the scientific research literature on reading and its implications for reading instruction.* Washington, DC: National Institute of Child Health and Human Development.

Paris, S. G., Wasik, D. A., & Turner, J. C. (1991). The development of strategic readers. In R. Barr, M. L. Kamil, P. B. Mosenthal, & P. D. Pearson (Eds.), *Handbook of reading research* (Vol. 2, pp. 609–640). New York: Longman.

Peterson. R., & Eeds, M. (2007). *Grand conversations: Literature groups in action* (updated ed). New York: Scholastic.

Pressley, M. (2000). What should comprehension instruction be instruction of? In M. L. Kamil, P. B. Mosenthal, P. D. Pearson, & R. Barr (Eds.), *Handbook of reading research* (Vol. 3, pp. 545–561). Mahwah, NJ: Erlbaum.

Rasinski, T. V. (2003). *The fluent reader.* New York: Scholastic.

Rosenblatt, L. M. (2004). The transactive theory of reading and writing. In R. B. Ruddell & N. J. Unrau (Eds.), *Theoretical models and processes of reading* (5th ed., pp. 1363–1398). Newark, DE: International Reading Association.

Rosenblatt, L. (2005). *Making meaning with texts: Selected essays*. Portsmouth, NH: Heinemann.

Shanahan, T. (1988). The reading-writing relationship: Seven instructional principles. *The Reading Teacher, 41*, 636–647.

Skillings, M. J., & Ferrell, R. (2000). Student-generated rubrics: Bringing students into the assessment process. *The Reading Teacher, 53*, 452–455.

Spandel, V. (2001). *Books, lessons, ideas for teaching the six traits*. Wilmington, MA: Great Source.

Spandel, V. (2005). *Creating writers through 6-trait writing assessment and instruction* (4th ed.). Boston: Allyn & Bacon.

Spivey, N. (1997). *The constructivist metaphor: Reading, writing, and the making of meaning*. New York: Academic Press.

Tierney, R. J. (1983). Writer-reader transactions: Defining the dimensions of negotiation. In P. L. Stock (Ed.), *Forum: Essays on theory and practice in the teaching of writing* (pp. 147–151). Upper Montclair, NJ: Boynton/Cook.

Tierney, R. J., & Shanahan, T. (1991). Research on the reading-writing relationship: Interactions, transactions, and outcomes. In R. Barr, M. L. Kamil, P. B. Mosenthal, & P. D. Pearson (Eds.), *Handbook of reading research* (Vol. 2, pp. 246–280). Mahwah, NJ: Erlbaum.

Weber, C. (2002). *Publishing with students: A comprehensive guide*. Portsmouth, NH: Heinemann.

Wilhelm, J. D. (2001). *Improving comprehension with think-aloud strategies*. New York: Scholastic.

Yaden, D. B., Jr. (1988). Understanding stories through repeated read-alouds: How many does it take? *The Reading Teacher, 41*, 556–560.

CHILDREN'S BOOK REFERENCES

Lowry, L. (2006a). *Gathering blue*. New York: Delacorte.

Lowry, L. (2006b). *The giver*. New York: Delacorte.

Lowry, L. (2006c). *The messenger*. New York: Delacorte.

O'Neill, M. (1990). *Hailstones and halibut bones*. New York: Doubleday.

Chapter 3

Assessing Students' Literacy Development

Mrs. McNeal Conducts
Second-Quarter Assessments

The end of the second quarter is approaching, and Mrs. McNeal is assessing her first-grade students. She collects four types of assessment data about her students' reading, writing, and spelling development. Then she uses the information to document children's achievement, verify that they're meeting state and district standards, determine report card grades, and make instructional plans for the next quarter.

Today, Mrs. McNeal assesses Seth, who is 6½ years old. He's a quiet, well-behaved child who regularly completes his work. She has a collection of Seth's writing and other papers he's done, but she wants to assess his current reading level. At the beginning of the school year, Mrs. McNeal considered him an average student, but in the past month, his reading progress has accelerated. She's anxious to see how much progress he's made.

Assessment 1: Determining Seth's Instructional Reading Level. Mrs. McNeal regularly takes running records as she listens to children reread familiar books

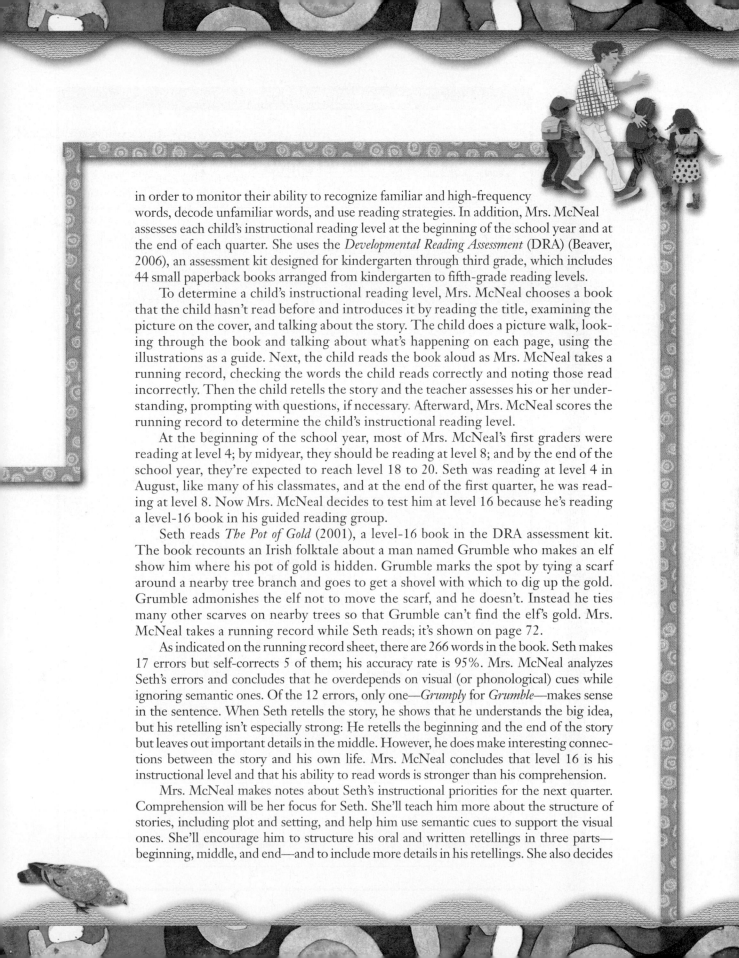

in order to monitor their ability to recognize familiar and high-frequency words, decode unfamiliar words, and use reading strategies. In addition, Mrs. McNeal assesses each child's instructional reading level at the beginning of the school year and at the end of each quarter. She uses the *Developmental Reading Assessment* (DRA) (Beaver, 2006), an assessment kit designed for kindergarten through third grade, which includes 44 small paperback books arranged from kindergarten to fifth-grade reading levels.

To determine a child's instructional reading level, Mrs. McNeal chooses a book that the child hasn't read before and introduces it by reading the title, examining the picture on the cover, and talking about the story. The child does a picture walk, looking through the book and talking about what's happening on each page, using the illustrations as a guide. Next, the child reads the book aloud as Mrs. McNeal takes a running record, checking the words the child reads correctly and noting those read incorrectly. Then the child retells the story and the teacher assesses his or her understanding, prompting with questions, if necessary. Afterward, Mrs. McNeal scores the running record to determine the child's instructional reading level.

At the beginning of the school year, most of Mrs. McNeal's first graders were reading at level 4; by midyear, they should be reading at level 8; and by the end of the school year, they're expected to reach level 18 to 20. Seth was reading at level 4 in August, like many of his classmates, and at the end of the first quarter, he was reading at level 8. Now Mrs. McNeal decides to test him at level 16 because he's reading a level-16 book in his guided reading group.

Seth reads *The Pot of Gold* (2001), a level-16 book in the DRA assessment kit. The book recounts an Irish folktale about a man named Grumble who makes an elf show him where his pot of gold is hidden. Grumble marks the spot by tying a scarf around a nearby tree branch and goes to get a shovel with which to dig up the gold. Grumble admonishes the elf not to move the scarf, and he doesn't. Instead he ties many other scarves on nearby trees so that Grumble can't find the elf's gold. Mrs. McNeal takes a running record while Seth reads; it's shown on page 72.

As indicated on the running record sheet, there are 266 words in the book. Seth makes 17 errors but self-corrects 5 of them; his accuracy rate is 95%. Mrs. McNeal analyzes Seth's errors and concludes that he overdepends on visual (or phonological) cues while ignoring semantic ones. Of the 12 errors, only one—*Grumply* for *Grumble*—makes sense in the sentence. When Seth retells the story, he shows that he understands the big idea, but his retelling isn't especially strong: He retells the beginning and the end of the story but leaves out important details in the middle. However, he does make interesting connections between the story and his own life. Mrs. McNeal concludes that level 16 is his instructional level and that his ability to read words is stronger than his comprehension.

Mrs. McNeal makes notes about Seth's instructional priorities for the next quarter. Comprehension will be her focus for Seth. She'll teach him more about the structure of stories, including plot and setting, and help him use semantic cues to support the visual ones. She'll encourage him to structure his oral and written retellings in three parts—beginning, middle, and end—and to include more details in his retellings. She also decides

A Running Record Scoring Sheet

Name __Seth__　　　　　　　　　　　Date __Jan. 18__

Level __16__　Title __The Pot of Gold__　　　Easy　(Instructional)　Hard

Running Record

	E	SC	E	SC
✓✓✓✓✓✓✓✓				
2 ✓ grumply|Grumble|T ✓✓✓✓✓✓✓	1		m s (v)	
✓✓✓✓✓ always|T A|T ✓✓✓✓✓	1			
✓✓✓✓✓✓✓✓✓✓				
✓✓✓✓✓✓✓✓✓✓				
✓✓✓✓✓✓ did not|didn't| ✓✓	1		(m)(s)v	
3 ✓✓✓✓✓✓✓✓✓✓				
✓✓✓✓✓✓✓✓✓✓				
✓✓✓✓✓✓				
✓✓✓✓✓✓✓✓✓				
4 ✓✓✓✓✓✓✓✓✓✓				
✓✓✓				
✓✓✓✓✓✓✓✓✓				
5 ✓✓✓✓✓✓ I|I'll| make|move| ✓✓	1 / 1		(m)(s)(v) / m s (v)	
✓✓✓✓✓✓✓✓✓✓				
safr|scarf| ✓✓✓✓✓ or|of| ✓✓	1 / 1		m s (v) / m s (v)	
✓✓✓✓✓✓ me|my| sc self|scarf|		1	m s (v)	(m)(s)(v)
6 ✓✓✓	1		m s (v)	
✓✓✓✓				
✓✓✓✓				
✓✓✓✓✓✓				
7 ✓✓✓✓✓✓✓✓				
✓✓✓✓✓✓✓✓✓				
✓✓✓✓✓✓✓✓✓✓				
8 ✓✓✓✓✓✓✓✓✓✓				
✓✓				
✓✓✓ take|taken| ✓ scafer|scarf| ✓✓✓	1 / 1		(m)s(v) / m s (v)	
9 ✓✓✓✓✓✓✓✓				
✓✓✓✓✓✓✓✓		1	m s (v)	(m)(s)(v)
10 ✓✓✓ they|that|sc R✓ ✓✓✓✓✓✓	1 / 1		m s (v) / m s (v)	
✓✓✓✓ maybe|may| sit|still| ✓✓				

Scoring	Picture Walk
12/266　95% accuracy	Gets gist of story
Types of Errors:　M　S　(V)	Oral Reading
Overdependent on V cues	Reads fluently
Self-correction Rate	Retelling/Questions
1:5	Tells BME but middle is brief

to introduce Seth to easy chapter books, such as Cynthia Rylant's Henry and Mudge series about the adventures of a boy named Henry and his dog, Mudge (e.g., *Henry and Mudge and the Big Sleepover*, 2007).

Assessment 2: Testing Seth's Knowledge of High-Frequency Words.

Mrs. McNeal's goal for her first graders is to recognize at least 75 of the 100 high-frequency words by the end of the school year. In August, most children could read at least 12 words; Seth read 16 correctly. Today, Mrs. McNeal asks Seth again to read the list of 100 high-frequency words, which is arranged in order of difficulty. She expects that he'll be able to read 50 to 60 of the words and when he misses 5 in a row, she'll stop, but Seth surprises her and reads the entire list! He misses only these 6 words: *don't*, *how*, *there*, *very*, *were*, and *would*. Seth's high score reinforces his results on the **running record**: He's a very good word reader.

Assessment 3: Checking Seth's Ability to Write and Spell Words.

Several days ago, Mrs. McNeal administered the "Words I Know" Test to the class: She asked the children to write as many words as they could in 10 minutes without copying from classroom charts. In August, most children could spell 15 to 20 words correctly; Mrs. McNeal's goal is that they be able to write 50 words by the end of the school year. Seth wrote 22 words in August, and on the recent test, he wrote 50 correctly spelled words. Seth's "Words I Know" test is shown here.

Seth's "Words I Know" Test

the im a can eat look took she play so he
man what han hat bat zadl got god cat
red in me at pig pl n see need ds and
night fight Dog come from sun run
ran going lettle fin will hill rat
srach ring ua fel tnees snow fun
CowBoys stop get no yes hors you

Mrs. McNeal reviews the list of words that Seth wrote and notices that most are one-syllable words with short vowels, such as *cat* and *fin*, but he's beginning to write words with more-complex spellings, such as *what*, *come*, and *night*, words with inflectional endings, such as *going*, and two-syllable words, such as *cowboys*. She concludes that Seth is making very good progress, both in terms of the number of words he can write and the complexity of the spelling patterns he's using.

Assessment 4: Scoring Seth's Compositions. Mrs. McNeal looks through Seth's journal and chooses several representative samples written in the past 3 weeks to score; one of the samples is shown below. Here is the text with conventional spelling and punctuation:

> *Last night I kept waking up. My dad slept with me. Then I fell fast asleep. Then dad went to bed.*

Using the school district's 6-point rubric, Mrs. McNeal scores the composition as a 4. A score of 5 is considered grade-level at the end of the school year, and Mrs. McNeal believes that Seth will reach that level before then. She notes that he's writing several sentences in an entry, even though he often omits punctuation at the ends of sentences. Seth writes fluently but sometimes omits a word or two. Mrs. McNeal plans to talk to him about the importance of rereading his writing to catch any omissions, add punctuation marks, and correct misspelled words.

Seth's Journal Entry

Seth correctly spells more than two thirds of the words he writes, and he uses invented spelling that generally represents beginning, middle, or ending sounds. In this entry, Seth wrote 21 words, spelling 13 of them correctly; this means that Seth spelled 71% correctly. He reversed the order of letters in three words (*lats* for *last*, *fli* for *fell*, *ot* for *to*) but didn't make any letter-order reversals in the other two samples that Mrs. McNeal evaluated. She recognizes that many first graders form letters backward and make letter-order reversals and isn't concerned about Seth's reversals because she thinks that he'll outgrow them.

Assessment 5: Measuring Seth's Phonics and Spelling Knowledge. Each week, the first graders craft two sentences for a dictation test. On Monday, they create the sentences and write them on chart paper that's displayed in the classroom. During the week, they practice writing the sentences on small dry-erase boards, and Mrs. McNeal uses the text for **minilessons** during which she draws children's attention to high-frequency words they've studied, the phonetic features of various words, and capitalization and punctuation rules applied in the sentences. Last week's sentences focused on the solar system and *The Magic School Bus Lost in the Solar System* (Cole, 1993), a book Mrs. McNeal read aloud to the class:

> *Their bus turned into a rocket ship. They wanted to visit all of the planets.*

After practicing the sentences all week, Mrs. McNeal dictates them for the students to write on Friday. She tells them to try to spell words correctly and to write all the sounds they hear in the words they don't know how to spell. Seth wrote:

> *The bus turd into a rocket ship they wande to vist all of the planis.*

Seth spelled 10 of the 15 words correctly and included 46 of 51 sounds in his writing. In addition, he omitted the period at the end of the first sentence and didn't capitalize the first word in the second sentence.

Mrs. McNeal uses this test to check students' phonics knowledge and ability to spell high-frequency words. Seth spelled most of the high-frequency words correctly, except that he wrote *the* for *their*. Seth's other errors involved the second syllable of the word or an inflectional ending. Mrs. McNeal concludes that Seth is making good progress in learning to spell high-frequency words and that he's ready to learn more about two-syllable words and inflectional endings.

Grading Seth's Reading, Writing, and Spelling Achievement.

Having collected these data, Mrs. McNeal is ready to complete Seth's report card. Seth and his classmates receive separate number grades in reading, writing, and spelling: The grades range from 1, not meeting grade-level standards, to 4, exceeding standards. Seth will receive a 3 in reading, writing, and spelling. A score of 3 means that Seth is meeting grade-level standards in all three areas. Even though his reading level is higher than average, his dependence on visual cues when decoding unfamiliar words and his weakness in comprehension keep him at level 3 in reading.

Assessment has become a priority in 21st-century schools. School districts and state and federal education agencies have increased their demands for accountability, and today, most students take annual high-stakes tests to judge their achievement. Teachers are collecting more assessment data now, and doing it more frequently than in the past. They're using the information to make instructional decisions, as Mrs. McNeal demonstrated in the vignette. Researchers explain that "a system of frequent assessment, coupled with strong content standards and effective reading instruction, helps ensure that teachers' . . . approaches are appropriate to each student's needs" (Kame'enui, Simmons, & Cornachione, 2000, p. 1). By linking assessment and instruction, teachers improve students' learning and their teaching.

As you continue reading, you'll notice that the term *assessment* is used much more often than *evaluation*. These terms are often considered interchangeable, but they're not. Assessment is formative; it's ongoing and provides immediate feedback to improve teaching and learning. It's usually authentic, based on the literacy activities in which students are engaged. Observations, conferences, and student work samples are examples of authentic assessment. In contrast, evaluation is summative; it's final, generally administered at the end of a unit or a school year, and used to judge quality. Tests are the most common type of evaluation, and they're used to compare one student's achievement against that of other students or against grade-level standards.

CLASSROOM-BASED READING ASSESSMENT

The purpose of classroom assessment is to collect meaningful information about what students know and do, and it takes many forms (Afflerbach, 2007a). Teachers use these four types of assessment to monitor and examine students' learning:

Teaching Struggling Readers and Writers

"Just Right" Books

Struggling readers need books they can read.

Too often, struggling readers pick up books that are too difficult, and when they attempt to read them, they give up in frustration. What students need are "just right" books that they can read fluently and can comprehend (Allington, 2006). When students read interesting books at their independent reading level, they're more successful. The "three-finger rule" is a quick way to determine whether a book is a good match for a student: Have the student turn to any page in the book, read it aloud, and raise a finger whenever there's an unknown word. If the student knows every word, it's too easy, but if there's one or two difficult words on a page, the book is probably an appropriate choice. If there are three or more difficult words on a page, the book's too difficult for independent reading.

◆ Kits of leveled books to determine students' reading levels
◆ Informal procedures, such as observations and conferences, to monitor student progress
◆ Tests to diagnose students' strengths and weaknesses in specific components of reading and writing
◆ Collections of work samples to document students' learning

Each type of assessment serves a different purpose, so it's important that teachers choose assessment tools carefully. Researchers recommend that teachers use a combination of informal and formal assessment tools to improve the fairness and effectiveness of classroom literacy assessment (Kuhs, Johnson, Agruso, & Monrad, 2001).

Determining Students' Reading Levels

Teachers match students with books at appropriate levels of difficulty because students are more likely to be successful when they're reading books that aren't too easy or too difficult. Books that are too easy don't provide enough challenge, and books that are too difficult frustrate students. Researchers have identified three reading levels that take into account students' ability to recognize words automatically, read fluently, and comprehend what they're reading:

Independent Reading Level. Students can read books at this level comfortably, on their own. They recognize almost all words; their accuracy rate is 95–100%. Their reading is fluent, and they comprehend what they're reading. Books at this level are only slightly easier than those at their instructional level, and they still engage students' interest.

Instructional Reading Level. Students can read and understand books at this level with support, but not on their own. They recognize most words; their accuracy rate is 90–94%. Their reading may be fluent, but sometimes it isn't. With support from the teacher or classmates, students comprehend what they're reading, but if they're reading independently, their understanding is limited. This level reflects Vygotsky's zone of proximal development, discussed in Chapter 1.

Frustration Reading Level. Books at this level are too difficult for students to read successfully, even with assistance. Students don't recognize enough words automatically; their accuracy is less than 90%. Students' reading is choppy and word by word, and it often doesn't make sense. In addition, students show little understanding of what's been read.

Students should be assessed regularly to determine their reading levels and monitor their progress.

These reading levels have important implications for instruction. Students read independent-level books when they're reading for pleasure and instructional-level books when they're participating in **guided reading** or another instructional activity. They shouldn't be expected to read books at their frustration level; when it's essential that struggling students experience grade-appropriate literature or learn content-area information, teachers should read the text aloud to students.

> Check the Compendium of Instructional Procedures, which follows Chapter 12, for more information on the highlighted terms.

Readability Formulas. For nearly a century, readability formulas have been used to estimate the ease with which reading materials, both trade books and textbooks, can be read. Readability scores serve as rough gauges of text difficulty and are traditionally reported as grade-level scores. If a book has a readability score of fifth grade, for example, teachers assume that average fifth graders will be able to read it. Sometimes readability scores are marked with *RL* and a grade level, such as *RL 5*, on books.

Readability scores are determined by correlating semantic and syntactic features in a text. Several passages from a text are identified for analysis, and then vocabulary sophistication is measured by counting the number of syllables in each word, and sentence complexity by the number of words in each sentence. The syllable counts and the word counts from each passage are averaged, and the readability score is calculated by plotting the averages on a graph. It seems reasonable to expect that texts with shorter words and sentences would be easier to read than others with longer words and sentences; however, readability formulas take into account only two text factors; they can't account for reader factors, including the experience and knowledge that readers bring to reading, their cognitive and linguistic backgrounds, or their motivation for reading.

One fairly quick and simple readability formula is the Fry Readability Graph, developed by Edward Fry (1968); it's presented in the Assessment Tools feature on page 78. This graph is used to predict the grade-level score for texts, ranging from first grade through college level. Teachers use a readability formula as an aid in evaluating textbook and trade-book selections for classroom use; however, they can't assume that materials rated as appropriate for a particular level will be appropriate for all students because students within a class typically vary three grade levels or more in their reading levels.

Just looking at a book isn't enough to determine its readability, because books that seem quite different sometimes score at the same level. For example, *Sarah, Plain and Tall* (MacLachlan, 2004), *Tales of a Fourth Grade Nothing* (Blume, 2007), *Bunnicula: A Rabbit-Tale of Mystery* (Howe & Howe, 2006), and *The Hundred Penny Box* (Mathis, 2006) are four novels that score at the third-grade reading level according to Fry's Readability Graph, even though their topics, use of illustrations, font sizes, and page length differ significantly.

Literacy Portraits:VIEWING GUIDE

Ms. Janusz regularly monitors the second graders' reading achievement. Working one-on-one, she introduces a leveled book and asks the student to read the first part aloud while she takes a running record on a separate sheet of paper. Then the student reads the rest of the book silently. She also asks questions after the student finishes reading orally and again after the student reaches the end of the book. Go to the Literacy Portraits section of MyEducationLab to watch Ms. Janusz assess Jimmy's reading in his October video clip and again in his March video clip. As you watch the videos, think about how Jimmy grew as a reader during the school year. Does he decode unfamiliar words, read fluently, and comprehend what he's read orally and silently? Next, reflect on how Ms. Janusz linked instruction and assessment when she took advantage of teachable moments while she assessed his reading.

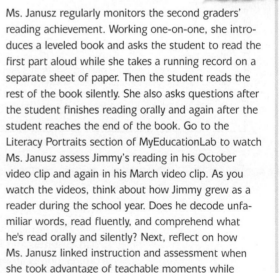

myeducationlab

Assessment Tools

The Fry Readability Graph

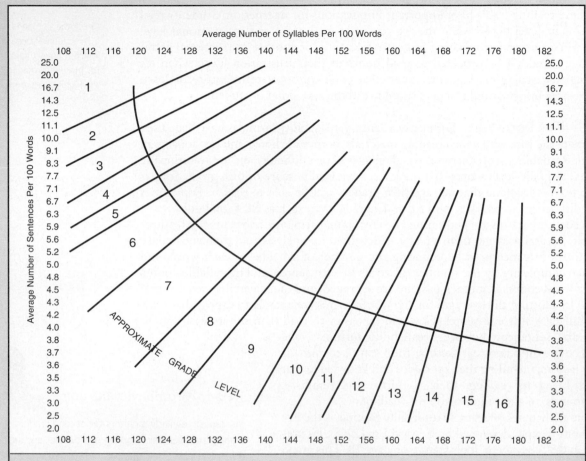

Average Number of Syllables Per 100 Words

Directions:
1. Select three 100-word passages from the book or other reading material.
2. Count the number of syllables in each 100-word passage and average them.
3. Count the number of sentences in each 100-word passage and average them.
4. Plot the averages on the graph to determine the difficulty level. If the score falls outside the lined area, it isn't valid.

From "A Readability Formula That Saves Time," by E. Fry, 1968, p. 587.

Leveled Books. Basal readers have traditionally been leveled according to grade levels, but grade-level designations, especially in kindergarten and first grade, are too broad. Fountas and Pinnell (2006b) developed a text gradient, or classification system that arranges books along a continuum from easiest to hardest, to match students to books in grades K–8. Their system is based on these 10 variables that influence reading difficulty:

♦ Genre and format of the book
♦ Organization and use of text structures

◆ Familiarity with and interest level of the content
◆ Complexity of ideas and themes
◆ Language and literary features
◆ Sentence length and complexity
◆ Sophistication of the vocabulary
◆ Word length and ease of decoding
◆ Relationship of illustrations to the text
◆ Length of the book, its layout, and other print features

Fountas and Pinnell used these criteria to identify 26 levels, labeled A through Z, for their text gradient, which teachers also can use to level books in their classrooms. More than 18,000 books have been leveled according to this text gradient. A sample trade book for each level is shown in Figure 3–1; other leveled books are listed in *The Fountas and Pinnell Leveled Book List, K–8* (Fountas & Pinnell, 2006a) and online at www.fountasandpinnellleveledbooks.com.

Figure 3–1 ◆ Books Leveled Using Fountas and Pinnell's Text Gradient

Level	Grade	Book
A	K	Burningham, J. (1985). *Colors*. New York: Crown.
B	K–1	Carle, E. (1997). *Have you seen my cat?* New York: Aladdin Books.
C	K–1	Martin, B., Jr. (2008). *Brown bear, brown bear, what do you see?* New York: Henry Holt.
D	1	Peek, M. (2006). *Mary wore her red dress*. New York: Clarion Books.
E	1	Hill, E. (2005). *Where's Spot?* New York: Putnam.
F	1	Hutchins, P. (2005). *Rosie's walk*. New York: Aladdin Books.
G	1	Shaw, N. (2006). *Sheep in a jeep*. Boston: Houghton Mifflin.
H	1–2	Kraus, R. (2005). *Whose mouse are you?* New York: Aladdin Books.
I	1–2	Wood, A. (2005). *The napping house*. San Diego: Harcourt.
J	2	Rylant, C. (1996). *Henry and Mudge and the bedtime thumps*. New York: Simon & Schuster.
K	2	Heller, R. (1999). *Chickens aren't the only ones*. New York: Putnam.
L	2–3	Marshall, J. (2000). *The three little pigs*. New York: Grosset & Dunlap.
M	2–3	Park, B. (2007). *Junie B. Jones and the stupid smelly bus*. New York: Random House.
N	3	Danziger, P. (2006). *Amber Brown is not a crayon*. New York: Puffin Books.
O	3–4	Cleary, B. (1992). *Ramona Quimby, age 8*. New York: HarperTrophy.
P	3–4	Mathis, S. B. (2006). *The hundred penny box*. New York: Puffin Books.
Q	4	Howe, D., & Howe, J. (2006). *Bunnicula: A rabbit-tale of mystery*. New York: Aladdin Books.
R	4	Paulsen, G. (2007). *Hatchet*. New York: Simon & Schuster.
S	4–5	Norton, M. (2003). *The borrowers*. San Diego: Odyssey Classics.
T	4–5	Curtis, C. P. (2004). *Bud, not Buddy*. New York: Laurel Leaf.
U	5	Lowry, L. (1998). *Number the stars*. New York: Yearling.
V	5–6	Sachar, L. (2003). *Holes*. New York: Yearling.
W	5–6	Choi, S. N. (1993). *Year of impossible goodbyes*. New York: Yearling.
X	6–8	Hesse, K. (1999). *Out of the dust*. New York: Scholastic.
Y	6–8	Lowry, L. (2006). *The giver*. New York: Delacorte.
Z	7–8	Hinton, S. E. (2006). *The outsiders*. New York: Puffin Books.

Fountas & Pinnell, 2006a.

The Lexile Framework. The newest approach to matching books to readers is the Lexile Framework, developed by MetaMetrics. This approach is different because it's used to measure both students' reading levels and the difficulty level of books. Word familiarity and sentence complexity are the two factors used to determine the difficulty level of books. Lexile scores range from 100 to 1300, representing kindergarten through 12th-grade reading levels. Figure 3–2 presents a list of books ranked according to the Lexile Framework.

Students' results on high-stakes tests are often linked to the Lexile Framework. Standardized achievement tests, including the Iowa Test of Basic Skills and the Stanford Achievement Test, report test results as Lexile scores, and a number of standards-based state reading tests, including the California English-Language Arts Standards Test, the North Carolina End-of-Grade Tests, and the Texas Assessment of Knowledge and Skills, do the same. With this information, students, parents, and teachers can match students to books by searching the online Lexile database to locate books at the student's reading level.

The Lexile Framework is a promising program, because the wide range of scores allows teachers to more closely match students and books. The availability of the online database with more than 44,000 leveled books that students, parents, and teachers can access makes it a very useful assessment tool; however, matching students to books is more complicated than determining a numerical score!

Figure 3–2 ◆ Books Ranked According to the Lexile Framework

Level	Grade	Book
100–149	K	Willems, M. (2003). *Don't let the pigeon drive the bus!* New York: Hyperion Books.
150–199	K–1	Marshall, E. (1999). *Fox all week*. New York: Puffin Books.
200–249	1	Bridwell, N. (2002). *Clifford the big red dog*. New York: Scholastic.
250–299	1	Kellogg, S. (2002). *Pinkerton, behave!* New York: Dial Books.
300–349	1–2	Allard, H. (1985). *Miss Nelson is missing!* Boston: Houghton Mifflin.
350–399	2	Bourgeois, P. (1997). *Franklin's bad day*. New York: Scholastic.
400–449	2	Coerr, E. (1989). *The Josefina story quilt*. New York: HarperTrophy.
450–499	2–3	Bunting, E. (1998). *Going home*. New York: HarperTrophy.
500–549	3	Rathmann, P. (1995). *Officer Buckle and Gloria*. New York: Putnam.
550–599	3–4	Sobol, D. (2008). *Encyclopedia Brown saves the day*. New York: Puffin Books.
600–649	3–4	Cole, J. (1994). *The magic school bus on the ocean floor*. New York: Scholastic.
650–699	4	Lowry, L. (1998). *Number the stars*. New York: Yearling.
700–749	4	Howe, D., & Howe, J. (2006). *Bunnicula: A rabbit-tale of mystery*. New York: Aladdin Books.
750–799	4–5	Creech, S. (2005). *Walk two moons*. New York: HarperTrophy.
800–849	5	Dahl, R. (2007). *Charlie and the chocolate factory*. New York: Puffin Books.
850–899	5–6	Naylor, P. (2000). *Shiloh*. New York: Aladdin Books.
900–949	6–7	Lewis, C. S. (2005). *The lion, the witch and the wardrobe*. New York: HarperCollins.
950–999	7	O'Dell, S. (2006). *The black pearl*. Boston: Houghton Mifflin.
1000–1049	8	Philbrick, R. (2001). *Freak the mighty*. New York: Scholastic.
1050–1099	9–10	Tolkien, J. R. R. (2007). *The hobbit*. Boston: Houghton Mifflin.
1100–1149	10–11	Freedman, R. (2006). *Freedom walkers: The story of the Montgomery bus boycott*. New York: Holiday House.
1150–1199	11–12	Brooks, B. (1995). *The moves make the man*. New York: HarperTrophy.
1200–1300	12	Alcott, L. M. (2004). *Little women*. New York: Signet Classics.

Assessment Tools

Determining Students' Reading Levels

Teachers use screening assessments to determine students' instructional reading levels, monitor their progress, and document student achievement through a school year and across grade levels. Here are three screening assessments:

◆ **Developmental Reading Assessment (DRA)** (Beaver, 2006)

The DRA is available as two kits, one for grades K–3 and the other for grades 4–8, to assess students' reading performance using leveled fiction and nonfiction books. The K–3 kit also includes an individualized diagnostic instrument to assess students' phonemic awareness and phonics knowledge. Teachers use an online system to manage students' scores and group students for instruction.

◆ **Fountas and Pinnell Benchmark Assessment System** (Fountas & Pinnell, 2007)

The Fountas and Pinnell Benchmark Assessment System is sold as two kits, one for grades K–2 and the other for grades 3–8. Each kit contains 30 leveled fiction and nonfiction books written specifically for the kit and CDs with assessment forms to manage students' scores. Teachers use the books in the kit to match students' reading levels to the Fountas and Pinnell 26-level text gradient.

For both of these assessments, teachers test students individually. The teacher selects an appropriate book for the student to read, and then introduces it; the student reads the book, and the teacher takes a running record of the student's reading. Then the student retells the text and answers comprehension questions. The teacher scores and analyzes the results, and testing continues until the teacher determines the student's instructional level.

◆ **Scholastic Reading Inventory (SRI)**

The SRI is a unique computer-adaptive assessment program for grades 1–12 that reports students' reading levels using Lexile scores. Students take this 20-minute computerized test individually. The student reads a narrative or informational passage on the computer screen and answers multiple-choice comprehension questions. This test is computer-adaptive because if the student answers a question correctly, the next one will be more difficult, and if the answer is wrong, the next one will be easier. Students read passages and answer questions until their reading level is determined. Students receive a customized take-home letter with their Lexile score and a personalized list of recommended books.

These assessments are usually administered at the beginning of the school year and periodically during the year to monitor students' progress. The results are also used to group students for guided reading and to identify students who need diagnostic testing.

Monitoring Students' Progress

Monitoring is vital to student success (Braunger & Lewis, 2006). Teachers monitor students' learning every day and use the results to make instructional decisions (Winograd & Arrington, 1999). As they monitor students' progress, teachers learn about their students, about themselves as teachers, and about the impact of their instructional program. Teachers use these informal, formative procedures to monitor students' progress:

Observations. Effective teachers are "kid watchers," a term Yetta Goodman (1978) coined to describe the "direct and informal observation of students" (p. 37). To be effective kid watchers, teachers must understand how children learn to read and write. The focus is on what students do as they read or write, not on whether they're behaving properly or working quietly. Of course, little learning can occur in disruptive situations, but during these observations, the focus is on literacy, not behavior. Observations should be planned. Teachers usually observe a specific group of students each day so that over the course of a week, they watch everyone in the class.

Anecdotal Notes. Teachers write brief notes in notebooks or on self-stick notes as they observe students (Boyd-Batstone, 2004). The most useful notes describe specific events, report rather than evaluate, and relate the events to other information about the student. Teachers make notes about students' reading and writing activities, the questions students ask, and the strategies and skills they use fluently and those they don't understand. These records monitor and document students' growth and pinpoint problem areas to address in future minilessons or conferences. A teacher's anecdotal notes about sixth-grade students participating in a literature circle on *Bunnicula: A Rabbit-Tale of Mystery* (Howe & Howe, 2006) appear in Figure 3–3.

Figure 3–3 ◆ Anecdotal Notes About a Literature Circle

March 7
Met with the *Bunnicula* literature circle as they started reading the book. They have their reading, writing, and discussion schedule set. Sari questioned how a dog could write the book. We reread the Editor's Note. She asked if Harold really wrote the book. She's the only one confused in the group. Is she always so literal? Mario pointed out that you have to know that Harold supposedly wrote the book to understand the first-person viewpoint of the book. Talked to Sari about fantasy. Told her she'll be laughing out loud as she reads this book. She doubts it.

March 8
Returned to *Bunnicula* literature circle for first grand conversation, especially to check on Sari. Annie, Mario, Ted, Rod, Laurie, and Belinda talked about their pets and imagined them taking over their homes. Sari is not getting into the book. She doesn't have any pets and can't imagine the pets doing these things. I asked if she wanted to change groups. Perhaps a realistic book would be better. She says no. Is that because Ted is in the group?

March 10
The group is reading chapters 4 and 5 today. Laurie asks questions about white vegetables and vampires. Rod goes to get an encyclopedia to find out about vampires. Mario asks about DDT. Everyone—even Sari—involved in reading.

March 13
During a grand conversation, students compare the characters Harold and Chester. The group plans to make a Venn diagram comparing the characters for the sharing on Friday. Students decide that character is the most important element, but Ted argues that humor is the most important element in the story. Other students say humor isn't an element. I asked what humor is a reaction to—characters or plot? I checked journals and all are up to date.

March 15
The group has finished reading the book. I share sequels from the class library. Sari grabs one to read. She's glad she stayed with the book. Ted wants to write his own sequel in writing workshop. Mario plans to write a letter to James Howe.

March 17
Ted and Sari talk about *Bunnicula* and share related books. Rod and Mario share the Venn diagram of characters. Annie reads her favorite part, and Laurie shows her collection of rabbits. Belinda hangs back. I wonder if she has been involved. I need to talk to her.

Conferences. Teachers talk with students to monitor their progress in reading and writing activities as well as to set goals and help them solve problems. Here are six types of conferences that teachers have with students:

> **On-the-Spot Conferences.** The teacher visits with students at their desks to monitor some aspect of the students' work or to check on progress. These conferences are brief, with the teacher often spending less than a minute with each student.
>
> **Planning Conferences.** The teacher and the student make plans for reading or writing at the conference. At a prereading conference, they may talk about information related to the book, difficult concepts or vocabulary words related to the book, or the reading log the student will keep. At a prewriting conference, they may discuss possible writing topics or how to narrow a broad topic.
>
> **Revising Conferences.** A small group of students meets with the teacher to share their rough drafts and get specific suggestions about how to revise them.
>
> **Book Discussion Conferences.** Students meet with the teacher to discuss the book they've read. They may share reading log entries, discuss plot or characters, or compare the story to others they've read.
>
> **Editing Conferences.** The teacher reviews students' proofread compositions and helps them correct spelling, punctuation, capitalization, and other mechanical errors.
>
> **Evaluation Conferences.** The teacher meets with students after they've completed an assignment or project to talk about their growth as readers and writers. Students reflect on their accomplishments and set goals.

Often these conferences are brief and impromptu, held at students' desks as the teacher moves around the classroom; however, at other times, the conferences are planned, and students meet with the teacher at a designated conference table.

Checklists. Checklists simplify assessment and enhance students' learning (Kuhs, Johnson, Agruso, & Monrad, 2001). Teachers identify the evaluation criteria in advance so students understand what's expected of them before they begin working. Grading is easier because teachers have already set the evaluation criteria, and it's

Assessment Tools

Book Talk Checklist

Name __Jaime__   Date __November 12__

Title __Cockroach Cooties__

Author __Laurence Yep__

- __✓__ Hold up the book to show to classmates.
- __✓__ State the title and author's name.
- __✓__ Interest classmates in the book by asking a question, reading an excerpt, or sharing some information.
- _____ Summarize the book, without giving away the ending.
- __✓__ Talk loud enough for everyone to hear you.
- __✓__ Look at the audience.
- _____ Limit the book talk to 3 minutes.

fairer, too, because teachers use the same criteria to grade all students' work. The Assessment Tools feature on page 83 shows a fourth-grade checklist for giving book talks. At the beginning of the school year, the teacher introduced book talks, modeled how to do one, and developed the checklist with the students. Students use the checklist whenever they're preparing to give a book talk, and the teacher uses it as a rating scale to evaluate the effectiveness of their book talks.

Rubrics. Rubrics are scoring guides that evaluate student performance in reading and writing according to specific criteria and levels of achievement (Afflerbach, 2007b). They're similar to checklists because they specify what students are expected to be able to do, but they go beyond checklists because they describe levels of achievement. A 4-level rubric for assessing sixth graders' independent reading during reading workshop is shown in the Assessment Tools feature below. Students complete the rubric at the end of each quarter. The quality levels, ranging from Outstanding (highest) to Beginning (lowest), are shown in the column on the far left, and the achievement categories are listed across the top row: number of books read during the quarter, reading level of the books, genres represented by the books, and students' interpretations. The Interpretation category assesses students' comprehension.

Assessment Tools

Independent Reading Rubric

Level	Books Read	Difficulty Level	Genres	Interpretation
Outstanding	Finishes 5 or more books	Reads "just right" books and tries "too hard" books sometimes	Reads books from three or more genres	Makes insightful interpretation with evidence from the book, author's style, and genre
Proficient	Finishes 3 or 4 books	Reads mostly "just right" books	Reads books from two genres	Shares accurate interpretation using a summary, inferences, and story structure
Developing	Finishes 2 or 3 books	Reads mostly "too easy" books	Tries a different genre once in a while	Provides literal interpretation by summarizing events and making personal connections
Beginning	Finishes 1 book	Always reads "too easy" books	Sticks with one genre	Offers incomplete or inaccurate response

Students' Work Samples. Teachers have students collect their work in folders to document their learning. Work samples might include reading logs, audiotapes of students' reading, photos of projects, videotapes of puppet shows and oral presentations, and books students have written. Students often choose some of these work samples to place in their portfolios.

Assessment Tools

Diagnostic Reading and Writing Assessments

Component	Test (With Recommended Grade Levels)	Where to Learn More
Concepts About Print	Observation Survey of Early Literacy Achievement (K–2)	Chapter 4, Working With the Youngest Readers and Writers, p. 113
Phonemic Awareness	Dynamic Indicators of Basic Early Literacy Skills (K–3) Phonological Awareness Literacy Screening (K–3) Yopp-Singer Test of Phonemic Segmentation (K)	Chapter 5, Cracking the Alphabetic Code, p. 154
Phonics	Dynamic Indicators of Basic Early Literacy Skills (K–3) The Names Test (3–8) Observation Survey of Early Literacy Achievement (K–2) The Tile Test (K–2)	Chapter 5, Cracking the Alphabetic Code, p. 166
Word Recognition	High-frequency word lists (K–3) Observation Survey of Early Literacy Achievement (K–2) Writing samples (K–3)	Chapter 6, Developing Fluent Readers and Writers, p. 196
Word Identification	Developmental Reading Assessment (K–8) The Names Test (3–8) Phonological Awareness Literacy Screening (K–3) Running records (K–8)	Chapter 6, Developing Fluent Readers and Writers, p. 207
Fluency	Dynamic Indicators of Basic Early Literacy Skills (K–3) Fluency checks (1–8) Informal reading inventories (2–8) Running records (K–8)	Chapter 6, Developing Fluent Readers and Writers, p. 216
Vocabulary	Expressive Vocabulary Test (K–8) Informal reading inventories (2–8) Peabody Picture Vocabulary Test (K–8)	Chapter 7, Expanding Students' Knowledge of Words, p. 248
Comprehension	Comprehension Thinking Strategies Assessment (1–8) Developmental Reading Assessment (K–8) Informal reading inventories (2–8)	Chapter 8, Facilitating Students' Comprehension: Reader Factors, p. 276
Writing	Rubrics (K–8)	Chapter 2, Teaching the Reading and Writing Processes, p. 64
Spelling	Developmental Spelling Analysis (K–8) Phonological Awareness Literacy Screening (K–3) Qualitative Spelling Inventory (K–8)	Chapter 5, Cracking the Alphabetic Code, p. 180

Diagnosing Students' Strengths and Weaknesses

Teachers use diagnostic reading assessments to identify students' strengths and weaknesses, examine any area of difficulty in more detail, and decide how to modify instruction to meet students' needs. They use a variety of diagnostic tests to examine students' achievement in phonemic awareness, phonics, fluency, vocabulary, comprehension, and other components of reading and writing. The Assessment Tools feature on page 85 lists the diagnostic tests recommended in this text and directs you to the chapter where you can learn more about how to use them.

Two of the assessments that teachers commonly use are running records and informal reading inventories. They're used to determine students' reading levels as well as to diagnose difficulties in word identification, fluency, and comprehension and to monitor students' growth as readers. Mrs. McNeal used running records in the vignette at the beginning of this chapter, and as you continue reading this text, you'll notice that they're referred to again and again.

Go to the Building Teaching Skills and Dispositions section of Chapter 3 on **MyEducationLab.com** to watch as Ms. Janusz conducts an assessment.

Running Records. Teachers often take **running records** of students' oral reading to assess their word identification and reading fluency (Clay, 2006). With a running record, teachers calculate the percentage of words the student reads correctly and then analyze the miscues or errors. They make a series of checkmarks on a sheet of paper as the student reads words correctly and use other marks to indicate words that the student substitutes, repeats, mispronounces, or doesn't know, as Mrs. McNeal did in the vignette. Although teachers can take the running record on a blank sheet of paper, it's much easier to make a copy of the page or pages the student will read and take the running record next to or on top of the actual text. Using a copy of the text is especially important when assessing older students who read more-complex texts and read them more quickly than younger children do.

After identifying the words the student misread, teachers calculate the percentage of words the student read correctly. They use this percentage to determine whether the book or other reading material is too easy, too difficult, or appropriate for the student at this time. If the student reads 95% or more of the words correctly, the book is easy, or at the independent reading level for that student. If the student reads 90–94% of the words correctly, the book is at his or her instructional level. If the student reads fewer than 90% of the words correctly, the book is too difficult: It's at the student's frustration level.

Teachers can categorize miscues according to the semantic, graphophonic, and syntactic cueing systems in order to examine what word-identification strategies students are using. As they categorize the miscues, teachers should ask themselves these questions:

◆ Does the reader self-correct the miscue?
◆ Does the miscue change the meaning of the sentence?
◆ Is the miscue phonologically similar to the word in the text?
◆ Is the miscue acceptable within the syntax (or structure) of the sentence?

The miscues that interfere with meaning and those that are syntactically unacceptable are the most serious because the student doesn't realize that reading should make sense. Miscues can be classified and charted; the Assessment Tools feature on the next page shows the analysis of Seth's miscues on the running record in the vignette at the beginning of the chapter. Only words that students mispronounce or substitute can be analyzed; repetitions and omissions are not calculated.

Mary Shea (2006) developed a modified procedure for using running records with fifth- through eighth-grade struggling readers. Instead of having these students read a complete text as younger children do, she recommends using a 1-minute probe: The student reads aloud for 1 minute from a text that's being used in class, and the teacher marks a copy of the text as the student reads. Afterward, the student retells what he or she has just read, and the teacher prompts the student about any ideas that aren't mentioned. Shea also suggests making an audio- or videotape of the student's reading and reviewing it to gain additional insights.

Assessment Tools

Miscue Analysis

Child ___Seth___ Date ___Jan. 18___

Text ___The Pot of Gold (Level 16)___

WORDS			MEANING	VISUAL	SYNTAX
Text	Child	Self-corrected?	Similar meaning?	Graphophonic similarity?	Grammatically acceptable?
Grumble	Grumply			✓	
always	–				
didn't	did not		✓	✓	✓
I'll	I		✓	✓	✓
move	make			✓	✓
scarf	safr			✓	
of	or			✓	
my	me	✓		✓	
scarf	self			✓	
taken	take		✓	✓	
scarf	scafer			✓	
that	they	✓		✓	
may	maybe			✓	
still	sit			✓	

Analysis: Seth overrelies on visual cues and rarely self-corrects.

Running records are an effective assessment tool because they are authentic (Shea, 2000). Students demonstrate how they read using their regular reading materials as teachers make a detailed account of their ability to read a book. Teachers collect valuable information about the strategies and skills students use to decode words and construct meaning.

Informal Reading Inventories. Teachers use commercial tests called *informal reading inventories* (IRIs) to evaluate students' reading performance. They can be used in first- through eighth-grade levels, but first-grade teachers often find that IRIs don't provide as much useful information about beginning readers as running records do. These popular reading tests are often used as a screening instrument to determine whether students are reading at grade level, but they're also a valuable diagnostic tool (Nilsson, 2008). Teachers can use IRIs to identify struggling students' instructional needs, particularly in the areas of word identification, oral reading fluency, and comprehension.

These individualized tests consist of two parts: graded word lists and passages ranging from first- to at least eighth-grade level. The word lists contain 10 to 20 words at each level, and students read the words until they become too difficult; this indicates an approximate level for students to begin reading the passages. Because students who can't read the words on their grade-level list may have a word-identification problem, teachers analyze the words students read incorrectly, looking for error patterns and deciding whether students rely on one cueing system.

The graded reading passages include both narrative and expository texts, presented in order of difficulty. Students read these passages orally or silently and then answer a series of comprehension questions. Three types of questions generally are used: They ask students to recall specific information, draw inferences, or explain the meaning of vocabulary words. When students read the passage orally, teachers assess their fluency. Students beyond third grade should be able to read the passages at their grade level fluently; if they can't, they may have a fluency problem. Teachers also examine students' comprehension. If students can't answer the questions after reading the passage at their grade level, they may have a comprehension problem, and teachers check to see if there's a pattern to the types of questions that students miss.

Teachers use scoring sheets to record students' performance data, and they calculate students' independent, instructional, and frustration reading levels. When students' reading level is below their grade-level placement, teachers also check their listening capacity; that is, their ability to understand passages that are read aloud to them. Knowing whether students can understand and learn from grade-level texts that are read aloud is crucial because that's a common way that teachers support struggling readers.

Nurturing English Learners

Teachers assess English learners' developing language proficiency as well as their progress in learning to read and write. It's more challenging to assess ELs than native English speakers, because when students aren't proficient in English, their scores don't accurately reflect what they know (Peregoy & Boyle, 2008). Their cultural and experiential backgrounds also contribute to making it more difficult to assure that assessment tools being used aren't biased.

Oral Language Assessment. Teachers assess students who speak a language other than English at home to determine their English language proficiency. They typically use commercial oral language tests to determine if students are proficient in English. If they're not, teachers place them in appropriate English language development programs and monitor their progress toward English language proficiency. Two widely used tests are the Language Assessment Scales, published by CTB/McGraw-Hill, and the IDEA Language Proficiency Test, published by Ballard and Tighe; both tests assess K–12 students' oral and written language (listening, speaking, reading, and writing) proficiency in English. Individual states have developed language assessments that are aligned with their English language proficiency standards; for example, the New York State English as a Second Language Achievement Test and the California English Language Development Test.

An authentic assessment tool that many teachers use is the Student Oral Language Observation Matrix (SOLOM), developed by the San Jose (CA) Area Bilingual Consortium. It's not a test per se; rather, the SOLOM is a rating scale that teachers use to assess students' command of English as they observe them talking and listening in real, day-to-day classroom activities. The SOLOM addresses five components of oral language:

- ◆ **Listening.** Teachers score students along a continuum from unable to comprehend simple statements to understanding everyday conversations.
- ◆ **Fluency.** Teachers score students along a continuum from halting, fragmentary speech to fluent speech, approximating that of native speakers.
- ◆ **Vocabulary.** Teachers score students along a continuum from extremely limited word knowledge to using words and idioms skillfully.
- ◆ **Pronunciation.** Teachers score students along a continuum from virtually unintelligible speech to using pronunciation and intonation proficiently, similar to native speakers.
- ◆ **Grammar.** Teachers score students along a continuum from excessive errors that make speech unintelligible to applying word order, grammar, and usage rules effectively.

Each component has a five-point range that's scored 1 to 5; the total score on the matrix is 25, and a score of 20 or higher indicates that students are fluent speakers of English. The SOLOM is available free of charge online at www.cal.org, at other websites, and in many professional books.

Reading Assessment. English learners face two challenges: They're learning to speak English at the same time they're learning to read. They learn to read the same way that native English speakers do, but they face additional challenges because their knowledge of English phonology, semantics, syntax, and pragmatics is limited and their background knowledge is different (Peregoy & Boyle, 2008). Some English learners are fluent readers in their home language (Garcia, 2000). These students already have substantial funds of knowledge about how written language works and about the reading process that they build on as they learn to read in English (Moll, 1994). Having this knowledge gives them a head start, but students also have to learn what transfers to English reading and what doesn't.

Teachers use the same assessments that they use for native English speakers to identify English learners' reading levels, monitor their growth, and document their learning. Peregoy and Boyle (2008) recommend using data from **running records** or informal reading inventories along with classroom-based informal assessments, such as observing and conferencing with students.

Because many English learners have less background knowledge about topics in books they're reading, it's important that teachers assess ELs' background knowledge before instruction so they can modify their teaching to meet students' needs. One of the best ways to accomplish this is with a **K-W-L chart**. As they work with students to complete the first two sections of the chart, teachers learn what students know about a topic and have an opportunity to build additional background knowledge and introduce related vocabulary. Later, when students complete the K-W-L chart, teachers get a clear picture of what they've learned and which vocabulary words they can use.

Another way teachers learn about ELs' development is by asking them to assess themselves as readers (Peregoy & Boyle, 2008). Teachers ask students, for example, what they do when they come to an unfamiliar word, what differences they've noticed between narrative and expository texts, which reading strategies they use, and what types of books they prefer. These quick assessments, commonly done during conferences at the end of a grading period, shed light on students' growth in a way that other assessments can't.

Writing Assessment. English learners' writing develops as their oral language grows and as they become more-fluent readers (Riches & Genesee, 2006). For beginning writers, fluency is the first priority. They move from writing strings of familiar words to grouping words into short sentences that often follow a pattern, much like young native English speakers do. As they develop some writing fluency, ELs begin to stick to a single focus, often repeating words and sentences to make their writing longer. Once they become fluent writers, ELs are usually able to organize their ideas more effectively and group them into paragraphs. They incorporate more-specific vocabulary and expand the length and variety of sentences. Their mechanical errors become less serious, and their writing is much easier to read. At this point, teachers begin teaching the qualities of good writing and choosing writing strategies and skills to teach based on the errors that students make.

Peregoy and Boyle (2008) explain that ELs' writing involves fluency, form, and correctness, and that teachers' assessment of students' writing should reflect these components:

◆ Teachers monitor students' ability to write quickly, easily, and comfortably.
◆ Teachers assess students' ability to apply writing genres, develop their topic, organize the presentation of ideas, and use sophisticated vocabulary and a variety of sentence structures.
◆ Teachers check that students control standard English grammar and usage, spell most words correctly, and use capitalization and punctuation conventions appropriately.

Teachers use **rubrics** to assess ELs' writing, and the rubrics address fluency, form, and correctness as well as the qualities of good writing that teachers have taught. They also conference with students about their writing and provide quick **minilessons**, as needed. To learn about students as writers, teachers observe them as they write, noticing how they move through the writing process, interact in **writing groups**, and share their writing from the author's chair. In addition, students document writing development by placing their best writing in portfolios.

Alternative Assessments. Because of the difficulties inherent in assessing English learners, it's important to use varied types of assessment that involve different language and literacy tasks and ways of demonstrating proficiency (Huerta-Macias, 1995). In addition to commercial tests, O'Malley and Pierce (1996) urge teachers to use authentic assessment tools, including oral performances, story retellings, oral interviews with students, writing samples, illustrations, diagrams, posters, and projects.

Assessment is especially important for students who are learning to speak English at the same time they're learning to read and write in English. Teachers use many of the same assessment tools that they use for their native English speakers but they also depend on alternative, more-authentic assessments because it's difficult to accurately measure these students' growth. Assessment results must be valid because teachers use them to make placement decisions, modify instruction, and document learning.

Documenting Students' Learning

Teachers routinely collect students' work samples, including cassette tapes of them reading aloud, lists of books they've read, reading logs, writing samples with rubrics, and photos of projects. They also keep students' test results and the anecdotal notes they make as they observe students and meet with them in conferences. Teachers use these data to document students' progress toward meeting grade-level standards as well as to evaluate their own teaching effectiveness. Students also collect their best work in portfolios to document their own learning and accomplishments.

PORTFOLIO ASSESSMENT

Portfolios are systematic and meaningful collections of artifacts documenting students' literacy development over a period of time (Hebert, 2001). These collections are dynamic and reflect students' day-to-day reading and writing activities as well as content-area activities. Students' work samples provide "windows" on the strategies they use as readers and writers. Not only do students select pieces to be placed in their portfolios, they also learn to establish criteria for their selections. Because of students' involvement in selecting pieces for their portfolios and reflecting on them, portfolio assessment respects students and their abilities. Portfolios help students, teachers, and parents see patterns of growth from one literacy milestone to another in ways that are not possible with other types of assessment.

Collecting Work in Portfolios

Portfolios are folders, large envelopes, or boxes that hold students' work. Teachers often have students label and decorate large folders and then store them in plastic crates or cardboard boxes. Students date and label items as they place them in their portfolios, and they often attach notes to the items to explain the context for the activity and why they selected a particular item. Students' portfolios should be stored in the classroom in a place where they are readily accessible; students like to review their portfolios periodically and add new pieces to them.

Students usually choose the items to place in their portfolios within the guidelines the teacher provides. Some students submit the original piece of work; others want to keep the original, so they place a copy in the portfolio instead. In addition to the reading and writing samples that go directly into portfolios, students can record oral language and drama samples on audiotapes and videotapes to place in their portfolios. Large-size art and writing projects can be photographed, and the photographs can be placed in the portfolio. Student work might include books, choral readings on audiotapes, reading logs and learning logs, graphic organizers, multigenre projects, lists of books read, and compositions. This variety of work samples reflects the students' literacy programs. Samples from literature focus units, literature circles, reading and writing workshop, basal reading programs, and content-area units can be included.

New Literacies
E-Portfolios

Instead of collecting papers with their writing samples, cassette tapes with their oral reading samples, photos of projects, and other artifacts in bulky folders that take up lots of space, students can create electronic portfolios to showcase their best work and document their learning. Their artwork and writing samples are scanned, reading samples are recorded, and artifacts are photographed using a digital camera. In addition, collaborative books and projects can be saved in each student's portfolio. Students add text boxes or video clips to provide context for the samples, reflect on their learning, and explain how their work demonstrates that they've met grade-level standards. They also insert hyperlinks to connect sections and enhance their e-portfolios by adding music and graphics.

Teachers create a template that lays out the design, including a title, table of contents, and collections of artifacts. Sometimes rubrics are included to show how the artifacts were assessed. Collections from each grade are saved in separate files within students' portfolios. Teachers can browse electronic portfolios that have been posted on the Web to get ideas about how to design and organize their students' collections of work samples.

E-portfolios are versatile assessment tools: They allow for the flexible input of a variety of multimodal items, incorporate a hierarchical organization, make searching for and retrieving items easy to do, and can be displayed for various audiences to view. Electronic portfolios are practical, too, especially if teachers and students know how to use computers, software, and related equipment, and if they're willing to devote the time needed to start up the portfolio system. They're quick and easy to access because they're stored on CD-ROMs or at the school's website. Web-based portfolios are sometimes called *webfolios*.

Even primary-grade students can assist in developing these technology-based collections, and older students who are more familiar with using computers, scanning writing samples, importing digital photos, and adding video clips can do more of the work themselves. Parent volunteers and cross-age tech buddies can teach students how to get started and provide support when they're adding work samples.

An exciting new online tool for creating portfolios is the KEEP Toolkit, developed by the Carnegie Foundation for the Advancement of Teaching. Its purpose is to provide an economical and accessible tool that teachers and students can use to create compact and engaging Web-based representations of teaching and learning that can be shared with others. Tools in the KEEP Toolkit are used to enter information, upload files, and create snapshots, single webpages or a linked series of webpages created using a template. These presentations can be added to or revised at any time. There's no charge to use this password-protected website. The files are stored on a server at the Carnegie Foundation and given a URL so others can access them. A collection of electronic portfolios created by elementary and secondary teachers and their students is displayed in the Gallery of Teaching and Learning section of the Carnegie Foundation's website (www.cfkeep.org).

Because the 21st century has a knowledge economy, students need to be able to express their knowledge. When teachers introduce e-portfolios in the primary grades and students are encouraged to use them effectively throughout their schooling, they're likely to continue using them in adult life to document and showcase their accomplishments.

Many teachers collect students' work in folders, and they assume that portfolios are basically the same as work folders; however, the two types of collections differ in several important ways. Perhaps the most important difference is that portfolios are student oriented, whereas work folders are usually teachers' collections—students choose which samples will be placed in portfolios, but teachers often place all completed assignments in work folders. Next, portfolios focus on students' strengths, not their weaknesses. Because students choose items for portfolios, they choose samples that best represent their literacy development. Another difference is that portfolios involve reflection (D'Aoust, 1992); through reflection, students pause and become aware of their strengths as readers and writers. They also use their work samples to identify the literacy procedures, strategies, and skills they already know and the ones they need to focus on.

Involving Students in Self-Assessment

Portfolios are a tool for engaging students in self-assessment and goal setting. Students learn to reflect on and assess their own reading and writing activities and their development as readers and writers (Stires, 1991). Teachers begin by asking students to think about their reading and writing in terms of contrasts. For reading, students identify the books they've read that they liked most and least, and they ask themselves what these choices suggest about themselves as readers. They also identify what they do well in reading and what they need to improve. In writing, students make similar contrasts: They identify their best compositions and others that weren't as good, and they think about what they do well when they write and what to improve. By making these comparisons, students begin to reflect on their literacy development.

Teachers use **minilessons** and conferences to teach about the characteristics of good readers and writers. In particular, they discuss these topics:

◆ What fluent reading is
◆ Which reading strategies and skills students use
◆ How students demonstrate their comprehension
◆ How students value books they've read
◆ What makes a good project to apply reading knowledge
◆ What makes an effective piece of writing
◆ Which writing strategies are most effective
◆ How to use writing rubrics
◆ How proofreading and correcting mechanical errors are a courtesy to readers

As students learn about what it means to be effective readers and writers, they acquire the tools they need to reflect on and evaluate their own reading and writing. They

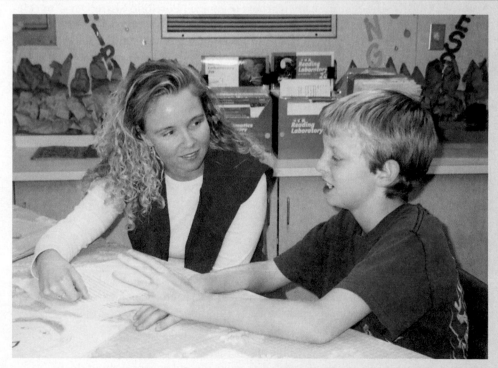

Conferences
This fourth grader meets with his teacher for 15 to 20 minutes to talk about his achievement at the end of the second grading period. Even though it's time-consuming, this teacher meets with each student at the end of every grading period to talk about the student's progress, identify standards-based accomplishments, select pieces to add to the portfolio, determine grades, and set goals for the next quarter. Through this process, teachers involve students in assessment, and students become more responsible for their own learning as they self-assess their progress and set goals for themselves.

learn how to think about themselves as readers and writers and acquire the vocabulary to use in their reflections, such as *goal*, *strategy*, and *rubric*.

Students write notes on items they choose to put into their portfolios. In these self-assessments, students explain the reasons for their choices and identify strengths and accomplishments in their work. In some classrooms, students write their reflections and other comments on index cards, and in other classrooms, they design special comment sheets that they attach to the items in their portfolios.

Teachers usually collect baseline reading and writing samples at the beginning of the school year and then conduct portfolio review conferences with students at the end of each grading period. At these conferences, the teacher and the student talk about the items being placed in the portfolio and the student's self-assessments. Students also talk about what they want to improve or what they want to accomplish during the next grading period, and these points become their goals for the next grading period.

Self-assessment can also be used for an assessment at the end of the school year. Coughlan (1988) asked his seventh-grade students to "show me what you have learned about writing this year" and to "explain how you have grown as a written language user, comparing what you knew in September to what you know now" (p. 375). These upper-grade students used a process approach to develop and refine their compositions, and they submitted all drafts with their final copies. Coughlan examined both the content of students' compositions and the strategies they used in thinking through the assignment and writing their responses. He found this "test" to be a very worthwhile project because it "forced the students to look within themselves . . . realize just how much they had learned" (p. 378). Moreover, students' compositions verified what they had learned about writing and that they could articulate their learning.

Showcasing Students' Portfolios

At the end of the school year, many teachers organize "Portfolio Share Days" to celebrate students' accomplishments and to provide an opportunity for students to share their portfolios with classmates and the wider community (Porter & Cleland, 1995). Often family members, local businesspeople, school administrators, local politicians, college students, and others are invited to attend. Students and community members form small groups, and students share their portfolios, pointing out their accomplishments and strengths. This activity is especially useful in involving community members in the school and showing them the types of literacy activities in which students are involved as well as how students are becoming effective readers and writers.

These sharing days also help students accept responsibility for their own learning—especially those students who have not been as motivated as their classmates. When less motivated students listen to their classmates talk about their work and how they have grown as readers and writers, they often decide to work harder the next year.

Why Are Portfolios Worthwhile?

Portfolios are used to document students' work, evaluate their progress, and showcase their best work (Afflerbach, 2007b). Collections of work samples add context to students' learning, and students become more reflective about the quality of their reading and writing. There are other benefits, too:

◆ Students feel ownership of their work.
◆ Students become more responsible about their work.
◆ Students set goals and are motivated to work toward accomplishing them.
◆ Students make connections between learning and assessing.

◆ Students' self-esteem is enhanced.
◆ Portfolios eliminate the need to grade all student work.
◆ Portfolios are used in student and parent conferences.
◆ Portfolios complement the information provided on report cards.

In schools where portfolios are used schoolwide, students overwhelmingly report that by using portfolios, they're better able to show their parents what they're learning and also better able to set goals for themselves (Kuhs, Johnson, Agruso, & Monrad, 2001). Teachers also find that portfolios enable them to assess their students more thoroughly, and students are better able to see their own progress.

HIGH-STAKES TESTING

Annual high-stakes testing is emphasized in American schools with the goal of improving the quality of reading instruction. These tests are designed to objectively measure students' knowledge according to grade-level standards. The current emphasis on testing and state-level standards are reform efforts that began in response to The National Commission on Education report *A Nation at Risk* (1983), which argued that American schools were failing miserably. The report stated that American students' test scores were dropping, comparing unfavorably with students' scores in other industrialized countries, and it concluded that the United States was in jeopardy of losing its global superiority. The No Child Left Behind Act, which promoted an increased focus on reading instruction to improve students' reading performance and narrow the racial and ethnic gaps in achievement, reinforced the call for annual standardized testing.

Researchers have repeatedly refuted these arguments (Bracey, 2004; McQuillan, 1998). Allington (2006) explained that average test scores have remained stable for 30 years despite the dramatic increases in federal funding over the past decade. He goes on to explain that reporting average scores obscures important findings, and it's necessary to examine subgroup data to discover that most students from middle-class families read well even though many students from low-income families lag behind. Despite a gap, he also notes that significant progress has been made in closing the achievement gap between white and minority students at the same time the number of minority students has grown tremendously. Finally, he points out that grade-level standards of achievement have increased in the last 50 years so that what was considered fifth-grade level is now fourth-grade level, and older readability formulas have been renormed to reflect today's higher grade-level standards. Nonetheless, the public's perception that schools are failing persists.

High-stakes testing is different than classroom assessment. The test scores typically provide little information for making day-to-day instructional decisions, but students, teachers, administrators, and schools are judged and held accountable by the results. The scores are used to make important educational decisions for students—to determine school placement and high school graduation, for example. These scores influence administrators' evaluations of teachers' effectiveness and even their salaries in some states, and they reward or sanction administrators, schools, and school districts.

Standardized tests are comprehensive with batteries of subtests, covering decoding, vocabulary, comprehension, writing mechanics, and spelling. Figure 3–4 presents an overview of the most commonly used tests. Most tests use multiple-choice test items, although a few are introducing open-ended questions that require students to write responses. Beginning in second grade, classroom teachers administer the tests to their students, typically in the spring. Most require multiple testing periods to administer all of the subtests.

Figure 3–4 ◆ Standardized Achievement Tests

Test	Purpose	Components	Special Features	Publisher
Iowa Test of Basic Skills (ITBS)	The ITBS provides information to improve instruction at grades K–8.	Phonics Vocabulary Comprehension Oral language Mechanics Spelling	The ITBS is the oldest statewide assessment program. It can be administered at the beginning of the school year to better inform instruction.	Iowa schools are served by the Iowa Testing Program; outside Iowa, the ITBS is available from the Riverside Publishing Company.
Metropolitan Achievement Test (MAT)	The MAT measures K–8 students using real-world content. Some items are multiple choice; others are performance-based tasks.	Emergent literacy Vocabulary Comprehension Mechanics Writing Spelling	Test items are aligned with the IRA/NCTE Language Arts Standards. The MAT also provides a Lexile measure of students' reading levels.	The MAT can be ordered from Pearson.
Stanford Achievement Test (SAT)	The SAT measures K–8 students' progress toward meeting the challenges set forth by the NCLB Act and state standards.	Phonemic awareness Phonics Vocabulary Comprehension Mechanics Writing Spelling	The SAT also provides a Lexile measure of students' reading levels.	The SAT is published by Pearson.
TerraNova Test (TNT)	The TNT is a standardized test that uses both multiple-choice and constructed-response items that allow students to write responses.	Word analysis Vocabulary Comprehension Mechanics Spelling	Lexile scores are reported so teachers can match students to books. Also, one version of the TNT is available as an online test.	The TNT is published by CTB/McGraw-Hill.

Problems With High-Stakes Testing

A number of problems are associated with high-stakes testing (IRA, 1999). Students feel the pressure of these tests, and researchers have confirmed what many teachers have noticed: Students don't try harder because of them (Hoffman, Assaf, & Paris, 2005). Struggling students, in particular, get discouraged and feel defeated, and over time, test pressure destroys their motivation and actually harms their achievement. In addition, student dropout rates are rising.

Teachers complain that they feel compelled to improve students' test scores at any price, and they lose valuable instructional time for test-taking and practice sessions (Hollingworth, 2007). Overemphasizing the test often leads teachers to abandon a balanced approach to instruction: Sometimes students spend more time completing practice tests than reading books and writing compositions. One of the most insidious side effects is that teachers are often directed to focus on certain groups of students, especially those scoring just below a cutoff point, in hopes of improving test scores.

Preparing for Standardized Tests

Standardized tests are a unique text genre, and they require readers and writers to do different things than they would normally, so teachers can't assume that students already know how to take reading tests. It's essential that teachers prepare students to take high-stakes tests without abandoning a balanced approach to instruction that's aligned to state standards (Calkins, Montgomery, & Santman, 1998). Greene and Melton (2007) agree; they maintain that teachers must prepare students for high-stakes tests without sacrificing their instructional program. Unfortunately, with the pressure to raise test scores, some teachers are having students take more multiple-choice tests while writing fewer essays and creating fewer projects.

Hollingworth (2007) recommends these five ways to prepare students for high-stakes tests without sacrificing the instructional program:

◆ Teachers check that their state's curriculum standards align with their instructional program and make any needed adjustments to ensure that they're teaching what's going to be on the test.
◆ Teachers set goals with students and use informal assessments to regularly monitor their progress.
◆ Teachers actively engage students in authentic literacy activities so that they become capable readers and writers.
◆ Teachers explain the purpose of the tests and how the results will be used, without making students anxious.
◆ Teachers stick with a balanced approach that combines explicit instruction and authentic application.

Other researchers advise that in addition to these recommendations, teachers prepare students to take standardized tests by teaching them how to read and answer test items and having them take practice tests to hone their test-taking strategies (McCabe, 2003). Preparing for tests involves explaining their purpose, examining the genre and format of multiple-choice tests, teaching the formal language of tests and test-taking strategies, and providing opportunities for students to take practice tests; and these lessons should be folded into the existing instructional program, not replace it. Greene and Melton (2007) organized test preparation into **minilessons** that they taught as part of reading workshop.

The Genre of Standardized Tests. Students need opportunities to examine old test forms to learn about the genre of standardized tests and how test questions are formatted. They'll notice that tests look different than other texts they've read; they're typically printed in black and white, the text is dense, and few illustrations are included. Sometimes words, phrases, and lines in the text are numbered, bolded, or underlined. Through this exploration, students begin to think about what makes one type of text harder to read than others, and with practice, they get used to how tests are formatted so that they're better able to read them.

The Language of Testing. Standardized reading tests use formal language that's unfamiliar to many students. For example, some tests use the word *passage* instead of *text* and *author's intent* instead of *main idea*. Test makers also use *locate, except, theme, reveal, inform, reason, in order to, provide suspense,* and other words that students may not understand. Greene and Melton (2007) call the language of testing "test talk" and explain that "students are helpless on standardized reading tests if they can't decipher test talk" (p. 8). Students need help understanding test talk so that high-stakes tests really measure what they know.

Test-Taking Strategies. Students vary the test-taking strategies they use according to the type of test they're taking. Most standardized tests employ multiple-choice questions. Here's a list of test-taking strategies that students use to answer multiple-choice questions:

Read the entire question first. Students read the entire question first to make sure they understand what it's asking. For questions about a reading passage, students read the questions first to guide their reading.

Look for key words in the question. Students identify key words in the question, such as *compare*, *except*, and *author's intent*, that will guide them to choose the correct answer.

Read all answer choices before choosing the correct answer. After students read the question, they stop and think about the answer before reading all the possible answers. Then they eliminate the unlikely answer choices and identify the correct answer.

Answer easier questions first. Students answer the questions they know, skipping the difficult ones, and then they go back and answer the questions they skipped.

Make smart guesses. When students don't know the answer to a question, they make a smart guess, unless there's a penalty for guessing. To make a smart guess, students eliminate the answer choices they're sure are wrong, think about what they know about the topic, and then pick the best remaining answer choice. The correct answer is often the longest one.

Stick with your first answer. Students shouldn't second-guess themselves; their first answer is probably right. They shouldn't change answers unless they're certain that their first answer was wrong.

Pace yourself. Students budget their time wisely so they'll be able to finish the test. They don't spend too much time on any one question.

Check your work carefully. Students check that they've answered every question, if they finish early.

Students use these test-taking strategies along with reading strategies, including determining importance, questioning, and rereading, when they're taking standardized tests. Teaching students about question-answer-relationships helps them to understand that sometimes answers to test questions can be found in a passage they've just read, or they have to use their own knowledge.

Preparing for tests should be embedded in literacy activities and not take up a great deal of instructional time. Teachers often teach test-taking strategies through minilessons where they explain the strategy, model its use, and provide opportunities for guided practice and discussion. Greene and Melton (2007) recommend teaching minilessons on test-taking strategies as well as the genre of tests, test formats, and the language of tests as part of reading workshop. They reported that their students, many of whom are English learners and struggling readers and writers, became more confident and empowered test-takers through test-preparation minilessons, and their test scores improved.

Practice Tests. Teachers design practice tests with the same types of items used on the standardized tests students will take. They use easy-to-read materials for practice tests so students can focus on practicing test-taking strategies without being challenged by the difficulty level of the text or the questions. They include a combination of unrelated narrative, poetic, and expository passages on the tests because all three types of texts are used on high-stakes tests. Teachers also provide answer sheets similar to those used on the standardized test so that students gain experience using them. So that students will be familiar with the testing conditions, teachers simulate them in the classroom or take students to where the test will be administered for practice sessions. Through these practice tests, students develop both confidence in their test-taking abilities and the stamina to persist through long tests.

Be Strategic!

Test-Taking Strategies

Students use these test-taking strategies to answer multiple-choice questions on standardized tests:

▶ Read the entire question first
▶ Look for key words in the question
▶ Read all answer choices before choosing the correct one
▶ Answer easier questions first
▶ Make smart guesses
▶ Stick with your first answer
▶ Pace yourself
▶ Check your work carefully

Students learn to use these strategies through test-prep lessons and practice tests.

Preparation for reading tests is especially important because when students aren't familiar with multiple-choice tests, they'll score lower than they otherwise would. Don't confuse test preparation with teaching to the test: Preparing for a test involves teaching students how to take a test, whereas teaching to the test is the unethical practice of drilling students on actual questions from old tests. The term "teaching to the test" is also used in a less pejorative way to describe when teachers tailor instruction to meet state-mandated standards.

 ## Nurturing English Learners

Researchers question the use of standardized achievement tests with English learners because these tests are often invalid, underestimating students' achievement (Peregoy & Boyle, 2008). It seems obvious that when students have limited English proficiency, their test performance would be affected; however, even students who do well in the classroom often score poorly on standardized achievement tests (Lindholm-Leary & Borsato, 2006). There are several reasons for this dichotomy. First, test-taking procedures are less familiar whereas classroom routines are more predictable and comfortable, and it's likely that ELs are more stressed by their unfamiliarity than native English speakers are. A second reason is that the language used in directions and test items is often complex, making comprehension more difficult for ELs. Another reason is cultural differences: English learners often lack background knowledge about the topics addressed in the reading passages and test questions.

Researchers believe that the best way to assess English learners more fairly is to provide accommodations, by modifying either the test or the testing procedure (Lindholm-Leary & Borsato, 2006). They've experimented with modifying tests by simplifying the language, translating the test into students' home language, or adding visual supports, and modifying the testing procedure by providing additional time, allowing students to use bilingual dictionaries, or translating or explaining the directions. Unfortunately, data are inconclusive about the effectiveness of these accommodations. Currently, there's renewed interest in rewriting test questions on high-stakes tests to avoid unnecessarily complex English syntactic structures and academic vocabulary so that ELs can actually demonstrate their knowledge.

Probably the best way to ameliorate the effects of ELs' potentially invalid test results is to use multiple measures, including some authentic assessments, to document English learners' language proficiency and literacy achievement. This accommodation, however, is unlikely to be implemented in today's educational climate where both students and teachers are being held accountable using the results from a single test.

The Politics of High-Stakes Testing

The debate over high-stakes testing is a politically charged issue (Casbarro, 2005). Test scores are being used as a means to reform schools, and although improving the quality of instruction and ensuring that all students have equal access to educational opportunities are essential, there are unwanted consequences for both students and teachers. Does high-stakes testing work? Proponents claim that schools are being reformed; however, although some gains in test scores for minority groups have been reported, many teachers feel that the improvement is the result of "teaching to the test." So far, no results indicate that students have actually become better readers and writers because of standardized achievement tests.

The goal of the No Child Left Behind Act is admirable, but test experts have argued that a single evaluation shouldn't be used to judge either students' learning or teachers' effectiveness. Braunger and Lewis (2006) point out that "ironically, the national focus on accountability . . . may leave little room for assessment linked to instruction that could actually improve literacy outcomes for students who are being left behind" (p. 130).

Chapter 3

Review

How Effective Teachers Assess Students' Literacy Development

▶ Teachers determine students' independent, instructional, and frustration reading levels.

▶ Teachers informally monitor students' progress in reading and writing.

▶ Teachers use diagnostic assessments to identify students' strengths and weaknesses and then provide instruction to address problem areas.

▶ Teachers have students document their learning in portfolios.

▶ Teachers prepare students for high-stakes tests without sacrificing their instructional programs.

myeducationlab
PEARSON
Where the Classroom Comes to Life

Go to MyEducationLab at www.myeducationlab.com to deepen your understanding of the concepts presented in this chapter:

▶ Expand your knowledge about assessing students' instructional reading levels by viewing video segments in the Literacy Portraits.
▶ Check your understanding of chapter concepts with the multiple-choice and essay quizzes in the Study Plan.
▶ Apply some of the main ideas discussed in the chapter in the Activities and Applications section of the website.
▶ Practice what you've learned in this chapter in Building Teaching Skills and Dispositions before applying the ideas in your own classroom.

PROFESSIONAL REFERENCES

Afflerbach, P. (2007a). Best practices in literacy assessment. In L. B. Gambrell, L. M. Morrow, & M. Pressley (Eds.), *Best practices in literacy instruction* (3rd ed., pp. 264–282). New York: Guilford Press.

Afflerbach, P. (2007b). *Understanding and using reading assessment, K–12*. Newark, DE: International Reading Association.

Allington, R. L. (2006). *What really matters for struggling readers: Designing research-based programs* (2nd ed.). Boston: Allyn & Bacon/Pearson.

Beaver, J. (2006). *Developmental reading assessment* (2nd ed.). Upper Saddle River, NJ: Celebration Press/Pearson.

Boyd-Batstone, P. (2004). Focused anecdotal records assessment: A tool for standards-based, authentic assessment. *The Reading Teacher, 58,* 230–239.

Bracey, G. W. (2004). *Setting the record straight: Responses to misconceptions about public education in the United States.* Portsmouth, NH: Heinemann.

Braunger, J., & Lewis, J. P. (2006). *Building a knowledge base in reading* (2nd ed.). Newark, DE: International Reading Association/National Council of Teachers of English.

Calkins, L., Montgomery, K., & Santman, D. (1998). *A teacher's guide to standardized reading tests: Knowledge is power.* Portsmouth, NH: Heinemann.

Casbarro, J. (2005, February). The politics of high-stakes testing. *Education Digest, 70*(6), 20–23.

Clay, M. M. (2006). *An observation survey of early literacy assessment* (2nd ed.). Portsmouth, NH: Heinemann.

Coughlan, M. (1988). Let the students show us what they know. *Language Arts, 65,* 375–378.

D'Aoust, C. (1992). Portfolios: Process for students and teachers. In K. B. Yancy (Ed.), *Portfolios in the writing classroom* (pp. 39–48). Urbana, IL: National Council of Teachers of English.

Fountas, I. C., & Pinnell, G. S. (2006a). *The Fountas and Pinnell leveled book list, K–8* (2006–2008 ed.). Portsmouth, NH: Heinemann.

Fountas, I. C., & Pinnell, G. S. (2006b). *Leveled books, K–8: Matching texts to readers for effective teaching.* Portsmouth, NH: Heinemann.

Fountas, I. C., & Pinnell, G. S. (2007). *The Fountas and Pinnell benchmark assessment system.* Portsmouth, NH: Heinemann.

Fry, E. (1968). A readability formula that saves time. *Journal of Reading, 11,* 587.

Garcia, G. E. (2000). Bilingual children's reading. In M. Kamil, P. Mosenthal, P. D. Pearson, & R. Barr (Eds.), *Handbook of reading research* (Vol. 3, pp. 813–834). Newark, DE: International Reading Association.

Goodman, Y. M. (1978). Kid watching: An alternative to testing. *The National Elementary Principal, 57,* 41–45.

Greene, A. H., & Melton, G. D. (2007). *Test talk: Integrating test preparation into reading workshop.* Portsmouth, ME: Stenhouse.

Hebert, E. A. (2001). *The power of portfolios: What children can teach us about learning and assessment.* San Francisco: Jossey-Bass.

Hoffman, J. V., Assaf, L. C., & Paris, S. G. (2005). High-stakes testing in reading: Today in Texas, tomorrow? In S. J. Barrentine & S. M. Stokes (Eds.), *Reading assessment: Principles and practices for elementary teachers* (2nd ed., pp. 108–120). Newark, DE: International Reading Association.

Hollingworth, L. (2007). Five ways to prepare for standardized tests without sacrificing best practice. *The Reading Teacher, 61,* 339–342.

Huerta-Macias, A. (1995). Alternative assessment: Responses to commonly asked questions. *TESOL Journal, 5,* 8–10.

International Reading Association (IRA). (1999). *High-stakes assessments in reading: A position statement.* Newark, DE: Author.

Kame'enui, E., Simmons, D., & Cornachione, C. (2000). *A practical guide to reading assessments.* Newark, DE: International Reading Association.

Kuhs, T. M., Johnson, R. L., Agruso, S. A., & Monrad, D. M. (2001). *Put to the test: Tools and techniques for classroom assessment.* Portsmouth, NH: Heinemann.

Lindholm-Leary, K., & Borsato, G. (2006). Academic achievement. In F. Genesee, K. Lindholm-Leary, W. M. Saunders, & D. Christian (Eds.), *Educating English language learners: A synthesis of research evidence* (pp. 176–222). New York: Cambridge University Press.

McCabe, P. P. (2003). Enhancing self-efficacy for high-stakes reading tests. *The Reading Teacher, 57,* 12–20.

McQuillan, J. (1998). *The literacy crisis: False claims, real solutions.* Portsmouth, NH: Heinemann.

Moll, L. (1994). Literacy research in community and class-rooms: A sociocultural approach. In R. R. Ruddell, M. R. Ruddell, & H. Singer (Eds.), *Theoretical models and processes of reading* (4th ed., pp. 197–207). Newark, DE: International Reading Association.

National Commission on Excellence in Education. (1983). *A nation at risk: The imperative for educational reform.* Washington, DC: U.S. Government Printing Office.

Nilsson, N. L. (2008). A critical analysis of eight informal reading inventories. *The Reading Teacher, 61,* 526–536.

O'Malley, J. M., & Pierce, L. V. (1996). *Authentic assessment for English language learners: Practical approaches for teachers.* Boston: Addison-Wesley.

Peregoy, S. F., & Boyle, O. F. (2008). *Reading, writing, and learning in ESL: A resource book for teaching K–12 English learners* (5th ed.). Boston: Allyn & Bacon/Pearson.

Peterson, B. (2001). *Literary pathways: Selecting books to support new readers.* Portsmouth, NH: Heinemann.

Porter, C., & Cleland, J. (1995). *The portfolio as a learning strategy.* Portsmouth, NH: Heinemann.

Riches, C., & Genesee, F. (2006). Literacy: Crosslinguistic and crossmodal issues. In F. Genesee, K. Lindholm-Leary, W. M. Saunders, & D. Christian (Eds.), *Educating English language learners: A synthesis of research evidence* (pp. 64–108). New York: Cambridge University Press.

Shea, M. (2000). *Taking running records.* New York: Scholastic.

Shea, M. (2006). *Where's the glitch? How to use running records with older readers, grades 5–8.* Portsmouth, NH: Heinemann.

Stires, S. (1991). Thinking through the process: Self-evaluation in writing. In B. M. Power & R. Hubbard (Eds.), *The Heinemann reader: Literacy in process* (pp. 295–310). Portsmouth, NH: Heinemann.

Winograd, P., & Arrington, H. J. (1999). Best practices in literacy assessment. In L. B. Gambrell, L. M. Morrow, S. B. Neuman, & M. Pressley (Eds.), *Best practices in literacy instruction* (pp. 210–241). New York: Guilford Press.

CHILDREN'S BOOK REFERENCES

Blume, J. (2007). *Tales of a fourth grade nothing.* New York: Puffin Books.

Cole, J. (1993). *The magic school bus lost in the solar system.* New York: Scholastic.

Howe, D., & Howe, J. (2006). *Bunnicula: A rabbit-tale of mystery.* New York: Aladdin Books.

MacLachlan, P. (2004). *Sarah, plain and tall.* New York: HarperTrophy.

Mathis, S. B. (2006). *The hundred penny box.* New York: Puffin Books.

Rylant, C. (2007). *Henry and Mudge and the big sleepover.* New York: Aladdin Books.

The pot of gold (an Irish folk tale). (2001). Upper Saddle River, NJ: Celebration Press/Pearson.

PART 2

Components of Literacy Development

Researchers have identified these components of literacy development that students need to learn to become effective readers and writers:

- **Alphabetic Code**
  Students learn phonemic awareness, phonics, and spelling to understand our sound-symbol system.

- **Fluency**
  Students learn to read fluently so that they have cognitive resources available for comprehension.

- **Vocabulary**
  Students acquire a wide vocabulary and learn how to unlock the meaning of new words.

- **Comprehension**
  Students learn to use strategies to direct their comprehension.

In this part opener, I'd like to introduce you to five students in Ms. Janusz's second-grade class. You'll learn about them and how they develop as readers and writers in their online Literacy Portraits—case study video clips and writing samples—located at the MyEducationLab website (www.myeducationlab.com). There you can track these students' development in phonics, fluency, vocabulary and comprehension. Four of them began second grade not meeting grade-level expectations, but the fifth student, Jimmy, exemplifies second-grade standards. I've included Jimmy's Literacy Portrait for a grade-level comparison. All five students have shown tremendous growth during second grade as they've become more-capable readers and writers.

Rakie

A minte leter I opened the door and Jojo was foze in a ice cobe.

Rakie's favorite color is pink, and she loves her cat, JoJo. She came to America from Africa when she was very young, and she's currently enrolled in the school's pull-out ESL program. Rakie enjoys reading books with her friends in the library area. Her favorite book is Doreen Cronin's *Click Clack Moo: Cows That Type* because she appreciates that troublesome duck. Rakie's a fluent reader, but she has difficulty understanding what she reads, mainly because of unfamiliar vocabulary, a common problem for English learners. Rakie's bright, and Ms. Janusz is pleased that she's making great strides!

Michael

Beep beep beep beep it was 9:00 am. I new I had to wacke up. I toock my first Step, Slip the flors were frozen Solid.

Michael is gregarious and loves fun in any size or shape. He takes karate lessons, and his Xbox video gaming system is a prized possession. In September, Michael, who is bilingual, was reading below grade level and couldn't stay on task, but after Ms. Janusz encouraged him to choose books that he wanted to read and to identify topics for writing, his motivation began to grow. Now, he's making rapid progress! He's not crazy about reading except for The Magic Tree House series of chapter books, but he really enjoys writing. He says that his stories are good because he uses wordplay effectively.

Rhiannon

Rhiannon, the youngest in Ms. Janusz's class, is a charmer. Her gusto for life is contagious! In September, she held books upside down, but she's made tremendous progress since then. Mo Willems is her favorite author; she loves his stories, including *Don't Let the Pigeon Drive the Bus!* She struggles to decode unfamiliar words, usually depending on the sound-it-out strategy. Rhiannon's passionate about writing. She creates inventive stories about her dogs, Taco and Tequila, and gets very animated when sharing them with classmates, but abbreviated spellings make her writing difficult to read.

I soD it to my DaD. B u D up! So I pot Logr clos on anD pas anD soD It to my DaD. B u D u p!

TRANSLATION:

I showed it to my Dad.
BUNDLE UP!
So I put longer clothes on and
pants and showed it to my Dad.
BUNDLE UP!

Curt'Lynn

Curt'Lynn enjoys playing with her buddies Leah and Audri at recess and spending time with her Granny. Her reading was at early-first-grade level at the beginning of second grade. She often "read" books to herself, telling the story through the illustrations. Now Curt'Lynn loves to read Dr. Seuss books because they're funny. Her focus is on decoding words, but she's beginning to think about whether the words she's reading make sense. Curt'Lynn recognizes that her reading has been improving this year because, as she explains, it's becoming easier to get the words right.

When I was just 4 years old, I was a CherLeedre Because I rill wueted to be a cherLeedre.

It was a haunted house! The door creKed opin "BOO!" said a ghost. And Lady was gone! "AAAA!" said Jim.

Jimmy

Jimmy's a big sports fan—he likes the Cleveland Indians and the Ohio State Buckeyes, in particular—but his real passion is World War II. He likes to play Army with his best friend, Sam. Jimmy often chooses nonfiction books on varied topics to read; recently, he read a biography about rock-and-roll idol Elvis Presley. Jimmy's a bright student who achieves at or above grade level in all subjects. He's eager to please and worries about making a mistake when he's sharing his writing or reading aloud. In September, Jimmy had trouble with comprehension, but now he's a confident, strategic reader.

To learn more about these students, go to the Literacy Portraits section of the MyEducationLab website and click on the Teacher Interviews to view Gail Tompkins's conversations with Ms. Janusz.

ChapTer 4

Working With the Youngest Readers and Writers

Ms. McCloskey's Students Become Readers and Writers

K indergarten through third-grade students sit together on the carpet for a shared reading lesson. They watch and listen intently as Ms. McCloskey prepares to read *Make Way for Ducklings* (McCloskey, 2001), the big-book version of an award-winning story about the dangers facing a family of ducks living in the city of Boston. She reads the title and the author's name, and some children recognize that the author's last name is the same as hers, but she points out that they aren't related. She reads the first page and asks the class to make predictions about what will happen in the story. During this first reading, Ms. McCloskey reads each page expressively and tracks the text, word by word, with a pointer as she reads. She clarifies the meaning as she talks about the illustrations on each page. A child helps balance the book on the easel and turn the pages for her. After she finishes, they talk about the story. Some of the English learners are initially hesitant, but others eagerly relate their own experiences to the story and ask questions to learn more.

The next day, Ms. McCloskey rereads *Make Way for Ducklings*. She begins by asking for volunteers to retell the story. Children take turns retelling each page, using the illustrations as clues. Ms. McCloskey includes this oral language activity because many of her students are English learners. The class is multilingual and multicultural: Approximately 45% of the children are Asian Americans who speak Hmong, Khmer, or Lao; 45% are Hispanics who speak Spanish or English at home; and the remaining 10% are African Americans and whites who speak English.

Next, Ms. McCloskey rereads the story, stopping several times to ask the class to think about the characters, draw inferences, and reflect on the theme. Her questions include: Why did the police officer help the ducks? What would have happened to the ducks if the police officer didn't help? Do you think that animals should live in cities? What was Robert McCloskey trying to say to us in this story? On the third day, Ms. McCloskey reads the story again, and the children take turns using the pointer to track the text and join in reading familiar words. After they finish, the children clap because rereading the now familiar story provides a sense of accomplishment.

Ms. McCloskey understands that her students are moving through three developmental stages—emergent, beginning, and fluent—as they learn to read and write. She monitors each child's development to provide instruction that meets his or her needs. As she reads the big book aloud, she uses a pointer to show the direction of print, from left to right and top to bottom on the page. She also moves the pointer across the lines of text, word by word, to demonstrate the relationship between the words on the page and the words she's reading aloud. These are concepts that many of the youngest, emergent-stage readers are learning.

Others are beginning readers who are learning to recognize high-frequency words and decode phonetically regular words. One day after rereading the story, Ms. McCloskey turns to one of the pages and asks the children to identify familiar high-frequency words (e.g., *don't*, *make*) and decode other CVC words (e.g., *run*, *big*). She also asks children to isolate individual sentences on the page and note the capital letter at the beginning and the punctuation that marks the end of the sentence.

The third group are fluent readers. Ms. McCloskey addresses their needs, too, as she rereads a page from the story: She asks several children to identify adjectives and notice inflectional endings on verbs. She also rereads the last sentence on the page and asks a child to explain why commas are used in it.

Ms. McCloskey draws the children's attention to the text as a natural part of **shared reading**. She demonstrates concepts; points out letters, words, and punctuation marks; models strategies; and asks questions about concepts of print. As they watch Ms. McCloskey and listen to their classmates, the children think about letters, words, and sentences and learn more about literacy.

Ms. McCloskey and her teaching partner, Mrs. Papaleo, share a large classroom and 38 students; despite the number of children present, the room feels spacious. Children's desks are arranged in clusters around the large, open area in the middle where children meet for whole-class activities. An easel to display big books is placed next to the teacher's chair. Several chart racks stand nearby; one rack holds Ms. McCloskey's morning messages and **interactive writing** texts that children have written, a second one holds charts with poems that the children use for **choral reading**, and a third rack holds a pocket chart with word cards and sentence strips.

On one side of the classroom is the library with books arranged in crates by topic. One crate has frog books, and others have books about the ocean, plants, and the five senses. Other crates contain books by authors who have been featured in author studies, including Eric Carle, Kevin Henkes, and Paula Danziger. Picture books and chapter books are neatly arranged in the crates; children take turns keeping the area neat. Sets of leveled books are arranged on a shelf above the children's reach for the teachers to use in **guided reading** lessons. A child-size sofa, a table and chairs, pillows, and rugs make the library area cozy and inviting. A listening center is set up at a nearby table with a tape player and headphones that accommodate six children at a time.

A **word wall** with high-frequency words fills a partition separating instructional areas. It's divided into sections for each letter of the alphabet. Arranged on it are nearly 100 words written on small cards cut into the shape of the words. The teachers introduce new words each week and post them on the word wall. The children often practice reading and writing the words as a center activity, and they refer to the word wall to spell words when they're writing.

A bank of computers with a printer are located on another side of the classroom. Everyone uses them, even the youngest children. Those who have stronger computer skills assist their classmates. They use word processing to publish their writing during writing workshop and monitor their independent reading practice on the computer using the Accelerated Reader® program. At other times, they search the Internet to find information related to topics they're studying in science and social studies, and use software programs to learn typing skills.

Literacy center materials are stored in another area. Clear plastic boxes hold sets of magnetic letters, puppets and other props, dry-erase boards and pens, puzzles and games, flash cards, and other manipulatives. The teachers choose materials to use during **minilessons**, and they also set boxes of materials out for children to use during center time.

Ms. McCloskey spends the morning teaching reading and writing using a variety of teacher-directed and student-choice activities. Her daily schedule is shown in the box on page 109. After **shared reading** and a minilesson, the children participate in reading and writing workshop.

The children write books during writing workshop. They pick up their writing folders and write independently at their desks. While most of them are working, Ms. McCloskey brings together a small group for a special activity: She conducts **interactive writing** lessons with emergent writers and teaches the writing process and revision strategies to more fluent writers. Today she's conferencing with six children who are beginning writers. Because they're writing longer compositions, Ms. McCloskey has decided to introduce revising. After each child reads his or her rough draft aloud to the group, classmates ask questions and offer compliments, and Ms. McCloskey encourages them to make a change in their writing so that their readers will understand it better. Anthony reads aloud a story about his soccer game, and after a classmate asks a question, he realizes that he needs to add more about how

Ms. McCloskey's Schedule		
Time	Activity	Description
8:10–8:20	Class Meeting	Children participate in opening activities, read the morning message from their teachers, and talk about plans for the day.
8:20–8:45	Shared Reading	The teachers read big books and poems written on charts; this activity often serves as a lead-in to the minilesson.
8:45–9:00	Minilesson	The teachers teach minilessons on literacy procedures, concepts, strategies, and skills.
9:00–9:45	Writing Workshop	Children write books while the teachers confer with individual children and small groups. They also do interactive writing activities.
9:45–10:00	Recess	
10:00–11:15	Reading Workshop	Children read self-selected books independently while the teachers do guided reading lessons with small groups.
11:15–11:30	Class Meeting	Children share their writing from the author's chair, and they review the morning's activities.
11:30–12:10	Lunch	
12:10–12:30	Read-Aloud	Teachers read aloud picture books and chapter books, and children discuss them in grand conversations.

he scored a goal. He moves back to his desk to revise. The group continues with children sharing their writing and beginning to make revisions. At the end of writing workshop, the children come together for author's chair. Each day, three children take turns sitting in the author's chair to read their writing to classmates.

During reading workshop, children read independently or with a buddy while Ms. McCloskey and her teaching partner conduct **guided reading** lessons. The children have access to a wide variety of books in the classroom library, including predictable books for emergent readers, decodable books for beginning readers, and easy-to-read chapter books for fluent readers. The children know how to choose books that they can read successfully so they're able to spend their time really reading. The children keep lists of the books they read in their workshop folders so that their teachers can monitor their progress.

Ms. McCloskey is working with a group of four emergent readers, and today they'll read *Playing* (Prince, 1999), a seven-page predictable book with one line of text on each page that uses the pattern "I like to _____." She begins by asking children what they like to do when they're playing. Der says, "I like to play with my brother, " and Ms. McCloskey writes that on a strip of paper. Some children say only a word or two, and she expands the words into a sentence for the child to repeat; then she writes the expanded sentence and reads it with the child. Next, she introduces the book and reads the title and the author's name. Ms. McCloskey does a picture walk, talking about the picture on each page and naming the activity the child is doing— running, jumping, sliding, and so on. She reviews the "I like to _____" pattern, and then the children read the book independently while Ms. McCloskey supervises and provides assistance as needed. The children eagerly reread the book several times, becoming more confident and excited with each reading.

Literacy Centers	
Center	Description
Bag a Story	Children use objects in a paper bag to create a story. They draw pictures or write sentences to tell the story they've created.
Clip Boards	Children search the classroom for words beginning with a particular letter or featuring a spelling pattern and write them on paper attached to clip boards.
Games	Children play alphabet, phonics, and other literacy card and board games with classmates.
Library	Children read books related to a thematic unit and write or draw about the books in reading logs.
Listening	Children listen to a tape of a story or informational book while they follow along in a copy of the book.
Making Words	Children practice a making words activity that they've previously done together as a class with teacher guidance.
Messages	Children write notes to classmates and the teachers and post them on a special "Message Center" bulletin board.
Poetry Frames	Children arrange word cards on a chart-sized poetry frame to create a poem and then practice reading it.
Reading the Room	Children use pointers to point to and reread big books, charts, signs, and other texts posted in the classroom.
Research	Children use the Internet, informational books, photos, and realia to learn more about topics in literature focus units and thematic units.
Story Reenactment	Children use small props, finger puppets, or flannel board figures to reenact familiar stories with classmates.
Word Sort	Children categorize high-frequency or thematic word cards displayed in a pocket chart.

Ms. McCloskey reviews the high-frequency words *I*, *like*, and *to*, and the children point them out on the classroom word wall. They use magnetic letters to spell the words and then write sentences that begin with *I like to . . .* on dry-erase boards. Then Ms. McCloskey cuts apart their sentence strips for them to sequence; afterward the children put their sentences into envelopes to practice another day. At the end of the lesson, the teacher suggests that the children might want to write "I like to ____ " books during writing workshop the next day.

During the last 30 minutes before lunch, the children work at literacy centers. Ms. McCloskey and Mrs. Papaleo have set out 12 centers, and the children are free to work at any one they choose. They're familiar with the routine and know what's expected of them at each center. The two teachers circulate around the classroom, monitoring children's work and taking advantage of teachable moments to clarify misunderstandings, reinforce previous lessons, and extend children's learning. A list of the literacy centers is presented in the box above.

After lunch, Ms. McCloskey reads aloud picture books and easy-to-read chapter books. Sometimes she reads books by a particular author, but at other times, she reads books related to a thematic unit. She uses these read-alouds to teach predicting, visualizing, and other reading strategies. This week, she's reading award-winning books, and today she reads aloud *The Stray Dog* (Simont, 2001), the story of a homeless dog that's taken in by a loving family. She uses the **interactive read-aloud** procedure to involve children in the book as she reads, and afterward they talk about it in a **grand conversation**. Ms. McCloskey asks them to share their connections to the story, and the teachers record them on a chart divided into three sections. Most comments are text-to-self connections, but several children make other types of connections. Rosario says, "I am thinking of a movie. It was 101 Dalmatians. It was about dogs, too." That's a text-to-text connection. Angelo offers a text-to-world connection: "You got to stay away from stray dogs. They can bite you, and they might have this bad disease called rabies—it can kill you."

Literacy is a process that begins in infancy and continues into adulthood, if not throughout life. It used to be that 5-year-old children came to kindergarten to be "readied" for reading and writing instruction, which formally began in first grade. The implication was that there's a point in children's development when it's time to teach them to read and write. For those not ready, a variety of "readiness" activities would prepare them. Since the 1970s, this view has been discredited because preschoolers have demonstrated that they could recognize signs and other environmental print, retell stories, scribble letters, invent printlike writing, and listen to stories read aloud (Morrow & Tracey, 2007). Some young children even teach themselves to read!

This perspective on how children become literate—that is, how they learn to read and write—is known as *emergent literacy*, a term that New Zealand educator Marie Clay coined. Studies from 1966 on have shaped the current outlook (McGee & Richgels, 2003; Morrow & Tracey, 2007). Now, researchers are looking at literacy learning from the child's point of view. Literacy development has been broadened to incorporate the cultural and social aspects of language learning, and children's experiences with and understandings about written language—both reading and writing—are included as part of emergent literacy.

FOSTERING AN INTEREST IN LITERACY

Young children's introduction to written language begins before they come to school. Parents and other caregivers read to them, and they learn to read signs and other environmental print in their community. They experiment with writing and have their parents write messages for them; they also observe adults writing. When young children come to school, their knowledge about written language expands quickly as they learn concepts about print and participate in meaningful experiences with reading and writing.

Concepts About Print

Through experiences in their homes and communities, young children learn that print carries meaning and that reading and writing are used for a variety of purposes (Clay, 2000a). They notice menus in restaurants, write and receive postcards and letters to communicate with friends and relatives, and listen to stories read aloud for enjoyment. Children also observe parents and teachers using written language for all these reasons.

Children's understanding about the purposes of reading and writing reflects how written language is used in their community. Although reading and writing are part of daily life for almost every family, families use written language for different purposes in different communities (Heath, 1983). Young children have a wide range of literacy experiences in both middle-class and working-class families, even though those experiences might not be the same (Taylor & Dorsey-Gaines, 1987). In some communities, written language is used mainly as a tool for practical purposes such as paying bills, whereas in others, reading and writing are also used for leisure-time activities. In still other communities, written language serves even wider functions, such as debating social and political issues.

Preschool and kindergarten teachers demonstrate the purposes of written language and provide opportunities for children to experiment with reading and writing in many ways:

Posting signs in the classroom

Making a list of classroom rules

Using reading and writing materials in literacy play centers

Exchanging messages with classmates

Reading and writing stories

Labeling classroom items

Drawing and writing in journals

Writing notes to parents

Young children learn other concepts about print through these activities, too: They learn book-orientation concepts, including how to hold a book and turn pages, and that the text, not the illustrations, carries the message. Children also learn directionality concepts—that print is written and read from left to right and from top to bottom on a page. They match voice to print, pointing word by word to the text as it is read aloud. Children also notice punctuation marks and learn their names and their purposes.

Check the Compendium of Instructional Procedures, which follows Chapter 12, for more information on the highlighted terms.

Assessing Children's Concepts About Print. Teachers observe children as they look at books and reread familiar ones. They also watch as children do pretend writing and write their names and other familiar words and phrases. They notice which concepts children understand and which ones they need to continue to talk about and demonstrate during shared reading.

Teachers use Marie Clay's Concepts About Print (CAP) Test (2006) to assess young children's understanding of these written language concepts, and it's explained in the Assessment Tools box on the next page. Teachers also create their own versions of the test to use with any story they're reading with a child. As they read aloud any big book or small book, teachers ask the child to point out book-orientation concepts, directionality concepts, and letter and word concepts. They can use the CAP Test scoring sheet shown in this same Assessment Tools feature or develop one of their own to monitor children's growing understanding of these concepts.

Assessment Tools

Concepts About Print

Teachers monitor children's growing awareness of the concepts about print as they observe them during shared reading and other reading and writing activities. The most widely used assessment is Marie Clay's Concepts About Print Test:

◆ **Concepts About Print (CAP) Test** (Clay, 2006)

The CAP Test assesses young children's understanding of three types of concepts about print: book-orientation concepts, directionality concepts, and letter and word concepts. The test has 24 items and is administered individually in about 10 minutes. The teacher reads a short book aloud while a child looks on. The child is asked to open the book, turn pages, and point out particular print features as the text is read. Four forms of the CAP Test booklet are available: *Sand* (Clay, 2007b), *Stones* (Clay, 2007c), *Follow Me, Moon* (Clay, 2000b), and *No Shoes* (Clay, 2007a), as well as a Spanish version. Teachers carefully observe children as they respond, and then mark their responses on a scoring sheet. The test is available for purchase from Heinemann Books.

Instead of using the test booklets, teachers can also administer the test using other books available in the classroom.

CAP Test Scoring Sheet

Name _____ Date _____

Title of Book _____

Check the items that the child demonstrates.

1. Book-Orientation Concepts
   - ☐ Shows the front of a book.
   - ☐ Turns to the first page of the story.
   - ☐ Shows where to start reading on a page.

2. Directionality Concepts
   - ☐ Shows the direction of print across a line of text.
   - ☐ Shows the direction of print on a page with more than one line of print.
   - ☐ Points to track words as the teacher reads.

3. Letter and Word Concepts
   - ☐ Points to any letter on a page.
   - ☐ Points to a particular letter on a page.
   - ☐ Puts fingers around any word on a page.
   - ☐ Puts fingers around a particular word on a page.
   - ☐ Puts fingers around any sentence on a page.
   - ☐ Points to the first and last letters of a word.
   - ☐ Points to a period or other punctuation mark.
   - ☐ Points to a capital letter.

Summary Comments:

Concepts About Words

At first, young children have only vague notions of literacy terms, such as *word, letter, sound*, and *sentence*, that teachers use in talking about reading and writing, but children develop an increasingly sophisticated understanding of these terms. Papandropoulou and Sinclair (1974) identified four stages of word consciousness. At first, young children don't differentiate between words and things. At the next level, they describe words as labels for things; children consider words that stand for objects as words, but they don't classify articles and prepositions as words because words such as *the* and *with* can't be represented with objects. At the third level, children understand that words carry meaning and that stories are built from words. Finally, more-fluent readers and writers describe words as autonomous elements having meanings of their own with definite semantic and syntactic relationships. Children might say, "You make words with letters." Also, children understand that words have different appearances: They can be spoken, listened to, read, and written. Invernizzi (2003) explains the importance of reaching the fourth level this way: "A concept of word allows children to hold onto the printed word in their mind's eye and scan it from left to right, noting every sound in the beginning, middle, and end" (p. 152).

Children develop concepts about words through active participation in literacy activities. They watch as teachers point to words in big books during shared reading, and they mimic the teacher and point to words as they reread familiar texts. After many, many shared reading experiences, children notice that word boundaries are marked with spaces, and they pick out familiar words. With experience, children's pointing becomes more exact, and they become more proficient at picking out specific words in the text, noticing that words at the beginning of sentences are marked with capital letters and words at the end of sentences are followed with punctuation marks.

Environmental Print. Young children begin reading by recognizing logos on fast-food restaurants, department stores, grocery stores, and commonly used household items within familiar contexts (Harste, Woodward, & Burke, 1984). They recognize the golden arches of McDonald's and say "McDonald's," but when they're shown the word *McDonald's* written on a sheet of paper without the familiar sign and restaurant setting, they can't read the word. At first, young children depend on context to read familiar words and memorized texts, but slowly, they develop relationships linking form and meaning as they gain more reading and writing experience.

Writing. As children begin to experiment with writing, they use scribbles and letter-like forms to represent words (Schickedanz & Casbergue, 2004). As they learn about letter names and phoneme-grapheme (sound-letter) correspondences, they use one, two, or three letters to stand for words. At first, they run their writing together, but they slowly learn to mark word boundaries by segmenting writing into words and leaving spaces between words. They sometimes add dots or lines as markers between words or draw circles around words. They also move from capitalizing words randomly to using capital letters at the beginning of sentences and marking proper nouns and adjectives. Similarly, children move from using a period at the end of each line of writing to marking the ends of sentences with periods.

Literacy Play Centers. Young children learn about the purposes of reading and writing as they use written language in their play: As they construct block buildings, children write signs and tape them on the buildings; as they play doctor, children

Writing Center
These first graders write in journals, make books, and compose notes to class-mates at the writing center. This center is stocked with writing supplies, a word wall with high-frequency words is displayed on a dry-erase board, and a message center (shown in the upper right-hand part of the photo) is available for children to post their notes. They keep their writing projects in folders stored nearby. Children work at this center while the teacher works with guided reading groups. Through this center activity, young chil-dren develop the indepen-dence they need for writing workshop.

write prescriptions on slips of paper; and as they play teacher, children read stories aloud to stuffed animal "students" (McGee, 2007). Young children use these activities to reenact familiar, everyday activities and to pretend to be someone else. Through these literacy play activities, children use reading and writing for a variety of purposes.

Kindergarten teachers add literacy materials to play centers to enhance their value for literacy learning. Housekeeping centers are probably the most common play cen-ters, and they can easily be transformed into a grocery store, a post office, or a medical center by changing the props. They become literacy play centers when materials for reading and writing are included: Food packages, price stickers, and play money are props in grocery store centers; letters, stamps, and mailboxes are props in post office centers; and appointment books, prescription pads, and folders for patient records are props in medical centers. A variety of literacy play centers can be set up in classrooms and coordinated with literature focus units and thematic units.

Concepts About the Alphabet

Young children also develop concepts about the alphabet and how letters are used to represent phonemes. Pinnell and Fountas (1998) identified these components of letter knowledge:

◆ The letter's name
◆ The formation of the letter in upper- and lowercase manuscript handwriting
◆ The features of the letter that distinguish it from other letters
◆ The direction the letter must be turned to distinguish it from other letters (e.g., *b* and *d*)
◆ The use of the letter in known words (e.g., names and common words)

◆ The sound the letter represents in isolation
◆ The sound the letter represents in combination with others (e.g., *ch*, *th*)
◆ The sound the letter represents in the context of a word (e.g., the *c* sounds in *cat*, *city*, and *chair*)

Children use this knowledge to decode unfamiliar words as they read and to create spellings for words as they write.

The most basic information children learn about the alphabet is how to identify and form the letters in handwriting. They notice letters in environmental print and learn to sing the ABC song. By the time children enter kindergarten, they usually recognize some letters, especially those in their own names, in names of family members and pets, and in common words in their homes and communities. Children also write some of these familiar letters.

Research suggests that children don't learn alphabet letter names in any particular order or by isolating letters from meaningful written language in skill-and-drill activities. McGee and Richgels (2008) conclude that learning letters of the alphabet requires many, many experiences with meaningful written language and recommend that teachers take these steps to encourage children's alphabet learning:

Capitalize on children's interests. Teachers provide letter activities that children enjoy, and they talk about letters when children are interested in talking about them. Teachers know what features to comment on because they observe children during reading and writing activities to find out which letters or features of letters children are exploring.

Talk about the role of letters in reading and writing. Teachers talk about how letters represent sounds and how letters combine to spell words and point out capital letters and lowercase letters. Teachers often talk about the role of letters as they write with children.

Provide a variety of opportunities for alphabet learning. Teachers use children's names and environmental print in literacy activities, do **interactive writing**, encourage children to use invented spelling, share alphabet books, and play letter games.

Teachers begin teaching letters of the alphabet using two sources of words—children's own names and environmental print. They teach the ABC song to provide children with a strategy for identifying the name of an unknown letter. Children learn to sing this song and point to each letter on an alphabet chart until they reach the unfamiliar one; this is a very useful strategy because it gives them a real sense of independence in identifying letters. Teachers also provide routines, activities, and games for talking about and manipulating letters. During these familiar, predictable activities, teachers and children say letter names, manipulate magnetic letters, and write letters on dry-erase boards. At first, the teacher structures and guides the activities, but with experience, the children internalize the routine and do it independently, often at a literacy center. Figure 4–1 presents 10 routines to teach the letters of the alphabet.

Being able to name the letters of the alphabet is a good predictor of beginning reading achievement, even though knowing the names of the letters doesn't directly affect a child's ability to read (Adams, 1990; Snow, Burns, & Griffin, 1998). A more likely explanation for this relationship between letter knowledge and reading is that children who have been actively involved in reading and writing activities before entering first grade know the names of the letters, and they're more likely to begin reading quickly. Simply teaching children to name the letters without the accompanying reading and writing experiences doesn't have this effect.

Figure 4–1 ◆ Routines to Teach the Letters of the Alphabet

Environmental Print
Children sort food labels, toy traffic signs, and other environmental print to find examples of a letter being studied.

Alphabet Books
Teachers read aloud alphabet books to build vocabulary, and later, children reread the books to find words when making books about a letter.

Magnetic Letters
Children pick all examples of one letter from a collection of magnetic letters or match upper- and lowercase letterforms of magnetic letters. They also arrange the letters in alphabetical order and use them to spell familiar words.

Letter Stamps
Children use letter stamps and ink pads to print letters on paper or in booklets. They also use letter-shaped sponges to paint letters and letter-shaped cookie cutters to cut out clay letters.

Alphabet Chart
Children point to letters and pictures on the alphabet chart as they recite the alphabet and the name of the picture, such as "A-airplane, B-baby, C-cat," and so on.

Letter Containers
Teachers collect coffee cans or shoe boxes, one for each letter, and place several familiar objects that represent the letter in each container. Teachers use these containers to introduce the letters, and children use them for sorting and matching activities.

Letter Frames
Teachers make circle-shaped letter frames from tagboard, collect large plastic bracelets, or shape pipe cleaners or Wikki-Stix (pipe cleaners covered in wax) into circles for students to use to highlight particular letters on charts or in big books.

Letter Books and Posters
Children make letter books with pictures of objects beginning with a particular letter on each page. They add letter stamps, stickers, or pictures cut from magazines. For posters, the teacher draws a large letterform on a chart and children add pictures, stickers, and letter stamps.

Letter Sorts
Children sort objects and pictures representing two or more letters and place them in containers marked with the specific letters.

Dry-Erase Boards
Children practice writing upper- and lowercase forms of a letter and familiar words on dry-erase boards.

OW CHILDREN DEVELOP AS READERS AND WRITERS

Young children move through three stages as they learn to read and write: emergent, beginning, and fluent (Juel, 1991). During the emergent stage, young children gain an understanding of the communicative purpose of print, and they move from pretend reading to reading predictable books and from using scribbles to simulate writing to writing patterned sentences, such as *I see a bird. I see a tree. I see a car*. The focus of the second stage, beginning reading and writing, is on children's growing ability to use phonics to "crack the alphabetic code" in order to decode and spell words. Children also learn to read and write many high-frequency words and write several sentences to develop a story or other composition. In the fluent stage, children are automatic, fluent readers, and in writing, they develop good handwriting skills, spell many high-frequency words correctly, and organize their writing into multiple-paragraph compositions. Figure 4–2 summarizes children's accomplishments in reading and writing development at each stage.

Figure 4–2 ◆ Young Children's Literacy Development

Stage	Reading	Writing
Emergent	Children: • notice environmental print • show interest in books • pretend to read • use picture cues and predictable patterns in books to retell the story • reread familiar books with predictable patterns • identify some letter names • recognize 5–20 familiar or high-frequency words	Children: • distinguish between writing and drawing • write letters and letterlike forms or scribble randomly on the page • develop an understanding of directionality • show interest in writing • write their first and last names • write 5–20 familiar or high-frequency words • use sentence frames to write a sentence
Beginning	Children: • identify letter names and sounds • match spoken words to written words • recognize 20–100 high-frequency words • use beginning, middle, and ending sounds to decode words • apply knowledge of the cueing systems to monitor reading • self-correct while reading • read slowly, word by word • read orally • point to words when reading • make reasonable predictions	Children: • write from left to right • print the upper- and lowercase letters • write one or more sentences • add a title • spell many words phonetically • spell 20–50 high-frequency words correctly • write single-draft compositions • use capital letters to begin sentences • use periods, question marks, and exclamation points to mark the end of sentences • can reread their writing
Fluent	Children: • identify most words automatically • read with expression • read at a rate of 100 words per minute or more • prefer to read silently • identify unfamiliar words using the cueing systems • recognize 100–300 high-frequency words • use a variety of strategies effectively • often read independently • use knowledge of text structure and genre to support comprehension • make inferences	Children: • use the writing process to write drafts and final copies • write compositions with one or more paragraphs • indent paragraphs • spell most of the 100 high-frequency words • use sophisticated and technical vocabulary • apply vowel patterns to spell words • add inflectional endings on words • apply capitalization rules • use commas, quotation marks, and other punctuation marks

Stage 1: Emergent Reading and Writing

Children gain an understanding of the communicative purpose of print and develop an interest in reading and writing during the emergent stage. They notice environmental print in the world around them and develop concepts about print as teachers read and write with them. As children dictate stories for the teacher to record, for example, they learn that their speech can be written down, and they observe how teachers write from left to right and top to bottom.

During the emergent stage, children accomplish the following:

◆ Develop an interest in reading and writing
◆ Acquire concepts about print

- ◆ Develop book-handling skills
- ◆ Learn to identify the letters of the alphabet
- ◆ Develop handwriting skills
- ◆ Learn to read and write some high-frequency words

Children are usually emergent readers and writers in kindergarten, but some children whose parents have read to them every day and provided a variety of literacy experiences do learn how to read before they come to school. Caroline, a 5-year-old emergent reader and writer in Ms. McCloskey's classroom, is presented in the spotlight feature on pages 120–121.

Young children make scribbles to represent writing. These scribbles may appear randomly on a page at first, but with experience, children line up the letters or scribbles from left to right on a line and from top to bottom on a page. Children also begin to "read," or tell what their writing says (Schickedanz & Casbergue, 2004). At first, they can reread their writing only immediately after writing, but with experience, they learn to remember what their writing says, and as their writing becomes more conventional, they're able to read it more easily.

Emergent readers and writers participate in a variety of literacy activities ranging from modeled and shared reading and writing, during which they watch as teachers read and write, to independent reading and writing that they do themselves. Ms. McCloskey's students, for example, listened to her read aloud books and read big books using shared reading, and they also participated in reading and writing workshop. When working with children at the emergent stage, however, teachers often use modeled and shared reading and writing activities because they are demonstrating what readers and writers do and teaching concepts about print.

Stage 2: Beginning Reading and Writing

This stage marks children's growing awareness of the alphabetic principle. Children learn about phoneme-grapheme correspondences, phonics rules in words such as *run*, *hand*, *this*, *make*, *day*, and *road*, and word families, including *-ill* (*fill*, *hill*, *will*) and *-ake* (*bake*, *make*, *take*). They also apply (and misapply) their developing phonics knowledge to spell words. For example, they spell *night* as *NIT* and *train* as *TRANE*. At the same time, they're learning to read and write high-frequency words, many of which can't be sounded out, such as *what*, *are*, and *there*.

During the beginning stage of reading and writing development, children accomplish the following:

- ◆ Learn phonics skills
- ◆ Recognize 20–100 high-frequency words
- ◆ Apply reading strategies, including cross-checking, predicting, and repairing
- ◆ Write five or more sentences, sometimes organized into a paragraph
- ◆ Spell phonetically
- ◆ Spell 20–50 high-frequency words
- ◆ Use capital letters to begin sentences
- ◆ Use punctuation marks to indicate the ends of sentences
- ◆ Reread their writing

Most first and second graders are beginning readers and writers, and with instruction in literacy strategies and skills and daily opportunities to read and write, children move through this stage to reach the fluent stage. Anthony, a 6-year-old beginning reader and writer in Ms. McCloskey's classroom, is presented in the spotlight feature on pages 122–123.

Spotlight on . . .

An Emergent Reader and Writer

Five-year-old Caroline is a friendly, eager child who is learning to speak English as she learns to read and write. Caroline's grandparents emigrated from Thailand to the United States; her family speaks Hmong at home, and she speaks English only at school. When her Hmong-speaking classmates start to talk in their native language, she admonishes them to speak English because "we learn English school."

When she came to kindergarten, Caroline didn't know any letters of the alphabet and had never held a pencil. She had not listened to stories read aloud and had no book-handling experience. She spoke barely a few words of English. The classroom culture and language were very different than those of her home, but Caroline was eager to learn. For the first few days, she stood back, observing her classmates; then she said "I do" and joined them.

Caroline has made remarkable growth in 5 months. She has been reading books with repetitive sentences on each page, but now at level 3, she is beginning to use phonics to sound out unfamiliar words. She knows the names of most letters and the sounds that the letters represent. She can read about 20 high-frequency words. She has developed good book-handling skills and follows the line of words on a page. She reads word by word and points at the text as she reads. She is learning consonant and vowel sounds, but because of her pronunciation of English sounds and lack of vocabulary, she has difficulty decoding words.

Caroline demonstrates that she understands the books she reads, and she makes text-to-self connections. Recently, she was reading a book about a child having a birthday, and she pointed to the picture of a young, blond mother wrapping a child's birthday present. She looked up at Ms. McCloskey and said,

Emergent Reader and Writer Characteristics That Caroline Exemplifies

Reading	Writing
• Shows great interest in reading	• Shows great interest in writing
• Has developed book-handling skills	• Writes from left to right and top to bottom on a page
• Identifies most of the letters of the alphabet	• Prints most of the letters of the alphabet
• Knows some letter sounds	• Writes 20 high-frequency words
• Sounds out a few CVC words	• Leaves spaces between words
• Reads 20 high-frequency words	• Writes sentences
• Uses predictable patterns in text to reread familiar books	• Begins sentences with a capital letter
• Makes text-to-self connections	• Puts periods at the ends of sentences
	• Rereads what she has written immediately afterward

"She no mom, she sister. This wrong." The woman in the picture looks nothing like her mother.

Caroline began participating in writing workshop on the first day of school, and for several weeks, she scribbled. Within a month, she learned how to print some letters because she wanted her writing to look like her classmates'. Soon she wrote her own name, copied classmates' names, and wrote words she saw posted in the classroom.

A month ago, Ms. McCloskey gave Caroline a ring for key words. Every few days, Caroline chooses a new word to add to her ring. Ms. McCloskey writes the word on a word card that is added to Caroline's ring. Caroline has 31 words now, including *you* and *birthday*. She flips through the cards to practice reading, and she uses the words when she writes sentences.

After 4 months of instruction, Caroline began writing sentences. Ms. McCloskey introduced the frame "I see a _____" and Caroline wrote sentences using familiar words, including some from her key words ring. Then, to make her writing longer, she wrote the same sentence over and over, as shown in the "Apple" writing sample.

Next, she began reading and writing color words, and she expanded her writing to two sentences. Her two-sentence writing sample, "Zebras," also is shown here. Most of the words that Caroline writes are spelled correctly because she uses key words and words she locates in a picture dictionary. Notice that Caroline puts a period at the end of each sentence; but recently she has noticed that some of her classmates put a period at the end of each line so she added periods at the end of each line in the "Zebra" sample, too. When she draws a picture to accompany a sentence, Caroline can usually read her writing

immediately after she has written it, but by the next day, she often doesn't remember what she has written.

Caroline has one of the thickest writing folders in the classroom, and she's very proud of her writing. Nearly 100 pages of writing are stuffed into the folder, tracing her development as a writer since the beginning of the school year.

In the 5 months she has been in kindergarten, Caroline has made excellent progress in learning to read and write. She is an emergent-stage reader and writer. She can read books with repetitive patterns and is learning phonics and high-frequency words. She can write words and craft sentences. A list of the emergent-stage characteristics that Caroline exemplifies is shown in the chart.

Spotlight on . . .

A Beginning Reader and Writer

Anthony, a first grader with a ready smile, is a beginning reader and writer. He's 6 years old, and he says that he likes to read and write. His best friend, Angel, is also in Ms. McCloskey's classroom, and they often sit together to read and write. (The photo shows Anthony, on the right, buddy-reading with his friend Angel.) The boys eat together in the lunchroom and always play together outside, too.

Anthony is a well-behaved child who is extremely competitive. He knows he's reading at level 12 now, and he announced to Ms. McCloskey that he wants to be reading at level 15. She explained that to do that, he needs to practice reading each night at home with his mom, and he's been taking several books home each night to practice. Ms. McCloskey predicts that Anthony will be reading at level 18 by the end of the year; level 18 is the school's benchmark for the end of first grade.

According to Ms. McCloskey's assessment of Anthony's reading at the end of the second quarter, he recognizes 80 of the 100 high-frequency words taught in first grade, and he can decode most one-syllable words with short and long vowel sounds, including words with consonant blends and digraphs, such as *shock*, *chest*, and *spike*. He's beginning to try to sound out some of the more-complex vowel digraphs and diphthongs (e.g., *loud*, *boil*, *soon*) and *r*-controlled vowels (e.g., *chart*, *snore*), and in the past month, Ms. McCloskey has noticed that his ability to decode words is growing and that about two thirds of the time, he can identify these words with more-complex vowel sounds in the context of a sentence. He also is decoding some two- and three-syllable words, such as *dinner*, *parents*, and *hospital*, in books he's reading.

Beginning Reader and Writer Characteristics That Anthony Exemplifies

Reading	Writing
• Likes to read	• Likes to write
• Reads orally	• Writes single-draft compositions
• Points to words when he reads challenging texts	• Adds a title
• Recognizes 80 high-frequency words	• Writes organized compositions on a single topic
• Uses phonics knowledge to decode unfamiliar words	• Writes more than five sentences in a composition
• Makes good predictions	• Has a beginning, middle, and end in his story
• Uses the cross-checking strategy	• Refers to the word wall to spell high-frequency words
• Retells what he reads	• Uses his knowledge of phonics to spell words
• Makes text-to-self and text-to-world connections	• Uses capital letters to mark the beginnings of sentences
	• Uses periods to mark the ends of sentences
	• Reads his writing to classmates

Anthony reads orally and points only when he reads challenging texts. He's beginning to chunk words into phrases as he reads, and he notices when something he is reading doesn't make sense. He uses the cross-checking strategy to make corrections and get back on track.

Anthony has read 17 books this month, according to his reading workshop log. He is increasingly choosing easy-to-read chapter books to read, including Syd Hoff's *Sammy the Seal* (2000b) and *Oliver* (2000a). After he reads, he often shares his books with his friend Angel, and they reread them together and talk about their favorite parts. He regularly uses the connecting strategy and shares his text-to-self and text-to-world connections with Angel and Ms. McCloskey. When he reads two or more books by the same author, he shares text-to-text comparisons and can explain to his teacher how these comparisons make him a better reader: "Now I think and read at the same time," he explains.

Anthony likes to write during writing workshop. He identified his "Being Sick" story as the very best one he's written, and Ms. McCloskey agrees. Anthony tells an interesting and complete story with a beginning, middle, and end. And, you can hear his voice clearly in the story. Anthony's story is shown in the box, and here is a translation of it:

Being Sick

Sometimes I go outside with no! jacket on and the air went in my ear. I went inside and stayed in the house. My ear started to hurt because I had pain. I went to see if Mom was there. I found her. I told her I have an ear ache. My mom put some ear ache stuff in my ear and it made it better.

Anthony's spelling errors are characteristic of phonetic spellers. He sounds out the spelling of many words, such as *sum tims* (*sometimes*) and *hrt* (*hurt*), and he's experimenting with final *e* markers at the end of *tolde* and *pane*, but ignores them on other words. He uses the word wall in the classroom and spells many high-frequency words correctly (e.g., *with*, *went*, *have*).

Anthony writes single-draft compositions in paragraph form, and he creates a title for his stories. He writes in sentences and includes simple, compound, and complex sentences in his writing. He uses capital letters to mark the beginnings of sentences and periods to mark the ends of sentences well, but he continues to randomly put capital letters at the beginnings of words.

Anthony is at the beginning stage of reading and writing development. He reads word by word, uses his finger to track text while reading, and stops to decode unfamiliar words. He's applying what he's learning about phonics to decode words when reading and to spell words when writing. He writes multisentence compositions with good sentence structure, but his phonetic spelling makes his writing difficult to read.

> Being Sick
> Sum tims I go autsid
> With No! JaKit on and the
> err went in my ere. I
> went insid and stad
> in the house. My ere
> Strdit to hrt becuase I had
> pane. I went to see if
> Mom Was ther. I fand
> her. I tolde her I have A Eer
> Fea. My Mom put Sum Ear
> Fea Stuf in My Ear. And it Mad
> it Betr.

Be Strategic!

Young Children's Reading Strategies

These are the first strategies that young children usually learn:

- ► Cross-check
- ► Predict
- ► Connect
- ► Monitor
- ► Repair

Children learn these reading strategies as they participate in shared and guided reading activities and interactive read-alouds.

Children usually read aloud slowly, in a word-by-word fashion, stopping often to sound out unfamiliar words. They point at each word as they read, but by the end of this stage, their reading becomes smoother and more fluent, and they point at words only when the text is especially challenging.

Although the emphasis in this stage is on decoding and recognizing words, children also learn that reading involves comprehension. They make predictions to guide their thinking about events in stories they read, and they make connections between what they're reading and their own lives and the world around them as they personalize the reading experience. They monitor their reading to recognize when it doesn't make sense, cross-check using phonological, semantic, syntactic, and pragmatic information in the text to figure out the problem, and repair or self-correct it (Fountas & Pinnell, 1996). They also learn about story structure, particularly that stories have a beginning, middle, and end, and use this knowledge to guide their reading and retelling.

Children move from writing one or two sentences to developing longer compositions, with five, eight, or more sentences organized into paragraphs, by the end of this stage. Their writing is better developed, too, because they're acquiring a sense of audience, and they want their classmates to like what they've written. Children continue to write single-draft compositions but begin to make a few revisions and editing corrections as they learn about the writing process toward the end of the stage.

Children apply what they're learning about phonics in their spelling, and they correctly spell many of the high-frequency words that they've learned to read. They know how to spell some high-frequency words and can locate others on **word walls** posted in the classroom. They learn to use capital letters to mark the beginnings of sentences and punctuation to mark the ends of sentences. Children are more adept at rereading their writing, both immediately afterward and days later, because they're able to read many of the words they've written.

Teachers plan activities for children at the beginning stage that range from modeled to independent reading and writing activities, but the emphasis is on interactive and guided activities. Through **interactive writing**, **choral reading**, and **guided reading**, teachers scaffold children as they read and write and use **minilessons** to provide strategy and skill instruction. For example, Ms. McCloskey's students were divided into small, homogeneous groups for guided reading lessons. The children met to read books at their reading levels, and Ms. McCloskey introduced new vocabulary words, taught reading strategies and skills, and assessed their comprehension.

Teachers introduce the writing process to beginning-stage writers once they develop a sense of audience and want to make their writing better so their classmates will like it. Children don't immediately begin writing rough drafts and final copies or doing both revising and editing: They often begin the writing process by rereading their compositions and adding a word or two, correcting a misspelled word, or capitalizing a lowercase letter. These changes are cosmetic, but the idea that the writing process doesn't end after the first draft is established. Next, children show interest in making a final copy that really looks good. They either recopy the composition by hand or use word processing and print out the final copy. Once children understand that writing involves a rough draft and a final copy, they're ready to learn more about revising and editing, and they usually reach this point at about the same time they become fluent writers.

Stage 3: Fluent Reading and Writing

The third stage marks children's move into fluent reading and writing. Fluent readers recognize hundreds and hundreds of words automatically and have the tools to identify unfamiliar words when reading. Fluent writers use the writing process to draft, revise, and publish their writing and participate in writing groups. They're familiar with a variety of genres and know how to organize their writing. They use conventional spelling and other written language conventions, including capital letters and punctuation marks.

Fluent readers and writers accomplish the following:

◆ Read fluently and with expression
◆ Recognize most one-syllable words automatically and can decode other words efficiently
◆ Use decoding and comprehension strategies effectively
◆ Write well-developed, multiparagraph compositions
◆ Use the writing process to draft and refine their writing
◆ Write stories, reports, letters, and other genres
◆ Spell most high-frequency and other one-syllable words correctly
◆ Use capital letters and punctuation marks correctly most of the time

Some second graders reach this stage, and all children should be fluent readers and writers by the end of third grade. Reaching this stage is an important milestone because it indicates that children are ready for the increased literacy demands of fourth grade, when they're expected to read longer chapter-book stories, use writing to respond to literature, read content-area textbooks, and write essays and reports. Jazmen, an 8-year-old fluent reader and writer in Ms. McCloskey's classroom, is profiled in the spotlight feature on pages 126–127.

The distinguishing characteristic of fluent readers is that they read words accurately, rapidly, and expressively. Fluent readers automatically recognize many words and can decode unfamiliar words efficiently. Their reading rate has increased to 100 words or more per minute; in addition, they can vary their speed according to the demands of the text they're reading.

Most fluent readers prefer to read silently because they can read more quickly than when they read orally. No longer do they point at words as they read. Children can read many books independently, actively making predictions, visualizing, monitoring their understanding, and making repairs when necessary. They have a range of strategies available and use them enhance their comprehension.

Fluent readers' comprehension is stronger, and they think more deeply about their reading than emergent and beginning readers do. It's likely that children's comprehension improves at this stage because they have more cognitive energy available for comprehension now; in contrast, beginning readers use much more cognitive energy to decode words. So, as children become fluent, they use less energy for word identification and have more cognitive resources available for comprehending what they read.

During this stage, children read longer, more sophisticated picture books and chapter books, but they generally prefer chapter books because they enjoy really getting into a story or digging deeply in an informational book. They learn more about the literary genres, their structural patterns, and literary devices, such as alliteration, personification, and symbolism. They participate in literature focus units featuring an author, genre, or book, in small-group literature circles where children read and discuss a book together, and in author studies where they read and compare several books

Spotlight on . . .

A Fluent Reader and Writer

Jazmen is a confident and articulate African American third grader. She's 8 years old, and she celebrated her birthday last fall with a family trip to the Magic Mountain amusement park in Southern California. She smiles easily and likes to shake her head so that her braided, beaded hair swirls around her head. Jazmen is a pro at using computers, and she often provides assistance to her classmates. When asked about her favorite school activity, Jazmen says that she likes using the computer best of all. In fact, she is interested in learning more about careers that involve computers because she knows that she always wants to work with them.

Ms. McCloskey identified Jazmen for this feature because she's made such remarkable progress this year. This is the second year that Jazmen has been in Ms. McCloskey's class. Last year, she seemed stuck in the beginning stage, not making too much progress, according to Ms. McCloskey, "but this year, it's like a light-bulb has been turned on!" She's now a fluent reader and writer.

Jazmen likes to read, and she reports that she has a lot of books at home. According to the Accelerated Reader® program, she is reading at 3.8 (third grade, eighth month) level, which means she is reading at or slightly above grade level. She enjoys reading the Marvin Redpost (e.g., *Marvin Redpost: A Magic Crystal?*, by Louis Sachar, 2000) and Zack Files (e.g., *Never Trust a Cat Who Wears Earrings*, by Dan Greenburg, 1997) series of easy-to-read paperback chapter books. She says that she enjoys these books because they're funny.

Currently she's reading Paula Danziger's series of chapter-book stories about a third grader named Amber Brown who deals with the realities of contemporary life, including adjusting to her parents' divorce. The first book in the series is *Amber Brown Is Not a Crayon* (2006), about Amber and her best friend, Justin, who moves away at the end of the book; other chapter books in the series are *Amber Brown Goes Fourth* (2007),

Fluent Reader and Writer Characteristics That Jazmen Exemplifies

Reading	Writing
• Recognizes most words automatically • Reads with expression • Reads more than 100 words per minute • Reads independently • Uses a variety of strategies • Makes connections when reading • Thinks inferentially • Applies knowledge of story structure and genre when reading	• Uses the writing process • Has a sense of audience and purpose • Writes a complete story with a beginning, middle, and end • Writes in paragraphs • Indents paragraphs • Uses sophisticated language • Spells most words correctly • Uses capital letters and punctuation to mark sentence boundaries

Amber Brown Is Feeling Blue (1999), *Amber Brown Sees Red* (1998), and *Amber Brown Is Green With Envy* (2004).

Jazmen reads well. She recognizes words automatically and reads with expression. She says that when you're reading to someone, you have to be interesting and that's why she reads the way she does. Her most outstanding achievement, according to Ms. McCloskey, is that she thinks inferentially about stories. She can juggle thinking about plot, characters, setting, and theme in order to make thoughtful connections and interpretations. She knows about various genres and literary elements, and she uses this knowledge as she reflects on her reading.

Jazmen likes to write. She gets her ideas for stories from television programs. She explains, "When I'm watching TV, I get these ideas and I draw pictures of them and that's how I think of a story." She's currently working on a story entitled "Lucky and the Color Purple," about a princess named Lucky who possesses magical qualities. Why are her stories interesting? Jazmen says, "Most important is that they are creative." She shares her stories with her classmates, and they agree that Jazmen is a good writer.

Jazmen is particularly pleased with her story "The Super Hero With the Long Hair," which is shown here. The story has a strong voice. Jazmen wanted her story to sound interesting, so she substituted *whined* and *grouched* for *said*. Ms. McCloskey explained that she likes the story because it's complete with a beginning, middle, and end, and because Jazmen uses dialogue (and quotation marks) effectively. The errors remaining on the final draft of the paper also suggest direction for future instruction. Jazmen spelled 95% of the words in her composition correctly. In particular, Jazmen appears ready to learn more about plurals and possessives and using commas within sentences.

During her third-grade year, Jazmen has become a fluent reader and writer, and she exemplifies the characteristics listed in the chart. In fact, her classmates look to her for leadership when they're working on reading and writing projects. They ask her assistance in choosing books and decoding difficult words. Jazmen's writing has become more polished this year, too. She's become a thoughtful writer, and she uses the writing process to draft and refine her writing. Her classmates ask her to respond to their writing, and they're eager to listen to her read her new stories from the author's chair.

The Super Hero With the Long Hair

One beutiful day Nancy woke up. When she realized her hair was more beutiful than ever. She started pumping n the bed.

After that she started brushing her hair. She kept on brushing and brushing and brushing. The finally her sister's got so jealous they got mad.

Then they asked. "Can we brush you're hair and give you a little S...T...Y...L...E?" "Sure," said Nancy. They brushed and brushed.

All of a sudden they started cutting her hair. "What kind of S...T...Y...L...E are you doing?" "A pretty hair style." "Of course pretty. Is it really really pretty?"

"Yes yes it's really really pretty." Kelly said in a diskusting way. Then Kelly was done–Nancy went to go look in the bathroom miron. She started to cry. Her sister's started to laugh.

Then the light started to glow on the phone. Niky answered it. It was the mayor. "Hello mayor yes we'll be right on our way. The mayor said townsvill's in trouble. There's a monster outside and he's distroying all of townsvill!" shouted Niky.

"Go without me." whined Nancy. "What?" ""We can't go without you. You're the leader." "Just go without me!" Grouched Nancy.

They left. She started to talk to her dad. She made up her mind about going. She also made up some joke's. She flew to the monster and told her joke's to him and he laughed so hard he flew all the way to Jupiter.

Her sister's said, "Are we even?" The she lazorbeeded her sister's hair and said, "Now were even."

They lived happily everaften.

by the same author and examine that author's writing style. They're able to explain why they liked a particular book and make recommendations to classmates.

Fluent writers understand that writing is a process, and they use the writing process stages—prewriting, drafting, revising, editing, and publishing. They make plans for writing and write both rough drafts and final copies. They reread their rough drafts and make revisions and editing changes that reflect their understanding of writing forms and their purpose for writing. They increasingly share their rough drafts with classmates and turn to them for advice on how to make their writing better.

Children get ideas for writing from books they've read and from television programs and movies they've viewed. They organize their writing into paragraphs, indent paragraphs, and focus on a single idea in each paragraph. They develop ideas more completely and use more-sophisticated vocabulary to express their ideas.

Fluent writers are aware of writing genres and organize their writing into stories, reports, letters, and poems. Their stories have a beginning, middle, and end, and the reports they write are structured using sequence, comparison, or cause-and-effect structures. Their letters reflect an understanding of the parts of a letter and how they're arranged on a page. Their poems incorporate alliteration, symbolism, rhyme, or other poetic devices to create vivid impressions.

Children's writing looks more conventional. They spell most of the 100 high-frequency words correctly and use phonics to spell other one-syllable words correctly. They add inflectional endings (e.g., *-s, -ed, -ing*) and experiment with spelling two-syllable and longer words. They've learned to capitalize the first word in sentences and names and to use punctuation marks correctly at the ends of sentences, although they're still experimenting with punctuation marks within sentences.

A list of instructional recommendations for each of the three stages of reading and writing development is presented in Figure 4–3.

INSTRUCTIONAL PRACTICES

Teachers who work with young readers and writers use many of the same instructional practices used with older students, such as reading aloud to children, doing **guided reading** with leveled books, teaching from basal reading textbooks, and providing opportunities for independent reading and writing in reading and writing workshop. Teachers adapt these approaches to provide enough scaffolding so that young children are successful. Other instructional practices have been developed specifically for young children and other novice readers and writers.

Morning Message

Morning message is a daily literacy routine that teachers use to teach literacy concepts, strategies, and skills (Payne & Schulman, 1999). Before the children arrive, teachers write a brief message on chart paper, usually in the form of a friendly letter, about what will happen that day; then the message is read at the beginning of the school day. Afterward, children reread it and count the letters, words, and sentences in the message. They also pick out familiar letters and words, words following a particular phonics pattern, high-frequency words, or capital letters and punctuation marks, depending on children's level of literacy development.

Figure 4–3 ◆ Instructional Recommendations for the Three Stages of Reading and Writing

Stage	Reading	Writing
Emergent	• Use environmental print. • Include literacy materials in play centers. • Read aloud to children. • Read big books and poems on charts using shared reading. • Introduce the title and author of books before reading. • Teach directionality and letter and word concepts using big books. • Encourage children to make predictions and text-to-self connections. • Have children retell and dramatize stories. • Have children respond to literature through talk and drawing. • Have children manipulate sounds using phonemic awareness activities. • Use alphabet-learning routines. • Take children's dictation using the Language Experience Approach. • Teach 20–24 high-frequency words. • Post words on a word wall.	• Have children use crayons for drawing and pencils for writing. • Encourage children to use scribble writing or write random letters if they can't do more conventional writing. • Teach handwriting skills. • Use interactive writing for whole-class and small-group writing projects. • Have children write their names on sign-in sheets each day. • Have children write their own names and names of classmates. • Have children inventory or make lists of words they know how to write. • Have children "write the classroom" by making lists of familiar words they find in the classroom. • Have children use frames such as "I like _____ " and "I see a _____ " to write sentences. • Encourage children to remember what they write so they can read it.
Beginning	• Read charts of poems and songs using choral reading. • Read leveled books using guided reading. • Provide daily opportunities to read and reread books independently. • Teach phonics concepts and rules. • Teach children to cross-check using the cueing systems. • Teach the 100 high-frequency words. • Point out whether texts are stories, informational books, or poems. • Teach predicting, connecting, cross-checking, and other strategies. • Teach the elements of story structure, particularly beginning, middle, and end. • Have children write in reading logs and participate in grand conversations. • Have children take books home to read with parents.	• Use interactive writing to teach concepts about print and spelling rules. • Provide daily opportunities to write for a variety of purposes and using different genres. • Introduce the writing process. • Teach children to develop a single idea in their compositions. • Teach children to proofread their compositions. • Teach children to spell the 100 high-frequency words. • Teach contractions. • Teach capitalization and punctuation skills. • Have children use computers to publish their writing. • Have children share their writing from the author's chair.
Fluent	• Have children participate in literature circles. • Have children participate in reading workshop. • Teach about genres and literary features. • Involve children in author studies. • Teach children to make text-to-self, text-to-world, and text-to-text connections. • Have children respond to literature through talk and writing.	• Have children participate in writing workshop. • Teach children to use the writing process. • Teach children to revise and edit their writing. • Teach paragraphing skills. • Teach spelling rules. • Teach homophones. • Teach synonyms. • Teach root words and affixes. • Teach children to use a dictionary and a thesaurus.

Teachers usually follow a predictable pattern in their messages each day to make it easier for children to read, as these two morning messages show:

Dear Kindergartners,
Today is Monday.
We will plant seeds.
We will make books
about plants.
  Love,
  Ms. Thao

Dear Kindergartners,
Today is Thursday.
We will measure the plants.
We will write about how
plants grow.
  Love,
  Ms. Thao

The morning messages that teachers write for first and second graders become gradually more complex, as this second-grade teacher's message demonstrates:

Good Morning!
Today is Monday, February 4, 2008.
New literature circles begin on Wednesday.
I'll tell you about the new book choices this
morning, and then you can sign up for your
favorite book. Who remembers what a
synonym is? Can you give an example?
  Love,
  Ms. Salazar

Teachers usually choose children to take the messages home to share with their families, either day by day or at the end of each week.

Teachers have adapted the morning message routine in a variety of ways to support their literacy programs. Here are three variations:

Fill-in-the-blank morning message. The teacher writes the morning message, omitting some words for children to fill in. The teacher reads the entire message once, and then during the second reading, children identify the missing words and write them in the blanks. Sometimes teachers write the missing words on cards and display them in a pocket chart to simplify the activity. Here's a first-grade class's morning message:

Mr. Diaz's Morning Message
Today is _____, October 15, 2008.
It is the _____ day of school. We love to _____
The Cat in the Hat by Dr. _____. We can read
words that rhyme with cat: _____, _____,
and _____.

The missing words are *Wednesday, 37th, read, Seuss, bat, hat*, and *rat*. After completing the chart, the children reread the message, count the sentences, circle high-frequency words they've learned, and think of additional rhyming words.

One child dictates a message to share with classmates. The children take turns creating a message to share personal news with classmates. The teacher writes the child's dictation on chart paper. Children usually read their own messages aloud to classmates, pointing to each word as they read, just like their teacher does. In this example, Ivan shares some big news:

Ivan's News
I have a new baby sister. Her name is
Ava. She sleeps all the time, and I have
to be very quiet so I won't wake her up.

After reading and rereading the message and examining individual words and punctuation marks, the children decide to write a welcome message to Ivan's sister at the bottom of the chart paper. They dictate it for the teacher to record and sign their names; then Ivan takes the chart paper home to share with his family.

New Literacies
Interactive Books

Technology is transforming literacy instruction, even for the youngest readers. Interactive books are one example of how young children can use technology as they learn concepts about print, read high-frequency words, develop reading fluency, expand vocabulary knowledge, and practice comprehension strategies. These electronic books have text and illustrations similar to traditional picture books, but they incorporate computer technology to enhance children's reading experience (Lefever-Davis & Pearman, 2005): They feature audio renditions of the entire text as children read along, pronunciations of individual words when children highlight them, and hotspots that children click to produce sound effects and graphic animations where characters talk and settings spring to life.

Many interactive books, based on high-quality books of children's literature, are available on CD-ROM. Here are some of the best ones:

- Dr. Seuss's rhyming stories *The Cat in the Hat* and *Green Eggs and Ham*, from the Learning Company
- H. A. Rey's *Curious George* stories about a hilarious little monkey, from Simon and Schuster
- Norman Bridwell's *Clifford* stories about a big red dog named Clifford, from Scholastic
- Stan and Jan Berenstain's adventures about a bear family in *Berenstain Bears*, from Broderbund
- Marc Brown's series about an aardvark named Arthur and his friends, from the Learning Company
- Janell Cannon's *Stellaluna*, a charming story about a bat named Stellaluna, from Living Books
- Mercer Mayer's *Just Grandma and Me*, a story about a little critter who takes a trip to the beach with his grandmother, from the Learning Company

Other interactive books for K–5 students are available from LeapFrog SchoolHouse: The Leveled Reading Series provides interactive books for independent reading practice, and the Language First! Program includes books for English learners at four levels of English proficiency with native-language audio support in Spanish, Vietnamese, Cantonese, Haitian Creole, and Hmong.

In addition to interactive books on CD-ROM, others are available at these websites:

Book Pals

www.storylineonline.net

Streaming video programs featuring Screen Actors Guild members reading popular children's books, including Mem Fox's *Wilfred Gordon McDonald Partridge*.

Dora the Explorer

www.nickjr.com

Interactive stories featuring Dora the Explorer from her Nickelodeon cable network series.

PBS Kids

www.pbskids.org

Interactive books from the Between the Lions PBS series, and stories featuring Arthur and Curious George.

Storytime Online

www.kennedy-center.org/multimedia/storytimeonline/

Streaming media presentations of Judith Viorst's *Alexander and the Terrible, Horrible, No Good, Very Bad Day* and other stories.

Tumble Books

www.tumblebooks.com

A collection of animated talking picture books for children, available by subscription.

Children appreciate the control they have in choosing how much support the interactive book provides while they're reading, and researchers have documented that children's word knowledge and comprehension are enhanced by these reading experiences (Lefever-Davis & Pearman, 2005). There's a potential drawback, however: Children can become dependent on the electronic support in decoding words that interactive books provide.

Children create a message collaboratively. Some teachers write class news at the end of the school day instead of morning messages. They discuss the day's activities and decide together what to write. Teachers use **interactive writing** so that children can do most of the writing. Here's an example of a first-grade class's news:

> *Room 3 News*
> *We are studying insects. Today we*
> *read <u>Diary of a Fly</u> by Doreen Cronin.*
> *It's a totally hilarious book! We learned*
> *that flies walk on walls, and they eat*
> *regurgitated food. That's so yucky!*

Through these adaptations, children learn about the format of friendly letters and other writing genres and the relationships between reading and writing. The writing is authentic, and children learn how to use writing to share information with others.

Shared Reading

Teachers use **shared reading** to read aloud books that are appropriate for children's interest level but too difficult for them to read for themselves (Parkes, 2000). Teachers use the five stages of the reading process in shared reading, as Ms. McCloskey did in the vignette at the beginning of the chapter. The steps in shared reading are presented in Figure 4–4, showing how the activities fit into the five stages of the reading process. Through the reading process, teachers model what fluent readers do as they involve children in enjoyable reading activities (Fountas & Pinnell, 1996). After the text is read several times, teachers use it to teach phonics and high-frequency words. Children also read small versions of the book with partners or independently, and the pattern or structure found in the text can be used for writing activities.

The books chosen for shared reading are available as big books and are close to children's reading level, but still beyond their ability to read independently. As an instructional strategy, shared reading differs from **interactive read-alouds** because they see the text as the teacher reads. Also, children often join in the reading of predictable refrains and rhyming words, and after listening to the teacher read the text several times, children often remember enough of the text to read along with the teacher. Through shared reading, teachers also demonstrate how print works, provide opportunities for children to make predictions, and increase children's confidence in their ability to read.

Big books are greatly enlarged picture books that teachers use in shared reading, most commonly with primary-grade students. In this technique, developed in New Zealand, teachers place an enlarged picture book on an easel or chart stand where all children can see it. They read it aloud, pointing to every word. Before long, children join in the reading, especially in repeating the refrain. Then teachers reread the book, inviting children to help with the reading. The next time the book is read, teachers read to the point that the text becomes predictable, such as the beginning of a refrain, and children supply the missing text; having them supply the missing words is important because it leads to independent reading. Once children are familiar with the text, they're invited to read the big book independently (Parkes, 2000).

Predictable Books. The stories and other books that teachers use for shared reading with young children often have repeated sentences, rhyme, or other patterns; books that incorporate these patterns are called *predictable books*. These are the four most common patterns:

Figure 4–4 ◆ How a Shared Reading Lesson Fits Into the Reading Process

1. **Prereading**
   - Activate or build background knowledge on a topic related to the book.
   - Show the cover of the book and read the title.
   - Talk about the author and the illustrator.
   - Have students make predictions.

2. **Reading**
   - Use a big book or text printed on a chart.
   - Use a pointer to track during reading.
   - Read expressively with very few stops during the first reading.
   - Highlight vocabulary and repetitive patterns.
   - Reread the book once or twice, and encourage students to join in the reading.

3. **Responding**
   - Discuss the book in a grand conversation.
   - Ask inferential and higher-level questions, such as "What would happen if . . .?" and "What did this book make you think of?"
   - Share the pen to write a sentence interactively about the book.
   - Have students draw and write in reading logs.

4. **Exploring**
   - Reread the book using small books.
   - Add important words to the word wall.
   - Teach minilessons on strategies and skills.
   - Present more information about the author and the illustrator.
   - Provide a text set with other books by the author or on the same topic.

5. **Applying**
   - Have students write a collaborative book to retell the story.
   - Have students write an innovation imitating the pattern used in the book.
   - Have students dramatize the story or use puppets to retell it.

Repetition. Authors repeat sentences to create a predictable pattern in many picture books. In *Barnyard Banter* (Fleming, 1997), for example, a white goose chases an elusive butterfly around a farm as the cows, roosters, and other animals call out their greetings using a predictable pattern.

Cumulative Sequence. Sentences are repeated and expanded in each episode in these books. For example, in *The Gingerbread Boy* (Galdone, 2008), the cookie repeats and expands his boast as he meets each character on his run away from the Little Old Man and the Little Old Woman.

Rhyme and Rhythm. Rhyme and rhythm are two poetic devices that authors use to add a musical quality to their writing. Many of the popular Dr. Seuss books, such as *Fox in Socks* (1965), use rhyme and rhythm. The sentences have a strong beat, and rhyme is used at the end of lines. Other books that incorporate rhyme and rhythm include familiar songs, such as *Shoo Fly!* (Trapani, 2000), and booklong verses, such as *Pattern Fish* (Harris, 2000).

Sequential Patterns. Some authors use a familiar sequence—such as the months of the year, days of the week, numbers 1 to 10, or letters of the alphabet—to structure their books. For example, in *The Very Hungry Caterpillar* (Carle, 2002), the author uses number and day-of-the-week sequences as the caterpillar eats through an amazing array of foods.

Figure 4–5 lists predictable books representing each category. These books are valuable for emergent readers because the repeated sentences, patterns, and sequences make it easier for children to predict the next sentence or episode (Tompkins & Webeler, 1983).

Language Experience Approach

The **Language Experience Approach** (LEA) is based on children's language and experiences (Ashton-Warner, 1986). In this approach, teachers do shared writing: Children dictate words and sentences about their experiences, and the teacher writes down what the children say; the text they develop becomes the reading material. Because the language comes from the children themselves and because the content is based on their experiences, they're usually able to read the text easily. Reading and writing are connected, because children are actively involved in reading what they've written.

Using this approach, children create individual booklets. They draw pictures on each page or cut pictures from magazines to glue on each page, and then they dictate the text that the teacher writes beside each illustration. Children can also make collaborative books, where each child creates one page to be added to a class book. For example, as part of the unit on "The Three Bears," a kindergarten class made a collaborative book on bears. Children each chose a fact about bears for their page; they drew an illustration and dictated the text for their teacher to record. One page from this class book is shown in Figure 4–6. The teacher took the children's dictation rather than having them write the book themselves because she wanted it to be written in conventional spelling so everyone in the classroom could read and reread the book.

When taking dictation, it's a great temptation to change the child's language to the teacher's own, in either word choice or grammar, but editing should be kept to a minimum

Figure 4–5 ◆ Predictable Books for Young Children

Repetition

Carle, E. (1997). *Have you seen my cat?* New York: Aladdin Books.

Guarino, D. (2004). *Is your mama a llama?* New York: Scholastic.

Martin, B., Jr. (2007). *Baby bear, baby bear, what do you see?* New York: Henry Holt.

Rathmann, P. (2000). *Good night, gorilla.* New York: Puffin Books.

Rosen, M. (2004). *We're going on a bear hunt.* New York: Candlewick Press.

Cumulative Sequence

Aylesworth, J. (1996). *The gingerbread man.* New York: Scholastic.

Fleming, D. (2006). *The cow who clucked.* New York: Henry Holt.

Pinkney, J. (2006). *The little red hen.* New York: Dial Books.

Taback, S. (2004). *The house that Jack built.* New York: Puffin Books.

Wood, A. (2007). *Silly Sally.* San Diego: Harcourt.

Rhyme and Rhythm

Fleming, D. (1995). *In the tall, tall grass.* New York: Henry Holt.

Hoberman, M. A. (2003). *Miss Mary Mack: A hand-clapping rhyme.* Boston: Little, Brown.

Hoberman, M. A. (2004). *The eensy-weensy spider.* Boston: Little, Brown.

Martin, B., Jr., & Archambault, J. (2000). *Chicka chicka boom boom.* New York: Aladdin Books.

Shaw, N. (2006). *Sheep in a jeep.* Boston: Houghton Mifflin.

Sequential Patterns

Baker, K. (2007). *Hickory dickory dock.* San Diego: Harcourt.

Carle, E. (1997). *Today is Monday.* New York: Putnam.

Carle, E. (2005). *A house for hermit crab.* New York: Aladdin Books.

Christelow, E. (2006). *Five little monkeys jumping on the bed.* New York: Clarion Books.

Wood, A. (2004). *Ten little fish.* New York: Blue Sky Press/Scholastic.

Figure 4-6 ◆ One Page From a Class Book About Bears

Polar bears live in
ice and snow.

Jesse

so that children don't get the impression that their language is inferior or inadequate. Also, as children become familiar with dictating to the teacher, they learn to pace their dictation to the teacher's writing speed. At first, children dictate as they think of ideas, but with experience, they watch as the teacher writes and supply the text word by word. This change also provides evidence of children's developing concepts about print.

Interactive Writing

In **interactive writing**, children and the teacher create a text together and "share the pen" as they write the text on chart paper (Button, Johnson, & Furgerson, 1996; McCarrier, Pinnell, & Fountas, 2000). The children compose the message together, and then the teacher guides them as they write it word by word on chart paper. Children take turns writing known letters and familiar words, adding punctuation marks, and leaving spaces between words. All children participate in creating and writing the text on chart paper, and they also write the text on small dry-erase boards or on paper as it is written on the chart paper. Afterward, children read and reread the text together with classmates and on their own.

Children use interactive writing to write class news, predictions before reading, retellings of stories, thank-you letters, reports, math story problems, and many other types of group writings (Tompkins & Collom, 2004). Two interactive writing samples are shown in Figure 4–7; the top sample was written by a kindergarten class during a health unit, and the second one is a story problem written by a first-grade class during math. After writing this story problem, children wrote other subtraction problems individually. The boxes drawn around some of the letters and words represent correction tape that was used to correct misspellings or poorly formed letters. In the kindergarten sample, children took turns writing individual letters; in the first-grade sample, children took turns writing entire words.

Go to the Building Teaching Skills and Dispositions section of Chapter 4 on **MyEducationLab.com** to see students participating in interactive writing.

Figure 4–7 ◆ Two Samples of Interactive Writing

Through interactive writing, children learn concepts about print, letter-sound relationships and spelling patterns, handwriting concepts, and capitalization and punctuation skills. Teachers model correct spelling and use of conventions of print, and children practice segmenting the sounds in words and spelling familiar words.

Teachers help children spell all words conventionally. They teach high-frequency words such as *the* and *of*, assist children in segmenting sounds and syllables in other words, point out unusual spelling patterns such as *pieces* and *germs*, and teach other conventions of print. Whenever children misspell a word or form a letter incorrectly, teachers use correction tape to cover the mistake and help them make the correction. For example, when a child wrote the numeral *8* to spell *ate* in the second sample in Figure 4–7, the teacher explained the *eight–ate* homophone, covered the numeral with correction tape, and helped the child spell the word, including the silent *e*. Teachers emphasize the importance of using conventional spelling as a courtesy to readers, not that a child made a mistake. In contrast to the emphasis on conventional spelling in interactive writing, children are encouraged to use invented spelling and other spelling strategies when writing independently. They learn to look for familiar words posted on classroom **word walls** or in books they have read, think about spelling patterns, or ask a classmate for help. Teachers also talk about purpose and explain that in personal writing and rough drafts, children do use invented spelling. Increasingly, however, children want to use conventional spelling and even ask to use the correction tape to fix errors they make as they write.

Manuscript Handwriting

Children enter kindergarten with different backgrounds of handwriting experience. Some 5-year-olds have never held a pencil, but many others have written cursivelike scribbles or manuscript letterlike lines and circles. Some have learned to print their names and even a few other letters. Handwriting instruction in kindergarten typically includes developing children's ability to hold pencils, refining their fine-motor control, and focusing on letter formation. Some people might argue that kindergartners are too young to learn handwriting skills, but young children should be encouraged to write from the first day of school. They write letters and words on labels, draw and write stories, keep journals, and write other types of messages. The more they write, the greater their need becomes for instruction in handwriting. Instruction is necessary so that children don't learn bad habits that later must be broken.

To teach children how to form letters, many kindergarten and first-grade teachers create brief directions for forming letters that they sing to a familiar tune; for example, to form a lowercase letter *a*, try "All around and make a tail" sung to the tune of "Row, Row, Row Your Boat." As teachers sing the directions, they model the formation of the letter in the air or on the chalkboard using large arm motions. Then children sing along and practice forming the letter in the air. Later, they practice writing letters using sponge paintbrushes dipped in water at the chalkboard or pens on dry-erase boards as well as in authentic paper-and-pencil writing activities.

Handwriting research suggests that moving models are much more effective than still models, which suggests that worksheets on the letters aren't very useful because children often don't form the letters correctly. Researchers recommend that children watch teachers to see how letters are formed and then practice forming them themselves. Also, teachers supervise children as they write so that they can correct those who form letters incorrectly. It's important that children write circles counterclockwise, starting from 1:00, and form most lines from top to bottom and left to right across the page. When children follow these guidelines, they're less likely to tear the paper they're writing on, and they'll have an easier transition to cursive handwriting.

Writing Centers

Writing centers are set up in kindergarten and first-grade classrooms so that children have a special place where they can go to write. The center should be located at a table with chairs, and a box of supplies, including pencils, crayons, a date stamp, different kinds of paper, journal notebooks, a stapler, blank books, notepaper, and envelopes, should be stored nearby. The alphabet, printed in upper- and lowercase letters, should be available on the table for children to refer to as they write. In addition, there should be a crate where children can file their work. When children come to the writing center, they draw and write in journals, compile books, and write messages to classmates (Tunks & Giles, 2007). Teachers assist children and provide information about letters, words, and sentences as needed, or aides, parent-volunteers, or older students can assist.

Figure 4–8 presents two reading log entries created by kindergartners and first graders at the writing center. The top piece shows a kindergartner's response to *If You Give a Mouse a Cookie* (Numeroff, 2000). The child's writing says, "I love chocolate chip cookies." The bottom piece was written by a first grader after reading *Are You My Mother?* (Eastman, 2005). The child wrote, "The bird said, 'Are you my mother, you big ole Snort?'" After children shared their log entries during a **grand conversation**, this child added, "The mommy said, 'Here is a worm. I am

Figure 4-8 ◆ Two Children's Reading Log Entries

here. I'm here.'" Notice that the part the mother says is written as though it were coming out of the bird's mouth and going up into the air.

Young children also make books at the writing center based on the books they have read. For example, they can use the same patterns as in *Baby Bear, Baby Bear, What Do You See?* (Martin, 2007), *If You Give a Mouse a Cookie* (Numeroff, 2000), and *Lunch* (Fleming, 1996) to create innovations, or new versions of familiar stories. A first grader's four-page book about a mouse named Jerry, written after reading *If You Give a Mouse a Cookie*, is shown in Figure 4–9. In these writing projects, children often use invented spelling, but they're encouraged to spell familiar words and words from the story correctly.

Children also write notes and letters to classmates at the writing center. They learn about the format of friendly letters and how to phrase the greeting and the closing. Then they apply what they're learning as they write to classmates to say hello, offer a compliment, share news, trade telephone numbers, and offer birthday wishes. As they write messages, the children practice writing their names, their classmates' names, and the words they're learning to read and spell. The classmates who receive the messages also gain practice reading the messages. Teachers participate, too, by regularly writing brief messages to children. Through their activities, they model how to write messages and how to read and respond to the messages they

Figure 4–9 ◆ A First Grader's Four-Page Innovation for *If You Give a Mouse a Cookie*

receive. To facilitate the sharing of these messages, teachers often set up a message bulletin board or individual mailboxes made from milk cartons or shoe boxes. This activity is especially valuable because children discover the social purposes of reading and writing as they write and receive notes and letters.

Chapter 4 Review

How Effective Teachers Support the Youngest Children's Literacy Development

▶ Teachers foster young children's interest in literacy and teach concepts about written language.

▶ Teachers understand that children move through the emergent, beginning, and fluent stages of literacy development.

▶ Teachers match instructional activities to children's stage of reading and writing development.

▶ Teachers monitor children's literacy development to ensure that they're moving through the three stages, and they intervene when children aren't making expected progress.

PEARSON
myeducationlab
Where the Classroom Comes to Life

Go to MyEducationLab at www.myeducationlab.com to deepen your understanding of the concepts presented in this chapter:

▶ Check your understanding of chapter concepts with the multiple-choice and essay quizzes in the Study Plan.
▶ Apply some of the main ideas discussed in the chapter in the Activities and Applications section of the website.
▶ Practice what you've learned in this chapter in Building Teaching Skills and Dispositions before applying the ideas in your own classroom.

PROFESSIONAL REFERENCES

Adams, M. J. (1990). *Beginning to read: Thinking and learning about print*. Cambridge, MA: MIT Press.

Ashton-Warner, S. (1986). *Teacher*. New York: Simon & Schuster.

Button, K., Johnson, M. J., & Furgerson, P. (1996). Interactive writing in a primary classroom. *The Reading Teacher, 49*, 446–454.

Clay, M. M. (2000a). *Concepts about print: What have children learned about the way we print language?* Portsmouth, NH: Heinemann.

Clay, M. M. (2000b). *Follow me, moon*. Portsmouth, NH: Heinemann.

Clay, M. M. (2006). *An observation survey of early literacy achievement* (2nd ed.). Portsmouth, NH: Heinemann.

Clay, M. M. (2007a). *No shoes*. Portsmouth, NH: Heinemann.

Clay, M. M. (2007b). *Sand*. Portsmouth, NH: Heinemann.

Clay, M. M. (2007c). *Stones*. Portsmouth, NH: Heinemann.

Fountas, I. C., & Pinnell, G. S. (1996). *Guided reading: Good first teaching for all children*. Portsmouth, NH: Heinemann.

Harste, J., Woodward, V., & Burke, C. (1984). *Language stories and literacy lessons*. Portsmouth, NH: Heinemann.

Heath, S. B. (1983). *Ways with words*. New York: Oxford University Press.

Invernizzi, M. (2003). Concepts, sounds, and the ABCs: A diet for a very young reader. In D. M. Barone & L. M. Morrow (Eds.), *Literacy and young children: Research-based practices* (pp. 140–156). New York: Guilford Press.

Juel, C. (1991). Beginning reading. In R. Barr, M. L. Kamil, P. Mosenthal, & P. D. Pearson (Eds.), *Handbook of reading research* (Vol. 2, pp. 759–788). New York: Longman.

Lefever-Davis, S., & Pearman, C. (2005). Early readers and electronic texts: CD-ROM storybook features that influence reading behaviors. *The Reading Teacher, 58*, 446–454.

McCarrier, A., Pinnell, G. S., & Fountas, I. C. (2000). *Interactive writing: How language and literacy come together, K–2*. Portsmouth, NH: Heinemann.

McGee, L. M. (2007). *Transforming literacy practices in preschool: Research-based practices that give all children the opportunity to reach their potential as learners*. New York: Scholastic.

McGee, L. M., & Richgels, D. J. (2003). *Designing early literacy programs: Strategies for at-risk preschool and kindergarten children*. New York: Guilford Press.

McGee, L. M., & Richgels, D. J. (2008). *Literacy's beginnings: Supporting young readers and writers* (5th ed.). Boston: Allyn & Bacon.

Morrow, L. M., & Tracey, D. H. (2007). Best practices in early literacy development in preschool, kindergarten, and first grade. In L. B. Gambrell, L. M. Morrow, & M.

Pressley (Eds.), *Best practices in literacy instruction* (3rd ed., pp. 57–82). New York: Guilford Press.

Papandropoulou, I., & Sinclair, H. (1974). What is a word? Experimental study of children's ideas on grammar. *Human Development, 17*, 241–258.

Parkes, B. (2000). *Read it again! Revisting shared reading*. Portland, ME: Stenhouse.

Payne, C. D., & Schulman, M. B. (1999). *Getting the most out of morning messages and other shared writing lessons*. New York: Scholastic.

Pinnell, G. S., & Fountas, I. C. (1998). *Word matters: Teaching phonics and spelling in the reading/writing classroom*. Portsmouth, NH: Heinemann.

Schickedanz, J., & Casbergue, R. (2004). *Writing in preschool: Learning to orchestrate meaning and marks*. Newark, DE: International Reading Association.

Snow, C. E., Burns, M. S., & Griffin, P. (Eds.). (1998). *Preventing reading difficulties in young children*. Washington, DC: National Academy Press.

Taylor, D., & Dorsey-Gaines, C. (1987). *Growing up literate: Learning from inner-city families*. Portsmouth, NH: Heinemann.

Tompkins, G. E., & Collom, S. (2004). *Sharing the pen: Interactive writing with young children*. Upper Saddle River, NJ: Merrill/Prentice Hall.

Tompkins, G. E., & Webeler, M. (1983). What will happen next? Using predictable books with young children. *The Reading Teacher, 36*, 498–502.

Tunks, K. W., & Giles, K. M. (2007). *Write now! Publishing with young authors, preK–grade 2*. Portsmouth, NH: Heinemann.

CHILDREN'S BOOK REFERENCES

Carle, E. (2002). *The very hungry caterpillar*. New York: Puffin Books.

Cronin, D. (2007). *Diary of a fly*. New York: HarperCollins.

Danziger, P. (1998). *Amber Brown sees red*. New York: Scholastic.

Danziger, P. (1999). *Amber Brown is feeling blue*. New York: Scholastic.

Danziger, P. (2004). *Amber Brown is green with envy*. New York: Scholastic.

Danziger, P. (2006). *Amber Brown is not a crayon*. New York: Scholastic.

Danziger, P. (2007). *Amber Brown goes fourth*. New York: Puffin Books.

Eastman, P. D. (2005). *Are you my mother?* New York: HarperCollins.

Fleming, D. (1996). *Lunch*. New York: Henry Holt.

Fleming, D. (1997). *Barnyard banter*. New York: Henry Holt.

Galdone, P. (2008). *The gingerbread boy*. New York: Clarion Books.

Greenburg, D. (1997). *Never trust a cat who wears earrings*. New York: Grosset & Dunlap.

Harris, T. (2000). *Pattern fish*. Brookfield, CT: Millbrook Press.

Hoff, S. (2000a). *Oliver*. New York: HarperTrophy.

Hoff, S. (2000b). *Sammy the seal*. New York: HarperTrophy.

Martin, B., Jr. (2007). *Baby bear, baby bear, what do you see?* New York: Henry Holt.

McCloskey, R. (2001). *Make way for ducklings*. New York: Viking.

Most, B. (1984). *If the dinosaurs came back*. San Diego: Harcourt Brace.

Numeroff, L. J. (2000). *If you give a mouse a cookie*. New York: HarperCollins.

Prince, S. (1999). *Playing*. Littleton, MA: Sundance.

Sachar, L. (2000). *Marvin Redpost: A magic crystal?* New York: Random House.

Seuss, Dr. (1965). *Fox in socks*. New York: Random House.

Simont, M. (2001). *The stray dog*. New York: Harper-Collins.

Trapani, I. (2000). *Shoo fly!* Watertown, MA: Charlesbridge.

CHAPTER 5

Cracking the Alphabetic Code

Mrs. Firpo Teaches Phonics Using a Basal Reading Program

It's 8:10 on Thursday morning, and the 19 first graders in Mrs. Firpo's classroom are gathered on the carpet for their phonics lesson that the teacher calls "word work." This week's topic is the long *i* and long *e* sounds for *y*: For example, in *my* and *multiply*, the *y* is pronounced as long *i*, and in *baby* and *sunny*, the *y* is pronounced as long *e*. She shows pictures representing words that end with *y*: *fly*, *baby*, *jelly*, *bunny*, and *sky*. The children identify each object and say its name slowly to isolate the final sound. Saleena goes first. She picks up the picture of a fly and says, "It's a fly: /f/ /l/ /ī/. It ends with the ī sound." Vincent is confused when it's his turn to identify the long *e* sound at the end of *bunny* so Mrs. Firpo demonstrates how to segment the sounds in the word: /b/ /ŭ/ /n/ /ē/. Then Vincent recognizes the long *e* sound at the end of the word. Next, the first graders sort the picture cards according to the final sound and place them in two columns in a nearby pocket chart. They add labels to the columns: *y* = ī and *y* = ē.

Mrs. Firpo begins her phonics lessons with an oral activity because she knows it's important to integrate phonemic awareness with phonics. In the oral activities, children focus on orally segmenting and blending the sounds they hear in words—

without worrying about phoneme-grapheme correspondences. Next, she introduces a set of cards with words ending in *y* for the children to read and classify. They take turns using phonics to sound out these words: *funny*, *my*, *try*, *happy*, *why*, *fussy*, *very*, *sticky*, *shy*, and *cry*. They add the word cards to the columns on the pocket chart. Then the teacher asks the children to suggest other words that end in *y*; Fernando names *yucky*, Crystal says *crunchy*, and Joel adds *dry*. Mrs. Firpo writes these words on small cards, too, and adds them to the pocket chart. Then Austin uses the pointer to point to each card in the pocket chart for the class to read aloud.

At the end of this 15-minute lesson, the children return to their desks and get out their dry-erase boards for spelling practice. This week's spelling words end in *y* pronounced as long *i*. Mrs. Firpo calls out each word, and the children practice writing it three times on their small dry-erase boards. If they need help spelling the word, they check the list of spelling words on the Focus Wall. As they write, Mrs. Firpo circulates around the classroom, modeling how to form letters, reminding Jordan and Kendra to leave a "two-finger" space between words, and checking that their spellings are correct.

Mrs. Firpo's Focus Wall is shown in the box on page 144. Each week, Mrs. Firpo posts the strategies and skills she'll be teaching, and the vocabulary words and spelling words are listed there, too. The vocabulary words are written on cards and displayed in a pocket chart attached to the Focus Wall so that they can be rearranged and used for various activities. Mrs. Firpo uses *Houghton Mifflin Reading* (Cooper & Pikulski, 2003), a basal reading textbook series; each week's topics are identified for her in the teacher's edition of the textbook. The reason why she posts these topics is to emphasize what she's teaching and what children are learning. In addition, Mrs. Firpo has her state's reading and writing standards for first grade listed on a chart next to the wall.

Next, Mrs. Firpo guides children as they complete several pages in the workbook that accompanies the basal reader. Some pages reinforce phonics and spelling concepts, and others focus on comprehension, vocabulary, grammar, and writing. Today, they begin on page 201. First the children examine the illustration at the top of the page, and then they write two sentences about the silly things they see in the picture on the lines at the bottom of the page. They talk about the illustration, identifying the silly things they see. Felicia says, "I see a bunny reading a book, and I think that's silly." Mrs. Firpo gives Felicia a "thumbs up" to compliment her. And Fernando comments, "I see something else. It's a bear up in a balloon." "Is the balloon up in the sky?" Mrs. Firpo asks because she wants to emphasize the phonics pattern of the week. Fernando agrees that it is, and he repeats, "I see a bear up in a balloon in the sky." He, too, gets a "thumbs up."

After children identify five or six silly things, they get ready to write. Mrs. Firpo reminds them to begin their sentences with capital letters and end them with periods. As they write their sentences, Alicia notices that she has written *bunny*—a word that ends in *y* and has an $\bar{e}$ sound. Mrs. Firpo congratulates her and encourages other children to point out when they write words that end in *y*. Joel waves his hand in the air, eager to report that he has written *sky*—a word that ends in *y* and has an $\bar{i}$ sound.

Then the children move on to page 202. On this page, there's a word bank with words that end in *y* and represent the $\bar{i}$ sound at the top and sentences with blanks at the

Mrs. Firpo's Focus Wall

| Theme 9: Special Friends | Week: 1 | Reading Level: 1.5 |

PHONICS FOCUS: Long i and long e sounds for y

WORD PATTERN: -ay

| say | day | way | bay | stay | gray |
| pay | may | lay | ray | pray | spray |

SPELLING CONCEPT: Long i sound at the end of a word spelled with y

COMPREHENSION STRATEGY: Monitoring

COMPREHENSION SKILL: Noting Details

GRAMMAR CONCEPT: is/are

WRITING GENRE: Friendly Letters

VOCABULARY WORDS

ocean	though	by
dance	talk	my
open	else	cry
ever	around	any
	Grandaddy	

SPELLING WORDS

1. by
2. my
3. fly
4. try
5. cry
6. why
7. pry
8. multiply

bottom. The children practice reading the words in the word bank. After reading the words several times, Vincent volunteers, "I get it! Look at these words: They all have *y* and they say ī." Mrs. Firpo is pleased and gives him a "thumbs up." Next, the teacher reads aloud the sentences at the bottom of the page and asks children to supply the missing words. Then they work independently to reread the sentences and complete them by filling in the missing words. Mrs. Firpo moves from one group of desks to the next as the children work, monitoring their work and providing assistance as needed.

Each week, the children receive take-home books that Mrs. Firpo has duplicated and stapled together; these books reinforce the week's phonics lesson and the vocabulary introduced in the reading textbook. The first graders read the books at school and use them for a phonics activity; then they take them home to practice reading with their families. Today's book is *I Spy*: It's eight pages long, with illustrations and text on each page. Mrs. Firpo introduces the book and reads it aloud once while the children follow along in their copies. They keep their books at their desks to use for a seatwork activity, and later they put the books in book bags that they take home each day. Already they've collected more than 75 books!

During the last 40 minutes of the reading period, Mrs. Firpo conducts **guided reading** groups. Her students' reading levels range from beginning first grade to the middle of second grade, with about half of them reading at grade level. She has grouped the first graders into four guided reading groups, and she meets with two groups each day. Children reading below grade level read leveled books, and those reading at and above grade level read easy-to-read chapter books, including Barbara Park's series of funny stories about a girl named Junie B. Jones (e.g., *Junie B., First Grader: Boss of Lunch* [2003]) and Mary Pope Osborne's Magic Tree House series of adventure stories (e.g., *High Tide in Hawaii* [2003]). Mrs. Firpo calls this period *differentiated instruction* because children participate in a variety of activities, based on their reading levels.

While Mrs. Firpo does guided reading with one group, the others are involved in seatwork and center activities. For the seatwork activity, children read their take-home book and highlight all the words in it ending in *y* pronounced as ī; they don't highlight *bunny*, *play*, and other words where the *y* is not pronounced as ī. They also work in small groups to cut out pictures and words that end in *y*, sort into *y* = ē, *y* = ī, and *y* = *other* categories, and paste them on a sheet of paper. The pictures and words for the activity include *puppy*, *city*, *they*, *buy*, *pretty*, *play*, *funny*, *dry*, *party*, *fifty*, *boy*, *sky*, *fly*, *today*, and *yummy*.

The first graders practice their spelling words using magnetic letters at the spelling center, practice the phonics focus and word pattern using letter cards and flip books at the phonics center, make books at the writing center, listen to the take-home books read aloud at the listening center, and read electronic books interactively at the computer center. The centers are arranged around the perimeter of the classroom; children know how to work at centers and understand what they're expected to do at each one.

After a 15-minute recess, children spend the last 55 minutes of literacy instruction in writing workshop. Each week, the class focuses on the genre specified in the basal reading program; this week's focus is on writing personal letters. First, Mrs. Firpo teaches a **minilesson** and guides children as they complete more pages in their workbooks. Today, she reviews how to use commas in a friendly letter. The children examine several letters hanging in the classroom that the class wrote earlier in the school year using **interactive writing**. After the class rereads each letter, Mrs. Firpo asks the children to mark the commas used in the letters with Vis-à-Vis pens (so their marks can be cleaned off afterward). Crystal points out that commas are used in the date, Saleena notices that a comma is used at the end of the greeting, and Luis marks the comma used after the closing. Next, children practice adding commas in the sample friendly letters on page 208 in their workbooks.

Then children spend the remaining 35 minutes of writing workshop working on the letters they're writing to their families this week. Mrs. Firpo works with five children on their letters while the others work independently. At the end of the writing time, Joel and Angelica sit in the author's chair to read their letters aloud to their classmates. Angelica's letter to her grandmother is shown in the box below.

Mrs. Firpo's students spend 3½ hours each morning involved in literacy instruction. Most of the goals, activities, and instructional materials come from the basal reading program, but Mrs. Firpo adapts some activities to meet her students' varied instructional needs. Through these phonemic awareness, phonics, and spelling activities, these first graders are learning to crack the alphabetic code.

Angelica's Letter to Her Grandmother

April 29, 2008

Dear Nanna Isabel,
I am writting you a letter. My birthday is in 35 days! Did you no that? I wud like to get a present. I want you to come to my party. It will be very funny.
Love,
Angelica

nglish is an alphabetic language, and children crack this code as they learn about phonemes (sounds), graphemes (letters), and graphophonemic (letter-sound) relationships. They learn about phonemes as they notice rhyming words, segment words into individual sounds, and invent silly words by playing with sounds, much like Dr. Seuss did. They learn about letters as they sing the ABC song, name the letters of the alphabet, and spell their own names. They learn graphophonemic relationships as they match letters and letter combinations to sounds, blend sounds to form words, and decode and spell vowel patterns. By third grade, most students have figured out the alphabetic code, and in fourth through eighth grades, students apply what they've learned to decode and spell multisyllabic words. You may think of all of this as phonics, but children actually develop three separate but related abilities about the alphabetic code:

◆ **Phonemic Awareness.** Children learn to notice and manipulate the sounds of oral language. Those who are phonemically aware understand that spoken words are made up of sounds, and they can segment and blend sounds in spoken words.

◆ **Phonics.** Children learn to convert letters into sounds and blend them to recognize words. Those who can apply phonics concepts understand that there are predictable sound-symbol correspondences in English, and they can use decoding strategies to figure out unfamiliar written words.

◆ **Spelling.** Children learn to segment spoken words into sounds and convert the sounds into letters to spell words. Those who have learned to spell conventionally understand English sound-symbol correspondences and spelling patterns, and they can use spelling strategies to spell unfamiliar words.

In the vignette, Mrs. Firpo incorporated all three components into her literacy program. She began the word work lesson on the long *e* and long *i* sounds of *y* with an oral phonemic awareness activity; next, she moved to a phonics activity where children read words that ended in *y* and categorized them on a pocket chart. Later, they practiced spelling words that ended with *y* on dry-erase boards. Teaching these graphophonemic relationships is not a complete reading program, but phonemic awareness, phonics, and spelling are integral to effective literacy instruction, especially for young children (National Reading Panel, 2000).

Go to the Building Teaching Skills and Dispositions section of Chapter 5 on **MyEducationLab.com** to see a kindergarten teacher and a speech therapist help children distinguish sounds.

PHONEMIC AWARENESS

Phonemic awareness is children's basic understanding that speech is composed of a series of individual sounds, and it provides the foundation for phonics and spelling (Armbruster, Lehr, & Osborn, 2001). When children can choose a duck as the animal whose name begins with /d/ from a collection of toy animals, identify *duck* and *luck* as rhyming words in a song, or blend the sounds /d/ /ŭ/ /k/ to pronounce *duck*, they are phonemically aware. Cunningham and Allington (2007) describe phonemic awareness as children's ability to "take words apart, put them back together again, and change them" (p. 37). The emphasis is on the sounds of spoken words, not on reading letters or pronouncing letter names. Developing phonemic awareness enables children to use sound-symbol correspondences to read and spell words (Gillon, 2004).

Phonemes are the smallest units of speech, and they're written as graphemes, or letters of the alphabet. In this book, phonemes are marked using diagonal lines (e.g., /d/) and graphemes are italicized (e.g., *d*). Sometimes phonemes (e.g., /k/ in *duck*) are spelled with two graphemes (*ck*).

Understanding that words are composed of smaller units—phonemes—is a significant achievement for young children because phonemes are abstract language units.

Phonemes carry no meaning, and children think of words according to their meanings, not their linguistic characteristics (Griffith & Olson, 1992). When children think about ducks, for example, they think of feathered animals that swim in ponds, fly through the air, and make noises we describe as "quacks"; they don't think of "duck" as a word with three phonemes or four graphemes, or as a word beginning with /d/ and rhyming with *luck*. Phonemic awareness requires that children treat speech as an object and that they shift their attention away from the meaning of words to the linguistic features of speech. This focus on phonemes is even more complicated because phonemes are not discrete units in speech: Often they are slurred or clipped in speech—think about the blended initial sound in *tree* and the ending sound in *eating*.

Be Strategic!

Phonemic Awareness Strategies

As students manipulate sounds orally, they learn to use these two strategies:

▶ Blend
▶ Segment

Students apply these oral strategies to written language for decoding and spelling words.

Phonemic Awareness Strategies

Children become phonemically aware by manipulating spoken language in these ways:

Identifying Sounds in Words. Children learn to identify a word that begins or ends with a particular sound. For example, when shown a brush, a car, and a doll, they can identify *doll* as the word that ends with /l/.

Categorizing Sounds in Words. Children learn to recognize the "odd" word in a set of three words; for example, when the teacher says *ring*, *rabbit*, and *sun*, they recognize that *sun* doesn't belong.

Substituting Sounds to Make New Words. Children learn to remove a sound from a word and substitute a different sound. Sometimes they substitute the beginning sound, changing *bar* to *car*, for example. Or, they change the middle sound, making *tip* from *top*, or substitute the ending sound, changing *gate* to *game*.

Blending Sounds to Form Words. Children learn to blend two, three, or four individual sounds to form a word; the teacher says /b/ /ĭ/ /g/, for example, and the children repeat the sounds, blending them to form the word *big*.

Segmenting a Word Into Sounds. Children learn to break a word into its beginning, middle, and ending sounds. For example, children segment the word *feet* into /f/ /ē/ /t/ and *go* into /g/ /ō/.

Children use these strategies, especially blending and segmenting, to decode and spell words. When children use phonics to sound out a word, for example, they say the sounds represented by each letter and blend them to read the word. Similarly, to spell a word, children say the word slowly to themselves, segmenting the sounds.

Teaching Phonemic Awareness

Teachers nurture children's phonemic awareness through the language-rich environments they create in the classroom. As they sing songs, chant rhymes, read aloud wordplay books, and play games, children have many opportunities to orally match, isolate, blend, and substitute sounds and to segment words into sounds (Griffith & Olson, 1992). Teachers often incorporate phonemic awareness into other oral language and literacy activities, but it's also important to teach lessons that focus specifically on the phonemic awareness strategies.

Phonemic awareness instruction should meet three criteria. First, the activities should be appropriate for 4-, 5-, and 6-year-old children. Activities involving songs, nursery rhymes, riddles, and wordplay books are good choices because they encourage children's playful experimentation with oral language. Second, the instruction should be planned and purposeful, not just incidental. Teachers need to choose instructional materials and plan activities that focus children's attention on the sound structure of oral language. Third, phonemic awareness activities should be integrated with other components of a balanced literacy program. It's crucial that children perceive the connection between oral and written language (Yopp & Yopp, 2000).

Many wordplay books are available for young children. A list of books is presented in Figure 5–1. Books such as *Cock-a-Doodle-Moo!* (Most, 1996) and *Rattletrap Car* (Root, 2004) stimulate children to experiment with sounds and to create nonsense words. Teachers often read wordplay books aloud more than once. During the first reading, children focus on comprehension or what interests them in the book. During a second reading, however, children's attention shifts to the wordplay elements, and teachers direct their attention to the way the author manipulated words and sounds by making comments and asking questions—"Did you notice how _____ and _____ rhyme?"—and encourage children to make similar comments themselves.

Teachers often incorporate wordplay books, songs, and games into the minilessons they teach. The feature on the next page presents a kindergarten teacher's minilesson on blending sounds into a word. The teacher reread Dr. Seuss's *Fox in Socks* (1965) and then asked children to identify words from the book that she pronounced sound by sound. This book is rich in wordplay: rhyming (e.g., *do, you, goo, chew*), initial consonant substitution (e.g., *trick, quick, slick*), vowel substitution (e.g., *blabber, blibber, blubber*), and alliteration (e.g., *Luke Luck likes lakes*).

Figure 5–1 ◆ Wordplay Books to Develop Phonemic Awareness

Crebbin, J. (1998). *Cows in the kitchen*. Cambridge, MA: Candlewick Press.

Degan, B. (1985). *Jamberry*. New York: HarperTrophy.

Deming, A. G. (1994). *Who is tapping at my window?* New York: Penguin.

Downey, L. (2000). *The flea's sneeze*. New York: Henry Holt.

Ehlert, L. (1993). *Eating the alphabet: Fruits and vegetables from A to Z*. San Diego: Voyager.

Gollub, M. (2000). *The jazz fly*. Santa Rosa, CA: Tortuga Press.

Hillenbrand, W. (2002). *Fiddle-I-fee*. San Diego: Gulliver Books.

Hoberman, M. A. (1998). *Miss Mary Mack*. Boston: Little, Brown.

Hoberman, M. A. (2003). *The lady with the alligator purse*. Boston: Little, Brown.

Hoberman, M. A. (2004). *The eensy-weensy spider*. Boston: Little, Brown.

Hutchins, P. (2002). *Don't forget the bacon!* New York: Red Fox Books.

Martin, B., Jr., & Archambault, J. (2000). *Chicka chicka boom boom*. New York: Aladdin Books.

Most, B. (1991). *A dinosaur named after me*. San Diego: Harcourt Brace.

Most, B. (1996). *Cock-a-doodle-moo!* San Diego: Harcourt Brace.

Most, B. (2003). *The cow that went oink*. San Diego: Voyager.

Prelutsky, J. (1989). *The baby uggs are hatching*. New York: Mulberry Books.

Raffi. (1988). *Down by the bay*. New York: Crown.

Raffi. (1990). *The wheels on the bus*. New York: Crown.

Root, P. (2003). *One duck stuck*. Cambridge, MA: Candlewick Press.

Seuss, Dr. (1963). *Hop on pop*. New York: Random House.

Shaw, N. (2006). *Sheep in a jeep*. Boston: Houghton Mifflin.

Slate, J. (1996). *Miss Bindergarten gets ready for kindergarten*. New York: Dutton.

Slepian, J., & Seidler, A. (2001). *The hungry thing*. New York: Scholastic.

Taback, S. (1997). *There was an old lady who swallowed a fly*. New York: Viking.

Taback, S. (2004). *This is the house that Jack built*. New York: Puffin Books.

Westcott, N. B. (2003). *I know an old lady who swallowed a fly*. Boston: Little, Brown.

Wilson, K. (2003). *A frog in a bag*. New York: McElderry.

MiniLesson

TOPIC: Blending Sounds Into Words
GRADE: Kindergarten
TIME: One 20-minute period

Ms. Lewis regularly includes a 20-minute lesson on phonemic awareness in her literacy block. She usually rereads a familiar wordplay book and plays a phonemic awareness game with the kindergartners that emphasizes one of the phonemic awareness strategies.

❶ Introduce the Topic

Ms. Lewis brings her 19 kindergartners together on the rug and explains that she's going to reread Dr. Seuss's *Fox in Socks* (1965). It's one of their favorite books, and they clap their pleasure. She explains that after reading, they're going to play a word game.

❷ Share Examples

Ms. Lewis reads aloud *Fox in Socks*, showing the pictures on each page as she reads. She encourages the children to read along. Sometimes she stops and invites the children to fill in the last rhyming word in a sentence or to echo read (repeating after her like an echo) the alliterative sentences. After they finish reading, she asks what they like best about the book. Pearl replies, "It's just a really funny book. That's why it is so good." "What makes it funny?" Ms. Lewis asks. Teri explains, "The words are funny. They make my tongue laugh. You know—*fox–socks–box–Knox*. That's funny on my tongue!" "Oh," Ms. Lewis clarifies, "your tongue likes to say rhyming words. I like to say them, too." Other children recall other rhyming words in the book: *clocks–tocks–blocks–box, noodle–poodle,* and *new–do–blue–goo.*

❸ Provide Information

"Let me tell you about our game," Ms. Lewis explains. "I'm going to say some of the words from the book, but I'm going to say them sound by sound, and I want you to blend the sounds together and guess the word." "Are they rhyming words?" Teri asks. "Sure," the teacher agrees. "I'll say two words that rhyme, sound by sound, for you to guess." She says the sounds /f/ /ŏ/ /x/ and /b/ /ŏ/ /x/ and the children correctly blend the sounds and say the words *fox* and *box*. She repeats the procedure for *clock–tock, come–dumb, big–pig, new–blue, rose–hose, game–lame,* and *slow–crow*. Ms. Lewis stops and talks about how to "bump" or blend the sounds to figure out the words. She models how she blends the sounds to form the word. "Make the words harder," several children say, and Ms. Lewis offers several more-difficult pairs of rhyming words, including *chick–trick* and *beetle–tweedle.*

❹ Guide Practice

Ms. Lewis continues playing the guessing game, but now she segments individual words. As each child correctly identifies a word, that child leaves the group and goes to work with the aide. Finally, six children remain who need additional practice. They continue blending *do, new,* and other two-sound words and some of the easier three-sound words, including *box, come,* and *like.*

❺ Assess Learning

Through the guided practice part of the lesson, Ms. Lewis informally checks to see which children need more practice blending sounds into words and provides additional practice for them.

Sound-Matching Activities. In sound matching, children choose one of several words beginning with a particular sound or say a word that begins with a particular sound (Yopp, 1992). For these games, teachers use familiar objects (e.g., feather, toothbrush, book) and toys (e.g., small plastic animals, toy trucks, artificial fruits and vegetables), as well as pictures of familiar objects.

Teachers can play a sound-matching guessing game (Lewkowicz, 1994). For this game, teachers collect two boxes and pairs of objects to place in the boxes (e.g., forks, mittens, erasers, combs, and books); one item from each pair is placed in each box. After the teacher shows children the objects in the boxes and they name them together, two children play the game. One child selects an object, holds it, and pronounces the initial (or medial or final) sound. The second child chooses the same object from the second box and holds it up. Classmates check to see if the two players are holding the same object.

Children also identify rhyming words as part of sound-matching activities: They name a word that rhymes with a given word and identify rhyming words from familiar songs and stories. As children listen to parents and teachers read Dr. Seuss books, such as *Fox in Socks* (1965) and *Hop on Pop* (1963), and other wordplay books, they refine their understanding of rhyme.

Sound-Isolation Activities. Teachers say a word and then children identify the sounds at the beginning, middle, or end of the word, or teachers and children isolate sounds as they sing familiar songs. Yopp (1992) created these new verses to the tune of "Old MacDonald Had a Farm":

> What's the sound that starts these words:
> Chicken, chin, and cheek?
> (wait for response)
>
> /ch/ is the sound that starts these words:
> Chicken, chin, and cheek.
> With a /ch/, /ch/ here, and a /ch/, /ch/ there,
> Here a /ch/, there a /ch/, everywhere a /ch/, /ch/.
>
> /ch/ is the sound that starts these words:
> Chicken, chin, and cheek. (p. 700)

Teachers change the question at the beginning of the verse to focus on medial and final sounds. For example:

> What's the sound in the middle of these words?
> Whale, game, and rain. (p. 700)

And for final sounds:

> What's the sound at the end of these words?
> Leaf, cough, and beef. (p. 700)

Teachers also set out trays of objects and ask children to choose the one object that doesn't belong because it begins with a different sound. For example, from a tray with a toy pig, a puppet, a teddy bear, and a pen, the teddy bear doesn't belong.

Sound-Blending Activities. Children blend sounds in order to combine them to form a word. For example, children blend the sounds /d/ /ŭ/ /k/ to form the word *duck*. Teachers play the "What am I thinking of?" guessing game with children by identifying several characteristics of the item and then saying its name, articulating each of the sounds slowly and separately (Yopp, 1992). Then children blend the sounds and identify the word, using the phonological and semantic information that the teacher provided. For example:

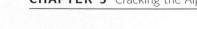

I'm thinking of a small animal that lives in the pond when it is young. When it is an adult, it lives on land and it is called a /f/ /r/ /ŏ/ /g/. What is it?

The children blend the sounds to pronounce the word *frog*. Then the teacher can move into phonics and spelling by setting out magnetic letters for children to arrange to spell *frog*. In this example, the teacher connects the game with a thematic unit, thereby making the game more meaningful for children.

Sound-Addition and -Substitution Activities. Children play with words and create nonsense words as they add or substitute sounds in words in songs they sing or in books that are read aloud to them. Teachers read wordplay books such as Pat Hutchins's *Don't Forget the Bacon!* (1989), in which a boy leaves for the store with a mental list of four items to buy. As he walks, he repeats his list, substituting words each time: "A cake for tea" changes to "a cape for me" and then to "a rake for leaves." Children suggest other substitutions, such as "a game for a bee."

Students substitute sounds in refrains of songs (Yopp, 1992). For example, students can change the "Ee-igh, ee-igh, oh!" refrain in "Old MacDonald Had a Farm" to "Bee-bigh, bee-bigh, boh!" to focus on the initial /b/ sound. Teachers can choose one sound, such as /sh/, and have children substitute it for the beginning sound in their names and in words for items in the classroom. For example, *Jimmy* becomes *Shimmy*, *José* becomes *Shosé*, and *clock* becomes *shock*.

Sound-Segmentation Activities. One of the more difficult phonemic awareness activities is segmentation, in which children isolate the sounds in a spoken word (Yopp, 1988). An introductory segmentation activity is to draw out the beginning sound in words. Children enjoy exaggerating the initial sound in their own names and other familiar words. For example, a pet guinea pig named Popsicle lives in Mrs. Firpo's classroom, and the children exaggerate the beginning sound of her name so that it is pronounced as "P-P-P-Popsicle." Children can also pick up objects or pictures of objects and identify the initial sound; a child who picks up a toy tiger says, "This is a truck and it starts with /t/."

From that beginning, children move to identifying all the sounds in a word. Using a toy truck again, the child would say, "This is a truck, /t/ /r/ /ŭ/ /k/." Yopp (1992) suggests singing a song to the tune of "Twinkle, Twinkle, Little Star" in which children segment entire words. Here is one example:

> Listen, listen
> To my word
> Then tell me all the sounds you heard: coat
> (slowly)
> /k/ is one sound
> /o–/ is two
> /t/ is last in coat
> It's true. (p. 702)

After several repetitions of the verse segmenting other words, the song ends this way:

> Thanks for listening
> To my words
> And telling all the sounds you heard! (p. 702)

Teachers also use Elkonin boxes to teach students to segment words; this activity comes from the work of Russian psychologist D. B. Elkonin (Clay, 2005a). As seen in Figure 5–2, the teacher shows an object or a picture of an object and draws a row of boxes, with one box for each sound in the name of the object or picture. Then the teacher or a child moves a marker into each box as the sound is pronounced. Children can move small markers onto cards on their desks, or the teacher can draw the boxes on

Figure 5–2 ◆ Ways to Use Elkonin Boxes

Type	Goal	Steps in the Activity
Phonemic Awareness	Segmenting sounds in a one-syllable word	1. Show children an object or a picture of an object with a one-syllable name, such as a duck, game, bee, or cup. 2. Prepare a diagram with a row of boxes, side-by-side, corresponding to the number of sounds heard in the name of the object. Draw the row of boxes on the chalkboard or on a small dry-erase board. For example, draw two boxes to represent the two sounds in *bee* or three boxes for the three sounds in *duck*. 3. Distribute coins or other small items to use as markers. 4. Say the name of the object slowly and move a marker into each box as the sound is pronounced. Then have children repeat the procedure.
	Segmenting syllables in a multisyllabic word	1. Show children an object or a picture of an object with a multisyllabic name, such as a butterfly, alligator, cowboy, or umbrella. 2. Prepare a diagram with a row of boxes, corresponding to the number of syllables in the name of the object. For example, draw four boxes to represent the four syllables in *alligator*. 3. Distribute markers. 4. Say the name of the object slowly and move a marker into each box as the syllable is pronounced. Then have children repeat the procedure.
Spelling	Representing sounds with letters	1. Draw a row of boxes corresponding to the number of sounds heard in a word. For example, draw two boxes for *go*, three boxes for *ship*, and four boxes for *frog*. 2. Pronounce the word, pointing to each box as the corresponding sound is pronounced. 3. Have the child write the letter or letters representing the sound in each box.
	Applying spelling patterns	1. Draw a row of boxes corresponding to the number of sounds heard in a word. For example, draw three boxes for the word *duck, game*, or *light*. 2. Pronounce the word, pointing to each box as the corresponding sound is pronounced. 3. Have the child write the letter or letters representing the sound in each box. 4. Pronounce the word again and examine how each sound is spelled. Insert additional unpronounced letters to complete the spelling patterns.

the chalkboard and use tape or small magnets to hold the larger markers in place. Elkonin boxes can also be used for spelling activities: When a child is trying to spell a word, such as *duck*, the teacher can draw three boxes, do the segmentation activity, and then have the child write the letters representing each sound in the boxes.

Children are experimenting with oral language in these activities. They stimulate children's interest in language and provide valuable experiences with books and words. Effective teachers recognize the importance of building this foundation as children are beginning to read and write. Guidelines for phonemic awareness activities are reviewed here.

Guidelines
for Teaching Phonemic Awareness

▶ Begin with oral activities using objects and pictures, but after children learn to identify the letters of the alphabet, add reading and writing components.

▶ Emphasize experimentation as children sing songs and play word games because these activities are intended to be fun.

▶ Read and reread wordplay books, and encourage children to experiment with rhyming words, alliteration, and other wordplay activities.

▶ Teach minilessons on manipulating words, moving from easier to more-complex levels.

▶ Emphasize blending and segmenting because children need these two strategies for phonics and spelling.

▶ Use small-group activities so children can be more actively involved in manipulating language.

▶ Teach phonemic awareness in the context of authentic reading and writing activities.

▶ Spend 20 hours teaching phonemic awareness strategies, but recognize that children develop phonemic awareness at different rates and that some children will need more or less instruction.

Nurturing English Learners

It's more difficult to develop English learners' phonemic awareness than native English speakers' because they're just learning to speak English; however, this training is worthwhile for English learners as long as familiar and meaningful words are used (Riches & Genesee, 2006). Teachers create a rich literacy environment and begin by reading books and poems aloud and singing songs so children can learn to recognize and pronounce English sound patterns.

To plan effective phonemic awareness instruction, teachers need to be familiar with English learners' home languages and understand how they differ from English (Peregoy & Boyle, 2008). Instruction should begin with sounds that children can pronounce easily and that don't conflict with those in their home language. Sounds that aren't present in children's home language or those that they don't perceive as unique, such as /ch/–/sh/ or /ĕ/–/ĭ/ for Spanish speakers, are more difficult. Children may need more time to practice producing and manipulating these difficult sounds.

Researchers recommend explicit instruction on phonemic awareness and practice opportunities for English learners (Snow, Burns, & Griffin, 1998). They sing familiar songs and play language games like native speakers do, but teachers also draw ELs' attention to pronouncing English sounds and words. Teachers often integrate phonemic awareness training, vocabulary instruction, and reading and writing activities to show how oral language sounds are represented by letters in written words (Peregoy & Boyle, 2008).

Phonemic awareness is a common underlying linguistic ability that transfers from one language to another (Riches & Genesee, 2006). Children who have learned to read in their home language are phonemically aware, and this knowledge supports their reading and writing development in English.

Assessing Children's Phonemic Awareness

Through phonemic awareness instruction, children learn strategies for segmenting, blending, and substituting sounds in words. Teachers often monitor their learning as

Assessment Tools

Phonemic Awareness

Kindergarten and first-grade teachers monitor children's learning by observing them during classroom activities, and they screen, monitor, diagnose, and document their growing phonemic awareness by administering these tests:

◆ **Dynamic Indicators of Basic Early Literacy Skills (DIBELS): Phoneme Segmentation Fluency Subtest** (Kaminski & Good, 1996)

This individually administered subtest assesses children's ability to segment words with two and three phonemes. Multiple forms are available so that this test can be used periodically to monitor children's progress. The test is available free of charge on the DIBELS website, but there is a charge for analyzing and reporting the test results.

◆ **Phonological Awareness Literacy Screening (PALS) System: Rhyme Awareness and Beginning Sound Subtests** (Invernizzi, Meier, & Juel, 2003)

The kindergarten level of PALS includes brief subtests to assess young children's phonemic awareness. Children look at pictures and supply rhyming words or produce the beginning sounds for picture names. The grades 1–3 tests also include phonemic awareness subtests for children who score below grade level on other tests. PALS is available from the University of Virginia; it's free for Virginia teachers, but teachers in other states pay for it.

◆ **Test of Phonological Awareness (TPA)** (Torgesen & Bryant, 2004)

This group test designed for children ages 5–8 measures their ability to isolate individual sounds in spoken words and understand the relationship between letters and phonemes. It takes 40 minutes. The TPA is available from LinguiSystems.

◆ **Yopp-Singer Test of Phonemic Segmentation** (Yopp, 1995)

This individually administered oral test for kindergartners measures their ability to accurately segment the phonemes in words; it contains 22 items and is administered in less than 10 minutes. The test is free; it can be found in the September 1995 issue of *The Reading Teacher* or online. A Spanish version is also available.

Information gained from classroom observations and these assessments is used to identify students who aren't yet phonemically aware, plan appropriate instruction, and monitor their progress.

they participate in phonemic awareness activities: When children sort picture cards according to beginning sounds or identify rhyming words in a familiar song, they're demonstrating their ability to manipulate sounds. Teachers also administer one of several readily available phonemic awareness tests to screen children's ability to use phonemic awareness strategies, monitor their progress, and document their learning. Four phonemic-awareness tests are described in the Assessment Tools feature on the preceding page.

Why Is Phonemic Awareness Important?

A clear connection exists between phonemic awareness and learning to read; researchers have concluded that phonemic awareness is a prerequisite for learning to read. As they become phonemically aware, children recognize that speech can be segmented into smaller units; this knowledge is very useful as they learn about sound-symbol correspondences and spelling patterns (Cunningham, 2007).

Children can be explicitly taught to segment and blend speech, and those who receive approximately 20 hours of training in phonemic awareness do better in both reading and spelling (Juel, Griffith, & Gough, 1986). Phonemic awareness is also nurtured in spontaneous ways by providing children with language-rich environments and emphasizing wordplay as teachers read books aloud and engage children in singing songs, chanting poems, and telling riddles.

Moreover, phonemic awareness has been shown to be the most powerful predictor of later reading achievement. Klesius, Griffith, and Zielonka (1991) found that children who began first grade with strong phonemic awareness did well regardless of the kind of reading instruction they received, and no one type of instruction was better for children who were low in phonemic awareness at the beginning of first grade.

PHONICS

Phonics is the set of relationships between phonology (the sounds in speech) and orthography (the spelling patterns of written language). The emphasis is on spelling patterns, not individual letters, because there isn't a one-to-one correspondence between phonemes and graphemes in English. Sounds are spelled in different ways. There are several reasons for this variety. One reason is that sounds, especially vowels, vary according to their location in a word (e.g., *go–got*). Adjacent letters often influence how letters are pronounced (e.g., *bed–bead*), as do vowel markers such as the final *e* (e.g., *bit–bite*) (Shefelbine, 1995).

Language origin, or etymology, of words also influences their pronunciation. For example, the *ch* digraph is pronounced in several ways; the three most common are /ch/ as in *chain* (English), /sh/ as in *chauffeur* (French), and /k/ as in *chaos* (Greek). Neither the location of the digraph within the word nor adjacent letters account for these pronunciation differences: In all three words, the *ch* digraph is at the beginning of the word and is followed by two vowels, the first of which is *a*. Some letters in words aren't pronounced, either. In words such as *write*, the *w* isn't pronounced, even though it probably was at one time. The same is true for the *k* in *knight*, *know*, and *knee*. "Silent" letters in words such as *sign* and *bomb* reflect their parent words, *signature* and *bombard*, and have been retained for semantic, not phonological, reasons (Venezky, 1999).

New Literacies
Online Games

Students practice phonics and spelling concepts they're learning as they play online games. These interactive games provide opportunities for students to match letters to pictures of objects illustrating their sounds, identify rhymes, sort words according to vowel pattern, and spell words, for example. They provide engaging practice opportunities because the colorful screen displays, sound effects, fast-paced action, and feedback about game performance grab students' attention, maintain their enthusiasm, and scaffold their learning (Chamberlain, 2005; Kinzer, 2005).

Teachers choose games based on concepts they're teaching and students' achievement levels. Teachers preview the games and bookmark those they want to use, and then students use the bookmarks to quickly access the game they'll play at the computer center. They play the games individually or with partners. Because most young children are experienced game-players and because many games have tutorial features, teachers don't have to spend much time introducing them, but it's helpful to have a parent-volunteer or older student available to assist when there are problems.

Here are some suggested websites with phonics and spelling games:

Game Goo: Learning That Sticks

www.earobics.com/gamegoo

Visit the Game Goo website to play games to practice letter recognition, phonics, synonym, antonym, and spelling concepts. The fast-action games are divided into three levels of difficulty.

Gamequarium

www.gamequarium.com

Check this mega-website with links to alphabet, phonics, and spelling games at other websites. Although hundreds of literacy-related games can be accessed through this site, Gamequarium is only a portal, so the quality of the games and computer requirements vary.

PBS Kids

www.pbskids.org

Play games and view video clips from the popular PBS series "Between the Lions," "Sesame Street," Reading Rainbow," "Word World," and "Super Why!" to learn letters of the alphabet, rhyming words, phonics, and spelling concepts.

RIF's Reading Planet Club

www.rif.org/readingplanet/

Join the Reading Planet Club at the Reading Is Fundamental website to play a variety of phonics, word-study, and spelling games at the Game Station, and be sure to check out the Book Zone and Express Yourself to read about featured authors and books and learn more about writing.

Scholastic Kids

www.scholastic.com

Check Scholastic's Learning Arcade to play concentration, make a word, word scrabble, and word find games featuring Clifford the Big Red Dog and other book characters. Also, visit the Homework Hub to create spelling scrambles and word searches using students' spelling words (up to 10 words).

Sesame Workshop

www.sesameworkshop.org

Try these interactive games about letters, consonant sounds, and rhyming words featuring Big Bird, Elmo, Grover, and the other familiar Sesame Street characters. These easy-to-play games engage young children without overwhelming them.

All of the games are free, but advertisements pop up at some sites.

When primary-grade teachers incorporate technology, such as interactive phonics and spelling games, into their literacy program, children are enhancing their traditional reading and writing competencies as well as their new 21st-century literacy.

Phonics Concepts

Phonics explains the relationships between phonemes and graphemes. There are 44 phonemes in English, and they are represented by the 26 letters. The alphabetic principle suggests that there should be a one-to-one correspondence between phonemes and graphemes, so that each sound is consistently represented by one letter. English, however, is an imperfect phonetic language, and there are more than 500 ways to represent the 44 phonemes using single letters or combinations of letters. Consider the word *day*: The two phonemes, /d/ and /ā/, are represented by three letters. The letter *d* is a consonant, and *a* and *y* are vowels. Interestingly, *y* isn't always a vowel; it's a consonant at the beginning of a word and a vowel at the end. When two vowels are side by side at the end of a word, they represent a long vowel sound. In *day*, the vowel sound is long *a*. Primary-grade students learn these phonics concepts to decode unfamiliar words.

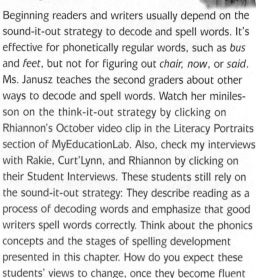

Literacy Portraits: VIEWING GUIDE

Beginning readers and writers usually depend on the sound-it-out strategy to decode and spell words. It's effective for phonetically regular words, such as *bus* and *feet*, but not for figuring out *chair, now,* or *said*. Ms. Janusz teaches the second graders about other ways to decode and spell words. Watch her minilesson on the think-it-out strategy by clicking on Rhiannon's October video clip in the Literacy Portraits section of MyEducationLab. Also, check my interviews with Rakie, Curt'Lynn, and Rhiannon by clicking on their Student Interviews. These students still rely on the sound-it-out strategy: They describe reading as a process of decoding words and emphasize that good writers spell words correctly. Think about the phonics concepts and the stages of spelling development presented in this chapter. How do you expect these students' views to change, once they become fluent readers and writers?

myeducationlab

Consonants. Phonemes are classified as either consonants or vowels. The consonants are *b, c, d, f, g, h, j, k, l, m, n, p, q, r, s, t, v, w, x, y,* and *z.* Most consonants represent a single sound consistently, but there are some exceptions. *C,* for example, doesn't represent a sound of its own: When it's followed by *a, o,* or *u,* it is pronounced /k/ (e.g., *castle, coffee, cut*), and when it's followed by *e, i,* or *y,* it is pronounced /s/ (e.g., *cell, city, cycle*). *G* represents two sounds, as the word *garbage* illustrates: It's usually pronounced /g/ (e.g., *glass, go, green, guppy*), but when *g* is followed by *e, i,* or *y,* it's pronounced /j/, as in *giant. X* is also pronounced differently according to its location in a word. At the beginning of a word, it's often pronounced /z/, as in *xylophone,* but sometimes the letter name is used, as in *x-ray.* At the end of a word, *x* is pronounced /ks/, as in *box.* The letters *w* and *y* are particularly interesting: At the beginning of a word or a syllable, they're consonants (e.g., *wind, yard*), but when they're in the middle or at the end, they are vowels (e.g., *saw, flown, day, by*).

Two kinds of combination consonants are blends and digraphs. Consonant blends occur when two or three consonants appear next to each other in words and their individual sounds are "blended" together, as in *grass, belt,* and *spring.* Consonant digraphs are letter combinations representing single sounds that aren't represented by either letter; the four most common are *ch* as in *chair* and *each, sh* as in *shell* and *wish, th* as in *father* and *both,* and *wh* as in *whale.* Another consonant digraph is *ph,* as in *photo* and *graph.*

Vowels. The remaining five letters—*a, e, i, o,* and *u*—represent vowels, and *w* and *y* are vowels when used in the middle and at the end of syllables and words. Vowels often represent several sounds. The two most common are short (marked with the symbol ˘, called a *breve*) and long sounds (marked with the symbol ‾, called a *macron*). The short vowel sounds are /ă/ as in *cat,* /ĕ/ as in *bed,* /ĭ/ as in *win,* /ŏ/ as in *hot,* and /ŭ/ as in *cup.* The long vowel sounds—/ā/, /ē/, /ī/, /ō/, and /ū/—are the same as the letter names, and they are illustrated in the words *make, feet, bike, coal,* and *rule.* Long vowel sounds are usually spelled with two vowels, except when the long vowel is at the end of a one-syllable word or a syllable, as in *she* or *secret* and *try* or *tribal.* When *y* is a vowel by itself at the end of a word, it's pronounced as long *e* or long *i,* depending on the length of the word. In one-syllable words such as *by* and *cry,* the *y* is pronounced as long *i,* but in longer words such as *baby* and *happy,* the *y* is usually pronounced as long *e.*

Vowel sounds are more complicated than consonant sounds, and there are many vowel combinations representing long vowels and other vowel sounds. Consider these combinations:

ai as in *nail*   *oa* as in *soap*
au as in *laugh* and *caught*   *oi* as in *oil*

aw as in *saw*
ea as in *peach* and *bread*
ew as in *sew* and *few*
ia as in *dial*
ie as in *cookie*

oo as in *cook* and *moon*
ou as in *house* and *through*
ow as in *now* and *snow*
oy as in *toy*

Most vowel combinations are vowel digraphs or diphthongs: When two vowels represent a single sound, the combination is a vowel digraph (e.g., *nail*, *snow*), and when the two vowels represent a glide from one sound to another, the combination is a diphthong. Two vowel combinations that are consistently diphthongs are *oi* and *oy*, but other combinations, such as *ou* as in *house* (but not in *through*) and *ow* as in *now* (but not in *snow*), are diphthongs when they represent a glided sound. In *through*, the *ou* represents the /ū/ sound as in *moon*, and in *snow*, the *ow* represents the /ō/ sound.

When one or more vowels in a word are followed by an *r*, it's called an *r-controlled vowel* because the *r* influences the pronunciation of the vowel sound. For example, read these words aloud: *start, award, nerve, squirt, horse, word, surf, square, stairs, pearl, beard, cheer, where, here, pier, wire, board, floor, scored, fourth,* and *cure.* Some words have a single vowel plus *r* and others have two vowels plus *r*, or the *r* is in between the vowels. Single vowels with *r* are more predictable than the other types. The most consistent *r*-controlled vowels are *ar* as in *car* and *shark* and *or* as in *fork* and *born.* The remaining single vowel + *r* combinations, *er, ir,* and *ur,* are difficult to spell because they're often pronounced /ûr/ in words, including *herd, father, girls, first, burn,* and *nurse.*

Three-letter spellings of *r*-controlled vowels are more complicated; they include *-are* (*care*), *-ear* (*fear*), *-ere* (*here*), *-oar* (*roar*), and *-our* (*your*). Consider these *-ear* words: *bears, beard, cleared, early, earth, hear, heard, heart, learner, pear, pearls, spear, wearing, yearly,* and *yearn.* The vowel sound is pronounced in four ways. The most common pronunciation for *ear* is /ûr/, as in *earth, learner,* and *pearls*; this pronunciation is used when *ear* is followed by a consonant, except in *heart* and *beard.* The next most common pronunciation is found in *cleared* and *spear,* where the vowel sounds like the word *ear.* In several words, including *bear* and *wearing,* the vowel sound is pronounced as in the word *air.* Finally, in *heart, ear* is pronounced as in *car.* Teachers usually introduce the more-predictable ways to decode *r*-controlled vowels, but students learn words with less common pronunciations, including *award, courage, flour, heart, here, very,* and *work,* in other ways.

The vowels in the unaccented syllables of multisyllabic words are often softened and pronounced "uh," as in the first syllable of *about* and *machine,* and the final syllable of *pencil, tunnel, zebra,* and *selection.* This vowel sound is called *schwa* and is represented in dictionaries with ə, which looks like an inverted *e.*

Blending Into Words. Readers blend or combine sounds in order to decode words. Even though children may identify each sound, one by one, they must also be able to blend them into a word. For example, to read the short-vowel word *best,* children identify /b/ /ĕ/ /s/ /t/ and then combine them to form the word. For long-vowel words, children must identify the vowel pattern as well as the surrounding letters. In *pancake,* for example, children identify /p/ /ă/ /n/ /k/ /ā/ /k/ and recognize that the *e* at the end of the word is silent and marks the preceding vowel as long. Shefelbine (1995) emphasizes the importance of blending and explains that students who have difficulty decoding words usually know the sound-symbol correspondences but can't blend the sounds into recognizable words. The ability to blend sounds into words is part of phonemic awareness, and students who haven't had practice blending speech sounds into words are likely to have trouble blending sounds into words in order to decode unfamiliar words.

Phonograms. One-syllable words and syllables in longer words can be divided into two parts, the onset and the rime: The onset is the consonant sound, if any, that precedes the vowel, and the rime is the vowel and any consonant sounds that follow it. For example, in *show*, *sh* is the onset and *ow* is the rime, and in *ball*, *b* is the onset and *all* is the rime. For *at* and *up*, there is no onset; the entire word is the rime. Research has shown that children make more errors decoding and spelling the rime than the onset and more errors on vowels than on consonants (Caldwell & Leslie, 2005). In fact, rimes may provide an important key to word identification.

Wylie and Durrell (1970) identified 37 rimes, including *-ay*, *-ing*, *-oke*, and *-ump*, that are found in nearly 500 common words; these rimes and some words using each one are presented in Figure 5–3. Knowing these rimes and recognizing common words made from them are very helpful for beginning readers because they can use the words to decode other words (Cunningham, 2009). For example, when children know the *-ay* rime and recognize *say*, they use this knowledge to pronounce *clay*: They identify the *-ay* rime and blend *cl* with *ay* to decode the word. This strategy is called *decoding by analogy*, and you'll read more about it in Chapter 6, "Developing Students' Reading and Writing Fluency."

Teachers refer to rimes as *phonograms* or *word families* when they teach them, even though *phonogram* is a misnomer; by definition, a *phonogram* is a letter or group of letters that represent a single sound. Two of the rimes, *-aw* and *-ay*, represent single sounds, but the other 35 don't.

Beginning readers often read and write words using each phonogram. First and second graders can read and write these words made using *-ain*: *brain*, *chain*, *drain*, *grain*, *main*, *pain*, *plain*, *rain*, *sprain*, *stain*, and *train*. Students must be familiar with consonant blends and digraphs to read and spell these words. Teachers often post these word lists on a word families **word wall**, as shown in Figure 5–4. Each phonogram and the words made using it are listed in a separate section of the word wall. Teachers use the words on the word wall for a variety of phonics activities, and students refer to it to spell words when they're writing.

> Check the Compendium of Instructional Procedures, which follows Chapter 12, for more information on the highlighted terms.

Figure 5–3 ◆ The 37 Rimes and Common Words Using Them

Rime	Examples	Rime	Examples
-ack	black, pack, quack, stack	-ide	bride, hide, ride, side
-ail	mail, nail, sail, tail	-ight	bright, fight, light, might
-ain	brain, chain, plain, rain	-ill	fill, hill, kill, will
-ake	cake, shake, take, wake	-in	chin, grin, pin, win
-ale	male, sale, tale, whale	-ine	fine, line, mine, nine
-ame	came, flame, game, name	-ing	king, sing, thing, wing
-an	can, man, pan, than	-ink	pink, sink, think, wink
-ank	bank, drank, sank, thank	-ip	drip, hip, lip, ship
-ap	cap, clap, map, slap	-it	bit, flit, quit, sit
-ash	cash, dash, flash, trash	-ock	block, clock, knock, sock
-at	bat, cat, rat, that	-oke	choke, joke, poke, woke
-ate	gate, hate, late, plate	-op	chop, drop, hop, shop
-aw	claw, draw, jaw, saw	-ore	chore, more, shore, store
-ay	day, play, say, way	-ot	dot, got, knot, trot
-eat	beat, heat, meat, wheat	-uck	duck, luck, suck, truck
-ell	bell, sell, shell, well	-ug	bug, drug, hug, rug
-est	best, chest, nest, west	-ump	bump, dump, hump, lump
-ice	mice, nice, rice, slice	-unk	bunk, dunk, junk, sunk
-ick	brick, pick, sick, thick		

Figure 5–4 ◆ Excerpt From a Word Wall of Phonograms

-ock		-oke		-old	
block	lock	broke	poke	bold	hold
clock	rock	Coke	smoke	cold	sold
dock	sock	choke	woke	fold	told
flock		joke		gold	
		*soak			

-op		-ore		-ot	
cop	pop	more	store	dot	lot
chop	plop	sore	tore	got	not
drop	shop	shore	wore	hot	shot
hop	stop	snore		knot	spot
mop	top				
		*door *pour *soar			
		*floor *your *war			

* = exceptions

Phonics Rules. Because English doesn't have a one-to-one correspondence between sounds and letters, linguists have created rules to clarify English spelling patterns. One rule is that *q* is followed by *u* and pronounced /kw/, as in *queen, quick,* and *earthquake*; *Iraq, Qantas,* and other names are exceptions. Another rule that has few exceptions relates to *r*-controlled vowels: *r* influences the preceding vowels so that they're neither long nor short. Examples are *car, wear,* and *four.* There are exceptions, however; one is *fire.*

Many rules aren't very useful because there are more exceptions than words that conform (Clymer, 1963). A good example is this long-vowel rule: When there are two adjacent vowels, the long vowel sound of the first one is pronounced and the second is silent; teachers sometimes call this the "when two vowels go walking, the first one does the talking" rule. Examples of conforming words are *meat, soap,* and *each.* There are many more exceptions, however, including *food, said, head, chief, bread, look, soup, does, too,* and *again.*

Only a few phonics rules have a high degree of utility for readers. Students should learn the ones that work most of the time because they're the most useful (Adams, 1990). Eight useful rules are listed in Figure 5–5. Even though they're fairly reliable, very few of them approach 100% utility. The rule about *r*-controlled vowels just mentioned has been calculated to be useful in 78% of words in which the letter *r* follows the vowel (Adams, 1990). Other commonly taught, useful rules have even lower percentages of utility. The CVC pattern rule—which says that when a one-syllable word has only one vowel and the vowel comes between two consonants, it is usually short, as in *bat, land,* and *cup*—is estimated to work only 62% of the time. Exceptions include *told, fall, fork,* and *birth.* The CVCe pattern rule—which says that when there are two vowels in a one-syllable word and one vowel is an *e* at the end of the word, the first vowel is long and the final *e* is silent—is estimated to work in 63% of CVCe words. Examples of conforming words are *came, hole,* and *pipe*; but three very common words—*have, come,* and *love*—are exceptions.

Figure 5–5 ◆ The Most Useful Phonics Rules		
Pattern	**Description**	**Examples**
Two sounds of *c*	The letter *c* can be pronounced as /k/ or /s/. When *c* is followed by *a, o,* or *u,* it's pronounced /k/—the hard *c* sound. When *c* is followed by *e, i,* or *y,* it's pronounced /s/—the soft *c* sound.	cat cent cough city cut cycle
Two sounds of *g*	The sound associated with the letter *g* depends on the letter following it. When *g* is followed by *a, o,* or *u,* it's pronounced as /g/—the hard *g* sound. When *g* is followed by *e, i,* or *y,* it's usually pronounced /j/—the soft *g* sound. Exceptions include *get* and *give*.	gate gentle go giant guess gypsy
CVC pattern	When a one-syllable word has only one vowel and the vowel comes between two consonants, it is usually short. One exception is *told*.	bat cup land
Final *e* or CVCe pattern	When there are two vowels in a one-syllable word and one of them is an *e* at the end of the word, the first vowel is long and the final *e* is silent. Three exceptions are *have, come,* and *love*.	home safe cute
CV pattern	When a vowel follows a consonant in a one-syllable word, the vowel is long. Exceptions include *the, to,* and *do*.	go be
r-controlled vowels	Vowels that are followed by the letter *r* are overpowered and are neither short nor long. One exception is *fire*.	car birth dear pair
-igh	When *gh* follows *i,* the *i* is long and the *gh* is silent. One exception is *neighbor*.	high night
kn- and *wr-*	In words beginning with *kn-* and *wr-,* the first letter is not pronounced.	knee write

Adapted from Clymer, 1963.

Teaching Phonics

The best way to teach phonics is through a combination of explicit instruction and authentic application activities. The National Reading Panel (2000) reviewed the research about phonics instruction and concluded that the most effective programs were systematic; that is, the most useful phonics skills are taught in a predetermined sequence. Most teachers begin with consonants and then introduce the short vowels so that children can read and spell consonant-vowel-consonant or CVC-pattern words, such as *dig* and *cup*. Then children learn about consonant blends and diagraphs and long vowels so that they can read and spell consonant-vowel-consonant-*e* or CVCe-pattern words, such as *broke* and *white*, and consonant-vowel-vowel-consonant or CVVC-pattern words, such as *clean*, *wheel*, and *snail*. Finally, children learn about the less common vowel diagraphs and diphthongs, such as *claw*, *bought*, *shook*, and *boil*, and *r*-controlled vowels, including *square*, *hard*, *four*, and *year*. Figure 5–6 details this sequence of phonics skills.

Children also learn strategies to use in identifying unfamiliar words (Mesmer & Griffith, 2005). Three of the most useful strategies are sounding out words, decoding by analogy, and applying phonics rules. When children sound out words, they convert letters and patterns of letters into sounds and blend them to pronounce the word; it's most effective when children are reading phonetically regular one-syllable words. In the second strategy, decoding by analogy, children apply their knowledge of phonograms to analyze the structure of an unfamiliar word (White, 2005). They use known words to recognize unfamiliar ones. For example, if children are familiar with will, they can use it to identify *grill*. They also apply phonics rules to identify unfamiliar words, such as *while* and *clean*. These strategies are especially useful when children don't recognize many words, but they become less important as readers gain more experience and can recognize most words automatically.

The second component of phonics instruction is daily opportunities for children to apply the phonics strategies and skills they're learning in authentic reading and writing activities (National Reading Panel, 2000). Cunningham and Cunningham (2002) estimate that the ratio of time spent on real reading and writing to time spent on phonics instruction should be 3 to 1. Without this meaningful application of what they are learning, phonics instruction is often ineffective (Dahl, Scharer, Lawson, & Grogan, 2001).

Phonics instruction begins in kindergarten when children learn to connect consonant and short vowel sounds to the letters, and it's completed by third grade because older students rarely benefit from it (Ivey & Baker, 2004; National Reading Panel, 2000). Guidelines for teaching phonics are presented here.

Be Strategic!

Phonics Strategies

Students apply their phonics knowledge to decode words when they use these strategies:

- ▶ Sound it out
- ▶ Decode by analogy
- ▶ Apply phonics rules

These strategies are most effective for decoding phonetically regular one-syllable words.

Guidelines
for Teaching Phonics

- ▶ Teach high-utility phonics concepts that are most useful for reading unfamiliar words.

- ▶ Follow a developmental continuum for systematic phonics instruction, beginning with rhyming and ending with phonics rules.

- ▶ Provide explicit instruction to teach phonics strategies and skills.

- ▶ Provide opportunities for students to apply what they are learning about phonics through word sorts, making words, interactive writing, and other literacy activities.

- ▶ Take advantage of teachable moments to clarify misunderstandings and infuse phonics instruction into literacy activities.

- ▶ Use oral activities to reinforce phonemic awareness strategies as students blend and segment written words during phonics and spelling instruction.

- ▶ Review phonics as part of spelling, when necessary, in the upper grades.

Figure 5–6 ◆ Sequence of Phonics Instruction

Grade	Skill	Description	Examples
K	More common consonants	Children identify consonant sounds, match sounds to letters, and substitute sounds in words.	/b/, /d/, /f/, /m/, /n/, /p/, /s/, /t/
K–1	Less common consonants	Children identify consonant sounds, match sounds to letters, and substitute sounds in words.	/g/, /h/, /j/, /k/, /l/, /q/, /v/, /w/, /x/, /y/, /z/
	Short vowels	Children identify the five short vowel sounds and match them to letters.	/ă/ = cat, /ĕ/ = bed, /ĭ/ = pig, /ŏ/ = hot, /ŭ/ = cut
	CVC pattern	Children read and spell CVC-pattern words.	dad, men, sit, hop, but
1	Consonant blends	Children identify and blend consonant sounds at the beginning and end of words.	/pl/ = plant /str/ = string
	Phonograms	Children break CVC words into onsets and rimes and use phonograms to form new words.	not: dot, shot, spot will: still, fill, drill
	Consonant digraphs	Children identify consonant diagraphs, match sounds to letters, and read and spell words with consonant digraphs.	/ch/ = chop /sh/ = dash /th/ = with /wh/ = when
	Long vowel sounds	Children identify the five long vowel sounds and match them to letters.	/ā/ = name, /ē/ = bee, /ī/ = ice, /ō/ = soap, /ū/ = tune
	CVCe pattern	Children read and spell CVCe-pattern words.	game, ride, stone
	Common long vowel digraphs	Children identify the vowel sound represented by common long vowel digraphs and read and spell words using them.	/ā/ = ai (rain), ay (day) /ē/ = ea (reach), ee (sweet) /ō/ = oa (soap), ow (know)
1–2	w and y	Children recognize when w and y are consonants and when they're vowels, and identify the sounds they represent.	window, yesterday y = /ī/ (by) y = /ē/ (baby)
	Phonograms	Children divide long-vowel words into onsets and rimes and use phonograms to form new words.	woke: joke, broke, smoke day: gray, day, stay
	Hard and soft consonant sounds	Children identify the hard and soft sounds represented by c and g, and read and spell words using them.	g = girl (hard), gem (soft) c = cat (hard), city (soft)
2–3	Less common vowel digraphs	Children identify the sounds of less common vowel digraphs and read and spell words using them.	/ô/ = al (walk), au (caught), aw (saw), ou (bought) /ā/ = ei (weigh) /ē/ = ey (key), ie (chief) /ī/ = ie (pie) /ŏŏ/ = oo (good), ou (could) /ū/ = oo (moon), ew (new), ue (blue), ui (fruit)
	Vowel diphthongs	Children identify the vowel diphthongs and read and write words using them.	/oi/ = oi (boil), oy (toy) /ou/ = ou (cloud), ow (down)
	Less common consonant digraphs	Children identify the sounds of less common consonant digraphs and read and write words using them.	ph = phone ng = sing gh = laugh tch = match
	r-controlled vowels	Children identify r-controlled vowel patterns and read and spell words using them.	/âr/ = hair, care, bear, there, their /ar/ = heart, star /er/ = clear, deer, here /or/ = born, more, warm /ûr/ = learn, first, work, burn

Explicit Instruction. Teachers present minilessons on phonics concepts to the whole class or to small groups of students, depending on the their instructional needs. They follow the minilesson format, explicitly presenting information about a phonics strategy or skill, demonstrating how to use it, and presenting words for students to use in guided practice, as Mrs. Firpo did in the vignette at the beginning of the chapter. During the minilesson, teachers use these activities to provide guided practice opportunities for students to manipulate sounds and read and write words:

◆ Sort objects, pictures, and word cards according to a phonics concept.
◆ Write letters or words on small dry-erase boards.
◆ Arrange magnetic letters or letter cards to spell words.
◆ Make class charts of words representing phonics concepts, such as the two sounds of *g* or the *-ore* phonogram.
◆ Make a poster or book of words representing a phonics concept.
◆ Locate other words exemplifying the spelling pattern in books students are reading.

The minilesson feature on the next page shows how a first-grade teacher teaches a minilesson on reading and spelling CVC-pattern words using final consonant blends.

Application Activities. Children apply the phonics concepts they're learning as they read and write and participate in teacher-directed activities. In interactive writing, for example, children segment words into sounds and take turns writing letters and sometimes whole words on the chart (McCarrier, Pinnell, & Fountas, 2000; Tompkins & Collom, 2004). Teachers help children correct any errors, and they take advantage of teachable moments to review consonant and vowel sounds and spelling patterns, as well as handwriting skills and rules for capitalization and punctuation. Making words, word ladders, and word sorts are other activities that children do to apply what they're learning about phoneme-grapheme correspondences, word families, and phonics rules.

Assessing Students' Phonics Knowledge

Primary teachers assess children's developing phonics knowledge using a combination of tests, observation, and reading and writing samples. They often use a test to screen children at the beginning of the school year, monitor their progress at midyear, and document their achievement at the end of the year. When children aren't making expected progress, teachers administer a test to diagnose the problem and plan for instruction. Four tests that assess children's phonics knowledge, including one designed for older, struggling readers, are described in the Assessment Tools feature on page 166.

Teaching Struggling Readers and Writers

Phonics

Struggling readers need to learn to decode words.

Phonics is a very useful tool for identifying unfamiliar words, and struggling readers need to learn to decode words. Most struggling students already know letter-sound relationships, but they guess at words based on the first letter or they sound out the letters, one by one, without blending the sounds or considering spelling patterns.

Instruction for students who can't decode words includes two components (Cunningham, 2009; McKenna, 2002): First, review word families, create a word wall divided into sections for words representing each phonogram, and teach students to decode by analogy. Second, teach spelling patterns and have students practice them using word sorts. Some teachers have students read decodable texts to practice particular phonics patterns. For example, this passage emphasizes /ă/ and the CVC pattern:

The cat sat on a mat. The cat was black. He sat and sat.
The black cat was sad. Too bad!

Even though publishers of these texts often tout their research base, Allington (2006) found no research to support their claims. Trade books at students' independent reading levels are more effective for decoding practice.

Sometimes teachers skip phonics instruction because they feel that struggling readers have been taught phonics without much benefit, but McKenna (2002) counters: "Unfortunately, there is no way to . . . bypass the decoding stage of reading development" (p. 9). Here's the reasoning: If students can't decode words, they won't become fluent readers; if they can't read fluently, they won't comprehend what they're reading; and if they can't comprehend, they won't become successful readers.

MiniLesson

TOPIC: Decoding CVC Words With Final Consonant Blends
GRADE: First Grade
TIME: One 30-minute period

Mrs. Nazir is teaching her first graders about consonant blends. She introduced initial consonant blends to the class, and children practiced reading and spelling words, such as *club, drop,* and *swim,* that were chosen from the selection they were reading in their basal readers. Then, in small groups, they completed workbook pages and made words using plastic tiles with onsets and rimes printed on them. For example, using the *-ip* phonogram, they made *clip, drip, flip, skip,* and *trip.* This is the fifth whole-class lesson in the series. Today, Mrs. Nazir is introducing final consonant blends.

❶ Introduce the Topic

Mrs. Nazir explains that blends are also used at the end of words. She writes these words on the chalkboard: *best, rang, hand, pink,* and *bump.* Together the children sound them out: They pronounce the initial consonant sound, the short vowel sound, and the final consonants. They blend the final consonants, then they blend the entire word and say it aloud. Children use the words in sentences to ensure that everyone understands them, and Dillon, T.J., Pauline, Cody, and Brittany circle the blends in the words on the chalkboard. The teacher points out that *st* is a familiar blend also used at the beginning of words, but that the other blends are used only at the end of words.

❷ Share Examples

Mrs. Nazir says these words: *must, wing, test, band, hang, sink, bend,* and *bump.* The first graders repeat each word, isolate the blend, and identify it. Carson says, "The word is *must*—/m/ /ŭ/ /s/ /t/—and the blend is *st* at the end." Bryan points out that Ng is his last name, and everyone claps because his name is so special. Several children volunteer additional words: Dillon suggests *blast,* and Henry adds *dump* and *string.* Then the teacher passes out word cards and children read the words, including *just, lamp, went,* and *hang.* They sound out each word carefully, pronouncing the initial consonant, the short vowel, and the final consonant blend. Then they blend the sounds and say the word.

❸ Provide Information

Mrs. Nazir posts a piece of chart paper, and labels it "The *-ink* Word Family." The children brainstorm these words with the *-ink* phonogram: *blink, sink, pink, rink, mink, stink,* and *wink,* and they take turns writing the words on the chart. They also suggest *twinkle* and *wrinkle,* and Mrs. Nazir adds them to the chart.

❹ Guide Practice

Children create other word family charts using *-and, -ang, -ank, -end, -ent, -est, -ing, -ump,* and *-ust.* Each group brainstorms at least five words and writes them on the chart. Mrs. Nazir monitors children's work and helps them think of additional words and correct spelling errors. Then children post their word family charts and share them with the class.

❺ Assess Learning

Mrs. Nazir observes the first graders as they brainstorm words, blend sounds, and spell the words. She notices several children who need more practice and will call them together for a follow-up lesson.

Assessment Tools

Phonics

Teachers monitor students' developing phonics knowledge by observing them during classroom activities and by administering these tests:

◆ **Observation Survey of Early Literacy Achievement (OS): Word Reading and Hearing and Recording Sounds in Words Subtests** (Clay, 2005b)

The OS includes six subtests. The Word Reading and Hearing and Recording Sounds in Words subtests are used to assess young children's ability to apply phonics concepts to decode and spell words. The subtests are administered individually, and children's scores for each subtest can be standardized and converted to stanines. The OS is published by Heinemann Books.

◆ **Dynamic Indicators of Basic Early Literacy Skills (DIBELS): Nonsense Word Fluency Subtest** (Kaminski & Good, 1996)

This individually administered subtest assesses young children's ability to apply phonics concepts to read two- and three-letter nonsense words (e.g., *ap, jid*). Multiple forms are available, so this test can be used to monitor children's progress during kindergarten and first grade. The test is available at the DIBELS website free of charge, but there's a charge for scoring tests and for reporting scores.

◆ **The Tile Test** (Norman & Calfee, 2004)

This individually administered test assesses K–2 students' knowledge of phonics. Children manipulate letter tiles to make words, and teachers also arrange tiles to spell words for them to read. The Tile Test can easily be administered in 10 to 15 minutes. It's available online, free of charge.

◆ **The Names Test: A Quick Assessment of Decoding Ability** (Cunningham, 1990; Duffelmeyer et al., 1994; Mather, Sammons, & Schwartz, 2006)

The Names Test measures older students' (grades 3–8) ability to decode words. The test is a list of names that illustrate phoneme-grapheme correspondences and phonics rules. As students read the names, teachers mark which ones they read correctly and which they mispronounce. Then teachers analyze the errors to determine which phonics concepts students haven't learned. This free assessment is available online.

These tests are useful assessment tools that teachers use to screen, monitor, diagnose, and document children's phonics knowledge and to make instructional decisions.

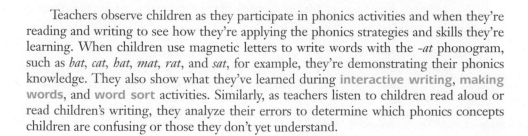

Teachers observe children as they participate in phonics activities and when they're reading and writing to see how they're applying the phonics strategies and skills they're learning. When children use magnetic letters to write words with the -*at* phonogram, such as *bat*, *cat*, *hat*, *mat*, *rat*, and *sat*, for example, they're demonstrating their phonics knowledge. They also show what they've learned during interactive writing, making words, and word sort activities. Similarly, as teachers listen to children read aloud or read children's writing, they analyze their errors to determine which phonics concepts children are confusing or those they don't yet understand.

What's the Role of Phonics in a Balanced Literacy Program?

Phonics is a controversial topic. Some parents and politicians, as well as even a few teachers, believe that most of our educational ills could be solved if children were taught to read using phonics. A few people still argue that phonics is a complete reading program, but that view ignores what we know about the interrelatedness of the four cueing systems. Reading is a complex process, and the phonological system works in conjunction with the semantic, syntactic, and pragmatic systems, not in isolation.

The controversy now centers on the best way to teach phonics. Marilyn Adams (1990), in her landmark review of the research on phonics instruction, recommends that phonics be taught within a balanced approach that integrates instruction in reading strategies and skills with meaningful opportunities for reading and writing. She emphasizes that phonics instruction should focus on the most useful information for identifying words, that it should be systematic and intensive, and that it should be completed by third grade.

SPELLING

Learning to spell is also part of "cracking the code." As children learn about phonics, they apply what they're learning through both reading and writing. Children's early spellings reflect what they know about phoneme-grapheme relationships, phonics rules, and spelling patterns. As their knowledge grows, their spelling increasingly approximates conventional spelling.

Students need to learn to spell words conventionally so that they can communicate effectively through writing. Learning phonics during the primary grades is part of spelling instruction, but students also need to learn other strategies and information about English orthography. In the past, weekly spelling tests were the main instructional approach; now, they're only one part of a comprehensive spelling program. Guidelines for spelling instruction are presented here.

Guidelines
for Teaching Spelling

▶ Analyze the errors in students' writing to provide appropriate spelling instruction based on their stage of development.

▶ Connect phonemic awareness, phonics, and spelling during minilessons by having students manipulate words orally and read and spell them.

▶ Guide students to use strategies to spell unfamiliar words.

▶ Teach students to spell high-frequency words before less common ones.

▶ Post words on word walls and use them for a variety of spelling activities.

▶ Involve students in making words, word ladders, word sorts, and other hands-on spelling activities.

▶ Consider spelling tests as only one part of an instructional program.

▶ Involve students in daily authentic reading and writing activities to apply their spelling knowledge.

Stages of Spelling Development

As young children begin to write, they create unique spellings, called *invented spelling*, based on their knowledge of phonology (Read, 1975). The children in Read's studies used letter names to spell words, such as *U* (*you*) and *R* (*are*), and they used consonant sounds rather consistently: *GRL* (*girl*), *TIGR* (*tiger*), and *NIT* (*night*). They used several unusual but phonetically based spelling patterns to represent affricates; for example, they replaced *tr* with *chr* (e.g., *CHRIBLES* for *troubles*) and *dr* with *jr* (e.g., *JRAGIN* for *dragon*). Words with long vowels were spelled using letter names: *MI* (*my*), *LADE* (*lady*), and *FEL* (*feel*). The children used several ingenious strategies to spell words with short vowels: The preschoolers selected letters to represent short vowels on the basis of place of articulation in the mouth. Short *i* was represented with *e*, as in *FES* (*fish*), short *e* with *a*, as in *LAFFT* (*left*), and short *o* with *i*, as in *CLIK* (*clock*). These spellings may seem odd to adults, but they are based on phonetic relationships.

Based on examinations of children's spellings, researchers have identified five stages that students move through on their way to becoming conventional spellers: emergent spelling, letter name-alphabetic spelling, within-word pattern spelling, syllables and affixes spelling, and derivational relations spelling (Bear, Invernizzi, Templeton, & Johnston, 2008). At each stage, students use different strategies and focus on particular aspects of spelling. The characteristics of the five stages are summarized in Figure 5–7.

Stage 1: Emergent Spelling. Children string scribbles, letters, and letterlike forms together, but they don't associate the marks they make with any specific phonemes. Spelling at this stage represents a natural, early expression of the alphabet and other written-language concepts. Children may write from left to right, right to left, top to bottom, or randomly across the page, but by the end of the stage, they have an understanding of directionality. Some emergent spellers have a large repertoire of letterforms to use in writing, whereas others repeat a small number of letters over and over. They use both upper- and lowercase letters but show a distinct preference for uppercase letters. Toward the end of the stage, children are beginning to discover how spelling works and that letters represent sounds in words. This stage is typical of 3- to 5-year-olds. During the emergent stage, children learn these concepts:

◆ The distinction between drawing and writing
◆ How to make letters
◆ The direction of writing on a page
◆ Some letter-sound matches

Stage 2: Letter Name-Alphabetic Spelling. Children learn to represent phonemes in words with letters. They develop an understanding of the alphabetic principle, that a link exists between letters and sounds. At first, the spellings are quite abbreviated and represent only the most prominent features in words. Children use only several letters of the alphabet to represent an entire word. Examples of early Stage 2 spelling are *D* (*dog*) and *KE* (*cookie*), and children may still be writing mainly with capital letters. Children slowly pronounce the word they want to spell, listening for familiar letter names and sounds.

In the middle of the letter name-alphabetic stage, children use most beginning and ending consonants and include a vowel in most syllables; they spell *like* as *lik* and *bed* as *bad*. By the end of the stage, they use consonant blends and digraphs and short-vowel patterns to spell *hat*, *get*, and *win*, but some still spell *ship* as *sep*. They can also spell

Figure 5–7 ◆ Stages of Spelling Development

Stage 1: Emergent Spelling

Children string scribbles, letters, and letterlike forms together, but they don't associate the marks they make with any specific phonemes. This stage is typical of 3- to 5-year-olds. Children learn these concepts:

- The distinction between drawing and writing
- How to make letters
- The direction of writing on a page
- Some letter-sound matches

Stage 2: Letter Name-Alphabetic Spelling

Children learn to represent phonemes in words with letters. At first, their spellings are quite abbreviated, but they learn to use consonant blends and digraphs and short-vowel patterns to spell many short-vowel words. Spellers are 5- to 7-year-olds. Children learn these concepts:

- The alphabetic principle
- Consonant sounds
- Short vowel sounds
- Consonant blends and digraphs

Stage 3: Within-Word Pattern Spelling

Students learn long-vowel patterns and *r*-controlled vowels, but they may confuse spelling patterns and spell *meet* as *mete*, and they reverse the order of letters, such as *form* for *from* and *gril* for *girl*. Spellers are 7- to 9-year-olds, and they learn these concepts:

- Long-vowel spelling patterns
- *r*-controlled vowels
- More-complex consonant patterns
- Diphthongs and other less common vowel patterns

Stage 4: Syllables and Affixes Spelling

Students apply what they have learned about one-syllable words to spell longer words, and they learn to break words into syllables. They also learn to add inflectional endings (e.g., *-es*, *-ed*, *-ing*) and to differentiate between homophones, such as *your–you're*. Spellers are often 9- to 11-year-olds, and they learn these concepts:

- Inflectional endings
- Rules for adding inflectional endings
- Syllabication
- Homophones

Stage 5: Derivational Relations Spelling

Students explore the relationship between spelling and meaning and learn that words with related meanings are often related in spelling despite changes in sound (e.g., *wise–wisdom*, *sign–signal*, *nation–national*). They also learn about Latin and Greek root words and derivational affixes (e.g., *amphi-*, *pre-*, *-able*, *-tion*). Spellers are 11- to 14-year-olds. Students learn these concepts:

- Consonant alternations
- Vowel alternations
- Latin affixes and root words
- Greek affixes and root words
- Etymologies

Adapted from Bear, Invernizzi, Templeton, & Johnston, 2008.

some CVCe words such as *name* correctly. Spellers at this stage are usually 5- to 7-year-olds. During the letter-name stage, children learn these concepts:

◆ The alphabetic principle
◆ Consonant sounds
◆ Short vowel sounds
◆ Consonant blends and digraphs

Stage 3: Within-Word Pattern Spelling. Students begin the within-word pattern stage when they can spell most one-syllable short-vowel words, and during this stage, they learn to spell long-vowel patterns and *r*-controlled vowels. They experiment with long-vowel patterns and learn that words such as *come* and *bread* are exceptions that don't fit the vowel patterns. Students may confuse spelling patterns and spell *meet* as *mete*, and they reverse the order of letters, such as *form* for *from* and *gril* for *girl*. They also learn about complex consonant sounds, including *-tch* (*match*) and *-dge* (*judge*), and less frequent vowel patterns, such as *oi/oy* (*boy*), *au* (*caught*), *aw* (*saw*), *ew* (*sew, few*), *ou* (*house*), and *ow* (*cow*). Students also become aware of homophones and compare long- and short-vowel combinations (*hope–hop*) as they experiment with vowel patterns. Students at this stage are 7- to 9-year-olds, and they learn these spelling concepts:

◆ Long-vowel spelling patterns
◆ *r*-controlled vowels
◆ More-complex consonant patterns
◆ Diphthongs and other less common vowel patterns

Stage 4: Syllables and Affixes Spelling. Students focus on syllables in this stage and apply what they've learned about one-syllable words to longer, multisyllabic words. They learn about inflectional endings (*-s, -es, -ed,* and *-ing*) and rules about consonant doubling, changing the final *y* to *i*, or dropping the final *e* before adding an inflectional suffix. They also learn about homophones and compound words and are introduced to some of the more-common prefixes and suffixes. Spellers in this stage are generally 9- to 11-year-olds. Students learn these concepts during the syllables and affixes stage of spelling development:

◆ Inflectional endings (*-s, -es, -ed, -ing*)
◆ Rules for adding inflectional endings
◆ Syllabication
◆ Homophones

Stage 5: Derivational Relations Spelling. Students explore the relationship between spelling and meaning during the derivational relations stage, and they learn that words with related meanings are often related in spelling despite changes in vowel and consonant sounds (e.g., *wise–wisdom, sign–signal, nation–national*). The focus in this stage is on morphemes, and students learn about Greek and Latin root words and affixes. They also begin to examine etymologies and the role of history in shaping how words are spelled. They learn about eponyms (words from people's names), such as *maverick* and *sandwich*. Spellers at this stage are 11- to 14-year-olds. Students learn these concepts at this stage of spelling development:

◆ Consonant alternations (e.g., *soft–soften, magic–magician*)
◆ Vowel alternations (e.g., *please–pleasant, define–definition, explain–explanation*)
◆ Greek and Latin affixes and root words
◆ Etymologies

Children's spelling provides evidence of their growing understanding of English orthography. The words they spell correctly show which phonics concepts, spelling patterns, and other language features they've learned to apply, and the words they invent and misspell show what they're still learning to use and those features of spelling that they haven't noticed or learned about. Invented spelling is sometimes criticized because it appears that students are learning bad habits by misspelling words, but researchers have confirmed that students grow more quickly in phonemic awareness, phonics, and spelling when they use invented spelling as long as they are also receiving spelling instruction (Snow, Burns, & Griffin, 1998). As students learn more about spelling, their invented spellings become more sophisticated to reflect their new knowledge, even if the words are still spelled incorrectly, and increasingly students spell more and more words correctly as they move through the stages of spelling development.

Nurturing English Learners

English learners move through the same five developmental stages that native English speakers do, but they move more slowly because they're less familiar with the letter-sound correspondences, spelling patterns, and grammar of English (Bear, Helman, Invernizzi, Templeton, & Johnston, 2007). Students' spelling development reflects their reading achievement, but it lags behind reading: When ELs learn a word, they begin by learning its meaning and how to pronounce it. Almost immediately, they're introduced to the word's written form, and with practice, they learn to recognize and read it. Soon they're writing the word, too. At first their spellings reflect what they know about the English spelling system, but with spelling instruction and reading and writing practice, they learn to spell words correctly. Because spelling is more demanding than reading, it's not surprising that students' knowledge about spelling grows this way.

It's essential that teachers learn about English learners' home language, especially about the ways it differs from English, and then they need to explicitly teach students about the contrasts because they're harder to learn than the similarities (Bear, Helman, Invernizzi, Templeton, & Johnston, 2007). Consider these written language differences, for example: Chinese uses syllable-length characters instead of letters; Arabic is written from right to left, and the way letters are formed varies according to their location within a word; and vowels aren't used in Croatian and Czech. Some languages, including Arabic, Spanish, Kiswahili (Swahili), and Russian, are more phonetically consistent than English; students who speak these languages are often confused by the number of ways a sound can be spelled in English. There are phonological differences, too: Many languages, including Korean, don't have the /th/ sound; there's no /p/ in Arabic, so Arabic speakers often substitute /b/ in English; and /l/ and /r/ sound alike to speakers of Asian languages. Vowels are particularly difficult for English learners because they're often pronounced differently in their home language. For example, Russian speakers don't differentiate between short and long vowels, and Spanish speakers often substitute /ĕ/ for /ā/ and /ō/ for /ŏ/. Many African and Asian languages, including Kiswahili, Punjabi, Chinese, and Thai, as well as Navajo, a Native American language, are tonal; in these languages, pitch, not spelling differences, is used to distinguish between words. In addition, there are syntactic differences that affect spelling: Hmong speakers don't add plural markers to nouns; Korean speakers add grammatical information to the end of verbs instead of using auxiliary verbs; and Chinese speakers aren't familiar with prefixes or suffixes because they're not used in their language.

Teachers base their instruction on English learners' stage of spelling development, and they emphasize the contrasts between students' home languages and English. At each developmental stage, teachers focus their instruction on concepts that confuse English learners, according to Bear and his colleagues (2007):

Emergent Stage. Students learn English letters, sounds, and words, and they learn that English is written from left to right and top to bottom, with spaces between words. Developing this awareness is more difficult for students whose home languages are not alphabetic.

Letter Name-Alphabetic Stage. Students learn that letters represent sounds, and the sounds that are the same in ELs' home languages and English are the easiest to learn. They learn both consonant and vowel sounds. Those consonant sounds that are more difficult include /d/, /j/, /r/, /sh/, and /th/. English learners often have difficulty pronouncing and spelling final consonant blends (e.g., -*st* as in *fast*, -*ng* as in *king*, -*mp* as in *stomp*, and -*rd* as in *board*). Long and short vowel sounds are especially hard because they're often pronounced differently than in students' home languages.

Within-Word Pattern Stage. Students move from representing individual sounds in words to using spelling patterns. They practice CVCe and CVVC spelling patterns and words that are exceptions to these rules; *r*-controlled vowels are especially tricky because they're found in common words, and sound often doesn't predict spelling (e.g., *bear/care/hair*, *bird/heard/fern/burst*). English learners also learn to spell homophones (e.g., *wear–where*, *to–too–two*) and contractions during this stage.

Syllables and Affixes Stage. Students learn spelling and grammar concepts together as they investigate verb forms (e.g., *talk–talked*, *take–took–taken*, *think–thought*), change adjectives to adverbs (e.g., *quick–quickly*), and add inflectional endings (e.g., *walks–walked–walking*) and comparatives and superlatives (e.g., *sunny–sunnier–sunniest*). They also learn to pronounce accented and unaccented syllables differently and to use the schwa sound in unaccented syllables.

Derivational Relations Stage. Students learn about Latin and Greek root words and vowel alternations in related words (e.g., *define–definition*). Some ELs use tonal changes to signal these relationships in their home languages, but they must learn that related words in English are signaled by similar spelling and changes in how the vowels are pronounced.

Spelling instruction for English learners is similar to that for native speakers: Teachers use a combination of explicit instruction, **word sorts** and other practice activities, and authentic reading and writing activities. The biggest difference is that ELs need more instruction on the English spelling concepts that confuse them, often because these features aren't used in their home languages.

Teaching Spelling

Perhaps the best-known way to teach spelling is through weekly spelling tests, but tests should never be considered a complete spelling program. To become good spellers, students need to learn about the English orthographic system and move through the stages of spelling development. They develop strategies to use in spelling unknown words and gain experience in using dictionaries and other resources. A complete spelling program includes the following components:

◆ Teaching spelling strategies
◆ Matching instruction to students' stage of spelling development
◆ Providing daily reading and writing opportunities
◆ Teaching students to learn to spell high-frequency words

Students learn spelling strategies that they can use to figure out the spelling of unfamiliar words. As students move through the stages of spelling development, they

Word Sorts
This second grader is participating in a phonics word sort: She's arranging letter cards to spell long *e* words that use the CVVC vowel pattern, including *mean*, *beat*, *peach*, *read*, and *cream*. Her teacher began the lesson by identifying specific words for the students to spell using small paper letter cards, and now they're rearranging them to spell other long *e* words that follow the CVVC pattern. Some students, including this girl, work independently while others collaborate with classmates for this spelling lesson. Afterward, the teacher will place several sets of these letter cards in a literacy center for students who need extra practice spelling long *e* words. Later, they'll examine other spelling patterns using word sorts.

become increasingly more sophisticated in their use of phonological, semantic, and historical knowledge to spell words; that is, they become more strategic. Important spelling strategies include the following:

◆ Segmenting the word and spelling each sound, often called *sound it out*
◆ Spelling unknown words by analogy to familiar words
◆ Applying affixes to root words
◆ Proofreading to locate spelling errors in a rough draft
◆ Locating the spelling of unfamiliar words in a dictionary

Teachers often give the traditional *sound it out* advice when young children ask how to spell an unfamiliar word, but teachers provide more useful information when they suggest that students use a strategic *think it out* approach. This advice reminds students that spelling involves more than phonological information and encourages them to think about spelling patterns, root words and affixes, and what the word looks like.

Two of the most important ways that students learn to spell are through daily reading and writing activities. Students who are good readers tend to be good spellers, too: As they read, students visualize words—the shape of the word and the configuration of letters within it—and they use this knowledge to spell many words correctly and to recognize when a word they've written doesn't look right. Through writing, of course, students gain valuable practice using the strategies they have learned to spell words. And, as teachers work with students to proofread and edit their writing, they learn more about spelling and other writing conventions.

In addition to reading and writing activities, students learn about the English orthographic system through **minilessons** about phonics, high-frequency words,

MiniLesson

TOPIC: Spelling -*at* Family Words
GRADE: First Grade
TIME: One 10-minute period

Mr. Cheng teaches phonics skills during guided reading lessons. He introduces, practices, and reviews phonics concepts using words from selections his first graders are reading. The children decode and spell words using letter and word cards, magnetic letters, and small dry-erase boards and pens.

❶ Introduce the Topic

Mr. Cheng holds up a copy of *At Home*, the small paperback level E book the children read yesterday, and asks them to reread the title. Then he asks the children to identify the first word, *at*. After they read the word, he hands a card with the word *at* written on it to each of the six children in the guided reading group. "Who can read this word?" he asks. Several children recognize it immediately, and others carefully sound out the two-letter word.

❷ Share Examples

Mr. Cheng asks children to think about rhyming words: "Who knows what rhyming words are?" Mike answers that rhyming words sound alike at the end—for example, *Mike, bike*, and *like*. The teacher explains that there are many words in English that rhyme, and that today, they are going to read and write words that rhyme with *at*. "One rhyming word is *cat*," he explains. Children name rhyming words, including *hat, fat*, and *bat*. Mr. Cheng helps each child in the group to name at least three rhyming words.

❸ Provide Information

Mr. Cheng explains that children can spell these *at* words by adding a consonant in front of *at*. For example, he places the foam letter *c* in front of his *at* card, and the children blend *c* to *at* to decode *cat*. Then he repeats the procedure by substituting other foam letters for the *c* to spell *bat, fat, hat, mat, pat, rat*, and *sat*. He continues the activity until every child successfully decodes one of the words.

❹ Guide Practice

Mr. Cheng passes out small plastic trays with foam letters to each child and asks them to add one of the letters to their *at* cards to spell the words as he pronounces them. He continues the activity until children have had several opportunities to spell each word, and they can quickly choose the correct initial consonant to spell it. Then Mr. Cheng collects the *at* cards and trays with foam letters.

❺ Assess Learning

Mr. Cheng passes out small dry-erase boards and pens. He asks the first graders to write the words as he says each one aloud: *cat, hat, mat, pat, rat, sat, bat, fat*. He carefully observes as each child segments the onset and rime to spell the word. The children hold up their boards to show him their spellings. Afterward, children erase the word and repeat the process, writing the next word. After children write all eight words, Mr. Cheng quickly jots a note about which children need additional practice with the -*at* word family before continuing with the guided reading lesson.

spelling rules, and spelling strategies. The minilesson feature on the preceding page shows how Mr. Cheng teaches his first graders to spell -*at* family words. Then in the following sections, you'll read about a number of spelling activities that expand students' spelling knowledge and help them move through the stages of spelling development.

Word Walls. Teachers use two types of word walls in their classrooms. One word wall features "important" words from books students are reading or thematic units. Words may be written on a large sheet of paper hanging in the classroom or on word cards and placed in a large pocket chart. Then students refer to these word walls when they're writing. Seeing the words posted on word walls and other charts in the classroom and using them in their writing help students learn to spell the words.

The second type of word wall displays high-frequency words. Researchers have identified the most commonly used words and recommend that students learn to spell 100 of these words because of their usefulness. The most frequently used words represent more than 50% of all the words children and adults write! Figure 5–8 lists the 100 most frequently used words.

Be Strategic!

Spelling Strategies

Students use these strategies to spell words and to verify that words they've written are spelled correctly:

► Sound it out
► Spell by analogy
► Apply affixes
► Proofread
► Check a dictionary

Sounding out spellings works best for spelling phonetically regular words in first and second grade; later, students learn more-effective strategies to think out correct spellings for longer words.

Figure 5–8 ◆ The 100 Most Frequently Used Words

A		B	C	D E	
a	and	back	came	day	do
about	are	be	can	did	don't
after	around	because	could	didn't	down
all	as	but			
am	at	by			
an					

F G		H		I J		K L
for		had	his	I	is	know
from		have	home	if	it	like
get		he	house	in	just	little
got		her	how	into		
		him				

M N		O		P Q R	S	
man	no	of	our	people	said	she
me	not	on	out	put	saw	so
mother	now	one	over		school	some
my		or			see	

T		U V	W X		Y Z
that	think	up	was	when	you
the	this	us	we	who	your
them	time	very	well	will	
then	to		went	with	
there	too		were	would	
they	two		what		
things					

Making Words. Teachers choose a five- to eight-letter word (or longer words for older students) and prepare sets of letter cards for a **making words** activity (Cunningham & Cunningham, 1992). Then students use the cards to practice spelling words and to review spelling patterns and rules. They arrange and rearrange the cards to spell one-letter words, two-letter words, three-letter words, and so forth, until they use all the letters to spell the original word. Second graders, for example, can create these words using the letters in *weather: a, at, we, he, the, are, art, ear, eat, hat, her, hear, here, hate, heart, wheat, there,* and *where.*

Word Sorts. Students use **word sorts** to explore, compare, and contrast word features as they sort a pack of word cards. Teachers prepare word cards for students to sort into two or more categories according to their spelling patterns or other criteria (Bear et al., 2008). Sometimes teachers tell students what categories to use, which makes the sort a closed sort; when students determine the categories themselves, the sort is an open sort. Students can sort word cards and then return them to an envelope for future use, or they can glue the cards onto a sheet of paper.

Interactive Writing. Teachers use **interactive writing** to teach spelling concepts as well as other concepts about written language. Because correct spelling and legible handwriting are courtesies for readers, they emphasize correct spelling as students take turns to collaboratively write a message. It is likely that students will misspell a few words as they write, so teachers take advantage of these "teachable moments" to clarify students' misunderstandings. Through interactive writing, students learn to use a variety of resources to correct misspelled words, including classroom word walls, books, classmates, and the dictionary.

Proofreading. Proofreading is a special kind of reading that students use to locate misspelled words and other mechanical errors in rough drafts. As students learn about the writing process, they are introduced to proofreading in the editing stage. More in-depth instruction about how to use proofreading to locate spelling errors and then correct these misspelled words is part of spelling instruction (Cramer, 1998). Through a series of minilessons, students can learn to proofread sample student papers and mark misspelled words. Then, working in pairs, students can correct the misspelled words.

Proofreading should be introduced in the primary grades. Young children and their teachers proofread **collaborative books** and dictated stories together, and students can be encouraged to read over their own compositions and make necessary corrections soon after they begin writing. This way, students accept proofreading as a natural part of writing. Proofreading activities are more valuable for teaching spelling than are dictation activities, in which teachers dictate sentences for students to write and correctly capitalize and punctuate. Few people use dictation in their daily lives, but we use proofreading skills every time we polish a piece of writing.

Dictionary Use. Students need to learn to locate the spelling of unfamiliar words in the dictionary. Although it is relatively easy to find a "known" word in the dictionary, it is hard to locate unfamiliar words, and students need to learn what to do when they don't know how to spell a word. One approach is to predict possible spellings for unknown words, then check the most probable spellings in a dictionary.

Students should be encouraged to check the spelling of words in a dictionary as well as to use a dictionary to check multiple meanings or etymology. Too often, students view consulting a dictionary as punishment; teachers must work to change this view. One way to do this is to appoint several students as dictionary checkers: These students keep dictionaries on their desks, and they're consulted whenever questions about spelling, a word's meaning, or word usage arise.

Spelling Options. In English, alternate spellings occur for many sounds because so many words borrowed from other languages retain their native spellings. There are many more options for vowel sounds than for consonants. Spelling options sometimes vary according to the letter's position in the word. For example, *ff* is found in the middle and at the end of words but not at the beginning (e.g., *muffin, cuff*), and *gh* represents /f/ only at the end of a syllable or word (e.g., *cough, laughter*).

Teachers point out spelling options as they write words on word walls and when students ask about the spelling of a word. They also can teach upper-grade students about these options in a series of minilessons. During each lesson, students can focus on one phoneme, such as /ō/ or /k/, and as a class or small group they can develop a list of the various ways the sound is spelled, giving examples of each spelling.

Weekly Spelling Tests

Many teachers question the usefulness of spelling tests, because research on invented spelling suggests that spelling is best learned through reading and writing (Gentry & Gillet, 1993). In addition, teachers complain that lists of spelling words are unrelated to the words students are reading and writing and that the 30 minutes of valuable instructional time spent each day in completing spelling activities is excessive. Even so, parents and school board members value spelling tests as evidence that spelling is being taught. Weekly spelling tests, when they are used, should be individualized so that students learn to spell the words they need for writing.

In the individualized approach to spelling instruction, students choose the words they'll study, many of which are words they use in their writing projects. Students study 5 to 10 specific words during the week using a study strategy; this approach places more responsibility on students for their own learning. Teachers develop a weekly word list of 20 or more words of varying difficulty from which students select words to study. Words for the master list include high-frequency words, words from the word wall related to literature focus units and thematic units, and words students needed for their writing projects during the previous week. Words from spelling programs can also be added to the list.

On Monday, the teacher administers a pretest using the master list of words, and students spell as many of the words as they can. Students correct their own pretests, and from the words they misspell they create individual spelling lists. They make two copies of their study list, using the numbers on the master list to make it easier to take the final test on Friday. Students use one copy of the list for study activities, and the teacher keeps the second copy.

Students spend approximately 5 to 10 minutes studying the words on their study lists each day during the week. Research shows that instead of "busy-work" activities such as using their spelling words in sentences or gluing yarn in the shape of the words, it's more effective for students to use this study strategy:

1. Look at the word and say it to yourself.
2. Say each letter in the word to yourself.
3. Close your eyes and spell the word to yourself.
4. Write the word, and check that you spelled it correctly.
5. Write the word again, and check that you spelled it correctly.

This strategy focuses on the whole word rather than on breaking the word apart into sounds or syllables. Teachers explain how to use the strategy during a minilesson at the beginning of the school year and then post a copy of it in the classroom. In addition, students often trade word lists on Wednesday to give each other a practice test.

A final test is administered on Friday. The teacher reads the master list, and students write only those words they've practiced during the week. To make the test easier to administer, students first list the numbers of the words they've practiced from their study lists on their test papers. Any words that students misspell should be included on their lists the following week.

Assessing Students' Spelling

The choices students make as they spell words are important indicators of their knowledge of both phonics and spelling. For example, a student who spells phonetically might spell *money* as *mune*, and others who are experimenting with long vowels might spell the word as *monye* or *monie*. Teachers classify and analyze the words students misspell in their writing to gauge their level of spelling development and to plan for instruction. The steps in determining a student's stage of spelling development are explained in this Assessment Tools feature. An analysis of a first grader's spelling development is shown in the Assessment Tools feature on the next page.

Teachers analyze the errors in students' compositions, analyze their errors on weekly spelling tests, and administer diagnostic tests. The Assessment Tools feature on page 180 lists tests that teachers use to determine their students' stage of spelling development.

Assessment Tools

How to Determine a Student's Stage of Spelling Development

1. **Choose a Writing Sample**
   Teachers choose a student's writing sample to analyze. In the primary grades, the sample should total at least 50 words, in the middle grades 100 words, and in the upper grades 200 words. Teachers must be able to decipher most words in the sample to analyze it.

2. **Identify Spelling Errors**
   Teachers read the writing sample to note the errors and identify the words the student was trying to spell. If necessary, teachers check with the writer to determine the intended word.

3. **Make a Spelling Analysis Chart**
   Teachers draw a chart with five columns, one for each stage of spelling development.

4. **Categorize the Spelling Errors**
   Teachers classify the student's spelling errors according to the stage of development. They list each error in one of the stages, ignoring proper nouns, capitalization errors, and grammar errors. Teachers ignore poorly formed letters or reversed letterforms in kindergarten and first grade, but these are significant errors when older students make them. To simplify the analysis, teachers write both the student's error and the correct spelling in parentheses.

5. **Tally the Errors**
   Teachers count the errors in each column, and the one with the most errors indicates the student's current stage of development.

6. **Identify Topics for Instruction**
   Teachers examine the student's errors to identify topics for instruction.

Assessment Tools

An Analysis of a First Grader's Spelling Development

Writing Sample

To bay a perezun at home kob uz anb seb that a bome wuz in or skuwl anb mab uz go at zib anb makbe uz wat a haf uf a awr anb it mab uz wazt or time on loren ee ing.

THE eNb

Translation

Today a person at home called us and said that a bomb was in our school and made us go outside and made us wait a half of an hour and it made us waste our time on learning. The end.

Spelling Analysis Chart

Emergent	Letter Name-Alphabetic	Within-Word Patterns	Syllables and Affixes	Derivational Relations
	kod (called)	bome (bomb)	peresun (person)	
	sed (said)	or (our)	loreneeing (learning)	
	wus (was)	skuwl (school)		
	mad (made)	makde (made)		
	at (out)	uf (of)		
	sid (side)	awr (hour)		
	wat (wait)	or (our)		
	haf (half)			
	mad (made)			
	wazt (waste)			

Conclusion

The student spelled 56% of the words correctly, and most of his spelling errors were in the Letter Name-Alphabetic and Within-Word Patterns stages, which is typical of first graders' spelling.

Topics for instruction

high-frequency words
CVCe vowel pattern
-ed inflectional ending

Assessment Tools

Spelling

Teachers assess students' spelling development by examining misspelled words in the compositions that students write. They classify students' spelling errors according to the stages of spelling development and plan instruction based on their analysis. Teachers also examine students' misspellings on weekly spelling tests and diagnostic tests. Here are three tests designed for classroom teachers to screen, monitor, diagnose, and document students' spelling development:

◆ **Developmental Spelling Analysis (DSA)** (Ganske, 2000)

The DSA is a dictated spelling inventory with two components: a Screening Inventory for determining students' stage of spelling development, and Feature Inventories to highlight students' knowledge of specific spelling concepts. The DSA with detailed guidelines is available in Ganske's book, *Word Journeys: Assessment-Guided Phonics, Spelling, and Vocabulary Instruction* (2000).

◆ **Phonological Awareness Literacy Screening (PALS) System: Spelling Subtest** (Invernizzi, Meier, & Juel, 2003)

The kindergarten-level battery of tests includes a brief spelling subtest in which children write the sounds they hear in CVC words. In the grades 1–3 tests, the spelling subtest includes words that exemplify phonics features that are appropriate for that grade level. Children receive credit for spelling the specific feature correctly and additional points for spelling the word correctly. The PALS test is available free for Virginia teachers from the University of Virginia, and it can be purchased by teachers in other states.

◆ **Qualitative Spelling Inventory (QSI)** (Bear et al., 2008)

The QSI has two forms, one for grades K–6 and another for grades 6–8. These tests each include 20 or 25 spelling words listed according to difficulty and can easily be administered to small groups or whole classes. The QSI is available in *Words Their Way: Word Study for Phonics, Vocabulary, and Spelling Instruction* (Bear et al., 2008).

Through these tests, teachers identify students' stage of spelling development and use this information to monitor their progress and plan for instruction.

What's the Controversy About Spelling Instruction?

The press and concerned parent groups periodically raise questions about invented spelling and the importance of weekly spelling tests. There is a misplaced public perception that today's children can't spell: Researchers who have examined the types of errors students make have noted that the number of misspellings increases in grades 1 through 4, as students write longer compositions, but that the percentage of errors decreases. The percentage continues to decline in the upper grades, although some students continue to make errors.

Chapter 5
Review

How Effective Teachers Assist Students in "Cracking the Code"

▶ Teachers teach students to "crack the code" through phonemic awareness, phonics, and spelling instruction.

▶ Teachers understand that phonemic awareness is the foundation for phonics instruction.

▶ Teachers teach high-utility phonics concepts, rules, phonograms, and spelling patterns.

▶ Teachers recognize that students' spelling errors are a measure of their understanding of phonics.

PEARSON myeducationlab
Where the Classroom Comes to Life

Go to MyEducationLab at www.myeducationlab.com to deepen your understanding of the concepts presented in this chapter:

▶ Analyze how second graders apply phonics knowledge in reading and spelling by viewing video segments in the Literacy Portraits.
▶ Check your understanding of chapter concepts with the multiple-choice and essay quizzes in the Study Plan.
▶ Apply some of the main ideas discussed in the chapter in the Activities and Applications section of the website.
▶ Practice what you've learned in this chapter in Building Teaching Skills and Dispositions before applying the ideas in your own classroom.

PROFESSIONAL REFERENCES

Adams, M. J. (1990). *Beginning to read: Thinking and learning about print.* Cambridge, MA: MIT Press.

Allington, R. L. (2006). *What really matters for struggling readers: Designing research-based programs* (2nd ed.). Boston: Allyn & Bacon.

Armbruster, B. B., Lehr, F., & Osborn, J. (2001). *Put reading first: The research building blocks for teaching children to read.* Urbana, IL: Center for the Improvement of Early Reading Achievement.

Bear, D. R., Helman, L., Invernizzi, M., Templeton, S., & Johnston, F. (2007). *Words their way with English learners: Word study for phonics, vocabulary, and spelling instruction.* Upper Saddle River, NJ: Merrill/Prentice Hall.

Bear, D. R., Invernizzi, M., Templeton, S., & Johnston, F. (2008). *Words their way: Word study for phonics, vocabulary,*

and spelling instruction (4th ed.). Upper Saddle River, NJ: Merrill/ Prentice Hall.

Caldwell, J. S., & Leslie, L. (2005). *Intervention strategies to follow informal reading inventory assessment: So what do I do now?* Boston: Allyn & Bacon/Pearson.

Chamberlain, C. J. (2005). Literacy and technology: A world of ideas. In R. A. Karchmer, M. H. Mallette, J. Kara-Soteriou, & D. J. Leu, Jr. (Eds.), *Innovative approaches to literacy education: Using the Internet to support new literacies* (pp. 44–64). Newark, DE: International Reading Association.

Clay, M. M. (2005a). *Literacy lessons: Designed for individuals, part 2: Teaching procedures.* Portsmouth, NH: Heinemann.

Clay, M. M. (2005b). *Observation survey of early literacy achievement* (2nd ed.). Portsmouth, NH: Heinemann.

Clymer, T. (1963). The utility of phonic generalizations in the primary grades. *The Reading Teacher, 16,* 252–258.

Cooper, J. D., & Pikulski, J. J. (2003). *Houghton Mifflin reading* (California ed.). Boston: Houghton Mifflin.

Cramer, R. L. (1998). *The spelling connection: Integrating reading, writing, and spelling instruction.* New York: Guilford Press.

Cunningham, P. (1990). The Names Test: A quick assessment of decoding ability. *The Reading Teacher, 44,* 124–129.

Cunningham, P. M. (2007). Best practices in teaching phonological awareness and phonics. In L. B. Gambrell, L. M. Morrow, & M. Pressley (Eds.), *Best practices in literacy instruction* (pp. 159–177). New York: Guilford Press.

Cunningham, P. M. (2009). *Phonics they use: Words for reading and writing* (5th ed.). Boston: Allyn & Bacon/Pearson.

Cunningham, P. M., & Allington, R. L. (2007). *Classrooms that work: They can all read and write* (4th ed.). Boston: Allyn & Bacon.

Cunningham, P. M., & Cunningham, J. W. (1992). Making words: Enhancing the invented spelling-decoding connection. *The Reading Teacher, 46,* 106–115.

Cunningham, P. M., & Cunningham, J. W. (2002). What we know about how to teach phonics. In A. E. Farstrup & S. J. Samuels (Eds.), *What research has to say about reading instruction* (3rd ed., pp. 87–109). Newark, DE: International Reading Association.

Dahl, K. L., Scharer, P. L., Lawson, L. L., & Grogan, P. R. (2001). *Rethinking phonics: Making the best teaching decisions.* Portsmouth, NH: Heinemann.

Duffelmeyer, F. A., Kruse, A. E. Merkley, D. J., & Fyfe, S. A. (1994). Further validation and enhancement of the Names Test. *The Reading Teacher, 48,* 118–128.

Ganske, K. (2000). *Word journeys: Assessment-guided phonics, spelling, and vocabulary instruction.* New York: Guilford Press.

Gentry, J. R., & Gillet, J. W. (1993). *Teaching kids to spell.* Portsmouth, NH: Heinemann.

Gillon, G. T. (2004). *Phonological awareness: From research to practice.* New York: Guilford Press.

Griffith, F., & Olson, M. (1992). Phonemic awareness helps beginning readers break the code. *The Reading Teacher, 45,* 516–523.

Hanna, P. R., Hanna, J. S., Hodges, R. E., & Rudorf, E. H. (1966). *Phoneme-grapheme correspondences as cues to spelling improvement.* Washington, DC: U.S. Government Printing Office.

Invernizzi, M., Meier, J. D., & Juel, C. (2003). *Phonological Awareness Literacy Screening System.* Charlottesville: University of Virginia Press.

Ivey, G., & Baker, M. I. (2004). Phonics instruction for older students? Just say no. *Educational Leadership, 61*(6), 35–39.

Juel, C., Griffith, P. L., & Gough, P. B. (1986). Acquisition of literacy: A longitudinal study of children in first and second grade. *Journal of Educational Psychology, 78,* 243–255.

Kaminski, R. A., & Good, R. H., III. (1996). *Dynamic Indicators of Basic Early Literacy Skills.* Eugene: University of Oregon Center on Teaching and Learning.

Kinzer, C. K. (2005). The intersection of schools, communities, and technology: Recognizing children's use of new literacies. In R. A. Karchmer, M. H. Mallette, J. Kara-Soteriou, & D. J. Leu, Jr. (Eds.), *Innovative approaches to literacy education: Using the Internet to support new literacies* (pp. 65–82). Newark, DE: International Reading Association.

Klesius, J. P., Griffith, P. L., & Zielonka, P. (1991). A whole language and traditional instruction comparison: Overall effectiveness and development of the alphabetic principle. *Reading Research and Instruction, 30,* 47–61.

Lewkowicz, N. K. (1994). The bag game: An activity to heighten phonemic awareness. *The Reading Teacher, 47,* 508–509.

Mather, N., Sammons, J., & Schwartz, J. (2006). Adaptations of the Names Test: Easy to use phonics assessments. *The Reading Teacher, 60,* 114–122.

McCarrier, A., Pinnell, G. S., & Fountas, I. C. (2000). *Interactive writing: How language and literacy come together, K–2.* Portsmouth, NH: Heinemann.

McKenna, M. C. (2002). *Help for struggling readers: Strategies for grades 3–8.* New York: Guilford Press.

Mesmer, H. A. E., & Griffith, P. L. (2005). Everybody's selling it—But just what is explicit, systematic phonics instruction? *The Reading Teacher, 59,* 366–376.

National Reading Panel. (2000). *Teaching children to read: An evidence-based assessment of the scientific research literature on reading and its implications for reading instruction.* Washington, DC: National Institute of Child Health and Human Development.

Norman, K. A., & Calfee, R. C. (2004). Tile Test: A hands-on approach for assessing phonics in the early grades. *The Reading Teacher 58,* 42–52.

Peregoy, S. F., & Boyle, W. F. (2008). *Reading, writing, and learning in ESL: A resource book for teaching K–12 English learners* (5th ed.). Boston: Allyn & Bacon/Pearson.

Read, C. (1975). *Children's categorization of speech sounds in English* (NCTE Research Report No. 17). Urbana, IL: National Council of Teachers of English.

Riches, C., & Genesee, F. (2006). Literacy: Crosslinguistic and crossmodal issues. In F. Genesee, K. Lindholm-Leary, W. M. Saunders, & D. Christian (Eds.), *Educating English language learners: A synthesis of research evidence* (pp. 64–108). New York: Cambridge University Press.

Shefelbine, J. (1995). *Learning and using phonics in beginning reading* (Literacy research paper; volume 10). New York: Scholastic.

Snow, C., Burns, M. W., & Griffin, P. (1998). *Preventing reading difficulties in young children.* Washington, DC: National Academy Press.

Tompkins, G. E., & Collom, S. (2004). *Sharing the pen: Interactive writing with young children*. Upper Saddle River, NJ: Merrill/Prentice Hall.

Torgesen, J. K., & Bryant, B. R. (2004). *Test of Phonological Awareness* (2nd ed.). East Moline, IL: LinguiSystems.

Venezky, R. L. (1999). *The American way of spelling: The structure and origins of American English orthography*. New York: Guilford Press.

White, T. G. (2005). Effects of systematic and strategic analogy-based phonics on grade 2 students' word reading and reading comprehension. *Reading Research Quarterly, 40*, 234–255.

Wylie, R. E., & Durrell, D. D. (1970). Teaching vowels through phonograms. *Elementary English, 47*, 787–791.

Yopp, H. K. (1988). The validity and reliability of phonemic awareness tests. *Reading Research Quarterly, 23*, 159–177.

Yopp, H. K. (1992). Developing phonemic awareness in young children. *The Reading Teacher, 45*, 696–703.

Yopp, H. K. (1995). Read-aloud books for developing phonemic awareness: An annotated bibliography. *The Reading Teacher, 48*, 538–542.

Yopp, H. K., & Yopp, R. H. (2000). Supporting phonemic awareness development in the classroom. *The Reading Teacher, 54*, 130–143.

CHILDREN'S BOOK REFERENCES

Hutchins, P. (1989). *Don't forget the bacon!* New York: HarperCollins.

Most, B. (1996). *Cock-a-doodle-moo!* San Diego: Harcourt Brace.

Osborne, M. P. (2003). *High tide in Hawaii*. New York: Random House.

Park, B. (2003). *Junie B., first grader: Boss of lunch*. New York: Random House.

Root, P. (2004). *Rattletrap car*. Cambridge, MA: Candlewick Press.

Seuss, Dr. (1963). *Hop on pop*. New York: Random House.

Seuss, Dr. (1965). *Fox in socks*. New York: Random House.

Chapter 6

Developing Fluent Readers and Writers

Ms. Williams's Students Learn High-Frequency Words

Ms. Williams's second graders are studying hermit crabs and their tide pool environments. A plastic habitat box with a hermit crab living inside sits in the center of each group of desks. As children care for their crustaceans, they observe the crabs. They've examined hermit crabs up close using magnifying glasses and identified the body parts. Ms. Williams helped them draw a diagram of a hermit crab on a large chart and label the body parts. They've compared hermit crabs to true crabs and examined their exoskeletons. They've also learned how to feed hermit crabs, how to get them to come out of their shells, and how they molt. And, they've conducted experiments to determine which environment hermit crabs prefer.

These second graders are using reading and writing as tools for learning. Eric Carle's *A House for Hermit Crab* (2005) is the featured book for this unit. Ms. Williams has read it aloud several times, and children are rereading it at the listening center. *Moving Day* (Kaplan, 1996), *Pagoo* (Holling, 1990), and other stories and informational books are available on a special shelf in the classroom library. Ms. Williams has read some aloud, and others children read independently or with buddies. Children make charts about hermit crabs that they post in the classroom and write about them in **learning logs**. One log entry is shown in the box below.

Ms. Williams and her second graders also write interesting and important vocabulary words related to hermit crabs on a **word wall** made on a sheet of butcher paper, divided into boxes for each letter. These words appear on their word wall:

coral	larvae	sea urchins
crustacean	molting	seaweed
eggs	pebbles	shells
enemies	pincers	shrimp
exoskeleton	regeneration	snails
lantern fish	scavenger	starfish
larva	sea anemone	tide pool

Then children refer to the words as they write about hermit crabs, and Ms. Williams uses them for various word study activities.

Ms. Williams integrates many components of reading instruction, including word recognition and fluency activities, into the unit on hermit crabs. To develop her second graders' ability to recognize many high-frequency words, she uses another word wall. This one differs from the hermit crab word wall, which contains only words related to these ocean animals. Her high-frequency word wall is a

A Student's Science Log Entry

brightly colored alphabet quilt with 26 blocks, one for each letter of the alphabet, displayed permanently on one wall of the classroom.

At the beginning of the school year, Ms. Williams and her students posted on the word wall the 70 high-frequency words that they were familiar with from first grade. Each word is written clearly on a small card, using print that's large enough so everyone can read it. Then each week, Ms. Williams adds three to five new words. At first, the words she chose were from her list of the 100 high-frequency words, and after finishing that list, she has begun choosing words from a list of the second 100 high-frequency words. She doesn't introduce the words in the order that they're presented in the list, but rather chooses words that she can connect to phonics lessons and literature focus units, and words that children misspell in their writing.

This week, Ms. Williams adds *soon*, *house*, *your*, and *you're* to the word wall. She chooses *soon* and *house* because these words are used in *A House for Hermit Crab* and because several children have recently asked her how to spell *house*. She chooses the homophones *your* and *you're* because children are confusing and misspelling these two words. She also has noticed that some children are confused about contractions, so she plans to review contractions, using *you're* as an example.

Ms. Williams has her students sit on the floor near the word wall to introduce and post the words on it. She uses a cookie sheet and large magnetic letters to introduce each new word. She explains that two of the new words—*house* and *soon*—are from *A House for Hermit Crab*. She scrambles the letters at the bottom of the cookie sheet and slowly builds the new word at the top of the sheet as children guess it. She begins with *h*, adds the *ou*, and several children call out "house." Ms. Williams continues adding letters, and when they are all in place, a chorus of voices says, "house." Then Kari places the new word card in the *H* square of the word wall, and children chant and clap as they say the word and spell it. Ms. Williams begins, "House, house, h-o-u-s-e," and children echo her chant. Then she calls on Enrique to begin the chant, and children echo him. Then Ms. Williams repeats the procedure with the three remaining words.

The next day, Ms. Williams and her students use **interactive writing** to compose sentences using each of the new words. They write these sentences:

> *The hermit crab has a good shell for a <u>house</u>. He likes it but <u>soon</u> he will move. "<u>You're</u> too small for me," he says. "I have to move, but I will always be <u>your</u> friend."*

Children take turns writing these sentences on a chart, and after rereading them, they underline the four new words. Each week, the children write sentences using the new word wall words. Ms. Williams and the children often reread the sentences they've written during previous weeks.

The next day, after children practice the new word wall words, Ms. Williams takes a few minutes to review contractions so that they understand that *you're* is a contraction of *you* and *are* and that the apostrophe indicates that a letter has been omitted. Then children volunteer other contractions. Michael identifies three: *I'm*, *can't*, and *don't*. The children use interactive writing to make a chart of contractions: They list the contractions and the two words that make up each one. Ms. Williams explains that she'll put the chart in the word work center and that they can use the information to make books about contractions.

After this practice with high-frequency words, children participate in activities at literacy centers while Ms. Williams meets with **guided reading** groups. Most of the center activities relate to the unit on hermit crabs and Eric Carle's book *A House for Hermit Crab*, but children also practice reading and writing high-frequency

Ms. Williams's Literacy Centers

Library Center
Children reread leveled books and other books about hermit crabs that were placed on a special shelf in the library. Ms. Williams includes *Moving Day* (Kaplan, 1996) (Level 7), *Hermit Crab* (Randell, 1994) (Level 8), and *Hermit's Shiny Shell* (Tuchman, 1997) (Level 10), three familiar books about hermit crabs, for children to reread.

Listening Center
Children use headphones to listen to an informational book about hermit crabs.

Retelling Center
Children sequence pictures of the events in the book and use them as a guide to retell the story.

Science Center
Children observe a hermit crab and make notes in their learning logs about its physical characteristics and eating habits.

Word Sort Center
Children sort words from *A House for Hermit Crab* into categories, including ocean animals and plants.

Word Wall Center
Children practice reading the word wall using pointers. Then they take a clipboard and a sheet of paper divided into 10 sections; the letters spelling h-e-r-m-i-t-c-r-a-b have been written in the sections. Children choose two words from the word wall beginning with each letter to write in each section on their papers.

Word Work Center
Children use magnetic letters to spell this week's high-frequency words—*house, soon, your*, and *you're*—and the words from the last 2 weeks. They also make a book of contractions with picture and sentence examples.

Writing Center
Children write "I Am a Hermit Crab" poems following the model posted at the center. They also write other books about hermit crabs.

words at two of the centers. The eight literacy centers in Ms. Williams's classroom are described above.

Each morning, a sixth-grade student aide comes to the classroom to monitor the children's work at the centers and provide assistance as needed. Ms. Williams worked with two sixth-grade teachers to train 10 students to serve as student aides, and they come to the classroom once every week or two on a rotating basis.

The second graders keep track of their work in centers using small booklets with eight sheets of paper that Ms. Williams calls their "center passports." The student aide marks their passports with stickers or stamps at each center after they finish the assignment, and children leave their written work in a basket at the center.

As a culminating activity, Ms. Williams and her students write a retelling of *A House for Hermit Crab*. The children compose the text, and Ms. Williams uses the **Language Experience Approach** to write their rough draft on chart paper so that everyone can see it. Children learn revision strategies as they fine-tune their retelling, and then Ms. Williams types the text on five sheets of paper, makes copies, and compiles booklets. Children each receive a copy of the booklet to read and illustrate. Later they'll take their booklets home to read to their families.

Ms. Williams reads their retelling aloud as children follow along and then join in the reading. They do **choral reading** as they read in small groups. The numbers on the left side indicate which group reads each sentence. As children read and reread the text aloud, they become increasingly fluent readers. Here's the last section of the class's retelling:

1   *Soon it was* January.
2   *Hermit Crab moved out of his house and the little crab moved in.*
3   *"Goodbye," said Hermit Crab.*
    "Be good to my friends."
4   *Soon Hermit Crab saw the perfect house.*
5   *It was a big, empty shell.*
1   *It looked a little plain but Hermit Crab didn't care.*
2   *He will decorate it*
3   *with sea urchins,*
4   *with sea anemones,*
5   *with coral,*
1   *with starfish,*
2   *with snails.*
ALL *So many possibilities!*

The underlined words are high-frequency words that are posted on the word wall in Ms. Williams's classroom; of the 68 words in this excerpt, 37 are high-frequency words! Also, two of the new words for this week, *soon* and *house*, are used twice.

As children learn to read, they move from word-by-word reading with little or no expression to fluent reading. Fluency is the ability to read quickly, accurately, and with expression, and to read fluently, they recognize most words automatically and identify unfamiliar words easily (Caldwell & Leslie, 2005). By third grade, most children have moved from word-by-word reading into fluent reading; however, 10–15% have difficulty learning to recognize words, and their learning to read is slowed (Allington, 2009). Fluency is an important component of reading instruction, especially in second and third grades, because researchers have found that fluent readers comprehend what they're reading better than less fluent readers do (National Reading Panel, 2000). Pikulski and Chard (2005) describe fluency as the bridge between decoding and comprehension.

Children become fluent readers through a combination of instruction and lots of reading experience. Through systematic phonics instruction, children learn how to identify unfamiliar words; as they read and reread hundreds of books during the primary grades, these words become familiar, and children learn to recognize them automatically. They also learn increasingly sophisticated strategies for identifying unfamiliar words, including syllabic and morphemic analysis, in which they break words into syllables and into root words and affixes.

At the same time children are becoming fluent readers, they're also becoming fluent writers. Through spelling instruction and lots of writing practice, children learn to spell many words automatically, apply capitalization and punctuation rules, and increase writing speed. They also learn strategies for spelling longer, multisyllabic words. Developing fluency is just as important for writers because both readers and writers must be able to focus their attention on meaning, not on decoding and spelling words.

LEARNING TO READ AND WRITE WORDS

Teachers have two goals as they teach children to read and write words. The first is to teach them to instantly recognize several hundred high-frequency words. Children need to be able to read and write these words automatically by the time they're third graders. The second is to equip them with strategies, or problem-solving techniques, that they can use to identify unfamiliar words—often longer, multisyllabic words— they come across during reading and need to spell during writing. Students learn and refine their use of these strategies between kindergarten and eighth grade.

Word Recognition

Students develop a large stock of words that they recognize automatically because it's impossible for them to analyze every word they encounter when reading or want to spell when writing; these recognizable words are called *sight words*. Through repeated reading and writing experiences, students develop automaticity, the ability to quickly recognize words they read and know how to spell words they're writing (LaBerge & Samuels, 1976; Samuels, 2004). The vital element in word recognition is learning each word's unique letter sequence.

High-Frequency Words. The most common words that readers and writers use again and again are called *high-frequency words*. There have been numerous attempts to identify specific lists of these words and to calculate their frequency in reading materials. Pinnell and Fountas (1998, p. 89) identified these 24 common words that kindergartners learn to read:

a	at	he	it	no	the
am	can	I	like	see	to
an	do	in	me	she	up
and	go	is	my	so	we

They also learn to write many of the words.

These words are part of the 100 high-frequency words, which account for more than half of the words people read and write. Children learn the rest of the 100 high-frequency words in first grade. Eldredge (2005) has identified the 300 highest-frequency words used in first-grade basal readers and trade books found in first-grade classrooms; these 300 words account for 72% of the words that beginning readers read. Figure 6–1 presents Eldredge's list of 300 high-frequency words; the 100 most common ones are marked with an asterisk. Children learn to read the last 200 words on the list during second and third grades.

It's essential that children learn to read and write high-frequency words, but many of these words are difficult to learn because they can't be easily decoded (Cunningham, 2009): Try sounding out *to*, *what*, and *could* and you'll see how difficult they are! Because these words can't be decoded easily, children learn to remember and recognize them automatically. A further complication is that many of these words are function words, so they don't carry much meaning. It's much easier to learn to recognize *whale* than *what*, because *whale* conjures up the image of the huge aquatic mammal, but *what* is abstract. *What*, however, is used much more frequently, and children must learn to recognize it.

Figure 6–1 ◆ The 300 High-Frequency Words

*a	children	great	looking	ran	through
*about	city	green	made	read	*time
*after	come	grow	make	red	*to
again	*could	*had	*man	ride	toad
*all	couldn't	hand	many	right	together
along	cried	happy	may	road	told
always	dad	has	maybe	room	*too
*am	dark	hat	*me	run	took
*an	*day	*have	mom	*said	top
*and	*did	*he	more	sat	tree
animals	*didn't	head	morning	*saw	truck
another	*do	hear	*mother	say	try
any	does	heard	mouse	*school	*two
*are	dog	help	Mr.	sea	under
*around	*don't	hen	Mrs.	*see	until
*as	door	*her	much	*she	*up
asked	*down	here	must	show	*us
*at	each	hill	*my	sister	*very
ate	eat	*him	name	sky	wait
away	end	*his	need	sleep	walk
baby	even	*home	never	small	walked
*back	ever	*house	new	*so	want
bad	every	*how	next	*some	wanted
ball	everyone	*I	nice	something	*was
*be	eyes	I'll	night	soon	water
bear	far	I'm	*no	started	way
*because	fast	*if	*not	stay	*we
bed	father	*in	nothing	still	*well
been	find	inside	*now	stop	*went
before	fine	*into	*of	stories	*were
began	first	*is	off	story	*what
behind	fish	*it	oh	sun	*when
best	fly	it's	old	take	where
better	*for	its	*on	tell	while
big	found	jump	once	than	*who
bird	fox	jumped	*one	*that	why
birds	friend	*just	only	that's	*will
blue	friends	keep	*or	*the	wind
book	frog	king	other	their	witch
books	*from	*know	*our	*them	*with
box	fun	last	*out	*then	wizard
boy	garden	left	*over	*there	woman
brown	gave	let	*people	these	words
*but	*get	let's	picture	*they	work
*by	girl	*like	pig	thing	*would
called	give	*little	place	*things	write
*came	go	live	play	*think	yes
*can	going	long	pulled	*this	*you
can't	good	look	*put	thought	your
cat	*got	looked	rabbit	three	*you're

From *Teach Decoding: How and Why* (2nd ed., pp. 119–120), by J. L. Eldredge, © 2005. Adapted by permission of Prentice Hall, Inc., Upper Saddle River, NJ.

*The first 100 most frequently used words, as shown in Figure 5–8 on p. 175.

Word Walls. Primary-grade teachers create word walls in their classrooms to display the high-frequency words the children are learning, as Ms. Williams did in the vignette at the beginning of the chapter. Some teachers use butcher paper or squares of construction paper for the word wall, and others use large pocket charts that they divide into sections for each letter of the alphabet. Word walls should be placed in a prominent, accessible location in the classroom so that everyone can see the words and new words can be added easily.

Teachers prepare word walls at the beginning of the school year and then add to them each week. Kindergarten teachers often begin by listing children's names on the word wall and then add the 24 highest-frequency words, one or two words per week, during the school year. First-grade teachers often begin with the 24 words introduced in kindergarten, and then add two to five words each week. Figure 6–2 presents a first-grade word wall with just over 100 words that were added during the school year. In second grade, teachers often begin the year with the easier half of the high-frequency words already on the word wall, and they add 100 more words during the school year. Third-grade teachers often test their students' knowledge of the 100 high-frequency words at the beginning of the year, add to the word wall any words that students can't read and write, and then continue with the next 200 high-frequency words so that everyone learns most of the 300 high-frequency words by the end of the school year.

> Check the Compendium of Instructional Procedures, which follows Chapter 12, for more information on the highlighted terms.

Figure 6–2 ◆ A First-Grade Word Wall

A	B	C	D	E
a are	be	call	did	each
about as	been	called	didn't	eat
after at	boy	can	do	
all	but	can't	does	
am	by	come	don't	
and		could	down	

F	G	H	I	J K
find	get	had here	I into	just
first	go	has him	if is	know
for	good	have his	in it	
from		he how		
		her		

L	M	N	O	P Q R
like	made must	no	of other	people
little	make my	not	on our	pretty
long	may	now	one out	
look	me		only over	
	more		or	

S	T	U V	W	X Y Z
said	than there	up	was where	you
saw	that these	us	water which	your
see	the they	very	way who	
she	their this		we will	
so	them to		were with	
some	then two		what words	
should			when would	

Teachers can create word walls for older students, too. To assist struggling readers, teachers can post the 100 high-frequency words or some of the 300 high-frequency words on a classroom word wall, or they can make individual word lists for these students. Teachers can type up a list of words in alphabetical order and make copies to cut into bookmarks, to glue on a file folder, or to create personal dictionaries. Teachers who work with students who read and write on grade level can also make word walls to display more difficult common words. Figure 6–3 presents a list of 100 common words that fourth- through eighth-grade students need to learn. Some of the words, such as *himself, finally,* and *remember,* are more appropriate for fourth and fifth graders, and others, such as *necessary, foreign,* and *throughout,* are more appropriate for sixth through eighth graders. Some of these are commonly used words that students confuse with other words, including *desert* and *dessert* and *quiet* and *quite.*

Figure 6–3 ◆ 100 High-Frequency Words for Older Students

A	B	C	D	E
a lot	beautiful	caught	decided	either
again	because	certain	desert	embarrassed
all right	belief	clothes	different	enough
although	believe	committee	discussed	especially
another	beneath	complete	doesn't	etc.
anything	between			everything
around	board			everywhere
	breathe			excellent
	brought			experience

F G	H	I J	K	L
familiar	heard	immediately	knew	language
favorite	height	interesting	know	lying
field	herself	its	knowledge	
finally	himself	it's		
foreign	humorous			
friends	hungry			
frighten				

M	N	O	P	Q R
maybe	necessary	once	particular	quiet
	neighbor	ourselves	peace	really
			people	receive
			piece	recommend
			please	remember
			possible	restaurant
			probably	

S	T	U V	W	X Y Z
safety	their	until	weight	your
school	there	usually	where	you're
separate	themselves		whether	
serious	they're		whole	
since	though			
special	thought			
something	through			
success	throughout			
	together			

Word Wall
These first graders participate in daily word wall activities. In this teacher-directed activity, the children read the high-frequency words posted on the word wall and write them on dry-erase boards. They apply phonics skills as they make up riddles about words for their classmates to guess. For example: "What word begins with /g/ and rhymes with *pet*?" Children take turns creating and sharing riddles. One child solves the riddle, and everyone writes it on dry-erase boards. Then they hold their boards up so the teacher can check their work.

Teaching Word Recognition. Teachers carefully select the high-frequency words they introduce each week. They choose words that students are familiar with and use in conversation but can't read or write. The selected words may have been introduced in **guided reading** lessons, or they may be words that students misspelled recently in their writing. Even though the words are listed alphabetically in Figures 6–2 and 6–3, they aren't taught in that order; in the vignette, for example, Ms. Williams chose *soon* and *house* from *A House for Hermit Crab* and the homophones *your* and *you're*, which children were confusing in their writing.

Teaching high-frequency words isn't easy, because many of them have little or no meaning when they're used in isolation. Cunningham (2009) recommends this chant-and-clap procedure to practice the words being placed on the word wall:

1. **Introduce the words in context.** Teachers introduce the new words using a familiar book or with pictures or objects. For example, to introduce the words *for* and *from*, teachers might show a gift box, wrapped and tied with a bow, and with an attached gift tag labeled "for" and "from." Then teachers pass out extra gift tags they've made, and children read the words *for* and *from* and briefly talk about gifts they've given and received. Teachers also clarify that *for* isn't the number *four* and show children where the number *four* is written on the number chart posted in the classroom.

2. **Have children chant and clap the words.** Teachers introduce the new word cards that will be placed on the word wall and read the words. Then they begin a chant, "For, for, f-o-r," and clap their hands. Then children repeat the chant. After several repetitions, teachers begin a second chant, "From, from, f-r-o-m," and the children repeat the chant and clap their hands as they chant. Children practice chanting and clapping the words each day that week.

3. **Have children practice reading and writing the words.** Children create sentences using the high-frequency words on sentence strips and read them to classmates. Later, they cut them apart and practice rearranging the words. They also search for the words in big books and on charts posted around the classroom.

They use dry-erase boards and magnetic letters to practice spelling the words. To emphasize the sequence of letters in a word, they also sort word cards. For example, the words *for, from, four, fun, fish, fast, free, from, for, four, free,* and *fun* are written on cards, and children sort them into three piles: one pile for *for,* a second pile for *from,* and a third pile for all other words. Teachers direct children in some of these activities, and children participate in others at literacy centers.

4. **Have children read and write the words.** Authentic reading and writing activities are the best ways to practice high-frequency words because these common words are likely to be used often. During sharing sessions after independent reading and writing, teachers often ask children to point out where they read or wrote the high-frequency words they've been practicing. Teachers also point out high-frequency words during interactive read-alouds, shared reading, interactive writing activities, and other literacy activities.

Through this chant-and-clap procedure, teachers make the high-frequency words more concrete, and easily confused words are clarified and practiced.

A minilesson showing how a first-grade teacher focuses her students' attention on high-frequency words is presented on the next page. These first graders are learning high-frequency words from big books they're reading. Activities involving word walls are an important way to teach word recognition; reading and writing are two other ways. Children develop automatic word recognition by reading words. They read words in the context of stories and other books, and they read them on word lists and on word cards. Practice makes students more fluent readers and even has an impact on their comprehension.

Students also practice word recognition through writing because they write high-frequency words again and again. For example, when a first-grade class was studying animals, the children wrote riddle books. One first grader wrote this riddle book, entitled "What Is It?":

Page 1: *It is a bird.*
Page 2: *It can't fly but it can swim.*
Page 3: *It is black and white.*
Page 4: *It eats fish.*
Page 5: *What is it?*
Page 6: *A penguin.*

Of the words that the child wrote, more than half are among the 24 highest-frequency words! (These words are underlined.) Students refer to the word wall when they're writing so that they can spell words conventionally and write fluently.

Assessing Word Recognition. Because word recognition is so important in beginning reading, teachers assess children's developing word recognition regularly (Snow, Burns, & Griffin, 1998). Primary-grade teachers screen children at the beginning of the school year, monitor their progress several times during the year, and document their achievement at the end of the year. How often they monitor children's progress depends on their reading level and on the progress they're making.

Assessing children's word recognition is easy: Teachers have children individually read the words posted on the word wall or read high-frequency words on word cards or word lists. Kindergartners are usually tested on the 24 most common words, first graders on the 100 high-frequency words, second and third graders on the 300 high-frequency words. In addition, teachers can use commercial tests. Check the Assessment Tools feature on page 196 for more information on word-recognition assessment tools.

TOPIC: Teaching High-Frequency Words
GRADE: First Grade
TIME: One 15-minute period

Miss Shapiro's goal is for her first graders to learn at least 75 of the 100 high-frequency words. She has a large word wall that's divided into sections for each letter. Each week, she introduces three new words and adds them to the word wall. She chooses words from the big book she's using for shared reading. On Monday, she introduces the new words and over the next four days, she focuses on them and reviews those she's introduced previously. To make the word study more authentic, the children often hunt for the word in reading materials available in the classroom; sometimes they look in familiar big books, in small books they're rereading, on charts of familiar poems and songs, or on Language Experience and interactive writing charts. On other days, the children create sentences using the words, which the teacher writes on sentence strips and displays in the classroom.

❶ Introduce the Topic

"Let's read the D words on the word wall," Miss Shapiro says. As she points to the words, the class reads them aloud. "Which word is new this week?" she asks. The children respond, "do." Next, they read the H words and identify *here* as a new word, and then the M words and identify *my* as a new word. She asks individual children to reread the D, H, and M words on the word wall.

❷ Share Examples

"Who can come up and point to our three new words for this week?" Miss Shapiro asks. Aaron eagerly comes to the word wall to point out *do, here*, and *my*. As he points to each word, Miss Shapiro writes it on the chalkboard, pronounces it, and spells it aloud. She and Aaron lead the class as they chant and clap the words: "Do, do, d-o, do!" "Here, here, h-e-r-e, here!" "My, my, m-y, my!"

❸ Provide Information

"Let's look for *do, here*, and *my* in these books," Miss Shapiro suggests as she passes out a familiar big book to the children at each table. In each group, the children reread the book, pointing out *do, here*, and *my* each time they occur. The teacher circulates around the classroom, checking that the children notice the words.

❹ Guide Practice

Miss Shapiro asks Aaron to choose three classmates to come to the chalkboard to spell the words with large magnetic letters; Daniel, Elizabeth, and Wills spell the words and read them aloud. Then Aaron passes out plastic bags with small magnetic letters and word cards to each pair of children. They read the word cards and spell the three words at their desks.

❺ Assess Learning

On Friday, Miss Shapiro works with the first graders in small groups, asking them to locate the words in sentences they've written and to read the words individually on word cards.

Assessment Tools

Word Recognition

Teachers monitor children's growing ability to recognize high-frequency words as they listen to them read aloud and through these classroom tests:

◆ **High-Frequency Word Lists**

Teachers regularly have children read lists of high-frequency words and keep a record of which words children can identify. Children can read the high-frequency words posted on word walls or use grade-level lists of the high-frequency words; kindergartners are expected to read 24 words, first graders 100 words, second graders 200 words, and third graders 300 words. The high-frequency word lists presented in this chapter can be used; other options are the Dolch list of 220 sight words and Fry's list of 300 instant words, both of which are available in *Assessment for Reading Instruction* (McKenna & Stahl, 2003).

◆ **Observation Survey of Early Literacy Achievement (OS): Word Reading and Writing Vocabulary Subtests** (Clay, 2005)

Two subtests of the OS are used to assess children's knowledge of high-frequency words. In the Word Reading subtest, children read a list of 15 words that were selected from a list of the 45 highest-frequency words used in first-grade basal readers, and in the Writing Vocabulary subtest, they write a list of all the words they know (within a 10-minute time limit). The Word Reading subtest is administered individually, but small groups or the entire class can complete the Writing Vocabulary subtest together. The subtests and directions for administering and scoring them are included in Clay's *Observation Survey of Early Literacy Achievement* (2005), which is available from Heinemann.

◆ **Writing Samples**

Teachers examine samples of children's writing to examine whether writers are using high-frequency words and spelling them correctly. They can use the same word lists used to monitor children's progress in reading high-frequency words to assess their progress in writing these words.

Once children can read and write all of the high-frequency words on grade-level lists or they've become fluent readers and writers, it's not necessary to continue to monitor their progress.

Once children read fluently, word-recognition assessments aren't needed any longer; however, teachers in fourth through eighth grade do assess students who read below the third-grade level because when they can't recognize some of the 300 high-frequency words, they need instruction on the words they don't know.

Teachers also assess children's ability to write high-frequency words because these common words are as essential for writers as they are for readers. Beginning in kindergarten, children learn to spell many of the same words, such as *the*, *I*, and *you*, that they're learning to read; however, spelling development lags behind because it's more demanding to learn the letter sequences in a word and form the letters correctly in writing than it is to remember the word itself. Children usually can write more than half of the high-frequency words they can read. The number of words reflects the instruction children have received and how much writing they do.

Teachers use writing samples or spelling tests to screen children's development at the beginning of the school year. They informally monitor children's growth during the year, usually by examining their writing. At the middle of the school year and again at the end of the year, teachers administer another spelling test or collect additional writing samples to document children's learning. This assessment also ends after third grade unless students have difficulty spelling high-frequency words correctly.

Word Identification

Beginning readers encounter many unfamiliar words, and even fluent readers come upon words that they don't immediately recognize. Students use word-identification strategies to identify these unfamiliar words. Young children often depend on phonics to sound out unfamiliar words, but older students develop other strategies that use phonological information as well as semantic, syntactic, and pragmatic cues to identify words.

— Be Strategic! —

Word-Identification Strategies

Students use these strategies to identify unfamiliar words when they're reading:

► Use phonic analysis
► Decode by analogy
► Divide into syllables
► Apply morphemic analysis

Students' choice of strategy depends on their knowledge about words and the complexity of the unfamiliar word.

The four strategies that students learn to use to identify unfamiliar words are *phonic analysis*, *decoding by analogy*, *syllabic analysis*, and *morphemic analysis*. Writers use these same strategies to spell words. As with reading, young children depend on phonics to spell many, many words, but as they want to spell multisyllabic words, they apply other strategies to spelling. These four word-identification strategies are summarized in Figure 6–4.

Phonic Analysis. Students use what they have learned about phoneme-grapheme correspondences, phonics rules, and spelling patterns to decode words when they're reading and to spell words when they're writing. Even though English isn't a perfectly phonetic language, phonic analysis is a very useful strategy because almost every word has some phonetically regular parts. The words *have* and *come*, for example, are considered irregular words because the vowel sounds aren't predictable; however, the initial and final consonant sounds in both words are regular.

Figure 6–4 ◆ Word-Identification Strategies

Strategy	Description	Examples
Phonic Analysis	Students apply their knowledge of sound-symbol correspondences, phonics rules, and spelling patterns to read or write a word.	*peach* *spring* *blaze* *chin*
Decoding by Analogy	Students use their knowledge of phonograms to deduce the pronunciation or spelling of an unfamiliar word.	*flat* from *cat* *creep* from *sheep* *think* from *pink* *claw* from *saw*
Syllabic Analysis	Students break a multisyllabic word into syllables and then use their knowledge of phonics and phonograms to decode the word, syllable by syllable.	*cul-prit* *neg-a-tive* *sea-weed* *bi-o-de-grad-a-ble*
Morphemic Analysis	Students apply their knowledge of root words and affixes to read or write an unfamiliar word.	*trans-port* *astro-naut* *bi-cycle* *centi-pede*

Beginning readers often try to identify words based on a partial word analysis (Gough, Juel, & Griffith, 1992): They may guess at a word using the beginning sound or look at its overall shape as a clue to word identification; however, these aren't effective techniques. Through phonics instruction, students learn to focus on the letter sequences in words so that they examine the entire word as they identify it (Adams, 1990).

Researchers report that the big difference between students who identify words effectively and those who don't is whether they survey the letters in the words and analyze the interior components (Stanovich, 1992). Capable readers notice all or almost all letters in a word, whereas less capable readers don't completely analyze the letter sequences of words. Struggling readers with limited phonics skills often try to decode words by sounding out the beginning sound and then guessing at the word without using the other cueing systems to verify their guesses (Gaskins, Ehri, Cress, O'Hara, & Donnelly, 1996/1997). And, as you might imagine, their guesses are usually wrong. Sometimes they don't even make sense in the context of the sentence.

Decoding by Analogy. Students identify some words by associating them with words they already know; this strategy is known as *decoding by analogy* (Cunningham, 2004). When readers come to an unfamiliar word, such as *fright*, they might notice the phonogram *-ight* and figure out the word by analogy. Students use analogies to figure out the spelling of unfamiliar words as well; they might use the familar word *game* (*-ame* phonogram) to help them spell *frame*, for example. This strategy accounts for students' common misspelling of *they* as *thay*, because *they* rhymes with *day* and *say*.

This word-identification strategy is dependent on students' knowledge of phonograms. Students who can break words into onsets and rimes and substitute sounds in words are more successful than those who can't. Moreover, researchers have found that only students who know many sight words use this strategy because they must be able to identify patterns in familiar words to associate with those in unfamiliar words (Ehri & Robbins, 1992).

Teachers introduce decoding by analogy when they have students read and write "word families" using familiar phonograms. Using the *-ill* phonogram, for example, students can read or write *bill*, *chill*, *fill*, *hill*, *kill*, *mill*, *pill*, *quill*, *spill*, *still*, and *will*. They can add inflectional endings to create even more words, including *filling*, *hills*, and *spilled*. Two-syllable words can also be created using these words: *killer*, *refill*, *chilly*, and *hilltop*. Students read word cards, write the words using **interactive writing**, and use magnetic letters to spell the words to learn more about substituting beginning sounds, breaking words into parts, and spelling word parts. Teachers also share picture books that include several words representing a particular phonogram (Caldwell & Leslie, 2005). In Denise Fleming's *In the Tall, Tall Grass* (1995), for example, children can locate *-um* words (*strum*, *drum*, and *hum*), and in her *In the Small, Small Pond* (1998), they can read *-are* words (*care* and *share*) and *-ay* words (*way* and *spray*). Figure 6–5 lists books with words representing common phonograms. It's a big step, however, for students to move from these structured activities to using this strategy independently to identify unfamiliar words.

Syllabic Analysis. During the middle grades, students learn to divide words into syllables in order to read and write multisyllabic words such as *biodegradable*, *admonition*, and *unforgettable*. Once a word is divided into syllables, students use phonic analysis and decoding by analogy to pronounce or spell it. Identifying syllable boundaries is important, because these affect the pronunciation of the vowel sound. For example, compare the vowel sound in the first syllables of *cabin* and *cable*. For *cabin*, the syllable boundary is after *b*, whereas for *cable*, the division is before *b*. We can predict that the *a* in *cabin* will be short because the syllable follows the CVC pattern, and that the *a* in *cable* will be long because the syllable follows the CV pattern.

Figure 6–5 ◆ Books With Words Representing a Phonogram	
Phonogram	**Books**
-ack	Shaw, N. E. (1996). *Sheep take a hike*. Boston: Houghton Mifflin.
-ail	Shaw, N. E. (1992). *Sheep on a ship*. Boston: Houghton Mifflin.
-are	Fleming, D. (1998). *In the small, small pond*. New York: Henry Holt.
-ash	Shaw, N. E. (2005). *Sheep eat out*. Boston: Houghton Mifflin.
-ay	Fleming, D. (1998). *In the small, small pond*. New York: Henry Holt.
-eep	Shaw, N. E. (1997). *Sheep in a jeep*. Boston: Houghton Mifflin.
-eet	Heiligman, D. (2005). *Fun dog, sun dog*. New York: Marshall Cavendish.
-ip	Fleming, D. (1995). *In the tall, tall grass*. New York: Henry Holt.
-og	Wood, A. (1992). *Silly Sally*. San Diego: Harcourt Brace.
-oose	Numeroff, L. J. (1991). *If you give a moose a muffin*. New York: HarperCollins.
-op	Shaw, N. E. (2005). *Sheep eat out*. Boston: Houghton Mifflin.
-ouse	Hoberman, M. A. (2007). *A house is a house for me*. New York: Puffin Books.
-own	Wood, A. (1992). *Silly Sally*. San Diego: Harcourt Brace.
-uck	Root, R. (2003). *One duck stuck*. Cambridge, MA: Candlewick Press.
-ug	Edwards, P. D. (1996). *Some smug slug*. New York: HarperCollins.
-um	Fleming, D. (1995). *In the tall, tall grass*. New York: Henry Holt.
-un	Heiligman, D. (2005). *Fun dog, sun dog*. New York: Marshall Cavendish.

The most basic rule about syllabication is that there's one vowel sound in each syllable. Consider the words *bit* and *bite*. *Bit* is a one-syllable word because there's one vowel letter representing one vowel sound. *Bite* is a one-syllable word, too, because even though there are two vowels, they represent one vowel sound. *Magic* and *curfew* are two-syllable words; there's one vowel letter and sound in each syllable in *magic*, but in the second syllable of *curfew*, the two vowels *ew* represent one vowel sound. Let's try a longer word: How many syllables are in *inconvenience*? There are six vowel letters representing four sounds in four syllables.

Syllabication rules are useful in teaching students how to divide words into syllables. Five of the most useful rules are listed in Figure 6–6. These 12 two-syllable words are from *A House for Hermit Crab* (Carle, 2005), the book Ms. Williams read in the vignette at the beginning of the chapter, and they illustrate all but one of the rules:

a-round	prom-ise	her-mit	with-out
pret-ty	ur-chin	nee-dles	cor-al
slow-ly	o-cean	ti-dy	com-plain

The first two rules focus on consonants, and the last three focus on vowels. The first rule, to divide between two consonants, is the most common rule; examples from the list include *her-mit* and *pret-ty*. The second rule deals with words where three consonants appear together in a word, such as *com-plain*: The word is divided

Figure 6–6 ◆ Syllabication Rules

Rules	Examples
• When two consonants come between two vowels in a word, divide syllables between the consonants.	cof-fee bor-der plas-tic jour-ney
• When there are more than two consonants together in a word, divide the syllables keeping the blends together.	em-ploy mon-ster en-trance bank-rupt
• When there is one consonant between two vowels in a word, divide the syllables after the first vowel.	ca-jole bo-nus plu-ral gla-cier
• If following the previous rule doesn't make a recognizable word, divide the syllables after the consonant that comes between the vowels.	doz-en ech-o meth-od cour-age
• When there are two vowels together that don't represent a long vowel sound or a diphthong, divide the syllables between the vowels.	cli-ent po-em cha-os li-on qui-et

between the *m* and the *p* in order to preserve the *pl* blend. The third and fourth rules involve the VCV pattern. Usually the syllable boundary comes after the first vowel, as in *ti-dy*, *o-cean*, and *a-round*; however, the division comes after the consonant in *cor-al* because dividing the word *co-ral* doesn't produce a recognizable word. The syllable boundary comes after the consonant in *without*, too, but this compound word has easily recognizable word parts. According to the fifth rule, words such as *qui-et* are divided between the two vowels because the vowels don't represent a vowel digraph or diphthong. This rule is the least common, and there were no examples of it in the story.

Teachers use **minilessons** to introduce syllabication and teach syllabication rules. During additional minilessons, students choose words from books they're reading and from thematic units for guided practice in breaking words into syllables. After identifying syllable boundaries, students pronounce and spell the words, syllable by syllable. Teachers also mark syllable boundaries on multisyllabic words on classroom word walls and create center activities in which students practice dividing words into syllables and building words using word parts. For example, after the word *compromise* came up in a social studies unit, a sixth-grade teacher developed a center activity in which students created two- and three-syllable words beginning with *com-* using syllable cards. Students created these words:

comic	*compliment*	*common*	*compromise*
companion	*complex*	*computer*	*comment*
complete	*commitment*	*complain*	*compartment*

After building these words, students brainstormed a list of additional words beginning with *com-*, including *complement, commuter, company, communicate, compass*, and *committee*.

Morphemic Analysis. Students examine the root word and affixes of longer unfamiliar words in order to identify them. A root word is a morpheme, the basic part of a word to which affixes are added. Many words are developed from a single root word; for example, the Latin words *portare* (to carry), *portus* (harbor), and *porta* (gate) are the sources of at least 12 English words: *deport, export, exporter, import, port, portable, porter, report, reporter, support, transport*, and *transportation*. Latin is the most common source of English root words; Greek and English are two other sources.

New Literacies
Visual Learning Software

Students use visual learning software to explore ideas and demonstrate their understanding through a combination of pictures and words. Inspiration® is a popular online graphics tool to help students visualize, think, organize, and learn (Silverman, 2005). It was developed for older students (grades 6–12), and a simpler version, Kidspiration®, was designed for children in kindergarten through fifth grade. Students use these software programs to practice strategies and skills they're learning in reading and across the curriculum. In word-identification activities, for example, they make maps and diagrams of words representing a phonogram, words with prefixes and suffixes, words sharing a root word, or etymological information about words (Gill, 2007). This software is especially useful for English learners: By visually representing information and adding links to show relationships, ELs convey their understanding more clearly than they could orally or in writing.

Kidspiration is an easy program for children to navigate. To begin, they choose the picture view on the starter screen and click on icons arranged on a tool bar to create graphic organizers, write words, search for appropriate images from the more than 3,000 pictures in the Symbol Library or create their own pictures, and add links to highlight relationships. There's a SuperGrouper tool that children use to categorize words, a word guide with a 13,000-word combined dictionary and thesaurus, and an audio feature that allows children to describe and document their work. In the writing view, their graphic organizers are transformed into skeleton compositions, and children expand the

words into sentences and paragraphs. Afterward, they can export the texts into multimodal projects or print them.

Inspiration is similar to Kidspiration. Students create diagrams using the Inspiration software that can be transformed into outlines and used for writing and Web-based projects. They use tool bars to navigate the program, choose images from the Symbol Library that's loaded with more than one million pictures or design their own, consult a word guide with a combined dictionary and thesaurus, and monitor their spelling with a spell checker. Students integrate video and sound clips, record their own audio, use a hyperlink tool to connect to research documents and websites, and export Inspiration documents to word processing, PowerPoint, or other programs.

Both software programs include templates and a template wizard that teachers use to modify the diagrams and create their own. Teacher guidebooks and online resources are also available; these resources include diagram archives, curriculum packets, training videos, and case studies with real-life stories about how K–8 teachers and students have used these visual learning software programs.

It's important that students become comfortable using 21st-century technology. As they work with visual learning software, students learn to navigate the programs, transform information from visual to written modes, and craft multimodal projects. Kidspiration and Inspiration software programs are compatible with other emerging classroom technologies, including interactive whiteboards and handheld devices. Teachers are invited to download Kidspiration or Inspiration software with their complete symbol palettes at www.inspiration.com for a free 30-day trial, and afterward the software's available for purchase online.

Some root words are whole words, and others are word parts. Some root words have become free morphemes and can be used as separate words, but others can't. For instance, *cent* comes from the Latin root word *cent*, meaning "hundred." English treats the word as a root word that can be used independently and in combination with affixes, as in *century*, *bicentennial*, and *centipede*. The words *cosmopolitan*, *cosmic*, and *microcosm* come from the Greek root word *cosmo*, meaning "universe"; it isn't an independent root word in English. A list of Latin and Greek root words appears in Figure 6–7. English words such as *eye*, *tree*, and *water* are root words, too. New words are formed through compounding—for example, *eyelash*, *treetop*, and *waterfall*—and other English root words, such as *read*, combine with affixes, as in *reader* and *unreadable*.

Affixes are bound morphemes that are added to words: Prefixes are added at the beginning, as in *replay*, and suffixes are added to the end, as in *playing*, *playful*, and *player*. Like root words, some affixes are English and others come from Latin and Greek. Affixes often change a word's meaning, such as adding *un-* to *happy* to form *unhappy*. Sometimes they change the part of speech, too; for example, when *-tion* is added to *attract* to form *attraction*, the verb *attract* becomes a noun.

There are two types of suffixes: inflectional and derivational. Inflectional suffixes are endings that indicate verb tense and person, plurals, possession, and comparison; these suffixes are English. They influence the syntax of sentences. Here are some examples:

the *-ed* in *walked*	the *-es* in *beaches*
the *-ing* in *singing*	the *-'s* in *girl's*
the *-s* in *asks*	the *-er* in *faster*
the *-s* in *dogs*	the *-est* in *sunniest*

In contrast, derivational suffixes show the relationship of the word to its root word. Consider these words containing the root word *friend*: *friendly*, *friendship*, and *friendless*.

When a word's affix is "peeled off," the remaining word is usually a real word. For example, when the prefix *pre-* is removed from *preview* or the suffix *-er* is removed from *viewer*, the word *view* can stand alone. Some words include letter sequences that might be affixes, but because the remaining words can't stand alone, they aren't affixes. For example, the *in-* at the beginning of *include* is not a prefix because *clude* isn't a word. Similarly, the *-ic* at the end of *magic* is not a suffix because *mag* isn't a word. Sometimes, however, Latin and Greek root words cannot stand alone. One example is *legible*: The *-ible* is a suffix, and *leg* is the root word even though it can't stand alone. Of course, *leg*—meaning part of the body—is a word, but the root word *leg-* from *legible* isn't: It's a Latin root word, meaning "to read."

A list of derivational prefixes and suffixes is presented in Figure 6–8. White, Sowell, and Yanagihara (1989) researched affixes and identified the most common ones; these are marked with an asterisk in Figure 6–8. White and his colleagues recommend teaching the common derivational affixes to students in grades 4–8 because of their usefulness. Some of the most common prefixes are confusing, however, because they have more than one meaning; the prefix *un-*, for example, can mean *not* (e.g., *unclear*) or it can reverse the meaning of a word (e.g., *tie–untie*).

Teaching Word Identification. Word-level learning is an essential part of a balanced literacy program (Hiebert, 1991), and teaching minilessons about analogies and phonic, syllabic, and morphemic analysis is a useful way to help students focus on words. Teachers choose words for minilessons from books students are reading, as Ms. Williams did in the vignette, or from thematic units. The minilesson feature on page 205 shows how Mr. Morales teaches his sixth graders about morphemic analysis as part of a thematic unit on ancient civilizations.

Figure 6–7 ◆ Latin and Greek Root Words

Root	Language	Meaning	Sample Words
ann/enn	Latin	year	anniversary, annual, centennial, millennium, perennial, semiannual
arch	Greek	ruler	anarchy, archbishop, architecture, hierarchy, monarchy, patriarch
astro	Greek	star	aster, asterisk, astrology, astronaut, astronomy, disaster
auto	Greek	self	autobiography, automatic, automobile, autopsy, semiautomatic
bio	Greek	life	biography, biohazard, biology, biodegradable, bionic, biosphere
capit/capt	Latin	head	capital, capitalize, capitol, captain, caption, decapitate, per capita
cent	Latin	hundred	bicentennial, cent, centennial, centigrade, centipede, century, percent
circ	Latin	around	circle, circular, circus, circumspect, circuit, circumference, circumstance
cosmo	Greek	universe	cosmic, cosmopolitan, cosmos, microcosm
cred	Latin	believe	credit, creed, creditable, discredit, incredulity
cycl	Greek	wheel	bicycle, cycle, cyclist, cyclone, recycle, tricycle
dict	Latin	speak	contradict, dictate, dictator, prediction, verdict
gram	Greek	letter	cardiogram, diagram, grammar, monogram, telegram
graph	Greek	write	autobiography, biographer, cryptograph, epigraph, graphic, paragraph
jus/jud/jur	Latin	law	injury, injustice, judge, juror, jury, justice, justify, prejudice
lum/lus/luc	Latin	light	illuminate, lucid, luminous, luster, translucent
man	Latin	hand	manacle, maneuver, manicure, manipulate, manual, manufacture
mar/mer	Latin	sea	aquamarine, marine, maritime, marshy, mermaid, submarine
meter	Greek	measure	centimeter, diameter, seismometer, speedometer, thermometer
mini	Latin	small	miniature, minibus, minimize, minor, minimum, minuscule, minute
mort	Latin	death	immortal, mortality, mortuary, postmortem
ped	Latin	foot	biped, impede, pedal, pedestrian, pedicure
phono	Greek	sound	earphone, microphone, phonics, phonograph, saxophone, symphony
photo	Greek	light	photograph, photographer, photosensitive, photosynthesis
pod/pus	Greek	foot	gastropod, octopus, podiatry, podium, tripod
port	Latin	carry	exporter, import, port, portable, porter, reporter, support, transportation
quer/ques/quis	Latin	seek	query, quest, question, inquisitive, request
scope	Latin	see	horoscope, kaleidoscope, microscope, periscope, telescope
scrib/scrip	Latin	write	describe, inscription, postscript, prescribe, scribble, scribe, script
sphere	Greek	ball	atmosphere, atmospheric, hemisphere, sphere, stratosphere
struct	Latin	build	construct, construction, destruction, indestructible, instruct, reconstruct
tele	Greek	far	telecast, telegram, telegraph, telephone, telescope, telethon, television
terr	Latin	land	subterranean, terrace, terrain, terrarium, terrier, territory
vers/vert	Latin	turn	advertise, anniversary, controversial, divert, reversible, versus
vict/vinc	Latin	conquer	convince, convict, evict, invincible, victim, victor, victory
vis/vid	Latin	see	improvise, invisible, revise, supervisor, television, video, vision, visitor
viv/vit	Latin	live	revive, survive, vital, vitamin, vivacious, vivid, viviparous
volv	Latin	roll	convolutions, evolve, evolution, involve, revolutionary, revolver, volume

Figure 6–8 ◆ Derivational Affixes

Language	Prefixes	Suffixes
English	*over- (too much): overflow self- (by oneself): self-employed *un- (not): unhappy *un- (reversal): untie under- (beneath): underground	-ful (full of): hopeful -ish (like): reddish -less (without): hopeless -ling (young): duckling *-ly (in the manner of): slowly *-ness (state or quality): kindness -ship (state of, art, or skill): friendship, seamanship -ster (one who): gangster -ward (direction): homeward *-y (full of): sleepy
Greek	a-/an- (not): atheist, anaerobic amphi- (both): amphibian anti- (against): antiseptic di- (two): dioxide hemi- (half): hemisphere hyper- (over): hyperactive hypo- (under): hypodermic micro- (small): microfilm mono- (one): monarch omni- (all): omnivorous poly- (many): polygon sym-/syn-/sys- (together): symbol, synonym, system	-ism (doctrine of): communism -ist (one who): artist -logy (the study of): zoology
Latin	bi- (two, twice): bifocal, biannual contra- (against): contradict de- (away): detract *dis- (not): disapprove *dis- (reversal): disinfect ex- (out): export *il-/im-/in-/ir- (not): illegible, impolite, inexpensive, irrational *in- (in, into): indoor inter- (between): intermission mille- (thousand): millennium *mis- (wrong): mistake multi- (many): multimillionaire non- (not): nonsense post- (after): postwar pre- (before): precede quad-/quart- (four): quadruple, quarter re- (again): repay *re-/retro- (back): replace, retroactive *sub- (under): submarine super- (above): supermarket trans- (across): transport tri- (three): triangle	-able/-ible (worthy of, can be): lovable, audible *-al/-ial (action, process): arrival, denial -ance/-ence (state or quality): annoyance, absence -ant (one who): servant -ary/-ory (person, place): secretary, laboratory -cule (very small): molecule -ee (one who is): trustee *-er/-or/-ar (one who): teacher, actor, liar -ic (characterized by): angelic -ify (to make): simplify -ment (state or quality): enjoyment -ous (full of): nervous *-sion/-tion (state or quality): tension, attraction -ure (state or quality): failure

From White, Sowell, & Yanagihara. Most commonly used affixes.

MiniLesson

TOPIC: Using Morphemic Analysis to Identify Words
GRADE: Sixth Grade
TIME: Three 30-minute periods

As part of a thematic unit on ancient civilizations, Mr. Morales introduces the concepts *democracy, monarchy, oligarchy,* and *theocracy* and adds the words to the word wall; however, he notices that many of his sixth graders have difficulty pronouncing the words and remembering what they mean even though they've read about them in the social studies textbook.

❶ Introduce the Topic

Mr. Morales looks over the ancient civilizations word wall and reads aloud these words: *democracy, monarchy, oligarchy,* and *theocracy.* Marcos volunteers that he thinks that the words have something to do with kings or rulers, but he's not sure.

❷ Share Examples

The teacher writes the words on the chalkboard, dividing them into syllables so that the sixth graders can pronounce them more easily. The students practice saying the words several times, but they're still puzzled about their meanings.

❸ Provide Information

Mr. Morales explains that he can help them figure out the meaning of the words. "The words are Greek," he says, "and they have two word parts. If you know the meaning of the word parts, you'll be able to figure out the meaning of the words." He writes the four words and breaks them into word parts this way:

democracy = demo + cracy   monarchy = mono + archy
oligarchy = olig + archy   theocracy = theo + cracy

Then he explains that Marcos was right—the words have to do with kings and rulers: They describe different kinds of government. *Cracy* means *government* and *archy* means *leader*. The first word part tells more about the kind of government; one of them means *gods*, and the others mean *one, people,* and *few*. The students work in small groups to figure out that *democracy* means government by the people, *monarchy* means one leader, *oligarchy* means rule by a few leaders, and *theocracy* means government by the gods.

❹ Guide Practice

The next day, Mr. Morales divides the class into four groups, and each group makes a poster to describe one of the four types of government. On each poster, students write the word, the two Greek word parts, and a definition. They also create an illustration based on what they've learned about this type of government. Afterward, students share their posters with the class and display them in the classroom.

❺ Assess Learning

On the third day, Mr. Morales passes out a list of six sentences about the types of government taken from the social studies textbook and asks them to identify the type. He encourages the sixth graders to refer to the posters the class made as they complete the assignment. Afterward, he reviews their papers to determine which students can use the words correctly to identify the four types of government.

Guidelines

for Teaching Students to Identify Words

▶ Post high-frequency words on word walls.

▶ Teach students to read and spell high-frequency words in minilessons.

▶ Practice reading and writing high-frequency words through authentic literacy activities.

▶ Introduce key words before reading, and teach other words during and after reading.

▶ Model how to use word-identification strategies during interactive read-alouds and shared reading.

▶ Teach students to use phonic analysis, decoding by analogy, syllabic analysis, and morphemic analysis word-identification strategies.

▶ Use words from reading selections as examples in minilessons on word-identification strategies.

▶ Encourage students to apply word-identification strategies to both reading and spelling.

Fluent readers develop a large repertoire of sight words and use word-identification strategies to decode unfamiliar words. Less capable readers, in contrast, can't read as many words and don't use as many strategies for decoding words. Researchers have concluded again and again that students who don't become fluent readers depend on explicit instruction to learn how to identify words (R. W. Gaskins et al., 1991). The guidelines for teaching word identification are summarized above.

Assessing Students' Word Identification. Teachers use a combination of informal assessment tools and classroom tests to monitor students' ability to identify unfamiliar words and to determine which word-identification strategies they can use successfully. Teachers can often gauge students' progress as they listen to them read aloud and notice how they figure out the unfamiliar words they come across. Teachers also use the graded word lists and running records to analyze their progress according to grade-level standards. Check the Assessment Tools feature on the next page for more information about word-identification assessment tools.

How students spell words also provides information about their ability to identify words. When students use word-identification strategies to spell words correctly, it's likely that they're also using the strategies for reading; and when students depend on their phonics knowledge to spell words, they're probably depending on phonics to figure out unfamiliar words when they're reading.

WHAT IS FLUENCY?

Go to the Building Teaching Skills and Dispositions section of Chapter 6 on **MyEducationLab.com** to watch and listen as students and their teacher discuss fluency.

Fluency is the ability to read efficiently, and it's a bridge to comprehension (Allington, 2009). Fluent readers are better able to comprehend what they read because they automatically recognize most words and can apply word-identification strategies when they come across unfamiliar words (LaBerge & Samuels, 1976). Their reading is faster, and they read expressively (Kuhn & Rasinski, 2007). It's a milestone in students' reading achievement! In contrast, students who aren't fluent readers often read slowly and hesitantly. They devote most of their mental energy to identifying words, leaving few cognitive resources available for comprehension.

Assessment Tools

Word Identification

Teachers use a variety of classroom tests to determine whether students can identify unfamiliar words in grade-level texts and which word-identification strategies they use successfully.

◆ **Developmental Reading Assessment, Grades K–3 (DRA)** (Beaver, 2006) and **Developmental Reading Assessment, Grades 4–8** (Beaver & Carter, 2003)

Two versions of DRA are available, one for the primary grades and the other for middle and upper grades. Each one contains a collection of leveled books to use in assessing students' reading levels. Students read leveled books aloud while teachers take running records to analyze their reading. To examine students' ability to use word-identification strategies, teachers analyze the unfamiliar words that students identify correctly and those they can't to determine which strategies they're applying successfully.

◆ **The Names Test: A Quick Assessment of Decoding Ability** (Cunningham, 1990; Duffelmeyer et al., 1994; Mather, Sammons, & Schwartz, 2006)

The Names Test focuses on decoding, one of four ways to identify unfamiliar words. It measures third through eighth graders' ability to apply phoneme-grapheme correspondences, phonics rules, and spelling patterns to decode unfamiliar words. The test is a list of names that students read aloud. Teachers record students' errors and then analyze them to determine which phonics concepts students haven't acquired to plan for future instruction. This no-cost assessment is available online.

◆ **Phonological Awareness Literacy Screening (PALS) System: Word Recognition in Isolation Subtest** (Invernizzi, Meier, & Juel, 2003)

This PALS subtest consists of graded word lists that children read aloud; the highest level where children can read at least 15 words correctly is the instructional level. First- through third-grade teachers use the subtest to monitor children's accurate and automatic recognition of words, and kindergarten teachers administer the test when they believe a child is already reading. The PALS test is available free for Virginia teachers from the University of Virginia, and it can be purchased by teachers in other states.

◆ **Running Records**

Teachers take running records (Clay, 2005) as children read aloud to analyze their ability to identify unfamiliar words, and afterward they categorize children's errors to determine which word-identification strategies children use effectively and which ones they don't.

These assessments are used to evaluate children's progress toward becoming fluent readers, but once readers can read fluently, they aren't needed any longer.

Writing fluency is similar to reading fluency: Students need to be able to write quickly and easily so that their hands and arms don't hurt. Slow, laborious handwriting interferes with the expression of ideas. In addition, students must be able to spell high-frequency words automatically so that they can focus on the ideas they're writing about.

Components of Fluency

Fluency involves three components: accuracy, speed, and prosody (Rasinski, 2003). Too often, reading quickly is equated with fluency, and some assessment tools use speed as their only measure of fluency, but accurately identifying words and reading expressively are also critical components.

Accuracy. Accuracy is the ability to recognize familiar words automatically, without any conscious thought, and to identify unfamiliar words almost as quickly. It's crucial that students immediately recognize most of the words they're reading. When students have to stop to decode words in every sentence, their reading isn't fluent; it's an indication that the selection is too difficult. The conventional wisdom is that students can read a text successfully when they know at least 95% of the words, which is 19 of every 20 words or 95 of every 100 words. Allington (2009) challenges this notion, suggesting that students need to know 98 or 99% of the words in a text to read it fluently; otherwise, stopping again and again to use word-identification strategies to figure out the unfamiliar words places too much of a burden on readers.

Reading Speed. Reading speed refers to the rate at which students read; to read fluently, students need to orally read at least 100 words per minute. Most students reach this reading speed by third grade, and their reading rate continues to grow. By the time they're sixth graders, they'll read 150 words per minute, and adults typically read 250 words per minute or more. Of course, both children and adults vary their reading speed depending on the difficulty of what they're reading and their purpose, but excessively slow or fast reading is often a characteristic of dysfluent readers.

Prosody. The third component, prosody, is the ability to orally read sentences expressively, with appropriate phrasing and intonation. Dowhower (1991) describes prosody as "the ability to read in expressive rhythmic and melodic patterns" (p. 166). Students move from word-by-word reading with little or no expression to chunking words into phrases, attending to punctuation, and applying appropriate syntactic emphases. Fluent readers' oral reading approximates speech, and for their reading to be expressive, they have to recognize accurately and automatically most of the words they're reading and read quickly.

Dysfluent Readers

Young children read slowly, pointing at each word as they pronounce it, but as they learn to recognize more words and gain experience, their reading becomes faster and smoother. In second grade, most children develop a large bank of sight words that they recognize instantly so they're able to chunk the the words they're reading into longer phrases and add more expression to their oral reading. They apply what they've learned by listening to parents and teachers read aloud. In third grade, students' reading becomes fluent. They usually can read 100 words or more per minute and vary the emphasis they place on particular words and phrases to make their reading more meaningful. Some students, however, don't become fluent readers. They exemplify some of these characteristics:

◆ Students read slowly or too quickly.
◆ Students try to sound out phonetically irregular words.
◆ Students guess at words based on the beginning sound.
◆ Students don't remember a word the second or third time it is used in a passage.
◆ Students don't break multisyllabic words into syllables or root words to decode them.
◆ Students point at words as they read.
◆ Students repeat words and phrases.
◆ Students read without expression.
◆ Students read in a word-by-word manner.
◆ Students ignore punctuation marks.
◆ Students don't remember or understand what they read.

Allington (2009) offers three reasons why some students struggle to become fluent readers. First, these students regularly read books that are too difficult, instead of those at their instructional and independent levels. Second, they do very little actual reading. Struggling readers typically do much less reading than more capable readers, even though increasing reading volume is necessary to become better readers. Third, teachers frequently ask struggling readers to read aloud and then immediately interrupt them when they misread a word, rather than giving them time to notice and correct their error. In time, these students become more tentative, word-by-word readers who depend on teachers to monitor their reading instead of monitoring it themselves. Teachers can ensure that all students become fluent readers by providing them with books at their reading levels, scheduling more time for them to read interesting texts, and modifying their interactions with struggling readers so that they interrupt them less often and nurture their strategic behaviors.

Promoting Reading Fluency

Nonfluent readers can learn to read fluently (Allington, 2009). They may need to work on their accuracy, reading speed, or prosody, or on all three components of fluency. They may also need more reading

Teaching Struggling Readers and Writers

Fluency
Struggling readers need to read fluently.

Many struggling readers don't read fluently, and their labored reading affects their comprehension. Allington (2006) examined the research about dysfluent readers and found that there's no single common problem; some have difficulty decoding words, whereas others read very slowly or in a monotone, ignoring phrasing and punctuation cues. Because struggling readers exhibit different fluency problems, it's essential to diagnose students and to plan instruction that's tailored to their instructional needs. To examine whether fluency is a problem, teachers listen to students read aloud in an appropriately leveled book and ask themselves these questions about their accuracy, reading speed, and prosody:
- *Does the student decode unfamiliar words quickly?*
- *Does the student know high-frequency words?*
- *Is the student's oral reading speed adequate for the text being read?*
- *Is the student's reading expressive?*

If struggling readers exhibit one or more problems, teachers provide instruction and involve them in activities, such as rereading familiar texts using repeated readings, using cross-age reading buddies for reading practice, and choral reading to develop reading speed and expression.

Teachers also ensure that struggling students have daily opportunities for independent reading in books that they can read comfortably. Too often, struggling readers try to read books like those that their classmates are reading, but they're usually too difficult. To increase reading volume, struggling readers need access to interesting books at their independent reading level and plenty of time to read, and to develop more interest in reading, students need to read fluently and comprehend what they're reading so they'll become confident that they're successful readers.

practice—daily opportunities to read books at their reading levels to develop reading stamina. Rasinski (2003) identified four principles of fluency instruction:

◆ Teachers model fluent reading for students.
◆ Teachers provide oral support while students are reading.
◆ Teachers have students do repeated readings of brief texts.
◆ Teachers focus students' attention on chunking words into meaningful phrases.

The instructional recommendations that follow embody these principles.

Enhancing Accuracy. To become fluent readers, students learn to accurately and automatically recognize two kinds of words during the primary grades—high-frequency words that often can't be sounded out and phonetically regular words. Students who aren't fluent may need instruction on one or both types of words, depending on which words they can read. To teach high-frequency words, teachers present minilessons on the words and post them on a word wall in the classroom, and to teach phonetically regular words, teachers present minilessons on phonics skills. Then students need daily opportunities to practice the words they're learning in reading and writing activities.

Literacy Portraits:VIEWING GUIDE

Most second graders move toward fluent reading, and Ms. Janusz spends a great deal of time talking about fluent reading, explaining its importance, teaching the components, and listening to her students read aloud to monitor their growth. Click on Rakie's December button to watch Ms. Janusz explain reading fluency during a guided reading lesson. Does she include the three components of fluency addressed in this chapter? Why do you think that she asks students to retell what they've just read? On this video clip, you can also listen to Rakie reading aloud. Next, click on Rakie's May button to listen to her reread *Click, Clack, Moo: Cows That Type*, by Doreen Cronin, and retell it to a classmate. It's one of her favorite books, and she's read it many times. Compare her accuracy, reading speed, and expression now with her fluency in December. Do you think that she's become a fluent reader?

myeducationlab

Improving Reading Speed. The best way to improve students' reading speed is repeated readings (Samuels, 1979), in which students practice reading aloud a book or an excerpt at their independent level three to five times, striving to improve their reading speed and decrease the number of errors with each reading. Teachers time students' reading and plot their speed on a graph so that improvements can be noted. Repeated readings also enhance students' ability to chunk words into meaningful phrases and read more expressively (Dowhower, 1989).

Teachers also have students reread passages as part of guided reading lessons when they want to improve students' reading speed. The teacher reads the passage aloud while students follow along or use echo reading, in which they repeat each phrase or sentence after the teacher reads it. After several repetitions, students read the passage one more time, this time independently. Teachers also set up rereading opportunities at a listening center; this activity is called Reading While Listening (Kuhn & Stahl, 2004). Students read along in a book as they listen to it read aloud.

Teaching Prosody. Schreider (1991) recommends teaching students how to phrase or chunk together parts of sentences in order to read with expression. Fluent readers seem to understand how to chunk parts of sentences into meaningful units, perhaps because they've been read to or have had many reading experiences themselves, but many struggling readers don't have this ability. Consider this sentence from *Sarah, Plain and Tall* (MacLachlan, 2004): "A few raindrops came, gentle at first, then stronger and louder, so that Caleb and I covered our ears and stared at each other without speaking" (p. 47). This sentence comes from the chapter describing a terrible storm that the pioneer family endured, huddled with their animals in their sturdy barn. Three commas help students read the first part of this sentence, but then they must decide how to chunk the second part.

Teachers work with nonfluent readers to break sentences into chunks and then read the sentences with expression. Teachers make copies of a page from a book students are reading so that they can mark pauses in longer sentences. Or, teachers can choose a sentence to write on the chalkboard, chunking it into phrases like this:

> A few raindrops came,
> gentle at first,
> then stronger and louder,
> so that Caleb and I
> covered our ears
> and stared at each other
> without speaking.

After chunking, students practice reading the sentence with classmates and individually. After working with one sentence, they work with a partner to choose another sentence to chunk and practice reading. Students who don't chunk words into phrases when they read aloud need many opportunities to practice chunking and rereading sentences.

Activities such as choral reading also help students improve their phrasing. In choral reading, students and the teacher take turns reading the text, as Ms. Williams and her students did in the vignette at the beginning of the chapter. Students provide support for each other because they're reading in small groups, and they learn to phrase sentences as they read together. Choral reading also improves students' reading speed because they read along with classmates.

One variation of choral reading is unison reading, in which the teacher and students read a text together (Reutzel & Cooter, 2008). The teacher is the leader and reads loudly enough to be heard above the group. Another variation is echo reading, in which the teacher reads a sentence with good phrasing and intonation, and then students read the same material again. If the students read confidently, the teacher moves to the next sentence. However, if students struggle to read the sentence, the teacher repeats the first sentence. These activities are especially useful for helping English learners to develop appropriate prosody.

Reading Practice. Students need many opportunities to practice reading and rereading books to develop fluency (Rasinski, 2003). The best books for reading practice are ones that students are interested in reading and that are written at their independent level; books for fluency practice should be neither too easy nor too difficult. Students should automatically recognize most words in the book, but if the book is extremely easy, it provides no challenge. And, when students read books that are too difficult, they read slowly because they stop again and again to identify unfamiliar words; this constant stopping reinforces nonfluent readers' already choppy reading style.

For reading practice, students often choose "pop" literature that's fun to read but rather ordinary. These books are often more effective than high-quality literature selections in helping children develop fluency because the vocabulary is more controlled, which allows students to be more successful. In addition, children like them because the stories are humorous or fantastic, or because they relate to their own lives. The popular Magic Tree House series, with coordinated stories and informational books, is written at the first- and second-grade reading levels, the time-travel stories in The Zack Files series at the second- and third-grade levels, and the hilarious Captain Underpants series at the third- and fourth-grade levels. A list of picture-book and chapter-book series written at the first- through fourth-grade levels is presented in Figure 6–9. More and more easy-to-read picture books and chapter books are becoming available each year, and many of them appeal to boys.

Teachers provide two types of daily opportunities for children to practice reading and rereading familiar stories and other books; some activities provide assisted practice, and others provide students with opportunities to read independently, without assistance. In assisted practice, students have a model to follow as they read or reread. Choral reading, readers theatre, and buddy reading are three examples. In choral reading, students experiment with different ways to read poems and other short texts (Rasinski, 2003). In readers theatre, students practice reading story scripts to develop fluency before reading the script to an audience of classmates. Researchers have found that practice reading using readers theatre scripts results in significant improvement in students' reading fluency (Griffith & Rasinski, 2004; Martinez, Roser, & Strecker, 1998/1999). In buddy reading, pairs of students who read at approximately the same level read or reread books together (Griffith & Rasinski, 2004). They choose a book that interests them and decide how they will read it. They may choose to read in unison or take turns reading aloud while the partner follows along. Sometimes when students are rereading familiar books, the student who isn't reading counts the errors that the reader makes and helps the reader with corrections afterward (Cunningham & Allington, 2007).

Figure 6–9 ◆ Popular Series of Picture Books and Chapter Books

Reading Level	Series	Description
1	Amelia Bedelia	Comical stories about a housekeeper who takes instructions literally.
	Fox and Friends	Stories about Fox, who likes to have everything his way.
	Pinky and Rex	Stories about two best friends, a boy named Pinky and a girl named Rex.
1–2	Arthur	Picture-book stories about an aardvark named Arthur.
	Henry and Mudge	Chapter-book stories about Henry and his 180-pound dog, Mudge.
	Junie B. Jones	Stories about a delightful girl who's always getting into trouble.
	The Magic Tree House	Stories about a magical tree house that transports children back in time and companion informational books.
	Third-Grade Detectives	Adventures featuring Todd and Noelle, two clever third graders.
2	Cam Jansen	Funny chapter books about a girl detective named Cam Jansen.
	Jigsaw Jones Mysteries	Stories featuring private eye Jigsaw Jones and his partner, Mila Yeh.
	Franklin	Picture-book stories featuring a gentle turtle-hero named Franklin.
	George and Martha	Stories about George and Martha, two hippo friends.
	Horrible Harry	Hilarious stories about Harry, who's a second-grade prankster.
	The Kids in Ms. Colman's Class	Chapter-book stories about a class of second graders.
2–3	Black Lagoon	Picture-book series deals with children's fears of the unknown.
	Marvin Redpost	Funny stories about third-grade Marvin Redpost.
	The Zack Files	Time-travel stories featuring a fifth grader named Zack.
	A to Z Mysteries	An alphabetical collection of mysteries.
3	Adventures of the Bailey School Kids	Chapter-book stories about the adventures of a diverse third-grade class.
	Hank the Cowdog	Fantastic chapter-book stories told by a cowdog named Hank.
	The Magic School Bus	Ms. Frizzle's adventures in her magic school bus.
	Secrets of the Droon	Fantasy adventures set in the magical world of Droon.
	Geronimo Stilton	Stories about Geronimo Stilton, a mouse who runs *The Rodent's Gazette*.
3–4	Amber Brown	Chapter-book stories about a spunky girl with a colorful name.
	Captain Underpants	Hilarious chapter-book stories about the superhero Captain Underpants.
	Time Warp Trio	Three friends travel back in time for adventure.

Developing Reading Stamina. Once students become fluent readers, the focus shifts to helping them develop reading stamina, or the strength to read silently for increasingly longer periods of time. Students develop this stamina through daily opportunities to read independently for extended periods. When students' reading is limited to reading basal reader selections, single chapters in novels, or magazine articles that can be completed in 15 or 20 minutes, they won't develop the endurance they need. Many teachers find that by sixth and seventh grades, their students can't read for more than 15 or 20 minutes at a time, or students complain about how tired they are or how hard reading is when they are asked to read for longer periods. It's crucial that students learn to read for longer periods of time so that they can handle novels and other chapter books and the lengthy texts they are asked to read on standardized tests.

Students develop this endurance through reading books at their independent level. Teachers typically include extended opportunities each day for independent reading of self-selected texts through Sustained Silent Reading at all grade levels. Kindergartners read for 5 to 10 minutes; in first grade, students begin by reading and rereading books for 10 to 15 minutes, and reach 20 minutes or more by the end of the school year. The time students spend reading gradually increases to at least 30 minutes a day in second and third grades, and students shift from oral to silent reading as they become fluent readers. In fourth and fifth grades, students' independent reading time increases to 40 or 45 minutes, and in sixth, seventh, and eighth grades, students spend 45 to 60 minutes a day reading. Students also benefit from doing additional independent reading at home.

Another way of looking at how students develop stamina is by the number of words they're expected to read. Many school districts now call for students to read 500,000 words in fourth grade and gradually increase the number of words until they read one million words in eighth grade. You may wonder how the number of words translates to books: Students in fourth, fifth, and sixth grades often read novels that are approximately 200 pages long, and these books typically have approximately 35,000 words; for example, *Esperanza Rising* (Ryan, 2000), *Loser* (Spinelli, 2002), and *Homeless Bird* (Whelan, 2000). Therefore, students need to read approximately 14 books to reach 500,000 words. Students who read two novels each month will reach the 500,000-word mark.

Students in seventh and eighth grades usually read longer books with 250 pages or more. Books with 250 pages, such as *Bud, Not Buddy* (Curtis, 1999), *Holes* (Sachar, 2003), and *Crispin: The Cross of Lead* (Avi, 2002), contain at least 50,000 words. Books containing more than 300 pages, such as *Harry Potter and the Chamber of Secrets* (Rowling, 1999), range from 75,000 to 100,000 words. Students need to read 10 to 20 books, depending on length, to reach one million words. So, students who read two books with 250 to 350 pages each month will reach the one million–word mark.

Why Is Round-Robin Reading No Longer Recommended?

Round-robin reading is an outmoded oral reading activity in which the teacher calls on children to read aloud, one after the other (Johns & Berglund, 2006). Some teachers used round-robin reading in small groups and others used the procedure with the whole class, but neither version is advocated today. According to Opitz and Rasinski (1998), many problems are associated with round-robin reading. First of all, students may develop an inaccurate view of reading because they are expected to read aloud to the class without having opportunities to rehearse. Next, they may develop inefficient reading habits because they alter their silent reading speed to match the various speeds of classmates when they read aloud. Students signal their inattention and boredom by misbehaving as classmates read aloud. In addition to these problems for students who are listening, round-robin reading causes problems for some students when they are called upon to read: Struggling readers are often anxious or embarrassed when they read aloud.

Researchers agree that round-robin reading wastes valuable classroom time that could be spent on more meaningful oral and silent reading activities (Allington, 2009). Instead of round-robin reading, students should read books independently if they're at their reading level. If the books are too difficult, they can read with buddies, participate in shared reading, or listen to the teacher or another fluent reader read aloud. Also, they might listen to the teacher read the material aloud and then try reading it with a buddy or independently.

urturing English Learners

To become fluent readers, English learners need to read words accurately, quickly, and expressively, like native speakers do. It's very unlikely that they'll become fluent readers, however, before they learn to speak English fluently, because their lack of oral language proficiency limits their recognition of high-frequency words and use of word-learning strategies, and it interferes with their ability to understand word meanings, string words together into sentences, and read expressively (Peregoy & Boyle, 2008).

Many ELs speak and read English with a native-language accent, but their differences in pronunciation and intonation shouldn't hamper their reading fluency. Everyone has an accent, even native English speakers, so ELs should never be expected to eliminate their accents to be considered fluent readers.

The same types of instruction and practice activities that are recommended for native speakers are effective with English learners; however, ELs often need more time because they're learning to speak English at the same time they're learning to read. Teachers continue teaching high-frequency words and word-learning strategies until students learn them, and ELs need to spend more time every day reading texts at their independent reading level. It's often helpful to have students reread Language Experience Approach stories and other familiar texts, participate in choral reading activities, and engage in oral reading practice with buddies to get all the practice they need.

Developing Writing Fluency

To become fluent writers, students must be able to rapidly form letters and spell words automatically. Just as nonfluent readers read word by word and have to stop and decode many words, nonfluent writers write slowly, word by word, and have to stop and check the spelling of many words. In fact, some nonfluent writers write so slowly that they forget the sentence they're writing! Through varied, daily writing activities, students develop the muscular control to form letters quickly and legibly. They write high-frequency words again and again until they can spell them automatically. Being able to write fluently usually coincides with being able to read fluently because reading and writing practice are mutually beneficial (Shanahan, 1988; Tierney, 1983).

Students become fluent writers as they practice writing, and they need opportunities for both assisted and unassisted practice. Writing on dry-erase boards during interactive writing lessons is one example of assisted writing practice (Tompkins, 2008). The teacher and classmates provide support for students.

Quickwriting. Peter Elbow (1998) recommends using quickwriting to develop writing fluency. In quickwriting, students write rapidly and without stopping as they explore an idea. As part of the unit on hermit crabs, Ms. Williams asked the second-grade students to do a quickwrite listing what they had learned about hermit crabs. Here is Arlette's quickwrite:

 Hermit crabs live in tide pools. They have pincers and 10 legs in all. They can pinch you very hard. Ouch! They are crabs and they molt to grow and grow. They have to buro [borrow] shells to live in becus other anmels [animals] will eat them. They like to eat fish and shrimp. Sea enomes [anemones] like to live on ther shells.

Arlette listed a great deal of information that she'd learned about hermit crabs. She misspelled five words; some correct spellings are given in brackets. Arlette was able to write such a long quickwrite and to misspell so few words because she is already a fluent writer. While she was writing, she checked the hermit crab word wall and the high-frequency word wall in the classroom in order to spell *pincers, shrimp,* and *other.* She knew how to spell the other words and wrote them automatically.

In contrast, Jeremy is not yet a fluent writer. Here is his quickwrite:

> *The hermit crab liv in a hues [house]*
> *he eat [eats] shimp [shrimp].*

Jeremy writes slowly and laboriously. He stops to think of an idea before writing each sentence and starts each sentence on a new line. He rarely refers to the word walls in the classroom and spells most words phonetically. Even though Jeremy's writing is not as fluent as Arlette's, quickwriting is a useful activity for him because he'll become more fluent through practice.

Ms. Williams has her students quickwrite several times each week. They quickwrite to respond to a story she's read aloud or to write about what they're learning in science. She reads and responds to the quickwrites, and she writes the correct form of misspelled words at the bottom of the page so that students will notice the correct spelling. Once in a while, she has students revise and edit their quickwrites and make a final, published copy, but her goal is to develop writing fluency, not polished compositions.

Why Is Copying From the Chalkboard No Longer Recommended?
Some teachers write sentences and poems on the chalkboard for students to copy in the hope that this activity will develop writing fluency. Copying isn't very effective, though, because students are passively recording letters, not actively creating sentences, breaking the sentences into words, and spelling the words. In fact, sometimes students are copying sentences they can't even read, so the activity becomes little more than handwriting practice. It's much more worthwhile for students to write sentences to express their own ideas and to practice spelling the high-frequency words they're using.

Assessing Students' Reading and Writing Fluency

Primary-grade teachers monitor children's developing reading and writing fluency by observing them as they read and write. They assess children's reading fluency by listening to them read aloud and considering these questions:

> Do students read most words automatically, or do they stop to decode many unfamiliar words?
>
> Do students read quickly enough to understand what they're reading, or do they read too slowly or too fast?
>
> Do students chunk words into phrases, or do they read word by word?
>
> Do students read with expressively, or do they read in a monotone?

Teachers assess students' writing fluency in a similar manner. They observe students as they write and consider these questions:

> Do students think of writing topics easily, or do they have trouble thinking of something to write?
>
> Do students write quickly enough to complete the assignment, or do they write slowly or try to avoid writing?
>
> Do students spell most words automatically, or do they stop to figure out the spelling of many words?
>
> Do students write easily, or do they complain that their hands hurt?

Teachers use running records, informal reading inventories, and classroom tests to determine whether students are fluent readers, and document their progress. This Assessment Tools feature lists the tests and other assessment tools for evaluating students' development toward becoming fluent readers.

Assessment Tools

Reading Fluency

Teachers use one or more of these assessment tools as well as informal observation to determine students' reading speed and monitor their reading fluency:

◆ **Dynamic Indicators of Basic Early Literacy Skills (DIBELS): Oral Reading Fluency Subtest** (Kaminski & Good, 1996)

The Oral Reading Fluency subtest is a collection of graded passages used to measure first through third graders' reading speed, one component of fluency. In this individually administered test, children read aloud for one minute, and teachers mark errors; children's oral reading rate is the number of words they read correctly in a grade-level passage in one minute. The test is available on the DIBELS website.

◆ **Fluency Checks** (Johns & Berglund, 2006)

Teachers use these graded passages to monitor students' growth toward fluent reading. First- through eighth-grade passages are included in this assessment tool. The authors recommend that students be tested several times during the school year. Teachers listen to students read aloud as much of a narrative or expository passage as they can in one minute and mark errors on a scoring sheet. They also ask comprehension questions related to the portion of the passage that students read. Afterward, teachers calculate students' reading speed and score it against grade-level standards, and they rate their phrasing, expression, and attention to punctuation marks from strong to weak.

◆ **Informal Reading Inventories (IRIs)**

Teachers listen to students in grades 2–8 read aloud grade-level passages in an IRI and mark accuracy and prosody errors on scoring sheets. Accuracy errors include substituted words, mispronounced words, and skipped words; prosody errors include pauses, phrasing, and expressiveness. In addition, teachers use a stopwatch to record the time it takes students to read the passage and then calculate their reading rate (words read correctly per minute). They also examine students' accuracy errors to determine their knowledge of high-frequency words and their use of word-identification strategies.

◆ **Running Records**

Teachers, especially those who teach in the primary grades, take running records as students read leveled books. They time students' reading, mark errors on a copy of the text, and evaluate their phrasing and expressiveness. They compare students' fluency when reading familiar and unfamiliar books or books at their reading level with those at their grade level to determine whether students meet grade-level standards.

Until students become fluent readers, it's crucial that teachers monitor their developing accuracy, reading speed, and prosody. When students aren't making expected progress, teachers determine the source of the problem and provide instruction to address it. Once students are fluent, less frequent assessments are needed, but sometimes fluent readers will read less proficiently when the text is unfamiliar or too difficult.

Chapter 6

Review

How Effective Teachers Develop Fluent Readers and Writers

▶ Teachers teach students to read and spell the 300 high-frequency words.

▶ Teachers teach four word-identification strategies—phonic analysis, decoding by analogy, syllabic analysis, and morphemic analysis.

▶ Teachers use instructional procedures, including repeated reading, choral reading, and independent reading, to develop students' reading fluency.

▶ Teachers use instructional procedures, including quickwriting and independent writing, to develop students' writing fluency.

▶ Teachers ensure that students become fluent readers and writers by third grade.

Go to MyEducationLab at www.myeducationlab.com to deepen your understanding of the concepts presented in this chapter:

▶ Watch second graders learn about fluency and become more fluent readers by viewing video segments in the Literacy Portraits.
▶ Check your understanding of chapter concepts with the multiple-choice and essay quizzes in the Study Plan.
▶ Apply some of the main ideas discussed in the chapter in the Activities and Applications section of the website.
▶ Practice what you've learned in this chapter in Building Teaching Skills and Dispositions before applying the ideas in your own classroom.

PROFESSIONAL REFERENCES

Adams, M. J. (1990). *Beginning to read: Thinking and learning about print.* Cambridge, MA: MIT Press.

Allington, R. L. (2006). *What really matters for struggling readers: Designing research-based programs* (2nd ed.). Boston: Allyn & Bacon/Pearson.

Allington, R. L. (2009). *What really matters in fluency: Research-based best practices across the curriculum.* Boston: Allyn & Bacon/Pearson.

Beaver, J. (2006). *Developmental reading assessment, grades K–3* (2nd ed.). Upper Saddle River, NJ: Celebration Press/Pearson.

Beaver, J., & Carter, M. (2003). *Developmental reading assessment, grades 4–8.* Upper Saddle River, NJ: Celebration Press/Pearson.

Caldwell, J. S., & Leslie, L. (2005). *Intervention strategies to follow informal reading inventory assessment: So what do I do now?* Boston: Allyn & Bacon/Pearson.

Clay, M. M. (2005). *An observation survey of early literacy achievement* (2nd ed.). Portsmouth, NH: Heinemann.

Cunningham, P. (1990). The Names Test: A quick assessment of decoding ability. *The Reading Teacher, 44,* 124–129.

Cunningham, P. M. (2009). *Phonics they use: Words for reading and writing* (5th ed.). Boston: Allyn & Bacon.

Cunningham, P. M., & Allington, R. L. (2007). *Classrooms that work: They can all read and write*. Boston: Allyn & Bacon.

Dolch, E. W. (1936). A basic sight vocabulary. *Elementary School Journal, 36,* 456–460.

Dowhower, S. L. (1989). Repeated reading: Research into practice. *The Reading Teacher, 42,* 502–507.

Dowhower, S. L. (1991). Speaking of prosody: Fluency's unattended bedfellow. *Theory Into Practice, 30,* 165–173.

Duffelmeyer, F. A., Kruse, A. E., Merkley, D. J., & Fyfe, S. A. (1994). Further validation and enhancement of the Names Test. *The Reading Teacher, 48,* 118–128.

Ehri, L. C., & Robbins, C. (1992). Beginners need some decoding skill to read words by analogy. *Reading Research Quarterly, 27,* 13–26.

Elbow, P. (1998). *Writing without teachers* (2nd ed.). New York: Oxford University Press.

Eldredge, J. L. (2005). *Teach decoding: How and why* (2nd ed.). Upper Saddle River, NJ: Merrill/Prentice Hall.

Fry, E. (1980). The new instant word list. *The Reading Teacher, 34,* 284–289.

Gaskins, I. W., Ehri, L. C., Cress, C., O'Hara, C., & Donnelly, K. (1996/1997). Procedures for word learning: Making discoveries about words. *The Reading Teacher, 50,* 312–326.

Gaskins, R. W., Gaskins, J. W., & Gaskins, I. W. (1991). A decoding program for poor readers—and the rest of the class, too! *Language Arts, 68,* 213–225.

Gill, S. R. (2007). Learning about word parts with Kidspiration. *The Reading Teacher, 61,* 79–84.

Griffith, L. W., & Rasinski, T. V. (2004). A focus on fluency: How one teacher incorporated fluency with her reading curriculum. *The Reading Teacher, 58,* 126–137.

Gough, P. B., Juel, C., & Griffith, P. L. (1992). Reading, spelling, and the orthographic cipher. In P. B. Gough, L. C. Ehri, & R. Treiman (Eds.), *Reading acquisition* (pp. 35–48). Hillsdale, NJ: Erlbaum.

Hiebert, E. H. (1991). The development of word-level strategies in authentic literacy tasks. *Language Arts, 68,* 234–240.

Invernizzi, M., Meier, J. D., & Juel, C. (2003). *Phonological awareness literacy screening (PALS)*. Charlottesville: University of Virginia Press.

Johns, J. L., & Berglund, R. L. (2006). *Fluency: Strategies and assessments* (3rd ed.). Newark, DE: International Reading Association and Kendall/Hunt.

Kaminski, R. A., & Good, R. H., III. (1996). *Dynamic Indicators of Basic Early Literacy Skills (DIBELS)*. Eugene: University of Oregon Center on Teaching and Learning.

Koskinen, P. S., & Blum, I. H. (1986). Paired repeated reading: A classroom strategy for developing fluent reading. *The Reading Teacher, 40,* 70–75.

Kuhn, M. R., & Rasinski, T. (2007). Best practices in fluency instruction. In L. B. Gambrell, L. M. Morrow, &

M. Pressley (Eds.), *Best practices in literacy instruction* (3rd ed., pp. 204–219). New York: Guilford Press.

Kuhn, M. R., & Stahl, S. A. (2004). Fluency: A review of developmental and remedial practices. In R. B. Ruddell & N. J. Unrau (Eds.), *Theoretical models and processes of reading* (5th ed., pp. 412–453). Newark, DE: International Reading Association.

LaBerge, D., & Samuels, S. J. (1976). Toward a theory of automatic information processing in reading. In H. Singer & R. Ruddell (Eds.), *Theoretical models and processes of reading* (pp. 548–579). Newark, DE: International Reading Association.

Martinez, M., Roser, N. L., & Strecker, S. (1998/1999). "I never thought I could be a star": A readers theatre ticket to fluency. *The Reading Teacher, 52,* 326–334.

Mather, N., Sammons, J., & Schwartz, J. (2006). Adaptations of the Names Test: Easy to use phonics assessments. *The Reading Teacher, 60,* 114–122.

McKenna, M. C., & Stahl, S. A. (2003). *Assessment for reading instruction*. New York: Guilford Press.

National Reading Panel. (2000). *Teaching children to read: An evidence-based assessment of the scientific research literature on reading and its implications for reading instruction*. Washington, DC: National Institute of Child Health and Human Development.

Opitz, M. F., & Rasinski, T. V. (1998). *Good-bye round robin: Twenty-five effective oral reading strategies*. Portsmouth, NH: Heinemann.

Peregoy, S. F., & Boyle, O. F. (2008). *Reading, writing, and learning in ESL: A resource book for teaching K–12 English learners* (5th ed.). Boston: Allyn & Bacon/Pearson.

Pikulski, J. J., & Chard, D. J. (2005). Fluency: Bridge between decoding and reading comprehension. *The Reading Teacher, 58,* 510–519.

Pinnell, G. S., & Fountas, I. C. (1998). *Word matters: Teaching phonics and spelling in the reading/writing classroom*. Portsmouth, NH: Heinemann.

Rasinski, T. V. (2000). Speed does matter in reading. *The Reading Teacher, 54,* 146–151.

Rasinski, T. V. (2003). *The fluent reader*. New York: Scholastic.

Rasinski, T. V. (2004). Creating fluent readers. *Educational Leadership, 61*(6), 146–151.

Reutzel, D. R., & Cooter, R. B. (2008). *Teaching children to read* (5th ed.). Upper Saddle River, NJ: Merrill/Prentice Hall.

Samuels, S. J. (1979). The method of repeated readings. *The Reading Teacher, 32,* 403–408.

Samuels, S. J. (2004). Toward a theory of automatic information processing in reading, revisited. In R. B. Ruddell & N. J. Unrau (Eds.), *Theoretical models and processes of reading* (5th ed., pp. 1127–1148). Newark, DE: International Reading Association.

Schreider, P. A. (1991). Understanding prosody's role in reading acquisition. *Theory Into Practice, 30,* 158–164.

Shanahan, T. (1988). The reading-writing relationship: Seven instructional principles. *The Reading Teacher, 41,* 636–647.

Silverman, S. (2005). Getting connected: My experience as a collaborative Internet project coordinator. In R. A. Karchmer, M. H. Mallette, J. Kara-Soteriou, & D. J. Leu, Jr. (Eds.), *Innovative approaches to literacy education: Using the Internet to support new literacies* (pp. 103–120). Newark, DE: International Reading Association.

Snow, C. E., Burns, M. S., & Griffin, P. (Eds.). (1998). *Preventing reading difficulties in young children.* Washington, DC: National Academy Press.

Stanovich, K. E. (1992). Speculations on the causes and consequences of individual differences in early reading acquisition. In P. B. Gough, L. C. Ehri, & R. Treiman (Eds.), *Reading acquisition* (pp. 307–342). Hillsdale, NJ: Erlbaum.

Tierney, R. J. (1983). Writer-reader transactions: Defining the dimensions of negotiation. In P. L. Stock (Ed.), *Forum: Essays on theory and practice in the teaching of writing* (pp. 147–151). Upper Montclair, NJ: Boynton/Cook.

Tompkins, G. E. (2008). *Teaching writing: Balancing process and product* (5th ed.). Upper Saddle River, NJ: Merrill/Prentice Hall.

White, T. G., Sowell, J., & Yanagihara, A. (1989). Teaching elementary students to use word-part clues. *The Reading Teacher, 42,* 302–308.

CHILDREN'S BOOK REFERENCES

Avi. (2002). *Crispin: The cross of lead.* New York: Hyperion Books.

Carle, E. (2005). *A house for hermit crab.* New York: Aladdin Books.

Curtis, C. P. (1999). *Bud, not Buddy.* New York: Delacorte.

Fleming, D. (1995). *In the tall, tall grass.* New York: Henry Holt.

Fleming, D. (1998). *In the small, small pond.* New York: Henry Holt.

Holling, H. C. (1990). *Pagoo.* Boston: Houghton Mifflin.

Kaplan, R. (1996). *Moving day.* New York: Greenwillow.

MacLachlan, P. (2004). *Sarah, plain and tall.* New York: HarperTrophy.

Randell, B. (1994). *Hermit crab.* Crystal Lake, IL: Rigby Books.

Rowling, J. K. (1999). *Harry Potter and the chamber of secrets.* New York: Scholastic.

Ryan, P. M. (2000). *Esperanza rising.* New York: Scholastic.

Sachar, L. (2003). *Holes.* New York: Yearling.

Spinelli, J. (2002). *Loser.* New York: HarperCollins.

Tuchman, G. (1997). *Hermit's shiny shell.* New York: Macmillan/McGraw-Hill.

Whelan, G. (2000). *Homeless bird.* New York: HarperCollins.

ChapTer 7

Expanding Students' Knowledge of Words

Mrs. Sanom's Word Wizards Club

Mrs. Sanom is the resource teacher at John Muir Elementary School, and she sponsors an after-school Word Wizards Club for fifth and sixth graders; the club meets for an hour on Wednesday afternoons. Nineteen students are club members this year; many of them are English learners. Mrs. Sanom teaches vocabulary lessons during the club meetings using costumes, books, and hands-on activities. She focuses on a different word-study topic each week; the topics include writing alliterations, choosing synonyms carefully, applying context clues to figure out unfamiliar words, using a dictionary and a thesaurus, understanding multiple meanings of words, choosing between homophones, adding prefixes and suffixes to words, and studying root words.

She devised this club because many students have limited vocabularies, which affects their reading achievement. She displays two banners in her classroom: "Expanding Your Vocabulary Leads to School Success" and "Knowing Words Makes You Powerful." In the letters that club members write to Mrs. Sanom at the end of the school year, they report paying more attention to words an author uses, and they're better at using context clues to figure out the meaning of unfamiliar words. Most importantly, the students say that participation in the Word Wizards

Club gives them an appreciation for words that will last a lifetime. Rosie writes:

I love being a Word Wizard. I learned lots of new words and that makes me smart. I have a favorite word that is <u>hypothesis</u>. Did you know that I am always looking for more new words to learn? My Tio Mario gave me a dictionary because I wanted it real bad. I like looking for words in the dictionary and I like words with lots of syllables the best. I want to be in the club next year in 6th grade. Ok?

At the first club meeting, Mrs. Sanom read aloud *Miss Alaineus: A Vocabulary Disaster* (Frasier, 2007), an outrageous yet touching story of a girl named Sage who loves words. In the story, Sage misunderstands the meaning of *miscellaneous*, but what begins as embarrassment turns into victory when she wins an award for her costume in the school's annual vocabulary parade. The students talked about the story in a **grand conversation**, and they decided that they want to dress in costumes and have a vocabulary parade themselves, just as Mrs. Sanom knew they would. They decided that they will have a vocabulary parade at the end of the year, and they'll invite their classmates to participate, too. "I like to dress in vocabulary costumes," Mrs. Sanom explained. "I plan to dress up in clothes or a hat that represents a vocabulary word at each club meeting." With that introduction, she reached into a shopping bag and pulled out an oversized, wrinkled shirt and put it on over her clothes. "Here is my costume," she announced. "Can you guess the word?" She modeled the shirt, trying to smooth the wrinkles, until a student guessed the word *wrinkled*.

The students talked about *wrinkle*, forms of the word (*wrinkled*, *unwrinkled*, and *wrinkling*), and the meanings. They checked the definitions of *wrinkle* in the dictionary. They understood the first meaning, "a crease or fold in clothes or skin," but the second meaning—"a clever idea or trick"—was more difficult. Mrs. Sanom called their idea to have a vocabulary parade "a new wrinkle" in her plans for the club, and then the students began to grasp the meaning.

The borders of each page in *Miss Alaineus* are decorated with words beginning with a specific letter; the first page has words beginning with A, the second page B, and so on. To immerse students in words, Mrs. Sanom asked them each to choose a letter from a box of plastic alphabet letters, turn to that page in the book, and then choose a word beginning with that letter from the border to use in an activity. The words they chose included *awesome, berserk, catastrophe,* and *dwindle*. Students wrote the word on the first page of their Word Wizard Notebooks (small, spiral-bound notebooks that Mrs. Sanom purchased for them), checked its meaning in a dictionary and wrote it beside the word, and then drew a picture to illustrate the meaning. While they worked, Mrs. Sanom wrote the words on the alphabetized **word wall** she posted in the classroom. Afterward, the students shared their words and illustrations in a **tea party** activity.

Mrs. Sanom has a collection of vocabulary books in her classroom library, and she gives brief **book talks** to introduce the books to the club members. She explains that the very best way to learn lots of words is to read every day, and she encourages students to choose a vocabulary book or another book from her library each week to read between club meetings. At the end of each meeting, she allows a few minutes for students to choose a book to take home to read.

At today's club meeting, Mrs. Sanom is wearing a broad-brimmed hat with two wrecked cars and a stop sign attached. The students check out Mrs. Sanom's costume because they know it represents a word—and that word is the topic of today's meeting. They quickly begin guessing words: "Is it *crash*?" Oscar asks. "I think the word is *accident*. My dad had a car accident last week," says Danielle. Ramon suggests, "Those cars are *wrecked*. Is that the word?" Mrs. Sanom commends the club members for their good guesses and says they're on the right track. To provide a little help, she draws a row of nine letter boxes on the chalkboard and fills in the first letter and the last four letters. Then Martha guesses it—*collision*. Mrs. Sanom begins a cluster on the chalkboard with the word *collision* written in the middle circle and related words on each ray. Students compare the noun *collision* and the verb *collide*. They also check the dictionary and a thesaurus for more information and write *crash, accident, wreck, hit, smashup*, and *collide* on the rays to complete the cluster. They talk about how and when to use *collide* and *collision*. Ramon offers, "I know a sentence: On 9-11, the terrorists' airplanes collided with the World Trade Center."

Mrs. Sanom explains that ships can be involved in collisions, too: A ship can hit another ship, or it can collide with something else in the water—an iceberg, for example. Several students know about the *Titanic*, and they share what they know about that ship's fateful ocean crossing. Mrs. Sanom selects *Story of the Titanic* (Kentley, 2001) from her text set of books about the *Titanic* and shows photos and drawings of the ship to provide more background information. They make a **K-W-L chart**, listing what they know in the K column and questions they want to find answers for in the W column. The students also make individual charts in their Word Wizard Notebooks.

Next, Mrs. Sanom presents a list of words using an overhead projector—some about the *Titanic* article they'll read and some not—for an **exclusion brainstorming** activity; the words include *unsinkable, crew, liner, passengers, voyage, airplane, catastrophe, ship, mountain, lifeboat*, and *general*. The students predict which words relate to the article and which don't. The word *general* stumps them because they think of it as an adjective meaning "having to do with the whole, not specific." A student checks the dictionary to learn about the second meaning—"a high-ranking military officer" (noun). The students are still confused, but after reading the article, they realize that the word *general* isn't related: The officer in charge of the *Titanic* (or any ship, for that matter) is called a *captain*.

Mrs. Sanom passes out copies of the one-page article and reads it aloud while students follow along. They discuss the article, talking and asking more questions about the needless tragedy. Then they complete the L section of the K-W-L chart and the exclusion brainstorming activity. Because the students are very interested in learning more about the disaster, Mrs. Sanom introduces her text set of narrative and informational books about the *Titanic*, including *Inside the Titanic* (Brewster, 1997), *Tonight on the Titanic* (Osborne & Osborne, 1995), *Titanic: A Nonfiction Companion to Tonight on the Titanic* (Osborne & Osborne, 2002), *On Board the Titanic: What It Was Like When the Great Liner Sank* (Tanaka, 1996), and *Voyage on the Great Titanic: The Diary of Margaret Ann Brady* (White, 1998). She invites the students to spend the last few minutes of the club meeting choosing a book from the text set to take home to read before the next meeting.

Mrs. Sanom wears a different costume or hat each week. Here are eight of her favorites:

bejeweled: A silky shirt with "jewels" glued across the front

champion: Racing shorts, tee shirt, and a medal on a ribbon worn around her neck

hocus-pocus: A black top hat with a stuffed rabbit stuck inside, white gloves, and a magic wand *international:* A dress decorated with the flags of many countries and a globe cut in half for a hat

mercury: A white sheet worn toga style and a baseball cap with wings on each side

slick: A black leather jacket, sunglasses, and hair slicked back with mousse

transparent: A clear plastic raincoat, clear plastic gloves, and a clear shower cap

vacant: A bird cage with a "for rent" sign worn as a hat with an artificial bird sitting on her shoulder

One week, however, Mrs. Sanom forgets to bring a costume, so after a bit of quick thinking, she decides to feature the word *ordinary*, and she wears her everyday clothes as her costume!

For their 17th weekly club meeting, Mrs. Sanom dressed as a queen with a flowing purple robe and a tiara on her head. The focus of the week was words beginning with Q, the 17th letter of the alphabet. They began by talking about queens—both historical queens such as Queen Isabella of Spain, who financed Christopher Columbus's voyage to the New World, and queens who are alive today. Next, Mrs. Sanom began a list of Q words with *queen*, and the students added words to it. They checked the Q page in alphabet books and examined dictionary entries for Q words. They chose interesting words, including *quadruped, quadruplet, qualify, quest,*

A Student's Square on *Quadruped* for the Q Quilt

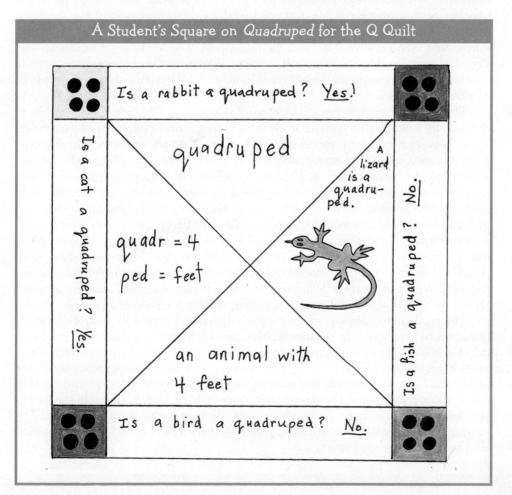

quarantine, quintet, quiver, quench, and *quotation*. After they had more than 20 words on their list, Mrs. Sanom asked each student to choose a Q word, study it, and make a square poster to share what he or she learned. Afterward, Mrs. Sanom collected the posters, made a quilt from them, and hung the quilt on the wall outside the classroom. One student's square about *quadruped* is presented in the box on page 223, and it documents the student's understanding of root words.

Last week's topic was homographs, two or more words that are spelled alike but pronounced differently, such as *record, bow, read*, and *dove*. Mrs. Sanom was dressed with a big red ribbon bow tied around her waist and smaller red bows tied on pigtails. At the beginning of the club meeting, she retied the bow at her waist and then she bowed to the students. Ramon quickly guessed that the word was *bow*, but the concept of homographs was new to him and the other club members. Mrs. Sanom introduced the word *homograph*, explained the definition, and offered examples. Then she shared several homograph riddles from *The Dove Dove: Funny Homograph Riddles* (Terban, 1992), including "The nurse *wrapped* the bandage around the *injury*." The students solve the riddle by identifying the homograph that can replace the two highlighted words; for this riddle, the answer is *wound*.

Next, Mrs. Sanom divided the students into small groups, and she gave each group a different homograph riddle from Terban's book to solve. Then they shared the riddles with the whole group. As they got more practice with homographs, the students became more confident at solving the riddles, but some were confused about homophones and homographs. Mrs. Sanom explained that homophones are words that sound alike but are spelled differently, such as *wood–would* and *there–their–they're*. The students used the last 10 minutes of the club meeting to write about homographs in their Word Wizard Notebooks. They also chose new books to take home and read.

The Word Wizards make and wear word bracelets to highlight special words; in October, for example, the students made word bracelets that spell the word they'd chosen to describe or represent themselves, such as *genius, ornery*, or *sincere*. Mrs. Sanom's word was *sassy*, and she demonstrated how to make a bracelet using small alphabet beads strung on an elastic string. Then students followed her steps to make their own bracelets, which they proudly wear to school and show off to their classmates. In February, they studied patriotic words, such as *allegiance, citizen, equality, independence*, and *republic*, and chose a word for a second bracelet. They chose words after reading books with patriotic themes, such as Lynne Cheney's *America: A Patriotic Primer* (2002) and *A Is for America: An American Alphabet* (Scillian, 2001). For their third word bracelet, they chose the most interesting word from all the words they've collected on the word wall and in their Word Wizard Notebooks, including *valiant, awesome, phenomenon, plethora, incredulous, cryptic, guffaw, mischievous*, and *razzle-dazzle*.

The vocabulary parade is the highlight of the year. Every club member creates a costume and participates in the parade. Mrs. Sanom dresses as a wizard—a word wizard, that is—and she leads the parade from classroom to classroom in the intermediate wing of the school. The students dress as *camouflage, victory, shimmer, monarch, liberty, uncomfortable, fortune, emerald*, and *twilight*, for example, and they carry word cards so that everyone will know the words they represent. As they tour each classroom, Mrs. Sanom and the students talk about their words and what they're learning. The club members' parents come to school to view the parade, and a local television station films the parade for the evening news.

S tudents learn the meanings of words by being immersed in an environment that's rich with words, through lots of daily independent reading and **interactive read-alouds**, and through explicit instruction. As they read, students learn many, many words incidentally, and teachers reinforce students' learning in several important ways: They explicitly teach some words and word-learning strategies, and they foster students' interest in words (Graves, 2006). In the vignette, Mrs. Sanom engaged her fifth and sixth graders with words as they participated in lively Word Wizard Club activities.

Vocabulary learning can't be left to chance because students' word knowledge affects whether they comprehend what they're reading, write effectively, and learn content-area information (Stahl & Nagy, 2006). Children come to school with varying levels of word knowledge, both in the number of words they know and in the depth of their understanding. Students from low-income homes have less than half of the vocabulary that more affluent children possess, and some researchers estimate that they know one quarter to one fifth of the words that their classmates do. To make matters worse, this gap widens each year (Cunningham, 2009). Therefore, it's essential that teachers recognize the impact of socioeconomic level on students' vocabulary knowledge, support all students' vocabulary growth, and emphasize word learning for students who know fewer words.

> Check the Compendium of Instructional Procedures, which follows Chapter 12, for more information on the highlighted terms.

HOW DO STUDENTS LEARN VOCABULARY WORDS?

Many students' vocabularies grow at an astonishing rate—about 3,000 words a year, or roughly 7 to 10 new words every day. By the time students graduate from high school, their vocabularies can reach 25,000 to 50,000 words or more. It seems obvious that to learn words at such a prolific rate, students learn words both in and outside of school, and they learn most words incidentally, not through explicit instruction. Reading has the greatest impact on students' vocabulary development, but other activities are important, too. For example, students learn words through family activities, hobbies, and vacations. Television also has a significant impact on vocabulary development, especially when students view educational programs and limit the amount of time they spend watching television each day.

Levels of Word Knowledge

Students develop knowledge about a word gradually, through repeated oral and written exposures to it. They move from not knowing a word at all to recognizing that they've seen the word before, and then to a level of partial knowledge where they have a general sense of the word or know one meaning. Finally, students know the word fully: They know multiple meanings of the word and can use it in a variety of ways (Nagy, 1988). Here are the four levels of word knowledge:

Unknown Word. Students don't recognize the word.

Initial Recognition. Students have seen or heard the word or can pronounce it, but they don't know the meaning.

Partial Word Knowledge. Students know one meaning of the word and can use it in a sentence.

Full Word Knowledge. Students know more than one meaning of the word and can use it in several ways. (Allen, 1999)

Once students reach the third level, they can usually understand the word in context and use it in writing. In fact, they don't reach the fourth level with every word they learn, but when they do develop full word knowledge, they're described as flexible word users because they understand the core meaning of a word and how it changes in different contexts (Stahl, 1999).

Incidental Word Learning

Students learn words incidentally, without explicit instruction, all the time, and because students learn so many words this way, teachers know that they don't have to teach the meaning of every unfamiliar word in a text. Students learn words from many sources, but researchers report that reading is the single largest source of vocabulary growth for students, especially after third grade (Swanborn & de Glopper, 1999). In addition, the amount of time students spend reading independently is the best predictor of vocabulary growth between second and fifth grades.

Independent Reading. Students need daily opportunities for independent reading in order to learn words, and they need to read books at their independent reading levels. If the books are too easy or too hard, students learn very few new words. The best way to provide opportunities for independent reading is reading workshop. Students choose books that they're interested in from age-appropriate and reading-level-suitable collections in their classroom libraries, and because they've chosen the books themselves, they're more likely to keep reading. Sustained Silent Reading (SSR) is another way to encourage wide reading. All students in a classroom or in the school spend 10 to 30 minutes or more silently reading appropriate books that they've chosen themselves. Even the teacher takes time to read, at the same time modeling how adults who enjoy reading make it part of their daily routine. Simply providing time for independent reading, however, doesn't guarantee that students will increase their vocabulary knowledge (Stahl & Nagy, 2006); students need to know how to use context clues and other word-learning strategies to figure out the meaning of unfamiliar words to increase their vocabulary. (Check pages 244–246 in this chapter to learn more about word-learning strategies.)

Reading Aloud to Students. Teachers also provide for incidental word learning when they read aloud stories, poems, and

---

Teaching Struggling Readers and Writers

Lots of Words

Struggling readers need to know more words.

One of the biggest challenges facing struggling readers is their limited word knowledge. Even though independent reading is an important way most students acquire a large vocabulary, it isn't enough for struggling students (Allington, 2006). Students who exhibit reading difficulties don't do as much reading as their classmates, and the books they read don't introduce them to grade-level vocabulary words. To expand students' vocabularies, it's essential that teachers provide both daily activities to draw students' attention to words and instruction on academic vocabulary and word-learning strategies. Cooper, Chard, and Kiger (2006) offer these instructional recommendations:

- *Nurture students' awareness of words using word walls, independent reading, and interactive read-alouds.*
- *Explicitly teach the meanings of 8–10 words each week by introducing key words before reading and providing worthwhile practice activities afterward.*
- *Develop students' ability to figure out the meaning of unfamiliar words.*

Teachers can accelerate students' vocabulary development by implementing a more-structured program with daily lessons based on these recommendations.

Sometimes teachers thwart students' vocabulary development. Allington (2006) identified three activities that waste instructional time: First, students shouldn't read books that are too difficult because they won't understand what they're reading. Next, teachers can't expect students to figure out the meaning of unfamiliar words when they're reading if they haven't been taught to use context clues or other word-learning strategies. Third, students shouldn't be given a list of words and asked to copy the definition for each word or write a sentence using it. These activities aren't recommended because they don't develop students' in-depth word knowledge.

Independent Reading
This third grader spends 30 minutes each day reading books she chooses herself from the classroom library. The books are interesting and appropriate for her reading level. So far this year, she's read 17 books! As she and her classmates read, they learn the meanings of hundreds of new words and additional meanings for familiar words incidentally. In addition, the third graders become more engaged in reading and feel their confidence soar. Students who participate in reading workshop, SSR, or another independent reading activity every day are more likely to become successful readers.

informational books. Daily read-aloud activities are important for students at all grade levels, kindergarten through eighth grade. Teachers use the interactive read-aloud procedure and focus on a few key words in the book, model how to use context clues to understand new words, and talk about the words after reading. Teachers use think-alouds when they model using context clues and other word-identification strategies. Two recent studies found that teachers enhance students' vocabulary knowledge and their comprehension when they add a focus on vocabulary to their read-alouds (Fisher, Frey, & Lapp, 2008; Santoro, Chard, Howard, & Baker, 2008).

Cunningham (2009) recommends that primary-grade teachers choose one picture book each week to read aloud and teach key vocabulary. Teachers read the book aloud one time and then present three new words from the book, each written on a word card. During the second reading, students listen for the words, and the teacher takes time to talk about each word's meaning using information available in the text and in the illustrations. Later, the teacher encourages students to practice using the new words when they talk and write about the book.

Although reading aloud is important for all students, it's especially important for struggling readers who typically read fewer books themselves, and because the books at their reading level have less sophisticated vocabulary words. In fact, researchers report that students learn as many words incidentally while listening to teachers read aloud as they do by reading themselves (Stahl, Richek, & Vandevier, 1991).

Why Is Vocabulary Knowledge Important?

Vocabulary knowledge and reading achievement are closely related: Students with larger vocabularies are more capable readers, and they know more strategies for figuring out the meanings of unfamiliar words than less capable readers do (Graves, 2006). Reading widely is the best way students learn new words, and that's one reason why capable readers have larger vocabularies: They simply do more reading, both in school and out of school.

The idea that capable readers learn more vocabulary because they read more is an example of the Matthew effect (Stanovich, 1986), which suggests that "the rich get richer and the poor get poorer" in vocabulary development and other components of reading. Capable readers become better readers because they read more, and the books they read are more challenging, with sophisticated vocabulary words. The gulf between more capable and less capable readers grows larger because less capable readers read less and the books they read aren't as challenging.

EACHING STUDENTS TO UNLOCK WORD MEANINGS

Vocabulary instruction plays an important role in balanced literacy classrooms. Baumann, Kame'enui, and Ash (2003) and Graves (2006) identified these components of vocabulary instruction:

- Immerse students in words through listening, talking, reading, and writing
- Teach specific words through active involvement and multiple encounters with words
- Teach word-learning strategies so students can figure out the meanings of unfamiliar words
- Develop students' word consciousness, their awareness of and interest in words

Teachers address all of these components when they teach vocabulary. Too often, vocabulary instruction has emphasized only the second component, teaching specific words, without considering how to develop students' ability to learn words

Guidelines
for Teaching Vocabulary

▶ Choose key words for vocabulary instruction from books students are reading and from thematic units and highlight them on word walls.

▶ Engage students in word-study activities, such as word posters, word maps, and word sorts, so they can deepen their understanding of specific words.

▶ Teach minilessons about the meanings of individual words, vocabulary concepts, and word-learning strategies.

▶ Scaffold students as they develop full word knowledge by learning multiple meanings, how root words and affixes affect meaning, synonyms, antonyms, word histories, and figurative meanings.

▶ During interactive read-alouds, focus on specific high-utility words.

▶ Teach students to use word-learning strategies to unlock new words.

▶ Develop students' word consciousness by demonstrating curiosity about words, teaching students about words, and involving them in wordplay activities.

▶ Provide daily opportunities for students to read independently—at least 15–30 minutes in grades 1–3 and 30–60 minutes in grades 4–8.

independently and use them effectively. The feature on the preceding page lists guidelines for teaching vocabulary.

Word-Study Concepts

It's not enough to have students memorize one definition of a word; to develop full word knowledge, they need to learn more about a word (Stahl & Nagy, 2006). Consider the word *brave*: It can be used as an adjective, a noun, or a verb. It often means "showing no fear," but it can also mean an "American Indian warrior" or "to challenge or defy." These forms are related to the first meaning: *braver, bravest, bravely*, and *bravery*. Synonyms related to the first meaning include *courageous, bold, fearless, daring, intrepid, heroic*, and *valiant*; antonyms include *cowardly* and *frightened*. Our word *brave* comes from the Italian word *bravo*. Interestingly, the Italian word *bravo* and a related form—*bravissimo*—have entered English directly, and they're used to express great approval; these words mean "excellent," an obsolete meaning of *brave*. In addition, there's *bravado*, a Spanish word that means "a pretense of courage." As students learn some of this information about *brave*, they're better able to understand the word and use it orally and in writing.

As students learn about a word, they acquire a wide range of information. They learn one or more meanings for a word and synonyms and antonyms to compare and contrast meanings. Sometimes they confuse a word they're learning with a homonym that sounds or is spelled the same. Students also learn about idioms and figurative sayings that make our language more colorful. A seventh grader's investigation of the word *vaporize* is shown in Figure 7–1.

Multiple Meanings of Words. Many words have more than one meaning. For some words, multiple meanings develop for the noun and verb forms, but sometimes additional meanings develop in other ways. The word *bank*, for example, has these meanings:

> a piled-up mass of snow or clouds
> the slope of land beside a lake or river
> the slope of a road on a turn
> the lateral tilting of an airplane in a turn
> to cover a fire with ashes for slow burning
> a business establishment that receives and lends money
> a container in which money is saved
> a supply for use in emergencies (e.g., a blood bank)
> a place for storage (e.g., a computer's memory bank)
> to count on
> similar things arranged in a row (e.g., a bank of elevators)
> to arrange things in a row

You may be surprised that there are at least a dozen meanings for this common word. Some are nouns and others are verbs, but grammatical form alone doesn't account for so many meanings.

The meanings of *bank* come from three sources. The first five meanings come from a Viking word, and they're related because they all deal with something slanted or making a slanted motion. The next five come from the Italian word *banca*, a money changer's table. These meanings deal with financial banking except for the 10th

Figure 7–1 ◆ A Seventh Grader's Investigation of *Vaporize*

Morphemic Analysis	Root Word	Suffix
vapor + ize	vapor	ize It is used to change a noun into a verb.

VAPORIZE

To change from a solid into a vapor (gas) (verb)

Word History	Related Words	Figurative Use
It became a word in the 1600's. It came from the Latin word "steam".	evaporate vaporizer vaporous	The boy's thoughts vaporized and he couldn't remember the answer.

meaning, "to count on," which requires a bit more thought. We use the saying "to bank on" figuratively to mean "to depend on," but it began more literally from the actual counting of money on a table. The last two meanings come from the French word *banc*, meaning "bench." Words acquired multiple meanings as society became more complex and finer shades of meaning were necessary; for example, the meanings of *bank* as an emergency supply and a storage place are fairly new. As with many words with multiple meanings, it's just a linguistic accident that three original words from different languages with related meanings came to be spelled the same way (Tompkins & Yaden, 1986). A list of other common words with more than five meanings is shown in Figure 7–2.

Students gradually acquire additional meanings for words, and they usually learn these new meanings through reading. When a familiar word is used in a new way, students often notice the new application and may be curious enough to check the meaning in a dictionary.

Synonyms: Words With the Same Meaning. Words that have nearly the same meaning as other words are *synonyms*. English has so many synonyms because numerous words have been borrowed from other languages. Synonyms are useful because they're more precise. Think of all the synonyms for the word *cold: cool, chilly, frigid, icy, frosty*, and *freezing*. Each word has a different shade of meaning: *Cool* means moderately cold; *chilly* is uncomfortably cold; *frigid* is intensely cold; *icy* means very cold; *frosty* means covered with frost; and *freezing* is so cold that water changes into ice. English would be limited if we had only the word *cold*.

Teachers should carefully articulate the differences among synonyms. Nagy (1988) emphasizes that teachers should focus on teaching concepts and related words, not just provide single-word definitions using synonyms. For example, to tell a student that *frigid* means *cold* provides only limited information. And, when a student says, "I want my sweater because it's frigid in here," it shows that he or she doesn't understand the different degrees of cold; there's a big difference between *chilly* and *frigid*.

Antonyms: Words That Mean the Opposite. Words that express opposite meanings are *antonyms*. For the word *loud*, some antonyms are *soft, subdued, quiet, silent, inaudible, sedate, somber, dull,* and *colorless*. These antonyms express shades of meaning just as synonyms do, and some opposites are more appropriate for one meaning of *loud* than for another. When *loud* means *gaudy*, for instance, antonyms are *somber, dull,* and *colorless*; when *loud* means *noisy*, the opposites are *quiet, silent,* and *inaudible*.

Students learn to use a thesaurus to locate both synonyms and antonyms. *A First Thesaurus* (Wittels, 2001), *Scholastic Children's Thesaurus* (Bollard, 2006), and *The American Heritage Children's Thesaurus* (Hellweg, 2006) are three excellent reference books. Students need to learn how to use these handy references to locate more-effective words when they're revising their writing and during word-study activities.

Homonyms: Words That Confuse. Homonyms are confusing because even though these words have different meanings, they're either pronounced the same or spelled the same as other words. Homophones are words that sound alike but are spelled differently, such as *right–write, air–heir, to–too–two,* and *there–their–they're*. A list of homophones is presented in Figure 7–3. Sometimes students confuse the meanings of

Figure 7–2 ◆ Common Words With More Than Five Meanings

act	drive	lay	place	set	strike
air	dry	leave	plant	sharp	stroke
away	dull	line	plate	shine	strong
bad	eye	low	play	shoot	stuff
bar	face	make	point	short	sweep
base	fail	man	post	side	sweet
black	fair	mark	print	sight	swing
blow	fall	mind	quiet	sign	take
boat	fast	mine	rain	sing	thick
break	fire	natural	raise	sink	thing
carry	fly	new	range	slip	think
case	good	nose	rear	small	throw
catch	green	note	rest	sound	tie
change	hand	now	return	spin	tight
charge	have	off	rich	spread	time
check	head	open	ride	spring	touch
clear	heel	out	right	square	tough
color	high	paper	ring	stamp	train
count	hold	part	rise	star	trip
cover	hot	pass	roll	stay	turn
crack	house	pay	rule	step	under
cross	keep	pick	run	stick	up
crown	key	picture	scale	stiff	watch
cut	knock	piece	score	stock	way
draw	know	pitch	serve	stop	wear

these words, but more often they confuse their spellings. Most homophones are linguistic accidents, but *stationary* and *stationery* share an interesting history: *Stationery*, meaning paper and books, developed from *stationary*. In medieval England, merchants traveled from town to town selling their wares. The merchant who sold paper goods was the first to set up shop in one town. His shop was "stationary" because it didn't move, and he came to be the "stationer." The spelling difference between the two words signifies the semantic difference. In contrast, words with identical spellings but different meanings and pronunciations, such as the noun and verb forms of *wind* and the noun and adjective forms of *minute*, are homographs. Other examples include *live, read, bow, conduct, present,* and *record*.

There are many books of homonyms designed for children, including Gwynne's *The King Who Rained* (2006) and *A Chocolate Moose for Dinner* (2005), Barretta's *Dear Deer: A Book of Homophones* (2007), *The Dove Dove: Funny Homograph Riddles* (Terban, 1992), and *Eight Ate: A Feast of Homonym Riddles* (Terban, 2007a). Sharing these books with students helps to develop their understanding of homophones and homographs.

Figure 7–3 ◆ Homophones, Words That Sound Alike But Are Spelled Differently

air–heir	creak–creek	hour–our	peace–piece	shoot–chute
allowed–aloud	days–daze	knead–need	peak–peek–pique	side–sighed
ant–aunt	dear–deer	knew–new	peal–peel	slay–sleigh
ate–eight	dew–do–due	knight–night	pedal–peddle–petal	soar–sore
ball–bawl	die–dye	knot–not	plain–plane	soared–sword
bare–bear	doe–dough	know–no	pleas–please	sole–soul
be–bee	ewe–you	lead–led	pole–poll	some–sum
beat–beet	eye–I	leak–leek	poor–pore–pour	son–sun
berry–bury	fair–fare	lie–lye	praise–prays–preys	stairs–stares
billed–build	feat–feet	loan–lone	presence–presents	stake–steak
blew–blue	fined–find	made–maid	pride–pried	stationary–stationery
boar–bore	fir–fur	mail–male	prince–prints	steal–steel
board–bored	flair–flare	main–mane	principal–principle	straight–strait
bough–bow	flea–flee	manner–manor	profit–prophet	suite–sweet
brake–break	flew–flu	marshal–martial	quarts–quartz	tail–tale
brews–bruise	flour–flower	meat–meet–mete	rain–reign–rein	taught–taut
bridal–bridle	for–fore–four	medal–meddle–metal	raise–rays–raze	tear–tier
brows–browse	forth–fourth	might–mite	rap–wrap	their–there–they're
buy–by–bye	foul–fowl	mind–mined	red–read	threw–through
capital–capitol	gorilla–guerrilla	miner–minor	reed–read	throne–thrown
ceiling–sealing	grate–great	missed–mist	right–rite–write	tide–tied
cell–sell	grill–grille	moan–mown	ring–wring	to–too–tow
cellar–seller	groan–grown	morning–mourning	road–rode–rowed	toad–toed–towed
cent–scent–sent	guessed–guest	muscle–mussel	role–roll	toe–tow
chews–choose	hair–hare	naval–navel	root–route	troop–troupe
chic–sheik	hall–haul	none–nun	rose–rows	vain–vane–vein
chili–chilly	hay–hey	oar–or–ore	rung–wrung	wade–weighed
choral–coral	heal–heel	one–won	sail–sale	waist–waste
chord–cord–cored	hear–here	pail–pale	scene–seen	wait–weight
cite–sight–site	heard–herd	pain–pane	sea–see	wares–wears
close–clothes	hi–high	pair–pare–pear	seam–seem	way–weigh
coarse–course	hoarse–horse	passed–past	serf–surf	weak–week
colonel–kernel	hole–whole	patience–patients	sew–so–sow	wood–would

Figure 7–4 ◆ A Sixth Grader's Homophone Poster

Primary-grade teachers introduce homonyms and teach the easier pairs, including *see–sea*, *I–eye*, *right–write*, and *dear–deer*. In the upper grades, teachers focus on homographs and the homophones that students continue to confuse, such as *there–their–they're* and the more-sophisticated pairs, including *morning–mourning*, *flair–flare*, and *complement–compliment*. Teachers teach minilessons to explain the concept of homophones and homographs and have students make charts of the homophones and homographs; calling students' attention to the differences in spelling, meaning, and pronunciation helps to clarify the words. This explicit instruction is especially important for English learners (Jacobson, Lapp, & Flood, 2007). Students can also make homonym posters, as shown in Figure 7–4. On the posters, students draw pictures and write sentences to contrast homophones and homographs. Displaying these posters in the classroom reminds students of the differences between the words.

Etymologies: The History of the English Language. Glimpses into the history of the English language provide interesting information about word meanings and spellings (Tompkins & Yaden, 1986). The English language began in A.D. 447 when Angles, Saxons, and other Germanic tribes invaded England. This Anglo-Saxon English was first written down by Latin missionaries in approximately A.D. 750. The English of the period from 450 to 1100 is known as Old English. During this time, English was a very phonetic language and followed many German syntactic patterns. Many loan words, including *ugly*, *window*, *egg*, *they*, *sky*, and *husband*, were contributed by the marauding Vikings who plundered villages along the English coast.

Middle English (1100–1500) began with the Norman Conquest in 1066. William, Duke of Normandy, invaded England and became the English king. William, his lords, and the royals who accompanied him spoke French, so it became the official language of England for nearly 200 years. Many French loan words were added to the language, and French spellings were substituted for Old English spellings. For example, *night* was spelled *niht* and *queen* was spelled *cwen* in Old English to reflect how they were pronounced; their modern spellings reflect changes made by French scribes. Loan words from Dutch, Latin, and other languages were added to English during this period, too.

The invention of the printing press marks the transition from Middle English to Modern English (1500–present). William Caxton brought the first printing press to England in 1476, and soon books and pamphlets were being mass-produced. Spelling became standardized as Samuel Johnson and other lexicographers compiled dictionaries, even though English pronunciation of words continued to evolve. Loan words continued to flow into English from almost every language in the world. Exploration and colonization in North America and around the world accounted for many of the loan words. For example, *canoe* and *moccasin* are from Native American languages; *bonanza*, *chocolate*, and *ranch* are from Mexican Spanish; and *cafeteria*, *prairie*, and *teenager* are American English. Other loan words include *zero* (Arabic), *tattoo* (Polynesian), *robot* (Czech), *yogurt* (Turkish), *restaurant* (French), *dollar* (German), *jungle* (Hindi), and *umbrella* (Italian). Some words, such as *electric*, *democracy*, and *astronaut*, were created using Greek word parts. New words continue to be added to English every year, and these words reflect new inventions and cultural practices. Many new words today, such as *e-mail*, relate to the Internet. The word *Internet* is a recent word, too; it's less than 25 years old!

Students use etymological information in dictionaries to learn how particular words evolved and what the words mean. Etymological information is included in brackets at the beginning or end of dictionary entries. Here's the etymological information for three words:

> *democracy [1576, < MF < LL < Gr demokratia, demos (people) + kratia (cracy = strength, power)]*

The etymological information explains that the word *democracy* entered English in 1576 through French, and the French word came from Latin and before that Greek. In Greek, the word *demokratia* means "power to the people."

> *house [bef. 900, ME hous, OE hus]*

According to the etymological information, *house* is an Old English word that entered English before 900. It was spelled *hus* in Old English and *hous* in Middle English.

> *moose [1603, < Algonquin, "he who strips bark"]*

The etymological information explains that the word *moose* is Native American—from an Algonquin tribe in the northeastern United States—and entered English in 1603. It comes from the Algonquin word for "he who strips bark."

Even though words have entered English from around the world, the three main sources of words are English, Latin, and Greek. Upper-grade students can learn to identify the languages that these words came from; knowing the language backgrounds helps students to predict the spellings and meanings (Venezky, 1999). English words are usually one- or two-syllable common words that may or may not be phonetically regular, such as *fox*, *arm*, *Monday*, *house*, *match*, *eleven*, *of*, *come*, *week*, *horse*, *brother*, and *dumb*. Words with *ch* (pronounced as /ch/), *sh*, *th*, and *wh* digraphs are usually English, as in *church*, *shell*, *bath*, and *what*. Many English words are compound words or use comparative and superlative forms, such as *starfish*, *toothache*, *fireplace*, *happier*, *fastest*.

Many words from Latin are similar to comparable words in French, Spanish, or Italian, such as *ancient, judicial, impossible,* and *officer.* Latin words have related words or derivatives, such as *courage, courageous, encourage, discourage,* and *encouragement.* Also, many Latin words have *-tion/-sion* suffixes: *imitation, corruption, attention, extension,* and *possession.*

Greek words are the most unusual. Many are long words, and their spellings seem unfamiliar. The digraph *ph* is pronounced /f/, and the digraph *ch* is pronounced /k/ in Greek loan words, as in *autograph, chaos,* and *architect.* Longer words with *th,* such as *thermometer* and *arithmetic,* are Greek. The suffix *-ology* is Greek, as in the words *biology, psychology,* and *geology.* The letter *y* is used in place of *i* in the middle of some words, such as *bicycle* and *myth.* Many Greek words are composed of two parts: *bibliotherapy, microscope, biosphere, hypodermic,* and *telephone.* Figure 7–5 presents lists of words from English, Latin, and Greek that teachers can use for **word sorts** and other vocabulary activities.

Conceptually related words have developed from English, Latin, and Greek sources. Consider the words *tooth, dentist,* and *orthodontist. Tooth* is an English word, which explains its irregular plural form, *teeth. Dentist* is a Latin word; *dent* means "tooth" in Latin, and the suffix *-ist* means "one who does." The word *orthodontist* is Greek. *Ortho* means "straighten" and *dont* means "tooth"; therefore, *orthodontist*

Figure 7–5 ◆ Words From English, Latin, and Greek

English	Latin	Greek
apple	addiction	ache
between	administer	arithmetic
bumblebee	advantage	astronomy
child	beautiful	atomic
cry	capital	biology
cuff	confession	chaos
earth	continent	chemical
fireplace	delicate	democracy
fourteen	discourage	disaster
freedom	erupt	elephant
Friday	explosion	geography
get	fraction	gymnastics
have	fragile	helicopter
horse	frequently	hemisphere
knight	heir	hieroglyphics
know	honest	kaleidoscope
ladybug	identify	myth
lamb	January	octopus
lip	journal	phenomenal
lock	junior	photosynthesis
mouth	nation	pseudonym
out	occupy	rhinoceros
quickly	organize	rhythm
ride	principal	sympathy
silly	procession	telescope
this	salute	theater
twin	special	thermometer
weather	uniform	trophy
whisper	vacation	zodiac
wild	vegetable	zoo

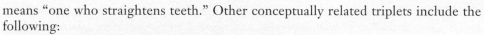

means "one who straightens teeth." Other conceptually related triplets include the following:

book: bookstore (E), bibliography (Gr), library (L)
eye: eyelash (E), optical (Gr), binoculars (L)
foot: foot-dragging (E), tripod (Gr), pedestrian (L)
great: greatest (E), megaphone (Gr), magnificent (L)
see: foresee (E), microscope (Gr), invisible (L)
star: starry (E), astronaut (Gr), constellation (L)
time: time-tested (E), chronological (Gr), contemporary (L)
water: watermelon (E), hydrate (Gr), aquarium (L)

When students understand English, Latin, and Greek root words, they appreciate the relationships among words and their meanings.

Figurative Meanings of Words. Many words have both literal and figurative meanings: Literal meanings are the explicit, dictionary meanings, and figurative meanings are metaphorical or use figures of speech. For example, to describe *winter* as the coldest season of the year is literal, but to say that "winter has icy breath" is figurative. Two types of figurative language are idioms and comparisons.

Idioms are groups of words, such as "in hot water," that have a special meaning. Idioms can be confusing because they must be interpreted figuratively. "In hot water" is an old expression meaning "to be in trouble." In the Middle Ages, people had to protect themselves from robbers. When a robber tried to break into a house, the homeowner might pour boiling water from a second-floor window onto the head of the robber, who would then be "in hot water." There are hundreds of idioms in English, which we use every day to create word pictures that make language more colorful. Some examples are "out in left field," "a skeleton in the closet," "raining cats and dogs," and "a chip off the old block." A variety of books that explain idioms are available for students to examine, including the *Scholastic Dictionary of Idioms* (Terban, 2006), *Mad as a Wet Hen!: And Other Funny Idioms* (Terban, 2007c), *In a Pickle and Other Funny Idioms* (Terban, 2007b), *My Teacher Likes to Say* (Brennan–Nelson, 2004), and *There's a Frog in My Throat! 440 Animal Sayings a Little Bird Told Me* (Leedy, 2003).

Because idioms are figurative sayings, many students—and especially those who are English learners—have difficulty understanding them (Palmer, Shackelford, Miller, & Leclere, 2006/2007). It's crucial that teachers provide explicit instruction so that students move beyond the literal meanings of phrases. One way to help students learn about figurative language is to have them create idiom posters showing both literal and figurative meanings, as illustrated in Figure 7–6.

Metaphors and similes are comparisons that liken something to something else. A simile is a comparison signaled by the use of *like* or *as*: "The crowd was as rowdy as a bunch of marauding monkeys" and "My apartment was like an oven after the air-conditioning broke" are two examples. In contrast, a metaphor compares two things by implying that one is the other, without using *like* or *as*: "The children were frisky puppies playing in the yard" is an example. Metaphors are stronger comparisons, as these examples show:

She's as cool as a cucumber.
She's a cool cucumber.

In the moonlight, the dead tree looked like a skeleton.
In the moonlight, the dead tree was a skeleton.

Differentiating between the terms *simile* and *metaphor* is less important than understanding the meaning of comparisons in books students read and having students use comparisons to make their writing more vivid. For example, a sixth-grade student

Figure 7–6 ◆ A Sixth Grader's Idiom Poster for "In Hot Water"

compared anger to a thunderstorm using a simile. She wrote, "Anger is like a thunderstorm, screaming with thunder-feelings and lightning-words." Another student compared anger to a volcano. Using a metaphor, he wrote, "Anger is a volcano, erupting with poisonous words and hot-lava actions."

Students begin by learning traditional comparisons such as "happy as a clam" and "high as a kite," and then they learn to notice and invent fresh, unexpected comparisons. To introduce traditional comparisons to young children, teachers often use Audrey Wood's *Quick as a Cricket* (1982). Middle- and upper-grade students can invent new comparisons for stale expressions such as "butterflies in your stomach." In *Anastasia Krupnik* (1984), for example, Lois Lowry substituted "ginger ale in her knees" for the trite "butterflies in her stomach" to describe how nervous Anastasia felt when she stood in front of the class to read her poem.

Words to Study

Teachers highlight many words related to literature focus units and thematic units. They post these words on word walls, use many of them in word-study activities, and carefully choose some to teach directly. Teachers choose words that are essential to understanding the book or the unit, words that confuse students, and general-utility words students will use as they read other books or study other topics. Teachers should avoid words that aren't related to the book or unit and words that are too conceptually difficult for students understand.

Teachers are usually relieved to learn that students don't have to know all of the words in a book to read and comprehend it or listen to it read aloud. Of course, students vary in the number of unfamiliar words they can tolerate, depending on the topic of the book, their purpose for reading or listening, and the role of the unfamiliar words. It's unrealistic to assume that students will learn every word in a book or expect to teach every word.

Choosing Words to Study. It's impossible for teachers to teach all of the unfamiliar words that students come across in books they're reading or about topics they're studying during thematic units. Beck, McKeown, and Kucan (2002) have devised a tool to assist teachers in choosing which words to study. The researchers divide vocabulary words into three tiers or levels, and recommend that teachers focus on the words in the second tier:

Tier 1: Basic Words. These common words are used socially, in informal conversation at home and on the playground. Examples include *animal, clean,* and *laughing.* Native English-speaking students rarely require instruction about the meanings of these words.

Tier 2: Academic Words. These words are used more frequently in writing than in oral language, and students should learn their meanings because they have wide application across the curriculum. Students often understand the general concept represented by the word, but they don't recognize the specific word. Adding these words to their vocabulary allows them to express ideas more precisely. Examples include *community, evidence,* and *greedy.* Teaching these words has a powerful impact on students' vocabulary development.

Tier 3: Specialized Words. These technical words are content-specific and abstract. Examples include *minuend, osmosis,* and *suffrage.* They aren't used frequently enough to devote time to teaching them except as part of thematic units.

As teachers choose words for instruction and word-study activities, they focus on Tier 2 words even though words representing all three levels are written on word walls. During a fifth-grade unit on America in the 20th century, students learned to sing Woody Guthrie's folk ballad "This Land Is Your Land" (Guthrie, 1998) and then read Bonnie Christensen's biography, *Woody Guthrie: Poet of the People* (2001). The fifth graders created a word wall that included these words about Woody Guthrie:

ballads	*Great Depression*	*nightmare*	*spirit*
celebrate	*guitar*	*ordinary*	*stock market*
criss-cross	*hardship*	*original*	*tragedy*
depression	*harmonica*	*rallies*	*unfair*
desperate	*hitchhiked*	*restless*	*unions*
devastated	*lonesome*	*scorn*	*unsanitary*
drought	*migrant*	*severe*	*wandering*
Dust Bowl	*migration*	*sorrow*	*worries*

From this list, their teacher identified some words from the word wall as Tier 1, 2, and 3 words:

Tier 1 words: *guitar, harmonica, worries, nightmare, unfair, celebrates*

Tier 2 words: *ordinary, spirit, desperate, original, sorrow, tragedy*

Tier 3 words: *drought, Dust Bowl, stock market, Great Depression, unions, unsanitary*

There was only one Tier 1 word that needed to be taught: Not all the students knew what a harmonica was, so the teacher invited a friend who played the instrument to visit the classroom and play the harmonica. He focused on teaching Tier 2 words, and the students connected each word to Woody Guthrie and other American icons they'd studied. Because this was a social studies unit, the students read in their social studies textbooks about the Great Depression and learned some of the Tier 3 words.

Spotlighting Words on Word Walls. Teachers post word walls in the classroom; usually they're made from large sheets of butcher paper and divided into sections for each letter of the alphabet. Students and the teacher write interesting, confusing, and important words representing all three tiers on the word wall. Usually students choose the words to write on the word wall and may even do the writing themselves. Teachers add other important words that students haven't chosen. Words are added to the word wall as they come up in books students are reading or during a thematic unit, not in advance. Janet Allen (2007) says that word walls should be "a living part of the classroom with new words being added each day" (p. 120). Word walls are useful resources: Students locate words on the word wall that they want to use during a grand conversation or check the spelling of a word they're writing, and teachers use the words for word-study activities.

Some teachers use large pocket charts and word cards instead of butcher paper for their word walls. This way, the word cards can easily be used for word-study activities, and they can be sorted and rearranged on the pocket chart. After the book or unit is completed, teachers punch holes in one end of the cards and hang them on a ring. Then the collection of word cards can be placed in the writing center for students to use when they're writing.

Students also make individual word walls by dividing a sheet of paper into 20–24 boxes and labeling the boxes with the letters of the alphabet; they can put several letters together in one box. Then students write important words and phrases in the boxes as they read and discuss a book. Figure 7–7 shows a sixth grader's word wall for *Hatchet* (2007), a wilderness survival story by Gary Paulsen.

Figure 7–7 ◆ A Sixth Grader's Alphabetized Word Wall for *Hatchet*

A	B	C	D
alone	bush plane	Canadian wilderness	divorce
absolutely terrified	Brian Robeson	controls	desperation
arrows	bruised	cockpit	destroyed
aluminum cookset	bow & arrow	crash	disappointment
		careless	devastating
		campsite	
E	**F**	**G**	**H**
engine	fire	gut cherries	hatchet
emergency	fuselage	get food	heart attack
emptiness	fish		hunger
exhaustion	foolbirds		hope
	foodshelf		
	54 days		
I J	**K L**	**M N**	**O P Q**
instruments	lake	memory	pilot
insane		mosquitoes	panic
incredible wealth		mistakes	painful
		matches	porcupine quills
		mental journal	patience
		moose	
R	**S T**	**U V**	**W X Y Z**
rudder pedals	stranded	visitation rights	wilderness
rescue	secret	viciously thirsty	windbreaker
radio	survival pack	valuable asset	wreck
relative comfort	search	vicious whine	woodpile
raspberries	sleeping bag	unbelievable riches	wolf
roaring bonfire	shelter		
raft	starved		

Even though 25, 50, or more words may be added to the word wall, not all of them are explicitly taught. As they plan, teachers create lists of words that will probably be written on word walls during the unit. From this list, teachers choose the words—usually Tier 2 words that are critical to understanding the book or the unit—and these are the words they teach.

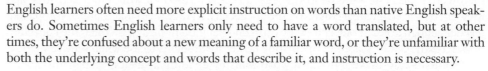

Nurturing English Learners

English learners often need more explicit instruction on words than native English speakers do. Sometimes English learners only need to have a word translated, but at other times, they're confused about a new meaning of a familiar word, or they're unfamiliar with both the underlying concept and words that describe it, and instruction is necessary.

Tier 1 Words. Tier 1 words are easier for English learners to learn because they often know these words in their native language; what they don't know are the equivalent English words. If teachers speak students' native language, they can translate the words and help students learn these English equivalents. English-speaking teachers often use pictures, pantomime, and demonstration to explain the words. It's often helpful for teachers to put together collections of small objects and pictures to share with students during literature focus units and thematic units.

Tier 2 Words. To build background knowledge, teachers preteach some unfamiliar words, including essential Tier 2 words, before students read a book or study a topic. Later, through explicit instruction and a variety of word-study activities, they teach other Tier 2 words. In addition, Calderon (2007) points out that ELs need to understand transition words and phrases, words with multiple meanings, and English words with cognates. Transition words, such as *consequently, yet, likewise, against, meanwhile, afterward*, and *finally*, are used to bridge ideas in sentences, paragraphs, and longer texts. Teachers can help ELs recognize these words and phrases, understand their meaning, and use them in their own writing.

Learning new meanings for familiar words is another Tier 2 activity. Some common words, such as *key, soft*, and *ready*, have less frequently used meanings that confuse English learners even though they're usually familiar with one or two of the meanings. Students also learn how to choose among related words. For example, *instrument* means a device for doing work; *tool* and *utensil* are also devices for doing work, but they don't mean exactly the same thing. *Instruments*, such as stethoscopes and scalpels, are used for doing complicated work; *tools*, such as hammers and screwdrivers, are used for skilled jobs, and *utensils* are simple devices, such as whisks and spoons, for working in the kitchen. Teachers also point out cognates, English words that are related to words in students' native language. Many Tier 2 words are Latin-based, so it's important to teach English learners who speak Spanish, Portuguese, Italian, and French to ask themselves whether an unfamiliar word is similar to a word in their native language.

Tier 3 Words. It's less important to teach these technical words because of their limited usefulness, and only a few words have cognates that students would know. Calderon (2007) recommends that teachers translate the words or briefly explain them. However, during thematic units, teachers do teach Tier 3 words that are important to understanding the big ideas being studied through a combination of instruction and word-study activities, including making word posters, doing **word sorts**, and completing **semantic feature analyses**.

Teaching Students About Words

Teachers explicitly teach students about specific words, usually Tier 2 words. McKeown and Beck (2004) emphasize that instruction should be rich, deep, and extended. That means that teachers provide multiple encounters with words; present a variety of information, including definitions, contexts, examples, and related words; and involve students in word-study activities so that they have multiple opportunities to interact with words. The procedure is time-consuming, but researchers report that students are more successful in learning and remembering word meanings this way (Beck, McKeown, & Kucan, 2002).

As teachers plan for instruction, they need to consider what students already know about a word. Sometimes the word is unfamiliar, or it represents a new concept. At other times, the word is familiar and students know one meaning, but they need to learn a new meaning. A word representing an unfamiliar concept usually takes the most time to teach, and a new meaning for a familiar word, the least.

Teachers use minilessons to teach students about specific words. They provide information about words, including both definitions and contextual information, and they engage students in activities to get them to think about and use words orally and in reading and writing. Sometimes teachers present minilessons before reading; at other times, they teach them after reading. The minilesson on page 242 shows how one teacher introduces vocabulary before reading a chapter in a content-area textbook.

Word-Study Activities

Students have opportunities to examine words and think more deeply about them as they participate in word-study activities (Allen, 2007). In some activities, they create visual representations of words, and in others, they categorize words or learn related words. Here's a list of word-study activities:

Word Posters. Students choose a word and write it on a small poster; then they draw and color a picture to illustrate it. They also use the word in a sentence on the poster. This is one way that students visualize the meaning of a word.

Word Maps. Students create a diagram to examine a word they're learning. They write the word, make a box around it, draw several lines from the box, and add information about the word in additional boxes they make at the end of each line. Three kinds of information typically included in a word map are a category for the word, examples, and characteristics or associations. Figure 7–8 shows a word map made by a fifth grader reading *Bunnicula: A Rabbit-Tale of Mystery* (Howe & Howe, 2006). Word maps are another way to visualize a word's meaning (Duffelmeyer & Banwart, 1992–1993).

Possible Sentences. To activate students' background knowledge about a topic and increase their curiosity before reading a book or a chapter in a content-area textbook, students write possible sentences using vocabulary words (Stahl & Kapinus, 1991). After reviewing the definitions of a set of 10 words, students work with classmates

Literacy Portraits: VIEWING GUIDE

The second graders in Ms. Janusz's class vary widely in their vocabulary knowledge. Some children have limited background knowledge and words to express ideas, but others are interested in many topics and know lots of words. Click on Jimmy's February button in the Literacy Profiles section of MyEducationLab at www.myeducationlab.com to watch a conference Ms. Janusz holds with him about a book he's reading during reading workshop. This informational book is about presidential elections. As they talk about the book, Jimmy uses sophisticated and technical vocabulary, including *democracy, electoral votes, snickering,* and *campaign slogan,* to discuss what he's learned. Most second graders aren't familiar with these concepts and don't use these words. How do you think Jimmy learned them? How does Ms. Janusz support his learning? Does his vocabulary knowledge correlate with his literacy level?

myeducationlab

Minilesson

TOPIC: Introducing Content-Area Vocabulary Words
GRADE: Fifth Grade
TIME: Three 30-minute periods

Mrs. Cramer's fifth-grade class is involved in a social studies unit on immigration. The class has already created a K-W-L chart on immigration to activate students' background knowledge, and students have written about how and when their families came to the United States. They've also marked their countries of origin on a world map in the classroom. In this 3-day minilesson, Mrs. Cramer introduces six key vocabulary words before students read a chapter in their social studies textbook. Because many of her students are English learners, she takes more time to practice vocabulary before reading the chapter.

❶ Introduce the Topic

Mrs. Cramer explains that after a week of studying immigration, the fifth graders are now getting ready to read the chapter about immigration in the social studies text. She places these five words written on word cards in a pocket chart and reads each one aloud: *culture, descendant, immigrant, prejudice,* and *pluralism.* She tells students that these words are used in the chapter and that it's important to be familiar with them before reading.

❷ Share Examples

Mrs. Cramer distributes anticipation guides for students to rate their knowledge of the new words. The guide has four columns; the new words are listed in the left column, and the other three columns have these headings: I know the word well, I've heard of it, I don't know this word. For each word, the students put a checkmark in the appropriate column. At the end of the unit, they'll again rate their knowledge of the words and compare the two ratings to assess their learning.

❸ Provide Information

Mrs. Cramer divides the students into small groups for a word sort. Each group receives a pack of 10 cards; the new vocabulary words are written on five of the cards and their definitions on the other cards. Students work together to match the words and definitions, and then Mrs. Cramer reviews the meaning of each word.

❹ Guide Practice

The next day, the students repeat the word sort activity to review the meanings of the words. Next, they work with partners to complete a cloze activity: Mrs. Cramer has prepared a list of sentences taken from the chapter with the new words omitted, and students write the correct word in each blank. Then she reviews the sentences, explaining any sentences completed incorrectly.

❺ Assess Learning

On the third day, Mrs. Cramer adds the new words to the word wall on immigration displayed in the classroom. Next, she models writing a quickwrite using the new words and other words from the word wall. Following the teacher's model, students write quickwrites using at least three of the new words and three other words from the word wall. Afterward, students use highlighters to mark the immigration-related words they've incorporated in their quickwrites. Later, Mrs. Cramer reads the quickwrites to assess the students' vocabulary knowledge.

to craft sentences using the words and afterward share them with the class. Then after reading, students review the sentences and revise those that aren't accurate.

Dramatizing Words. Students each choose a word and dramatize it for classmates, who then try to guess it. Sometimes an action is a more effective way to explain a word than a verbal definition. For example, a teacher teaching a literature focus unit on *Chrysanthemum* (Henkes, 1996), the story of a little girl who didn't like her name, dramatized the word *wilted* for her second graders when they didn't understand how a girl could wilt. Other words in *Chrysanthemum* that can easily be acted out include *humorous*, *sprouted*, *dainty*, and *wildly*. Dramatization is an especially effective activity for English learners.

Word Sorts. Students sort a collection of words taken from the word wall into two or more categories in a word sort (Bear, Invernizzi, Templeton, & Johnston, 2008). Usually students choose the categories they use for the sort, but sometimes the teacher chooses them. For example, words from a story might be sorted by character, or words from a thematic unit on machines might be sorted according to type of machine. The words can be written on cards, and then students sort a pack of word cards into piles. Or, students can cut apart a list of words, sort them into categories, and then paste the grouped words together on a sheet of paper.

Word Chains. Students choose a word and then identify three or four words to sequence before or after it to make a chain. For example, the word *tadpole* can be chained this way: *egg, tadpole, frog*; and the word *aggravate* can be chained like this: *irritate, bother, aggravate, annoy*. Students can draw and write their chains on a sheet of paper, or they can make a chain out of construction paper and write a word on each link.

Semantic Feature Analysis. Students learn the meanings of words that are conceptually related by examining their characteristics in a semantic feature analysis (Allen, 2007). Teachers select a group of related words, such as animals and plants in the rain forest or planets in the solar system, and then make a grid to classify them according to distinguishing characteristics (Pittelman, Heimlich, Berglund, & French, 1991; Rickelman & Taylor, 2006). Students analyze each

Figure 7–8 ❖ A Word Map for *Glistened*

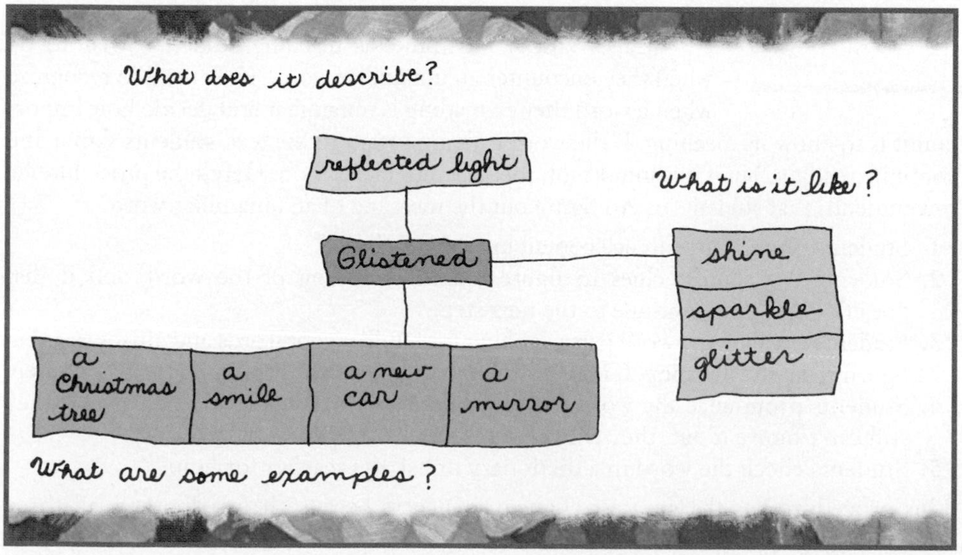

word, characteristic by characteristic, and they put checkmarks, circles, and question marks in each cell to indicate whether the word represents that characteristic. For example, on a semantic feature analysis about the rain forest, animals, plants, and people living in the rain forest are listed on one side of the grid and characteristics on the other. For the word *sloth*, students would add checkmarks in the grid to indicate that it is a mammal, lives in the canopy, goes to the forest floor, and has camouflage. They would add circles to indicate that a sloth is not colorful, not dangerous to people, not a plant, and not a bird or insect. If they aren't sure whether sloths are used to make medicine, they use a question mark.

These word-study activities provide opportunities for students to deepen their understanding of words listed on word walls, other words related to books they're reading, and words they're learning during thematic units. Students develop concepts, learn one or more meanings of words, and make associations among words through these activities. None of them require students to simply write words and their definitions or to use the words in sentences or a contrived story.

Word-Learning Strategies

When students come across an unfamiliar word while reading, there are a variety of things they can do: They can reread the sentence, analyze root words and affixes in the word, check a dictionary, sound out the word, look for context clues in the sentence, skip the word and keep reading, or ask the teacher or a classmate for help, for example (Allen, 1999). Some techniques, however, work better than others. After studying the research on ways to deal with unfamiliar words, Michael Graves (2006) has identified these three effective word-learning strategies:

Be Strategic!

Word-Learning Strategies

When students are reading and come across an unfamiliar word, they use these strategies to figure out the word's meaning:

- ▶ Use context clues
- ▶ Analyze word parts
- ▶ Check a dictionary

These three strategies are effective when students know how to apply them and are interested in learning new words.

- ◆ Using context clues
- ◆ Analyzing word parts
- ◆ Checking a dictionary

Capable readers know and use these strategies to figure out the meaning of unfamiliar words as they read. In contrast, less capable readers have fewer strategies available: They often depend on just one or two less effective strategies, such as sounding out the word or skipping it.

Graves (2006) recommends teaching students what to do when they encounter an unfamiliar word. They need to recognize when a word they're reading is unfamiliar and decide how important it is to know its meaning. If the word isn't important to the text, students skip it and continue reading, but if it is important, they need to take action. Here's the procedure he recommends that students use to figure out the meaning of an unfamiliar word:

1. Students reread the sentence containing the word.
2. Students use context clues to figure out the meaning of the word, and if that doesn't work, they continue to the next step.
3. Students examine the word parts, looking for familiar root words and affixes to aid in figuring out the meaning. If they're still not successful, they continue to the next step.
4. Students pronounce the word to see if they recognize it when they say it. If they still can't figure it out, they continue to the next step.
5. Students check the word in a dictionary or ask the teacher for help.

This procedure has the greatest chance of success because it incorporates all three word-learning strategies.

Using Context Clues. Students learn many words from context as they read. The surrounding words and sentences offer context clues; some clues provide information about the meaning of the word, and others provide information about the part of speech and how the word is used in a sentence. This contextual information helps students infer the meaning of the unfamiliar word. Illustrations also provide contextual information that helps readers identify words. The different types of context clues that readers use are presented in Figure 7–9. Interestingly, two or three types of contextual information are often found in the same sentence.

Nagy, Anderson, and Herman (1987) found that students who read books at their grade level have a 1 in 20 chance of learning the meaning of a word from context. Although that might seem insignificant, if students read 20,000 words a year and learn 1 of every 20 words from context, they will learn 1,000 words, or one third of their annual vocabulary growth. That's significant! How much time does it take to read 20,000 words? Nagy (1988) estimated that if teachers provide 30 minutes of daily reading time, students will learn an additional 1,000 words a year! It's interesting to note that both capable and less capable readers learn from context at about the same rate (Stahl, 1999).

The best way to teach students about context clues is by modeling. When teachers read aloud, they stop at a difficult word and do a **think-aloud** to show students how they use context clues to figure out its meaning. When the context provides enough information, teachers use the information and continue reading, but when the rest of the sentence or paragraph doesn't provide enough information, teachers use another strategy to figure out the meaning of the word.

Analyzing Word Parts. Students use their knowledge of prefixes, suffixes, and root words to unlock many multisyllabic words when they understand how word parts function. For example, *omnivorous, carnivorous,* and *herbivorous* relate to the foods that animals eat: *Omni* means "all," *carno* means "flesh," and *herb* means "vegetation." The common word part *vorous* comes from the Latin *vorare,* meaning "to swallow up." When students know *carnivorous* or *carnivore,* they use morphemic analysis to figure out the other words.

Go to the Building Teaching Skills and Dispositions section of Chapter 7 on **MyEducationLab.com** to hear second grader Michael discuss the strategies he uses to determine the meaning of unfamiliar words.

Figure 7–9 ◆ Six Types of Context Clues

Clue	Description	Sample Sentence
Definition	Readers use the definition in the sentence to understand the unknown word.	Some spiders spin silk with tiny organs called *spinnerets*.
Example-Illustration	Readers use an example or illustration to understand the unknown word.	Toads, frogs, and some birds are *predators* that hunt and eat spiders.
Contrast	Readers understand the unknown word because it's compared or contrasted with another word in the sentence.	Most spiders live for about one year, but *tarantulas* sometimes live for 20 years or more!
Logic	Readers think about the rest of the sentence to understand the unknown word.	An *exoskeleton* acts like a suit of armor to protect the spider.
Root Words and Affixes	Readers use their knowledge of root words and affixes to figure out the unknown word.	People who are terrified of spiders have *arachnophobia*.
Grammar	Readers use the word's function in the sentence or its part of speech to figure out the unknown word.	Most spiders *molt* five to ten times.

Teaching derivational prefixes and suffixes and non-English root words in fourth through eighth grades improves students' ability to unlock the meaning of unfamiliar words (Baumann, Edwards, Font, Tereshinski, Kame'enui, & Olejnik, 2002; Baumann, Font, Edwards, & Boland, 2005). For example, when students recognize that the Latin roots *-ann* and *-enn* mean "year," they can figure out the meanings of many of these words: *annual, biennial, perennial, centennial, bicentennial, millennium*, and *sesquicentennial*. Graves (2006) recommends that teachers teach morphemic analysis when non-English root words appear in books students are reading and during thematic units. Teachers break apart the words and discuss the word parts when they're posted on the word wall and through minilessons.

Checking the Dictionary. Looking up unfamiliar words in the dictionary is often frustrating because the definitions don't provide enough useful information or because words used in the definition are forms of the word being defined (Allen, 1999). Sometimes the definition that students choose—usually the first one—is the wrong one. Or, the definition doesn't make sense. For example, the word *pollution* is usually defined as "the act of polluting"—not a useful definition. Students could look for an entry for *polluting*, but they won't find it. They might notice an entry for *pollute*, where the first definition is "to make impure." The second definition is "to make unclean, especially with man-made waste," but even this definition may be difficult to understand.

Because dictionary definitions are most useful when a person is vaguely familiar with the word's meaning, teachers play an important role in dictionary work: They teach students how to read a dictionary entry and decide which definitions make sense, and they model the strategy when they're reading aloud and come across a word that's unfamiliar to most students. They also assist students by explaining the definitions that students locate, providing sample sentences, and comparing the word to related words and opposites.

Word Consciousness

Another component of vocabulary instruction is developing students' word consciousness, their interest in learning and using words (Graves & Watts-Taffe, 2002). According to Scott and Nagy (2004), word consciousness is "essential for vocabulary growth and comprehending the language of schooling" (p. 201). Students who have word consciousness exemplify these characteristics:

- ◆ Students use words skillfully, understanding the nuances of word meanings.
- ◆ Students gain a deep appreciation of words and value them.
- ◆ Students are aware of differences between social and academic language.
- ◆ Students understand the power of word choice.
- ◆ Students are motivated to learn the meaning of unfamiliar words.

Word consciousness is important because vocabulary knowledge is generative—that is, it transfers to and enhances students' learning of other words (Scott & Nagy, 2004).

The goal is for students to become more aware of words, manipulate them playfully, and appreciate their power. Teachers foster word consciousness in a variety of ways, as Mrs. Sanom did in the vignette at the beginning of the chapter. Most importantly, they model interest in words and precise use of vocabulary (Graves, 2006). To encourage students' interest in words, teachers share books about words, including *Max's Words* (Banks, 2006), *Word Wizard* (Falwell, 2006), and *The Boy Who Loved Words* (Schotter, 2006) with primary-grade students; and *Miss Alaineus: A Vocabulary Disaster* (Fraiser, 2007), *Baloney (Henry P.)* (Scieszka, 2005), and *Mom and Dad Are Palindromes* (Shulman, 2006) with older students. Next, they call students' attention to words by highlighting words of the day, posting words on word walls, and having students collect words from books they're reading. They promote wordplay by sharing riddles, jokes, puns, songs, and poems and encouraging students to experiment with words and use them in new ways. Figure 7–10 lists the types of wordplay. Through these activities, students become more powerful word users.

Assessing Students' Vocabulary Knowledge

It's difficult to assess students' vocabulary knowledge. There aren't any grade-level standards to indicate which words students should know or even how many words they need to learn. In addition, it's complicated because students learn words gradually,

Figure 7–10 ◆ Types of Wordplay

Type	Description	Examples
Alliteration	Repetition of a beginning consonant or vowel in neighboring words within a phrase or sentence. Sometimes sentences are called *tongue twisters*.	now or never do or die Peter Piper picked a peck of pickled peppers
Eponym	A person's name that has become a word.	teddy bear sandwich pasteurization
Hyperbole	An exaggerated statement.	I almost died laughing my feet are killing me I'm so hungry I could eat a horse
Onomatopoeia	A word that imitates a sound.	tick-tock kerplunk sizzling
Oxymoron	The combination of two normally contradictory words.	jumbo shrimp pretty ugly deafening silence
Palindrome	A word or phrase that reads the same forward or backward.	mom civic a man, a plan, a canal—Panama
Personification	A figure of speech that endows human traits or abilities to inanimate objects.	the old VW's engine coughed raindrops danced on my umbrella fear knocked on the door
Pig Latin	A language game where a speaker rearranges the sounds in words: The initial consonant sound of each word is moved to the end and *ay* is added after it; but when the word begins with a vowel, the initial sound isn't moved, but *ay* is added at the end.	cat = at-cay ice cream = ice-ay eam-cray pig Latin is fun = ig-pay atin-lay is-ay un-fay
Portmanteau	A word created by fusing two words to combine the meaning of both words. This wordplay was invented by Lewis Carroll in *Jabberwocky*.	spork (spoon + fork) brunch (breakfast + lunch) smog (smoke + fog)
Spoonerism	A tangle of words in which sounds are switched, often with a humorous effect. These "slips of the tongue," named for Reverend William Spooner (1844–1930), usually occur when a person is speaking quickly.	butterfly—flutterby go and take a shower—go and shake a tower save the whales—wave the sails

moving to deeper levels of "knowing" a word. Teachers typically monitor students' independent reading and use informal measures to evaluate their word knowledge, but several tests are available to measure students' vocabulary, and they're described in the Assessment Tools feature below.

Teachers often choose more-authentic measures of students' vocabulary knowledge because they're more useful than formal tests (Bean & Swan, 2006). These informal assessment tools show whether students have learned the words that were taught as well as the depth of their knowledge:

Observations. Teachers watch how students use new words during word-study activities, minilessons, and discussions. They also notice how students apply word-learning strategies during guided reading and when they're reading aloud.

Conferences. Teachers talk with students about the words they've used in word-study activities and in their writing. They also ask what students do when they come across an unfamiliar word and talk about word-learning strategies.

Assessment Tools

Vocabulary

Both informal assessments and standardized tests can be used to measure students' vocabulary knowledge, but tests often equate word knowledge with recognizing or being able to state a single definition of a word rather than assessing the depth of students' knowledge. Here are several norm-referenced vocabulary tests:

◆ **Peabody Picture Vocabulary Test-4 (PPVT-4)** (Dunn, Dunn, & Dunn, 2006)

The PPVT-4 is an individually administered assessment to screen students' vocabulary knowledge. The test can be used with K–8 students, but it's most commonly used with K–2 students showing limited verbal fluency. The PPVT-4 measures receptive vocabulary: The teacher says a word and asks the student to look at four pictures and identify the one that best illustrates the meaning of the word. Unfortunately, this test takes 10–15 minutes to administer, which makes it too time-consuming for regular classroom use. The PPVT-4 is available for purchase from the American Guidance Service.

◆ **Expressive Vocabulary Test-2 (EVT-2)** (Williams, 2006)

The EVT-2 is also an individual test that's used to screen K–8 students' knowledge of words. The EVT-2 is the expressive counterpart of the PPVT-4: The teacher points to a picture and asks the student to say a word that labels the picture or to provide a synonym for a word that's illustrated in the picture. This test is also very time-consuming for classroom teachers to use. It's available from the American Guidance Service.

◆ **Informal Reading Inventories (IRIs)**

Sometimes teachers in grades 2–8 use IRIs to assess students' vocabulary knowledge. One or two comprehension questions at each grade level focus on the meaning of words selected from the passage students have read. The usefulness of this assessment is limited, however, because so few questions deal with vocabulary and because students who read below grade level aren't tested on age-appropriate words.

Even though these tests aren't very useful in classroom settings, they are helpful in diagnosing struggling readers and English learners with limited word knowledge.

Rubrics. Teachers include items about vocabulary on **rubrics** to emphasize its importance. For oral-presentation rubrics, teachers emphasize the use of technical words related to the topic, and for writing, they emphasize precise vocabulary.

Tests. Teachers also create a variety of paper-and-pencil tests to monitor students' vocabulary knowledge. For example, they can have students complete a **cloze** passage using newly learned words, **quickwrite** about a word, create a word map or word chain about a word, or draw a picture to represent a word's meaning.

These informal assessments go beyond simply providing a definition or using a word in a sentence because students are actively involved in using the word in context.

Students also self-assess their word knowledge. Cunningham and Allington (2007) suggest having students self-assess their knowledge of specific words, using the levels of word knowledge. Teachers develop a list of five levels of word knowledge using language that's appropriate for their students and post it in the classroom. Here's a list developed by a sixth-grade teacher:

1 = I don't know this word at all.
2 = I've heard this word before, but I don't know the meaning.
3 = I think I know what this word means.
4 = I know one meaning for this word, and I can use it in a sentence.
5 = I know several meanings or other things about this word.

Teachers give students a list of words related to a book they're going to read or at the beginning of a thematic unit; students assess their word knowledge by writing a number to indicate their level of knowledge beside each word, and then they repeat the assessment at the end to see how their knowledge has grown. Or, before introducing a new word, teachers can informally ask students to raise their hands and show the number of fingers that corresponds with their level of knowledge about the word.

Chapter 7 Review

How Effective Teachers Expand Students' Knowledge of Words

▶ Teachers provide daily opportunities for students to read books independently and listen to them read aloud.

▶ Teachers categorize unfamiliar words into three tiers—basic words, academic words, and specialized words.

▶ Teachers teach Tier 2 words using explicit instruction and a variety of word-study activities.

▶ Teachers support students' development of word-learning strategies.

▶ Teachers nurture students' word consciousness.

Go to MyEducationLab at www.myeducationlab.com to deepen your understanding of the concepts presented in this chapter:

► Investigate the second graders' growing knowledge of word-identification strategies by viewing video segments in the Literacy Portraits.
► Check your understanding of chapter concepts with the multiple-choice and essay quizzes in the Study Plan.
► Apply some of the main ideas discussed in the chapter in the Activities and Applications section of the website.
► Practice what you've learned in this chapter in Building Teaching Skills and Dispositions before applying the ideas in your own classroom.

PROFESSIONAL REFERENCES

Allen, J. (1999). *Words, words, words*. Portsmouth, NH: Heinemann.

Allen, J. (2007). *Inside words: Tools for teaching academic vocabulary, grades 4–12*. Portland, ME: Stenhouse.

Allington, R. L. (2006). *What really matters for struggling readers* (2nd ed.). Boston: Allyn & Bacon/Pearson.

Baumann, J. F., Edwards, E. C., Font, G., Tereshinski, C. A., Kame'enui, E. J., & Olejnik, S. (2002). Teaching morphemic and contextual analysis to fifth grade students. *Reading Research Quarterly, 37*, 150–176.

Baumann, J. F., Font, G., Edwards, E. C., & Boland, E. (2005). Strategies for teaching middle-grade students to use word-part and context clues to expand reading vocabulary. In E. Hiebert & M. L. Kamil (Eds.), *Teaching and learning vocabulary: Bringing research to practice* (pp. 179–205). Mahwah, NJ: Erlbaum.

Baumann, J. F., Kame'enui, E. J., & Ash, G. (2003). Research on vocabulary instruction: Voltaire redux. In J. Flood, D. Lapp, J. R. Squire, & J. M. Jensen (Eds.), *Handbook of research on teaching the English language arts* (2nd ed., pp. 752–785). Mahwah, NJ: Erlbaum.

Bean, R. M., & Swan, A. (2006). Vocabulary assessment: A key to planning vocabulary instruction. In C. C. Block & J. N. Mangieri (Eds.), *The vocabulary-enriched classroom: Practices for improving the reading performance of all students in grades 3 and up* (pp. 164–187). New York: Scholastic.

Bear, D. R., Invernizzi, M., Templeton, S., & Johnston, F. (2008). *Words their way: Word study for phonics, vocabulary, and spelling instruction* (4th ed.). Upper Saddle River, NJ: Merrill/Pearson.

Beck, I. L., McKeown, M. G., & Kucan, L. (2002). *Bringing words to life: Robust vocabulary instruction*. New York: Guilford Press.

Calderon, M. (2007). *Teaching reading to English language learners, grades 6–12*. Thousand Oaks, CA: Corwin Press.

Cooper, J. D., Chard, D. J., & Kiger, N. D. (2006). *The struggling reader: Interventions that work*. New York: Scholastic.

Cunningham, P. M. (2009). *What really matters in vocabulary: Research-based practices across the curriculum*. Boston: Allyn & Bacon/Pearson.

Cunningham, P. M., & Allington, R. L. (2007). *Classrooms at work: They can all read and write*. Boston: Allyn & Bacon.

Duffelmeyer, F. A., & Banwart, B. H. (1992–1993). Word maps for adjectives and verbs. *The Reading Teacher, 46*, 351–353.

Dunn, D. M., Dunn, L. W., & Dunn, L. M. (2006). *Peabody picture vocabulary test-4*. Bloomington, MN: American Guidance Service/Pearson.

Fisher, D., Frey, N., & Lapp, D. (2008). Shared readings: Modeling comprehension, vocabulary, text structures, and text features for older readers. *The Reading Teacher, 61*, 548–556.

Graves, M. F. (2006). *The vocabulary book: Learning and instruction*. New York: Teachers College Press.

Graves, M. F., & Watts-Taffe, S. M. (2002). The place of word consciousness in a research-based vocabulary program. In S. J. Samuels & A. E. Farstrup (Eds.), *What research has to say about reading instruction* (3rd ed., pp. 140–165). Newark, DE: International Reading Association.

Jacobson, J., Lapp, D., & Flood, J. (2007). A seven-step instructional plan for teaching English-language learners to comprehend and use homonyms, homophones, and homographs. *Journal of Adolescent and Adult Literacy, 51*, 98–111.

McKeown, M. G., & Beck, I. L. (2004). Direct and rich vocabulary instruction. In J. F. Baumann & E. B. Kame'enui (Eds.), *Vocabulary instruction: Research to practice* (pp. 13–27). New York: Guilford Press.

Nagy, W. E. (1988). *Teaching vocabulary to improve reading comprehension*. Urbana, IL: ERIC Clearinghouse on Reading and Communication Skills and the National Council of Teachers of English and the International Reading Association.

Nagy, W. E., Anderson, R. C., & Herman, P. A. (1987). Learning word meanings from context during normal reading. *American Educational Research Journal, 24*, 237–270.

Palmer, B. C., Shackelford, V. S., Miller, S. C., & Leclere, J. T. (2006/2007). Bridging two worlds: Reading comprehension, figurative language instruction, and the English-language learner. *Journal of Adolescent and Adult Literacy, 50*, 258–267.

Pittelman, S. D., Heimlich, J. E., Berglund, R. L., & French, M. P. (1991). *Semantic feature analysis: Classroom applications*. Newark, DE: International Reading Association.

Rickelman, R. J., & Taylor, D. B. (2006). Teaching vocabulary by learning content-area words. In C. C. Block & J. N. Mangieri (Eds.), *The vocabulary-enriched classroom: Practices for improving the reading performance of all students in grades 3 and up* (pp. 54–73). New York: Scholastic.

Santoro, L. E., Chard, D. J., Howard, L., & Baker, S. K. (2008). Making the *very* most of classroom read-alouds to promote comprehension and vocabulary. *The Reading Teacher, 61*, 396–408.

Scott, J. A., & Nagy, W. E. (2004). Developing word consciousness. In J. F. Baumann & E. J. Kame'enui (Eds.), *Vocabulary instruction: Theory to practice* (pp. 210–217). New York: Guilford Press.

Stahl, S. A. (1999). *Vocabulary development*. Cambridge, MA: Brookline Books.

Stahl, S. A., & Kapinus, B. (1991). Possible sentences: Predicting word meanings to teach content area vocabulary. *The Reading Teacher, 45*, 36–43.

Stahl, S. A., & Nagy, W. E. (2006). *Teaching word meanings*. Mahwah, NJ: Erlbaum.

Stahl, S. A., Richek, M. G., & Vandevier, R. (1991). Learning word meanings through listening: A sixth grade replication. In J. Zutell & S. McCormick (Eds.), *Learning factors/teacher factors: Issues in literacy research. Fortieth yearbook of the National Reading Conference* (pp. 185–192). Chicago: National Reading Conference.

Stanovich, K. E. (1986). Matthew effects in reading: Some consequences of individual differences in the acquisition of literacy. *Reading Research Quarterly, 21*, 360–406.

Swanborn, M. S. W., & de Glopper, K. (1999). Incidental word learning while reading: A meta-analysis. *Review of Educational Research, 69*, 261–285.

Tompkins, G. E., & Yaden, D. B., Jr. (1986). *Answering students' questions about words*. Urbana, IL: ERIC Clearinghouse on Reading and Communication Skills and the National Council of Teachers of English.

Venezky, R. L. (1999). *The American way of spelling: The structure and origins of American English orthography*. New York: Guilford Press.

Williams, K. T. (2006). *Expressive vocabulary test-2*. Bloomington, MN: American Guidance Service/Pearson.

CHILDREN'S BOOK REFERENCES

Banks, K. (2006). *Max's words*. New York: Farrar, Straus & Giroux.

Barretta, G. (2007). *Dear deer: A book of homophones*. New York: Holt.

Bollard, J. K. (2006). *Scholastic children's thesaurus*. New York: Scholastic.

Brennan-Nelson, D. (2004), *My teacher likes to say*. Chelsea, MI: Sleeping Bear Press.

Brewster, H. (1997). *Inside the Titanic*. Boston: Little, Brown.

Cheney, L. (2002). *America: A patriotic primer*. New York: Simon & Schuster.

Christensen, B. (2001). *Woody Guthrie: Poet of the people*. New York: Knopf.

Cole, J. (1997). *The magic school bus and the electric field trip*. New York: Scholastic.

Falwell, C. (2006). *Word wizard*. New York: Clarion Books.

Frasier, D. (2007). *Miss Alaineus: A vocabulary disaster*. New York: HarperCollins/Voyager Books.

Guthrie, W. (1998). *This land is your land*. New York: Little, Brown.

Gwynne, F. (2005). *A chocolate moose for dinner*. New York: Aladdin Books.

Gwynne, F. (2006). *The king who rained*. New York: Aladdin Books.

Hellweg, P. (2006). *The American Heritage children's thesaurus*. Boston: Houghton Mifflin.

Henkes, K. (1996). *Chrysanthemum*. New York: HarperTrophy.

Howe, D., & Howe, J. (2006). *Bunnicula: A rabbit-tale of mystery*. New York: Aladdin Books.

Kentley, E. (2001). *Story of the Titanic*. London: Dorling Kindersley.

Leedy, L. (2003). *There's a frog in my throat! 440 animal sayings a little bird told me*. New York: Holiday House.

Lowry, L. (1984). *Anastasia Krupnik*. New York: Yearling.

Osborne, W., & Osborne, M. P. (1995). *Tonight on the Titanic*. New York: Random House.

Osborne, W., & Osborne, M. P. (2002). *Titanic: A nonfiction companion to Tonight on the Titanic*. New York: Random House.

Paulsen, G. (2007). *Hatchet*. New York: Simon & Schuster.

Schotter, R. (2006). *The boy who loved words*. New York: Random House/Schwartz & Wade.

Scieszka, J. (2005). *Baloney (Henry P.)*. New York: Puffin Books.

Scillian, D. (2001). *A is for America*. Chelsea, MI: Sleeping Bear Press.

Shulman, M. (2006). *Mom and dad are palindromes*. San Francisco: Chronicle Books.

Tanaka, S. (1996). *On board the Titanic: What it was like when the great liner sank*. New York: Hyperion Books.

Terban, M. (1992). *The dove dove: Funny homograph riddles*. New York: Clarion Books.

Terban, M. (2006). *Scholastic dictionary of idioms*. New York: Scholastic.

Terban, M. (2007a). *Eight ate: A feast of homonym riddles*. New York: Clarion Books.

Terban, M. (2007b). *In a pickle and other funny idioms*. New York: Clarion Books.

Terban, M. (2007c). *Mad as a wet hen!: And other funny idioms*. New York: Clarion Books.

White, E. E. (1998). *Voyage on the great Titanic: The diary of Margaret Ann Brady*. New York: Scholastic.

Wittels, H. (2001). *A first thesaurus*. New York: Golden Books.

Wood, A. (1982). *Quick as a cricket*. London: Child's Play.

Chapter 8

Facilitating Students' Comprehension: Reader Factors

Mrs. Donnelly Teaches Comprehension Strategies

Posters about comprehension strategies, including connecting, questioning, repairing, and summarizing, hang on the wall in Mrs. Donnelly's classroom. She introduced comprehension strategies by explaining that sixth graders think while they read, and they do different kinds of thinking. These kinds of thinking are called *strategies*. Her students made the posters as they studied each strategy. Tanner, Vincente, and Ashante's poster for monitoring is shown in the box on the next page.

One of the first strategies that Mrs. Donnelly taught was predicting, and even though her students were familiar with it, they didn't know why they were using it. She explained that predictions guide their thinking. Together they made a chart about the strategy and practiced making predictions as Mrs. Donnelly read *The Garden of Abdul Gasazi* (Van Allsburg, 1993), the story of an evil magician who hates dogs. The students made predictions about *The Garden of Abdul Gasazi* based on the title and the cover illustration, but making predictions got harder in the middle of the surrealistic story because they didn't know whether the dog would escape the magician's garden after he was turned into a duck. Mrs. Donnelly emphasized the importance of continuing to think about the story and to make predictions when it gets confusing. She stopped reading and talked first about why the dog was likely to be successful and then why he wouldn't be. Only about two thirds of the students predicted he would make it home safely, but he did.

The next day, they read *La Mariposa* (Jiménez, 1998), the autobiographical picture-book story about a migrant child with exceptional artistic ability. The title, which means "the butterfly," and the illustration on the cover of a boy flying toward the sun didn't provide enough information on which to base a prediction, so the students learned that sometimes they have to read a few pages before they can make useful predictions. After reading about Spanish-speaking Francisco's difficult first day of school in an English-only classroom, Norma figured out that the caterpillar the boy is watching in the classroom will become a butterfly, and that the boy on the front cover is flying like a butterfly, but she didn't know why that connection was important. Several students pointed out that the butterfly might symbolize freedom. Moises predicted that the boy will be rescued from the migrant tent city where he and his family live, and Lizette suggested that he will move to a bilingual classroom where his teacher will understand him and he will make friends. Even though those predictions were wrong, the students became more engaged in the story and were eager for their teacher to continue reading. Mrs. Donnelly wrote their predictions on small self-stick notes and attached them to the edge of the pages as she read. She modeled how to use these notes because she wanted to make their thinking more visible, and she explained that she wants them to use self-stick notes, too: "I want you to show me your thinking."

Sixth Graders' Strategy Poster	
Monitoring	
What is it?	It is checking that you are understanding what you are reading.
Why use it?	Monitoring helps you solve problems so you can be successful.
When?	You should use this strategy while you are reading.

What do you do?	1. Keep asking: Does this make sense?
	   If you are understanding, keep reading, but if it doesn't make sense, take action to solve the problem.
	2. Try these solutions:
	   • Go back several pages or to the beginning of the chapter and reread.
	   • Keep reading one or two more pages.
	   • Reread the last prediction, connection, or summary you wrote.
	   • Talk to a friend about the problem.
	   • Write a quickwrite about the problem.
	   • Talk to Mrs. Donnelly.

Next, she taught the connecting strategy using *So Far From the Sea* (Bunting, 1998), a story about life at a Japanese relocation camp during World War II. She explained that readers make three kinds of connections—text-to-self, text-to-world, and text-to-text. As she read each book aloud, she modeled making connections and encouraged the sixth graders to share their connections. Each time they made a connection, Mrs. Donnelly wrote it on a self-stick note; after she finished reading the book, she collected the notes, had the students sort them according to the kind of connection, and posted them in text-to-self, text-to-world, and text-to-text columns on a chart. The chart for *So Far From the Sea* is shown here.

Mrs. Donnelly reviewed each comprehension strategy because she wanted the sixth graders to be familiar with all of them. Next, she introduced *Joey Pigza Loses Control*, a Newbery Honor book by Jack Gantos (2005), so that students could practice integrating their use of the comprehension strategies in an authentic reading experience. Mrs. Donnelly explained that readers rarely use only one strategy; instead, they use many of them at the same time.

Mrs. Donnelly introduced the book: "This is a story about a boy named Joey who is about your age. His parents are divorced, and he's going to spend the summer with his dad. Joey is ADHD. His mother says he's 'wired,' and he uses medicine patches to

The Connections Chart About *So Far From the Sea*

Text-to-Self	Text-to-World	Text-to-Text
My grandmother takes flowers when she goes to the cemetery because one of her husbands died.	I know that in World War II, Americans were fighting the Japanese because of Pearl Harbor, and they were fighting Hitler and the Germans, too.	This story is like <u>The Bracelet</u>. That girl and her family were taken to a camp in the desert. It was miserable there and she didn't deserve to have to go.
My great-granddad had to go too, and it wasn't fair because he was a loyal American, but his parents were from Japan.	In the book it's World War II, but I'm thinking about our war in Iraq.	Another book I know is <u>Journey to Topaz</u>. Topaz was another war relocation center and it was a terrible prison, too.
I know how to make origami birds. My cousin and I learned last summer.		I've heard about a book called <u>Anne Frank</u>. She was Jewish and this sorta happened to her in Germany and she died, too.
We have an American flag on our car so everyone knows we love America.		

control his behavior. He doesn't know his dad very well, so he doesn't know what to expect. His mom tells him not to expect too much." She asks the sixth graders to think about what they know about divorced parents, summer vacations, and ADHD kids. They talk about what they know about each topic, and then they brainstorm these questions to stimulate their thinking about the story:

What is Joey's dad like?

Will they have fun together?

Will Joey be in the way?

Does he hope his parents will get back together?

Does Joey's dad love him?

Will Joey's dad disappoint him?

Will Joey disappoint his dad?

Will Joey's medicine work or will he be "wired"?

Will Joey's mom be lonely without him?

Will Joey stay with his dad all summer or come back home sooner?

Mrs. Donnelly passes out copies of the book and stacks of small self-stick notes for students to use to record their thinking as they read. They read the first chapter together, and then students continue to read on their own or with a partner. The book is contemporary realism, and it's easy reading for most students. Mrs. Donnelly chose it because it would be interesting but easy to read, so they'd have the cognitive resources available while reading to concentrate on their strategy use.

After reading the first chapter, the students come together to talk about it in a **grand conversation**. They begin by talking about what they remember from the chapter, and then Mrs. Donnelly reads the sentence from page 10 where Joey says this to his mom about the dad he doesn't know very well: "I just want him to love me as much as I already love him." She asks, "How do parents show that they love their children?" She hangs up a sheet of chart paper, divides it into two columns, and writes the question at the top of the first column. The students suggest a number of ways, including giving them presents, taking care of them, spending time with them, taking them to church, keeping them safe, and having dinner with them. Mrs. Donnelly writes their ideas under the question in the first column of the chart. Then she narrows the question and asks, "What do you think Joey is looking for from his dad?" Ashante says, "He wants his dad to pay attention to him." Leticia suggests, "He wants him to say 'I love you, son,' tell him he's missed him, and play basketball with him." Students continue to offer ideas, which Mrs. Donnelly adds to the chart. Then she asks, "How do kids show love to their parents?" and she writes the question at the top of the second column. The students suggest that children show their love by behaving, making their parents proud, being responsible, and doing their chores; she writes these answers under the question in the second column. Finally, Mrs. Donnelly asks, "What is Joey's dad expecting from his son?" It's much harder for the students to put themselves in this role. Henry offers, "I think he just wants to have him live with him every day." The sixth graders also reflect on their strategy use. Several students talk about predictions they made, and others share how they monitored their reading and made connections while they were reading.

After reading and discussing each chapter, the students collect the self-stick notes they've used to keep track of their thinking, and they write about the strategies they've used in a **double-entry journal**. Normally, double-entry journals have two columns, but Mrs. Donnelly asks the students to include three columns—she's calling it a triple-entry journal: They write what was happening in the text or copy a quote from the text in the first column, explain their thinking in the second column, and identify the strategy they used in the third column. Excerpts from Tanner's triple-entry thinking journal are shown below.

The students continue to read, discuss, and write about their strategy use as they read *Joey Pigza Loses Control*. After they've read half the book, Mrs. Donnelly brings the class together for a **minilesson**. She explains that she's reviewed their thinking journals and has noticed that students weren't summarizing very much. They talk about the summarizing strategy and how, when, and why they should use it. Mrs. Donnelly demonstrates how to summarize as she reads the beginning of the next chapter aloud, and then she encourages students to try to use the strategy as they read the next chapter.

Excerpts From Tanner's Triple-Entry Thinking Journal

Chapter	The Text	Your Thinking	The Strategy
1	Joey's mom warns him that his dad is wired like he is.	I'm thinking that this book is about a kid who doesn't know his dad and he's going to be disappointed by him. His Mom doesn't think it's going to be a good vacation.	Identifying big ideas
4	Joey's dad doesn't act like a dad and his Grandma doesn't act like a grandma.	My stomach feels queasy. Joey doesn't belong with these people. His dad doesn't stop talking to listen to him and his grandma doesn't even like him. I predict bad things are going to happen.	Predicting
7	After the game they go to the mall to see Leezy.	My mind is asking questions. Why would Carter let Joey drive the car to the mall? Why would his dad tell him it's OK to steal money out of the wishing pond? Is the author trying to show us what a terrible dad he is? We already know that.	Questioning
8	His dad thinks Joey doesn't need the patches and he won't let him have them.	What is wrong with his dad? The patch is medicine that he needs. I am so mad at his dad. That's all I can think. I'm glad my parents take good care of me.	Connecting
14	Joey calls his mom to come get him at the mall.	I think Joey is really a smart kid. He knows how to save himself. He calls his mom and she comes to get him. Joey is right to call his dad a J-E-R-K because that's what he is. The visit was a fiasco just like I predicted. This is a really great book and I want to read it all over again.	Evaluating

After they finish reading the book, the students have another **grand conversation**. They talk about how Joey's mom rescues him and how disillusioned Joey is about his dad. Next, they return to the list of questions they brainstormed before they began reading and talk about the questions and answers. Jake answers the question "Does Joey's dad love him?" this way: "I think his dad does love him but it's a strange kind of love because his dad is selfish. He loves him as much as he can, but it's not very good love." Lizette answers these two questions: "Will Joey's dad disappoint him?" and "Will Joey disappoint his dad?" She says, "I'm positive that Joey's dad disappointed him. His dad wasn't a good dad. The second question is harder to answer. I know Joey tried to be a good son, but it's impossible to satisfy his dad. His dad made him hyper and then got mad at him for being hyper."

Then they reread the chart they began after reading the first chapter about parents showing their love for their children and children showing their love for their parents. They talk about the things they learned that Joey wanted from his dad: for his dad to listen to him, to take care of him, to be responsible for him. They also talk about what Joey's dad wanted from him. Dillan explains, "I think Joey's dad wanted Joey to be his friend and to take care of him. I think Joey would be a better dad than his dad was." Then Mrs. Donnelly asks about Joey's mom: "Does Joey's mom love him?" Everyone agrees that she does, and they name many ways that she shows her love, including giving him money so he can call her, listening to him, worrying about him, hugging him, and telling him she loves him. They complete the chart by adding the new suggestions and then circling the behaviors that his dad exemplified in blue, his mom's in green, and Joey's in red. Later, students will use the information on this chart as they write an essay about how parents and children show their love for one another.

As they reflect on their strategy use, the students are amazed that they remember so much from the story and how well they understand it. Jake says, "I was thinking all the time in this story. I guess that's why I know so much about it. This thinking is a good idea." Richard agrees, saying, "I don't even have to remember to use strategies now. I just naturally think that way." Mrs. Donnelly smiles at Richard's comment. Her goal is for her students to use comprehension strategies independently. She'll continue to emphasize strategies and remind the sixth graders to use self-stick notes to track their thinking for several more months, but she'll gradually remove this scaffold once she sees that they've become strategic readers.

omprehension is the goal of reading; it's the reason why people read. Students must understand what they're reading to learn from the experience; they must make sense of the words in the text to maintain interest; and they must enjoy reading to become lifelong readers. Mrs. Donnelly was teaching her students to use comprehension strategies in the vignette because strategic readers are more likely to comprehend what they're reading. Struggling readers, in contrast, are frustrated; they don't understand what they're reading, don't like to read, and aren't likely to read in the future.

Comprehension involves different levels of thinking, from literal to inferential, critical, and evaluative. The most basic level is literal comprehension: Readers pick out main ideas, sequence details, notice similarities and differences, and identify explicitly stated reasons. The higher levels differ from literal comprehension because readers use their own knowledge along with the information presented in the text. The second level is inferential comprehension. Readers use clues in the text, implied information, and their background knowledge to draw inferences. They make predictions, recognize cause and effect, and determine the author's purpose. Critical comprehension is next: Readers analyze symbolic meanings, distinguish fact from opinion, and draw conclusions. The most sophisticated level is evaluative comprehension: Readers judge the value of a text using generally accepted criteria and personal standards. They detect bias, identify faulty reasoning, determine the effectiveness of persuasive techniques, and assess the quality of a text. These levels point out the range of thinking readers do. Because it's important to involve students in higher-level thinking, teachers ask questions and involve students in activities that require them to use inferential, critical, and evaluative comprehension.

WHAT IS COMPREHENSION?

Comprehension is a creative, multifaceted thinking process in which students engage with the text (Tierney, 1990). You've read about the word *process* before—both reading and writing have been described as processes. A process is more complicated than a single action: It involves a series of behaviors that occur over time. The comprehension process begins during prereading as students activate their background knowledge and preview the text, and it continues to develop as students read, respond, explore, and apply their reading. Readers construct a mental "picture" or representation of the text and its interpretation through the comprehension process (Van Den Broek & Kremer, 2000).

Judith Irwin (1991) defines comprehension as a reader's process of using prior experiences and the author's text to construct meaning that's useful to that reader for a specific purpose. This definition emphasizes that comprehension depends on two factors: the reader and the text that's being read. Whether comprehension is successful, according to Sweet and Snow (2003), depends on the interaction of reader factors and text factors.

Reader and Text Factors

Readers are actively engaged with the text; they think about many things as they read to comprehend the text. For example, they do the following:

    Activate prior knowledge
    Examine the text to uncover its organization
    Make predictions
    Connect to their own experiences
    Create mental images
    Draw inferences
    Notice symbols and other literary devices
    Monitor their understanding

These activities can be categorized as reader and text factors (National Reading Panel, 2000). Reader factors include the background knowledge that readers bring to the reading process as well as the strategies they use while reading and their motivation and engagement during reading. Text factors include the author's ideas, the words the author uses to express those ideas, and how the ideas are organized and presented. Both reader factors and text factors affect comprehension. Figure 8–1 presents an

Figure 8–1 ◆ Overview of the Comprehension Factors		
Type	**Factor**	**Role in Comprehension**
Reader	Background Knowledge	Students activate their world and literary knowledge to link what they know to what they're reading.
	Vocabulary	Students recognize the meaning of familiar words and apply word-learning strategies to understand what they're reading.
	Fluency	Students have adequate cognitive resources available to understand what they're reading when they read fluently.
	Comprehension Strategies	Students actively direct their reading, monitor their understanding, and troubleshoot problems when they occur.
	Comprehension Skills	Students automatically note details that support main ideas, sequence ideas, and use other skills.
	Motivation	Motivated students are more engaged in reading, more confident, and more likely to comprehend successfully.
Text	Genres	Genres have unique characteristics, and students' knowledge of them provides a scaffold for comprehension.
	Text Structures	Students recognize the important ideas more easily when they understand the patterns that authors use to organize text.
	Text Features	Students apply their knowledge of the conventions and literary devices used in texts to deepen their understanding.

overview of these two factors. This chapter focuses on reader factors, and Chapter 9 addresses text factors.

Prerequisites for Comprehension

In addition to reader and text factors, comprehension depends on three prerequisites: having adequate background knowledge about the topic and the genre, being familiar with most words in the text, and being able to read it fluently (Allington, 2006). When one of these requirements is lacking, students are unlikely to comprehend what they're reading (Cooper, Chard, & Kiger, 2006). Teachers can ameliorate students' difficulties through their instruction to increase the likelihood that students will be successful.

Background Knowledge. Having adequate background knowledge is a prerequisite because when students have both world knowledge and literary knowledge, it provides a bridge to a new text (Braunger & Lewis, 2006). When students don't have adequate background knowledge, the topic or genre of the text is unfamiliar and many words are new, they're likely to find the text very challenging, and it's unlikely that they'll be successful. Teachers use prereading activities to build students' background knowledge; first they determine whether students need world or literary knowledge and then provide experiences and information to develop their schema. They use a combination of experiences, visual representations, and talk to build knowledge. Involving students in authentic experiences such as taking field trips, participating in dramatizations, and examining artifacts is the best way to build background knowledge, but photos and pictures, picture books, websites, videos, and other visual representations can also be used. Talk is often the least effective way, especially for English learners, but sometimes explaining a concept or listing the characteristics of a genre does provide enough information.

Vocabulary. Students' knowledge of words plays a tremendous role in comprehension because it's difficult to comprehend a text that's loaded with unknown words. It's also possible that when students don't know many words related to a topic, they don't have adequate background knowledge either. Blachowicz and Fisher (2007) recommend creating a word-rich classroom environment to immerse students in words and teaching word-learning strategies so they can figure out the meaning of new words. In addition, teachers preteach key words when they're building background knowledge using **K-W-L charts**, graphic organizers, **anticipation guides**, and other prereading activities.

Fluency. Fluent readers read quickly and efficiently. Because they recognize most words automatically, their cognitive resources aren't depleted by decoding unfamiliar words, and they can devote their attention to comprehension (Pressley, 2002a). In the primary grades, developing reading fluency is an important component of comprehension instruction because children need to learn to recognize words automatically so they can concentrate on comprehending what they're reading (Samuels, 2002). For many struggling readers, their lack of fluency severely affects their ability to understand what they read. Teachers help older struggling readers who aren't fluent readers by teaching or reteaching word-identification strategies, having students do repeated readings, and providing students with books at their reading levels so that they can be successful. When teachers use grade-level texts that are too difficult for struggling students, they read them aloud so that everyone can comprehend and participate in related activities.

Comprehension Strategies

Comprehension strategies are thoughtful behaviors that students use to facilitate their understanding as they read (Afflerbach, Pearson, & Paris, 2008). Some strategies are *cognitive*—they involve thinking; others are *metacognitive*—students reflect on their thinking. For example, readers make predictions about a story when they begin reading: They wonder what will happen to the characters and whether they'll enjoy the story. Predicting is a cognitive strategy because it involves thinking. Readers also monitor their reading, and monitoring is a metacognitive strategy. They notice whether they're understanding; and if they're confused, they take action to solve the problem. For exam-

Check the Compendium of Instructional Procedures, which follows Chapter 12, for more information on the highlighted terms.

Literacy Portraits:VIEWING GUIDE

Ms. Janusz regularly teaches her second graders about comprehension strategies, including predicting, connecting, visualizing, asking questions, and repairing. She introduces a strategy and demonstrates how to use it in a minilesson; next, she encourages students to practice using it as she reads books aloud. Then students start using the strategy themselves during guided reading lessons and reading workshop. Ms. Janusz monitors the students' strategy use as she observes and conferences with them. To see how Ms. Janusz works with Curt'Lynn as she's learning to make personal connections, go to the Literacy Profiles section of the MyEducationLab website and click on Curt'Lynn's November button. How does Ms. Janusz scaffold Curt'Lynn's learning? You might also check the student interviews to see Curt'Lynn and her classmates talk about comprehension strategies and their ability to use them.

myeducationlab

ple, they may go back and reread or talk to a classmate to clarify their confusion. Students are being metacognitive when they are alert to the possibility that they might get confused, and they know several ways to solve the problem (Pressley, 2002b).

Students learn to use a variety of cognitive and metacognitive strategies to ensure that they comprehend what they're reading. Here's a list of the most important comprehension strategies:

- Activating background knowledge
- Connecting
- Determining importance
- Drawing inferences
- Evaluating
- Monitoring
- Predicting
- Questioning
- Repairing
- Setting a purpose
- Summarizing
- Visualizing

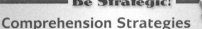

Be Strategic!

Comprehension Strategies

Students use these strategies to understand texts they're reading:

- Activate background knowledge
- Connect
- Determine importance
- Draw inferences
- Evaluate

- Monitor
- Predict
- Question
- Repair
- Set a purpose
- Summarize
- Visualize

These 12 strategies emphasize how readers think during the reading process; they're reader factors.

Students use these comprehension strategies not only to understand what they're reading, but also for understanding while they're listening to books read aloud and when they're writing. For example, students use the determining importance strategy when they're listening or reading to identify the big ideas, and when they're writing, they organize their writing around the big ideas so that readers also will comprehend what they're reading. Figure 8–2 presents an overview of the comprehension strategies and explains how readers use them.

Activating Background Knowledge. Readers bring their background knowledge to every reading experience; in fact, they read a text differently depending on their prior experiences. Zimmermann and Hutchins (2003) explain that "the meaning you get from a piece is intertwined with the meaning you bring to it" (p. 45). Readers think about the topic before they begin reading and call up relevant information and related vocabulary to use while reading. The more background knowledge and prior experiences readers have about a topic, the more likely they are to successfully comprehend what they're reading (Harvey & Goudvis, 2007).

Teachers use a variety of prereading activities to scaffold students as they learn to activate their background knowledge, such as **anticipation guides**, **exclusion brainstorming**, graphic organizers, **K-W-L charts**, and **prereading plans**. Through these activities, students think about the topic they'll read about, use related vocabulary, and get interested in reading the text.

Connecting. Readers make three types of connections between the text and their background knowledge: text-to-self, text-to-world, and text-to-text connections (Harvey & Goudvis, 2007). In text-to-self connections, students link the ideas they're reading about to events in their own lives; these are personal connections. A story event or character may remind them of something or someone in their own lives, and information in a nonfiction book may remind them of a past experience. In text-to-world connections, students relate what they're reading to their "world" knowledge, learned both in and out of school. When students make text-to-text connections, they link the text or an element of it to another text they've read or to a familiar film or television program. Students often compare different versions of familiar folktales, novels and their sequels, and sets of books by the same author. Text-to-text connections require higher-level thinking, and they are often the most difficult, especially for students who have done less reading or who know less about literature.

Figure 8–2 ◆ Overview of the Comprehension Strategies

Strategy	What Readers Do	How It Aids Comprehension
Activating Background Knowledge	Readers make connections between what they already know and the information in the text.	Readers use their background knowledge to fill in gaps in the text and enhance their comprehension.
Connecting	Readers make text-to-self, text-to-world, and text-to-text links.	Readers personalize their reading by relating what they're reading to their background knowledge.
Determining Importance	Readers notice the big ideas in the text and the relationships among them.	Readers focus on the big ideas so they don't become overwhelmed with details.
Drawing Inferences	Readers use background knowledge and clues in the text to "read between the lines."	Readers move beyond literal thinking to grasp meaning that isn't explicitly stated in the text.
Evaluating	Readers evaluate both the text itself and their reading experience.	Readers assume responsibility for their own strategy use.
Monitoring	Readers supervise their reading experience, checking that they're understanding the text.	Readers expect the text to make sense, and they recognize when it doesn't so they can take action.
Predicting	Readers make thoughtful "guesses" about what will happen and then read to confirm their predictions.	Readers become more engaged in the reading experience and want to continue reading.
Questioning	Readers ask themselves literal and inferential questions about the text.	Readers use questions to direct their reading, clarify confusions, and make inferences.
Repairing	Readers identify a problem interfering with comprehension and then solve it.	Readers solve problems to regain comprehension and continue reading.
Setting a Purpose	Readers identify a broad focus to direct their reading through the text.	Readers focus their attention as they read according to the purpose they've set.
Summarizing	Readers paraphrase the big ideas to create a concise statement.	Readers have better recall of the big ideas when they summarize.
Visualizing	Readers create mental images of what they're reading.	Readers use the mental images to make the text more memorable.

One way that teachers teach this strategy is by making connection charts with three columns labeled *text-to-self*, *text-to-world*, and *text-to-text*. Then students write connections that they've made on small self-stick notes and post them in the correct column of the chart, as Mrs. Donnelly did in the vignette at the beginning of the chapter. Students can also make connection charts in their reading logs and write connections in each column. Later in the reading process, during the exploring and applying stages, students make connections as they assume the role of a character and are interviewed by classmates during hot seat, create open-mind portraits to share the character's thinking, or write simulated journals from the viewpoint of a character, for example.

Determining Importance. Readers sift through the text to identify the important ideas as they read because it isn't possible to remember everything (Harvey &

Goudvis, 2007; Keene & Zimmermann, 2007). Students learn to distinguish the big ideas and the details and to recognize what's important as they read and talk about the books they've read. This comprehension strategy is important because students need to be able to identify the big ideas in order to summarize.

Teachers often direct students toward the big ideas when they encourage them to make predictions. The way they introduce the text also influences students' thinking about what's important in the book they're about to read. Mrs. Donnelly's introduction of *Joey Pigza Loses Control* (Gantos, 2005), for instance, directed her sixth graders' thinking about the story and its theme. When students read stories, they make diagrams about the plot, characters, and setting, and these graphic organizers emphasize the big ideas. Similarly, students make diagrams that reflect the structure of the text when they read informational articles and books and chapters in content-area textbooks. Sometimes teachers provide the diagrams with the big ideas highlighted, but students often analyze the text to determine the big ideas and then create their own graphic organizers.

Drawing Inferences. Readers seem to "read between the lines" to draw inferences, but what they actually do is synthesize their background knowledge with the author's clues to ask questions that point toward inferences. Keene and Zimmermann (2007) explain that when readers draw inferences, they have "an opportunity to sense a meaning not explicit in the text, but which derives or flows from it" (p. 145). Readers make both unconscious and conscious inferences about characters in a story and its theme, the big ideas in a newspaper, magazine article, or informational book, and the author's purpose in a poem (Pressley, 2002a). In fact, readers may not even be aware that they're drawing inferences, but when they wonder why the author included this or omitted that information, they probably are.

Students often have to read a picture-book story or an excerpt from a chapter of a novel two or three times in order to draw inferences because at first they focused on literal comprehension, which has to precede higher-level thinking. Very capable students draw inferences on their own as they read, but other students don't notice opportunities to make them. Sometimes students do draw inferences when prompted by the teacher, but it's important to teach students how to draw inferences so that they can think more deeply when they read independently.

Teachers begin by explaining what inferences are, how inferential thinking differs from literal thinking, and why they're important. Then they teach these four steps in drawing inferences:

1. Activate background knowledge about topics related to the text.
2. Look for the author's clues as you read.
3. Ask questions, tying together background knowledge and the author's clues.
4. Draw inferences by answering the questions.

Teachers can create charts to make the steps more visible as students practice making inferences. Figure 8–3 shows an inference chart developed by a seventh-grade class as they read and analyzed *The Wretched Stone* (Van Allsburg, 1991). The story, told in diary format, is about a ship's crew that picks up a strange, glowing stone on a sea voyage. The stone captivates the sailors and has a terrible transforming effect on them. After reading the story and talking about what they understood and what confused them, students began making the chart. First, they completed the "background knowledge" column. The students thought about what they needed to know about to understand the story: the meaning of the word *wretched*, sailors, the author/illustrator Chris Van Allsburg, and the fantasy genre because fantasies are

Figure 8–3 ◆ The Seventh Graders' Inference Chart About *The Wretched Stone*

Background Knowledge	Clues in the Story	Questions	Inferences
• The word <u>wretched</u> means "causing misery." • The people who work on a ship are sailors or the crew. Usually they're hard workers but not readers and musicians. • Chris Van Allsburg writes and illustrates fantasy picture books. He has brown hair and a beard. He wears glasses. • In fantasies, magic and other impossible things happen.	• The captain's last name is Hope. • The crew can read, play music, and tell stories. • It's odd that the island isn't on any maps. • The odor on the island seems sweet at first, but then it stinks. • The crew stare at the glowing stone. They lose interest in reading and stop working. • The crew change into monkeys because they watch the stone. • Capt. Hope looks just like Chris Van Allsburg. • Sailors who could read recovered the quickest.	• Why did Chris Van Allsburg make himself the captain? • Was it a real island or was it magic? • What is the wretched stone? • Why did the sailors turn into monkeys? • Why did the sailors who could read get well faster?	• Chris Van Allsburg wrote this book with hope for kids. • The wretched stone is television. • This book is a warning that watching too much TV is bad for you. • He wants kids to spend more time reading books because reading is good for you. • He wants kids to watch less TV. • Watching television is like the odor on the island. It's sweet at first, but too much of it stinks and isn't good for you.

different from other types of stories. Then they reread the story, searching for clues that might affect the meaning. They noticed that the ship captain's name was Hope, the island was uncharted, and the sailors who could read recovered faster, and they wrote these clues in the second column. Next, they thought about questions they had about the story and wrote them in the third column of the chart. Finally, the teacher reread the book one more time; this time, students listened more confidently, recognizing clues and drawing the inferences they had missed earlier. Finally, they completed the last column of the chart with their inferences.

Evaluating. Readers reflect on their reading experience and evaluate the text and what they're learning (Owocki, 2003). As with the other comprehension strategies, students use the evaluating strategy throughout the reading process. They monitor their interest from the moment they pick up the book and judge their success in solving reading problems when they arise. They evaluate their reading experience, including these aspects:

Their ease in reading the text
The adequacy of their background knowledge
Their use of comprehension strategies
How they solved reading problems
Their interest and attention during reading

They also consider the text:

Whether they like the text
Their opinions about the author

The world knowledge they gain

How they'll use what they're learning

Students usually write about their reflections in **reading log** entries and talk about their evaluations in conferences with the teacher. Evaluating is important because it helps students assume more responsibility for their own learning.

New Literacies
Online Comprehension Strategies

Websites are dynamic learning contexts that create new challenges for readers because online texts differ from books, magazines, and other print texts in significant ways (Castek, Bevans-Mangelson, & Goldstone, 2006). Print texts are linear and unchanging; they contain a finite number of pages with information arranged in predictable narrative, informational, and poetic formats. Internet texts, in contrast, are multilayered, with unlimited multimodal information available through hypertext links.

Students use traditional comprehension strategies to read Web-based texts, but they use them in new ways (Coiro & Dobler, 2007; Leu, Kinzer, Coiro, & Cammack, 2004). Students use these five comprehension strategies to read online texts:

Activating Background Knowledge. Readers activate background knowledge about topics and text structures when they're reading both print and online texts. For Web-based texts, however, readers also need to know about informational websites and how to navigate search engines to locate useful ones.

Predicting. Students use predicting differently for online reading. When they're making choices about which hyperlinks to click on, readers predict which ones will be most useful. Making these predictions is important; otherwise, students get distracted or waste time finding their way back from unproductive links.

Evaluating. Students evaluate their reading experience and the text they're reading, no matter whether they're reading a print or a Web-based text, but when they're reading online, students use this strategy to determine the accuracy, objectivity, relevance, and quality of information at websites. It's crucial for Internet reading because anyone can post erroneous and biased information on the Web.

Monitoring. Students monitor their reading to determine whether what they're reading makes sense and so they can take action if they're confused. When they're reading online, students also monitor their navigational choices and decide whether the links they've clicked on are useful.

Repairing. Readers use the repairing strategy to fix comprehension problems when they're reading print and Web-based texts. For Internet reading, students also use this strategy to correct poor navigational choices and return to useful websites.

As researchers learn more about online reading, it's likely that they'll identify more ways students adapt traditional comprehension strategies.

Readers also learn new comprehension strategies that address the unique characteristics and complex applications of online texts (Coiro, 2003). In the New Literacies feature in Chapter 1, you read about coauthoring, a comprehension strategy that readers use to impose an organization on the information they read online (Leu, Kinzer, Coiro, & Cammack, 2004). More recently, Coiro and Dobler (2007) examined the strategies that sixth graders used for Internet reading and found that these students use a self-directed process of text construction. In this strategy routine, readers make a series of decisions as they move from one link to another, searching for information. They plan, predict, monitor, and evaluate each time they make a navigational choice. More than 25 years ago, Tierney and Pearson (1983) asserted that reading is a composing process, and these comprehension strategies emphasize the interrelatedness of reading and writing.

It's essential that teachers prepare students to use new 21st-century technology. Online reading isn't just a technology issue; websites have unique reader and text factors that affect comprehension (Henry, 2006). Students need to understand how print and Web-based texts differ so they can adjust how they apply traditional comprehension strategies and learn new ones to use for Internet texts.

Go to the Building Teaching Skills and Dispositions section of Chapter 8 on **MyEducationLab.com** to hear second grader Jimmy discuss the ways in which he monitors his comprehension.

Monitoring. Readers monitor their understanding as they read, although they may be aware that they're using this strategy only when their comprehension breaks down and they have to take action to solve their problem. Harvey and Goudvis (2007) describe monitoring as the inner conversation that students carry on in their heads with the text as they read—expressing wonder, making connections, asking questions, reacting to information, drawing conclusions, noticing confusions, for example.

Monitoring involves regulating reader and text factors at the same time. Readers often ask themselves these questions:

◆ What's my purpose for reading?
◆ Is this book too difficult for me to read on my own?
◆ Do I need to read the entire book or only parts of it?
◆ What's special about the genre of this book?
◆ How does the author use text structure?
◆ What is the author's viewpoint?
◆ Do I understand the meaning of the words I'm reading? (Pressley, 2002b)

Once students detect a problem, they shift into problem-solving mode to repair their comprehension.

Teachers use think-alouds to demonstrate the monitoring strategy during minilessons and when they're reading aloud to students. They show that capable readers ask themselves if they're understanding what they're reading or if they realize that they don't remember what they've just read and what they do when they run into difficulty. Students also write about their thinking on small self-stick notes and place them in their books, next to text that stimulated their thinking. Later, students share their notes during a discussion about how students monitor their reading.

Predicting. Readers make thoughtful "guesses" or predictions about what will happen or what they'll learn in the book they're reading. These guesses are based on what students already know about the topic and genre or on what they've read thus far. Students often make a prediction before beginning to read and several others at pivotal points in a text—no matter whether they're reading stories, informational books, or poems—and then as they read, they either confirm or revise their predictions. Predictions about nonfiction are different than for stories and poems; here students are generating questions about the topic that they would like to find answers to as they read.

When teachers share a big book with young children using shared reading, they prompt children to make predictions at the beginning of the book and again at key points during the reading. They model how to make reasonable predictions and use think-alouds to explain their thinking. When older students are reading novels, they often write their predictions on small self-stick notes while they're reading and stick them in their books to share with classmates in a discussion afterward.

Questioning. Readers ask themselves questions about the text as they read (Duke & Pearson, 2002). They ask self-questions out of curiosity, and as they use this strategy, they become more engaged with the text and want to keep reading to find answers (Harvey & Goudvis, 2007). These questions often lead to making predictions and drawing inferences. Students also ask themselves questions to clarify misunderstandings as they read. Students use this strategy throughout the reading process—to activate background knowledge and make predictions before reading, to engage with the text and clarify confusions during reading, and to evaluate and reflect on the text after reading.

Traditionally, teachers have been the question-askers and students have been the question-answerers, but when students learn to generate questions about the text, their comprehension improves. In fact, students comprehend better when they generate their own questions than when teachers ask questions (Duke & Pearson, 2002). Many students don't know how to ask questions to guide their reading, so it's important that teachers teach students how to do so. They model generating questions and then encourage students to do the same. Tovani (2000) suggests having students brainstorm a list of "I wonder" questions on a topic because they need to learn how to generate questions; in the vignette at the beginning of the chapter, for example, Mrs. Donnelly's sixth graders brainstormed questions before they began reading *Joey Pigza Loses Control* (Gantos, 2005).

The questions students ask shape their comprehension: If they ask literal questions, their comprehension will be literal, but if students generate inferential, critical, and evaluative questions, their comprehension will be higher-level. **Question-Answer-Relationships** (QARs) (Raphael, Highfield, & Au, 2006) is an effective way to teach students about the different types of questions they can ask about a text. QARs was developed for analyzing the end-of-chapter questions in content-area textbooks, but it's also useful for teaching students to categorize questions and ultimately to ask higher-level questions.

Repairing. Readers use repairing to fix comprehension problems that arise while reading (Zimmermann & Hutchins, 2003). When students notice that they're confused or bored, can't remember what they just read, or aren't asking questions, they need to use this strategy (Tovani, 2000). Repairing involves figuring out what the problem is and taking action to solve it; Sometimes students go back and reread or skip ahead and read, or they try questioning or another strategy that might help. At other times, they check the meaning of an unfamiliar word, examine the structure of a confusing sentence, learn more about an unfamiliar topic related to the text, or ask the teacher for assistance. These solutions are often referred to as *fix-up strategies*.

Setting a Purpose. Readers read for different reasons—for entertainment, to learn about a topic, for directions to accomplish a task, or to find the answer to a specific question, for instance—and the purposes they set direct their attention during reading (Tovani, 2000). Setting a purpose activates a mental blueprint, which aids in determining how readers focus their attention and how

Teaching Struggling Readers and Writers

Strategic Readers

Struggling students need to become strategic readers.

Struggling readers often complain that they don't understand what they're reading. Comprehension difficulties are due to a variety of problems, but one of the most common is that students don't read strategically (Cooper, Chard, & Kiger, 2006). They read passively, without using comprehension strategies to think about what they're reading. Without learning to thoughtfully engage in the reading process, it's unlikely that students who struggle with comprehension will improve very much.

The good news is that teachers can help struggling students become better readers by teaching them to use comprehension strategies to be more thoughtful readers (Allington, 2006). The most important comprehension strategies for struggling readers are activating background knowledge, determining importance, summarizing, questioning, visualizing, and monitoring.

As teachers teach comprehension strategies, they explain each strategy, including how, when, and why to use it, and they make the strategy visible by demonstrating how to use it during minilessons, interactive read-alouds, and guided reading lessons. They use think-alouds to show that capable readers are active thinkers while they're reading. Students participate in small-group and partner activities as they practice using the strategy and verbalize their thinking. At first, teachers provide lots of support, and they withdraw it slowly as students become responsible for using the strategy independently. Once students have learned to apply two or three strategies, they begin to use them together. Integrating strategy use is important because capable readers don't depend on a single comprehension strategy; instead, they have a repertoire of strategies available that they use as needed while they're reading (Allington, 2006).

they sort relevant from irrelevant information as they read (Blanton, Wood, & Moorman, 1990). Before they begin to read, students identify a single, fairly broad purpose that they sustain while reading the entire text; it must fit both students' reason for reading and the text. Students can ask themselves "Why am I going to read this text?" or "What do I need to learn from this book?" to help them set a purpose. It's important that students have a purpose when they read, because readers vary how they read and what they remember according to their purpose. When students don't have a purpose, they are likely to misdirect their attention and focus on unimportant ideas.

Summarizing. Readers pick out the most important ideas and the relationships among them and briefly restate them so they can be remembered (Harvey & Goudvis, 2007). It's crucial that students determine which ideas are the most important because if they focus on tangential ideas or details, their comprehension is compromised. To create effective summaries, students need to learn to paraphrase, or restate ideas in their own words.

Summarizing is a difficult task, but instruction and practice improve not only students' ability to summarize but their overall comprehension as well (Duke & Pearson, 2002). One way to teach students to summarize is to have them create graphic organizers after reading a chapter in a novel or a content-area textbook: They emphasize the big ideas and relationships among them in their diagram, and then they use the information to write a brief summary statement.

Visualizing. Readers create mental images of what they're reading (Harvey & Goudvis, 2007; Keene & Zimmermann, 2007). They often place themselves in the images they create, becoming a character in the story they're reading, traveling to that setting, or facing the conflict situations the characters face. Teachers sometimes ask students to close their eyes to help visualize the story or to draw pictures of the scenes and characters they visualize. How well students use visualization often becomes clear when they view film versions of books they've read: Students who are good visualizers are often disappointed with the film version and the actors who perform as the characters, but those who don't visualize are often amazed by the film and prefer it to the book.

Students use comprehension strategies at every stage in the reading process, but their activities vary from stage to stage, depending on the strategy being used. Figure 8–4 explains what readers do to comprehend at each stage and the strategies they use. Sometimes strategies are grouped into before reading, during reading, and after reading strategies, but that categorization doesn't work: Although setting a purpose is almost always a prereading strategy and monitoring and repairing are usually reading-stage strategies, students use connecting, drawing inferences, questioning, and other strategies in more than one stage.

Comprehension Skills

"interesting" ✱

Even though there's controversy regarding the differences between comprehension strategies and skills, it's possible to identify some comprehension skills that students need to learn to become successful readers. These skills are related to strategies, but the big difference is that skills involve literal thinking. They're like questions to which there's one correct answer. One group of skills focus on main ideas and details. Students use the determining importance strategy to identify main ideas, and they use these related skills:

Figure 8–4 ◆ How the Comprehension Strategies Fit Into the Reading Process

Stage	What Readers Do	Strategies Readers Use
Prereading	Students prepare to read by setting purposes, thinking about the topic and genre of the text, and planning for the reading experience.	Activating background knowledge Predicting Questioning Setting a purpose
Reading	Students read the text silently or orally, thinking about it as they read, monitoring their understanding, and solving problems as they arise.	Monitoring Repairing All other strategies
Responding	Students share their reactions, making tentative and exploratory comments, asking questions, and clarifying confusions, by talking with classmates and the teacher and writing in reading logs.	Connecting Determining importance Drawing inferences Evaluating Questioning Visualizing
Exploring	Students reread parts of the text, examine it more analytically, and study the genre and author's craft.	Determining importance Drawing inferences Evaluating Summarizing
Applying	Students create projects to deepen their understanding of the text they've read and reflect on their reading experience.	Connecting Evaluating Questioning

Recognizing details
Noticing similarities and differences
Identifying topic sentences
Comparing and contrasting main ideas and details
Matching causes with effects
Sequencing details
Paraphrasing ideas
Choosing a good title for a text

In contrast, when main ideas and relationships among them aren't explicitly stated in the text, students use the drawing inferences strategy to comprehend them because higher-level thinking is required. Another group of comprehension skills are related to the evaluating strategy:

Recognizing the author's purpose
Detecting propaganda
Distinguishing between fact and opinion

Teachers teach these skills and students practice them until they become automatic procedures that don't require conscious thought or interpretation.

TEACHING STUDENTS ABOUT READER FACTORS

Comprehension instruction involves teaching students about comprehension and the strategies they use to understand what they're reading. The three components are explicit instruction, reading, and writing (Duke & Pearson, 2002). Researchers emphasize the need to establish the expectation that the books students read and the compositions they write will make sense (Duke & Pearson, 2002). Teachers create an expectation of comprehension in these ways:

- ◆ Involving students in authentic reading and writing activities every day
- ◆ Providing access to well-stocked classroom libraries
- ◆ Teaching students to use comprehension strategies
- ◆ Ensuring that students are fluent readers
- ◆ Providing opportunities for students to talk about the books they read
- ◆ Linking vocabulary instruction to underlying concepts

Teachers can't assume that students will learn to comprehend simply by doing lots of reading; instead, students develop an understanding of comprehension and what readers do to be successful through a combination of instruction and authentic reading activities (Block & Pressley, 2007). Guidelines for teaching comprehension are presented below.

Explicit Comprehension Instruction

The fact that comprehension is an invisible mental process makes it difficult to teach; however, through explicit instruction, teachers can make comprehension more visible. They explain what comprehension is and why it's important, and they model how they do it, by thinking aloud. Next, teachers encourage students to direct their thinking as they read, gradually releasing responsibility to students through guided and independent

Guidelines
for Teaching Comprehension

- ▶ Teach students about both reader and text factors.

- ▶ Teach comprehension strategies using a combination of explanations, demonstrations, think-alouds, and practice activities.

- ▶ Demonstrate how to use strategies through interactive read-alouds.

- ▶ Have students apply strategies in literacy activities as well as in thematic units.

- ▶ Teach groups of strategies in routines so that students learn to orchestrate their use of multiple strategies.

- ▶ Ask students to reflect on their use of individual strategies and strategy routines.

- ▶ Hang charts in the classroom of the strategies and strategy routines students are learning.

- ▶ Differentiate between strategies and skills so that students understand that strategies are problem-solving tactics and skills are automatic behaviors.

practice. Finally, they move students from focusing on a single comprehension strategy to integrating several strategies in routines. Mrs. Donnelly demonstrated the concept of gradual release in the vignette at the beginning of the chapter as she reviewed each comprehension strategy and had the students practice it as they read picture books; then she had them apply all the strategies as they read *Joey Pigza Loses Control* (Gantos, 2005).

Teaching Comprehension Strategies. Teachers teach individual comprehension strategies and then show students how to integrate several strategies simultaneously (Block & Pressley, 2007). They introduce each comprehension strategy in a series of minilessons. Teachers describe the strategy, model it for students as they read a text aloud, use it collaboratively with students, and provide opportunities for guided and then independent practice (Duke & Pearson, 2002); the independent practice is important because it's motivational. The minilesson feature on page 272 shows how Mrs. Macadangdang teaches her third graders to use the questioning strategy.

Teachers also support students' learning about comprehension strategies in other ways: Figure 8–5 suggests several activities for each strategy. Second graders practice questioning by asking questions instead of giving answers during a **grand conversation**, for example, and sixth graders practice connecting when they write favorite quotes in one column of a double-entry journal and then explain in the second column why each quote is meaningful. When teachers involve students in these activities, it's important to explain that students will be practicing a particular strategy as they complete an activity so that they think about what they're doing and how it's helping them to comprehend better.

Teaching Comprehension Routines. Once students know how to use individual strategies, they need to learn how to use routines or combinations of strategies because capable readers rarely use comprehension strategies one at a time (Duke & Pearson, 2002). In the vignette at the beginning of the chapter, for example, Mrs. Donnelly was teaching her sixth graders to use multiple strategies as they read *Joey Pigza Loses Control* (Gantos, 2005) and reflected on their strategy use in their thinking logs.

One of the most effective comprehension routines is *reciprocal teaching* (Palincsar & Brown, 1986). Students use predicting, questioning, clarifying, and summarizing strategies to figure out the meaning of a text, paragraph by paragraph. Teachers can use this instructional procedure with the whole class when students are reading chapters in content-area textbooks or in small groups, such as literature circles when students are reading novels (Oczkus, 2003).

Developing Comprehension Through Reading

Students need to spend lots of time reading authentic texts independently and talking about their reading with classmates and teachers. Having students read interesting books written at their reading level is the best way for them to apply comprehension strategies. As they read and discuss their reading, students are practicing what they're learning about comprehension. Reading a selection in a basal reader each week is not enough; instead, students need to read many, many books representing a range of genres during reading workshop or Sustained Silent Reading.

In addition to providing opportunities for students to read independently, teachers read books aloud to young children who are not yet fluent readers and to struggling readers who can't read age-appropriate books themselves. When teachers do the reading, students have more cognitive resources available to focus on comprehension.

MiniLesson

TOPIC: Teaching Students to Ask Self-Questions
GRADE: Third Grade
TIME: Three 30-minute periods

Mrs. Macadangdang (the students call her Mrs. Mac) introduced questioning by talking about why people ask questions and by asking questions about stories they were reading. She encouraged the third graders to ask questions, too. They made a list of questions for each chapter of *Chang's Paper Pony* (Coerr, 1993), a story set in the California gold rush era, as she read it aloud, and then they evaluated their questions, choosing the ones that focus on the big ideas and helped them understand the story better. Now all of her students can generate questions, so she's ready to introduce the questioning strategy.

❶ Introduce the Topic

Mrs. Mac reads the list of comprehension strategies posted in the classroom that they've learned to use and explains, "Today, we're going to learn a new thinking strategy—questioning. Readers ask themselves questions while they're reading to help them think about the book." She adds "Questioning" to the list.

❷ Share Examples

The teacher introduces *The Josefina Story Quilt* (Coerr, 1989), the story of a pioneer family going to California in a covered wagon. She reads aloud the first chapter, thinking aloud and generating questions about the story. Each time she says a question, she places in a pocket chart a sentence strip on which the question has already been written. Here are the questions: Why is Faith excited? Why are they going in a covered wagon? Who is Josefina? Can a chicken be a pet? Can Josefina do anything useful? Why is Faith crying?

❸ Provide Information

Mrs. Mac explains, "Questions really turn your thinking on! I know it's important to think while I'm reading because it helps me understand. I like to ask questions about things I think are important and things that don't make sense to me." They reread the questions in the pocket chart and talk about the most helpful questions. Many students thought the question about the covered wagon was important, but as they continue reading, they'll learn that Josefina does indeed do something useful—she turns out to be a "humdinger of a watch dog" (p. 54)! Then Mrs. Mac reads aloud the second chapter, stopping often for students to generate questions. The students write their questions on sentence strips and add them to the pocket chart.

❹ Guide Practice

The following day, Mrs. Mac reviews the questioning strategy, and students reread the questions for chapters 1 and 2. Then the students form pairs, get copies of the book, and read the next two chapters of *The Josefina Story Quilt* together, generating questions as they read. They write their questions on small self-stick notes and place them in the book. Mrs. Mac monitors students, noticing which ones need additional practice. Then the class comes together to share their questions and talk about the chapters they've read. On the third day, they read the last two chapters and generate more questions.

❺ Assess Learning

As she monitored the students, Mrs. Mac made a list of students who needed more practice generating questions, and she'll work with them as they read another book together.

Figure 8–5 ◆ Ways to Teach the Comprehension Strategies

Strategy	Instructional Procedures
Activating Background Knowledge	• Students complete an anticipation guide. • Students do an exclusion brainstorming activity. • Students develop a K-W-L chart.
Connecting	• Students add text-to-self, text-to-world, and text-to-text connections to a class chart. • Students write a double-entry journal with quotes and reflections about each one. • Students become a character and participate in a hot seat activity.
Determining Importance	• Students create graphic organizers. • Students make posters highlighting the big ideas.
Drawing Inferences	• Students use small self-stick notes to mark clues in the text. • Students create charts with author's clues, questions, and inferences. • Students quickwrite about an inference they've made.
Evaluating	• Students write reflections and evaluations in reading logs. • Students conference with the teacher about a book they've read.
Monitoring	• Students think aloud to demonstrate how they monitor their reading. • Students write about their strategy use on small self-stick notes and in reading logs.
Predicting	• Students make and share predictions during read-alouds. • Students write a double-entry journal with predictions in one column and summaries in the other. • Students make predictions during guided reading lessons.
Questioning	• Students brainstorm a list of questions before reading. • Students ask questions during grand conversations and other discussions. • Students analyze the questions they pose using the QAR levels.
Repairing	• Students make personal charts of the ways they solve comprehension problems. • Students think aloud to demonstrate how they use the repairing strategy. • Students write about their repairs on small self-stick notes and place them in a book they're reading.
Setting a Purpose	• Students identify their purpose in a discussion before beginning to read. • Students write about their purpose in a reading log entry before beginning to read.
Summarizing	• Students write a summary using interactive writing. • Students create visual summaries on charts using words, diagrams, and pictures.
Visualizing	• Students create open-mind portraits of characters. • Students draw pictures of episodes from a book they're reading. • Students role-play episodes from a book they're reading.

Grand Conversations
These students have gathered together for a grand conversation to talk about chapters 6, 7, and 8 in a novel they're reading. The sixth graders share ideas, ask questions, and read and comment on excerpts from the book. Without raising their hands to be called on, the students take turns making comments. The teacher participates in the conversation to share her insights, ask questions, and clarify misconceptions. Later in the discussion, she'll focus on story elements and draw students' attention to the characters and talk about the similarities and differences among them.

Teachers often read books aloud when they introduce comprehension strategies so that they can model procedures and scaffold students' thinking.

Students also develop their comprehension abilities when they discuss the stories they're reading in grand conversations and informational books and chapters in content-area textbooks in other discussions. As students talk about their reading, draw inferences, ask questions to clarify confusions, and reflect on their use of the comprehension strategies, they elaborate and refine their comprehension.

Nurturing English Learners

Comprehension is often difficult for English learners, and there are a number of reasons why (Bouchard, 2005). Many ELs lack the background knowledge that's necessary for understanding the book they're attempting to read. Sometimes they lack culturally based knowledge, and at other times, they're unfamiliar with a genre or can't understand the meaning of figurative vocabulary. There can be a mismatch between the level of students' English proficiency and the reading level of the book too: Like all students, ELs won't understand what they're reading if the book is too difficult.

Teachers can address these issues by carefully choosing books that are appropriate for English learners, building their world and literary knowledge, and introducing key vocabulary words in advance. Peregoy and Boyle (2008) also point out that many ELs read texts passively, as if they were waiting for the information they're reading to organize itself and highlight the big ideas. To help these students become more active readers, teachers explicitly teach the comprehension strategies. During the lessons, teachers explain each strategy, including why it will help students become better readers and how and when to use it. They spend more time modeling how to apply each strategy and thinking aloud to share their thoughts. Next, teachers provide guided practice with the students working together in small groups and with partners, and they assist students as they use the strategy. Finally, students use the strategy independently and apply it in new ways.

Assessing Students' Comprehension

Teachers assess students' comprehension informally every day. They listen to the comments students make during **grand conversations**, conference with students about books they're reading, and examine their entries in **reading logs**, for example. They use informal assessment procedures such as the following to monitor students' use of comprehension strategies and their understanding of books they're reading:

Cloze Procedure. Teachers examine students' understanding of a text using the **cloze procedure**, in which students supply the deleted words in a passage taken from a text they've read. Although filling in the blanks may seem like a simple activity, it isn't because students need to consider the content of the passage, vocabulary words, and sentence structure to choose the exact word that was deleted.

Story Retellings. Teachers often have young children retell stories they've read or listened to read aloud to assess their literal comprehension (Morrow, 2002). Students' **retellings** should be coherent and well organized and should include the big ideas and important details. When teachers prompt students with questions and encourage them to "tell me more," they're known as *aided retellings*; otherwise they're *unaided retellings*. Teachers often use checklists and **rubrics** to score students' story retellings.

Running Records. Teachers use **running records** (Clay, 2007) to examine children's oral reading behaviors, analyze their comprehension, and determine their reading levels. Although they're most commonly used with young children, running records can also be used with older students. Children read a book, and afterward they orally retell it. Teachers encourage children to recall as much detail as possible, ask questions to prompt their recall, when necessary, and sometimes pose other comprehension questions to probe the depth of their understanding. Finally, they evaluate the completeness of the child's retelling.

Think-Alouds. Teachers assess students' ability to apply comprehension strategies by having them **think aloud** and share their thinking as they read a passage (Wilhelm, 2001). Students usually think aloud orally, but they can also write their thoughts on small self-stick notes that they place beside sections of text, write entries in **reading logs**, and do **quickwrites**.

Teachers also use other assessment tools, including tests, to evaluate students' comprehension; the Assessment Tools feature on page 276 presents more information about comprehension tests. No matter whether teachers are using informal assessments or tests to examine students' comprehension, they need to consider whether they're assessing literal, inferential, critical, or evaluative thinking. The emphasis in both assessment and instruction should be on higher-level comprehension.

Assessment Tools

Comprehension

Teachers use a combination of informal assessment procedures, including retelling and think-alouds, and commercially available tests to measure students' comprehension. Here are several tests that are commonly used in K–8 classrooms:

◆ **Comprehension Thinking Strategies Assessment** (Keene, 2006)

The Comprehension Thinking Strategies Assessment examines first through eighth graders' ability to use these strategies to think about fiction and nonfiction texts they're reading: activating background knowledge, determining importance, drawing inferences, noticing text structure, questioning, setting a purpose, and visualizing. As students read a passage, they pause and reflect on their strategy use. Teachers score students' responses using a rubric. This 30-minute test can be administered to individuals or to the class, depending on whether students' responses are oral or written. This flexible assessment tool can be used to evaluate students' learning after teaching a strategy, to survey progress at the beginning of the school year, or to document achievement at the end of the year. It's available from Shell Education.

◆ **Developmental Reading Assessment, Grades K–3 (DRA)** (Beaver, 2006)
Developmental Reading Assessment, Grades 4–8 (Beaver & Carter, 2003)

K–8 teachers use the DRA to determine students' reading levels, assess their strengths and weaknesses in word identification, fluency, and comprehension, and make instructional decisions. To measure comprehension, students read a leveled book and then retell what they've read. Their retellings are scored using a 4-point rubric. Both DRA levels are available from Celebration Press/Pearson.

◆ **Informal Reading Inventories (IRIs)**

Teachers use individually administered IRIs to assess students' comprehension of narrative and informational texts. Comprehension is measured by students' ability to retell what they've read and to answer questions about the passage. The questions examine how well students use literal and higher-level thinking and their knowledge about word meanings. A number of commercially published IRIs are available, including the following:

> Analytical Reading Inventory (Woods & Moe, 2007)
> Comprehensive Reading Inventory (Cooter, Flynt, & Cooter, 2007)
> Critical Reading Inventory (Applegate, Quinn, & Applegate, 2008)
> Qualitative Reading Inventory (Leslie & Caldwell, 2006)

These IRIs can be purchased from Pearson. Other IRIs accompany basal reading series. IRIs typically are designed for grades 1–8, but first- and second-grade teachers often find that running records provide more-useful information about beginning readers.

These tests provide valuable information about whether students meet grade-level comprehension standards.

OTIVATION

Motivation is intrinsic, the innate curiosity that makes us want to figure things out. It involves feeling self-confident, believing you'll succeed, and viewing the activity as pleasurable (Guthrie & Wigfield, 2000). It's based on the engagement theory that you read about in the first chapter. Motivation is social, too: People want to socialize, share ideas, and participate in group activities. Motivation is more than one characteristic, however; it's a network of interacting factors (Alderman, 1999). Often students' motivation to become better readers and writers diminishes as they reach the middle grades, and struggling students demonstrate significantly less enthusiasm for reading and writing than other students do.

Many factors contribute to students' engagement or involvement in reading and writing. Some focus on teachers' role—what they believe and do—and others focus on students (Pressley, Dolezal, Raphael, Mohan, Roehrig, & Bogner, 2003; Unrau, 2004). Figure 8–6 summarizes the factors affecting students' engagement in literacy activities and what teachers can do to nurture students' interest.

Figure 8–6 ◆ Factors Affecting Students' Motivation

Roles	Factors	What Teachers Do
Teachers	Attitude	• Show students that you care about them. • Display excitement and enthusiasm about what you're teaching. • Stimulate students' curiosity and desire to learn.
	Community	• Create a nurturing and inclusive classroom community. • Insist that students treat classmates with respect.
	Instruction	• Focus on students' long-term learning. • Teach students to be strategic readers and writers. • Engage students in authentic activities. • Offer students choices of activities and reading materials.
	Rewards	• Employ specific praise and positive feedback. • Use external rewards only when students' interest is very low.
Students	Expectations	• Expect students to be successful. • Teach students to set realistic goals.
	Collaboration	• Encourage students to work collaboratively. • Minimize competition. • Allow students to participate in making plans and choices.
	Reading and Writing Competence	• Teach students to use reading and writing strategies. • Provide guided reading lessons for struggling readers. • Use interactive writing to teach writing skills to struggling writers. • Provide daily reading and writing opportunities.
	Choices	• Have students complete interest inventories. • Teach students to choose books at their reading levels. • Encourage students to write about topics that interest them.

Teachers' Role

Everything teachers do affects their students' interest and engagement with literacy, but four of the most important factors are teachers' attitude, the community teachers create, the instructional approaches they use, and their reward systems:

Attitude. It seems obvious that when teachers show that they care about their students and exhibit excitement and enthusiasm for learning, students are more likely to become engaged. Effective teachers also stimulate students' curiosity and encourage them to explore ideas. They emphasize intrinsic over extrinsic motivation because they understand that students' intrinsic desire to learn is more powerful than grades, rewards, and other extrinsic motivators.

Community. Students are more likely to engage in reading and writing when their classroom is a learning community that respects and nurtures everyone. Students and the teacher show respect for each other, and students learn how to work well with classmates in small groups. In a community of learners, students enjoy social interaction and feel connected to their classmates and their teacher.

Instruction. The types of literacy activities in which students are involved affect their interest and motivation. Turner and Paris (1995) compared authentic literacy activities such as reading and writing workshop with skills-based reading programs and concluded that students' motivation was determined by the daily classroom activities. They found that open-ended activities and projects in which students were in control of the processes they used and the products they created were the most successful.

Rewards. Many teachers consider using rewards to encourage students to do more reading and writing, but Alfie Kohn (2001) and others believe that extrinsic incentives are harmful because they undermine students' intrinsic motivation. Incentives such as pizzas, free time, or "money" to spend in a classroom "store" are most effective when students' interest is very low and they are reluctant to participate in literacy activities. Once students become more interested, teachers withdraw these incentives and use less tangible ones, including positive feedback and praise (Stipek, 2002).

Students' Role

Motivation isn't something that teachers or parents can force on students; rather, it's an innate, intrinsic desire that students must develop themselves. They're more likely to become engaged with reading and writing when they expect to be successful, when they work collaboratively with classmates, when they're competent readers and writers, and when they have opportunities to make choices and develop ownership of their work. Here are four factors that influence students' motivation:

Expectations. Students who feel they have little hope of success are unlikely to become engaged in literacy activities. Teachers play a big role in shaping students' expectations, and teacher expectations are often self-fulfilling (Brophy, 2004): If teachers believe that their students can be successful, it's more likely that they will be. Stipek (2002) found that in classrooms where teachers take a personal interest in their students and expect that all of them can learn, the students are more successful.

Collaboration. When students work with classmates in pairs and in small groups, they're often more interested and engaged in activities than when they read and write alone. Collaborative groups support students because they have opportunities to share ideas, learn from each other, and enjoy the collegiality of their classmates. Competition, in contrast, doesn't develop intrinsic motivation; instead, it decreases many students' interest in learning.

Reading and Writing Competence. Not surprisingly, students' competence in reading and writing affects their motivation: Students who read well are more likely to be motivated to read than those who read less well, and the same is true for writers. Teaching students how to read and write is an essential factor in developing their motivation. Teachers find that once struggling students improve their reading and writing performance, they become more interested.

Choices. Students want to have a say in which books they read and which topics they write about. By making choices, students develop more responsibility for their work and ownership of their accomplishments. Reading and writing workshop are instructional approaches that honor students' choices: In reading workshop, students choose books they're interested in reading and that are written at their reading level, and in writing workshop, students write about topics that interest them.

How to Engage Students in Reading and Writing

Oldfather (1995) conducted a 4-year study to examine the factors influencing students' motivation. She found that students were more highly motivated when they had opportunities for authentic self-expression as part of literacy activities. The students she interviewed reported that they were more highly motivated when they had ownership of the learning activities. Specific activities they mentioned included opportunities to do the following:

Express their own ideas and opinions
Choose topics for writing and books for reading
Talk about books they're reading
Share their writing with classmates
Pursue authentic activities—not worksheets—using reading, writing, listening, and talking

Ivey and Broaddus (2001) reported similar conclusions from their study of the factors that influence sixth graders' desire to read. Three of their conclusions are noteworthy. First, students are more interested in reading when their teachers make them feel confident and successful; a nurturing classroom community is an important factor. Second, students are more intrinsically motivated when they have ownership of their literacy learning. Students place great value on being allowed to choose interesting books and other reading materials. Third, students become more engaged with books when they have time for independent reading and opportunities to listen to the teacher read aloud. Students reported that they enjoy listening to teachers read aloud because teachers make books more comprehensible and more interesting through the background knowledge they provide.

Some students aren't strongly motivated to learn to read and write, and they adopt defensive tactics for avoiding failure rather than strategies for being successful (Paris, Wasik, & Turner, 1991). Unmotivated readers give up or remain passive, uninvolved in reading. Some students feign interest or pretend to be involved even though they aren't. Others don't think reading is important, and they choose to focus on other curricular areas—math or sports, for instance. Some students complain about feeling ill or that classmates are bothering them. They place the blame anywhere but on themselves.

Other students avoid reading and writing entirely; they just don't do it. Still others read books that are too easy for them or write short pieces so that they don't have to exert much effort. Even though these strategies are self-serving, students use them because they lead to short-term success. The long-term result, however, is devastating because these students fail to learn to read and write well. Because it takes quite a bit of effort to read and write strategically, it's especially important that students experience personal ownership of the literacy activities going on in their classrooms and know how to manage their own reading and writing behaviors.

Assessing Students' Motivation

Because students' motivation and engagement affect their success in reading as well as writing, it's important that teachers learn about their students and work to ensure that they're motivated and have positive attitudes about literacy. Teachers observe students and conference with them and their parents to understand students' reading and writing habits at home, their interests and hobbies, and their view of themselves as readers and writers. There are also surveys that teachers can administer to quickly estimate students' motivation toward reading and writing; these surveys are described in the Assessment Tools feature on the next page.

Comparing Capable and Less Capable Readers and Writers

Researchers have compared students who are capable readers and writers with other students who are less successful and have found some striking differences (Baker & Brown, 1984; Faigley, Cherry, Jolliffe, & Skinner, 1985; Paris, Wasik, & Turner, 1991). The researchers have found that more capable readers do the following:

- ◆ Read fluently
- ◆ View reading as a process of creating meaning
- ◆ Decode rapidly
- ◆ Have large vocabularies
- ◆ Understand the organization of stories, plays, informational books, poems, and other texts
- ◆ Use comprehension strategies
- ◆ Monitor their understanding as they read

Similarly, capable writers do the following:

- ◆ Vary how they write depending on the purpose for writing and the audience that will read the composition
- ◆ Use the writing process flexibly
- ◆ Focus on developing ideas and communicating effectively
- ◆ Turn to classmates for feedback on how they are communicating
- ◆ Monitor how well they are communicating in the piece of writing
- ◆ Use formats and structures for stories, poems, letters, and other texts
- ◆ Postpone attention to mechanical correctness until the end of the writing process

All of these characteristics of capable readers and writers relate to comprehension, and because these students know and use them, they are better readers and writers than students who don't use them.

A comparison of the characteristics of capable and less capable readers and writers is presented in Figure 8–7. Young children who are learning to read and write often exemplify many of the characteristics of less capable readers and writers, but older students who are less successful readers and writers also exemplify them.

Less successful readers exemplify few of the characteristics of capable readers or behave differently when they are reading and writing. Perhaps the most remarkable difference is that more capable readers view reading as a process of comprehending or creating meaning, whereas less capable readers focus on decoding. In writing, less capable writers make cosmetic changes when they revise, rather than changes to communicate

Assessment Tools

Motivation

Teachers assess students' motivation in several ways. They observe students as they read and write, read entries in their reading logs, and conference with them about their interests and attitudes. At the beginning of the school year, teachers often have students create interest inventories with lists of things they're interested in, types of books they like to read, and favorite authors. Teachers also administer attitude surveys. These surveys assess students' motivation:

◆ **Elementary Reading Attitude Survey** (McKenna & Kear, 1990)

The Elementary Reading Attitude Survey assesses first- through sixth-grade students' attitudes toward reading at home and in school. The 20 items begin with the stem "How do you feel . . ." and students mark one of four pictures of Garfield, the cartoon cat; each picture depicts a different emotional state, ranging from positive to negative. This survey enables teachers to quickly estimate their students' attitudes.

◆ **Motivation to Read Profile** (Gambrell, Palmer, Codling, & Mazzoni, 1996)

The Motivation to Read Profile consists of two parts, a group test and an individual interview. The test is a survey with 20 items about self-concept as a reader and the value of reading that students respond to using a 4-point Likert scale. The interview is a series of open-ended questions about the types of books students like best and where they get reading materials. Each part takes about 15 minutes to administer.

◆ **Reader Self-Perception Scale** (Henk & Melnick, 1995)

The Reader Self-Perception Scale measures how students feel about reading and about themselves as readers. It's designed for third to sixth graders. Students respond to "I think I am a good reader" and other statements using a 5-point Likert scale where responses range from "strongly agree" to "strongly disagree." Teachers score students' responses and interpret the results to determine both overall and specific attitude levels.

◆ **Writing Attitude Survey** (Kear, Coffman, McKenna, & Ambrosio, 2000)

The Writing Attitude Survey examines students' feelings about the writing process and types of writing. It has 28 items, including "How would you feel if your classmates talked to you about making your writing better?" It features Garfield, the cartoon cat, as in the Elementary Reading Attitude Survey. Students indicate their response by marking the picture of Garfield that best illustrates their feelings.

◆ **Writer Self-Perception Scale** (Bottomley, Henk, & Melnick, 1997/1998)

The Writer Self-Perception Scale assesses third through sixth graders' attitudes about writing and how they perceive themselves as writers. Students respond to statements such as "I write better than my classmates do," using the same 5-point Likert scale that the Reader Self-Perception Scale uses.

These attitude surveys were originally published in *The Reading Teacher* and are readily available at libraries, online, and in collections of assessment instruments, such as *Assessment for Reading Instruction* (McKenna & Stahl, 2003).

Figure 8–7 ◆ Capable and Less Capable Readers and Writers

Components	Reader Characteristics	Writer Characteristics
Belief Systems	Capable readers view reading as a comprehending process, but less capable readers view reading as a decoding process.	Capable writers view writing as communicating ideas, but less capable writers see writing as putting words on paper.
Purpose	Capable readers adjust their reading according to purpose, but less capable readers approach all reading tasks the same way.	Capable writers adapt their writing to meet demands of audience, purpose, and form, but less capable writers don't.
Fluency	Capable readers read fluently, whereas less capable readers read word by word, don't chunk words into phrases, and sometimes point at words as they read.	Capable writers sustain their writing for longer periods of time and pause as they draft to think and reread what they've written, whereas less capable writers write less and without pausing.
Background Knowledge	Capable readers relate what they're reading to their background knowledge, but less capable readers don't make this connection.	Capable writers gather and organize ideas before writing, but less capable writers don't plan before beginning to write.
Decoding/ Spelling	Capable readers identify unfamiliar words efficiently, but less capable readers make nonsensical guesses or skip over unfamiliar words and invent what they think is a reasonable text when they're reading.	Capable writers spell many words conventionally and use the dictionary to spell unfamiliar words, but less capable writers can't spell many high-frequency words, and they depend on phonics to spell unfamiliar words.
Vocabulary	Capable readers have larger vocabularies than less capable readers do.	Capable writers use more sophisticated words and figurative language than less capable writers do.
Strategies	Capable readers use a variety of strategies as they read, but less capable readers use fewer strategies or less effective ones.	Capable writers use many strategies effectively, but less capable writers use fewer strategies or less effective ones.
Monitoring	Capable readers monitor their comprehension, but less capable readers don't realize or take action when they don't understand.	Capable writers monitor that their writing makes sense, and they turn to classmates for revising suggestions, but less capable writers don't.

Adapted from Faigley, Cherry, Jolliffe, & Skinner, 1985; Paris, Wasik, & Turner, 1991.

meaning more effectively. These important differences indicate that capable students focus on comprehension and the strategies readers and writers use to understand what they read and to make sure that what they write will be comprehensible to others.

Another important difference between capable and less capable readers and writers is that those who are less successful aren't strategic. They are naive. They seem reluctant to use unfamiliar strategies or those that require much effort. They don't seem to be motivated or to expect that they'll be successful. Less capable readers and writers don't understand or use all stages of the reading and writing processes effectively. They don't monitor their reading and writing (Keene & Zimmermann, 2007). Or, if they do use strategies, they remain dependent on primitive ones. For example, as they read, less successful readers seldom look ahead or back into the text to clarify misunderstandings or make plans. Or, when they come to an unfamiliar word, they often stop reading, unsure of what to do. They may try to sound out an unfamiliar word, but if that's unsuccessful, they give up. In contrast, capable readers know a variety of strategies, and if one strategy isn't successful, they try another.

Less capable writers move through the writing process in a lockstep, linear approach. They use a limited number of strategies, most often a "knowledge-telling" strategy in which they write everything they know about a topic with little thought to choosing information to meet the needs of their readers or to organizing the information to put related ideas together (Faigley et al., 1985). In contrast, capable writers understand the recursive nature of the writing process and turn to classmates for feedback about how well they're communicating. They are more responsive to the needs of the audience that will read their writing, and they work to organize their writing in a cohesive manner.

This research on capable and less capable readers and writers has focused on comprehension differences and students' use of strategies. It's noteworthy that all research comparing readers and writers focuses on how students use strategies, not on their use of reading and writing skills.

Chapter 8 Review

How Effective Teachers Facilitate Students' Comprehension of Reader Factors

▶ Teachers understand that comprehension is a process involving both reader factors and text factors.

▶ Teachers ensure that students have adequate background knowledge, vocabulary, and fluency, the prerequisites for comprehension.

▶ Teachers understand how comprehension strategies support students' understanding of texts they're reading.

▶ Teachers teach students how to use comprehension strategies and skills.

▶ Teachers nurture students' motivation and engagement in literacy activities.

myeducationlab
Where the Classroom Comes to Life

Go to MyEducationLab at www.myeducationlab.com to deepen your understanding of the concepts presented in this chapter:

▶ Identify the comprehension strategies that Ms. Janusz's second graders have learned by viewing video segments in the Literacy Portraits.

▶ Check your understanding of chapter concepts with the multiple-choice and essay quizzes in the Study Plan.

▶ Apply some of the main ideas discussed in the chapter in the Activities and Applications section of the website.

▶ Practice what you've learned in this chapter in Building Teaching Skills and Dispositions before applying the ideas in your own classroom.

PROFESSIONAL REFERENCES

Afflerbach, P., Pearson, P. D., & Paris, S. G. (2008). Clarifying differences between reading skills and strategies. *The Reading Teacher, 61,* 364–373.

Alderman, M. K. (1999). *Motivation for achievement: Possibilities for teaching and learning.* Mahwah, NJ: Erlbaum.

Allington, R. L. (2006). *What really matters for struggling readers: Designing research-based programs* (2nd ed.). Boston: Allyn & Bacon/Pearson.

Applegate, M. D., Quinn, K. B., & Applegate, A. J. (2008). *The critical reading inventory: Assessing students' reading and thinking* (2nd ed.). Upper Saddle River. NJ: Merrill/Prentice Hall.

Baker, L., & Brown, A. (1984). Metacognitive skills of reading. In P. D. Pearson, M. Kamil, P. Mosenthal, & R. Barr (Eds.), *Handbook of reading research* (pp. 353–394). New York: Longman.

Beaver, J. (2006). *Developmental reading assessment, grades K–3* (2nd ed.). Upper Saddle River, NJ: Celebration Press/Pearson.

Beaver, J., & Carter, M. (2003). *Developmental reading assessment, grades 4–8.* Upper Saddle River, NJ: Celebration Press/Pearson.

Blachowicz, C. L. Z., & Fisher, P. J. (2007). Best practices in vocabulary instruction. In L. B. Gambrell, L. M. Morrow, & M. Pressley (Eds.), *Best practices in literacy instruction* (3rd ed., pp. 178–203). New York: Guilford Press.

Blanton, W. E., Wood, K. D., & Moorman, G. B. (1990). The role of purpose in reading instruction. *The Reading Teacher, 43,* 486–493.

Block, C. C., & Pressley, M. (2007). Best practices in teaching comprehension. In L. B. Gambrell, L. M. Morrow, & M. Pressley (Eds.), *Best practices in literacy instruction* (3rd ed., pp. 220–242). New York: Guilford Press.

Bottomley, D. M., Henk, W. A., & Melnick, S. A. (1997/1998). Assessing children's views about themselves as writers using the Writer Self-Perception Scale. *The Reading Teacher, 51,* 286–296.

Bouchard, M. (2005). *Comprehension strategies for English language learners.* New York: Scholastic.

Braunger, J., & Lewis, J. P. (2006). *Building a knowledge base in reading* (2nd ed.). Newark, DE: International Reading Association/National Council of Teachers of English.

Brophy, J. (2004). *Motivating students to learn* (2nd ed.). Mahwah, NJ: Erlbaum.

Castek, J., Bevans-Mangelson, J., & Goldstone, B. (2006). Reading adventures online: Five ways to introduce the new literacies of the Internet through children's literature. *The Reading Teacher, 59,* 714–728.

Clay, M. M. (2007). *An observation survey of early literacy achievement* (rev. ed.). Portsmouth. NH: Heinemann.

Coiro, J. (2003). Reading comprehension on the Internet: Expanding our understanding of reading comprehension to encompass new literacies. *The Reading Teacher, 56,* 458–464.

Coiro, J., & Dobler, E. (2007). Exploring the online reading comprehension strategies used by sixth-grade skilled readers to search for and locate information on the Internet. *Reading Research Quarterly, 42,* 214–257.

Cooper, J. D., Chard, D. J., & Kiger, N. D. (2006). *The struggling reader: Interventions that work.* New York: Scholastic.

Cooter, R. B., Jr., Flynt, E. S., & Cooter, K. S. (2007). *Comprehensive reading inventory.* Upper Saddle River. NJ: Merrill/Prentice Hall.

Cunningham, J. W. (1982). Generating interactions between schemata and text. In J. A. Niles & L. A. Harris (Eds.), *New inquiries in reading research and instruction* (pp. 42–47). Rochester, NY: National Reading Conference.

Duke, N. K., & Pearson, P. D. (2002). Effective practices for developing reading comprehension. In A. E. Farstrup & S. J. Samuels (Eds.), *What research has to say about reading instruction* (3rd ed., pp. 205–242). Newark, DE: International Reading Association.

Faigley, L., Cherry, R. D., Jolliffe, D. A., & Skinner, A. M. (1985). *Assessing writers' knowledge and processes of composing.* Norwood, NJ: Ablex.

Gambrell, L. B., Palmer, B. M., Codling, R. M., & Mazzoni, S. A. (1996). Assessing motivation to read. *The Reading Teacher, 49,* 518–533.

Guthrie, J. T., & Wigfield, A. (2000). Engagement and motivation in reading. In M. L. Kamil, P. B. Mosenthal, P. D. Pearson, & R. Barr (Eds.), *Handbook of reading research* (Vol. 3, pp. 403–422). New York: Erlbaum.

Harvey, S., & Goudvis, A. (2007). *Strategies that work: Teaching comprehension for understanding and engagement* (2nd ed.). Portland, ME: Stenhouse.

Henk, W. A., & Melnick, S. A. (1995). The Reader Self-Perception Scale (RSPS): A new tool for measuring how children feel about themselves as readers. *The Reading Teacher, 48,* 470–482.

Henry, L. A. (2006). SEARCHing for an answer: The critical role of new literacies while reading on the Internet. *The Reading Teacher, 59,* 614–627.

Irwin, J. W. (1991). *Teaching reading comprehension processes* (2nd ed). Boston: Allyn & Bacon.

Ivey, G., & Broaddus, K. (2001). "Just plain reading": A survey of what makes students want to read in middle school classrooms. *Reading Research Quarterly, 36,* 350–377.

Kear, D. J., Coffman, G. A., McKenna, M. C., & Ambrosio, A. L. (2000). Measuring attitude toward writing: A new tool for teachers. *The Reading Teacher, 54,* 10–23.

Keene, E. (2006). *Assessing comprehension thinking strategies.* Huntington Beach, CA: Shell Education.

Keene, E. O., & Zimmermann, S. (2007). *Mosaic of thought: The power of comprehension strategy instruction* (2nd ed.). Portsmouth, NH: Heinemann.

Kohn, A. (2001). *Punished by rewards: The trouble with gold stars, incentive plans, A's, praise, and other bribes.* Boston: Houghton Mifflin.

Leslie, L., & Caldwell, J. (2006). *Qualitative reading inventory* (4th ed.). Boston: Allyn & Bacon/Pearson.

Leu, D. J., Jr., Kinzer, C. K., Coiro, J., & Cammack, D. W. (2004). Toward a theory of new literacies emerging from the Internet and other communication technologies. In R. Ruddell & N. Unrau (Eds.), *Theoretical models and processes of reading* (5th ed., pp. 1570–1613). Newark, DE: International Reading Association.

McKenna, M. C., & Kear, D. J. (1990). Measuring attitudes toward reading: A new tool for teachers. *The Reading Teacher, 43,* 626–639.

McKenna, M. C., & Stahl, S. A. (2003). *Assessment for reading instruction.* New York: Guilford Press.

Morrow, L. M. (2002). *Organizing and managing the language arts block.* New York: Guilford Press.

National Reading Panel. (2000). *Teaching children to read: An evidence-based assessment of the scientific research literature on reading and its implications for reading instruction.* Washington, DC: National Institute of Child Health and Human Development.

Oczkus, L. D. (2003). *Reciprocal teaching at work: Strategies for improving reading comprehension.* Newark, DE: International Reading Association.

Oldfather, P. (1995). Commentary: What's needed to maintain and extend motivation for literacy in the middle grades. *Journal of Reading, 38,* 420–422.

Owocki, G. (2003). *Comprehension: Strategic instruction for K–3 students.* Portsmouth, NH: Heinemann.

Palinscar, A. S., & Brown, A. L. (1986). Interactive teaching to promote independent learning from text. *The Reading Teacher, 39,* 771–777.

Paris, S. G., Wasik, B. A., & Turner, J. C. (1991). The development of strategic readers. In R. Barr, M. L. Kamil, P. B. Mosenthal, & P. D. Pearson (Eds.), *Handbook of reading research* (Vol. 2, pp. 609–640). New York: Longman.

Peregoy, S. F., & Boyle, W. F. (2008). *Reading, writing, and learning in ESL: A resource book for teaching K–12 English learners* (5th ed.). Boston: Allyn & Bacon/Pearson.

Pressley, M. (2002a). Comprehension strategies instruction: A turn-of-the-century status report. In C. C. Block & M. Pressley (Eds.), *Comprehension instruction: Research-based best practices* (pp. 11–27). New York: Guilford Press.

Pressley, M. (2002b). Metacognition and self-regulated comprehension. In A. E. Farstrup & S. J. Samuels (Eds.), *What research has to say about reading instruction* (3rd ed., pp. 291–309). Newark, DE: International Reading Association.

Pressley, M., Dolezal, S. E., Raphael, L. M., Mohan, L., Roehrig, A. D., & Bogner, K. (2003). *Motivating primary-grade students.* New York: Guilford Press.

Raphael, T. E., Highfield, K., & Au, K. H. (2006). *QAR now: A powerful and practical framework that develops comprehension and higher-level thinking in all students.* New York: Scholastic.

Samuels, S. J. (2002). Reading fluency: Its development and assessment. In A. E. Farstrup & S. J. Samuels (Eds.), *What research has to say about reading instruction* (3rd ed., pp. 166–185). Newark, DE: International Reading Association.

Stipek, D. J. (2002). *Motivation to learn: Integrating theory and practice* (4th ed.). Boston: Allyn & Bacon.

Sweet, A. P., & Snow, C. E. (2003). Reading for comprehension. In A. P. Sweet & C. E. Snow (Eds.), *Rethinking reading comprehension* (pp. 1–11). New York: Guilford Press.

Tierney, R. J. (1990). Redefining reading comprehension. *Educational Leadership, 47,* 37–42.

Tierney, R., & Pearson, P. D. (1983). Toward a composing model of reading. *Language Arts, 60,* 568–580.

Tovani, C. (2000). *I read it, but I don't get it: Comprehension strategies for adolescent readers.* Portland, ME: Stenhouse.

Turner, J., & Paris, S. G. (1995). How literacy tasks influence children's motivation for literacy. *The Reading Teacher, 48,* 662–673.

Unrau, N. (2004). *Content area reading and writing: Fostering literacies in middle and high school cultures.* Upper Saddle River, NJ: Merrill/Prentice Hall.

Van Den Broek, P., & Kremer, K. E. (2000). The mind in action: What it means to comprehend during reading. In B. M. Taylor, M. F. Graves, & P. Van Den Broek (Eds.), *Reading for meaning: Fostering comprehension in the middle grades* (pp. 1–31). New York: Teachers College Press.

Wilhelm, J. D. (2001). *Improving comprehension with think-aloud strategies.* New York: Scholastic.

Woods, M. L., & Moe, A. J. (2007). *Analytical reading inventory* (8th ed.). Upper Saddle River. NJ: Merrill/Prentice Hall.

Zimmermann, S., & Hutchins, C. (2003). *Seven keys to comprehension: How to help your kids read it and get it!* New York: Three Rivers Press.

CHILDREN'S BOOK REFERENCES

Bunting, E. (1998). *So far from the sea.* Boston: Houghton Mifflin.

Coerr, E. (1989). *The Josefina story quilt.* New York: HarperCollins.

Coerr, E. (1993). *Chang's paper pony.* New York: HarperCollins.

Gantos, J. (2005). *Joey Pigza loses control.* New York: HarperCollins.

Jiménez, F. (1998). *La mariposa.* Boston: Houghton Mifflin.

Van Allsburg, C. (1991). *The wretched stone.* Boston: Houghton Mifflin.

Van Allsburg, C. (1993). *The garden of Abdul Gasazi.* Boston: Houghton Mifflin.

CHapTeR 9

Facilitating Students' Comprehension: Text Factors

Mr. Abrams's Fourth Graders Learn About Frogs

The fourth graders in Mr. Abrams's class are studying frogs. They began by making a class **K-W-L chart** (Ogle, 1986), listing what they already know about frogs in the "K: What We Know" column and things they want to learn in the "W: What We Wonder" column. At the end of the unit, students will finish the chart by listing what they've learned in the "L: What We Have Learned" column. The fourth graders want to know how frogs and toads are different and if it is true that you get warts from frogs. Mr. Abrams assures them that they will learn the answers to many of their questions and makes a mental note to find the answer to their question about warts.

Aquariums with frogs and frog spawn are arranged in one area in the classroom. Mr. Abrams has brought in five aquariums and filled them with frogs he collected in his backyard and others he "rented" from a local pet store, and he has also brought in frog spawn from a nearby pond. The fourth graders are observing the frogs and the frog spawn daily and drawing diagrams and making notes in their **learning logs**.

Mr. Abrams sets out a text set with books about frogs representing the three genres—stories, informational books, and poetry books—on a special shelf in the classroom library. He reads many of the books aloud to the class. When he begins, he reads the title and shows students several pages and asks them whether the book is a story, an informational book, or a poem. After they determine the genre, they talk about their purpose for listening. For an informational book, the teacher writes a question or two on the chalkboard to guide their listening. After reading, the students answer the questions as part of their discussion. Students also read and reread many of these books during an independent reading time.

Mr. Abrams also has a class set of *Amazing Frogs and Toads* (Clarke, 1990), a nonfiction book with striking photograph illustrations and well-organized presentations of information. He reads it once with the whole class using shared reading, and they discuss the interesting information in the book. He divides the class into small groups, and each group chooses a question about frogs to research in the book. Students reread the book, hunting for the answer to their question. Mr. Abrams has already taught the students to use the table of contents and the index to locate facts in an informational book. After they locate and reread the information, they use the writing process to develop a poster to answer the question and share what they've learned. He meets with each group to help them organize their posters and revise and edit their writing.

From the vast amount of information in *Amazing Frogs and Toads*, Mr. Abrams chooses nine questions, which he designs to address some of the questions on the "W: What We Wonder" section of the K-W-L chart, to highlight important information in the text, and to focus on the five expository text structures, the organizational patterns used for nonfiction texts that students read and write. Mr. Abrams is teaching the fourth graders that informational books, like stories, have special organizational elements. Here are his questions organized according to the expository structures:

What are amphibians? (Description)

What do frogs look like? (Description)

What is the life cycle of a frog? (Sequence)

How do frogs eat? (Sequence)

How are frogs and toads alike and different? (Comparison)

Why do frogs hibernate? (Cause and Effect)

How do frogs croak? (Cause and Effect)

How do frogs use their eyes and eyelids? (Problem and Solution)

How do frogs escape from their enemies? (Problem and Solution)

After the students complete their posters, they share them with the class through brief presentations, and the posters are displayed in the classroom. Two of the students' posters are shown on page 288; the life cycle poster emphasizes the sequence structure, and the "Frogs Have Big Eyes" poster explains that the frog's eyes help it solve problems—finding food, hiding from enemies, and seeing underwater.

Two Posters About Frogs

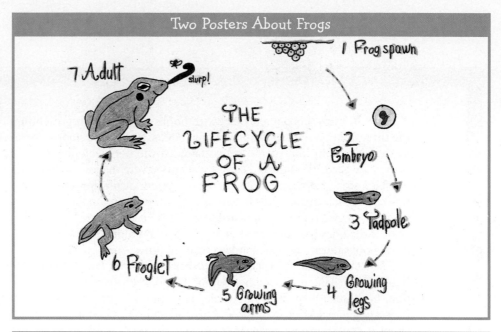

Mr. Abrams's students use the information in the posters to write books about frogs. Students choose three posters and write one- to three-paragraph chapters to report the information from the poster. Students meet in **writing groups** to revise their rough drafts and then edit with a classmate and with Mr. Abrams. Finally, students word process their final copies and add illustrations, a title page, and a table of contents. Then they compile their books and "publish" them by sharing them with classmates from the author's chair.

Armin wrote this chapter on "Hibernation" in his book:

> *Hibernation means that an animal sleeps all winter long. Frogs hibernate because they are cold blooded and they might freeze to death if they didn't. They find a good place to sleep like a hole in the ground, or in a log, or under some leaves. They go to sleep and they do not eat, or drink, or go to the bathroom.*

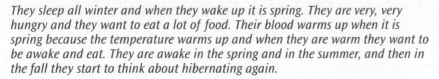

They sleep all winter and when they wake up it is spring. They are very, very hungry and they want to eat a lot of food. Their blood warms up when it is spring because the temperature warms up and when they are warm they want to be awake and eat. They are awake in the spring and in the summer, and then in the fall they start to think about hibernating again.

Jessica wrote this chapter on "The Differences Between Frogs and Toads" for her book:

You might think that frogs and toads are the same but you would be wrong. They are really different but they are both amphibians. I am going to tell you three ways they are different.

First of all, frogs really love water so they stay in the water or pretty close to it. Toads don't love water. They usually live where it is dry. This is a big difference between frogs and toads.

Second, you should look at frogs and toads. They look different. Frogs are slender and thin but toads are fat. Their skin is different, too. Frogs have smooth skin and toads have bumpy skin. I would say that toads are not pretty to look at.

Third, frogs have long legs but toads have short legs. That probably is the reason why frogs are wonderful jumpers and toads can't. They move slowly. They just hop. When you watch them move, you can tell that they are very different.

Frogs and toads are different kinds of amphibians. They live in different places, they look different, and they move in different ways. You can see these differences when you look at them and it is very interesting to study them.

Mr. Abrams helps his students develop a **rubric** to assess their books. The rubric addresses the following points about the chapters:

- The title describes the chapter.
- The information in each chapter is presented clearly.
- Vocabulary from the **word wall** is used in each chapter.
- The information in each chapter is written in one or more indented paragraphs.
- The information in each chapter has very few spelling, capitalization, and punctuation errors.
- There is a useful illustration in each chapter.

Other points on the rubric consider the book as a whole:

- The title page lists the title and the author's name.
- All pages in the book are numbered.
- The table of contents lists the chapters and the pages for each chapter.
- The title is written on the cover of the book.
- The illustrations on the cover of the book relate to frogs.

The students evaluate their books using a 4-point scale; Mr. Abrams also uses the rubric to assess their writing. He conferences with students and shares his scoring with them. Also, he helps the students set goals for their next writing project.

To end the unit, Mr. Abrams asks his students to finish the K-W-L chart. In the third column, "L: What We Have Learned," students list some of the information they have learned:

Tadpoles breathe through gills but frogs breathe through lungs.
Tadpoles are vegetarians but frogs eat worms and insects.
Snakes, rats, birds, and foxes are the frogs' enemies.

Some frogs in the rainforest are brightly colored and poisonous, too.
Some frogs are hard to see because they camouflage coloring.
Male frogs puff up their air sacs to croak and make sounds.
Frogs have teeth but they swallow their food whole.
Frogs have two sets of eyelids and one set is clear so frogs can see when they are underwater.
Frogs can jump ten times their body length but toads can't—they're hoppers.

Mr. Abrams stands back to reread the fourth graders' comments. "I can tell how much you've learned when I read the detailed information you've added in the L column," he remarks with a smile. He knows that one reason why his students are successful is because he taught them to use text structure as a tool for learning.

What readers know and do during reading has a tremendous impact on how well they comprehend, but comprehension involves more than just reader factors: It also involves text factors. Stories, informational books, and poems can be easier or more difficult to read depending on factors that are inherent in them (Harvey & Goudvis, 2007). Here are the three most important types of text factors:

Genres. The three broad categories of literature are stories, informational books or nonfiction, and poetry, and there are subgenres within each category. For example, science fiction, folktales, and historical fiction are subgenres of stories.

Text Structures. Authors use text structures to organize texts and emphasize the most important ideas. Sequence, comparison, and cause and effect, for example, are three internal patterns used to organize nonfiction texts.

Text Features. Authors use text features to achieve a particular effect in their writing. Literary devices and conventions include symbolism and tone in stories, headings and indexes in informational books, and page layout for poems.

When students understand how authors organize and present their ideas in texts, this knowledge about text factors serves as a scaffold, making comprehension easier (Meyer & Poon, 2004; Sweet & Snow, 2003). Text factors make a similar contribution to students' writing; students apply what they've learned about genres, text structures, and text features when they're writing (Mooney, 2001).

TEXT FACTORS OF STORIES

Stories are narratives about characters trying to overcome problems or deal with difficulties. They've been described as "waking dreams" that people use to find meaning in their lives. Children develop an understanding of what constitutes a story beginning in the preschool years when their parents read aloud to them, and they refine and expand their understanding of stories through literacy instruction at school (Applebee, 1978; Appleyard, 1994). Students learn about the subgenres of stories and read stories representing each one, examine the structural patterns that authors use to organize stories, and point out the narrative devices that authors use to breathe life into their stories.

Formats of Stories

Stories are available in picture-book and chapter-book formats. Picture books have brief texts, usually spread over 32 pages, in which text and illustrations combine to tell a story. The text is minimal, and the illustrations supplement the sparse text. The illustrations in many picture books are striking. Many picture books, such as *Rosie's Walk* (Hutchins, 2005), about a clever hen who outwits a fox, are for primary-grade students, but others, such as *Show Way* (Woodson, 2005), a multimedia story about the generations of women in the author's family, from slavery to the Civil Rights movement to the present, were written with middle-grade students in mind. Others are wordless picture books, such as *Flotsam* (Wiesner, 2006) and *The Red Book* (Lehman, 2004), in which the story is told entirely through the illustrations.

Novels are longer stories written in a chapter format. Most are written for older students, but Dan Greenburg's adventure series, The Zack Files, including *Just Add Water . . . and Scream!* (2003), is for students reading at the second- and third-grade levels. Chapter books for middle-grade students include *Shiloh* (Naylor, 2000) and *Esperanza Rising* (Ryan, 2002). Complex stories such as *Holes* (Sachar, 2003) are more suitable for upper-grade students. Chapter books have few illustrations, if any, because they don't usually play an integral role in the story.

Narrative Genres

Stories can be categorized in different ways, one of which is according to genres (Buss & Karnowski, 2000). Three general subcategories are folklore, fantasies, and realistic fiction. Figure 9–1 presents an overview of these narrative genres.

Folklore. Stories that began hundreds of years ago and were passed down from generation to generation by storytellers before being written down are *folk literature*. These stories, including fables, folktales, and myths, are an important part of our cultural heritage. Fables are brief narratives designed to teach a moral. The story format makes the lesson easier to understand, and the moral is usually stated at the end. Fables exemplify these characteristics:

◆ They are short, often less than a page long.
◆ The characters are usually animals.
◆ The characters are one-dimensional: strong or weak, wise or foolish.
◆ The setting is barely sketched; the stories could take place anywhere.
◆ The theme is usually stated as a moral at the end of the story.

The best-known fables, including "The Hare and the Tortoise" and "The Ant and the Grasshopper," are believed to have been written by a Greek slave named Aesop in the 6th century B.C. Individual fables hare been retold as picture-book stories, including *The Hare and the Tortoise* (Ward, 1999) and *The Lion and the Rat* (Wildsmith, 2007).

Folktales began as oral stories, told and retold by medieval storytellers as they traveled from town to town. The problem in a folktale usually revolves around one of four situations: a journey from home to perform a task, a journey to confront a monster, the miraculous change from a harsh home to a secure home, or a confrontation between a wise beast and a foolish beast. Here are other characteristics:

◆ The story often begins with the phrase "Once upon a time . . ."
◆ The setting is generalized and could be located anywhere.
◆ The plot structure is simple and straightforward.
◆ Characters are one-dimensional: good or bad, stupid or clever, industrious or lazy.
◆ The end is happy, and everyone lives "happily ever after."

Figure 9–1 ◆ Narrative Genres

Category	Genre	Description
Folklore	Fables	Brief tales told to point out a moral. For example: *Town Mouse, Country Mouse* (Brett, 2003) and *The Boy Who Cried Wolf* (Hennessy, 2006).
	Folktales	Stories in which heroes demonstrate virtues to triumph over adversity. For example: *Jouanah: A Hmong Cinderella* (Coburn, 1996) and *Rumpelstiltskin* (Zelinsky, 1996).
	Myths	Stories created by ancient peoples to explain natural phenomena. For example: *Why Mosquitoes Buzz in People's Ears* (Aardema, 2004) and *Raven* (McDermott, 2001).
	Legends	Stories, including hero tales and tall tales, that recount the courageous deeds of people who struggled against each other or against gods and monsters. For example: *John Henry* (Lester, 1999) and *The Adventures of Robin Hood* (Williams, 2007).
Fantasy	Modern Literary Tales	Stories written by modern authors that are similar to folktales. For example: *The Ugly Duckling* (Mitchell, 2007) and *Sylvester and the Magic Pebble* (Steig, 2006).
	Fantastic Stories	Imaginative stories that explore alternate realities and contain elements not found in the natural world. For example: *Jeremy Thatcher, Dragon Hatcher* (Coville, 2007b) and *Poppy* (Avi, 2005).
	Science Fiction	Stories that explore scientific possibilities. For example: *Aliens Ate My Homework* (Coville, 2007a) and *The Giver* (Lowry, 2006).
	High Fantasy	Stories that focus on the conflict between good and evil and often involve quests. For example: the Harry Potter series and *The Lion, the Witch and the Wardrobe* (Lewis, 2005).
Realistic Fiction	Contemporary Stories	Stories that portray today's society. For example: *Going Home* (Bunting, 1998) and *Seedfolks* (Fleischman, 2004b).
	Historical Stories	Realistic stories set in the past. For example: *Sarah, Plain and Tall* (MacLachlan, 2004) and *Roll of Thunder, Hear My Cry* (Taylor, 2001).

Some folktales are cumulative tales, such as *The Gingerbread Boy* (Galdone, 2008); these stories are built around the repetition of words and events. Others are talking animal stories; in these stories, such as *The Three Little Pigs* (Kellogg, 2002), animals act and talk like humans. The best-known folktales are fairy tales. They have motifs or small recurring elements, including magical powers, transformations, enchantments, magical objects, trickery, and wishes that are granted, and they feature witches, giants, fairy godmothers, and other fantastic characters. Well-known examples are *Cinderella* (Ehrlich, 2004) and *Jack and the Beanstalk* (Kellogg, 1997).

People around the world have created myths to explain natural phenomena. Some explain the seasons, the sun, the moon, and the constellations, and others tell how the mountains and other physical features of the earth were created. Ancient peoples used myths to explain many things that have since been explained by scientific investigations. Myths exemplify these characteristics:

◆ Myths explain creations.
◆ Characters are often heroes with supernatural powers.
◆ The setting is barely sketched.
◆ Magical powers are required.

For example, the Greek myth *King Midas: The Golden Touch* (Demi, 2002) tells about the king's greed, and the Native American myth *The Legend of the Bluebonnet* (dePaola, 1996) recounts how these flowers came to beautify the countryside. Other myths tell how animals came to be or why they look the way they do. Legends are myths about heroes who have done something important enough to be remembered in a story; they may have some basis in history but aren't verifiable. Stories about Robin Hood and King Arthur, for example, are legends. American legends about Johnny Appleseed, Paul Bunyan, and Pecos Bill are known as *tall tales*.

Fantasies. Fantasies are imaginative stories. Authors create new worlds for their characters, but these worlds must be based in reality so that readers will believe they exist. One of the most beloved fantasies is *Charlotte's Web* (White, 2004). Four types of fantasies are modern literary tales, fantastic stories, science fiction, and high fantasy.

Modern literary tales are related to folktales and fairy tales because they often incorporate many characteristics and conventions of traditional literature, but they've been written more recently and have identifiable authors. The best-known author of modern literary tales is Hans Christian Andersen, a Danish writer of the 1800s who wrote *The Snow Queen* (Ehrlich, 2006) and *The Ugly Duckling* (Mitchell, 2007). Other examples of modern literary tales include *Alexander and the Wind-Up Mouse* (Lionni, 2006) and *The Wolf's Chicken Stew* (Kasza, 1996).

Fantastic stories are realistic in most details, but some events require readers to suspend disbelief. Fantasies exemplify these characteristics:

◆ The events in the story are extraordinary; things that could not happen in today's world.
◆ The setting is realistic.
◆ Main characters are people or personified animals.
◆ Themes often deal with the conflict between good and evil.

Some are animal fantasies, such as *Babe: The Gallant Pig* (King-Smith, 2005). The main characters in these stories are animals endowed with human traits. Students often realize that the animals symbolize human beings and that these stories explore human relationships. Some are toy fantasies, such as *The Miraculous Journey of Edward Tulane* (DiCamillo, 2006). Toy fantasies are similar to animal fantasies except that the main characters are talking toys, usually stuffed animals or dolls. Other fantasies involve enchanted journeys during which wondrous things happen. The journey must have a purpose, but it is usually overshadowed by the thrill and delight of the fantastic world, as in Roald Dahl's *Charlie and the Chocolate Factory* (2007).

In science fiction stories, authors create a world in which science interacts with society. Many stories involve traveling through space to distant galaxies or meeting alien societies. Authors hypothesize scientific advancements and imagine technology of the future to create the plot. Science fiction exemplifies these characteristics:

◆ The story is set in the future.
◆ Conflict is usually between the characters and natural or mechanical forces, such as robots.
◆ The characters believe in the advanced technology.
◆ A detailed description of scientific facts is provided.

Time-warp stories in which the characters move forward and back in time are also classified as science fiction. Jon Scieszka's Time Warp Trio stories, including *Knights of the Kitchen Table* (2004), are popular with middle-grade students.

New Literacies
A New Generation of Books

Many of the best books for children and adolescents published since 2000 defy conventions, blur the lines between genres, and incorporate innovative forms. Because these texts require different reading strategies, they support students' learning about new literacies (Kiefer, Price-Dennis, & Ryan, 2006). *The Invention of Hugo Cabret* (Selznick, 2007), the first novel to win the Caldecott Medal, is a good example. Selznick combined storytelling, meticulous charcoal drawings, and cinematic techniques to create a touching story about Hugo, a 12-year-old orphan who lived in a Paris train station a century ago. Half of the 500-page novel is told through full-page illustrations, and to comprehend this story, readers must read the illustrations as carefully as they do the text.

Sometimes authors combine genres. *Love That Dog* (Creech, 2001), about a boy who learns the power of poetry, and *Becoming Joe Di Maggio* (Testa, 2005), about an Italian American kid who escapes his difficult life by listening to baseball games with his grandfather, are poetic narratives—stories told in verse. Students focus on the characters and the plot, but they're aware of the unique page layout and appreciate the figurative qualities of poetic language as they read.

Other authors invent multiple voices to develop their stories. *Day of Tears: A Novel in Dialogue* (Lester, 2005) tells about an 1859 slave auction in Georgia using different voices to emphasize the anguish of slave families and the greed of owners, and *Good Masters! Sweet Ladies! Voices From a Medieval Village* (Schlitz, 2007) is an award-winning collection of 23 monologues, each featuring a person living in and around an English manor in 1255. Students read flexibly, adjusting to a new viewpoint in each chapter. These stories can be read conventionally or presented as a reader's theatre or a play.

Book-length comics called *graphic novels* are a new genre, appealing to students of all ages and gaining respect from teachers and librarians. Babymouse is a sassy young mouse featured in *Babymouse: Queen of the World* (Holm, 2005) and numerous sequels. Fone Bone and his cousins engage in battles of good versus evil in *Bone: Out of Boneville* (Smith, 2005) and other books in this fantasy series. The wildly popular *Diary of a Wimpy Kid* (Kinney, 2007) and its sequels about Greg Heffley's trials and tribulations in middle school combine text and graphics. When students read graphic novels, they learn to examine all the details of every illustration and use their imagination to understand what's happening between frames.

Some wordless picture books incorporate the characteristics of graphic novels. *The Arrival* (Tan, 2007), for example, is a compelling story about an immigrant's journey to build a better future. Although the plot is straightforward, readers must study the illustrations to develop a sense of the immigrant's isolation, recognize the visual metaphors, and appreciate the themes.

Primary source materials are also being used to craft multigenre stories. *Middle School Is Worse Than Meatloaf: A Year Told Through Stuff* (Holm, 2007) incorporates diary entries, refrigerator notes, IM screen messages, and cards from grandpa to recount a girl's day-to-day experiences; and *The Wall: Growing Up Behind the Iron Curtain* (Sís, 2007) combines drawings, diary entries, and photographs to create a powerful graphic memoir of the author's childhood in Soviet-ruled Prague, where children were encouraged to report on their parents and public displays of loyalty were required.

As 21st-century authors transform children's and adolescent literature, students are learning new strategies for exploring books that they can also use on the Internet. They learn to use a combination of visual and textual information to comprehend what they're reading and make connections across genres, text structures, and conventions.

Heroes confront evil for the good of humanity in high fantasy. The primary characteristic is the focus on the conflict between good and evil, as in C. S. Lewis's *The Lion, the Witch and the Wardrobe* (2005) and J. K. Rowling's Harry Potter stories. High fantasy is related to folk literature in that it's characterized by motifs and themes. Most stories include magical kingdoms, quests, tests of courage, magical powers, and super-human characters.

Realistic Fiction. These stories are lifelike and believable. The outcome is reasonable, and the story is a representation of action that seems truthful. Realistic fiction helps students discover that their problems aren't unique and that they aren't alone in experiencing certain feelings and situations. Realistic fiction also broadens students' horizons and allows them to experience new adventures. Two types are contemporary stories and historical stories.

Readers identify with characters who are their own age and have similar interests and problems in contemporary stories. In *The Higher Power of Lucky* (Patron, 2006), for example, students read about an eccentric 10-year-old girl named Lucky who finally comes to terms with her mother's death and finds stability in her life. Here are the characteristics of contemporary fiction:

◆ Characters act like real people or like real animals.
◆ The setting is in the world as we know it today.
◆ Stories deal with everyday occurrences or "relevant subjects."

Other contemporary stories include *Granny Torrelli Makes Soup* (Creech, 2005) and *I Am Not Joey Pigza* (Gantos, 2007).

In contrast, historical stories are set in the past. Details about food, clothing, and culture must be typical of the era in which the story is set because the setting influences the plot. These are the characteristics of this genre:

◆ The setting is historically accurate.
◆ Conflict is often between characters or between a character and society.
◆ The language is appropriate to the setting.
◆ Themes are universal, both for the historical period of the book and for today.

Examples of historical fiction include *Witness* (Hesse, 2001) and *Crispin: The Cross of Lead* (Avi, 2002). In these stories, students are immersed in historical events, they appreciate the contributions of people who have lived before them, and they learn about human relationships.

Elements of Story Structure

Stories have unique structural elements that distinguish them from other genres. The most important story elements are plot, characters, setting, point of view, and theme. They work together to structure a story, and authors manipulate them to develop their stories.

Plot. Plot is the sequence of events involving characters in conflict situations. It's based on the goals of one or more characters and the processes they go through to attain them (Lukens, 2006). The main characters want to achieve the goal, and other characters are introduced to prevent them from being successful. The story events are set in motion by characters as they attempt to overcome conflict and solve their problems. Figure 9–2 presents a list of stories with well-developed plots and other elements of story structure.

The most basic aspect of plot is the division of the main events into the beginning, middle, and end. In *The Tale of Peter Rabbit* (Potter, 2006), for instance, the three story parts are easy to pick out. As the story begins, Mrs. Rabbit sends her children out to play after warning them not to go into Mr. McGregor's garden. In the middle, Peter goes to Mr. McGregor's garden and is almost caught. Then Peter finds his way out of

Figure 9–2 ◆ Stories Illustrating the Elements of Story Structure

Plot

Brett, J. (2000). *Hedgie's surprise*. New York: Putnam. (P)

Fleming, D. (2003). *Buster*. New York: Henry Holt. (P)

Paulsen, G. (2007). *Hatchet*. New York: Simon & Schuster. (U)

Sachar, L. (2003). *Holes*. New York: Yearling. (U)

Steig, W. (2006). *Sylvester and the magic pebble*. New York: Aladdin Books. (P–M)

Characters

Cushman, K. (1994). *Catherine, called Birdy*. New York: HarperCollins. (U)

Dahl, R. (2007). *James and the giant peach*. New York: Puffin Books. (M–U)

Henkes, K. (1996). *Lilly's purple plastic purse*. New York: Greenwillow. (P)

Look, L. (2004). *Ruby Lu, brave and true*. New York: Atheneum. (P–M)

Lowry, L. (2006). *The giver*. New York: Delacorte. (U)

Setting

Bunting, E. (2006). *Pop's bridge*. San Diego: Harcourt. (P–M)

Curtis, C. P. (2000). *The Watsons go to Birmingham—1963*. New York: Laurel Leaf. (M–U)

Hale, S. (2005). *Princess Academy*. New York: Bloomsbury. (M–U)

Lowry, L. (1998). *Number the stars*. New York: Laurel Leaf. (M–U)

Patron, S. (2006). *The higher power of lucky*. New York: Atheneum. (U)

Point of View

Bunting, E. (2006). *One green apple*. New York: Clarion Books. (P–M)

Hesse, K. (2001). *Witness*. New York: Scholastic. (U)

Lewis, C. S. (2005). *The lion, the witch and the wardrobe*. New York: HarperCollins. (U)

MacLachlan, P. (2004). *Sarah, plain and tall*. New York: HarperTrophy. (M)

Pinkney, J. (2006). *The little red hen*. New York: Dial Books. (P)

Theme

Babbitt, N. (2007). *Tuck everlasting*. New York: Square Fish Books. (U)

Bunting, E. (1999). *Smoky night*. San Diego: Harcourt Brace. (M)

DiCamillo, K. (2006). *The miraculous journey of Edward Tulane*. Cambridge, MA: Candlewick Press. (M–U)

Naylor, P. R. (2000). *Shiloh*. New York: Aladdin Books. (M–U)

Woodson, J. (2001). *The other side*. New York: Putnam. (P–M)

P = primary grades (K–2); M = middle grades (3–5); U = upper grades (6–8)

---

the garden and gets home safely—the end of the story. Students can make a story map of the beginning-middle-end of a story using words and pictures, as the story map for *The Tale of Peter Rabbit* in Figure 9–3 shows.

Specific types of information are included in each part. In the beginning, the author introduces the characters, describes the setting, and presents a problem. Together, the characters, setting, and events develop the plot and sustain the theme through the story. In the middle, the plot unfolds, with each event preparing readers for what follows. Conflict heightens as the characters face roadblocks that keep them from solving their problems; how the characters tackle these problems adds suspense to keep readers interested. In the end, all is reconciled, and readers learn whether the characters' struggles are successful.

Conflict is the tension or opposition between forces in the plot, and it's what interests readers enough to continue reading the story (Lukens, 2006). Conflict occurs in these four ways:

Between a Character and Nature. Conflict between a character and nature occurs in stories in which severe weather plays an important role and in stories set in isolated geographic locations, such as *Holes* (Sachar, 2003), in which Stanley struggles to survive at Camp Green Lake, a boys' juvenile detention center.

Between a Character and Society. Sometimes the main character's activities and beliefs differ from those of others, and conflict arises between that character and society. In *The Witch of Blackbird Pond* (Speare, 2001), for example, Kit Tyler is accused of being a witch because she continues activities in a New England Puritan community that were acceptable in the Caribbean community where she grew up but aren't in her new home.

Between Characters. Conflict between characters is very common in children's literature. In *Tales of a Fourth Grade Nothing* (Blume, 2007), for instance, the never-ending conflict between Peter and his little brother, Fudge, is what makes the story entertaining.

Within a Character. The main character struggles to overcome challenges in his or her own life. In *Esperanza Rising* (Ryan, 2002), the title character must come to terms with her new life as a migrant worker after she leaves her family's ranch in Mexico.

Plot is developed through conflict that's introduced at the beginning, expanded in the middle, and finally resolved at the end. The development of the plot involves these components:

◆ A problem that introduces conflict is presented at the beginning of the story.
◆ Characters face roadblocks in attempting to solve the problem in the middle.
◆ The high point in the action occurs when the problem is about to be solved. This high point separates the middle and the end.
◆ The problem is solved and the roadblocks are overcome at the end of the story.

Figure 9–4 presents a plot diagram shaped like a mountain that incorporates these four components, which fifth graders completed after reading *Esperanza Rising* (Ryan, 2002). The problem in *Esperanza Rising* is that Esperanza and her mother must create a new life for themselves in California because they can't remain at their Mexican ranch home any longer. Certainly, there's conflict between characters here and conflict with society, too, but the most important conflict is within Esperanza as she leaves her comfortable life in Mexico to become a migrant laborer in California. Esperanza and her mother face many roadblocks. They become farm laborers, and the work is very difficult. Esperanza wants to bring her grandmother to join them, but they don't have enough money for her travel expenses. Then Esperanza's mother becomes ill, and Esperanza takes over her mother's work. Finally, Esperanza saves enough money to

Figure 9–3 ◆ A Beginning-Middle-End Story Map for *The Tale of Peter Rabbit*

Figure 9–4 ◆ A Plot Diagram for *Esperanza Rising*

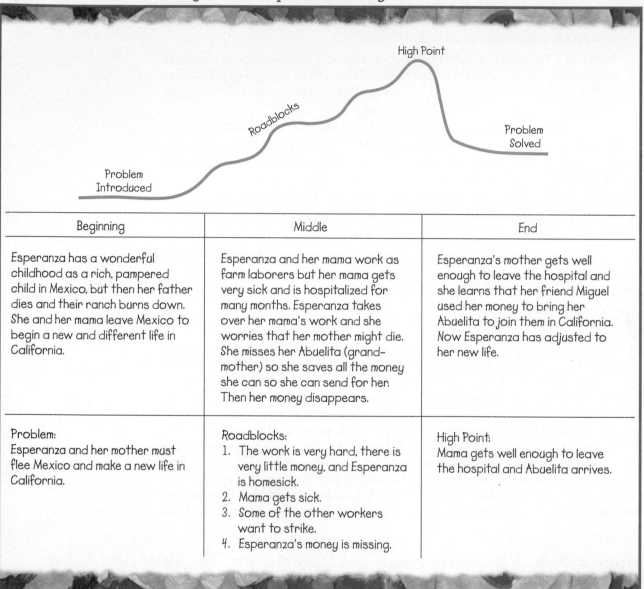

Beginning	Middle	End
Esperanza has a wonderful childhood as a rich, pampered child in Mexico, but then her father dies and their ranch burns down. She and her mama leave Mexico to begin a new and different life in California.	Esperanza and her mama work as farm laborers but her mama gets very sick and is hospitalized for many months. Esperanza takes over her mama's work and she worries that her mother might die. She misses her Abuelita (grandmother) so she saves all the money she can so she can send for her. Then her money disappears.	Esperanza's mother gets well enough to leave the hospital and she learns that her friend Miguel used her money to bring her Abuelita to join them in California. Now Esperanza has adjusted to her new life.
Problem: Esperanza and her mother must flee Mexico and make a new life in California.	Roadblocks: 1. The work is very hard, there is very little money, and Esperanza is homesick. 2. Mama gets sick. 3. Some of the other workers want to strike. 4. Esperanza's money is missing.	High Point: Mama gets well enough to leave the hospital and Abuelita arrives.

bring her grandmother to California, but her money disappears. The high point of the action occurs when Esperanza's mother recovers enough to return to the farm labor camp, and it turns out that her money wasn't stolen after all: Esperanza's friend Miguel used it to bring her grandmother to California. As the story ends, the problem is solved: Esperanza adjusts to her new life in California with her mother and grandmother. *Esperanza* means "hope" in Spanish, and readers have reason to be optimistic that the girl and her family will create a good life for themselves.

Characters. Characters are the people or personified animals in the story. Characters are the most important structural element when stories are centered on a character or group of characters. Main characters have many character traits, both good and bad;

that is to say, they have all the characteristics of real people. Inferring a character's traits is an important part of comprehension: Through character traits, readers get to know a character well, and the character seems to come to life. A list of stories with fully developed main characters is included in Figure 9–2. Characters are developed in four ways:

Appearance. Readers learn about characters by the description of their facial features, body shapes, habits of dress, mannerisms, and gestures. On the first page of *Tacky the Penguin* (Lester, 1990), the illustration of Tacky wearing a bright floral shirt and a purple-and-white tie suggests to readers that Tacky is an "odd bird"! Lester confirms this impression as she describes how Tacky behaves.

Action. The best way to learn about characters is through their actions. In Van Allsburg's *The Stranger* (1986), readers deduce that the stranger is Jack Frost because of what he does: He watches geese flying south for the winter, blows a cold wind, labors long hours without becoming tired, has an unusual rapport with wild animals, and is unfamiliar with modern conveniences.

Dialogue. Authors use dialogue to breathe life into characters, develop their personalities, and spark reader interest. Also, dialogue is an effective way to move a story forward.

Monologue. Authors provide insight into characters by revealing their thoughts. In *Sylvester and the Magic Pebble* (Steig, 2006), thoughts and wishes are central to the story. Sylvester, a foolish donkey, wishes to become a rock, and he spends a miserable winter that way. Steig shares the donkey's thinking with readers: He thinks about his parents, who are frantic with worry, and readers learn how Sylvester feels in the spring when his parents picnic on the rock he has become.

Setting. The setting is generally thought of as the location where the story takes place, but it's only one aspect. There are the four aspects of setting:

Location. Many stories take place in predictable settings that don't contribute to a story's effectiveness, but sometimes the location is integral. For instance, the Boston Commons in *Make Way for Ducklings* (McCloskey, 2001) and the Alaskan North Slope in *Julie of the Wolves* (George, 2005) are artfully described and add uniqueness to the story.

Weather. Severe weather, such as a blizzard, a rainstorm, or a tornado, is crucial in some stories. A rainstorm is essential to the plot development in *Bridge to Terabithia* (Paterson, 2005), but in other books, the weather isn't mentioned because it doesn't affect the outcome of the story. Many stories take place on warm, sunny days.

Time Period. For stories set in the past or in the future, the time period is important. If *The Witch of Blackbird Pond* (Speare, 2001) and *Number the Stars* (Lowry, 1998) were set in different eras, for example, they would lose much of their impact. Today, few people would believe that Kit Tyler is a witch or that Jewish people are the focus of government persecution.

Time. This dimension involves both the time of day and the passage of time. Most stories take place during the day, except for scary stories that are set after dark. Many stories span a brief period of time. *Hatchet* (Paulsen, 2007) takes place in less than 2 months. Other stories, such as *The Ugly Duckling* (Mitchell, 2007), span a year—long enough for the main character to grow to maturity.

In some stories, the setting is barely sketched; these are called *backdrop settings*. The setting in many folktales, for instance, is relatively unimportant, and the convention "Once upon a time . . ." is enough to set the stage. In other stories, the setting is elaborated and essential to the story's effectiveness; these settings are called *integral settings* (Lukens, 2006). Stories with integral settings also are listed in Figure 9–2.

Point of View. Stories are written from a particular viewpoint, and this perspective determines to a great extent readers' understanding of the characters and events of the story (Lukens, 2006). Stories written from different viewpoints are presented in Figure 9–2. Here are the points of view:

First-Person Viewpoint. This point of view is used to tell a story through the eyes of one character using the first-person pronoun "I." The narrator, usually the main character, speaks as an eyewitness and a participant in the events. For example, in *The True Story of the 3 Little Pigs!* (Scieszka, 1996), the wolf tries to explain away his bad image in his version of the familiar folktale.

Omniscient Viewpoint. The author is godlike, seeing and knowing all. The author tells readers about the thought processes of each character without worrying about how the information is obtained. *Doctor De Soto* (Steig, 1990), a story about a mouse dentist who outwits a fox with a toothache, is told from the omniscient viewpoint. Steig lets readers know that the fox wants to eat the dentist as soon as his toothache is cured and that the mouse dentist is aware of the fox's thoughts and plans a clever trick.

Limited Omniscient Viewpoint. This viewpoint is used so that readers know the thoughts of one character. It's told in third person, and the author concentrates on the thoughts, feelings, and experiences of the main character or another important character. Gary Paulsen used this viewpoint for *Hatchet* (2007) to be able to explore both Brian's thoughts as he struggled to survive in the wilderness and his coming to terms with his parents' divorce.

Objective Viewpoint. Readers are eyewitnesses to the story and are confined to the immediate scene. They learn only what is visible and audible and are not aware of what any characters think. Most fairy tales, such as *Rumpelstiltskin* (Zelinski, 1996), are told from the objective viewpoint. The focus is on recounting events, not on developing the personalities of the characters.

Some stories are told from multiple viewpoints, such as *Seedfolks* (Fleischman, 2004b), the story of a community garden that brings hope to a blighted neighborhood, and *Witness* (Hesse, 2001), the story of what happened in 1924 when the Ku Klux Klan moved into a Vermont town. Each chapter is told from a first-person viewpoint by a different character.

Theme. Theme is the underlying meaning of a story; it embodies general truths about human nature (Lehr, 1991; Lukens, 2006). Themes usually deal with the characters' emotions and values, and can be stated either explicitly or implicitly: Explicit themes are stated clearly in the story, whereas implicit themes must be inferred. In a fable, the theme is often stated explicitly at the end, but in most stories, the theme emerges through the thoughts, speech, and actions of the characters as they try to overcome the obstacles that prevent them from reaching their goals. In *A Chair for My Mother* (Williams, 1993), for example, a young girl demonstrates the importance of sacrificing personal wants for her family's welfare as she and her mother collect money to buy a new chair after they lose all of their belongings in a fire.

Stories usually have more than one theme, and their themes generally can't be articulated with a single word. *Charlotte's Web* (White, 2004), for example, has several "friendship" themes, one explicitly stated and others that must be inferred. Friendship is a multidimensional theme—qualities of a good friend, unlikely friends, and sacrificing for a friend, for instance. Teachers probe students' thinking as they work to construct a theme and move beyond simplistic one-word labels. The minilesson featured on page 302 demonstrates how Mrs. Miller, a seventh-grade teacher, reviewed the concept of theme. Afterward, her students analyzed the theme of books they were reading in literature circles.

Check the Compendium of Instructional Procedures, which follows Chapter 12, for more information on the highlighted terms.

Narrative Devices

Authors use narrative devices to make their writing more vivid and memorable (Lukens, 2006). Figure 9–5 presents a list of literary devices used in stories. Imagery is probably the most commonly used convention; many authors use it as they paint rich word pictures that bring their characters and settings to life. Flashbacks are commonly used in stories, such as the Time Warp Trio series by Jon Scieszka and the Magic Tree House series by Mary Pope Osborne, where readers travel back in time for adventures. Authors also create symbols as they use one thing to represent something else. In Chris Van Allsburg's *The Wretched Stone* (1991), for example, the glowing stone that distracts the crew from reading, from spending time with their friends, and from doing their jobs symbolizes television or computers. To understand the theme of many stories, students must recognize symbols and what they represent. The author's style conveys the tone or overall feeling: Some stories are

Figure 9–5 ◆ Narrative Devices	
Dialogue	Written conversation where characters speak to each other. Authors use dialogue to move the story forward while bringing the characters to life.
Flashback	An interruption, often taking readers back to the beginning of the story. Authors use flashbacks in time-warp stories where characters travel back in time to a particular historical period.
Foreshadowing	Hinting at events to come later in the story to build readers' expectations. Authors often use foreshadowing in the beginning of a story.
Imagery	Descriptive words and phrases used to create a picture in readers' minds. Authors also use metaphors and similes as they craft images.
Suspense	An excited uncertainty about the outcome of conflict in a story. Authors use suspense in the middle of the story as characters attempt to thwart one roadblock after another.
Symbolism	A person, place, or thing used to represent something else. For example, a lion often symbolizes courage and a dove symbolizes peace. Authors use symbols to enhance the theme of a story.
Tone	The overall feeling or mood in a story, ranging from humorous to serious and sad. Authors create the tone through their choice of words and use of other narrative devices.

TOPIC: Analyzing the Theme
GRADE: Seventh Grade
TIME: 20 minutes

Mrs. Miller's seventh graders are studying the Middle Ages and are reading novels set in that period, such as *Catherine, Called Birdy* (Cushman, 1994), in literature circles. Mrs. Miller brings the class together to teach a minilesson on theme before asking the students in each literature circle to analyze the theme of the book they're reading.

❶ Introduce the Topic

"It's time to talk about theme because most of you are reaching the end of the book you're reading," Mrs. Miller begins. "Before, I asked you to focus on the setting to learn more about medieval life as you were reading and discussing the book. Now, I want you to think about your book in a different way: I want you to think about the theme. Let's review: Theme is the universal message in the book. It might be about friendship, courage, acceptance, determination, or some other important quality."

❷ Share Examples

Mrs. Miller uses *Hatchet* (Paulsen, 2007), a survival story that students read in September, as an example. "Did Brian save himself?" the teacher asks. Everyone agrees that he did. "So what is the theme of the story?" Mrs. Miller asks. Students identify survival as the theme, and Mrs. Miller asks them to explain it in a sentence. Jared suggests, "Sometimes you have to do a lot of disgusting things if you want to survive." Mrs. Miller agrees. Carole offers, "I think the theme is that you may not think that you have the guts and the brains to survive, but if you get trapped in the wilderness, you will find that you do." Again she agrees. Jo-Jo expresses the theme another way: "It's like in the movie *Castaway*. Brian has to get mad—really mad and a little crazy, too, but he gets mad enough to survive. You have to stand up and prove to yourself that you can survive." Again she agrees. Mrs. Miller draws a cluster on the chalkboard and writes *survival* in the center circle. Then she draws out rays and writes on them the sentences that the students offered.

❸ Provide Information

"Theme isn't obvious the way plot, characters, and setting are," Mrs. Miller explains. She tells the class that in order to uncover the theme, they need to think about the conflicts facing the character and how the character goes about solving the problem. "Then you have to answer the question: 'What is the author trying to tell me about life?'"

❹ Guide Practice

The minilesson ends as the students return to their literature circles to talk about the theme of their book. Mrs. Miller asks them to think of one or more one-word qualities and then to draw out at least three possible sentence-long themes. As they analyze the theme, they draw clusters on chart paper.

❺ Assess Learning

Mrs. Miller moves from group to group, talking with students about theme. She checks their clusters and helps them draw out additional themes to add to the cluster.

humorous, some are uplifting celebrations of life, and others are sobering commentaries on society.

Looking at the Text Factors in a Story

Project Mulberry (Park, 2005) is a contemporary realistic novel about Julie Song, a seventh-grade Korean American girl, and her friend, Patrick, who team up to create a project to win a blue ribbon at the state fair. This multicultural novel is appropriate for fourth through eighth graders, and the reading level is fifth grade. Newbery Medal–winning author Linda Sue Park has written a lively, engaging first-person narrative. Julie is a compelling character, and her thoughts and actions drive the story forward. Her mother suggests that she and Patrick raise silkworms for their state fair project, but at first Julie isn't interested because she thinks it's too Korean; instead, she wants to do something "American."

Self-acceptance is the most important theme in this story. The conflict is within Julie as she struggles to fit in while honoring her Korean heritage. Another theme is prejudice: Julie fears that her mother may be racist because she doesn't want her to spend time with Mr. Dixon, the African American man who gives her mulberry leaves to feed to the silkworms. The story emphasizes the importance of doing small things to increase tolerance.

The most interesting feature in the book is a series of conversations between Julie and the book's author that are inserted between chapters. In these exchanges, Julie complains about her character and asks questions about how Ms. Park thinks of ideas and writes books. These witty conservations provide useful insights about the writing process. Most students will enjoy reading them, but those who don't can easily skip over them because they're set off from the rest of the story.

EXT FACTORS OF INFORMATIONAL BOOKS

Stories have been the principal genre for reading and writing instruction in the primary grades because it's been assumed that constructing stories in the mind is a fundamental way of learning; however, many students prefer to read informational books, and they're able to understand them as well as they do stories (Stead & Duke, 2005). Certainly, students are interested in learning about their world—about the difference between dolphins and whales, how a road is built, threats to the environment of Antarctica, or Amelia Earhart's ill-fated flight around the world—and informational books provide this knowledge. Even young children read informational books to learn about the world around them.

Nonfiction Genres

Informational books provide facts about just about any topic you can think of. Consider, for example: *Flick a Switch: How Electricity Gets to Your Home* (Seuling, 2003), *Taj Mahal* (Arnold & Comora, 2007), *Saguaro Moon: A Desert Journal* (Pratt-Serafini, 2002), *The Brain* (Simon, 2006), *Groundhog Day!* (Gibbons, 2007), *Ancient Inca* (Gruber, 2006), and *Right Dog for the Job: Ira's Path From Service Dog to Guide Dog* (Patent, 2004). Some of these books are picture books that use a combination of text and illustrations to present information, and others are chapter books that depend primarily on the text to provide information.

Other books present information within a story context; the Magic School Bus series is perhaps the best known. In *The Magic School Bus and the Science Fair Expedition* (Cole, 2006), for example, Ms. Frizzle and her class travel through time to learn how scientific thinking developed. The page layout is innovative, with charts and reports containing factual information presented at the outside edges of most pages.

Alphabet Books. Many alphabet books are designed for young children who are learning to identify the letters of the alphabet. Some are predictable, featuring a letter and an illustration of a familiar object on each page, but others, such as *Alphabet Adventure* (Wood, 2001) and *The Alphabet Room* (Pinto, 2003), are more imaginative presentations. Other alphabet books are intended for older students. *The Alphabet From A to Y With Bonus Letter Z!* (Martin & Chast, 2007) is a clever wordplay book, and others, such as *SuperHero ABC* (McLeod, 2006) and *Q Is for Quark: A Science Alphabet Book* (Schwartz, 2001), provide a wealth of information about various topics. In these books, words representing each letter are explained in paragraph-long entries.

Biographies. Students read biographies to learn about a person's life. A wide range of biographies are available for children today, from those featuring well-known personalities, such as *Eleanor Roosevelt: A Life of Discovery* (Freedman, 1997), *Muhammad* (Demi, 2003), *Escape! The Story of the Great Houdini* (Fleischman, 2006), and *Isaac Newton* (Krull, 2006), to those about unsung heroes, such as *Delivering Justice: W. W. Law and the Fight for Civil Rights* (Haskins, 2006). These books are individual biographies because they focus on a single person; others are collective biographies with short vignettes about a group of people who are related in some way, such as *American Heroes* (Delano, 2005) and *Honky-Tonk Heroes and Hillbilly Angels: The Pioneers of Country and Western Music* (George-Warren, 2006). Only a few autobiographies are available for students, but the Meet the Author series of autobiographies for kindergarten through fifth-grade students and the Author at Work series for older students, from Richard C. Owen Publisher, are interesting to students who have read these authors' books. These autobiographies of contemporary authors, including Janet S. Wong's *Before It Wriggles Away* (2006) and Ralph Fletcher's *Reflections* (2007), include information about their lives and insights about their writing.

Expository Text Structures

Informational books are organized in particular ways called *expository text structures* (McGee & Richgels, 1985). Figure 9–6 describes these patterns, presents sample passages and cue words that signal use of each pattern, and suggests a graphic organizer for each structure. When readers are aware of these patterns, it's easier to understand what they're reading, and when writers use these structures to organize their writing, it's easier for readers to understand. Sometimes the pattern is signaled through the title, a topic sentence, or cue words, but sometimes it isn't. Here are the most common expository text structures:

Description. The author describes a topic by listing characteristics, features, and examples. Phrases such as *for example* and *characteristics are* cue this structure. When students delineate any topic, such as the Mississippi River, eagles, or Alaska, they use description.

Sequence. The author lists or explains items or events in numerical, chronological, or alphabetical order. Cue words for sequence include *first*, *second*, *third*, *next*, *then*, and *finally*. Students use this pattern to write directions for completing a math problem or the stages in an animal's life cycle. The events in a biography are often written in the sequence pattern, too.

Figure 9–6 ◆ The Five Expository Text Structures

Pattern	Graphic Organizer	Sample Passage
Description The author describes a topic by listing characteristics and examples. Cue words include *for example* and *characteristics are.*		The Olympic symbol consists of five interlocking rings. The rings represent the five continents from which athletes come to compete in the games. The rings are colored black, blue, green, red, and yellow. At least one of these colors is found in the flag of every country sending athletes to compete in the Olympic games.
Sequence The author lists items or events in numerical or chronological order. Cue words include *first, second, third, next, then,* and *finally.*	1. _____ 2. _____ 3. _____ 4. _____ 5. _____	The Olympic games began as athletic festivals to honor the Greek gods. The most important festival honored Zeus, the king of the gods, and this festival became the Olympic games in 776 B.C. They ended in A.D. 394, and no games were held for more than 1,500 years. Then the modern Olympics began in 1896. Almost 300 male athletes competed in the first modern Olympics. In the 1900 games, female athletes also competed. The games have continued every four years since 1896 except during World War II.
Comparison The author explains how two or more things are alike and/or how they're different. Cue words include *different, in contrast, alike, same as,* and *on the other hand.*	Alike	Different	The modern Olympics is very different than the ancient games. While there were no swimming races, for example, there were chariot races. There were no female contestants, and all athletes competed in the nude. Of course, the ancient and modern Olympics are also alike in many ways. Some events, such as the javelin and discus throws, are the same. Some people say that cheating, professionalism, and nationalism in the modern games are a disgrace to the Olympic tradition, but according to ancient Greek writers, cheating, nationalism, and professionalism existed in their Olympics, too.
Cause and Effect The author lists one or more causes and the resulting effect or effects. Cue words include *reasons why, if . . . then, as a result, therefore,* and *because.*	Cause → Effect #1, Effect #2, Effect #3	There are several reasons why so many people attend the Olympic games or watch them on television. One reason is tradition. The name *Olympics* and the torch and flame remind people of the ancient games. People escape the ordinariness of daily life by attending or watching the Olympics. They like to identify with someone else's accomplishment. National pride is another reason, and an athlete's hard-earned victory becomes a nation's victory. There are national medal counts, and people keep track of how many medals their country's team has won.
Problem and Solution The author states a problem and lists one or more solutions. A variation is the question-and-answer format. Cue words include *problem is, dilemma is, puzzle is, solved,* and *question . . .answer.*	Problem → Solution	One problem with the modern Olympics games is that they're very expensive to operate. A stadium, pools, and playing fields must be built for the athletic events, and housing is needed for the athletes. And these facilities are used for only 2 weeks! In 1984, Los Angeles solved these problems by charging a fee for companies to be official sponsors. Many buildings that were already built in the Los Angeles area were also used. The Coliseum where the 1932 games were held was used again, and many local colleges became playing and living sites.

Figure 9–7 ◆ Informational Books Representing the Expository Text Structures

Description

Cooper, M. L. (2007). *Jamestown, 1607*. New York: Holiday House. (M–U)

Floca, B. (2007). *Lightship*. New York: Atheneum. (P–M)

Gibbons, G. (2007). *Groundhog day!* New York: Holiday House. (P)

Simon, S. (2007). *Snakes*. New York: HarperCollins. (M)

Sequence

Cole, J. (2006). *The magic school bus and the science fair expedition*. New York: Scholastic. (M)

Kelly, I. (2007). *It's a butterfly's life*. New York: Holiday House. (P)

Minor, W. (2006). *Yankee Doodle America: The spirit of 1776 from A to Z*. New York: Putnam. (M)

Royston, A. (2006). *The life and times of a drop of water: The water cycle*. Chicago: Raintree. (M)

Comparison

Bidner, J. (2007). *Is my cat a tiger? How your cat compares to its wild cousins*. New York: Lark Books. (M)

Jenkins, S. (2007). *Dogs and cats*. Boston: Houghton Mifflin. (M–U)

Munro, R. (2001). *The inside-outside book of Washington, DC*. San Francisco: Chronicle Books. (M–U)

Thomas, I. (2006). *Scorpion vs. tarantula*. Chicago: Raintree. (M)

Cause-Effect

Brown, C. L. (2006). *The day the dinosaurs died*. New York: HarperCollins. (P)

Burns, L. G. (2007). *Tracking trash: Flotsam, jetsam, and the science of ocean movement*. Boston: Houghton Mifflin. (M–U)

Collins, A. (2006). *Violent weather: Thunderstorms, tornadoes, and hurricanes*. Washington, DC: National Geographic. (M)

Rockwell, A. (2006). *Why are the ice caps melting? The dangers of global warming*. New York: HarperCollins. (P–M)

Problem-Solution

Bledsoe, L. J. (2006). *How to survive in Antarctica*. New York: Holiday House. (M–U)

Calmenson, S. (2007). *May I pet your dog? The how-to guide for kids meeting dogs (and dogs meeting kids)*. New York: Clarion Books. (P–M)

Morrison, M. (2006). *Mysteries of the sea: How divers explore the ocean depths*. Washington, DC: National Geographic. (M)

Thimmesh, C. (2006). *Team moon: How 400,000 people landed Apollo 11 on the moon*. Boston: Houghton Mifflin. (M–U)

Comparison. The author compares two or more things. *Different, in contrast, alike,* and *on the other hand* are cue words and phrases that signal this structure. When students compare and contrast book and movie versions of a story, reptiles and amphibians, or life in ancient Greece with life in ancient Egypt, they use this organizational pattern.

Cause and Effect. The author explains one or more causes and the resulting effect or effects. *Reasons why, if . . . then, as a result, therefore,* and *because* are words and phrases that cue this structure. Explanations of why dinosaurs became extinct, the effects of pollution, or the causes of the Civil War use this pattern.

Problem and Solution. The author states a problem and offers one or more solutions. A variation is the question-and-answer format, in which the writer poses a question and then answers it. Cue words and phrases include *the problem is, the puzzle is, solve,* and *question . . . answer*. Students use this structure when they write about why money was invented, why endangered animals should be saved, or why dams are needed to ensure a permanent water supply.

Figure 9–7 lists books exemplifying each of the expository text structures.

Nonfiction Features

Informational books have unique text features that stories and books of poetry normally don't have, such as margin notes and glossaries. The purpose of these features is to make text easier to read and to facilitate students' comprehension. Here's a list of nonfiction text features:

◆ Headings and subheadings to direct readers' attention to the big ideas
◆ Photographs and drawings to illustrate the big ideas
◆ Figures, maps, and tables to provide diagrams and detailed information visually
◆ Margin notes that provide supplemental information or direct readers to additional information on a topic
◆ Highlighted vocabulary words to identify key terms
◆ A glossary to assist readers in pronouncing and defining key terms
◆ Review sections or charts at the end of chapters or the entire book
◆ An index to assist readers in locating specific information

It's important that students understand these nonfiction text features so they can use them to make their reading more effective and improve their comprehension (Harvey & Goudvis, 2007).

Looking at the Text Factors in an Informational Book

The Down-to-Earth Guide to Global Warming (David & Gordon, 2007) is a 112-page paperback nonfiction book that explains global warming and its disastrous consequences using examples that students can relate to. It's organized into four sections: The first section explains global warming, the second examines weather changes, the next addresses extinction of plants and animals, and the fourth is a call to action. The authors present serious information in an entertaining way using concrete examples, and they provide practical suggestions to show students how they can help combat global warming in their homes and communities.

This informational book is reader-friendly; it incorporates most of the conventions of the nonfiction genre. Readers will find a table of contents and a "dear reader" letter at the beginning. Margin notes are used again and again to highlight important information and to add interesting facts. Key terms and important facts are printed in color and in a font that's larger than the surrounding text. Photos and cartoon illustrations add interest, and diagrams, pie charts, and maps make the information being presented easier to understand. In the back of the book are a glossary, an index, a bibliography, and suggestions for further reading, including websites for students to check out.

The authors use a problem-and-solution organizational structure: The problem is global warming, and the authors suggest ways that children can help to solve the problem, including recycling, conserving power, replacing conventional light bulbs with compact fluorescent light bulbs, using canvas bags instead of paper or plastic bags, and pursuing a career in the environmental field. Other text structures are also used within chapters. For example, the authors describe global warming, explain the water cycle, and identify effects of global warming that children can appreciate, such as worse allergies and less maple syrup for pancakes.

This brightly colored, inviting paperback book is appropriate for third through sixth graders, both for students who are interested in learning more about global warming and for those who are collecting information for a report or other project.

TEXT FACTORS OF POETRY

It's easy to recognize a poem because the text looks different than a page from a story or an informational book. Layout, or the arrangement of words on a page, is an important text factor. Poems are written in a variety of poetic forms, ranging from free verse to haiku, and poets use poetic devices to make their writing more effective. Janeczko (2003) explains that it's important to point out poetic forms and devices to establish a common vocabulary for talking about poems, and because poems are shorter than other types of text, it's often easier for students to examine the text, notice differences in poetic forms, and find examples of poetic devices that authors have used.

Formats of Poetry Books

Three types of poetry books are published for children. Picture-book versions of *The Midnight Ride of Paul Revere* (Longfellow, 2001) and other classic poems are the first type. In these books, each line or stanza is presented and illustrated on a page. Others are specialized collections of poems, either written by a single poet or related to a single theme, such as *Tour America: A Journey Through Poems and Art* (Siebert, 2006). Comprehensive anthologies are the third type, and these books feature 50 to 500 or more poems arranged by category. One of the best is Jack Prelutsky's *The Random House Book of Poetry for Children* (2000). A list of poetry books that includes examples of each format is presented in Figure 9–8.

Sometimes authors use narrative poems, usually free verse, to tell their stories. Karen Hesse's Newbery Medal–winning story, *Out of the Dust* (1999), focuses on the grim realities of living in the Oklahoma dust bowl, and *Witness* (2003) recounts the Ku Klux Klan infiltration into a sleepy Vermont town, told through 12 people's viewpoints. In *Locomotion* (2004), Jacqueline Woodson uses a collection of 60 poems to tell the sad but hopeful story of a New York City fifth grader who grieves and then slowly recovers after his parents are killed in a house fire. Sharon Creech's *Love That Dog* (2001) is a sweet novel written in the form of a boy's journal as he discovers the power and pleasures of poetry.

Figure 9–8 ◆ Collections of Poetry

Picture-Book Versions of Single Poems

Carroll, L. (2007). *Jabberwocky* (C. Myers, illus.). New York: Jump at the Sun. (U)

Frost, R. (2001). *Stopping by woods on a snowy evening* (S. Jeffers, illus.). New York: Dutton. (M–U)

Thayer, E. L. (2006). *Casey at the bat.* Tonawanda, NY: Kids Can Press. (M–U)

Westcott, N. B. (2003). *The lady with the alligator purse.* New York: Little, Brown. (P)

Specialized Collections

Florian, D. (2007). *Comets, stars, the moon, and Mars: Space poems and paintings.* Orlando, FL: Harcourt. (M–U)

Havill, J. (2006). *I heard it from Alice Zucchini: Poems about the garden.* San Francisco: Chronicle Books. (P–M)

Issa, K. (2007). *Today and today.* New York: Scholastic. (M–U)

Kuskin, K. (2003). *Moon, have you met my mother? The collected poems of Karla Kuskin.* New York: HarperCollins. (P–M–U)

Larios, J. (2006). *Yellow elephant: A bright bestiary.* Orlando, FL: Harcourt. (P–M)

Prelutsky, J. (2006). *Behold the bold umbrellaphant and other poems.* New York: Greenwillow. (P–M)

Sidman, J. (2006). *Butterfly eyes and other secrets of the meadow.* Boston: Houghton Mifflin. (M–U)

Soto, G. (2006). *A fire in my hands.* Orlando, FL: Harcourt. (U)

Comprehensive Anthologies

Driscoll, M., & Hamilton, M. (Sels.). (2003). *A child's introduction to poetry.* New York: Black Dog & Leventhal. (P–M)

Paschem, E., & Raccah, D. (Sels.). (2005). *Poetry speaks to children.* Naperville, IL: Sourcebooks MediaFusion. (M)

Prelutsky, J. (Sel.). (2000). *The Random House book of poetry for children.* New York: Random House. (P–M–U)

Sword, E. H. (Sel.). (2007). *A child's anthology of poetry.* New York: HarperCollins/Ecco. (M–U)

Poetic Forms

Poets who write for K–8 students employ a variety of poetic forms; some are conventional, but others are innovative. Here are some of the more commonly used poetic forms:

Rhymed Verse. The most common type of poetry is rhymed verse, as in *My Parents Think I'm Sleeping* (Prelutsky, 2007) and *Today at the Bluebird Café: A Branchful of Birds* (Ruddell, 2007). Poets use various rhyme schemes, including limericks, and the effect of the rhyming words is a poem that's fun to read and listen to when it's read aloud.

Narrative Poems. Poems that tell a story are *narrative poems*. Perhaps our best-known narrative poem is Clement Moore's classic, "The Night Before Christmas." Other examples include Longfellow's *The Midnight Ride of Paul Revere* (2001), illustrated by Christopher Bing, and *Casey at the Bat* (Thayer, 2006).

Haiku. Haiku is a Japanese poetic form that contains just 17 syllables arranged in three lines of 5, 7, and 5 syllables. It's a concise form, much like a telegram, and the poems normally deal with nature, presenting a single clear image. Books of haiku to share with students include *Dogku* (Clements, 2007) and *Cool Melons— Turn to Frogs! The Life and Poems of Issa* (Gollub, 2004). The artwork in these picture books may give students ideas for illustrating their own haiku poems.

Free Verse. Unrhymed poetry is *free verse*. Word choice and visual images take on greater importance in free verse, and rhythm is less important than in other types of poetry. *The Friendly Four* (Greenfield, 2006) and *Canto Familiar* (Soto, 2007) are two collections of free verse. Poems for two voices are a unique form of free verse, written in two columns, side by side, and the columns are read simultaneously by two readers. The best-known collection is Paul Fleischman's Newbery Award–winning *Joyful Noise: Poems for Two Voices* (2004a).

Odes. These poems celebrate everyday objects, especially those things that aren't usually appreciated. The unrhymed poem, written directly to that object, tells what's good about the thing and why it's valued. The ode is a venerable poetic form, going back to ancient Greece. Traditionally, odes were sophisticated lyrical verses, such as Keats's "Ode to a Nightingale," but Chilean poet Pablo Neruda (2000) introduced this contemporary variation that's more informal. The best collection of odes for students is Gary Soto's *Neighborhood Odes* (2005), which celebrates everyday things, such as water sprinklers and tennis shoes, in the Mexican American community in Fresno, California, where he grew up.

Concrete Poems. The words and lines in concrete poems are arranged on the page to help convey the meaning. When the words and lines form a picture or outline the objects they describe, they're called *shape poems*. Sometimes the layout of words, lines, and stanzas is spread across a page or two to emphasize the meaning. *A Poke in the I: A Collection of Concrete Poems* (Janeczko, 2005) and *Doodle Dandies: Poems That Take Shape* (Lewis, 2002) are two collections of concrete poems.

To learn about other poetic forms, check *Handbook of Poetic Forms* (Padgett, 2007). Students use some of these forms when they write their own poems, including odes and concrete poems.

Go to the Building Teaching Skills and Dispositions section of Chapter 9 on **MyEducationLab.com** to watch second graders Rakie and Michael write an acrostic poem together.

Poetry Unit
These fifth graders are studying Jack Prelutsky and reading his poems. They especially enjoy his CD of *The New Kid on the Block*. The students pick favorite poems and copy them on chart paper. Next, they choose a familiar tune, such as "Twinkle, Twinkle, Little Star" or "I've Been Working on the Railroad," that fits the cadence of the poem and sing the poem to that tune. Singing poems is a favorite daily activity. They're also writing their own verses collaboratively using Prelutsky's poetic forms, such as "My Fish Can Ride a Bicycle," that they will make into class books.

Poetic Devices

Poetic devices are especially important tools because poets express their ideas very concisely. Every word counts! Here are some of the poetic devices they use:

◆ Assonance: the type of alliteration where vowel sounds are repeated in nearby words.
◆ Consonance: the type of alliteration where consonant sounds are repeated in nearby words.
◆ Imagery: words and phrases that appeal to the senses and evoke mental pictures.
◆ Metaphor: a comparison between two unlikely things, without using *like* or *as*.
◆ Onomatopoeia: words that imitate sounds.
◆ Repetition: words, phrases, or lines that are repeated for special effect.
◆ Rhyme: words that end with similar sounds used at the end of the lines.
◆ Rhythm: the internal beat in a poem that's felt when poetry is read aloud.
◆ Simile: a comparison incorporating the word *like* or *as*.

Narrative and poetic devices are similar, and many of them, such as imagery and metaphor, are important in both genres.

Poets use other conventions, too. Capitalization and punctuation are used differently; poets choose where to use capital letters and whether or when to add punctuation marks. They think about the meaning they're conveying and the rhythm of their writing as they decide how to break poems into lines and whether to divide the lines into stanzas. Layout is another consideration: The arrangement of lines on the page is especially important in concrete poems, but it matters for all poems.

Looking at the Text Factors in a Book of Poetry

This Is Just to Say: Poems of Apology and Forgiveness (Sidman, 2007) is presented as a collection of poems written and compiled by Mrs. Merz's sixth graders at the Florence Scribner School as part of a poetry unit. In the introduction, student-editor Anthony K. explains that he and his classmates wrote the apology poems using William Carlos Williams's poem "This Is Just to Say" as a model, and then the recipients wrote poems of forgiveness back to the students.

The book is arranged in two parts. The first part, Apologies, contains the sixth graders' apology poems, with each student's poem featured on a separate page with a drawing of the student-author and other illustrations related to the content of the poem. Readers are told that the line drawings and mixed-media illustrations were created by Bao Vang, an artistic student in the class. The second part, Responses, contains the forgiveness poems that the sixth graders received. These poems are arranged in the same order as the apology poems, with each one on a separate page and accompanied by Bao's whimsical illustrations.

Short poems written on a wide variety of topics are included in this captivating anthology; some are humorous, and others heartfelt or sad. José, for example, wrote an apology to his dad for throwing a rock and breaking the garage window. Other topics include stealing brownies, the death of a pet, insensitive comments, and rough play during a dodge ball game. José's dad responds, telling him to forget about the broken window and expressing his pride in his son's accomplishments. Other recipients' poems convey feelings of love, grief, and acceptance.

Most of the poems follow the pattern of William Carlos Williams's model poem, but many of the students modified it to fit their ideas and words. A handful use different forms, including haiku, poems for two voices, odes, found poems, and free verse. The poems are typed in different fonts, and their arrangement on the page varies, too. The most striking feature of the poems is the range of voices: Some sound as if they were written by sixth-grade girls, some by boys, and others by siblings, parents, and grandparents.

In the author biography, Joyce Sidman confesses that she assumed the personas of the students and the recipients and wrote the poems in this book. Years before, she'd written an apology poem with a class of fourth graders and sent it to her mother who responded with a letter of forgiveness, and the idea for this book was born! This collection of poems is appropriate for third through sixth graders. Many of the poems can be used as models for students' writing, and teachers may want to have their students write their own collections of apology and forgiveness poems.

TEACHING STUDENTS ABOUT TEXT FACTORS

Researchers have documented that when teachers teach students about text factors, their comprehension increases (Fisher, Frey, & Lapp, 2008; Sweet & Snow, 2003). In addition, when students are familiar with the genres, organizational patterns, and literary devices in books they're reading, they're better able to create those text factors in their own writing (Buss & Karnowski, 2002). It's not enough to focus on stories, however; students need to learn about a variety of genres. In the vignette at the beginning of the chapter, Mr. Abrams used text factors to scaffold his students' learning about frogs. He taught them about the unique characteristics of informational books, emphasized text structures through the questions he asked, and used graphic organizers to help students visualize big ideas.

Minilessons

Teachers teach students about text factors directly—often through **minilessons** (Simon, 2005). They highlight a genre, explain its characteristics, and then read aloud books representing that genre, modeling their thinking about text factors. Later, students make charts of the information they're learning and hang them in the classroom. Similarly, teachers introduce structural patterns and have students examine how authors use them to organize a book or an excerpt from a book they're reading. Students often create graphic organizers to visualize the structure of informational books they're reading and appreciate how the organization emphasizes the big ideas (Opitz, Ford, & Zbaracki, 2006). Teachers also focus on the literary devices that authors use to make their writing more vivid and the conventions that make a text more reader-friendly. Students often collect sentences with narrative devices from stories they're reading and lines of poetry with poetic devices from poems to share with classmates, and they create charts with nonfiction features they've found in books to incorporate in reports they're writing.

Comprehension Strategies

It's not enough that students can name the characteristics of a myth, identify cue words that signal expository text structures, or define *metaphor* or *assonance*. The goal is for students to actually use what they've learned about text factors when they're reading and writing. The comprehension strategy they use when they're applying what they've learned is called *noticing text factors*; it involves considering genre, recognizing text structure, and attending to literary devices. Lattimer (2003) explains the strategy this way: Students need to think about "what to expect from a text, how to approach it, and what to take away from it" (p. 12). Teachers teach students about text factors through minilessons and other activities, but the last step is to help students internalize the information and apply it when they're reading and writing. One way teachers do this is by demonstrating how they use the strategy as they read books aloud using **think-alouds** (Harvey & Goudvis, 2007). Teachers also use think-alouds to demonstrate this strategy as they do modeled and shared writing.

Reading and Writing Activities

Students need opportunities to read books and listen to teachers read books aloud while they're learning about text factors. Lattimer (2003) recommends teaching genre studies where students learn about a genre while they're reading and exploring books representing that genre and then apply what they're learning through writing. For example, a small group of fifth graders wrote this poem for two voices as a project after reading *Number the Stars* (Lowry, 1998), the story of the friendship between two Danish girls, a Christian and a Jew, during World War II:

Literacy Portraits:VIEWING GUIDE

Ms. Janusz's classroom is filled with stories and informational books. She uses these books for instructional purposes, and plenty of books are available for students to read independently. These second graders know about genres. They can identify books representing each genre and talk about the differences between them. Ms. Janusz teaches minilessons on genres and points out the genre of books she's reading aloud. She doesn't call all books "stories." Go to the Literacy Profiles section of the MyEducationLab website and click on Rhiannon's Student Interview to watch her compare fiction and nonfiction. As you listen to Rhiannon, think about the information provided in this chapter. What conclusions can you draw about what Ms. Janusz has taught about text factors? Also, look at other video clips of Rhiannon to see how she applies her knowledge about genres in both reading and writing.

I am Annemarie, a Christian.

I hate this war.

The Nazis want to kill my friend.
Why?
I want to help my friend.

My mother will take you to my uncle.
He's a fisherman.

He will hide you on his ship.

He will take you to Sweden.
To freedom.
I am Annemarie, a Christian.

I want to help my friend.

I hate this war.

I am Ellen, a Jew.
I hate this war.
The Nazis want to kill me.

Why?

Can you help me?

Your uncle is a fisherman?

He will hide me on his ship?

To freedom.

I am Ellen, a Jew.

I need the help of my friends
or I will die.
I hate this war.

The fifth graders' choice of this poetic form is especially appropriate because it highlights one of the story's themes: These characters are very much alike even though one is Christian and the other is Jewish. The students knew how to write poems for two voices because they participated in a genre study about poetry several months earlier.

Assessing Students' Knowledge of Text Factors

Although there aren't formal tests to assess students' knowledge of text factors, students demonstrate their knowledge in a variety of ways:

◆ Talk about the characteristics of the genre in **book talks** and **grand conversations**
◆ Use their understanding of story elements to explain themes in **reading log** entries
◆ Apply their knowledge of genre when writing in response to prompts for district and state writing assessments
◆ Document their understanding of text structures as they make graphic organizers
◆ Write poems that are patterned after poems they've read
◆ Choose sentences with literary devices when asked to share favorite sentences with the class from a book they're reading
◆ Incorporate literary devices in their own writing

It's up to teachers to notice how students are applying their knowledge about text factors, and to find new ways for students to share their understanding.

Be Strategic!

Comprehension Strategies

Students apply what they've learned about text factors when they use these comprehension strategies:

▶ Consider genre
▶ Recognize text structure
▶ Attend to literary devices

When students notice text factors, they're better able to understand what they're reading.

Chapter 9
Review

How Effective Teachers Facilitate Students' Comprehension of Text Factors

▶ Teachers teach students that stories have unique text factors: narrative genres, story elements, and narrative devices.

▶ Teachers teach students that informational books have unique text factors: nonfiction genres, expository text structures, and nonfiction features.

▶ Teachers teach students that poems have unique text factors: book formats, poetic forms, and poetic devices.

▶ Teachers encourage students to apply their knowledge of text factors when they're reading and writing.

PEARSON
myeducationlab
Where the Classroom Comes to Life

Go to MyEducationLab at www.myeducationlab.com to deepen your understanding of the concepts presented in this chapter:

▶ Evaluate the second graders' developing knowledge about fiction and nonfiction genres by viewing video segments in the Literacy Portraits.
▶ Check your understanding of chapter concepts with the multiple-choice and essay quizzes in the Study Plan.
▶ Apply some of the main ideas discussed in the chapter in the Activities and Applications section of the website.
▶ Practice what you've learned in this chapter in Building Teaching Skills and Dispositions before applying the ideas in your own classroom.

PROFESSIONAL REFERENCES

Applebee, A. N. (1978). *Child's concept of story: Ages 2–17.* Chicago: University of Chicago Press.

Appleyard, J. A. (1994) *Becoming a reader: The experience of fiction from childhood to adulthood.* New York: Cambridge University Press.

Buss, K., & Karnowski, L. (2000). *Reading and writing literary genres.* Newark, DE: International Reading Association.

Fisher, D., Frey, N., & Lapp, D. (2008). Shared readings: Modeling comprehension, vocabulary, text structures, and text features for older readers. *The Reading Teacher, 61,* 548–556.

Harvey, S., & Goudvis, A. (2007). *Strategies that work: Teaching comprehension for understanding and engagement* (2nd ed.). York, ME: Stenhouse.

Janeczko, P. B. (2003). *Opening a door: Reading poetry in the middle school classroom.* New York: Scholastic.

Kiefer, B. Z., Price-Dennis, D., & Ryan, C. L. (2006). Children's books in a multimodal age. *Language Arts, 84,* 92–98.

Lattimer, H. (2003). *Thinking through genre.* Portland, ME: Stenhouse.

Lehr, S. S. (1991). *The child's developing sense of theme: Responses to literature.* New York: Teachers College Press.

Lukens, R. J. (2006). *A critical handbook of children's literature* (8th ed.). Boston: Allyn & Bacon.

McGee, L. M., & Richgels, D. J. (1985). Teaching expository text structures to elementary students. *The Reading Teacher, 38,* 739–745.

Meyer, B. J. F., & Poon, L. W. (2004). Effects of structure strategy training and signaling on recall of text. In R. B. Ruddell & N. J. Unrau (Eds.), *Theoretical models and processes of reading* (5th ed., pp. 810–850). Newark, DE: International Reading Association.

Mooney, M. E. (2001). *Text forms and features: A resource for intentional teaching*. Katonah, NY: Richard C. Owen.

Neruda, P. (2000). *Selected odes of Pablo Neruda*. Berkeley: University of California Press.

Ogle, D. M. (1986). K-W-L: A teaching model that develops active reading of expository text. *The Reading Teacher, 39,* 564–570.

Opitz, M. F., Ford, M. P., & Zbaracki, M. D. (2006). *Books and beyond: New ways to reach readers*. Portsmouth, NH: Heinemann.

Padgett, R. (2007). *Handbook of poetic forms* (2nd ed.). New York: Teachers & Writers Collaborative.

Simon, L. (2005). *Write as an expert: Explicit teaching of genres*. Portsmouth, NH: Heinemann.

Stead, T., & Duke, N. K. (2005). *Reality checks: Teaching reading comprehension with nonfiction, K–5*. York, ME: Stenhouse.

Sweet, A. P., & Snow, C. E. (2003). Reading for comprehension. In C. E. Snow & A. P. Sweet (Eds.), *Rethinking reading comprehension* (pp. 1–11). New York: Guilford Press.

CHILDREN'S BOOK REFERENCES

Aardema, V. (2004). *Why mosquitoes buzz in people's ears*. New York: Puffin Books.

Arnold, C., & Comora, M. (2007). *Taj Mahal*. Minneapolis: Carolrhoda.

Avi. (2002). *Crispin: The cross of lead*. New York: Hyperion Books.

Avi. (2005). *Poppy*. New York: HarperTrophy.

Blume, J. (2007). *Tales of a fourth grade nothing*. New York: Puffin Books.

Brett, J. (2003). *Town mouse, country mouse*. New York: Putnam.

Bunting, E. (1998). *Going home*. New York: HarperTrophy.

Clarke, B. (1990). *Amazing frogs and toads*. New York: Knopf.

Clements, A. (2007). *Dogku*. New York: Simon & Schuster.

Coburn, J. R. (1996). *Jouanah: A Hmong Cinderella*. San Francisco: Shen's Books.

Cole, J. (2006). *The magic school bus and the science fair expedition*. New York: Scholastic.

Coville, B. (2007a). *Aliens ate my homework*. New York: Aladdin Books.

Coville, B. (2007b). *Jeremy Thatcher, dragon hatcher*. San Diego: Harcourt/Magic Carpet Books.

Creech, S. (2001). *Love that dog*. New York: HarperCollins.

Creech, S. (2005). *Granny Torrelli makes soup*. New York: HarperTrophy.

Cushman, K. (1994). *Catherine, called Birdy*. New York: HarperCollins.

Dahl, R. (2007). *Charlie and the chocolate factory*. New York: Puffin Books.

David, L., & Gordon, C. (2007). *The down-to-earth guide to global warming*. New York: Orchard/Scholastic.

Delano, M. F. (2005). *American heroes*. Washington, DC: National Geographic Society.

Demi. (2002). *King Midas: The golden touch*. New York: McElderry.

Demi. (2003). *Muhammad*. New York: McElderry.

dePaola, T. (1996). *The legend of the bluebonnet*. New York: Putnam.

DiCamillo, K. (2006). *The miraculous journey of Edward Tulane*. Cambridge, MA: Candlewick Press.

Ehrlich, A. (2004). *Cinderella*. New York: Dutton.

Ehrlich, A. (2006). *The snow queen*. New York: Dutton.

Fleischman, P. (2004a). *Joyful noise: Poems for two voices*. New York: HarperCollins.

Fleischman, P. (2004b). *Seedfolks*. New York: HarperTrophy.

Fleischman, S. (2006). *Escape! The story of the Great Houdini*. New York: Greenwillow.

Fletcher, R. (2007). *Reflections*. Katonah, NY: Richard C. Owen.

Freedman, R. (1997). *Eleanor Roosevelt: A life of discovery*. New York: Clarion Books.

Galdone, P. (2008). *The gingerbread boy*. New York: Clarion Books.

Gantos, J. (2007). *I am not Joey Pigza*. New York: Farrar, Straus & Giroux.

Gardiner, J. R. (1980). *Stone Fox*. New York: HarperTrophy.

George, J. C. (2005). *Julie of the wolves*. New York: HarperTrophy.

George-Warren, H. (2006). *Honky-tonk heroes and hillbilly angels: The pioneers of country and western music*. Boston: Houghton Mifflin.

Gibbons, G. (2007). *Groundhog Day!* New York: Holiday House.

Gollub, M. (2004). *Cool melons—turn to frogs! The life and poems of Issa*. New York: Lee & Low.

Greenburg, D. (2003). *Just add water . . . and scream!* New York: Grosset & Dunlap.

Greenfield, E. (2006). *The friendly four*. New York: HarperCollins.

Gruber, B. (2006). *Ancient Inca*. Washington, DC: National Geographic Children's Books.

Haskins, J. (2006). *Delivering justice: W. W. Law and the fight for civil rights*. Cambridge, MA: Candlewick Press.

Hennessy, B. G. (2006). *The boy who cried wolf*. New York: Simon & Schuster.

Hesse, K. (1999). *Out of the dust*. New York: Scholastic.

Hesse, K. (2001). *Witness*. New York: Scholastic.

Holm, J. L. (2005). *Babymouse: Queen of the world*. New York: Random House.

Holm, J. L. (2007). *Middle school is worse than meatloaf: A year told through stuff*. New York: Ginee Seo Books/Simon & Schuster.

Hutchins, P. (2005). *Rosie's walk*. New York: Aladdin Books.

Janeczko, P. B. (2005). *A poke in the I: A collection of concrete poems*. Cambridge, MA: Candlewick Press.

Kasza, K. (1996). *The wolf's chicken stew*. New York: Putnam.

Kellogg, S. (1997). *Jack and the beanstalk*. New York: HarperTrophy.

Kellogg, S. (2002). *The three little pigs*. New York: HarperTrophy.

King-Smith, D. (2005). *Babe the gallant pig*. New York: Knopf.

Kinney, J. (2007). *Diary of a wimpy kid*. New York: Abrams.

Krull, K. (2006). *Isaac Newton*. New York: Viking.

Lehman, B. (2004). *The red book*. Boston: Houghton Mifflin.

Lester, H. (1990). *Tacky the penguin*. Boston: Houghton Mifflin.

Lester, J. (1999). *John Henry*. New York: Puffin Books.

Lester, J. (2005). *Day of tears: A novel in dialogue*. New York: Hyperion Books.

Lewis, C. S. (2005). *The lion, the witch and the wardrobe*. New York: HarperCollins.

Lewis, J. P. (2002). *Doodle dandies! Poems that take shape*. New York: Aladdin Books.

Lionni, L. (2006). *Alexander and the wind-up mouse*. New York: Knopf.

Longfellow, H. W. (2001). *The midnight ride of Paul Revere* (C. Bing, Illus.). Brooklyn, NY: Handprint Books.

Lowry, L. (1998). *Number the stars*. New York: Laurel Leaf.

Lowry, L. (2006). *The giver*. New York: Delacorte.

MacLachlan, P. (2004). *Sarah, plain and tall*. New York: HarperTrophy.

Martin, S., & Chast, R. (2007). *The alphabet from A to Y with bonus letter Z!* New York: Flying Dolphin Press.

McCloskey, R. (2001). *Make way for ducklings*. New York: Viking.

McDermott, G. (2001). *Raven*. San Diego: Voyager.

McLeod, B. (2006). *Superhero ABC*. New York: HarperCollins.

Mitchell, S. (2007). *The ugly duckling*. Cambridge, MA: Candlewick Press.

Naylor, P. R. (2000). *Shiloh*. New York: Aladdin Books.

Park, L. S. (2005). *Project mulberry*. New York: Clarion Books.

Patent, D. H. (2004). *Right dog for the job: Ira's path from service dog to guide dog*. New York: Walker.

Paterson, K. (2005). *Bridge to Terabithia*. New York: HarperTrophy.

Patron, S. (2006). *The higher power of Lucky*. New York: Atheneum.

Paulsen, G. (2007). *Hatchet*. New York: Simon & Schuster.

Pinto, S. (2003). *The alphabet room*. New York: Bloomsbury.

Potter, B. (2006). *The tale of Peter Rabbit*. New York: Warne.

Pratt-Serafini, K. J. (2002). *Saguaro moon: A desert journal*. Nevada City, CA: Dawn.

Prelutsky, J. (Sel.). (2000). *The Random House book of poetry for children*. New York: Random House.

Prelutsky, J. (2007). *My parents think I'm sleeping*. New York: Greenwillow.

Ruddell, D. (2007). *Today at the Bluebird Café: A branchful of birds*. New York: McElderry.

Ryan, P. M. (2002). *Esperanza rising*. New York: Scholastic.

Sachar, L. (2003). *Holes*. New York: Yearling.

Schlitz, L. A. (2007). *Good masters! Sweet ladies! Voices from a medieval village*. Cambridge, MA: Candlewick Press.

Schwartz, D. M. (2001). *Q is for quark: A science alphabet book*. Berkeley, CA: Tricycle Press.

Scieszka, J. (1996). *The true story of the 3 little pigs!* New York: Puffin Books.

Scieszka, J. (2004). *Knights of the kitchen table*. New York: Puffin Books.

Selznick, B. (2007). *The invention of Hugo Cabret*. New York: Scholastic.

Seuling, B. (2003). *Flick a switch: How electricity gets to your home*. New York: Holiday House.

Sidman, J. (2007). *This is just to say: Poems of apology and forgiveness*. Boston: Houghton Mifflin.

Siebert, D. (2006). *Tour America: A journey through poems and art*. San Francisco: Chronicle Books.

Simon, S. (2003). *Spiders*. New York: HarperCollins.

Simon, S. (2006). *The brain: Our nervous system*. New York: HarperCollins.

Sís, P. (2007). *The wall: Growing up behind the iron curtain*. New York: Farrar, Straus & Giroux.

Smith, J. (2005). *Bone: Out of Boneville*. New York: Scholastic/Graphix.

Soto, G. (2005). *Neighborhood odes*. San Diego: Harcourt.

Soto, G. (2007). *Canto familiar*. San Diego: Harcourt.

Speare, E. G. (2001). *The witch of Blackbird Pond*. Boston: Houghton Mifflin.

Steig, W. (1990). *Doctor De Soto*. New York: Farrar, Straus & Giroux.

Steig, W. (2006). *Sylvester and the magic pebble*. New York: Aladdin Books.

Tan, S. (2007). *The arrival*. New York: Arthur A. Levine/Scholastic.

Taylor, M. D. (2001). *Roll of thunder, hear my cry*. New York: Dial Books.

Testa, M. (2005). *Becoming Joe Di Maggio*. Cambridge, MA: Candlewick Press.

Thayer, E. L. (2006). *Casey at the bat*. Tonawanda, NY: Kids Can Press.

Van Allsburg, C. (1986). *The stranger*. Boston: Houghton Mifflin.

Van Allsburg, C. (1991). *The wretched stone*. Boston: Houghton Mifflin.

Ward, C. (1999). *The hare and the tortoise*. New York: Millbrook Press.

White, E. B. (2004). *Charlotte's web*. New York: HarperTrophy.

Wiesner, D. (2006). *Flotsam*. New York: Clarion Books.

Wildsmith, B. (2007). *The lion and the rat*. New York: Oxford University Press.

Williams, M. (2007). *The adventures of Robin Hood*. New York: Walker.

Williams, V. B. (1993). *A chair for my mother*. New York: HarperTrophy.

Wong, J. S. (2006). *Before it wriggles away*. Katonah, NY: Richard C. Owen.

Wood, A. (2001). *Alphabet adventure*. New York: Blue Sky Press.

Woodson, J. (2004). *Locomotion*. New York: Puffin Books.

Woodson, J. (2005). *Show way*. New York: Putnam.

Zelinsky, P. O. (1996). *Rumpelstiltskin*. New York: Puffin Books.

PaRT 3

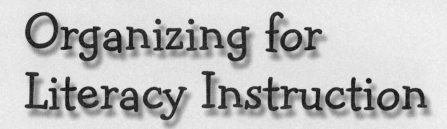

Organizing for Literacy Instruction

Teachers generally use one or more of these instructional approaches to teach reading and writing:

▶ **Basal reading programs**
▶ **Literature focus units**
▶ **Literature circles**
▶ **Reading and writing workshop**

None of the instructional approaches has been found to be significantly more effective than the others, so teachers combine approaches or components from several approaches to ensure that students receive both explicit instruction and opportunities for authentic reading and writing. Many teachers add guided reading or another instructional program to address their students' needs or to comply with district requirements. In addition, they teach students how to use reading and writing as tools for learning through thematic units that focus on social studies and science topics.

These instructional approaches differ in significant ways. Probably the most important difference is theoretical orientation: Basal reading programs reflect behaviorism; literature circles, in contrast, reflect sociolinguistics. The instructional materials differ, too: Students primarily read textbooks in basal reader programs, but they read trade books in the other approaches. Teachers organize for literacy instruction according to their beliefs about how children learn, district expectations, and the available materials.

In this part opener, you see how Ms. Boland teaches a thematic unit on the Middle Ages. Her seventh graders read one of several novels set in this historical period, along with their social studies textbook. Then they investigate a topic that interests them and apply what they learn as they create an interactive museum that includes technology.

Becca is reading Karen Cushman's *Catherine, Called Birdy*, a novel written as a diary. Catherine, the diary's author, is a young noblewoman in 1290, and her diary provides fascinating details about medieval life. The book's humorous tone makes it very popular. ▶

Students meet in literature circles to talk about the novel, and Ms. Boland sits in to help them focus on both the story events and the historical information they're learning.

Working in small groups, the seventh graders read about the Middle Ages in their social studies textbook. Then they create a graphic organizer about one of the big ideas and present what they've learned to the class.

Group Roles

Students assume these roles in their research groups:

- **Facilitator**—keeps the group on task and solves problems
- **Research coordinator**—makes sure group members are investigating their topics
- **Troubleshooter**—assists group members with the Internet
- **Harmonizer**—helps the group work together smoothly
- **Supply person**—gets needed materials from the library and from Ms. Boland

The culminating project is an interactive museum about medieval life. The students form research groups to investigate topics, including cathedrals, the life of a knight, and the crusades.

Jeremy and Connor are creating a website about the life of a knight for their museum display.

Museum Rubric

	Excellent	Very Good	Good	Inadequate
Talk	Insightful talk about ideas and relationships.	Entertaining presentation focusing on the big ideas.	Useful presentation of information.	Presentation is very brief or unfocused.
Visuals	3–4 visuals extend visitors' knowledge.	2–3 visuals enrich the display.	1–2 visuals present information.	Visuals aren't used.
Artifacts	3+ artifacts are used interactively.	3+ artifacts are integrated into the display.	1–3 realistic artifacts can be examined.	Artifacts aren't available.
Technology	Computer is used in 2–3 ways.	Computer is integrated into the display.	Computer is used to review information.	A computer isn't used.
Overall Impression	Impressive display challenges visitors to think in new ways.	Inviting display engages visitors in hands-on activities.	Informative display enhances visitors' knowledge.	Display isn't useful.

On museum day, students, parents, and school board members visit the museum, listen to costumed students share what they've learned, and participate in interactive activities. Afterward, the students and Ms. Boland grade the displays using the rubric.

CHAPTER 10

Organizing for Instruction

Fourth Graders Participate in a Yearlong Author Study

There's a busy hum in Miss Paniccia's fourth-grade classroom. The students are involved in a 40-minute writing workshop; it's the time when students develop and refine pieces of writing on topics they've chosen themselves. They work with classmates to revise and edit their rough drafts and then use AlphaSmart® keyboards for word processing. Next, they transfer their compositions to a classroom computer and print out clean copies of their drafts for a final editing conference with Miss Paniccia. Afterward, they print out the finished copies.

Today, the fourth graders are putting the finishing touches on the collections of stories they've worked on for months. Each student has written at least seven stories, and now they're publishing them by pasting them into bound books with blank pages. The spring back-to-school night is 2 days away, and everyone is eager for parents to read their newly published books.

The class has been involved in an ambitious yearlong project on Chris Van Allsburg, the popular author and illustrator of award-winning fantasy picture books, including *Probuditi* (2006) and *The Polar Express* (2005). The students have read some of these stories in their basal readers and during literature circles, and Miss Paniccia has read others aloud. The stories they've been writing accompany the illustrations in *The Mysteries of Harris Burdick* (Van Allsburg, 1996).

The Chris Van Allsburg unit began in September when Miss Paniccia read aloud *Jumanji* (Van Allsburg, 1982), the story of two children who play a jungle adventure board game that comes to life. She also read aloud the sequel, *Zathura* (2002), about a space adventure board game, and students watched the movie version. They also made board games and wrote directions for playing them. She used the story to emphasize the importance of listening to directions in the classroom, following parents' directions at home, and reading directions on state achievement tests.

Miss Paniccia regularly teaches minilessons on writing strategies that students then apply in their own writing. She began with a series of lessons on revising and proofreading that students use in writing workshop. Next, she taught lessons about the elements of story structure. Posters about each story element hang in the classroom, testimony to the learning taking place there. Students apply what they've learned as they craft their own stories. They use the writing process, as shown in the box on page 322, to draft and refine their stories. Last year, these students took an afterschool touchtyping course, so they know the fundamentals of finger placement on the keyboard and are developing typing fluency as they use the AlphaSmart® word processing machines.

Month after month, the students have been writing stories. Seth's story for the illustration entitled "Mr. Linden's Library" is shown in the box on page 323. The illustration depicts a girl sleeping in bed with an open book beside her; vines are growing out of the book and spreading across her bed. As you read Seth's story, you'll see how his story developed from the illustration and how he applied what he's learned about story structure.

Today during writing workshop, Miss Paniccia is meeting with Alfonso, Martha, and Yimleej to proofread their stories and correct errors. Other students are word processing their last stories or printing out final copies and gluing them into their books. Miguel and Lindsey have finished their books, so they're helping classmates word process, transfer to the computer, and print out their stories. Miss Paniccia's optimistic that everyone will be finished by lunchtime tomorrow. She plans to start author's chair during writing workshop tomorrow: Students will take turns reading their favorite stories aloud to classmates. Author's chair is a popular classroom activity; most students are eager to share their stories, and their classmates enjoy listening to them because they've learned how to read with expression and hold their classmates' interest.

Last week, the students created this introductory page for their story collections:

> Thirty years ago a man named Harris Burdick came by Peter Wenders's publishing office. Mr. Burdick claimed that he had written 15 stories and illustrated them. All he brought with him on that day were the illustrations with titles. The next day Harris Burdick was going to bring the stories to Mr. Wenders, but he never returned. In fact, Harris Burdick was never seen again.
>
> Chris Van Allsburg met with Mr. Wenders and that is where he came across the illustrations. Mr. Wenders handed Mr. Van Allsburg a dust-covered box full of

Stage	Activity	Description
Prewriting	Story Cards	Students create story cards to develop their ideas, characters, setting, problem, climax, and solution.
	One-On-One	Students meet with a classmate to share their story cards and talk out their ideas.
Drafting	Rough Drafts	Students write their rough drafts in pencil, working from their story cards.
Revising	Writing Groups	Students meet with two classmates to share their rough drafts, getting feedback about their stories. Then they make revisions based on the feedback they received.
	Conference With Miss P.	They recopy their drafts in pen and have Miss Paniccia read and respond to their stories. Students make more revisions based on their teacher's feedback.
Editing	Proofreading	Students proofread their drafts and correct the errors they notice. Then they have two classmates proofread their drafts to identify and correct remaining spelling, capitalization, punctuation, and grammar errors.
	Word Processing	Students word process their stories using word processing machines. Then they transfer their stories to the classroom computer, put them into their own files, and print out a copy in a legible font.
	Conference With Miss P.	Students meet with Miss Paniccia to proofread and correct the remaining errors.
Publishing	Final Copy	Students print out a final copy, glue the pages into a book, and add illustrations.

Students' Writing Process Activities

drawings, and Chris Van Allsburg was inspired to reproduce them for children across the nation.

Right here in room 30, we have worked hard all year creating stories for the illustrations. Even though we have completed our stories, the mystery of Harris Burdick still remains.

It's a class collaboration: Miss Paniccia and the students developed the introduction together, and copies were made for each student. By collaborating, the teacher ensured that they had a useful introduction for their books.

After beginning the author study in September, Miss Paniccia continued to read stories each month. In October, she and her students read *The Stranger* (Van Allsburg, 1986), a story included in their basal readers. In the story, the Baileys take in an injured stranger, a man who doesn't speak or seem to know who he is, but he appears to be attuned with the seasons and has an amazing connection with wild animals. The stranger is Jack Frost, although it's never explicitly stated in the story. They take several days to read the story. On the first day, the teacher introduced the key vocabulary

---

Seth's Story About "Mr. Linden's Library"

"I would like to check out this book," Sally Olger said. The book that she wanted to check out was called <u>Adventures in the Wild</u>. She had skipped as she had gone up to the counter. Sally loved to go to this library. It was owned by Mr. Linden, so everybody just called it Mr. Linden's library.

The expression on the man at the counter's face changed when he saw the book that Sally was holding. The man warned Sally that if she left the book out on one page for over an hour, something dangerous would come out of the book.

Sally didn't really hear or care about what the man said. She checked out the book and started reading it in bed that night. The book was really interesting. It had tons of short stories in it. At 12:00 midnight, Sally turned the page to a story called "Lost in the Jungle," yawned, and fell asleep. At 1:00 A.M. vines started to grow out of the book. He had warned her about the book. Now it was too late. Soon Sally's whole room was covered in vines. By 2:00, they were making their way up the stairs.

BBBRRRRIIIIINNNNNNGGGGGG! went Sally's alarm clock.

"AAAAAAAHHHHHHHH!" screamed Sally. Now the whole house was covered in vines. Sally slowly made her way to her parents' bedroom through the vines and woke them up. They screamed too. As quickly as possible (which wasn't very fast) the Olgers got out of their house, got in their car and drove to the library. They told the man at the desk what had happened. He said that the only way to get rid of the vines was to cut their roots (they would be sticking right out of the book) and then haul all of the vines off to the dump. Luckily, the town dump wasn't very far away from the Olgers' house.

By the time Mr. Olger had found and cut the roots away from the book, Sally and Mrs. Olger had rounded up the whole neighborhood to help take the vines to the dump. By 5:00 P.M. in the afternoon they had cleared away all of the vines. Sally had learned her lesson to listen when someone warns you about something.

---

words, including *autumn*, *etched*, and *peculiar*, and the class previewed the story, examining the illustrations and making predictions. Miss Paniccia used a shared reading procedure: The students listened to the story read aloud on the professional CD that accompanies the textbook and followed along in their textbooks. Some inferred that the stranger is Jack Frost, but others didn't. That's when the teacher introduced the drawing inferences strategy, which she called "reading between the lines."

They read the story a second time, searching for clues that led their classmates to guess that the stranger is Jack Frost, and afterward made a cluster, a spider web–like diagram, with the clues. They wrote the words *The Stranger* in the center circle, drew out rays from this circle, and wrote these clues at the end of each one: he wears odd clothing, is confused by buttons, and works hard but doesn't get tired. Afterward, they completed page 156 in the Practice Book that accompanies the textbook as well as other pages that emphasize comprehension. Then Miss Paniccia asked students to closely examine the illustrations in the story. They noticed how the perspective in the illustrations varies to draw readers into the scenes and create the mood. The students read the story a third time with partners, talking about how Chris Van Allsburg used viewpoint in the illustrations.

In November, students read other books by Chris Van Allsburg in literature circles. Miss Paniccia presented book talks about these four books: *Two Bad Ants* (Van Allsburg, 1988), *Just a Dream* (Van Allsburg, 1990), *The Sweetest Fig* (Van Allsburg, 1993b), and *The Wreck of the Zephyr* (Van Allsburg, 1983). Then students formed small groups to read one of the books. They assumed roles and took on responsibilities in the small groups as they read and discussed the book. Then students read another of the books during a second literature circle in January.

Miss Paniccia read aloud the award-winning holiday story *The Polar Express* (Van Allsburg, 2005) in December. In the story, being able to hear Santa's bells jiggle represents belief in the magic of Christmas, so Miss Paniccia gave each student a small bell to jiggle each time it was mentioned in the story. The students discussed the story in a grand conversation; much of their discussion focused on the theme and how the author states it explicitly at the end of the story. "What an awesome story!" Hunter concluded, and his classmates agreed. They also talked about their own holiday traditions and wrote about them during writing workshop.

They continued to read other books by Chris Van Allsburg: In February, Miss Paniccia read *The Garden of Abdul Gasazi* (Van Allsburg, 1993a), and in March, she read *The Wretched Stone* (Van Allsburg, 1991). These books are difficult for students to comprehend because they have to make inferences: In *The Garden of Abdul Gasazi*, readers have to decide whether the magician really changes the dog into a duck, and in *The Wretched Stone*, they need to understand that the stone is a symbol, representing television, computers, or video games. Miss Paniccia taught a series of minilessons on drawing inferences, and she modeled the strategy as she reread the stories, showing the fourth graders how to use their background knowledge, the clues in the story, and self-questions to read between the lines. Then students reread the stories with partners, talked about clues in the stories, and made inferences as their teacher had.

In March, Miss Paniccia also taught a series of minilessons on the fantasy genre. Then students divided into small groups to reread the Chris Van Allsburg books and examine them for fantasy characteristics. They developed a chart with the titles of the books written across the top and the characteristics of fantasies written down the left side. Then they completed the chart by indicating how the characteristics are represented in each book.

This month, students are reading Chris Van Allsburg's books independently; some students are reading those they haven't yet read, and others are rereading favorite ones. As they read, they search for the white dog that Van Allsburg includes in each book. In some books, such as *The Garden of Abdul Gasazi*, the dog is alive, but in others, he's a puppet, a hood ornament, or a picture. In several books, only a small part of him shows; in *The Wretched Stone*, for example, you see only his tail on one page. In addition, they continue to notice the fantasy elements of the stories, they draw inferences when needed, and they reflect on Van Allsburg's use of perspective in his illustrations.

There's no one best way to teach reading and writing. Instead, teachers create a balanced literacy program using two or more approaches. Four of the most commonly used literacy programs for kindergarten through eighth grade are basal reading programs, literature focus units, literature circles, and reading and writing workshop. Miss Paniccia's author study in the vignette was successful because her literacy program was balanced with a combination of explicit instruction, small-group and whole-class literacy activities, and independent reading and writing opportunities.

By combining several instructional approaches, Miss Paniccia juggled the district's adopted basal reading program with other instructional approaches that enriched and extended her students' literacy learning.

TEACHING WITH BASAL READING PROGRAMS

Commercial reading programs, commonly called *basal readers*, have been a staple in reading instruction for 150 years. Before 1850, William Holmes McGuffey wrote the McGuffey Readers, the first textbooks published with increasingly challenging books designed for each grade level. The lessons featured literature selections that emphasized religious and patriotic values. Students used phonics to sound out words, studied vocabulary words in the context of stories, and practiced proper enunciation as they read aloud to classmates. These books were widely used until the beginning of the 20th century. The Scott Foresman basal reading program, introduced in 1930 and used through the 1960s, is probably the most famous; the first-grade textbooks featured stories about two children named Dick and Jane, their little sister Sally, their pets Puff and Spot, and their parents. The first-grade books relied on the repetition of words through contrived sentences such as "See Jane. See Sally. See Jane and Sally." to teach words. Students were expected to memorize words rather than use phonics to decode them. This whole-word method was known as "look and say." The Scott Foresman program has been criticized for its lack of phonics instruction as well as for centering stories on an "ideal" middle-class white family.

Today's basal readers include more authentic literature selections that celebrate diverse cultures, and they emphasize an organized presentation of strategies and skills, especially phonics in the primary grades. Kate Walsh (2003) reviewed five widely used series and found that they all provide visually stimulating artwork to engage students, similar methods of teaching decoding and comprehension, and teachers' guides with detailed lesson plans. She also uncovered a common problem: None of the programs provided for the sustained development of students' background knowledge, but when students don't develop a strong foundation of world and word knowledge, they have difficulty reading and understanding more conceptually demanding books, beginning at fourth-grade level. This drop in achievement is known as the "fourth-grade slump," and children from economically disadvantaged families are more likely to fall behind their classmates (Chall, Jacobs, & Baldwin, 1991).

Publishers of basal reading textbooks tout their programs as complete literacy programs containing all the materials needed for students to become successful readers. The accessibility of reading materials is one advantage: Teachers have copies of grade-level textbooks for every student. The instructional program is planned for them; teachers follow step-by-step directions to teach strategies and skills, and workbooks provide practice materials. An overview of basal reading programs is presented on page 326. It's unrealistic, however, to assume that any commercial reading program could be a complete literacy program. Teachers who have students reading above or below grade level need reading materials at their students' levels. In addition, students need many more opportunities to listen to books read aloud and to read and reread books than are provided in a basal reading program. In addition, a complete literacy program involves more than reading; students need opportunities to learn the writing process, draft and refine compositions, and learn writing strategies and skills.

Basal Reading Programs

TOPIC	DESCRIPTION
Purpose	To teach the strategies and skills that successful readers need using an organized program that includes grade-level reading selections, workbook practice assignments, and frequent testing.
Components	Basal reading programs involve five components: reading the selections in the grade-level textbook, instruction on strategies and skills, workbook assignments, independent reading opportunities, and a management plan that includes flexible grouping and regular assessment.
Theory Base	Basal reading programs are based on behaviorism because teachers provide explicit instruction and students are passive rather than active learners.
Applications	Basal reading programs organize instruction into units with weeklong lessons that include reading, strategy and skill instruction, and workbook activities. They should be used with other instructional approaches to ensure that students read books at their instructional levels and have opportunities to participate in writing projects.
Strengths	• Textbooks are aligned with grade-level standards. • Students read selections at their grade level. • Teachers teach strategies and skills in a sequential program, and students practice them through reading and workbook assignments. • The teacher's guide provides detailed instructions for teaching reading. • Assessment materials are included in the program.
Limitations	• Selections may be too difficult for some students and too easy for others. • Selections may lack the authenticity of good literature or not include a variety of genres. • Programs include many workbook assignments. • Most instruction is presented to the whole class.

Components of Basal Reading Programs

Even though there are a number of commercial programs available today, most include these components:

◆ Selections in grade-level textbooks
◆ Instruction about decoding and comprehension strategies and skills
◆ Workbook assignments
◆ Independent reading opportunities

Basal readers are recognized for their strong skills component: Teachers teach skills in a predetermined sequence, and students apply what they're learning in the textbook selections they read and the workbook assignments they complete.

Selections in Grade-Level Textbooks. Basal reading programs are organized into units on topics such as challenges, folktales, and friends. Each unit includes four to six weeklong lessons, each with a featured selection. The selections in the kindergarten and first-grade textbooks contain decodable text so that children can apply the phonics skills they're learning, but as students develop stronger word-identification skills and a bank of familiar high-frequency words, textbooks transition to literature selections that were originally published as trade books.

Everyone reads the same selections in the grade-level textbook each week, no matter their reading level. These commercial programs argue that it's important to expose all students to grade-level instruction because some students, especially minority students, have been denied equal access to instruction. The teacher's guide provides suggestions for supporting struggling readers and English learners. Many programs also provide video, audio, and Internet resources. Audiotapes of the selections, which teachers often play as students follow along in their copies of the textbook, are an especially useful resource. After this shared reading experience, some less successful readers can then read the selection, but many teachers complain that a few students can't read the selections no matter how much support they provide.

Instruction in Strategies and Skills. Teachers use basal reading programs to deliver explicit and systematic instruction that is aligned with state literacy outcomes and standards. Most textbooks include instruction in phonemic awareness, phonics, high-frequency words, word-identification skills, spelling, grammar, and writing mechanics (capitalization and punctuation). The programs also emphasize comprehension strategies, including evaluating, monitoring, predicting, questioning, summarizing, and visualizing.

The teacher's guide provides detailed lesson plans for teaching strategies and skills with each selection. Teachers explain the strategies and skills and model their use as they read with students, then students apply them as they read selections and complete workbook pages. Scope-and-sequence charts for each grade level that are included in the teacher's guide show the order for teaching strategies and skills and explain how they're introduced at one grade level and reinforced and expanded at the next level. These programs claim that it's their explicit, systematic instruction that ensures success.

Workbook Assignments. Students complete workbook pages before, during, and after reading each selection to reinforce instruction; 10 to 12 workbook pages that focus on phonics, vocabulary, comprehension, grammar, spelling, and writing accompany each selection. On these pages, students write words, letters, or sentences, match words and sentences, or complete graphic organizers.

Teachers vary how they use the workbook pages. Once students know how to complete a workbook page, such as the pages that focus on practicing spelling words, they work independently or with partners. However, for more-challenging assignments, such as those dealing with comprehension strategies or newly introduced skills, teachers have the whole class do the assignment together at their direction. Teachers also devise various approaches for monitoring students' completion of workbook assignments: They may have students check their own work, or they may grade the assignments themselves.

Independent Reading Opportunities. Most basal reading programs include a collection of easy, on-grade-level, and challenging paperback books for students to read independently. There are multiple copies of each book, and teachers set out some of these books for students to read after finishing each selection. Some of these books, especially in the primary grades, have been written to reinforce phonics skills and vocabulary words, but others are trade books. The goal is for the collection to meet the needs of all students, but sometimes teachers still need to supplement with much easier books for English learners or struggling readers.

Check the Compendium of Instructional Procedures, which follows Chapter 12, for more information on the highlighted terms.

When teachers implement basal reading programs, they use the reading process, even though many activities are different than in other approaches:

Prereading. Teachers follow directions in the teacher's guide to activate and build students' background knowledge, introduce vocabulary, teach word-identification and comprehension strategies, and preview the selection.

Reading. Students read the selection independently, but if it's too difficult, teachers read it aloud or play an audiotape before students read it themselves.

Responding. Teachers follow directions in the teacher's guide to enhance students' comprehension by asking questions about the author's purpose, modeling **think-alouds**, encouraging students to draw inferences, and summarizing the selection. Students also complete workbook assignments that focus on comprehension.

Exploring. Teachers teach phonics, word analysis, spelling, and grammar skills, and students practice the skills by completing workbook assignments. They also teach students about authors, genres, and text structures.

Applying. Students read related selections in the basal reader or in other books that accompany the program and participate in writing activities related to the selection or genre being studied.

One of the most striking differences is that students complete practice activities in workbooks during several of the stages rather than applying what they're learning in more authentic ways.

Materials Included in Basal Reading Programs

At the center of a basal reading program is the student textbook or anthology. In the primary grades, two or more books are provided at each grade level, and in fourth through sixth grades, there's usually one book. Most basal reading programs end in sixth grade. The books are colorful and inviting, often featuring pictures of children and animals on the covers of primary-level books and exciting adventures and fanciful locations on the covers of books for grades 4 through 6. The selections are grouped into units, and each unit includes stories, poems, and informational articles. Many multicultural selections have been added, and illustrations usually feature ethnically diverse people. Information about authors and illustrators is provided for many selections. Textbooks contain a table of contents and a glossary.

Commercial reading programs provide a wide variety of materials to support student learning. Consumable workbooks are probably the best-known support material; students write letters, words, and sentences in these books to practice phonics, comprehension, and vocabulary strategies and skills. Big books and kits with letter and word cards, wall charts, and manipulatives are available for kindergarten and first-grade programs. Black-line masters of parent letters are also available.

Some multimedia materials, including audiocassettes, CD-ROMs, and videos, are included, which teachers can use at listening centers and computer centers. Collections of trade books are available for each grade level to provide supplemental reading materials. In the primary grades, many books have decodable text to provide practice on phonics skills and high-frequency words; in the upper grades, the books are related to unit topics.

Basal reading programs also offer a variety of assessment tools. Teachers use placement evaluations or informal reading inventories to determine students' reading levels and for placement in reading groups. They use **running records** to informally monitor students' reading. There are also selection and unit tests to determine students' phonics, vocabulary, and comprehension achievement. Information is provided on how to administer the assessments and analyze the results.

A teacher's instructional guidebook is provided for each grade level. This oversize handbook gives comprehensive information about how to plan lessons, teach the selections, and assess students' progress. The selections are shown in reduced size in the guidebook, and each page includes background information about the selection, instructions for reading the selections, and ideas for coordinating skill and strategy instruction. In addition, information is presented about which supplemental books to use with each selection and how to assess students' learning. Figure 10–1 summarizes the materials provided in most basal reading programs.

Managing a Basal Reading Program

The teacher's guide provides a management plan for the basal reading program. Daily and weekly lesson plans are included with suggestions for pacing for each unit, ideas for flexible grouping, and regular assessment activities. There are letters to send home

Figure 10–1 ◆ Materials in Basal Reading Programs

Materials	Description
Textbook or Anthology	The student's book of reading selections. The selections are organized thematically and include literature from trade books. Often the textbook is available in a series of softcover books or a single hardcover book.
Big Books	Enlarged copies of books for shared reading. These books are used in kindergarten and first grade.
Supplemental Books	Collections of trade books for each grade level. Kindergarten-level books often feature familiar songs and wordless stories. First- and second-grade books often include decodable words for practicing phonics skills and high-frequency words. In grades 3 to 6, books are often related to unit themes.
Workbooks	Consumable books of phonics, comprehension, vocabulary, spelling, and grammar worksheets.
Transparencies	Color transparencies to use in teaching skills and strategies.
Black-Line Masters	Worksheets that teachers duplicate and use to teach skills and provide additional reading practice.
Kits	Alphabet cards, word cards, and other instructional materials. These kits are used in kindergarten through second grade.
Teacher's Guide	An oversize book that presents comprehensive information about how to teach reading using the basal reading program. The selections are shown in reduced size, and background information about the selection, instructions for teaching the selections, and instructions on coordinating skill and strategy instruction are given on each page. In addition, information is presented about which supplemental books to use with each selection and how to assess students' learning.
Parent Materials	Black-line masters that teachers duplicate and send home to parents. Information about the reading program and lists of ways parents can work with their children are included. These materials are available in English, Spanish, and several other languages.
Assessment Materials	A variety of assessments, including selection and unit tests, running records, and phonics inventories, are available along with teacher's guides.
Multimedia	Audiocassettes and CDs of some selections, related videos, and website connections are provided.

to parents at the beginning of each unit, usually available in several languages, as well as a variety of assessment materials, including phonics tests, end-of-lesson and end-of-unit tests, writing rubrics, and observation guidelines. Teachers are encouraged to assess students' learning regularly to monitor their progress and to evaluate the effectiveness of the instructional program.

TEACHING WITH LITERATURE FOCUS UNITS

Teachers plan literature focus units featuring popular and award-winning stories, informational books, or books of poetry. Some literature focus units feature a single book, either a picture book or a chapter book, whereas others feature several books for a genre unit or an author study. Teachers guide and direct students as they read and respond to a book, but the emphasis in this instructional approach is on teaching students about literature and developing lifelong readers. An overview of this instructional approach is shown on the next page.

Literature focus units include activities incorporating the five stages of the reading process:

Prereading. Teachers involve students in activities to build background knowledge and interest them in reading the book, including sharing book boxes, reading related books, showing DVDs, and talking about related topics.

Reading. Students read the featured selection independently, or the teacher reads it aloud or uses shared reading if it's too difficult for students to read themselves.

Responding. Students participate in grand conversations to talk about the book and write entries in reading logs to deepen their understanding.

Exploring. Students post vocabulary on word walls, participate in word-study activities, learn comprehension strategies, examine text factors, and research the book's author or related topics.

Applying. Students apply their learning as they create oral and written projects and share them with their classmates.

Through these activities, teachers guide students as they read and respond to high-quality literature.

Steps in Developing a Unit

Teachers develop a literature focus unit through a series of steps, beginning with choosing the literature and setting goals, then identifying and scheduling activities, and finally deciding how to assess students' learning. Effective teachers don't simply follow directions in literature focus unit planning guides that are available for purchase in school supply stories; rather, they do the planning themselves because they're the ones who are most knowledgeable about their students, the time available for the unit, the strategies and skills they need to teach, and the activities they want to develop.

Usually literature focus units featuring a picture book are completed in 1 week, and units featuring a novel or other longer book are completed in 3 or 4 weeks. Genre and author units often last 3 or 4 weeks. Rarely, if ever, do literature focus units continue for more than a month. When teachers drag out a unit, they risk killing students' interest in that particular book or, worse yet, their interest in literature and reading.

Go to the Building Teaching Skills and Dispositions section of Chapter 10 on **MyEducationLab.com** to see an upper elementary class participating in a literature focus unit.

OVERVIEW OF THE INSTRUCTIONAL APPROACH

Literature Focus Units

TOPIC	DESCRIPTION
Purpose	To teach reading through literature, using high-quality, grade-appropriate picture books and novels.
Components	Teachers involve students in three activities: Students read and respond to a trade book together as a class; the teacher teaches minilessons on phonics, vocabulary, and comprehension using the book they're reading; and students create projects to extend their understanding of the book.
Theory Base	Literature focus units represent a transition between teacher-centered and student-centered learning because the teacher guides students as they read a book. This approach reflects cognitive/information processing theory because teachers develop students' background knowledge, read aloud when students can't read fluently, and teach vocabulary words and comprehension strategies. It also reflects Rosenblatt's transactive theory because students participate in grand conversations and write in reading logs to deepen their comprehension, and critical literacy theory because issues of social justice often arise in the trade books.
Applications	Teachers teach units featuring a picture book or a novel, generally using books on a district-approved list, or units featuring a genre or author. Literature focus units are often alternated with another approach where students read books at their own reading levels.
Strengths	• Teachers select award-winning literature for these units. • Teachers scaffold students' comprehension as they read with the class or small groups. • Teachers teach minilessons on reading strategies and skills. • Students learn vocabulary through word walls and other activities. • Students learn about genres, story structure, and literary devices.
Limitations	• All students read the same book whether or not they like it and whether or not it's written at their reading level. • Many activities are teacher directed.

Step 1: Select the Literature. Teachers select the book for the literature focus unit—a picture-book story, a novel, an informational book, or a book of poetry. Teachers collect multiple copies so students will each have their own copy to read. Many school districts have class sets of selected books available; however, sometimes teachers have to ask administrators to purchase multiple copies or buy books themselves through book clubs.

Teachers collect related books for the text set, too, including other versions of the same story, sequels, other books written by the same author, or other books in the same genre. Teachers collect one or two copies of 10, 20, 30, or more books for the text set and add them to the classroom library for the unit. Books for the text set are placed on a special shelf or in a crate in the library center. At the beginning of the unit, teachers introduce the books and provide opportunities for students read them during independent reading time.

Teachers also identify and collect supplemental materials related to the featured selection, including puppets, stuffed animals, and toys; charts and diagrams; book boxes of materials to use in introducing the book; and information about the author and the illustrator. For many picture books, big-book versions are also available that can be used for shared reading. Teachers also locate multimedia resources, including videotapes of the featured selection, DVDs to provide background knowledge on the topic, and Internet sites about the author and the illustrator.

Step 2: Set Goals. Teachers decide what they want their students to learn during the unit, and they connect the goals they set with state standards that their students are expected to learn.

Step 3: Develop a Unit Plan. Teachers read or reread the selected book and then think about the focus they will use for the unit. Sometimes teachers focus on an element of story structure, the historical setting, wordplay, the author or genre, or a topic related to the book, such as weather or desert life. After determining the focus, they choose activities to use at each of the five stages of the reading process. Teachers often jot notes on a chart divided into sections for each stage; then they use the ideas they've brainstormed as they plan the unit. Generally, not all of the brainstormed activities will be used, but teachers select the most important ones according to their focus and the time available.

Step 4: Coordinate Grouping Patterns With Activities. Teachers think about how to incorporate whole-class, small-group, partner, and individual activities into their unit plans. It's important that students have opportunities to read and write independently as well as to work with small groups and to come together as a class. If the book will be read together as a class, then students need opportunities to reread it with a buddy or to read related books independently. These grouping patterns should be alternated during various activities in the unit. Teachers often go back to their planning sheet and highlight activities with colored markers according to grouping patterns.

Step 5: Create a Time Schedule. Teachers create a schedule that provides sufficient time for students to move through the five stages of the reading process and to complete the activities planned for the unit. They also plan minilessons to teach reading and writing strategies and skills identified in their goals and those needed for students to complete the unit activities. Teachers usually have a set time for minilessons in their weekly schedule, but sometimes they arrange their schedules to teach minilessons just before they introduce specific activities or assignments.

Step 6: Assessing Students. Teachers often distribute unit folders in which students keep all their work. Keeping all the materials together makes the unit easier for both students and teachers to manage. Teachers also plan ways to document students' learning and assign grades. One type of record keeping is an assignment checklist, which is developed with students and distributed at the beginning of the literature focus unit. Students keep track of their work during the unit and sometimes negotiate to change the checklist as the unit evolves. Students keep the lists in their unit folders and mark off each item as it's completed. At the end of the unit, students turn in their assignment checklist and other completed work. Although this list doesn't include every activity students were involved in, it identifies those that will be graded.

Units Featuring a Picture Book

In literature focus units featuring picture books, younger children read predictable picture books or books with very little text, such as *Rosie's Walk* (Hutchins, 2005), a humorous story about a hen who walks leisurely around the barnyard, unwittingly leading the fox who is following her into one mishap after another; older students read more-sophisticated picture books with more-elaborate story lines, such as *Train to Somewhere* (Bunting, 2000), a story about an orphan train taking children to adoptive families in the West in the late 1800s. Teachers use the same six-step approach for developing units featuring a picture book for younger and older students.

Units Featuring a Novel

Teachers develop literature focus units using novels, such as *Bunnicula: A Rabbit-Tale of Mystery* (Howe & Howe, 2006), *Sarah, Plain and Tall* (MacLachlan, 2004), and *Number the Stars* (Lowry, 1998). The biggest difference between picture-book stories and novels is their length, and when teachers plan literature focus units featuring a novel, they need to decide how to schedule the reading of the book. Will students read one or two chapters each day? How often will they respond in reading logs or grand conversations? It's important that teachers reread the book to note the length of chapters and identify key points in the book where students will want time to explore and respond to the ideas presented there.

Figure 10–2 presents a 4-week lesson plan for Lois Lowry's *Number the Stars*, a story of friendship and courage set in Nazi-occupied Denmark during World War II. The daily routine during the first 2 weeks is as follows:

Reading. Students and the teacher read two chapters using shared reading.

Responding After Reading. Students participate in a grand conversation about the chapters they've read, write in reading logs, and add important words to the class word wall.

Minilesson. The teacher teaches a minilesson on a reading strategy or presents information about World War II or about the author.

More Reading. Students read related books from the text set independently.

The schedule for the last 2 weeks is different. During the third week, students choose a class project (interviewing people who were alive during World War II) and individual projects. They work in teams on activities related to the book and continue to read other books about the war. During the final week, students finish the class interview project and share their completed individual projects.

Units Featuring a Genre

During a genre unit, students learn about a particular genre, such as folktales, science fiction, or biographies. Students read several books illustrating the genre, participate in a variety of activities to deepen their knowledge about the genre's text factors, and sometimes apply what they've learned through a writing project. For example, after reading and comparing Cinderella tales from around the world, third graders often create picture books to retell their favorite version, and seventh graders who are studying the Middle Ages often write stories incorporating details that they've learned about the historical period. During a genre unit on biographies, fifth graders choose a person to research, read a biography, do more research on the Internet, and then write a biography to share what they've learned; or during a genre unit on poetry, students write poems applying the forms of the poetry they've read.

Units Featuring an Author

During an author study, students learn about an author's life and read one or more books he or she has written. Most authors post websites where they share information about

Figure 10–2 ◆ A Lesson Plan for *Number the Stars*

	Monday	Tuesday	Wednesday	Thursday	Friday
Week 1	Build background on World War II The Resistance movement ML: Reading maps of Nazi-occupied Europe Read aloud The Lily Cupboard	Introduce NTS Begin word wall Read Ch. 1 & 2 Grand conversation Reading log Add to word wall Book talk on text set	Read Ch. 3 & 4 Grand conversation Reading log Word wall ML: Connecting with a character Read text set books	Read Ch. 5 Grand conversation Reading log Word wall ML: Visualizing Nazis in apartment (use drama)	Read Ch. 6 & 7 Grand conversation Reading log Word wall ML: Information about the author and why she wrote the book
Week 2	Read Ch. 8 & 9 Grand conversation Reading log Word wall ML: Compare home front and war front Read text set books →	Read Ch. 10 & 11 Grand conversation Reading log Word wall ML: Visualizing the wake (use drama) →	Read Ch. 12 & 13 Grand conversation Reading log Word wall ML: Compare characters – make Venn diagram →	Read Ch. 14 & 15 Grand conversation Reading log Word wall ML: Make word maps of key words →	Finish book Grand conversation Reading log Word wall ML: Theme of book →
Week 3	Plan class interview project Choose individual projects Independent reading/projects →	Activities at Centers: 1. Story map 2. Word sort 3. Plot profile 4. Quilt →	→		→
Week 4	Revise interviews Independent reading/projects →		Edit interviews Share projects →	Make final copies →	Compile interview book →

Author Study
These sixth graders participate in an author study featuring books by Gary Paulsen. They begin by reading *Hatchet*, a coming-of-age story about a boy who survives alone in the wilderness after a plane crash. Then they read other adventure stories by Gary Paulsen, including two sequels to *Hatchet*. For each book, they participate in grand conversations to discuss the book and write in reading logs. Their teacher also taught them about the contemporary realism genre and helped them analyze the author's writing style. During writing workshop, the students write adventure stories using some of Gary Paulsen's techniques.

themselves, their books, and how they write, and each year more authors are writing autobiographies. As students learn about authors, they develop a concept of author; this awareness is important so that students will think of them as real people who eat breakfast, ride bikes, and take out the garbage, just as they do. When students think of authors as real people, they view reading in a more personal way. This awareness also carries over to their writing: Students gain a new perspective as they realize that they, too, can write books. They learn about the writing process that authors use, too.

In first grade, for example, many children read Eric Carle's books and experiment with his illustration techniques, and in the vignette at the beginning of the chapter, Miss Pannicia's students participated in a yearlong author study on Chris Van Allsburg. They read his fantasy picture books, hunted for the picture of the white dog that he includes in every book, and wrote their own fantasy stories based on *The Mysteries of Harris Burdick* (Van Allsburg, 1996). Figure 10–3 presents a list of recommended authors for author studies; the list is divided into primary-, middle-, and upper-grade levels, but many authors are appropriate for students at more than one level. Jerry Spinelli, for instance, writes books that appeal to both middle- and upper-grade students.

Managing Literature Focus Units

Literature focus units are somewhat teacher directed, and teachers play several important roles. They share their love of literature and direct students' attention to comprehension strategies and text factors. They model the strategies that capable readers use and guide students to read more strategically. They also scaffold students, providing

Figure 10–3 ◆ Recommended Authors for Author Studies

Primary Grades	Middle Grades	Upper Grades
Caroline Arnold	Eve Bunting	Avi
Jan Brett	Joanna Cole	Sharon Creech
Ashley Bryan	Gail Gibbons	Christopher Paul Curtis
Eric Carle	Nikki Giovanni	Paul Fleischman
Doreen Cronin	Eric Kimmel	Karen Hesse
Tomie dePaola	Patricia MacLachlan	Lois Lowry
Arthur Dorros	Phyllis Reynolds Naylor	Walter Dean Myers
Lois Ehlert	Patricia Polacco	Linda Sue Park
Denise Fleming	Pam Muñoz Ryan	Gary Paulsen
Kevin Henkes	Jon Scieszka	J. K. Rowling
Steven Kellogg	Jerry Spinelli	Louis Sachar
Patricia McKissack	Janet Stevens	Gary Soto
Rosemary Wells	Chris Van Allsburg	Suzanne Fisher Staples
Mo Willems	Carole Boston Weatherford	Jacqueline Woodson
Audrey Wood	David Wiesner	Laurence Yep

support and guidance so that students can be successful. Through this instruction and support, students learn about reading and literature, and they apply what they've learned as they participate in literature circles and reading workshop, two more student-centered approaches.

ORCHESTRATING LITERATURE CIRCLES

One of the best ways to nurture students' love of reading and ensure that they become lifelong readers is through literature circles—small, student-led book discussion groups that meet regularly in the classroom (Daniels, 2001). Sometimes literature circles are called *book clubs*. The reading materials are quality books of children's literature, including stories, poems, biographies, and other informational books, and what matters most is that students are reading something that interests them and is manageable. Students choose the books to read and form temporary groups. Next, they set a reading and discussion schedule. Then they read independently or with buddies and come together to talk about their reading in discussions that are like **grand conversations**. Sometimes the teacher meets with the group, and at other times, the group meets independently. A literature circle on one book may last from several days to a week or two, depending on the length of the book and the age of the students.

Key Features of Literature Circles

The three key features of literature circles are choice, literature, and response. As teachers organize for literature circles, they make decisions about these features: They structure the program so that students can make choices about what to read, and they develop a plan for response so that students can think deeply about books they're reading and respond to them.

Choice. Students make many choices in literature circles. They choose the books they'll read and the groups in which they participate. They share in setting the schedule for reading and discussing the book, and they choose the roles they assume in the discussions. They also choose how they will share the book with classmates. Teachers structure literature circles so that students have these opportunities, but even more important, they prepare students for making choices by creating a community of learners in their classrooms in which students assume responsibility for their learning and can work collaboratively with classmates.

Literature. The books chosen for literature circles should be interesting to students and at their reading level. The books must seem manageable to the students, especially during their first literature circles. Samway and Whang (1996) recommend choosing shorter books or picture books at first so that students don't become bogged down. It's also important that teachers have read and liked the books because otherwise they won't be able to do convincing **book talks** when they introduce them. In addition, they won't be able to contribute to the book discussions.

Students typically read stories during literature circles, but they can also read informational books or informational books paired with stories (Heller, 2006; Stien & Beed, 2004). Students read informational books related to thematic units or biographies during a genre unit. Second graders often choose books from the Magic Tree House series of easy-to-read chapter books that features pairs of fiction and nonfiction books, including *Hour of the Olympics* (Osborne, 1998) and *Olympics of Ancient Greece* (Osborne & Boyce, 2004), or the popular Magic School Bus picture-book series, including *The Magic School Bus Explores the Senses* (Cole, 1999).

Response. Students meet several times during a literature circle to discuss the book. Through these discussions, students summarize their reading, make connections, learn vocabulary, and explore the author's use of text factors. They learn that comprehension develops in layers. From an initial comprehension gained through reading, students deepen their understanding through the discussions. They learn to return to the text to reread sentences and paragraphs in order to clarify a point or state an opinion. Gilles (1998) examined children's talk during literature circle discussions and identified four types of talk, which are presented in Figure 10–4.

Karen Smith (1998) describes the discussions her students have as "intensive study," often involving several group meetings. At the first session, students share personal responses. They talk about the characters and events of the story, share favorite parts, and ask questions to clarify confusions. At the end of the first session, students and the teacher decide what they want to study at the next session, such as an element of story structure. Students prepare for the second discussion by rereading excerpts from the book related to the chosen focus. Then, during the second session, students talk about how the author used that element of story structure, and they often make charts and diagrams, such as an **open-mind portrait**, to organize their thoughts.

Students need many opportunities to respond to literature before they'll be successful in literature circles. One of the best ways to prepare students is by reading aloud to them and involving them in **grand conversations** (Peterson & Eeds, 2007). Teachers demonstrate ways to respond that are reflective and thoughtful, encourage students to respond to the books, and reinforce students' comments when they share their thoughts and feelings and talk about their use of comprehension strategies as they listened to the teacher reading aloud.

Some teachers have students assume roles and complete assignments in preparation for discussion group meetings (Daniels, 2001). One student is the discussion director, and he or she assumes the leadership role and directs the discussion. This student chooses topics and formulates questions to guide the discussion. Other students prepare by selecting a passage to read aloud, drawing a picture or making a graphic related to the book, or investigating a topic connected to the book. The roles are detailed in Figure 10–5. Although having students assume specific roles may seem artificial, it teaches them about the ways they can respond in literature circles.

Teachers often prepare assignment sheets for each of the roles their students assume during a literature circle and then pass out copies before students begin reading. Students complete one of the assignment sheets before each discussion. Figure 10–6 shows a "word wizard" assignment sheet that an eighth grader completed as he read *Holes* (Sachar, 2003), the story of a boy named Stanley Yelnats who is sent to a hellish

Figure 10–4 ◆ Types of Talk During Literature Circle Discussions

Talk About the Book

Students summarize their reading and talk about the book by applying what they've learned about text factors as they do the following:

- Retell events or big ideas
- Examine the theme or genre
- Explore the organizational elements or patterns the author used
- Find examples of literary devices

Talk About Connections

Students make connections between the book and their own lives, the world, and other literature they've read in these ways:

- Explain connections to their lives
- Compare this book to another book
- Make connections to a film or television show they've viewed

Talk About the Reading Process

Students think metacognitively and reflect on the strategies they used to read the book as they do the following:

- Reflect on how they used strategies
- Explain their reading problems and how they solved them
- Identify sections that they reread and why they reread them
- Talk about their thinking as they were reading
- Identify parts they understood or misunderstood

Talk About Group Process and Social Issues

Students use talk to organize the literature circle and maintain the discussion. They also examine social issues and current events related to the book, such as homelessness and divorce, as they do the following:

- Decide who will be group leader
- Determine the schedule, roles, and responsibilities
- Draw in nonparticipating students
- Bring the conversation back to the topic
- Extend the discussion to social issues and current events

Figure 10–5 ◆ Roles Students Play in Literature Circles	
Role	Responsibilities
Discussion Director	The discussion director guides the group's discussion and keeps the group on task. To get the discussion started or to redirect it, the student may ask: • What did the reading make you think of? • What questions do you have about the reading? • What do you predict will happen next?
Passage Master	The passage master focuses on the literary merits of the book. This student chooses several memorable passages to share with the group and tells why each one wash chosen
Word Wizard	The word wizard is responsible for vocabulary. This student identifies four to six important, unfamiliar words from the reading and looks them up in the dictionary. He or she selects the most appropriate meaning and other interesting information about the word to share with the group.
Connector	The connector makes connections between the book and the students' lives. These connections might include happenings at school or in the community, current events or historical events from around the world, or something from the connector's own life. Or the connector can make comparisons with other books by the same author or on the same topic.
Summarizer	The summarizer prepares a brief summary of the reading to convey the big ideas to share with the group. This student often begins the discussion by reading the summary aloud to the group.
Illustrator	The illustrator draws a picture or diagram related to the reading. The illustration might relate to a character, an exciting event, or a prediction. The student shares the illustration with the group, and the group talks about it before the illustrator explains it.
Investigator	The investigator locates some information about the book, the author, or a related topic to share with the group. This student may search the Internet, check an encyclopedia or library book, or interview a person with special expertise on the topic.

Adapted from Daniels, 2001; Daniels & Bizar, 1998.

correctional camp where he finds a real friend, a treasure, and a new sense of himself. As word wizard, this student chose important words from the story to study. In the first column on the assignment sheet, he wrote the words and the pages on which they were found. Next, he checked the dictionary for each word's meaning, and in the second column listed several meanings when possible and placed checkmarks next to the appropriate meanings for how a word was used in the book. The student also checked the etymology of the word in the dictionary, and in the third column, he listed the language the word came from and when it entered English.

During the discussion about the second section of *Holes*, the word *callused* became important. The "word wizard" explained that *callused* means "toughened" and "hardened," and that in the story, Stanley and the other boys' hands became callused from

Figure 10–6 ◆ An Eighth Grader's Literature Circle Role Sheet

Word Wizard

Name *Ray*   Date *Dec. 7*   Book *Holes*

You are the Word Wizard in this literature circle. Your job is to look for important words in the book and learn about them. Complete this chart before your literature circle meets.

Word and Page Number	Meanings	Etymology
callused p. 80 "his callused hands"	✓ to toughen ✓ to make hard ? unsympathetic	Latin 1565
penetrating p. 82 "a penetrating stare"	? to enter ✓ sharp or piercing	Latin 1520
condemned p. 88 "a condemned man"	✓ found guilty	Latin 1300
writhed p. 91 "his body writhed with pain"	✓ to twist the body in pain	English 900

digging holes. He continued to say that the third meaning, "unsympathetic," didn't make sense. This comment provided an opportunity for the teacher to explain how *callused* could mean "unsympathetic," and students decided to make a chart to categorize characters in the story who had callused hands and those who were unsympathetic. The group concluded that the boys with callused hands were sympathetic to each other, but the adults at the correctional camp who didn't have callused hands were often unsympathetic and had callused hearts. Talking about the meaning of a single word—*callused*—led to a new and different way of looking at the characters in the story.

Literature circles are an effective instructional approach because of the three key features—choice, literature, and response. As students read and discuss books with classmates, they often become more engaged and motivated than in more teacher-directed approaches. The feature on page 341 presents an overview of literature circles.

Implementing Literature Circles

Teachers organize literature circles using a six-step series of activities.

Step 1: Select Books. Teachers prepare text sets with five to seven related titles and collect six or seven copies of each book. They give a brief **book talk** to introduce the books, and then students sign up for the one they want to read. Students need time to preview the books, and then they decide what to read after considering the topic and the difficulty level. Once in a while, students don't get to read their first choice, but they can always read it another time, perhaps during another literature circle or during reading workshop.

Step 2: Form Literature Circles. Students get together to read each book; usually no more than six students participate in a group. They begin by setting a schedule for reading and discussing the book within the time limits set by the teacher. Students also choose discussion roles so that they can prepare for the discussion after reading.

Step 3: Read the Book. Students read all or part of the book independently or with a partner, depending on the book's difficulty level. Afterward, students prepare for the discussion by doing the assignment for the role they assumed.

Step 4: Participate in a Discussion. Students meet to talk about the book; these **grand conversations** usually last about 30 minutes. The discussion director or another student who has been chosen as the leader begins the discussion, and then classmates continue as in any other grand conversation. They take turns sharing their responses according to the roles they assumed. The talk is meaningful because students talk about what interests them in the book.

Step 5: Teach Minilessons. Teachers teach **minilessons** before or after group meetings on a variety of topics, including asking insightful questions, completing role sheets, using comprehension strategies, and examining text factors (Daniels & Steineke, 2004). Teachers address the procedures that students use in small-group discussions as well as literary concepts and strategies and skills.

Step 6: Share With the Class. Students in each literature circle share the book they've read with their classmates through a **book talk** or another presentation.

OVERVIEW OF THE INSTRUCTIONAL APPROACH

Literature Circles

TOPIC	DESCRIPTION
Purpose	To provide students with opportunities for authentic reading and literary analysis.
Components	Students form literature circles to read and discuss books that they choose themselves. They often assume roles for the book discussion.
Theory Base	Literature circles reflect sociolinguistic, transactive, and critical literacy theories because students work in small, supportive groups to read and discuss books, and the books they read often involve cultural and social issues that require students to think critically.
Applications	Teachers often use literature circles in conjunction with a basal reading program or with literature focus units so students have opportunities to do independent reading and literary analysis.
Strengths	• Books are available at a variety of reading levels. • Students are more strongly motivated because they choose the books they read. • Students have opportunities to work with their classmates. • Students participate in authentic literacy experiences. • Students learn how to respond to literature. • Teachers may participate in discussions to help students clarify misunderstandings and think more critically about the book.
Limitations	• Teachers often feel a loss of control because students are reading different books. • Students must learn to be task oriented and to use time wisely to be successful. • Sometimes students choose books that are too difficult or too easy for them.

As students participate in literature circles, they're involved in activities representing all five stages of the reading process:

Prereading. Teachers give book talks, and then students choose books to read, form groups, and get ready to read by making schedules and choosing roles.

Reading. Students read the book independently or with a partner, and prepare for the group meeting.

Responding. Students talk about the book and take responsibility to come to the discussion prepared to participate actively.

Exploring. Teachers teach minilessons to rehearse literature circle procedures, learn comprehension strategies, and examine text factors.

Applying. Students give brief presentations to the class about the books they've read.

As students make choices and move through the reading process, they assume increasingly more responsibility for their own learning.

Using Literature Circles With Young Children

First and second graders can meet in small groups to read and discuss books, just as older, more experienced readers do (Frank, Dixon, & Brandts, 2001; Marriott, 2002; Martinez-Roldan & Lopez-Robertson, 1999/2000). These young children choose books at their reading levels, listen to the teacher read a book aloud, or participate in a shared reading activity. Children probably benefit from listening to a book read aloud two times or reading it several times before participating in the discussion. In preparation for the literature circle, children often draw and write reading log entries to share with the group. Or, they can write a letter to their group telling about the book. The literature circle often begins with one child sharing a reading log entry or letter with the small group.

Children meet with the teacher to talk about a book. The teacher guides the discussion at first and models how to share ideas and to participate in a discussion. The talk is meaningful because children share what interests them in the book, make text-to-self, text-to-world, and text-to-text connections, point out illustrations and other book features, ask questions, and discuss themes. Young children don't usually assume roles as older students do, but teachers often notice a few of the first and second graders beginning to take on leadership roles. During a literature circle, the other children in the classroom are usually reading books or writing in reading logs in preparation for their upcoming literature circle meeting with the teacher.

Managing Literature Circles

When teachers introduce literature circles, they teach students how to participate in small-group discussions and respond to literature. At first, many teachers participate in discussions, but they quickly step back as students become comfortable with the procedures and get engaged in the discussions.

Unfortunately, groups don't always work well. Sometimes conversations get off track because of disruptive behavior, or students monopolize the discussion, hurl insults at classmates, or exclude certain students. Clarke and Holwadel (2007) describe an inner-city sixth-grade classroom where literature circles deteriorated because of race, gender, and class tensions. They identified students' negative feelings toward classmates and their limited conversational skills as two problems they could address, and they improved the quality of literature circles in this classroom through these activities:

◆ **Minilessons.** The teachers taught minilessons to develop more-positive relationships among group members and build more-effective discussion skills, including learning how to listen to each other and take turns when talking (Daniels & Steineke, 2004).

◆ **Videotapes.** The teachers videotaped students participating in a literature circle and viewed it with group members to make them more aware of how their behavior affected their discussions. They talked about how the discussions went, identified problems, and brainstormed ways to solve them.

◆ **Books.** The teachers reconsidered the books they'd chosen and looked for books that might relate better to students' lives and inspire more-powerful discussions. These books were especially effective in this classroom: *Sang Spell* (Naylor, 1998), *Hush* (Woodson, 2002), *Slave Dancer* (Fox, 2001), and *Stargirl* (Spinelli, 2004).

◆ **Coaching.** The teachers became coaches to guide students in becoming more-effective participants. They modeled positive group behavior and appropriate discussion skills and demonstrated how to use their responses to deepen their understanding of a book. At times, they assumed the teacher role to ensure that everyone participated and to keep the discussion on track.

Even though some problems persisted, Clarke and Holwadel improved the quality of their students' literature circles. The classroom environment became more respectful, and students' improved conversation skills transferred to other discussions. And, once students became more successful, their interest in reading increased, too.

IMPLEMENTING READING AND WRITING WORKSHOP

Students are involved in authentic reading and writing projects during reading and writing workshop. This approach involves three key characteristics: time, choice, and response. First, students have large chunks of time and the opportunity to read and write. Instead of being add-ons for after students finish assignments, reading and writing become the core of the literacy curriculum.

Second, students assume ownership of their learning through self-selection of books they read and their topics for writing. Instead of reading books that the teacher has selected or reading the same book together as a group or class, students choose the books they want to read, books that are suitable to their interests and reading levels. Usually students choose whatever book they want to read—a story, a collection of poems, or an informational book—but sometimes teachers set parameters. For example, during a genre unit on science fiction, teachers ask students to select a science fiction story to read. During writing workshop, students plan their writing projects: They choose topics related to hobbies, content-area units, and other interests, and they also select the format for their writing. Often they choose to publish their writing as books.

The third characteristic is response. Students respond to books they're reading in reading logs that they share during conferences with the teacher. They also do book talks to share books they've finished reading with classmates. Similarly, in writing workshop, students share with classmates rough drafts of books and other compositions they're writing, and they share their completed and published compositions with genuine audiences.

Reading workshop and writing workshop are different types of workshops. Reading workshop fosters real reading of self-selected books. Students read hundreds of books during reading workshop. At the first-grade level, students might read or reread three or four books each day, totaling close to a thousand books during the school year, and older students read fewer, longer books. Even so, upper-grade teachers report that their students read between 25 and 100 books during the school year.

Similarly, writing workshop fosters real writing (and the use of the writing process) for genuine purposes and for authentic audiences. Each student writes and publishes as many as 50 to 100 short books in the primary grades and 20 to 25 longer books in the middle and upper grades. As they write, students come to see themselves as authors and become interested in learning about the authors of the books they read.

Teachers often use both workshops, or if their schedule doesn't allow, they may alternate the two. Schedules for reading and writing workshop at the first-, third-, sixth-, and eighth-grade levels are presented in Figure 10–7. Kindergarten teachers can implement reading and writing workshop in their classrooms, too (Cunningham & Shagoury, 2005); even though they do more of the reading and writing themselves, teachers involve 5-year-olds in authentic literacy experiences and teach them about comprehension strategies and text factors.

Reading and writing workshop can be used as the primary instructional approach in a classroom, or it can be used along with other instructional approaches to provide authentic opportunities for students to read and write. This approach is student centered because students make many choices and work independently as they read and write. Providing authentic activities and independent work opportunities reflects the constructivist theory, which emphasizes that learners create their own knowledge through exploration and experimentation.

Reading Workshop

Nancie Atwell introduced reading workshop in 1987 as an alternative to traditional reading instruction. In reading workshop, students read books that they choose themselves and respond to books through writing in **reading logs** and conferencing with teachers and classmates (Atwell, 1998). This approach represented a change in what teachers believe about how children learn and how literature should be used in the classroom. Whereas traditional reading programs emphasized dependence on a teacher's guide to determine how and when particular strategies and skills should be taught, reading workshop is an individualized reading program. Atwell developed reading workshop with her middle school students, but it's been adapted and used successfully at every grade level, first through eighth. There are several versions of reading workshop, but they usually contain five components: reading, responding, sharing, teaching minilessons, and reading aloud to students.

Reading. Students spend 30 to 60 minutes independently reading books. Students choose the books they read, often using recommendations from classmates. They also choose books on favorite topics—horses, science fiction, and dinosaurs, for example— or written by favorite authors, such as Audrey Wood, Chris Van Allsburg, and Louis Sachar. It's crucial that students be able to read the books they choose. Ohlhausen and Jepsen (1992) developed a strategy for choosing books called the *Goldilocks Strategy*. These teachers created three categories of books—"Too Easy" books, "Too Hard"

Figure 10–7 ◆ Schedules for Reading and Writing Workshop

First Grade

9:00–9:10	The teacher rereads several familiar big books. Then the teacher introduces a new big book and reads it aloud.
9:10–9:30	Children read matching small books independently and reread other familiar books.
9:30–9:40	Children choose one of the books they've read or reread during independent reading to draw and write a quickwrite.
9:40–9:50	Children share the favorite book and quickwrite.
9:50–10:05	The teacher teaches a reading/writing minilesson.
10:05–10:30	Children write independently on self-selected topics and conference with the teacher.
10:30–10:40	Children share their published books with classmates.
10:40–10:45	The class uses choral reading to enjoy poems and charts hanging in the classroom.

Third Grade

10:30–11:00	Students read self-selected books and respond to them in reading logs.
11:00–11:15	Students share with classmates books they have finished reading and do informal book talks about them. Students often pass the "good" books to classmates who want to read them next.
11:15–11:30	The teacher teaches a reading/writing minilesson.
11:30–11:55	The teacher reads aloud and afterward, students participate in a grand conversation. —Continued after lunch—
12:45–1:15	Students write books independently.
1:15–1:30	Students share their published books with classmates.

Sixth Grade

8:20–8:45	The teacher reads aloud a chapter book, and students talk about it in a grand conversation.
8:45–9:30	Students write independently and conference with the teacher.
9:30–9:40	The teacher teaches a reading/writing minilesson.
9:40–10:25	Students read self-selected books independently.
10:25–10:40	Students share published writings and give book talks about books they've read.

Eighth Grade

During alternating months, students participate in reading or writing workshop.

1:00–1:45	Students read or write independently.
1:45–2:05	The teacher presents a minilesson on a reading or writing procedure, concept, strategy, or skill.
2:05–2:15	Students share the books they've read or compositions they've published.

books, and "Just Right" books—using "The Three Bears" folktale as their model. The books in the "Too Easy" category were those students had read before or could read fluently; "Too Hard" books were unfamiliar and confusing; and books in the "Just Right" category were interesting, with just a few unfamiliar words. The books in each category vary according to the student's reading level. This approach works at any grade level. Figure 10–8 presents a chart about choosing books using the Goldilocks Strategy.

Classroom libraries need to contain literally hundreds of books, including books written at a range of reading levels, so that every student can find books to read. Primary teachers often worry about finding books that their students can handle independently. Predictable books, leveled books, easy-to-read books, and books that have been read aloud several times are often the most accessible for young children. Teachers need to introduce students—especially reluctant readers—to the books in the classroom library so that they can more effectively choose books to read. The best way to preview books is using a very brief book talk to interest students in the book. Teachers tell a little about the book, show the cover, and perhaps read the first paragraph or two.

Teachers often read their own books or a book of children's literature during reading workshop; through their example, they model the importance of reading. Teachers also conference with students about the books they're reading while the rest of the class reads. As they conference, they talk briefly and quietly with students about their reading. Students may also read aloud favorite quotes or an interesting passage to the teacher.

Responding. Students usually keep reading logs in which they write their initial responses to the books they're reading. Sometimes students dialogue with the teacher about the book they're reading; a journal allows for ongoing written conversation

Figure 10–8　◆　The Goldilocks Strategy

How to Choose the Best Books for YOU

"Too Easy" Books
1. The book is short.
2. The print is big.
3. You have read the book before.
4. You know all the words in the book.
5. The book has a lot of pictures.
6. You are an expert on this topic.

"Just Right" Books
1. The book looks interesting.
2. You can decode most of the words.
3. Mrs. Reeves has read this book aloud to you.
4. You have read other books by this author.
5. There's someone to give you help if you need it.
6. You know something about this topic.

"Too Hard" Books
1. The book is long.
2. The print is small.
3. There aren't many pictures in the book.
4. There are a lot of words that you can't decode.
5. There's no one to help you read this book.
6. You don't know much about this topic.

Figure 10–9 ◆ Response Patterns

Category	Pattern	Description
Immersion Responses	Understanding	Students write about their understanding of characters and plot. Their responses include personal interpretation as well as summarizing.
	Character Introspection	Students share their insights into the feelings and motives of a character. They often begin their comments with "I think . . ."
	Predicting	Students speculate about what will happen later in the story and confirm predictions they made previously.
	Questioning	Students ask "I wonder why" questions and write about confusions.
Involvement Responses	Character Identification	Students show personal identification with a character, sometimes writing "If I were ____, I would. . ." They express empathy, share related experiences from their own lives, and sometimes give advice to the character.
	Character Assessment	Students judge a character's actions and often use evaluative terms, such as *nice* or *dumb*.
	Story Involvement	Students reveal their involvement as they express satisfaction with how the story's developing. They may comment on their desire to continue reading or use terms such as *disgusting, weird,* or *awesome* to react to sensory aspects of the story.
Literary Connections	Connections	Students make text-to-self, text-to-world, text-to-text, and text-to-media (TV shows and movies) connections.
	Literary Evaluation	Students evaluate part or all of the book. They may offer "I liked/I didn't like" opinions and praise or condemn an author's style.

Adapted from Hancock, 2007.

between the teacher and individual students (Atwell, 1998). Responses often demonstrate students' reading strategies and offer insights into their thinking about literature. Seeing how students think about their reading helps teachers guide their learning.

Teachers play an important role in helping students expand and enrich their responses to literature. They collect students' reading logs periodically to monitor their responses. They write back and forth with students, with the idea that students write more if the teacher responds. However, because responding to students' journals is very time-consuming, teachers should keep their responses brief and not respond to every entry.

Hancock (2007) identified three types of response as students write about stories they're reading: immersion responses, involvement responses, and literary evaluation. The categories and the various patterns that exemplify each one are summarized in Figure 10–9. In most reading log entries, students write responses that address several patterns as they reflect on the story and explore their understanding.

In the first category, immersion responses, students indicate whether the book is making sense to them. They make inferences about characters, offer predictions, ask questions, or discuss confusions. Here are some responses excerpted from sixth graders' reading logs about *Bunnicula: A Rabbit-Tale of Mystery* (Howe & Howe, 2006):

 I think the Monroes will find out what Chester and Harold are doing.

Can a bunny be a vampire? I don't think so. A bunny couldn't suck the blood out of a vegetable. They don't even have blood.

I guess Bunnicula really is a vampire.

I was right! I knew Harold and Chester would try to take care of Bunnicula. What I didn't know was that the Monroes would come home early.

I wonder why the vegetables are turning white. I know it's not Bunnicula but I don't know why.

In the second category, involvement responses, students show that they are personally involved with a character, often giving advice or judging a character's actions. They reveal their own involvement in the story as they express satisfaction with how the story is developing. Here are some examples:

I know how Chester and Harold feel. It's like when I got a new baby sister and everyone paid attention to her. I got ignored a lot.

If I were Bunnicula, I'd run away. He's just not safe in that house!

Gross!!! The vegetables are all white and there are two little fang holes in each one.

I just can't stop reading. This book is so cool. And it's funny, too.

In the third category, literary connections, students make connections and evaluate the book. They offer opinions, sometimes saying "I liked . . ." or "I didn't like . . ." and compare the book to others they've read. Here are some examples:

My dog is a lot like Harold. He gets on my bed with me and he loves snacks, but you should never feed a dog chocolate.

This is a great book! I know stuff like this couldn't happen but it would be awesome if it could. It's just fantasy but it's like I believe it.

This book is like <u>Charlotte's Web</u> because the animals can talk and have a whole life that the people in the story don't know about. But the books are different because <u>Bunnicula</u> is much funner than <u>Charlotte's Web</u>. It made me laugh and <u>Charlotte's Web</u> made me cry.

When students use only a few types of responses, teachers can teach **minilessons** to model the types of responses that students aren't using and ask questions to prompt students to think in new ways about the story they're reading.

Some students write minimal responses in journals. It's important that students choose books to read that they find personally interesting and that they feel free to share their thoughts, feelings, and questions with a trusted audience—usually the teacher. Sometimes writing entries on a computer and using e-mail to share them with students in another class or with other interested readers increase students' interest in writing more-elaborated responses.

During reading and responding, there's little or no talking because students are engrossed in reading and writing independently. Rarely do students interrupt classmates, go to the rest room, or get drinks of water, except in case of emergency, nor do they use reading workshop time to do homework or other schoolwork.

Sharing. For the last 15 minutes of reading workshop, the class gathers together to discuss books they've finished reading. Students talk about a book and why they liked it. Sometimes they read a brief excerpt aloud or formally pass the book to a classmate who wants to read it. Sharing is important because it helps students become a community to value and celebrate each other's accomplishments.

Minilessons. The teacher also spends 5 to 15 minutes teaching **minilessons** on reading workshop procedures, comprehension strategies, and text factors. Sometimes minilessons are taught to the whole class, and at other times, they're taught to small groups. At the beginning of the school year, teachers teach minilessons to the whole class on choosing books to read and other reading workshop procedures; later in the year, they teach minilessons on drawing inferences and other comprehension strategies and text factors. Teachers teach minilessons on particular authors when they introduce their books to the whole class and on literary genres when they set out collections of books representing a genre in the classroom library.

Reading Aloud to Students. Teachers use the **interactive read-aloud** procedure to read picture books and chapter books to the class as part of reading workshop. They choose high-quality literature that students might not be able to read themselves, award-winning books that they believe every student should be exposed to, or books that relate to a thematic unit. After reading, students talk about the book and share the reading experience. This activity is important because students listen to a book read aloud and respond to it together as a community of learners, not as individuals.

Even though reading workshop is different from other instructional approaches, students work through the same five stages of the reading process:

Prereading. Students choose books at their reading level to read and activate background knowledge as they look at the cover and think about the title.

Reading. Students read the books they've selected independently, at their own pace.

Responding. Students talk about the books they're reading when they conference with the teacher, and they often write responses in **reading logs**.

Exploring. Teachers teach students about text factors, authors, and comprehension strategies through **minilessons**.

Applying. Students often give **book talks** to their classmates about the books they've finished reading.

Is Sustained Silent Reading the Same as Reading Workshop? Sustained Silent Reading (SSR) is an independent reading time set aside during the school day for students in one class or the entire school to silently read self-selected books. It's used to increase the amount of reading students do and to encourage students to develop the habit of daily reading (Pilgreen, 2000). Reading workshop and SSR are similar. The goal of both programs is to provide opportunities for students to read self-selected books independently. Both programs work best in classrooms that are communities of learners. It seems obvious that students need to feel relaxed and comfortable in order to read for pleasure, and a community of learners is a place where students do feel comfortable because they are respected and valued by classmates and the teacher.

There are important differences, however. Reading workshop has five components—reading, responding, sharing, teaching minilessons, and reading aloud to students—whereas SSR has only one—reading. Reading workshop is recognized as an instructional approach because it includes both independent reading and instruction through minilessons. In contrast, SSR is a supplemental program without an instructional component.

Writing Workshop

Writing workshop is the best way to implement the writing process (Atwell, 1998; Fletcher & Portalupi, 2001). Students write on topics that they choose themselves and assume ownership of their writing and learning. At the same time, the teacher's role changes from being a provider of knowledge to serving as a facilitator and guide. The classroom becomes a community of writers who write and share their writing. There's a spirit of pride and acceptance in the classroom.

Students have writing folders in which they keep all papers related to the writing project they're working on. They also keep writing notebooks in which they jot down images, impressions, dialogue, and experiences that they can build upon for writing

Literacy Portraits: VIEWING GUIDE

The second graders in Ms. Janusz's classroom participate in writing workshop every morning. They use
the writing process as they craft stories, poems, and
informational books, usually on topics they've chosen
themselves. Visit the Literacy Profiles section of the
MyEducationLab website (www.myeducationlab.com),
and click on Rakie's March button to watch her participate in writing workshop. Recently, Ms. Janusz
taught a minilesson about how to write about a
memory, and now Rakie's writing about a memory—
a trip she took to Africa with her mom and sister. As
you view the clip, try to identify some of the writing
workshop activities that are described in this chapter.
Since it's not possible to see every activity in one
video clip, think about what might be going on during the other activities. Also, watch the video clip
again to identify the stages of the writing process
that Rakie's using.

myeducationlab

projects (Calkins, 1994). Students have access to different kinds of paper, some lined and some unlined, as well as writing instruments, including pencils and red and blue pens. They also have access to the classroom library because many times, students' writing grows out of books they've read. They may write a sequel to a book or retell a story from a different viewpoint. Primary-grade students often use patterns from books they've read to structure books they're writing.

As they write, students sit at desks or tables arranged in small groups. The teacher circulates around the classroom, conferencing briefly with students, and the classroom atmosphere is free enough that students converse quietly with classmates and move around to assist each other or share ideas. There's space for students to meet for writing groups, and often a sign-up sheet for writing groups is posted in the classroom. A table is available for the teacher to meet with individual students or small groups for conferences, writing groups, proofreading, and minilessons.

Writing workshop is a 60- to 90-minute period scheduled each day. During this time, students are involved in three components: writing, sharing, and minilessons. Sometimes a fourth activity, reading aloud to students, is added when it's not used in conjunction with reading workshop. The feature on page 351 presents an overview of the workshop approach.

Writing. Students spend 30 to 45 minutes or longer working independently on writing projects. Just as students in reading workshop choose books and read at their own pace, in writing workshop, they work at their own pace on writing projects they've chosen themselves. Most students move at their own pace through all five stages of the writing process, but young children often use an abbreviated process consisting of prewriting, drafting, and publishing.

Teachers conference with students as they write. Many teachers prefer moving around the classroom to meet with students rather than having students come to a table to meet with them: Too often, a line forms as students wait, and they lose precious writing time. Some teachers move around the classroom in a regular pattern, meeting with one fifth of the students each day. In this way, they are sure to conference with everyone during the week.

Other teachers spend the first 15 to 20 minutes of writing workshop stopping briefly to check on 10 or more students each day. Many use a zigzag pattern to get to all parts of the classroom each day. These teachers often kneel down beside each student, sit on the edge of the student's seat, or carry their own stool around to each student's desk. During the 1- or 2-minute conferences, teachers ask students what they're writing, listen to them read a paragraph or two, and then ask what they plan to do next. Then these teachers use the remaining time during writing workshop to conference more formally with students who are revising and editing their compositions. They identify strengths in students' writing, ask questions, and discover possibilities during revising conferences. Some teachers like to read the pieces themselves, and others like to listen to students read their papers aloud. As they interact with students, teachers model the kinds of responses that students are learning to give to each other.

As students meet to share their writing during revising and editing, they continue to develop as a community of writers. They share their rough drafts in **writing groups** composed of four or five students. Sometimes teachers join in, but students normally run the groups themselves. They take turns reading their rough drafts to each other

OVERVIEW OF THE INSTRUCTIONAL APPROACH

Reading and Writing Workshop

TOPIC	DESCRIPTION
Purpose	To provide students with opportunities for authentic reading and writing activities.
Components	Reading workshop involves reading, responding, sharing, teaching minilessons, and reading aloud to students. Writing workshop consists of writing, sharing, and teaching minilessons.
Theory Base	The workshop approach reflects sociolinguistic and cognitive/information processing theories because students participate in authentic activities that encourage them to become lifelong readers and writers.
Applications	Teachers often use reading workshop in conjunction with a basal reading program or with literature focus units so students have opportunities to do independent reading. They often add writing workshop to any of the other instructional approaches so students have more sustained opportunities to use the writing process to develop and refine compositions.
Strengths	• Students read books that are appropriate for their reading levels. • Students are more motivated because they choose the books to read that interest them. • Students work through the stages of the writing process. • Activities are student directed, and students work at their own pace. • Teachers have opportunities to work individually with students during conferences.
Limitations	• Teachers often feel a loss of control because students are reading different books and working at different stages of the writing process. • Teachers have responsibility to teach minilessons on strategies and skills, in both whole-class groups and small groups. • Students must learn to be task oriented and to use time wisely to be successful.

and listen as their classmates offer compliments and suggestions for revision. Students also participate in revising and editing centers that are set up in the classroom. They know how to work at each center and the importance of working with classmates to make their writing better.

After proofreading their drafts with a classmate and then meeting with the teacher for final editing, students make the final copy of their writings. They often want to print out their writing on the computer so that it looks professional. Many times, students compile their final copies to make books, but sometimes they attach their writing to artwork, make posters, write letters that will be mailed, or perform scripts as skits or puppet shows. Not every piece is necessarily published; sometimes students decide not to continue with a piece of writing, and they file that piece in their writing folders and start something new.

Sharing. For the last 10 to 15 minutes of writing workshop, the class gathers together to share their new publications. Younger students often sit in a circle or gather together on a rug for sharing time. If an author's chair is available, each student sits in the special chair to read his or her composition aloud. After each sharing, classmates clap and offer compliments. They may also make other comments and suggestions, but the focus is on celebrating completed writing projects, not on revising the composition to make it better.

Minilessons. During this 5- to 30-minute period, teachers provide minilessons on writing workshop procedures, qualities of good writing, and writing strategies and skills, such as organizing ideas, proofreading, and using quotation marks to mark dialogue (Fletcher & Portalupi, 2007). In the middle and upper grades, teachers often display an anonymous piece of writing (perhaps from a student in another class or from a previous year). Students read the writing, and the teacher uses it to teach the lesson, which may focus on giving suggestions for revision, combining sentences, proofreading, or writing a stronger lead sentence. Teachers also select excerpts from books students are reading for minilessons to show how published authors use writing skills and strategies.

Writing workshop is the best way for students to apply the writing process: Teachers teach students how to complete the activities during each stage of the writing process, and then students practice what they have learned during writing workshop. Students move through the five stages of the writing process as they plan, draft, revise, edit, and, finally, publish their writing:

Prewriting. Students choose topics and set their own purposes for writing. Then they gather and organize ideas, often drawing pictures, making graphic organizers, or talking out their ideas with classmates.

Drafting. Students work independently to write their rough drafts.

Revising. Students participate in writing groups to share their rough drafts and get feedback to help them revise their writing.

Editing. Students work with classmates to proofread and correct mechanical errors in their writing, and they also meet with the teacher for a final editing.

Publishing. Students prepare a final "published" copy of their writing, and sit in the author's chair to read it to classmates.

As students participate in writing workshop, they gain valuable experience using the writing process.

Managing a Workshop Classroom

It takes time to establish a workshop approach because students need to develop new ways of working and learning, and they have to form a community of readers and writers in the classroom (Gillet & Beverly, 2001). For reading workshop, students need to know how to select books and other reading workshop procedures. For writing workshop, students need to know how to use the writing process to develop and refine a piece of writing, how to make books for their compositions, and other writing workshop procedures. Sometimes students complain that they don't know what to write about, but in time, they learn how to brainstorm possible topics and to keep a list of topics in their author's notebooks.

Teachers establish the workshop environment in their classroom, beginning on the first day of the school year. They provide time for students to read and write and teach them how to respond to books and to their classmates' writing. Through their interactions with students, the respect they show to students, and the way they model reading and writing, teachers establish the classroom as a community of learners.

Teachers develop a schedule for reading and writing workshop with time allocated for each component, as was shown in Figure 10–7. In their schedules, teachers allot as much time as possible for students to read and write. After developing the schedule, teachers post it in the classroom and talk with students about the activities and their expectations. Teachers teach the workshop procedures and continue to model them until students become comfortable with the routines. As students gain experience with the workshop approach, their enthusiasm grows and the workshop approach is successful.

Many teachers use a classroom chart, which Nancie Atwell (1998) calls "status of the class," to monitor students' work. At the beginning of reading workshop, students (or the teacher) record what book they are reading or if they're writing in a reading log, waiting to conference with the teacher, or browsing in the classroom library.

For writing workshop, students identify the stage of the writing process they're involved in. A sample writing workshop chart is shown in the Assessment Tools feature below. Teachers can also use the chart to award weekly "effort" grades, to have students indicate their need to conference with the teacher, or to have students announce that they are ready to share the book they've read or publish their writing. Teachers can review students' progress and note which students they need to meet with. When students fill in the chart themselves, they develop responsibility and a stronger desire to accomplish tasks they set for themselves.

Teachers take time during reading and writing workshop to observe students as they work together in small groups. Researchers who have observed in reading and writing workshop classrooms report that some students, even as young as first graders, are excluded from group activities because of gender, ethnicity, or socioeconomic status (Henkin, 1995); the socialization patterns in classrooms seem to reflect society's. Henkin recommends that teachers be alert to the possibility that boys might share books only with other boys or that some students won't find anyone willing to be their editing partner. If teachers see instances of discrimination, they should confront the situation directly and work to foster a classroom environment where students treat each other equitably.

Many teachers fear that when they implement the workshop approach in their classrooms, students' scores on standardized achievement tests will decline, even though teachers have reported either an increase in test scores or no change at all. Swift (1993) reported the results of a yearlong study comparing two groups of her students; one group read basal reader selections, and the other participated in reading workshop. The reading workshop group showed significantly greater improvement, and Swift also reported that students participating in reading workshop showed more-positive attitudes toward reading.

Assessment Tools

"Status of the Class" Chart

Names	Dates							
	3/15	3/16	3/17	3/18	3/19	3/22	3/23	3/24
Antonio	4	5	5	5	5	1	1	1 2
Bella	2	2	2 3	2	2	4	5	5
Charles	3	3 1	1	2	2 3	4	5	5
Dina	4 5	5	5	1	1	1	1	2 3
Dustin	3	3	4	4	4	5	5 1	1
Eddie	2 3	2	2 4	5	5	1	1 2	2 3
Elizabeth	2	3	3	4	4	4 5	5	1 2
Elsa	1 2	3 4	4 5	5	5	1	2	2

Code:
1 = Prewriting   2 = Drafting   3 = Revising   4 = Editing   5 = Publishing

Chapter 10 Review

How Effective Teachers Organize for Instruction

► Teachers use a combination of instructional approaches to provide effective literacy instruction because they understand that no one approach is a complete program.

► Teachers recognize that basal reading programs have strong skill components.

► Teachers present literature focus units to teach students about award-winning books.

► Teachers incorporate choice, literature, and response into literature circles.

► Teachers provide opportunities for students to read self-selected books during reading workshop and write on self-selected topics during writing workshop.

PEARSON
myeducationlab
Where the Classroom Comes to Life

Go to MyEducationLab at www.myeducationlab.com to deepen your understanding of the concepts presented in this chapter:

► Analyze how Ms. Janusz organizes writing workshop by viewing video segments in the Literacy Portraits.
► Check your understanding of chapter concepts with the multiple-choice and essay quizzes in the Study Plan.
► Apply some of the main ideas discussed in the chapter in the Activities and Applications section of the website.
► Practice what you've learned in this chapter in Building Teaching Skills and Dispositions before applying the ideas in your own classroom.

PROFESSIONAL REFERENCES

Atwell, N. (1998). *In the middle: New understandings about reading and writing with adolescents* (2nd ed.). Upper Montclair, NJ: Boynton/Cook.

Calkins, L. M. (1994). *Teaching writing* (rev. ed.). Portsmouth, NH: Heinemann.

Chall, J. S., Jacobs, V. A., & Baldwin, L. E. (1991). *The reading crisis: Why poor children fall behind.* Cambridge, MA: Harvard University Press.

Clarke, L. W., & Holwadel, J. (2007). "Help! What is wrong with these literature circles and how can we fix them?" *The Reading Teacher, 61,* 20–29.

Cunningham, A., & Shagoury, R. (2005). *Starting with comprehension: Reading strategies for the youngest learners.* Portland, ME: Stenhouse.

Daniels, H. (2001). *Literature circles: Voice and choice in book clubs and reading groups.* York, ME: Stenhouse.

Daniels, H., & Bizar, M. (1998). *Methods that matter: Six structures for best practice classrooms.* York, ME: Stenhouse.

Daniels, H., & Steineke, N. (2004). *Mini-lessons for literature circles.* Portsmouth, NH: Heinemann.

Fletcher, R., & Portalupi, J. (2001). *Writing workshop: The essential guide.* Portsmouth, NH: Heinemann.

Fletcher, R., & Portalupi, J. (2007). *Craft lessons: Teaching writing K–8* (2nd ed.). York, ME: Stenhouse.

Frank, C. R., Dixon, C. N., & Brandts, L. R. (2001). Bears, trolls, and pagemasters: Learning about learners in book clubs. *The Reading Teacher, 54,* 448–462.

Gilles, C. (1998). Collaborative literacy strategies: "We don't need a circle to have a group." In K. G. Short & K. M. Pierce (Eds.), *Talking about books: Literature discussion groups in K–8 classrooms* (pp. 55–68). Portsmouth, NH: Heinemann.

Gillet, J. W., & Beverly, L. (2001). *Directing the writing workshop: An elementary teacher's handbook.* New York: Guilford Press.

Hancock, M. R. (2007). *Language arts: Extending the possibilities.* Upper Saddle River, NJ: Merrill/Prentice Hall.

Heller, M. F. (2006). Telling stories and talking facts: First graders' engagement in a nonfiction book club. *The Reading Teacher, 60,* 358–369.

Henkin, R. (1995). Insiders and outsiders in first-grade writing workshops: Gender and equity issues. *Language Arts, 72,* 429–434.

Marriott, D. (2002). *Comprehension right from the start: How to organize and manage book clubs for young readers.* Portsmouth, NH: Heinemann.

Martinez-Roldan, C. M., & Lopez-Robertson, J. M. (1999/2000). Initiating literature circles in a first grade bilingual classroom. *The Reading Teacher, 53,* 270–281.

Ohlhausen, M. M., & Jepsen, M. (1992). Lessons from Goldilocks: "Somebody's been choosing my books but I can make my own choices now!" *The New Advocate, 5,* 31–46.

Peterson, R., & Eeds, M. (2007). *Grand conversations: Literature groups in action.* New York: Scholastic.

Pilgreen, J. L. (2000). *The SSR handbook: How to organize and manage a sustained silent reading program.* Portsmouth, NH: Boynton/Cook/Heinemann.

Samway, K. D., & Whang, G. (1996). *Literature study circles in a multicultural classroom.* York, ME: Stenhouse.

Smith, K. (1998). Entertaining a text: A reciprocal process. In K. G. Short & K. M. Pierce (Eds.), *Talking about books: Literature discussion groups in K–8 classrooms* (pp. 17–31). Portsmouth, NH: Heinemann.

Stien, D., & Beed, P. L. (2004). Bridging the gap between fiction and nonfiction in the literature circle setting. *The Reading Teacher, 57,* 510–518.

Swift, K. (1993). Try reading workshop in your classroom. *The Reading Teacher, 46,* 366–371.

Walsh, K. (2003, Spring). Basal readers: The lost opportunity to build the knowledge that propels comprehension. *American Educator, 27,* 24–27.

CHILDREN'S BOOK REFERENCES

Bunting, E. (2000). *Train to somewhere.* New York: Clarion Books.

Cole, J. (1999). *The magic school bus explores the senses.* New York: Scholastic.

Fox, P. (2001). *Slave dancer.* New York: Atheneum.

Howe, D., & Howe, J. (2006). *Bunnicula: A rabbit-tale of mystery.* New York: Aladdin Books.

Hutchins, P. (2005). *Rosie's walk.* New York: Aladdin Books.

Lowry, L. (1998). *Number the stars.* New York: Laurel Leaf.

MacLachlan, P. (2004). *Sarah, plain and tall.* New York: HarperTrophy.

Naylor, P. R. (1998). *Sang spell.* New York: Atheneum.

Osborne, M. P. (1998). *Hour of the Olympics.* New York: Random House.

Osborne, M. P., & Boyce, N. P. (2004). *Olympics of Ancient Greece.* New York: Random House.

Sachar, L. (2003). *Holes.* New York: Yearling.

Spinelli, J. (2004). *Stargirl.* New York: Laurel Leaf.

Van Allsburg, C. (1982). *Jumanji.* Boston: Houghton Mifflin.

Van Allsburg, C. (1983). *Wreck of the Zephyr.* Boston: Houghton Mifflin.

Van Allsburg, C. (1986). *The stranger.* Boston: Houghton Mifflin.

Van Allsburg, C. (1988). *Two bad ants.* Boston: Houghton Mifflin.

Van Allsburg, C. (1990). *Just a dream.* Boston: Houghton Mifflin.

Van Allsburg, C. (1991). *The wretched stone.* Boston: Houghton Mifflin.

Van Allsburg, C. (1993a). *The garden of Abdul Gasazi.* Boston: Houghton Mifflin.

Van Allsburg, C. (1993b). *The sweetest fig.* Boston: Houghton Mifflin.

Van Allsburg, C. (1996). *The mysteries of Harris Burdick.* Boston: Houghton Mifflin.

Van Allsburg, C. (2002). *Zathura.* Boston: Houghton Mifflin.

Van Allsburg, C. (2005). *The polar express.* Boston: Houghton Mifflin.

Van Allsburg, C. (2006). *Probuditi.* Boston: Houghton Mifflin.

Woodson, J. (2002). *Hush.* New York: Scholastic.

CHAPTER 11

Differentiating Reading and Writing Instruction

Mrs. Shasky Differentiates Instruction

The 31 students in Mrs. Shasky's sixth-grade class are reading *The Breadwinner* (Ellis, 2001), the story of a girl who seeks work disguised as a boy so that she can support her family during the Taliban era in Afghanistan. Before students began reading the novel, they participated in a webquest activity about Afghan culture at www.literacynet.org/cortez/ to learn basic information about Afghanistan and listen to an interview with the novel's author.

Today, some of the students are sitting on a sofa or lounging on floor pillows in the reading area in the back of the classroom; they're reading independently. Others are clustered around Mrs. Shasky, listening as she reads the same book aloud. She reads softly to avoid distracting the students reading in the back of the classroom. Some of the students close to Mrs. Shasky follow along in their copies, but others look at Mrs. Shasky, listening intently.

Mrs. Shasky provides two ways to read the novel because her students have a broad range of reading levels, from third through seventh grade. Her students who read at the fifth-, sixth-, and seventh-grade levels can read the book independently, but her 10 struggling readers who read at the third- and fourth-grade levels need extra support; that's why she reads the book aloud to them.

After she finishes reading the chapter, the class comes together for a **grand conversation**. Because the students have many questions about Afghanistan and life under Taliban rule, Mrs. Shasky often takes more of the discussion time than she would like to answer their questions, but gradually the students are developing the background knowledge they need to understand the story. This is the time when Mrs. Shasky teaches comprehension, so she asks inferential questions that require students to go beyond literal information. For example, she asks, "Why did the Taliban arrest Parvana's father?" Hector quickly answers with what he remembers reading in the novel: "Because he went to college in another country, and they don't want teachers to do that." Mrs. Shasky persists, "Why doesn't the Taliban want teachers or other people to study in another country?" No one has an idea, so Mrs. Shasky asks the question another way: "Lots of teachers in America go to other countries to study. You know that I went to visit schools in China last summer. Why is that a good idea?" The students offer several reasons—to learn about other people, to learn new things, and to learn new ways of teaching. "Wouldn't the Taliban want teachers to do these things, too?" Mrs. Shasky asks. Marisela replies, "No, the Taliban closed the schools because they want to control everyone. They don't like teachers who have new ideas because they could make trouble." "How could they make trouble?" Mrs. Shasky continues. Jared suggests, "Parvana's father and the other teachers could tell people that there is a better way to live, and then everyone could get together and fight the Taliban and kill them and have a free country like ours."

As they talk, several students add new words to the **word wall** posted on a nearby wall. The words they add include *burqa*, *hospitable*, *turban*, *chador*, *nan*, *exhaustion*, and *toshak*. Mrs. Shasky refers students to the word wall, and they use some of these words later in the morning during their word study period.

Literature study is only one part of Mrs. Shasky's literacy block; her schedule is shown on page 358. She differentiates instruction in several ways during the literacy block to ensure that her students are successful.

Mrs. Shasky begins the literacy block each morning with Accelerated Reader™. All students read independently in leveled books for 30 minutes, using books at their reading level, and complete online comprehension checks after each book. Mrs. Shasky supervises students as they read, moving from desk to desk and listening to individual students read. She also monitors their progress on the comprehension checks. A chart is posted in the classroom so students can track their reading growth.

Next, students participate in a literature study of a novel. Books are usually chosen from the district's recommended reading list for sixth grade, and Mrs. Shasky supplements with other books such as *The Breadwinner* that are timely or

Ways Mrs. Shasky Differentiates Instruction		
Schedule	Grade-Level Students	Struggling Students
8:30–9:00 Accelerated Reader	Students read books at their reading level and check their comprehension online.	Students read books at their reading level and check their comprehension online.
9:00–10:00 Literature Study	Students read the featured novel independently and participate in grand conversations.	Students listen to the teacher read the featured novel aloud and participate in grand conversations.
10:00–10:15 Minilesson	Mrs. Shasky presents whole-class minilessons on grade-level literacy topics.	Mrs. Shasky presents whole-class minilessons on grade-level literacy topics and other minilessons for small groups according to need.
10:15–11:15 Activities/ Guided Reading	Students are involved in activities related to the featured novel.	Students participate in guided reading groups and work in small groups to do activities related to the featured novel.
11:15–11:45 Word Study	Students participate in whole-class and small-group word-study activities and lessons. They use an individualized approach to spelling.	Students participate in whole-class and small-group word-study activities and lessons. They use an individualized approach to spelling.

that she thinks would appeal to her students. The novel becomes a vehicle for teaching reading strategies and literary analysis.

The third activity is a **minilesson**. Mrs. Shasky teaches minilessons on comprehension strategies, literary analysis, and other grade-level standards; sometimes the whole class participates, and at other times, the lesson is designed for a specific group of students. She ties lessons to the novel they're reading, and her focus for this novel is on how authors use elements of story structure to develop theme. Right now, the students are overwhelmed by the devastating effects of war, but later during the unit, Mrs. Shasky redirects the focus to human rights. Today, she reviews character development with the whole class and explains that authors develop characters in four ways: through appearance, actions, talking, and thinking. She asks students to think about Parvana, the main character in *The Breadwinner*, and how the author, Deborah Ellis, developed her. As the students share ideas, Mrs. Shasky draws a weblike diagram on chart paper and writes Parvana's name in the center circle. She divides the diagram into four sections and writes *appearance*, *actions*, *talking*, and *thinking* in each section. Next, she writes a sentence or two that students have suggested in each section. Mrs. Shasky steps back and rereads the chart, and then she asks, "Which of the four ways of character development is most important in *The Breadwinner*? What is Deborah Ellis trying to tell us?" The students are torn between "appearance" and "actions." Nita says, "It's her clothes. She has to dress like a boy." Javier disagrees, "No, it's what she's doing. She is pretending to be a boy to help her family. That's what matters." With more discussion, most students agree with Javier. A student's copy of the character development diagram is shown on the next page.

Most of the students return to their desks to write in **reading logs** or work on activities, but Mrs. Shasky keeps a group of struggling readers who need more

A Character Diagram About Parvana

When she was a girl she kept her face covered and tried to be envisible. She cut her hair and pretended to be a boy. *Appearance*	She dressed as a boy to go to the markut and buy food. She was a reader and writer. She dug up graves. *Actions*
Talking (Parvana) *Thinking*	
"I can do this". "I am working to get my family back".	She dident like the hard work but she did it to help her family. She was very lonely.

practice writing summaries with her to write a summary statement about character development. She uses the Language Experience Approach to take the students' dictation quickly as they develop this summary statement, which they'll share with the whole class:

> *Deborah Ellis tells us about Parvana in four ways: appearance, actions, talking, and thinking. The most important way we learn about Parvana is by her actions. She pretends she is a boy to make money so her family doesn't starve.*

Next week, Mrs. Shasky will introduce human rights with his scenario: Imagine that when you wake up tomorrow morning, life as you know it is totally different—it's like Parvana's life. What will be different? How will you feel? What will you do? What won't you be able to do? Students will talk, draw, and write about the ways their lives would change. Mrs. Shasky will explain what human rights are, talk about the rights discussed in the Declaration of Independence and guaranteed in the Constitution's Bill of Rights, and have students play an interactive online game about human rights. Next, students will participate in differentiated activities to think more deeply about the human rights they enjoy and those denied to Parvana.

While students are working on activities, Mrs. Shasky meets with small groups of struggling readers for guided reading lessons. One group is reading at early third-grade level (Level M), the second group is reading at late third-grade/early fourth-grade level (Level P), and the third group is reading at fourth-grade level (Level R). She usually meets with two groups each day for 25 to 30 minutes each and they read short chapter books at their reading levels; they read and discuss one or two chapters each day, and then they are to reread the chapters independently or with a buddy before they meet again.

The group at the early third-grade level is reading Greenburg's wacky series, The Zack Files, about an amazing fifth grader named Zack. In the book they've just finished reading, *How I Went From Bad to Verse* (Greenburg, 2000), Zack is bitten by an insect and catches Rhyme Disease. He speaks only in rhyme, and worse yet, he floats above the ground and turns blue. Finally, his science teacher, Mrs. Coleman-Levin, cures him and his life returns to normal—at least until the next book. The students silently reread the last two chapters, and they talk again about Zack's weird symptoms and Mrs. Coleman-Levin's unusual cures.

Mrs. Shasky draws a chart about symptoms and cures on a dry-erase board beside her, and the students list the three symptoms that Zack exhibited (rhyming, floating, and blue skin) on the chart; then they explain how Mrs. Coleman-Levin cured each symptom. The students return to Chapter 8 to check that they remember the cures (wearing a reversible jacket, reciting a poem backward, and thinking happy thoughts) and then complete the chart.

These students also go through a ceremonial process of listing the book on a chart of the books they've read as a group. *How I Went From Bad to Verse* is number 28 on the list, and the students are amazed! "I've never read so many books before in my life," Ana comments, and the group agrees. "I told my Tio Roberto that I am a good reader now," Mark says. The students will take the book home tonight to read to their parents, a sibling, a grandparent, or a neighbor.

After conducting another guided reading group, Mrs. Shasky moves the class to the last segment of the literacy block: word study. Students do a combination of vocabulary and individualized spelling activities during word study. On Monday, Mrs. Shasky takes the entire 30 minutes for spelling. She administers the pretest, and students check it themselves. Then they choose the words they will study during the week and make two copies of their word list, one for themselves and one for Mrs. Shasky to keep. Because she's implemented an individualized spelling program, students study different words, depending on their developmental levels. The students practice their spelling words each day, and on Friday, they take the final test.

On Tuesday, Wednesday, and Thursday, students participate in vocabulary lessons to study the meanings of specific words, examine root words and affixes, and learn to use a dictionary and a thesaurus. They use words from the **word wall** for most activities. Over the past 5 weeks, Mrs. Shasky has taught lessons on these root words:

ann/enn (*year*): *annual, anniversary, millennium*
graph (*write*): *paragraph, autobiography, photograph*
mar/mer (*sea*): *mermaid, submarine, marsh*
tele (*far*): *telecast, telephone, telethon*
volv (*roll*): *revolution, evolution, revolver*

The students have made posters about these root words and brainstormed lists of words using them on chart paper, and they're displayed around the classroom. Today, students are examining words from the word wall to identify other root words.

Because Mrs. Shasky wants to do more to help her struggling readers, she developed a twice-a-week after-school intervention that she calls Shasky's Reading Club. She invited the 10 students reading at third- and fourth-grade levels to stay after school each Tuesday and Thursday to participate in the club. She began the club after parent conferences in early October; she explained the importance of providing these struggling readers with additional instruction and time for reading. All parents agreed to pick up their children after the reading club and to provide 30 minutes of independent reading time at home 4 days a week.

During the 45-minute reading club meeting, students read self-selected books independently and participate in guided reading groups. Mrs. Shasky is pleased to see these students' growth over the 4 months the club has been operating. She's noticed that her struggling students behave like her grade-level readers do during the school day: Instead of being reticent and unsure of themselves as they sometimes are during

the school day, they participate willingly in discussions and confidently assume leadership roles.

As the club meeting begins, the 10 students have picked up books they're reading and settled on the sofa and on floor pillows in the back of the classroom. Mrs. Shasky checks that everyone has an appropriate book to read, and then she calls a group of 4 students reading at Level P (late third-/early fourth-grade level); they're reading Jon Scieszka's The Time Warp Trio series of easy-reading chapter books. In these stories, three modern-day friends warp back into history and find themselves in adventures. These students have already read *Your Mother Was a Neanderthal* (2004c) and *Tut Tut* (2004b).

Now they're reading *Knights of the Kitchen Table* (2004a), in which the boys travel back to the days of King Arthur. A giant and a dragon threaten Camelot, and the boys help King Arthur and his knights. The first few chapters were difficult because the students didn't know the King Arthur stories, but Mrs. Shasky told the stories to build their background knowledge. The vocabulary was unfamiliar, too—*vile knaves*, *methinks*, and *foul-mouthed enchanters*, for example—but now the group is into the story. They read about the boys reaching Camelot and meeting King Arthur, Queen Guenevere, and Merlin when they read Chapter 5 today in class. They begin by rereading the chapter and doing a read-around, where they take turns randomly reading aloud their favorite sentences from the chapter. Then Mrs. Shasky takes them on a text walk of Chapter 6, and they examine a full-page illustration of the giant. Hector predicts, "I think Sir Joe the Magnificent will kill the giant and the dragon." "You should say he will *slay* them. *Slay* means to kill," explains Jesus. Mrs. Shasky asks how the students might slay the giant and the dragon, and the boys quickly suggest using swords or guns, but the illustrations in Chapter 6 don't provide any clues.

Mrs. Shasky explains that this riddle is going to be important in the chapter: *Why did the giant wear red suspenders?* The students aren't familiar with suspenders, so Mrs. Shasky shows them a pair of her husband's. She models them and explains that sometimes her husband wears suspenders instead of a belt to hold his pants up.

Marisela, who has been listening quietly while the boys eagerly talked about slaying dragons and giants, asks, "Why did the giant wear suspenders?" The teacher explains that they'll learn the answer as they read the chapter, and then Marisela predicts, "You have to be smart to know the answer to a riddle, so I think those boys will use their brains to save Camelot." Mrs. Shasky smiles in agreement and says, "Let's read Chapter 6 to see if Marisela's prediction is right."

The students read the five-page chapter in less than 10 minutes, and while they're reading, Mrs. Shasky helps students decode several unfamiliar words and explains a confusing section when two boys ask about it. The group now knows the answer to the riddle: *Why did the giant wear red suspenders? To hold his pants up.* They like the riddle and show interest in reading more riddles. Mrs. Shasky says that she'll get some riddle books for them tomorrow. They continue to discuss the chapter, and Jesus sums up the group's feelings by saying, "Bleob [the giant] should be dead and gone by now. I just want to keep reading and find out what happens." Because the giant and the dragon do destroy themselves in the next chapter, Mrs. Shasky lets them take their books back to the reading corner and read the next chapter to find out what happens.

Then Mrs. Shasky calls a second group for a guided reading lesson while the other two groups continue reading on their own. The second group finishes reading with Mrs. Shasky when only several minutes remain before the reading club ends, so Mrs. Shasky joins the group in the back of the classroom and asks each student to briefly tell what he or she has been reading.

eachers know that their students vary—in their interests and motivation, their background knowledge and prior experiences, and their culture and language proficiency as well as their reading and writing achievement—so it's important to take these individual differences into account as they plan for instruction. Differentiated instruction is based on this understanding that students differ in important ways. According to Tomlinson (2001), differentiated instruction "means 'shaking up' what goes on in the classroom so that students have multiple options for taking in information, making sense of ideas, and expressing what they learn" (p. 1). Differentiating instruction is especially important for struggling readers and writers who haven't been successful and who can't read grade-level textbooks and other reading materials.

In the vignette, for example, Mrs. Shasky modified her instruction to meet her students' needs and provided support for her struggling readers and writers so that they could be successful. First, she provided additional support for struggling students during regular classroom reading and writing activities: During the literature focus unit, Mrs. Shasky read aloud to students who couldn't read the featured novel independently. Second, she provided additional instruction for her struggling students: During the activities period, Mrs. Shasky taught **guided reading** lessons for those students. Third, she provided an after-school intervention program: Mrs. Shasky met with her struggling readers twice a week for Shasky's Reading Club and got these students' parents to commit to providing time for independent reading at home.

> Check the Compendium of Instructional Procedures, which follows Chapter 12, for more information on the highlighted terms.

WAYS TO DIFFERENTIATE INSTRUCTION

The expectation that all students are to meet the same literacy standards at each grade level implies that all students should receive the same instructional program, but teachers know that some of their students are working at grade level but others are struggling or advanced. Because students' achievement levels differ and their interests and preferred ways of learning vary, teachers modify their instructional programs so that all students can be successful. Tomlinson (2001) explains that in differentiated classrooms, "teachers provide specific ways for students to learn as deeply as possible and as quickly as possible without assuming one student's road map for learning is identical to anyone else's" (p. 2). Heacox (2002) characterizes differentiated instruction as rigorous, relevant, flexible, and complex:

Rigorous means that teachers provide challenging instruction that encourages students' active engagement in learning.

Relevant means that teachers address literacy standards to assure that students learn essential knowledge, strategies, and skills.

Flexible means that teachers use a variety of instructional procedures and grouping techniques to support students.

Complex means that teachers engage students in thinking deeply about books they're reading, compositions they're writing, and concepts they're learning.

It's crucial that teachers recognize the diversity of learners in 21st-century classrooms and understand that students don't need to participate in the same learning activities or read and write in whole-class groups all day long. A list of the characteristics of differentiated instruction is presented in Figure 11–1.

Figure 11–1 ◆ Characteristics of Differentiated Instruction

High Standards

Teachers maintain a commitment to meeting grade-level standards for all students.

Assessment-Instruction Link

Teachers use assessment procedures to diagnose students' needs and plan instruction to address those needs.

Flexible Grouping

Teachers have students work individually, in small groups and as a class, and they change grouping arrangements to reflect students' achievement levels and interests.

Reading Materials

Teachers teach with collections of books and other reading materials, written at varying difficulty levels.

Varied Instructional Activities

Teachers design activities with multiple options to meet students' instructional levels.

Instructional Modifications

Teachers modify instruction to respond to students' specific learning needs and continue to make adjustments during instruction to ensure that all students are successful.

Respect

Teachers respect students and value their work.

Academic Achievement

Teachers focus on individual students' academic achievement and success.

Adapted from Heacox, 2002; Robb, 2008; Tomlinson, 2001.

Teachers modify instruction in three ways: They modify the *content* that students need to learn, the instructional *process* used to teach students, and the *products* students create to demonstrate their learning (Heacox, 2002; Tomlinson, 2001):

Differentiating the Content. The content is the "what" of teaching, the literacy knowledge, strategies, and skills that students are expected to learn at each grade level. The content reflects state-mandated grade-level standards. Teachers concentrate on teaching the essential content, and to meet students' needs, they provide more instruction and practice for some students and less for others. For those who are already familiar with the content, they increase the complexity of instructional activities. Teachers decide how they will differentiate the content by assessing students' knowledge before they begin teaching, and then they match students with appropriate activities.

Differentiating the Process. The process is the "how" of teaching, the instruction that teachers provide, the instructional materials they use, and the activities in which students are involved to ensure that they're successful. Teachers group students for instruction and choose reading materials at appropriate levels of difficulty. They also make decisions about involving students in activities that allow them to process what they're learning through oral, written, or visual means.

Differentiating the Product. The product is the end result of learning; it demonstrates what students understand and how well they can apply what they've learned. Students usually create projects, such as posters, multimodal reports, board games, puppet shows, and new versions of stories. Teachers often vary the complexity of the projects they ask students to create by changing the level of thinking that's required to complete the project.

New Literacies
Computer-Based Reading Programs

Scholastic's Reading Counts! and Renaissance Learning's Accelerated Reader™ are two popular K–12 computer-based reading programs that manage students' daily reading practice. They are consistent with differentiated instruction because students choose books to read from a leveled collection and read at their own pace during an independent reading period. Afterward, students take computer-generated quizzes to check their comprehension, and the teacher retrieves computer-generated reports to track students' progress. More than half of the schools in the United States use one of these programs.

These programs provide students with daily opportunities for independent reading practice, and reading volume is related to achievement (Snow, Burns, & Griffin, 1998; Topping & Paul, 1999). Students who do more reading are better readers than those who do less reading. The programs are predicated on these principles:

● Students read authentic books at their reading levels.
● The quizzes provide frequent monitoring of students' comprehension.
● Teachers use the test results to quickly intervene with struggling students.
● Students' motivation grows as they read books and score well on the accompanying quizzes.

These principles reflect the balanced approach to reading instruction.

More than 100,000 books—stories, informational books, and magazine articles—are included in the Accelerated Reader collection, and approximately half that many are included in the Reading Counts! collection. Books in both programs have been leveled, and the reading level is clearly marked on each book. One potential problem is that a limited number of appropriate books are available for older struggling students because these students don't want to read childish books. Sometimes the book collections are housed in a special part of the school library, or teachers set out smaller collections of books at their students' reading levels in their classrooms.

Students take computer-generated quizzes after reading each book. Each quiz has 5 to 20 multiple-choice items, depending on the book's reading level; the questions focus on literal comprehension. The minimum passing score is 60%, and the optimal score is 85%. Students receive the results immediately after taking a quiz so they can learn from their errors and alert the teacher if they're having difficulty. The software provides information about students' comprehension, reading rates, and amount of reading they've done to assist teachers in monitoring their progress. The software also generates classroom, school, and district reports.

Researchers have found that students participating in these computer-based reading programs score higher on standardized tests than students in schools not using the programs; nonetheless, the programs are controversial for several reasons (Holmes & Brown, 2003; Schmidt, 2008). First, the quizzes focus on literal comprehension, not higher-level thinking. Proponents counter that the purpose is to determine whether students have read a book, not to assess higher-level comprehension. Next, detractors argue that students are limited in which books they can choose to read because they can read only those books in the collection that match their reading level, but proponents say that these programs involve only one independent reading time and that students can read any books they want at other times. Third, detractors contend that students often read the book with the goal of passing the quiz, rather than for enjoyment or to learn about an interesting topic, but proponents point out that students need to learn to read for a variety of purposes. Many teachers report liking the program because they can effectively manage students' independent reading and monitor their progress.

Teachers create a classroom culture that promotes acceptance of individual differences and is conducive to matching instruction to individual students. Having a classroom community where students respect their classmates and can work collaboratively is vital. They learn that students don't always do the same activity or read the same book, and they focus on their own work rather than on what their classmates are doing. Students become more responsible for their own learning and develop more confidence in their ability to learn.

Grouping for Instruction

Teachers use three grouping patterns: Sometimes students work together as a whole class, and at other times, they work in small groups or individually. Deciding which type of grouping to use depends on the teacher's purpose, the complexity of the activity, and students' specific learning needs. Small groups should be used flexibly to provide a better instructional match between students and their needs. In differentiated classrooms, students are grouped and regrouped often; they aren't always grouped according to achievement levels or with the same classmates.

Teachers use a combination of the three grouping patterns in each instructional program, but basal reading programs and literature focus units use primarily whole-class groups, literature circles are predominantly small-group programs, and reading and writing workshop feature mostly individual reading and writing activities. Nonetheless, each instructional program incorporates all three grouping patterns. The activities involved in each instructional program are categorized in Figure 11–2.

Teachers use the three types of groups for a variety of activities. Whole-class activities typically include **interactive read-alouds** and **word walls**. **Guided reading** and **shared reading** are small-group activities. Other activities, including the **Language Experience Approach**, **open-mind portraits**, and **reading logs**, are often done individually. Some activities, such as **minilessons** and **interactive writing**, are used with more than one type of group. In addition, when teachers introduce an activity, they have students work together as a class to learn the steps involved; then, once students understand the procedure, they work in small groups or individually.

Guided Reading. Teachers use **guided reading** to work with small groups of students who are reading books at their instructional level, with approximately 90–94% accuracy (Fountas & Pinnell, 1996, 2001). Students do the actual reading themselves,

Figure 11–2 ◆ The Grouping Patterns in Four Literacy Programs

Program	Whole Class	Small Groups	Individuals
Basal Readers	Introduce the book Teach vocabulary Teach strategies and skills Read the featured selection	Reread the selection Practice vocabulary and skills Work at centers	Complete workbook assignments Read related books
Literature Focus Units	Read a featured book Participate in grand conversations Teach minilessons Do word-study activities Learn about author and genre Create projects	Participate in grand conversations Teach minilessons Create projects	Respond in reading logs Read related books Create projects

Literature Circles	Introduce books	Read and discuss a book
		  together
			Choose a book to read
			Assume roles to contribute
			  to group discussions

Reading Workshop	Read aloud to students Teach minilessons Share books	Teach minilessons	Read self-selected books Conference with the teacher
Writing Workshop	Read aloud to students Teach minilessons Share writing from the author's chair	Teach minilessons Participate in writing groups Edit with a partner	Write on self-selected topics Conference with the teacher

although the teacher may read aloud with students to get them started on the first page or two. Beginning readers often mumble the words softly as they read, which helps the teacher keep track of students' reading and the decoding and comprehension strategies they're using and their level of fluency. Older students who are more fluent readers usually read silently during guided reading.

Teachers choose the books that students read during guided reading; the books are carefully chosen to reflect students' reading levels and their ability to use reading strategies. Teachers read the book in preparation for the lesson and plan how they'll teach it, considering how to develop students' background knowledge and which concepts and vocabulary to teach before students begin reading. They choose a strategy to teach, prepare for word-study activities, and plan other after-reading activities. Many teachers mark important teaching points in the book with little self-stick notes.

Guided reading lessons usually last approximately 20–30 minutes, and teachers meet with several groups each day. Primary-grade students read a book over a day or two, but older students often take a week or longer to complete a book.

Guided reading was developed to use with beginning readers, but teachers also use it with older students, especially English learners and struggling readers who need more teacher support to decode and comprehend books they're reading, learn reading strategies, and become independent readers. Sometimes guided reading is confused with round-robin reading and literature circles, but these three small-group instructional activities are different. In round-robin reading, an approach that's no longer recommended, students take turns reading aloud to the group rather than doing their own reading. In literature circles, students read books on their own with very limited teacher guidance.

Text Sets of Reading Materials

Teachers create text sets of books and other reading materials for students to read during literature focus units and thematic units. These collections include reading materials representing several genres, bookmarked Internet resources, and books that vary in difficulty level. If teachers can't locate a wide enough range of reading materials, they can create them with students to add to the text set. Figure 11–3 presents Mrs. Shasky's text set of books and Internet resources related to *The Breadwinner* (Ellis, 2001), Afghanistan, Muslim religious holidays, and Arab immigrants. The list includes all three books in Deborah Ellis's trilogy of stories about Parvana, and it features two books of poetry by Naomi Shihab Nye (2002a, 2002b), an esteemed Arab American poet and anthologist. Teachers use **book talks** to introduce books at the beginning of the unit and then display the books on a special shelf in the classroom library. They often read some of the books aloud to the class, have students read other books in literature circles, and encourage students to read additional books during reading workshop.

Text sets are only a small part of well-stocked classroom libraries. Teachers set out collections of stories, informational books, magazines, and books of poetry, written at a range of levels for students to read independently. They also make available lots of other books that are interesting, familiar, and easy enough for reluctant

Literacy Portraits: VIEWING GUIDE

Ms. Janusz uses flexible groups—whole class, small groups, buddies, and individuals—for instruction. Go to the Literacy Profiles section of MyEducationLab and watch these four video clips: Click on Michael's November button to see him reading a poem to the class; Rakie's December button to watch her participate in a guided reading group; Rhiannon's December button to view her reading individually with the teacher; and Curt'Lynn's March button to watch her read with a classmate. As you view these video segments, think about why Ms. Janusz grouped the students as she did. It's not enough to use varied grouping patterns; what matters most is that when students participate in a group, their learning is enhanced. When they set up groups, teachers consider their instructional goal, the activity, and group membership. How do you think Ms. Janusz's grouping patterns benefited these students' learning?

myeducationlab

Figure 11–3 ◆ A Text Set for *The Breadwinner*

Stories

Bunting, E. (2006). *One green apple*. New York: Clarion Books.

Ellis, D. (2001). *The breadwinner*. Toronto: Groundwood Books.

Ellis, D. (2003). *Parvana's journey*. Toronto: Groundwood Books.

Ellis, D. (2004). *Mud city*. Toronto: Groundwood Books.

Khan, R. (2004). *The roses in my carpets*. Markham, ON: Fitzhenry & Whiteside.

Oppenheim, S. L. (1997). *The hundredth name*. Honesdale, PA: Boyds Mills Press.

Informational Books

Banting, E. (2003). *Afghanistan: The culture*. Minneapolis, MN: Crabtree.

Banting, E. (2003). *Afghanistan: The land*. Minneapolis, MN: Crabtree.

Banting, E. (2003). *Afghanistan: The people*. Minneapolis, MN: Crabtree.

Haskins, J., & Benson, K. (2006). *Count your way through Afghanistan*. Minneapolis, MN: Millbrook Press.

Mobin-Uddin, A. (2007). *The best Eid ever*. Honesdale, PA: Boyds Mills Press.

Whitfield, S. (2008). *National Geographic countries of the world: Afghanistan*. Washington, DC: National Geographic Children's Books.

Wolf, B. (2003). *Coming to America: A Muslim family's story*. New York: Lee & Low.

Zucker, J. (2004). *Fasting and dates: A Ramadan and Eid-ul-Fitr story*. New York: Barron's.

Poetry

Nye, N. S. (Compiler). (2002). *The flag of childhood: Poems from the Middle East*. New York: Aladdin Books.

Nye, N. S. (2002). *19 varieties of gazelle: Poems of the Middle East*. New York: Greenwillow.

Websites and Webquests

Afghanistan for Kids

http://www.public.asu.edu/~apnilsen/afghanistan4kids/index2.html

The Breadwinner: A Prereading Webquest Activity for Grades 4–7

www.literacynet.org/cortez/

Kids in Afghanistan Scavenger Hunt

http://teacher.scholastic.com/scholasticnews/indepth/afghanistan/

No Music, no TV

http://www.timeforkids.com/TFK/kids/wr/article/0,28391,94545,00.html

Understanding Afghanistan: Land in Crisis

http://www.nationalgeographic.com/landincrisis/

and struggling students to read and reread on their own, including books they read the previous year.

Tiered Activities

To match students' needs, teachers create several tiered or related activities that focus on the same essential knowledge but vary in complexity (Robb, 2008). These activities are alternative ways of reaching the same goal because "one-size-fits-all" activities can't benefit on-grade-level students, support struggling readers, and challenge advanced students. Creating tiered lessons, according to Tomlinson (2001), increases the likelihood that all students will be successful. Even though the activities are different, they should be interesting and engaging and require the same amount of effort from students.

Teachers vary activities in several ways. First, they vary them by complexity of thinking. In recall-level activities, students identify, retell, or summarize; in analysis-level activities, they compare and categorize; and in synthesis-level activities, students evaluate, draw conclusions, and invent. Second, teachers vary activities according to the level of reading materials. They use books and other print and online materials written at students' reading level, or they vary the way the materials are shared with students. Third, teachers vary activities by the form of expression. Students are involved in visual, oral, and written expression as they complete an activity: Examples of visual expression

Tiered Activities
Teachers use tiered activities to maximize students' learning. These fourth graders are working on a tiered activity—a poster report about stagecoaches—based on Pam Muñoz Ryan's *Riding Freedom* (1998), the story of Charlotte Parkhurst, a legendary stagecoach driver during the California Gold Rush. The students have researched the vehicles and downloaded pictures from the Internet for their report. Today, they're revising their captions to include more facts. Later, they'll print out a "clean" copy, cut the captions apart, and attach them next to the pictures they've already glued on a poster.

are charts, posters, and dioramas; examples of oral expression are dramatizations, oral reports, and choral readings; and examples of written expression are stories, poems, and reports. Some activities require a combination of forms of expression; for example, students might write a poem from the viewpoint of a book character (written) and dress up as the character (visual) to read the poem aloud to the class (oral). Creating tiered activities doesn't mean that some students do more work and others do less; each activity must be equally interesting and challenging to the students.

Tomlinson (2001) suggests that teachers follow these steps to develop a tiered activity:

1. **Design an activity.** Teachers design an interesting activity that focuses on elemental knowledge and requires high-level thinking.
2. **Visualize a ladder.** Teachers visualize a ladder where the top rung represents advanced students, the middle rung on-grade-level students, and the bottom rung struggling students, and then they decide where the activity they've created fits on the ladder.
3. **Create other versions of the activity.** Teachers create one, two, or three versions of the activity at different levels of difficulty to meet the needs of their students. Versions can vary according to the difficulty level of reading materials they use, thinking levels, or forms of expression.
4. **Match activities to students.** Teachers decide which students will do each version of the activity.

It's important to make tiering invisible. Heacox (2002) recommends that teachers alternate the order in which activities are introduced to students, show similar enthusiasm for each one, and use neutral ways of identifying groups of students who will pursue each activity.

One of the literacy standards that Mrs. Shasky addressed as her sixth graders read and responded to *The Breadwinner* (Ellis, 2001) was to analyze the theme conveyed through the characters and the plot. She decided to explore the theme of human rights and, in particular, what happens when they're denied. She began by talking about human rights during a **grand conversation** as the class discussed the book, and students looked for examples of human rights that the Taliban denied to Parvana and her family. Later, students worked in small groups to create lists of human rights, including religious freedom, the right to safe food and drinking water, the right to speak your mind, the right to education, freedom to work and earn a living, civil rights, and equal rights for all people. They played the interactive game "Save the Bill of Rights" at the National Constitution Center's website (www.constitutioncenter.org/BillOf RightsGame) to learn more about the rights that Americans are guaranteed.

Once students understood what human rights were and could find examples of these rights and freedoms being denied in *The Breadwinner*, Mrs. Shasky designed this activity:

> *Information, please! Create a Venn diagram on chart paper to compare the human rights we have in America to those Parvana and her family had in Taliban-controlled Afghanistan. Then create a statement to summarize the information presented in the Venn diagram and write it underneath the diagram.*

Mrs. Shasky decided that this graphic activity was appropriate for her on-grade-level students. Here's the version she developed for her struggling students:

> *A celebration of human rights! Choose the human right that you value most and create a quilt square using color, images, and words to describe this right. Then we'll connect the squares and create a human rights quilt.*

Finally, Mrs. Shasky designed this activity for her advanced students:

> *Let's get involved! Students in our class are passionate about human rights and want to help people like Parvana and her family. Find a way for us to get involved, and create a brochure about your idea to share with everyone.*

The advanced students researched organizations that aid refugees and promote human rights, including UNICEF, Habitat for Humanity, Heifer International, and Doctors Without Borders, before they heard about Greg Mortenson's work building schools in Afghanistan that's described in *Three Cups of Tea: One Man's Mission to Promote Peace . . . One School at a Time* (Mortenson & Relin, 2007). The group proposed that that their class raise money to build a school through the Pennies for Peace program (www.penniesforpeace.org), and before long, the class had gotten the entire school and their local community involved!

Literacy Centers

Literacy centers contain meaningful, purposeful literacy activities that students can work at in small groups. Students practice phonics skills at the phonics center, sort word cards at the vocabulary center, or listen to books related to a book they're reading at the listening center. Figure 11–4 describes 20 literacy centers. Centers are usually organized in special places in the classroom or at groups of tables (Fountas & Pinnell, 1996).

Although literacy centers are generally associated with primary classrooms, they can be used effectively at all grade levels, even in seventh and eighth grades, to differentiate instruction. In most classrooms, the teacher works with a small group of students while the others work at centers, but sometimes all students work at centers at the same time.

The activities in these literacy centers relate to concepts, strategies, and skills that the teacher recently taught in minilessons, and they vary from simple to complex. Other center activities relate to books students are reading and to thematic units. Students manipulate objects, sort word cards, reread books, complete graphic organizers related to books, and practice skills in centers. Some literacy centers, such as reading and writing centers, are permanent, but others change according to the books students are reading and the activities planned. Teachers provide clear directions at the center so students know what to do and what they should do after they finish an activity.

Figure 11–4 ◆ Literacy Centers

Center	Description
Alphabet	Young children sing the ABC song, sort upper- and lowercase letters, read alphabet books, and practice other activities the teacher has introduced.
Author	Students examine information about authors they're studying, and interested students write letters to them.
Collaborative Books	Students write pages for a class book following the format indicated at the center, and the teacher compiles and binds the pages into a book afterward.
Computer	Students do word processing, read interactive books, complete webquests, search the Internet, and play online games.
Dramatic Play	Students work with puppets, small manipulative materials related to books they're reading, and book boxes as they retell stories and create sequels.
Grammar	Students examine grammar concepts, such as identifying parts of speech and marking capitalization and punctuation on sample compositions.
Informational Books	Students read nonfiction books on a special topic, complete graphic organizers emphasizing the big ideas, and examine genres and nonfiction features.
Library	Students look at books and magazines, choose appropriate books to read from text sets, read books classmates have written, and reread favorite books.
Listening	Students use a tape player and headphones to listen to stories and other books read aloud. Often copies of the books are available so students can read along.
Making Words	Students arrange letter cards to spell words using the procedure their teacher has taught them.
Message	Kindergartners write notes to classmates and post them on a message board. They also check for messages their classmates and the teacher have written to them.
Phonics	Children practice phonics concepts the teacher has introduced using a variety of small objects, picture cards, and games.
Pocket Charts	Children arrange sentence strips for a familiar poem or song in the pocket chart, and then they read or sing it. They also write new versions on sentence strips.
Poetry	Students read poems and locate examples of poetic devices. They also write poems, referring to charts describing various poetic formulas posted in the center.
Proofreading	Students proofread with partners and then use spellcheckers, high-frequency word lists, and dictionaries to correct mechanical errors in their rough drafts.
Sequencing	Students retell stories by sequencing story boards (made by cutting apart two copies of a picture book) or illustrations students have drawn.
Spelling	Students practice spelling words, do word sorts to review spelling concepts, and play spelling games at the center.
Stories	Students use copies of diagrams available at the center to examine story elements, narrative genres, and literary devices in stories they're reading.
Vocabulary	Students learn about idioms; match synonyms, homophones, or antonyms; make word posters or maps; and sort words according to meaning or structural form.
Writing	Students locate needed writing materials, work on writing projects, get feedback from classmates about their writing, and make books.

In some classrooms, students flow freely from one center to another according to their interests; in other classrooms, students are assigned to centers or are required to work at some "assigned" centers and choose among other "choice" centers. Students can sign attendance sheets when they work at each center or mark off their names on a class list posted there. Rarely do students move from center to center in a lockstep approach every 15 to 30 minutes; instead, they move from one center to the next when they finish what they're doing.

This Assessment Tools feature shows a checklist that eighth graders used as they worked at centers as part of a unit on the Constitution. Some centers are required;

Assessment Tools

An Eighth-Grade Centers Checklist

US Constitution Centers Checklist			
Center	Activity	Student's Check	Teacher's Check
Word Wall	Choose three words from the word wall and make word-study cards for each word.		
Puzzle Center	Complete the "Branches of Government" puzzle.		
Library Center	Use the informational books at the center to complete the Constitution time line.		
Internet Center	Research the Constitution on the Internet and complete the study guide.		
Writing Center	Study Howard Christy's painting "The Signing of the Constitution" and write a poem or descriptive essay about it.		
*Legislative Branch Center	Complete activities at this student-developed center.		
*Executive Branch Center	Complete activities at this student-developed center.		
*Judicial Branch Center	Complete activities at this student-developed center.		
*The Bill of Rights Center	Complete activities at this student-developed center.		
*Alphabet Book Center	Choose a letter and create a page for the Class Constitution Alphabet Book.		

they're marked with an asterisk. Students are expected to complete the "required" centers and two others of their choice. They put a checkmark in the "Student's Check" column when they finish work there. Students keep their checklists in their unit folders, and they add any worksheets or papers they do at the center. Having a checklist or another approach to monitor students' progress helps them develop responsibility for completing their assignments.

Differentiated Projects

Go to the Building Teaching Skills and Dispositions section of Chapter 11 on **MyEducationLab.com** to see the ways in which a teacher uses differentiated projects.

Students often create projects at the end of a unit to apply what they've learned and to bring closure to the unit. Possible projects include charts, murals, and other visual representations; poems, essays, and other compositions; PowerPoint reports, **readers theatre** productions, and other oral presentations; websites and other Internet products; and community-based projects that reflect students' synthesis of the big ideas and high-quality workmanship. Projects are an important part of differentiated instruction because students follow their interests, demonstrate what they've learned in authentic ways, and feel successful (Yatvin, 2004).

At the end of some units, students work together on a class project. When fifth graders are studying idioms, for example, they often create a collection of posters or write and compile a collaborative book about idioms, showing their literal and figurative meanings. Most of the time, however, students choose their own projects. Some students work independently or with a partner, and others work in small groups.

Projects are especially valuable for advanced students and struggling students (Yatvin, 2004). Advanced students have opportunities to pursue special interests and extend their learning beyond the classroom when they create projects. For example, they often choose to get involved in community and social issues that they're passionate about, such as homelessness, global warming, and disaster relief, through the projects they do. Similarly, struggling students are often more successful in demonstrating their learning when they work with classmates in small, collaborative groups and use their special talents and expertise, such as drawing, making oral presentations, and using computers, to create a high-quality project.

STRUGGLING READERS AND WRITERS

Why are some students more successful than others in learning to read and write? Researchers report that young children with strong oral language skills and in families where parents read aloud to them and provide other early literacy experiences are more likely to be successful in school. They've also found that children who aren't fluent English speakers, children whose parents had difficulty learning to read and write, and children from low-SES communities are more likely to have difficulty reaching grade-level proficiency in reading and writing (Strickland, 2002).

Struggling Readers

It's crucial to identify students at risk for reading problems early so these problems can be addressed quickly, before they're compounded. Fink (2006) identified these factors that predict early reading difficulty in kindergarten or first grade:

- Difficulty developing concepts about print, phonemic awareness, letter names, sound-symbol correspondences
- Slower response than classmates when asked to name letters and identify words
- Behavior that deviates from school norms

In addition, children with a family history of reading problems are more likely to experience difficulty in learning to read.

It's common for young children to make letter and word reversals (Fink, 2006); they often reverse the lowercase letters *b* and *d* and the words *was* and *saw*, for example. These reversals don't signify that students have a reading problem unless they persist beyond second grade.

Although many struggling readers are identified in the primary grades, other students who have been successful begin to exhibit reading problems in fourth or fifth grade. This phenomenon is known as the "fourth-grade slump" (Chall & Jacobs, 2003). Many teachers attribute this problem to the growing use of informational books and content-area textbooks that may be poorly written or that present unfamiliar topics using new vocabulary words.

Struggling readers exhibit a variety of difficulties. Some have ineffective decoding skills or don't read fluently, and others have insufficient vocabulary knowledge or difficulty understanding and remembering the author's message. Still others struggle because they're unfamiliar with English language structures. Figure 11–5 identifies some of the problems that struggling readers face and suggests ways to solve each one. When teachers suspect that a student is struggling, they take action and assess him or her to diagnose any problems, and they intervene if problems are present because expert instruction helps overcome reading difficulties (Snow, Burns, & Griffin, 1998).

Struggling Writers

Many students struggle with writing. It's easy to notice some of their problems when you examine the quality of their compositions: Some students have difficulty developing and organizing ideas, some struggle with word choice and writing complete sentences and effective transitions, and others have problems with spelling, capitalization, punctuation, and grammar skills. Other students struggle with the writing process and using writing strategies effectively. They may be unsure about what writers do as they develop and refine their compositions or the thinking that goes on during writing (Christenson, 2002). There are some students, too, who complain that their hands and arms hurt when they write, some who show little interest and do the bare minimum, and others who are so frustrated with writing that they refuse to write at all. Figure 11–6 lists some of the problems that struggling writers face and suggests ways to address each problem.

Struggling students need to learn more about writing and have more opportunities to practice writing in order to build their confidence and become more successful. Teachers address students' specific problem areas in their instruction, but high-quality instruction usually includes these five components:

Minilessons. Teachers teach students about the writing process, writing strategies and skills, qualities of good writing, and writing genres through **minilessons**. Students often examine anonymous student samples saved from previous years as part of their lessons, use **rubrics** to score these samples, and revise and edit weaker papers to apply what they're learning in the lesson. As part of minilessons, teachers also model how they write and think aloud about how to use writing strategies.

Interactive Writing. Teachers use **interactive writing** to craft a composition that's well developed and mechanically correct. As students take turns writing words and sentences on chart paper, the teacher reviews strategies and skills and monitors each student's knowledge. Students make their own copy as the composition is written on chart paper, which reinforces what they're learning.

Daily Opportunities to Write. Students need opportunities to apply what they're learning about writers and writing and to develop the stamina to see a

Figure 11–5 ◆ Ways to Address Struggling Readers' Problems

Component	Problem	Solutions
Concepts About Print	Student doesn't understand print concepts.	Use the Language Experience Approach to record the student's language and demonstrate concepts about print. Use shared reading and have the student point out examples of print concepts in big books. Have the student dictate and write messages.
Alphabet Knowledge	Student can't name letters or match upper- and lowercase letters.	Examine alphabet books with the student. Identify letters in the student's name and in environmental print. Teach the student to use the ABC song to identify specific letters. Teach the student to use an alphabet chart to identify matching letters. Play matching games with the student. Have the student sort upper- and lowercase letters. Compile an ABC book with the student.
Phonemic Awareness	Student can't manipulate speech sounds.	Sing songs, read poems, and have the student identify rhyming words. Have the student match rhyming picture cards. Pronounce individual sounds in a word and have the student orally blend them into words. Have the student orally segment words into individual sounds using Elkonin boxes. Have the student substitute beginning, medial, and ending sounds in words.
Decoding	Student can't identify high-frequency words.	Make a personal word wall with words the student recognizes. Use a routine to teach and practice high-frequency words. Have the student look for high-frequency words in familiar books. Have the student write words using magnetic letters or on a dry-erase board.
	Student can't identify consonant and vowel sounds.	Have the student sort objects or picture cards according to sounds. Have the student play phonics games, including those online. Have the student substitute initial consonants to create a list of words using a phonogram. Do interactive writing with the student.
	Student can't decode one-syllable words.	Involve the student in making words activities and word ladder games. Have the student spell words using magnetic letters or on a dry-erase board. Teach the student about vowel patterns. Have the student sort word cards according to vowel patterns. Teach the student to decode by analogy. Have the student read and write lists of words created from one phonogram. Do interactive writing with the student.
	Student can't identify multisyllabic words.	Teach a procedure for decoding multisyllabic words. Have the student remove prefixes and suffixes to identify the root word. Brainstorm lists of words from a single root word. Have the student write words with prefixes and suffixes on a dry-erase board. Do interactive writing with the student.
Fluency	Student omits, substitutes, or repeats words when reading.	Teach high-frequency words that the student doesn't know. Ensure that the level of reading materials is appropriate for the student. Have the student read the text quietly before reading it aloud. Have the student reread familiar texts, including big books and classroom charts. Use choral reading in small groups.

	Student reads word by word, without expression.	Have the student practice rereading easier texts to develop fluency. Have the student echo read, imitating the teacher's expression. Have the student do repeated readings. Break the text into phrases for the student to read aloud. Do choral reading in small groups.
Vocabulary	Student doesn't understand the meanings of words.	Create a K-W-L chart or do an anticipation guide before reading. Teach key vocabulary before reading. Have the student sort words from a book being read or a thematic unit. Have the student make diagrams and posters about key words. Read books aloud every day to build the student's vocabulary. Teach idioms, synonyms and antonyms, and word-learning strategies. Use tea party and semantic feature analysis to learn about words.
Comprehension	Student can't retell or answer questions after reading.	Build the student's background knowledge before reading. Ensure that the book is appropriate for the student. Read the book aloud instead of having the student read it. Teach the student how to retell a story. Have the student sequence story boards and use them to retell the story. Set a purpose for reading by having the student read a brief text to find the answer to one literal-level question.
	Student can't draw inferences or do higher-level thinking.	Read the book aloud instead of having the student read it. Do think-alouds to model drawing inferences and higher-level thinking. Teach comprehension strategies. Teach the student about text structure. Use the Questioning the Author procedure. Use QARs to teach the student about types of questions. Involve the student in small-group grand conversations and literature circles.
	Student is a passive reader.	Use the interactive read-aloud procedure. Teach the student to self-select books using the Goldilocks strategy. Teach the comprehension strategies. Have the student read a book with a partner or in a literature circle. To stimulate interest, have the student view the movie version before reading a novel. Involve the student in hot seat, grand conversations, and other participatory activities. Use the Questioning the Author procedure.
Study Skills	Student can't locate information in reference materials.	Teach the student to use an index to locate information. Have the student practice locating information in TV guides, dictionaries, almanacs, and other reference materials. Teach the student to skim and scan to find information in a text. Teach the student to navigate the Web to locate information online.
	Student can't take notes.	Demonstrate how to take notes using a graphic organizer or small self-stick notes. Make a copy of a text and have the student mark the big ideas with a highlighter pen. Have the student identify big ideas and create a graphic organizer to represent them. Have the student work with a partner to take notes on small self-stick notes.

Adapted from McKenna, 2002; Shanker & Cockrum, 2009.

Figure 11–6 ◆ Ways to Address Struggling Writers' Problems

Component	Problem	Solutions
Ideas	Student complains, "I don't know what to write."	Have the student • brainstorm a list of ideas and pick the most promising one. • talk with classmates to get ideas. • draw a picture to develop an idea. Suggest to the student several specific situations related to the assigned topic.
	Composition lacks focus.	After writing a draft, have the student highlight sentences that pertain to the focus, cut the other parts, and elaborate the highlighted ideas. Give the student a very focused assignment. In a minilesson, share samples of unfocused writing for the student to revise.
	Composition lacks interesting details.	Have the student • brainstorm words related to each of the five senses and then add some of the words to the composition. • draw a picture related to the topic of the composition and then add details reflected in the picture. In minilessons, • teach vivid verbs and adjectives. • teach the visualization strategy.
Organization	Composition lacks organization.	Help the student decide on paragraph organization before beginning to write. In minilessons, • teach the concept of "big idea" using many types of texts. • have the student examine the structure of sample compositions.
	Composition is divided into paragraphs, but some sentences in the paragraph don't belong.	Have the student • reread each paragraph, checking that each sentence belongs. • work with a partner to check sentences in each paragraph. In minilessons, • teach paragraph structure. • have the student examine paragraphs and locate sentences that don't belong.
	Composition lacks an exciting lead.	Have the student • try several leads with an experience, a question, a quotation, or a comparison. • get feedback about the effectiveness of the lead in a writing group. In a minilesson, have the student examine the leads in stories and informational books.
	Ideas in the composition aren't sequenced.	Write the sentences on sentence strips for the student to sequence. In a minilesson, teach sequence words, such as *first, next, last*, and *finally*.
	Composition follows a circular pattern.	Have the student create a graphic organizer before beginning to write. Assist the student in identifying the big idea for each paragraph before beginning to write. In a minilesson, teach sequence of ideas.
Word Choice	Composition lacks interesting vocabulary.	Have the student • refer to word walls posted in the classroom for vocabulary. • focus on adding more-interesting vocabulary words during revising. In a minilesson, have the student revise sample compositions to add interesting vocabulary.
Writing Process	Student doesn't reread or revise composition.	In minilessons, • model revision with sample compositions. • compare the quality of unrevised and revised compositions. Include revision as a requirement in the assessment rubric.

	Student doesn't make constructive revisions.	Use writing groups. Conference with the student to examine the revisions during the revising stage. Include substantive revision as a requirement on the assessment rubric. In minilessons, teach and model the types of revision.
	Student plagiarizes.	Use the writing process. Make the student accountable for clusters, graphic organizers, or note cards. Have the student do the research and writing in class, not at home. In a minilesson, teach the student how to take notes and develop a composition.
Mechanics	Composition is difficult to read because of misspelled words.	Have the student • refer to high-frequency and content-area word walls when writing. • edit with a partner. Conference with the student to correct remaining errors in the editing stage. Set high expectations. In minilessons, • teach the student to proofread. • have the student examine and correct errors in sample compositions. Encourage the student to do more reading.
	Composition is difficult to read because of capitalization and punctuation errors.	Have editing partners identify and correct capitalization and punctuation errors. Conference with the student to identify and correct remaining errors during editing. In minilessons, • teach capitalization and punctuation skills. • have the student examine sample compositions for errors and correct them.
	Composition is difficult to read because of grammar errors.	Have editing partners identify and correct grammar errors during the editing stage. Conference with the student to correct remaining errors during editing. In minilessons, • teach grammar concepts. • have the student examine and correct errors in sample compositions.
	Composition has weak sentence structure.	Have editing partners address sentence structure during the editing stage. In minilessons, • teach sentence structure. • teach sentence combining and then have the student practice it.
	Composition is difficult to read because of poor handwriting or messiness.	Have the student • use word processing. • use manuscript rather than cursive handwriting. • try various types of paper and writing instruments. Take the student's dictation, if necessary.
Motivation	Student does the bare minimum.	Conference with the student to determine why he/she is hesitant. Brainstorm ideas with the student during prewriting. In minilessons, • model how to expand a sentence into a paragraph. • have the student practice expanding a brief composition into a better-developed one.
	Student is too dependent on teacher approval.	Have the student • check with a classmate before coming to the teacher. • sign up for conferences with the teacher. Make sure the student understands expectations and procedures.
	Student refuses to write.	Conference with the student to determine and address the problem. Try Language Experience Approach and interactive writing. Have the student write a collaborative composition with a small group or a partner. Keep first writing assignments very short to ensure success.

composition from beginning to end. They also use writing as a tool for learning as they write in reading logs about books they're reading and in learning logs as part of thematic units.

Conferences. Teachers meet with individual students to talk about their writing, the writing process they use, and how they view themselves as writers. They ask questions such as these:

- What's one important thing you've learned about writing?
- What part of writing is easy for you? hard for you?
- How do you decide what changes to make in your writing?
- What would you like to learn next?
- Do you think of yourself as a good writer? Why? Why not?

Through these conversations, students learn to think metacognitively and reflect on the progress they've made.

Daily Opportunities to Read. Students need time to read books at their own reading level, and opportunities to listen to the teacher read aloud high-quality stories and informational books that they can't read independently to develop background knowledge, examine genres, become more strategic, and deepen their knowledge of vocabulary words.

Through a combination of instruction and practice, struggling students become more confident writers, develop stamina, and learn to craft well-organized and interesting compositions that are more mechanically correct.

Working With Struggling Students

Struggling students have significant difficulty learning to read and write. Some students are at risk for reading and writing problems in kindergarten and first grade, but others develop difficulties in fourth or fifth grade or even later. The best way to help these students is to prevent their difficulties in the first place by providing high-quality classroom instruction and adding an intervention, if it's needed (Cooper, Chard, & Kiger, 2006). Unfortunately, there's no quick fix for low-achieving students. Helping struggling students requires both high-quality classroom instruction and "a comprehensive and sustained intervention effort" (Allington, 2006, p. 141).

High-Quality Classroom Instruction. Teachers use a balanced approach to literacy that combines explicit instruction in decoding, fluency, vocabulary, comprehension, and writing along with daily opportunities for students to apply what they're learning in authentic literacy activities (Allington, 2006). It's standards driven and incorporates research-based procedures and activities. Teachers address these four components to enhance the literacy development of all students, including struggling readers and writers:

Differentiate instruction. Teachers adjust their instructional programs to match student needs using flexible grouping, tiered activities, and respectful tasks (Opitz & Ford, 2008). Results of ongoing assessment are used to vary instructional content, process, and assignments according to students' developmental levels, interests, and learning styles.

Use appropriate instructional materials. Most of the time, students read interesting books written at their reading levels in small groups or individually. Teachers usually have plenty of books available for on-grade-level readers, but finding appropriate books for struggling readers can be difficult. Figure 11–7 presents a list of easy-to-read paperback series for older struggling students. Teachers also choose award-winning books for literature focus units, but even though these "teaching-texts" are important, Allington (2006) recommends using a single text with the whole class only 25% of the time because students need more opportunities to read books at their reading levels.

Expand teachers' expertise. Teachers continue to grow professionally during their careers (Allington, 2006): They join professional organizations, participate in professional book clubs, attend workshops and conferences, and find answers to questions that puzzle them through teacher-inquiry projects. Figure 11–8 outlines some ways that teachers stretch their knowledge and teaching expertise.

Collaborate with literacy coaches. Literacy coaches are experienced teachers with special expertise in working with struggling readers and writers who support teachers (Casey, 2006). They work alongside teachers in their classrooms, demonstrating instructional procedures and evaluation techniques, and they collaborate with teachers to design instruction to address students' needs. Toll (2005) explains that "literacy coaching is not about telling others what to do, but rather bringing out the best in others" (p. 6). Through their efforts, teachers are becoming more expert, and schools are becoming better learning environments.

The quality of classroom instruction has a tremendous impact on how well students learn to read and write, and studies of exemplary teachers indicate that teaching expertise is the critical factor (Block, Oakar, & Hurt, 2002).

Interventions. Schools use intervention programs to address low-achieving students' reading and writing difficulties and accelerate their literacy learning (Cooper, Chard, & Kiger, 2006). They're used in addition to regular classroom instruction, not as a replacement for it. The classroom teacher or a specially trained reading teacher meets with struggling students on a daily basis. Using paraprofessionals is a widespread practice but not recommended because they aren't as effective as certified teachers (Allington, 2006). During interventions, teachers provide intensive, expert instruction to individuals or very small groups of no more than three students. Interventions take various forms: They can be provided by adding a second lesson during the regular school day, offering extra instruction in an after-school program, or holding extended-school-year programs during the summer. Figure 11–9 summarizes the recommendations for effective intervention programs.

Until recently, most interventions were designed for students in fourth through eighth grades who were already failing; now the focus has changed to early intervention to eliminate the pattern of school failure that begins early and persists throughout some students' lives (Strickland, 2002). Three types of interventions for preschoolers and students in the primary grades have been developed:

◆ Preventive programs to create more-effective early-childhood programs
◆ Family-focused programs to develop young children's awareness of literacy, parents' literacy, and parenting skills
◆ Early interventions to resolve reading and writing problems and accelerate literacy development for low-achieving K–3 students

Intervention programs still exist, of course, for older low-achieving students, but teachers are optimistic that earlier and more-intensive intervention will solve many of the difficulties that older students exhibit today.

Figure 11-7 ◆ Easy-to-Read Paperback Series

Reading Level	Series	Genre
2	A to Z Mysteries by Ron Roy (Random House)	Mystery
	Andrew Lost by J. C. Greenburg (Random House)	Informational
	Cam Jansen by David A. Adler (Puffin)	Adventure
	Jigsaw Jones Mysteries by James Preller (Scholastic)	Mystery
	Magic Tree House by Mary Pope Osborne (Random House)	Adventure
	Marvin Redpost by Louis Sachar (Random House)	Adventure
	Ricky Ricotta's Mighty Robots by Dav Pilkey (Scholastic)	Science Fiction
	Scooby-Do Mysteries by James Golsey (Scholastic)	Mystery
	The Zack Files (some are third-grade level) by Dan Greenburg (Grosset & Dunlap)	Fantasy
3	Abracadabra! by Peter Lerangis (Scholastic)	Mystery
	The Adventures of the Bailey School Kids by Debbie Dadey and Marcia Thornton Jones (Scholastic)	Adventure
	The Boxcar Children by Gertrude Chandler Warner (Albert Whitman)	Mystery
	Captain Underpants by Dav Pilkey (Scholastic)	Humor
	Hank the Cowdog by John R. Erickson (Puffin)	Fantasy
	The Magic School Bus Chapter Books by Joanna Cole (Scholastic)	Informational
	The Secrets of Droon by Tony Abbott (Scholastic)	Fantasy
	Sports by Matt Christopher (Little, Brown)	Sports
	The Unicorn's Secret by Kathleen Duey (Aladdin)	Fantasy
	The Zack Files (some are second-grade level) by Dan Greenburg (Grosset & Dunlap)	Fantasy
4	Animal Ark by Ben M. Baglio (Scholastic)	Animals
	The Babysitters Club by Ann M. Martin (Scholastic)	Adventure
	Deltora Quest by Emily Rodda (Scholastic)	Fantasy
	Dolphin Diaries by Ben M. Baglio (Scholastic)	Animals
	Encyclopedia Brown by Donald J. Sobol (Dutton)	Mystery
	Goosebumps by R. L. Stine (Scholastic)	Horror
	Guardians of Ga'hoole by Kathryn Lasky (Scholastic)	Fantasy
	Island/Everest/Dive Series by Gordon Korman (Scholastic)	Adventure
	Pyrates by Chris Archer (Scholastic)	Adventure
	The Time Warp Trio by Jon Scieszka (Puffin)	Fantasy
5	The Amazing Days of Abby Hayes by Anne Mazer (Scholastic)	Contemporary
	Animorphs by K. A. Applegate (Scholastic)	Science Fiction
	The Black Stallion by Walter Farley (Random House)	Animals
	Dinotopia by Peter David (Random House)	Science Fiction
	From the Files of Madison Finn by Laura Dower (Hyperion)	Contemporary
	Heartland by Lauren Brooke (Scholastic)	Animals
	The Saddle Club by Bonnie Bryant (Random House)	Animals
	Thoroughbred by Joanna Campbell (HarperCollins)	Animals

To prevent literacy problems and break the cycle of poverty in the United States, the federal government directs two early-intervention programs for economically disadvantaged children and their parents. The best-known program is Head Start, which began more than 40 years ago as part of President Lyndon Johnson's War on Poverty. It currently serves nearly one million children and their families each year. Young children grow rapidly in their knowledge of concepts about print and their understanding of literacy behaviors, but these remarkable gains aren't usually sustained after children start school. A newer program that began as part of the No Child Left Behind legislation is the Even Start Family Literacy Program, which integrates early-childhood education and literacy instruction for parents into one program.

Figure 11–8 ◆ Ways to Develop Professional Knowledge and Expertise

Professional Organizations

International Reading Association (IRA)
www.reading.org

National Council of Teachers of English (NCTE)
www.ncte.org

Teachers of English to Speakers of Other Languages (TESOL)
www.tesol.org

Journals

Journal of Adolescent and Adult Literacy (IRA)
Reading Online (www.readingonline.org) (IRA)
The Reading Teacher (IRA)

Language Arts (NCTE)
Voices From the Middle (NCTE)

Essential Teacher (TESOL)
The Internet TESOL Journal (iteslj.org) (TESOL)

Professional Books

Teachers read books about research-based instructional strategies, current issues, and innovative practices published by IRA, NCTE, TESOL, Heinemann, Scholastic, Stenhouse, and other publishers.

Literacy Workshops and Conferences

Teachers attend local, state, and national conferences sponsored by IRA, NCTE, and TESOL to learn more about teaching reading and writing, and they also attend workshops sponsored by local sites affiliated with the National Writing Project (NWP).

Collaboration

Teachers at one grade level or at one school can participate in teacher book clubs, view videos about classroom practices, and discuss ways to improve teaching and meet the needs of their students.

Teacher-Inquiry Projects

To learn how to conduct teacher research, consult one of these books: *The Art of Classroom Inquiry: A Handbook for Teacher-Researchers* (Hubbard & Power, 2003), *The Power of Questions: A Guide to Teacher and Student Research* (Falk & Blumenreich, 2005), and *What Works? A Practical Guide for Teacher Research* (Chiseri-Strater & Sunstein, 2006).

National Writing Project

Teachers attend programs at local National Writing Project sites and apply to participate at invitational summer institutes. To locate the nearest NWP site, check their website at www.nwp.org.

Figure 11–9 ◆ High-Quality Interventions

Scheduling
Interventions take place daily for 20–45 minutes, depending on students' age and instructional needs. Classroom teachers often provide the interventions as second reading lessons in the classroom or during after-school programs, but at other times, specially trained reading teachers provide the interventions.

Grouping
Teachers work with students individually or in small groups of no more than three students; larger groups of students, even when they exhibit the same reading or writing problems, aren't as effective.

Reading Materials
Teachers match students to books at their instructional level for lessons and at their independent level for voluntary reading. The reading materials should engage students and provide some challenge without frustrating them.

Instruction
Teachers provide lessons that generally include rereading familiar books, reading new books, word study (phonics, word identification, and vocabulary), and writing activities. The content of the lessons varies according to students' identified areas of difficulty.

Reading and Writing Practice
Teachers provide additional opportunities for students to spend time reading and writing to practice and apply what they're learning.

Assessment
Teachers monitor progress on an ongoing basis by observing students and collecting work samples. They also use diagnostic tests to document students' learning according to grade-level standards.

Professional Development
Teachers continue their professional development to improve their teaching expertise, and they ensure that the aides and volunteers who work in their classroom are well trained.

Home–School Partnerships
Teachers keep parents informed about students' progress and involve them in supporting independent reading and writing at home.

Two important school-based interventions are Reading Recovery® and Response to Intervention. These are early interventions that quickly identify students who are at risk of failing to avoid long-term reading and writing problems.

Reading Recovery is the most widely known intervention program for the lowest-achieving first graders (Clay, 1993, 2005a, 2005b). It involves 30-minute daily one-on-one tutoring by specifically trained and supervised teachers for 12 to 30 weeks. Reading Recovery lessons involve these components:

Rereading familiar books
Independently reading the book introduced in the previous lesson
Teaching decoding and comprehension strategies
Writing sentences
Reading a new book with teacher support

Once students reach grade-level standards and demonstrate that they can work independently in their classroom, they leave the program. The results of the intervention are impressive: 75% of students who complete the Reading Recovery program meet grade-level literacy standards and continue to be successful.

Response to Intervention (RTI) is a promising schoolwide initiative to identify struggling students quickly, promote effective classroom instruction, provide interventions, and increase the likelihood that students will be successful (Mellard & Johnson, 2008). It involves three tiers:

Tier 1: Screening and Prevention. Teachers provide high-quality instruction that's supported by scientifically based research, screen students to identify those at risk for academic failure, and monitor their progress. If students don't make adequate progress toward meeting grade-level standards, they move to Tier 2.

Tier 2: Early Intervention. Trained reading teachers provide enhanced, individualized instruction targeting students' specific areas of difficulty. If the intervention is successful and students' reading problems are resolved, they return to Tier 1; if they make some progress but need additional instruction, they remain in Tier 2; and if they don't show improvement, they move to Tier 3, where the intensity of intervention increases.

Tier 3: Intensive Intervention. Special education teachers provide more-intensive intervention to individual students and small groups and more-frequent progress monitoring. They focus on remedying students' problem areas and teaching compensatory strategies.

This schoolwide instruction and assessment program incorporates data-driven decision making, and special education teachers are optimistic that it will be a better way to diagnose learning-disabled students.

Improving classroom instruction, diagnosing students' specific reading and writing difficulties, and implementing intensive intervention programs to remedy students' literacy problems are three important ways that teachers work more effectively with struggling students. Research-based interventions, such as Reading Recovery and Response to Intervention, are changing the ways teachers work with students who struggle.

Chapter 11 Review

How Effective Teachers Differentiate Literacy Instruction

▶ Teachers differentiate instruction to meet the needs of all students, including those who struggle.

▶ Teachers understand that struggling readers have difficulties in decoding, fluency, vocabulary, and/or comprehension.

▶ Teachers understand that struggling writers lack knowledge about the qualities of good writing and the process that writers use.

▶ Teachers use a balanced approach to teach struggling students that incorporates explicit instruction, materials at students' reading levels, and more time for reading and writing.

▶ Teachers understand that interventions are additional instructional programs to remedy students' reading and writing difficulties.

Go to MyEducationLab at www.myeducationlab.com to deepen your understanding of the concepts presented in this chapter:

► Examine how Ms. Janusz uses grouping to enhance learning in her second-grade classroom by viewing video segments in the Literacy Portraits.
► Check your understanding of chapter concepts with the multiple-choice and essay quizzes in the Study Plan.
► Apply some of the main ideas discussed in the chapter in the Activities and Applications section of the website.
► Practice what you've learned in this chapter in Building Teaching Skills and Dispositions before applying the ideas in your own classroom.

PROFESSIONAL REFERENCES

Allington, R. L. (2006). *What really matter for struggling readers: Designing research-based programs* (2nd ed.). Boston: Allyn & Bacon.

Block, C., Oakar, M., & Hurt, N. (2002). The expertise of literacy teachers: A continuum from preschool–grade 5. *Reading Research Quarterly, 37,* 178–206.

Casey, K. (2006). *Literacy coaching: The essentials.* Portsmouth, NH: Heinemann.

Chall, J. S., & Jacobs, V. A. (2003). Poor children's fourth-grade slump. *American Educator, 27*(1), 14–15, 44.

Chiseri-Strater, E., & Sunstein, B. S. (2006). *What works? A practical guide for teacher research.* Portsmouth, NH: Heinemann.

Christenson, T. A. (2002). *Supporting struggling writers in the elementary classroom.* Newark, DE: International Reading Association.

Clay, M. M. (1993). *Reading Recovery: A guidebook for teachers in training.* Portsmouth, NH: Heinemann.

Clay, M. M. (2005a). *Literacy lessons: Designed for individuals (Part 1: Why? when? and how?).* Portsmouth, NH: Heinemann.

Clay, M. M. (2005b). *Literacy lessons: Designed for individuals (Part 2: Teaching procedures).* Portsmouth, NH: Heinemann.

Cooper, J. D., Chard, D. J., & Kiger, N. D. (2006). *The struggling reader: Interventions that work.* New York: Scholastic.

Falk, B., & Blumenreich, M. (2005). *The power of questions: A guide to teacher and student research.* Portsmouth, NH: Heinemann.

Fink, R. (2006). *Why Jane and John couldn't read—and how they learned: A new look at striving readers.* Newark, DE: International Reading Association.

Fountas, I. C., & Pinnell, G. S. (1996). *Guided reading: Good first teaching for all children.* Portsmouth, NH: Heinemann.

Fountas, I. C., & Pinnell, G. S. (2001). *Guiding readers and writers, grades 3–6.* Portsmouth, NH. Heinemann.

Heacox, D. (2002). *Differentiating instruction in the regular classroom: How to reach and teach all learners, grades 3–12.* Minneapolis, MN: Free Spirit Publishing.

Holmes, C. T., & Brown, C. L. (2003). *A controlled evaluation of a total school improvement process, School Renaissance* (Technical report). Athens: University of Georgia.

Hubbard, R. S., & Power, B. M. (2003). *The art of classroom inquiry: A handbook for teacher-researchers* (rev. ed.). Portsmouth, NH: Heinemann.

McKenna, M. C. (2002). *Help for struggling readers: Strategies for grades 3–8.* New York: Guilford Press.

Mellard, D. F., & Johnson, E. (2008). *RTI: A practitioner's guide to implementing Response to Intervention.* Thousand Oaks, CA: Corwin Press and the National Association of Elementary School Principals.

Mortenson, G., & Relin, D. O. (2007). *Three cups of tea: One man's mission to promote peace . . . one school at a time.* New York: Penguin.

Opitz, M. F., & Ford, M. P. (2008). *Do-able differentiation: Varying groups, texts, and supports to reach readers.* Portsmouth, NH: Heinemann.

Robb, L. (2008). *Differentiating reading instruction: How to teach reading to meet the needs of each student.* New York: Scholastic.

Schmidt, R. (2008). Really reading: What does Accelerated Reader teach adults and children? *Language Arts, 85,* 202–211.

Shanker, J. L., & Cockrum W. (2009). *Locating and correcting reading difficulties* (9th ed.). Boston: Allyn & Bacon/Pearson.

Snow, C., Burns, S., & Griffin, P. (Eds.). (1998). *Preventing reading difficulties in young children.* Washington, DC: National Academy Press.

Strickland, D. S. (2002). The importance of effective early intervention. In A. E. Farstrup & S. J. Samuels (Eds.), *What research has to say about reading instruction* (3rd ed., pp. 261–290). Newark, DE: International Reading Association.

Toll, C. A. (2005). *The literacy coach's survival guide: Essential questions and practical answers*. Newark, DE: International Reading Association.

Tomlinson, C. A. (2001). *The differentiated classroom: Responding to the needs of all learners* (2nd ed.). Alexandria, VA: Association for Supervision and Curriculum Development.

Topping, K. J., & Paul, T. D. (1999). Computer-assisted assessment of practice at reading: A large scale survey using Accelerated Reader data. *Reading & Writing Quarterly, 15,* 213–231.

Yatvin, J. (2004). *A room with a differentiated view: How to serve ALL children as individual learners*. Portsmouth, NH: Heinemann.

CHILDREN'S BOOK REFERENCES

Ellis, D. (2001). *The breadwinner*. Toronto: Groundwood Books.

Greenburg, D. (2000). *How I went from bad to verse*. New York: Grosset & Dunlap.

Nye, N. S. (Compiler). (2002a). *The flag of childhood: Poems from the Middle East*. New York: Aladdin Books.

Nye, N. S. (2002b). *19 varieties of gazelle: Poems of the Middle East*. New York: Greenwillow.

Ryan, P. M. (1998). *Riding Freedom*. New York: Scholastic.

Scieszka, J. (2004a). *Knights of the kitchen table*. New York: Puffin Books.

Scieszka, J. (2004b). *Tut tut*. New York: Puffin Books.

Scieszka, J. (2004c). *Your mother was a neanderthal*. New York: Puffin Books.

CHAPTER 12

Reading and Writing in the Content Areas

Mrs. Zumwalt's Third Graders Create Multigenre Projects

Mrs. Zumwalt's third graders are studying ocean animals, and her focus is adaptation: How do animals adapt to survive in the ocean? As her students learn about ocean life, they take special notice of how individual animals adapt. For example, Alyssa learns that whelks have hard shells to protect them, Aidan knows that some small fish travel together in schools, Cody reports that clams burrow into the sand to be safe, and Christopher read that sea otters have thick fur to keep them warm in the cold ocean water. Students add what they're learning about adaptation to a chart hanging in the classroom.

A month ago, Mrs. Zumwalt began the thematic unit by passing out a collection of informational picture books from the text set on ocean animals for students to peruse. After they examined the books and read excerpts for 30 minutes or so, she brought them together to begin a **K-W-L chart**. This huge chart covers half of the back wall of the classroom; three sheets of poster paper hang vertically, side by side. The sheet on the left is labeled "K—What We Know About Ocean Animals." The middle sheet is labeled "W—What We Wonder About Ocean Animals," and the one on the right is labeled "L—What We Learned About

Ocean Animals." Mrs. Zumwalt asked what students already knew about ocean animals, and they offered many facts, including "sea stars can grow a lot of arms," "sharks have three rows of teeth," and "jellyfish and puffer fish are poisonous," which Mrs. Zumwalt recorded in the K column. They also asked questions, including "How can an animal live inside a jellyfish?" "Is it true that father seahorses give birth?" and "How do some fish light up?" which she wrote in the W column. Students continued to think of questions for several days, and Mrs. Zumwalt added them to the W column. At the end of the unit, students will add facts they've learned to the L column.

Mrs. Zumwalt talked about the six ocean habitats—seashore, open ocean, deep ocean, seabed, coral reefs, and polar seas—and the animals living in each one. She began with the seashore, and the students took a field trip to the Monterey Bay Aquarium to learn about the animals that live at the seashore. She focused on several animals in each habitat, reading aloud books and emphasizing how animals have adapted. For each habitat, they made a class chart about it, and students recorded information in their learning logs. They hung the charts in the classroom, and after all six habitats were introduced, Mrs. Zumwalt set out a pack of cards with names of animals and pictures of them for students to sort according to habitat. The box on page 388 shows the habitat sort.

Students have **learning logs** with 20 sheets of lined paper for writing, 10 sheets of unlined paper for drawing and charting, and 15 information sheets about ocean animals. There's also a page for a personal word wall that's divided into nine boxes and labeled with letters of the alphabet; students record words from the class **word wall** on their personal word walls. Mrs. Zumwalt introduces new words during her presentations and as she reads aloud books from the text set on ocean animals; then she adds them to the word wall.

Eight of her 20 third graders come from homes where Spanish is spoken, and these students struggle with oral and written English. Mrs. Zumwalt brings them together most days for an extra lesson while their classmates work on other activities. She either previews the next lesson she'll teach or the next book she'll read or reviews her last lesson or the last book she read. In this small-group setting, students talk about what they're learning, ask questions, examine artifacts and pictures, and practice vocabulary. They often create **interactive writing** charts to share what they've discussed with their classmates. Here is their chart about schools of fish:

> *There are two kinds of schools. Kids go to school to be smart and little fish travel in groups that are called "schools." Fish are safer when they stick together in schools.*

Once the class became familiar with a variety of ocean animals, each student picked a favorite animal to study. They chose sting rays, dolphins, squids, sea anenomes, sand dollars, great white sharks, seals, penguins, sea turtles, jellyfish, octopuses, seahorses, pelicans, killer whales, barracudas, tunas, electric eels, lobsters, manatees, and squid. They researched their animals using the Internet and books in the text set; one of their best

Ocean Habitat Sort

Seashore	Open Ocean	Deep Ocean	Seabed	Coral Reefs	Polar Seas
shrimp	puffer fish	nautilus	sting ray	sea fan	penguin
sea gull	swordfish	sperm whale	nurse shark	coral	narwhal
sea otter	sea turtles		clam	barracuda	elephant seal
crab	manta ray		scallop		walrus
lobster	porpoise		sponge		leopard seal
octopus	dolphin		whelk		krill
pelican	squid				

resources was the 11-volume encyclopedia *Aquatic Life of the World* (2001). Once they became experts, Mrs. Zumwalt introduced the idea of developing multigenre projects about the animals they'd studied. In multigenre projects, students create a variety of items representing different genres and package them in a box, on a display board, or in a notebook. Earlier in the year, the students worked collaboratively to develop a class multigenre project, so they were familiar with the procedure and format.

The students decided to create four items for their multigenre projects: an informational book with chapters about their animal's physical traits, diet, habitat, and enemies together with three other items. Other possible items included an adaptation poster, a life-cycle chart, a poem, an alliterative sentence, a diagram of the animal, and a pack of true/false cards about the animal. They plan to package their projects in cereal boxes brought from home and decorated with pictures, interesting information, and a big idea statement about how that animal has adapted to ocean life.

The third graders used the writing process to prepare their informational books. These students know how writers develop, draft, and refine their writing, and earlier in the year, they developed charts describing each stage of the writing process that now hang in the classroom. For prewriting, they used large, multicolored index cards to jot notes; the green one is for "Physical Traits," the yellow one is for "Diet," the blue one is for "Habitat," the purple one is for "Enemies," and the pink one is for other interesting information.

After students took notes using book resources from the text set and Internet resources, they shared the information they'd gathered one-on-one with classmates, who asked questions about things that confused them and encouraged the students to add more information about incomplete topics. Next, students wrote rough drafts and shared them with the partners they worked with earlier. Then they met in **writing groups** with Mrs. Zumwalt and several classmates and refined their drafts using the feedback they received from their group.

Now students are proofreading and correcting their revised drafts and creating published books. Once they correct the mechanical errors and meet with Mrs. Zumwalt for an editing conference, they recopy their drafts in their best handwriting, add illustrations, and compile the pages into a hardbound book. They're also preparing their boxes and the other items for their multigenre projects.

Christian researched pelicans; his informational book is shown here. For his other three items, he drew a life-cycle chart showing a pelican egg, a newly hatched bird in the nest, a young adult bird flapping its wings, and an older adult diving into the ocean for food; he made a Venn diagram comparing white and brown pelicans; and he wrote an alliterative sentence about pelicans using only words that begin with *p*. His multigenre project box is decorated with pictures of pelicans and interesting information he collected, including "their wings are nine feet long" and "pelicans can live to be 25 years old." The adaptation statement on his multigenre box reads, "Pelicans have web feet and they can dive underwater to catch their food to eat. That's how they can survive at the seashore."

Today, the students finish the **K-W-L chart** by adding comments about what they've learned about ocean animals. Cody offers that "octopuses can change shape

---

Christian's Informational Book About Pelicans

Chapter 1
Introduction
Pelicans are birds that live on the seashore. They have web feet for walking on sand and swimming. They can dive underwater to catch their food. That's how they live near the ocean.

Chapter 2
Physical Traits
Pelicans have some interesting physical traits. The pelican is easy to identify. They have big pouches and you can tell them by their big necks and plump bodies. The pelican has big legs and colors brown and white.

Chapter 3
Diet
Diet is what an animal eats. The pelican swallows a lot of fish. Pelicans gobble up meat. Pelicans attack sea stars and they chomp on seahorses.

Chapter 4
Habitat
A habitat is where an animal lives. The pelican lives in many countries. Pelicans are found where there's air and where it's warm. Some pelicans are now living in Monterey. Pelicans live by water, too.

Chapter 5
Enemies
Most animals are both prey and predator. That means animals are usually both the hunted and the hunter. The pelican eats seahorses and sea stars. Pelicans are hunted by sharks and people. Why do people hurt these birds? People dump waste into the water and it kills the fishes that the pelicans eat!

Chapter 6
Conclusion
I hope pelicans will always live in Monterey Bay but they could die if people dump pollution into the ocean and that would be very sad.

and color to camouflage themselves," Hernan reports that "dolphins' tails go up and down and fishes' tails go side to side," and Carlos adds that "jellyfish are related to sea anemones because neither one has teeth."

Next Monday afternoon, the third graders will share their completed multigenre boxes one-on-one with second graders, and that evening, they'll share them with their parents at back-to-school night. In preparation for this sharing, the students have been taking turns sharing their projects in the classroom. Each day, three students sit in the author's chair to show their projects and read their informational books aloud to the class.

S tudents read and write all through the school day as they learn science, social studies, and other content areas. Just as Mrs. Zumwalt's third graders learned about ocean animals through reading and writing, students at all grade levels— even kindergartners and first graders—use reading and writing as tools to learn about insects, the water cycle, pioneers, astronomy, and World War II. Teachers organize content-area study into thematic units and identify big ideas to investigate. Units are time-consuming because student-constructed learning takes time. Teachers can't try to cover every topic; if they do, their students will learn very little. Instead, teachers make careful choices as they plan units, because only a relatively few topics can be presented in depth during a school year. During thematic units, students need opportunities to question, discuss, explore, and apply what they're learning (Harvey, 1998).

Content-area textbooks are important resources that students use to learn about social studies, science, and other content areas, but they aren't a complete instructional program. Students need to know how to read content-area textbooks because these books differ from other reading materials: They have unique conventions and structures that students use as aids in reading and remembering the big ideas. Because many students find textbooks more challenging to read than other books, teachers need to know how to support their students' reading so that they will be successful.

CONNECTING READING AND WRITING

Reading and writing should be connected because reading has a powerful impact on writing, and vice versa (Tierney & Shanahan, 1996): When students read about a topic before writing, their writing is enhanced because of what they learn about the topic, and when they write about the ideas in a book they're reading, their comprehension is deepened because they're exploring big ideas and relationships among ideas. Making this connection is especially important when students are learning content-area information because of the added challenges that unfamiliar topics and technical vocabulary present.

There are other reasons for connecting reading and writing, too. Making meaning is the goal of both reading and writing: Students activate background knowledge, set purposes, and use many of the same strategies for reading and writing. In addition, the reading and writing processes are remarkably similar.

Reading Trade Books

A wide variety of high-quality picture books and chapter books are available today for teachers to use in teaching thematic units. Two outstanding science-related trade books, for example, are *Team Moon: How 400,000 People Landed Apollo 11 on the Moon* (Thimmesh, 2006), a stunning book that highlights the contributions of the people working behind the scenes on that space mission, and *Oh, Rats! The Story of Rats and People* (Marrin, 2006), a riveting book of facts about a champion of survival. Two notable trade books on social studies topics are *Freedom Riders: John Lewis and Jim Zwerg on the Front Lines of the Civil Rights Movement* (Bausum, 2006), a powerful book that contrasts black America and white America in the 1960s by tracing the journeys of two young men, and *One Thousand Tracings: Healing the Wounds of World War II* (Judge, 2007), a moving picture-book story of an American family who started a relief effort that reached 3,000 people in war-ravaged Europe. These books are entertaining and informative, and the authors' engaging writing styles and formats keep readers interested. They're relevant, too, because many students make connections to their own life experiences and background knowledge as they read these books, and teachers use them to build students' background knowledge at the beginning of a thematic unit.

Teachers share these trade books with students in many ways. They use **interactive read-alouds** to share some books that are too difficult for students to read on their own, and they feature others in literature focus units. They use related books at a range of reading levels for literature circles, and others for students to read independently during reading workshop. Because many books on social studies and science topics are available at a range of reading levels, teachers can find good books, many at their students' reading levels, to use in teaching in the content areas.

> Check the Compendium of Instructional Procedures, which follows this chapter, for more information on the highlighted terms.

Text Sets. Teachers collect text sets of books and other reading materials on topics to use in teaching thematic units, as Mrs. Zumwalt did in the vignette at the beginning of the chapter. Materials for text sets are carefully chosen to include different genres, a range of reading levels to meet the needs of all students in the class, and multimedia resources that present a variety of perspectives. It's especially important to include plenty of books and other materials that English learners and struggling readers can read (Robb, 2002).

Teachers collect as many different types of materials as possible, for example:

stories	newspaper articles
informational books	magazines
poems and songs	photographs
reference books	copies of primary source materials
encyclopedias	atlases and maps
websites and webquests	brochures and pamphlets
films and videos	models and diagrams

They collect single copies of some books and multiple copies of others to use for literature focus units and literature circles. Too often, teachers don't think about using magazines to teach social studies and science, but many excellent magazines are available, including *Click* and *National Geographic Explorer* for young children and *Cobblestone* and *Time for Kids* for older students. Some magazines are also available online, including *Time for Kids*. Figure 12–1 presents a list of print and online magazines for K–8 students.

Mentor Texts. Teachers use stories, informational books, and poems that students are familiar with to model quality writing (Dorfman & Cappelli, 2007). Picture books are especially useful mentor texts because they're short enough to be reread quickly. Teachers begin by rereading a mentor text and pointing out a specific feature such as adding punch with strong verbs, writing from a different perspective, or changing the tone by placing adjectives after nouns. Then students imitate the feature in brief collaborative compositions and in their own writing. Students have opportunities to experiment with literary devices, imitate sentence and book structures, try out new genres, or explore different page arrangements.

Informational books are often used as mentor texts to teach students about new genres, organizational structures, and page formats. For example, *Gone Wild: An Endangered Animal Alphabet* (McLimans, 2006) is a graphic masterpiece where letters

Figure 12–1 ◆ Magazines for Children and Adolescents	
Format	**Magazines**
Print	*Appleseeds* (social studies) (M–U)
	Calliope (history) (M–U)
	Click (science) (P)
	Cobblestone (history) (M–U)
	Cricket (stories) (M–U)
	Dig (archeology) (M–U)
	Faces: People, Places, Cultures (multicultural) (M–U)
	Kids Discover (science and history themes) (M–U)
	Ladybug (stories, poems, and songs) (P)
	Muse (science and the arts) (M–U)
	National Geographic Explorer (geography and culture) (P)
	National Geographic for Kids (geography and culture) (M–U)
	Odyssey (science) (M–U)
	OWL (science) (U)
	Ranger Rick (nature) (M)
	Skipping Stones (multicultural) (M–U)
	Spider (stories and poems) (P–M)
	Sports Illustrated for Kids (sports) (M–U)
	Time for Kids (current events) (M–U)
	Your Big Backyard (nature) (P)
Online	*CobblestoneOnline.net* www.cobblestoneonline.net (history, social studies, science) (M–U)
	Dig www.digonsite.com (archeology) (M–U)
	Kids Newsroom www.kidsnewsroom.org (current events) (P–M)
	KidsPost www.washingtonpost.com/wp-srv/kidspost/orbit/kidspost.html (current events) (M–U)
	National Geographic for Kids www.kids.nationalgeographic.com (geography and culture) (M–U)
	Odyssey www.odysseymagazine.com (science) (M)
	OWL owlkids.com/ (science) (M–U)
	Ranger Rick www.nwf.org/rangerrick/ (nature) (M)
	Sports Illustrated for Kids www.sikids.com/ (sports) (M–U)
	Time for Kids www.timeforkids.com/ (current events) (M–U)
	Your Big Backyard www.nwf.org/kidzone/ (nature) (P)
P = primary grades (K–2); M = middle grades (3–5); U = upper grades (6–8)	

Text Sets
These eighth graders are reading a novel as part of a text set about the Civil War. As they read, they enjoy the story and learn information at the same time. Other books in the text set include informational books and their social studies textbook. After finishing the novel, the students will preview the unit in their textbook, read other books in the text set, and then return to the textbook to read it thoroughly. The text set helps students expand their knowledge base about the Civil War, prepares them to read the textbook, and extends their learning.

of the alphabet are transformed into vulnerable animals and text boxes accompanying each letter provide information about the animal. Students can use the format of *Gone Wild* to write a class alphabet book during a science or social studies unit. Another excellent mentor text is *Good Masters! Sweet Ladies! Voices From a Medieval Village* (Schlitz, 2007), a collection of 23 first-person character sketches of young people living in an English village in 1255. Each character has a distinct personality and societal role, and historical notes are included in the margins. This book was designed as a play or a **readers theatre** presentation. During a unit on ancient Rome or World War II, for example, students can use this mentor text to write their own collection of character sketches and present them for students in other classrooms or their parents.

Teachers use mentor texts in **minilessons** to teach students how to make their writing more powerful, and students use these books as springboards for writing as part of thematic units. Dorfman and Cappelli (2007) explain that "mentor texts serve as snapshots into the future. They help students envision the kind of writers they can become" (p. 3).

Writing as a Learning Tool

Students use writing as a tool for learning during thematic units to take notes, categorize ideas, draw graphic organizers, and write summaries. The focus is on using writing to help students think and learn, not on spelling every word correctly. Nevertheless, students should use classroom resources, such as **word walls**, to spell most words correctly and write as neatly as possible so that they can reread their own writing. Armbruster, McCarthey, and Cummins (2005) also point out that writing to learn serves two other purposes as well: When students write about what they're learning, it helps them become better writers, and teachers can use students' writing to assess their learning.

Figure 12–2 ◆ A Page From a Second Grader's
Learning Log on Penguins

Learning Logs. Students use learning logs to record and react to what they are learning in social studies, science, or other content areas. Laura Robb (2003) explains that learning logs are "a place to think on paper" (p. 60). Students write in these journals to discover gaps in their knowledge and to explore relationships between what they're learning and their past experiences. Through these activities, students practice taking notes, writing descriptions and directions, and making graphic organizers. Figure 12–2 presents a page from a second grader's learning log about penguins. The chart shows that penguins have three enemies—leopard seals, skua gulls, and people.

Double-Entry Journals. Double-entry journals are just what the name suggests: Students divide their journal pages into two parts and write different types of information in each part (Daniels & Zemelman, 2004). They write important facts in one column and their reactions to the facts in the other column, or questions about the topic in the left column and answers in the right column. Figure 12–3 shows a sixth grader's double-entry journal written during a unit on drug prevention. In the left column, the student wrote information she was learning, and in the right column, she made personal connections to the information.

Simulated Journals. In some stories, such as *Catherine, Called Birdy* (Cushman, 1994), the author assumes the role of a character and writes a series of diary entries from the character's point of view. Here is an excerpt from one of Birdy's entries, which describes life in the Middle Ages:

12th Day of October

No more sewing and spinning and goose fat for me! Today my life is changed. How it came about is this:

We arrived at the abbey soon after dinner, stopping just outside the entry gate at the guest-house next to the mill. The jouncing cart did my stomach no kindness after jellied eel and potted lamb, so I was most relieved to alight. (Cushman, 1994, p. 25)

These books can be called *simulated journals*. They are rich with historical details and feature examples of both the vocabulary and the sentence structure of the period.

Figure 12–3 ◆ A Page From a Sixth Grader's Double-Entry Journal

DRUGS

Take notes

pot affects your brain
mariquania is a ilegal drug and does things to your lungs makes you forget things.
Affects your brain

Crack and coacain is illegal a small pipeful can cause death. It can cause heart atachs.
is very dangerous
It doesent make you cool. It makes you a dummy. you and your friends might think so but others think your a dummy. people are stupid if they attemp to take drugs. The ansew is no, no, no, no.

Make Notes

How long does it take to affect your brain?
how long, does it last?
Could it make you forget how to drive?

Like basketball players?

Why do people use drugs?

How do people get the seeds to grow drugs?

At the end of the book, authors often include information about how they researched the period and explanations about the liberties they took with the characters or events that are recorded.

Scholastic has created two series of historical journals; one is for girls, and the other is for boys. *I Walk in Dread: The Diary of Deliverance Trembly, Witness to the Salem Witch Trials* (Fraustino, 2004), *A Picture of Freedom: The Diary of Clotee, a Slave Girl* (McKissack, 1997), and *Survival in the Storm: The Dust Bowl Diary of Grace Edwards* (Janke, 2002) are from the Dear America series; each book provides a glimpse into American history from a young girl's perspective. The My Name Is America series features books written from a boy's point of view. Three examples are *The Journal of Patrick Seamus Flaherty: United States Marine Corps* (White, 2002), *The Journal of Ben Uchida: Citizen 13559, Mirror Lake Internment Camp* (Denenberg, 1999), and *The Journal of Jesse Smoke: A Cherokee Boy, Trail of Tears, 1838* (Bruchac, 2001). These books are handsomely bound to look like old journals with heavy paper rough cut around the edges.

Students, too, can write simulated journals by assuming the role of another person and writing from that person's viewpoint. They assume the role of a historical figure when they read biographies or as part of social studies units. As they read stories, students assume the role of a character in the story. In this way, they gain insight into other people's lives and into historical events. When students write from the viewpoint of a famous person, they begin by making a "life line," a time line of the person's life. Then they pick key dates in the person's life and write entries about those dates. A look at a series of diary entries written by a fifth grader who has assumed the role of Benjamin Franklin shows how the student chose the important dates for each entry and wove in factual information:

 December 10, 1719

Dear Diary,

My brother James is so mad at me. He just figured out that I'm the one who wrote the articles for his newspaper and signed them Mistress Silence Dogood. He says I can't do any more of them. I don't understand why. My articles are funny. Everyone reads them.
I bet he won't sell as many newspapers anymore. Now I have to just do the printing.

 February 15, 1735

Dear Diary,

I have printed my third "Poor Richard's Almanack." It is the most popular book in America and now I am famous. Everyone reads it. I pretend that somebody named Richard Saunders writes it, but it's really me. I also put my wise sayings in it. My favorite wise saying is "Early to bed, early to rise, makes a man healthy, wealthy, and wise."

 June 22, 1763

Dear Diary,

I've been an inventor for many years now. There are a lot of things I have invented like the Franklin stove (named after me) and bifocal glasses, and the lightning rod, and a long arm to get books off of the high shelves. That's how I work. I see something that we don't have and if it is needed, I figure out how to do it. I guess I just have the knack for inventing.

May 25, 1776

Dear Diary,

Tom Jefferson and I are working on the Declaration of Independence. The patriots at the Continental Congress chose us to do it but it is dangerous business. The Red Coats will call us traitors and kill us if they can. I like young Tom from Virginia. He'll make a good king of America some day.

April 16, 1790

Dear Diary,

I am dying. I only have a day or two to live. But it's OK because I am 84 years old. Not very many people live as long as I have or do so many things in a life. I was a printer by trade but I have also been a scientist, an inventor, a writer, and a statesman. I have lived to see the Philadelphia that I love so very much become part of a new country. Good-bye to my family and everyone who loves me.

Students can use simulated journals in two ways: as a journal or as a refined and polished composition—a demonstration-of-learning project. When students use simulated journals as a tool for learning, they write the entries as they are reading a book in order to get to know the character better, or during a thematic unit as they are learning about the historical period. In these entries, students are exploring concepts and making connections between what they are learning and what they already know. These journal entries are less polished than when students write a simulated journal as a culminating project for a unit. For a project, students plan out their journals carefully, choose important dates, and use the writing process to draft, revise, edit, and publish their journals. They often add covers typical of the historical period. For example, a simulated journal written as part of a unit on ancient Greece might be written on a long sheet of butcher paper and rolled like a scroll, or a pioneer journal might be backed with paper cut from a brown grocery bag to resemble an animal hide.

Quickwriting. Teachers use **quickwriting** during thematic units to activate background knowledge, monitor students' learning, and review big ideas (Readence, Moore, & Rickelman, 2000). Students write on a topic for 5 to 10 minutes, letting thoughts flow from their minds to their pens without focusing on mechanics or revisions. Young children often draw pictures or use a combination of drawing and writing to explore ideas.

Toward the end of a thematic unit on the solar system, for example, fourth graders each chose a word from the **word wall** for a quickwrite, and then they shared their writing with classmates. This is one student's quickwrite on Mars:

Mars is known as the red planet. Mars is Earth's neighbor. Mars is a lot like Earth. On Mars one day lasts 24 hours. It is the fourth planet in the solar system. Mars may have life forms. Two Viking ships landed on Mars. Mars has a dusty and rocky surface. The Viking ships found no life forms. Mars' surface shows signs of water long ago. Mars has no water now. Mars has no rings.

Quickwrites provide a good way of checking on what students are learning and an opportunity to clarify misconceptions. After students write, they usually share their quickwrites in small groups, and then one student in each group shares with the class. Sharing also takes about 10 minutes, so the entire activity can be completed in 20 minutes or less.

Figure 12–4 ◆ A Fifth Grader's Poster About Bees

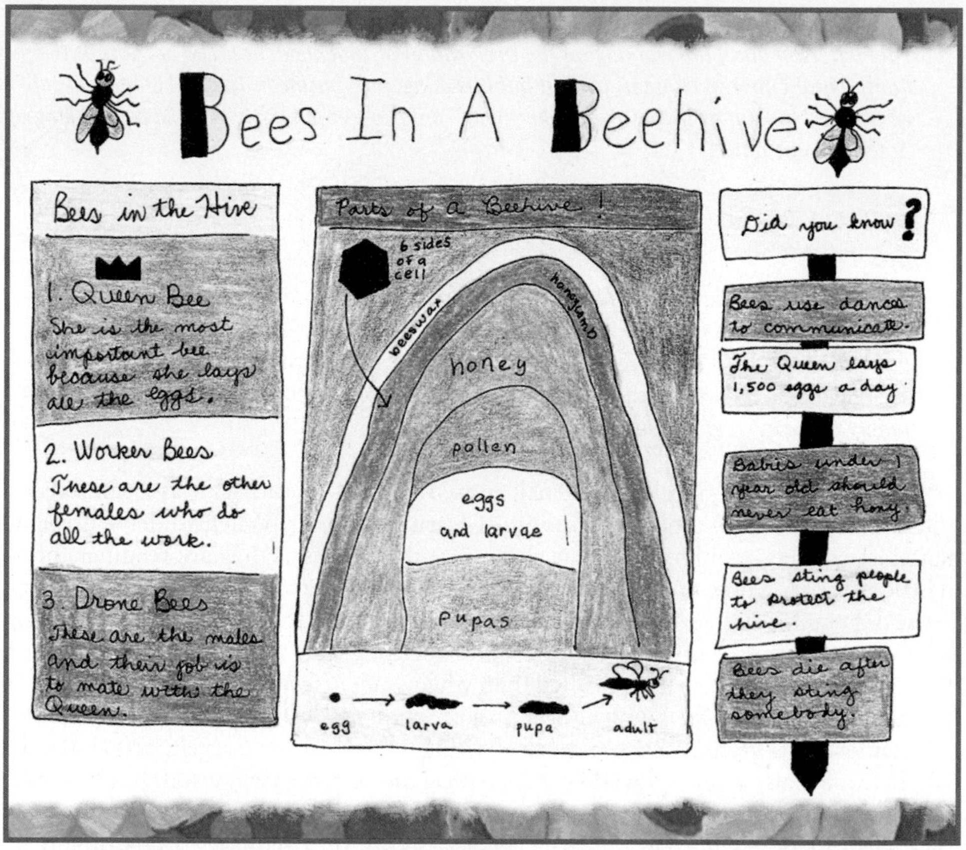

Writing to Demonstrate Learning

Students research topics and then use writing to demonstrate their learning. This writing is more formal, and students use the writing process to revise and edit their writing before making a final copy. Four types of writing to demonstrate learning are reports, essays, poems, and multigenre projects.

Reports. Reports are the best-known type of writing to demonstrate learning; students write many types of reports, ranging from posters to collaborative books and individual reports. Too often, students aren't exposed to report writing until they are faced with writing a term paper in high school, and then they're overwhelmed with learning how to take notes on note cards, organize information, write the paper, and compile a bibliography. There's absolutely no reason to postpone report writing; early, successful experiences with informative writing teach students about content-area topics as well as how to share information (Harvey, 1998; Tompkins, 2008). Here are five types of reports:

Posters. Students combine visual and verbal elements when they make posters (Moline, 1995). They draw pictures and diagrams and write labels and commentary. For example, students draw diagrams of the inner and outer planets in the solar system, identify the parts of a complex machine, label the clothing a Revolutionary War soldier wore and the supplies he carried, identify important events of a person's life on a life line, or chart the explorers' voyages to America and around the world on a map. Students plan the information they want to include in the poster and consider how to devise an attention-getting display using headings, illustrations, captions, boxes, and rules. They prepare a rough draft of their posters, section by section, and then revise and edit each section. Then they make a final copy of each section, glue the sections onto a sheet of posterboard, and share their posters with classmates as they would share finished pieces of writing. As part of a reading and writing workshop focusing on informational books, a fifth grader read *The Magic School Bus Inside a Beehive* (Cole, 1996) and created the poster shown in Figure 12–4 to share what he had learned.

"All About . . ." Books. The first reports that young children write are "All About . . ." books, in which they provide information about familiar topics, such as "Signs of Fall" and "Sea Creatures." Young children write an entire booklet on a single topic. Usually one piece of information and an illustration appear on each page. A page from a first grader's "All About Penguins" book is shown in Figure 12–5.

Alphabet Books. Students use the letters of the alphabet to organize the information they want to share in an alphabet book. These collaborative books

Figure 12–5 ◆ A Page From a First Grader's "All About Penguins" Book

incorporate the sequence structure, because the pages are arranged in alphabetical order. Alphabet books such as *Z Is for Zamboni: A Hockey Alphabet* (Napier, 2002) and *The Queen's Progress: An Elizabethan Alphabet* (Mannis, 2003) can be used as models. Students begin by brainstorming information related to the topic being studied and identify a word or fact for each letter of the alphabet. Then they work individually, in pairs, or in small groups to compose pages for the book. The format for the pages is similar to the one used in alphabet books written by professional authors: Students write the letter in one corner of the page, draw an illustration, and write a sentence or paragraph to describe the word or fact. The text usually begins "_____ is for _____," and then a sentence or paragraph description follows. The "U" page from a fourth-grade class's alphabet book on the California missions is shown in Figure 12–6.

Class Collaborations. Students work together to write **collaborative books**. Sometimes students each write one page for the report, or they can work together in small groups to write chapters. Students create collaborative reports on almost any science or social studies topic. They write collaborative biographies; each student or small group writes about one event or accomplishment in the subject's life, and then the pages are assembled in chronological order. Or, students work in small groups to write chapters for a collaborative report on the planets in the solar system, ancient Egypt, or the Oregon Trail.

Individual Reports. Students also write individual reports during thematic units. They do "authentic" research, in which they explore topics that interest them or hunt for answers to questions that puzzle them (Harvey, 1998; Stead, 2002). Students read books and interview people with special knowledge to learn about their topics, and increasingly they're turning to the Internet for information. After learning about their topics, students write reports, using the writing process, to share their new knowledge.

Essays. Students write essays to explain, analyze, and persuade; sometimes their topics are personal, such as the death of a parent or adjusting to a new school, and at other times, they address national and international issues such as gun control, famine, and global warming. These compositions are short, usually no longer than two pages. They're classified as nonfiction but often include some story elements, especially in personal essays. Students write essays from their own viewpoints, and their voices should come clearly through the writing (Pryle, 2007). They learn to write personal essays, in which they recount an experience, shaping it to illustrate a theme or generalization; comparisons essays, in which they compare two or more things to emphasize important differences and sometimes offer an opinion; and persuasive essays, in which they try to persuade readers to accept an idea, agree with an opinion, or take a course of action.

Another type is the five-paragraph essay; it's tightly structured with the introduction, body, and conclusion divided into five paragraphs, as the name suggests. In the first paragraph, the writer introduces the topic, often using a thesis statement. In the next three paragraphs, the writer presents three ideas with supporting evidence and examples, one in each paragraph. In the last paragraph, the writer summarizes the ideas and restates the thesis. Use of the five-paragraph essay is very controversial: Proponents argue that it teaches students how to organize their thoughts, and opponents counter that its rigid structure limits thinking. In addition, essays can't always be organized into a predetermined number of paragraphs; instead, the topic and the

Figure 12–6 ◆ The "U" Page From a Fourth-Grade Class's Alphabet Book

writer's ideas drive the organization and determine the number of paragraphs (Robb, 2004). Because of its limitations, use of this type of essay isn't recommended.

Poetry. Students often write poems as projects after reading books and as part of thematic units. They write formula poems by beginning each line or stanza with a word or line, they create free-form poems, and they follow the structure of model poems as they create their own poems. Here are three poetry forms that students use to demonstrate content-area learning:

"I Am" Poems. Students assume the role of a person and write a poem from that person's viewpoint. They begin and end the poem (or each stanza) with "I am ____" and begin all the other lines with "I." For example, an eighth grader wrote an "I am" poem from the viewpoint of John F. Kennedy after reading a biography about the 35th president:

I am John Fitzgerald Kennedy.
I commanded a PT boat in World War II.
I saved my crew after a Japanese ship hit us.
I became a politician because that's
what my dad wanted me to do.
I was elected the 35th president of the United States.
I said, "Ask not what your country can do for you—
ask what you can do for your country."
I believed in equal rights for blacks and whites.
I began the Peace Corps to help the world live free.
I cried the tears of assassination because
Lee Harvey Oswald shot me dead.
I left my young family in America's love.
I am John Fitzgerald Kennedy.

Poems for Two Voices. Students take on two, often contrasting, roles to write poems for two voices. This unique form of free verse is arranged in two columns, side by side. The columns are read together by two readers or two groups of readers: One reader reads the left column, and the other reader reads the right column. When both readers have words—either the same words or different words—written on the same line, they read them simultaneously so that the poem sounds like a musical duet. The best-known book of poems for two voices is Paul Fleischman's Newbery Award–winning collection of insect poems, *Joyful Noise: Poems for Two Voices* (2004). Two eighth graders wrote the following poem during a unit on slavery, after learning about Harriet Tubman and her work with the Underground Railroad. The left column is written from the slave's perspective, and the right column from the conductor's.

FREEDOM!	*FREEDOM!*
	I hide slaves in my house;
	It is my moral duty.
I dodge the law wherever I go;	
I follow the north star.	
	I feed them until they get
	to the next stop.
I hide in closets and cellars	
and sleep whenever I can.	
	It is a big risk.
I am in grave danger.	
BUT IT'S WORTH IT!	*BUT IT'S WORTH IT!*
Harriet Tubman is the Moses	
of our people.	
	I am a conductor,
	helping her and her passengers
	along the way.
Once we reach Canada,	
we're free.	
Will freedom be sweet?	
	Oh, yes it will.
FREE AT LAST!	*FREE AT LAST!*

New Literacies
Webquests

Webquests are inquiry-oriented online projects that enhance students' learning by scaffolding their thinking and involving them in meaningful activities. In addition, these projects foster students' ability to use the Internet to search and retrieve information from websites and understand multimodal presentations of information (Ikpeze & Boyd, 2007). Too often, students waste time searching for Internet resources, but in webquests, the resources have been bookmarked so students can locate them easily. Webquests have these six components:

- **Introduction.** An engaging scenario is presented with background information and descriptions of the roles that students will assume, such as time traveler, botanist, superhero, or archeologist.
- **Task.** A description of the creative activity that students will accomplish during the webquest is provided, including open-ended questions to answer. Possible activities include making brochures, maps, graphs, or posters; writing poems, newspaper articles, letters, or songs; or creating board games or video-diaries.
- **Process.** The steps that students will follow to complete the task are presented.
- **Resources.** The bookmarked websites and any other resources that students will need are listed.
- **Evaluation.** A rubric is provided for students to use to self-assess their work. Teachers also use it to assess the quality of students' work.
- **Conclusion.** Opportunities are presented for students to share their experience, reflect on their learning, and pursue extensions.

These online learning projects were created by Bernie Dodge of San Diego State University in 1995. His website at http://webquest.org/ provides useful information about locating teacher-made webquests and creating your own online inquiry projects.

Webquests are quickly becoming popular. Teachers have created hundreds on a wide range of literature, social studies, science, and math topics that are available without charge on the Internet. A few websites are available for young children, but most are for older students. For example, in one webquest, students who have read *Hatchet* (Paulsen, 2006) embark on a wilderness journey and answer scavenger-hunt questions as they learn survival skills, and in another, students who are studying ancient Egypt travel back to 1250 B.C. to find King Tut's burial mask and decode the message hidden inside it. In these online inquiry projects, students assume roles, work in small groups to read Web-based information, and complete authentic tasks. Other webquest topics include roller coasters, chocolate, biomes, voting, polygons, World War II, and hurricanes, as well as picture books and novels that teachers often use in literature focus units, such as *The Outsiders* (Hinton, 2007) and *Whirligig* (Fleischman, 1999).

Most online resources for webquests are informational websites related to the topic, and most include multimodal features such as graphics, photos, maps, video clips, sound, and interactive activities. It's more difficult to locate good online resources for webquests featuring literature selections, but they generally include websites about the author and topics related to the story's characters, setting, or theme, such as gangs (*The Outsiders*) and drunk driving (*Whirligig*).

As with any instructional materials, teachers must carefully evaluate webquests before using them (Leu, Leu, & Coiro, 2004). Not surprisingly, some are much better than others. The webquests that teachers choose to use in their classrooms should include all six components described here, and resource links must still be active, or teachers need to replace them with new ones. In addition, teachers evaluate their quality: Will the webquest enhance students' understanding of the topic? promote higher-level thinking, including analysis and evaluation? develop new literacies?

Found Poems. Students create poems by culling words and phrases from a book they're reading and arranging the words and phrases into a free-form poem. Fourth graders created this poem about a Saguaro cactus after reading *Cactus Hotel* (Guiberson, 2007):

A young cactus sprouts up.

After 10 years only four inches high,

after 25 years two feet tall,

after 50 years 10 feet all.

A welcoming signal across the desert.

A Gila woodpecker,

a white-winged dove,

an elf owl

decide to stay.

After 60 years an arm grows,

the cactus hotel is 18 feet tall.

After 150 years 7 long branches

and holes of every size

in the cactus hotel.

Multigenre Projects. Students explore a science or social studies topic through several genres in a multigenre project (Allen, 2001). They combine content-area study with writing in significant and meaningful ways. Romano (2000) explains that the benefit of this approach is that each genre offers ways of learning and understanding that the others don't; students gain different understandings, for example, by writing a simulated journal entry, an alphabet book, and a time line. Teachers or students identify a *repetend*, a common thread or unifying feature for the project, which helps students move beyond the level of remembering facts to a higher, more analytical level of understanding. In the vignette at the beginning of the chapter, Mrs. Zumwalt's repetend was adaptation; in their multigenre projects, her students highlighted how the animal they studied adapted to life in the ocean.

Depending on the information they want to present and their repetend, students use a variety of genres such as these for their projects:

acrostics	found poems	websites
riddles	quotes	questions and answers
cartoons	songs	biographical sketches
reports	essays	simulated journals
letters	posters	videos
maps	word sorts	"I am" poems
photo galleries	Venn diagrams	alphabet books
time lines	book boxes	double-entry journals

Students generally use three or more genres in a multigenre project and include both textual and visual genres. What matters most is that the genres amplify and extend the repetend.

Not only can students create multigenre projects, but some authors use the technique in trade books; *The Magic School Bus and the Electric Field Trip* (Cole, 1999) and others in the Magic School Bus series are examples of multigenre books. Each book features a story about Ms. Frizzle and her students on a fantastic science adventure, and on the side panels of pages, a variety of explanations, charts, diagrams, and essays are presented. Together the story and informational side panels present a more complete, multigenre presentation or project. Other multigenre books for older students are *To Be a Slave* (Lester, 2005), *Nothing But the Truth* (Avi, 1993), *Lemony Snicket: The Unauthorized Autobiography* (Snicket, 2003), *Middle School Is Worse Than Meatloaf* (Holms, 2007), and *Ernest L. Thayer's Casey at the Bat: A Ballad of the Republic Sung in the Year 1888* (Bing, 2000).

CONTENT-AREA TEXTBOOKS

Textbooks have traditionally been the centerpiece of social studies and science classes, but these textbooks have shortcomings that limit their effectiveness. Too often, content-area textbooks are unappealing and too difficult for students to read and understand, and they cover too many topics superficially. It's up to teachers to plan instruction to make content-area textbooks more comprehensible and to supplement students' learning with other reading and writing activities during thematic units. A list of guidelines for using content-area textbooks is presented here.

Guidelines
for Using Content-Area Textbooks

▶ Teach students about the unique conventions of textbooks, and show how to use them as comprehension aids.

▶ Have students create questions before reading each section of a chapter and then read to find the answers.

▶ Introduce key terms before students read the textbook assignment.

▶ Have students focus on the big ideas instead of trying to remember lots of facts.

▶ Have students complete graphic organizers as they read because these visual representations emphasize the big ideas and the connections among them.

▶ Include small-group activities to make textbooks more comprehensible.

▶ Teach students to take notes about the big ideas as they read.

▶ Encourage students to be active readers, to ask themselves questions and to monitor their reading.

▶ Use the listen-read-discuss format when textbook assignments are too difficult for students to read on their own.

▶ Create text sets to supplement content-area textbooks.

Go to the Building Teaching Skills and Dispositions section of Chapter 12 on **MyEducationLab.com** to observe the ways in which students use the features of content-area textbooks to improve their comprehension.

Features of Content-Area Textbooks

Content-area textbooks look different than other types of books and have unique conventions, such as the following:

Headings and subheadings to direct readers' attention to the big ideas

Photographs and drawings to illustrate the big ideas

Charts and maps to provide detailed information visually

Margin notes to provide supplemental information or to direct readers to additional information on a topic

Highlighted words to identify key vocabulary

An index for locating specific information

A glossary to assist readers in pronouncing and defining technical words

Study questions at the end of the chapter to check readers' comprehension

These features make the textbook easier to read. It's essential that students learn to use them to make reading content-area textbooks more effective and improve their comprehension (Harvey & Goudvis, 2000). Teachers teach **minilessons** about these features and demonstrate how to use them to read more effectively.

Making Content-Area Textbooks More Comprehensible

Teachers use a variety of activities during each stage of the reading process to make content-area textbooks more "reader friendly" and to improve students' comprehension of what they've read. Figure 12–7 lists ways teachers can make content-area textbooks more comprehensible at each stage of the reading process. Teachers choose one or more activities at each stage to support their students' reading but never try to do all of the activities listed in the figure during a single reading assignment.

Stage 1: Prereading. Teachers prepare students to read the chapter and nurture their interest in the topic. There are four purposes:

◆ Activate and build students' background knowledge about the topic
◆ Introduce big ideas and technical words
◆ Set purposes for reading
◆ Preview the text

Teachers use a variety of activities to activate and build students' background knowledge about the topic, including developing **K-W-L charts**, reading aloud stories and informational books, reading information on websites, and viewing videos and DVDs. They also use the gamelike formats of anticipation guides and exclusion brainstorming to heighten students' interest. In **anticipation guides**, teachers introduce a set of statements on the topic of the chapter, students agree or disagree with each statement, and then they read the assignment to see if they were right. In **exclusion brainstorming**, students examine a list of words and decide which ones they think are related to the textbook chapter and then read the chapter to check their predictions.

Teachers introduce the big ideas in a chapter when they create a **prereading plan** in which they present an idea discussed in the chapter and then have students brainstorm words and ideas related to it. They begin a **word wall** with some key words. Another activity is possible sentences, in which students compose sentences that might be in the textbook chapter using two or more vocabulary words from the chapter. Later, as they read the chapter, students check to see if their sentences are included or are accurate enough so that they could be used in the chapter.

Students are more successful when they have a purpose for reading. Teachers set the purpose through prereading activities, and they also can have students read the questions at the end of the chapter, assume responsibility for finding the answer to a specific question, and then read to find the answer. After reading, students share their answers with the class. To preview the chapter, teachers take students on a "text walk" page by page through the chapter, noting main headings, looking at illustrations, and reading diagrams and charts. Sometimes students turn the main headings into questions and prepare to read to find the answers to the questions or check the questions at the end of the chapter to determine the **question-answer-relationships**.

Teaching Struggling Readers and Writers

Content-Area Textbooks

Struggling readers need to know how to read content-area textbooks.

Struggling readers approach all reading assignments the same way—they open to the first page and read straight through—and afterward complain that they don't remember anything. This approach isn't successful because students aren't actively involved in the reading experience, and they're not taking advantage of the special features used in content-area textbooks, including headings, highlighted words, illustrations, end-of-chapter questions, and a glossary, that make the books easier to read.

Successful readers think about the text while they're reading, and the textbook features encourage students' active engagement. Before beginning to read, students activate their background knowledge by previewing the chapter. They read the introduction, the headings, the conclusion, and the end-of-chapter questions and examine photos and illustrations. They locate highlighted vocabulary words, use context clues to figure out the meaning of some words, and check the meaning of others in the glossary. Now they're thinking about the topic. As they read, students try to identify the big ideas and the relationships among them. They stop after reading each section to add information to a graphic organizer, take notes using small self-stick notes, or talk about the section with a classmate. After students finish reading the entire chapter, they make sure they can answer the end-of-chapter questions.

Teachers need to teach students how to read a content-area textbook, pointing out the special features and demonstrating how to use them. Next, students work in small groups or with partners as they practice using the features to engage their thinking and improve their comprehension. With guided practice and opportunities to work collaboratively with classmates, students can become more successful readers.

Stage 2: Reading. Students read the textbook chapter. There are three purposes:

◆ Ensure that students can read the assignment
◆ Assist students in identifying the big ideas
◆ Help students organize ideas and details

It's essential that students can read the chapter. Sometimes the prereading activities provide enough scaffolding so that students can read the assignment successfully, but sometimes they need more support. When students can't read the chapter, teachers have several options. They can read the chapter aloud before students read it independently, or students can read with a buddy. Teachers also can divide the chapter into sections and assign groups of students to read each section and report back to

Figure 12–7 ◆ Ways to Make Content-Area Textbooks More Comprehensible		
Stage	**Activities**	
Prereading	K-W-L charts	Possible sentences
	Text set of books	Prereading plan
	Websites, videos, and DVDs	Question-answer-relationships
	Anticipation guides	Text walk
	Exclusion brainstorming	Word walls
Reading	Interactive read-aloud	Reciprocal questioning
	Buddy reading	Note taking
	Small-group read and share	Graphic organizers
Responding	Discussions	Learning logs
	Think-pair-square-share	Double-entry journals
	Graphic organizers	Quickwriting
Exploring	Word walls	Semantic feature analysis
	Word sorts	Hot seat
	Data charts	Tea party
Applying	Webquests	Multigenre projects
	PowerPoint presentations	Oral reports
	RAFT	Essays

the class; in this way, the reading assignment is shorter, and students can read along with their group members. Students learn the material from the entire chapter as they listen to classmates share their sections. After this sharing experience, students may then be able to go back and read the chapter.

Teachers help students identify and organize the big ideas in a variety of ways. Three of the best ways are **reciprocal questioning**, when students and the teacher ask questions and talk about each big idea as they read the chapter, taking notes about the big ideas, and completing graphic organizers that focus on the big ideas as they read.

Stage 3: Responding. Teachers help students develop and refine their comprehension in this stage as they think, talk, and write about the information they've read. There are three purposes:

◆ Clarify students' misunderstandings
◆ Help students summarize the big ideas
◆ Make connections to students' lives

Students talk about the big ideas, ask questions to clarify confusions, and make connections as they participate in class discussions. They also talk about the chapter in small groups. One popular technique is think-pair-square-share, in which students think about a topic individually for several minutes; then they pair up with classmates to share their thoughts and hear other points of view. Next, each pair of students gets together with another pair, forming a square, to share their thinking. Finally, students come back together as a class to discuss the topic.

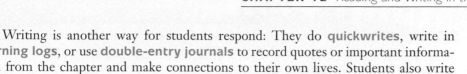

Writing is another way for students respond: They do **quickwrites**, write in **learning logs**, or use **double-entry journals** to record quotes or important information from the chapter and make connections to their own lives. Students also write summaries in which they synthesize the big ideas and describe the relationships among them. Summary writing requires students to think strategically as they analyze what they've read to determine which ideas are important. The minilesson feature on page 410 shows how Mr. Surabian teaches his fourth graders to write summaries.

Stage 4: Exploring. Teachers ask students to dig into the text during the exploring stage to focus on vocabulary, examine the text, and analyze the big ideas. There are three purposes:

◆ Have students study vocabulary words
◆ Review the big ideas in the chapter
◆ Help students to connect the big ideas and details

As they study the technical words in the chapter, students post them on **word walls**, make posters to study their meaning, and do **word sorts** to emphasize the relationships among the big ideas. To focus on the big ideas, students make data charts to record information according to the big ideas or create a **semantic feature analysis** chart to classify important information Figure 12–8 shows an excerpt from a data chart that fourth graders made as they studied the regions of their state. Students often keep these charts and refer to them to write reports or create other projects. They also participate in **hot seat** and **tea party** to talk about what they're learning.

Stage 5: Applying. Teachers support students as they apply what they've learned by creating projects. There are three purposes:

◆ Expand students' knowledge about the topic
◆ Personalize students' learning
◆ Expect students to share their knowledge

Students participate in webquests, read additional books from the text set, conduct research online, and interview people to expand their knowledge, and then they share what they've learned by writing reports and essays, creating PowerPoint presentations and multigenre projects, presenting oral reports, and doing other projects.

Learning How to Study

Students are often asked to remember content-area material that they've read for a discussion, to take a test, or for an oral or written project. The traditional way to study is to memorize a list of facts, but it's more effective to use strategies that require students to think critically and to elaborate ideas. As they study, students need to do the following:

◆ Restate the big ideas in their own words
◆ Make connections among the big ideas
◆ Add details to each of the big ideas
◆ Ask questions about the importance of the ideas
◆ Monitor whether they understand the ideas

Minilesson

TOPIC: Writing Summaries of Informational Articles
GRADE: Fourth Grade
TIME: Five 30-minute sessions

Mr. Surabian plans to teach his students how to write a summary; only a few of his students seem familiar with the term *summary writing*, and no one knows how to write one. Writing a summary is one of the state's fourth-grade standards, and the prompt for the writing assessment often requires summary writing. The teacher recognizes that his students need both instruction in how to write a summary and many opportunities to practice summary writing if they are to be successful on the state's achievement tests.

❶ Introduce the Topic

Mr. Surabian explains that a summary is a brief statement of the main points of an article. He presents a poster with these characteristics of a summary:

▶ A summary tells the big ideas.

▶ A summary is organized to show connections between the big ideas.

▶ A summary has a generalization or a conclusion.

▶ A summary is written in a student's own words.

▶ A summary is brief.

❷ Share Examples

Mr. Surabian shares a one-page article about Wilbur and Orville Wright and the summary he has written about it. The students check that the summary meets all of the characteristics on the poster. Then he shares a second article about mummification, and the students pick out the big ideas and highlight them. Next, Mr. Surabian draws a diagram to show the relationships among the ideas, and they develop a generalization or conclusion statement. Then he shares his summary, and the fourth graders check that he included the big ideas and that the summary meets all of the characteristics on the poster.

❸ Provide Information

The next day, Mr. Surabian reviews the characteristics of a summary and shares an article about motorcycles. The students read it, identify and highlight the big ideas, draw a diagram to illustrate the relationships among the ideas, and create a generalization. After this preparation, they write a summary of the article. They check that their summary meets the characteristics listed on the classroom poster. On the third day, Mr. Surabian's students repeat the process with an article about rain forests.

❹ Guide Practice

On the fourth day, Mr. Surabian shares an article about the Mississippi River. The students read and discuss it, identifying the big ideas, relationships among them, and possible conclusions. Then the teacher divides the students into small groups, and each group writes a summary. Afterward, they share their summaries and check them against the poster. The class repeats this activity the next day; this time, they read about porpoises. Mr. Surabian shortens the time spent discussing the article and identifying the big ideas and conclusions so that students must assume more responsibility for developing and writing the summary.

❺ Assess Learning

Mr. Surabian assesses students' learning by monitoring them as they work in small groups. He identifies several students who need practice, and he plans additional minilessons with them.

Figure 12–8 ◆ An Excerpt From a Data Chart on California

REGION	VEGETATION	ANIMALS	PLACES	HISTORY	ECONOMY
North	Redwood tres	Grizzly Bears Salmon	Eureka Napa Valley	Sutter's Fort GOLD!	Logging Wine
North Coast	Redwood trees Giant sequoia tres	seals Sea Otters Monarch Butterflies	San Francisco	Chinatown Cable Cars Earthquake	Computers Ghirardelli chocolate Levis
South Coast	Palm tres Orange tres	Gray whales Condors	Los Angeles Hollywood	El Camino Real missions O.J. Simpson Earthquake	Disneyland TV + movies airplanes
Central Valley	Poppies	Quail	Fresno Sacramento	capital Pony Express Railroad	grapes Peaches Cotton Almond
Sierra Nevada	Giant Sequoia Lupine	Mule Deer Golden eagles Black Baers	Yosemite	John Muir	skiing

Students use these five strategies as they study class notes, complete graphic organizers to highlight the big ideas, and orally rehearse by explaining the big ideas to themselves.

Taking Notes. When students take notes, they identify what is most important and then restate it in their own words. They select and organize the big ideas, identify organizational patterns, paraphrase and summarize information, and use abbreviations and symbols to take notes more quickly. Copying information verbatim is less effective than restating information because students are less actively involved in understanding what they're reading.

Students take notes in different ways: They can make outlines or bulleted lists; draw flow charts, webs, and other graphic organizers; or make **double-entry journals** with notes in one column and interpretations in the other column. Or, if students can mark on the text they're reading, they underline or highlight the big ideas and write notes in the margin.

Too often, teachers encourage students to take notes without teaching them how to do it. It's important that teachers share copies of notes they've taken so students see different styles of note taking, and that they demonstrate note taking—identifying the big ideas, organizing them, and restating information in their own words—as students read an article or an excerpt from a content-area textbook. Once students understand how to identify the big ideas and to state them in their own words, they need opportunities to practice note taking. First, they work in small groups to take notes collaboratively, and then they work with a partner.

Teachers often use study guides to direct students toward the big ideas when they read content-area textbooks. Teachers create the study guides using diagrams, charts, lists, and sentences, and students complete them as they read using information and vocabulary from the chapter. Afterward, they review their completed study guides with partners, small groups, or the whole class and check that their work is correct.

It's also important that teachers teach students how to review notes to study for quizzes and tests. Too often, students think they're done with notes once they've written them because they don't understand that the notes are a study tool.

Question-Answer-Relationships. Students use Taffy Raphael's **question-answer-relationships** (QARs) technique (1986) to understand how to answer questions written at the end of content-area textbook chapters. The technique teaches students to become aware of whether they are likely to find the answer to a question "right there" on the page, between the lines, or beyond the information provided in the text. By being aware of the requirements posed by a question, students are in a better position to answer it correctly and to use the activity as a study strategy.

The SQ3R Study Strategy. Students in the seventh and eighth grades also learn how to use the SQ3R study strategy, a five-step technique in which students survey, question, read, recite, and review as they study a content-area reading assignment. This study strategy, which incorporates before-, during-, and after-reading components, was devised in the 1930s and has been researched and thoroughly documented as a very effective technique (Topping & McManus, 2002).

Teachers introduce SQ3R and provide opportunities for students to practice each step. At first, students can work together as a class as they use the strategy with a text the teacher is reading to them. Then they can work with partners and in small groups before using the strategy individually. Teachers need to emphasize that if students simply begin reading the first page of the assignment without doing the first two steps, they won't be able to remember as much of what they read. When students are in a hurry and skip some of the steps, the strategy will not be as successful.

Why Aren't Content-Area Textbooks Enough?

Sometimes content-area textbooks are used as the entire instructional program in social studies or science, but that's not a good idea. Textbooks typically only survey topics; other instructional materials are needed to provide depth and understanding. Students need to read, write, and discuss topics. It is most effective to use the reading process and then extend students' learning with projects. Developing thematic units with content-area textbooks as one resource is a much better idea than using content-area textbooks as the only reading material.

THEMATIC UNITS

Thematic units are interdisciplinary units that integrate reading and writing with social studies, science, and other curricular areas. Students are often involved in planning the thematic units and identifying some of the questions they want to explore and the activities that interest them. Textbooks are used as a resource, but only one of many. Students explore topics that interest them and research answers to questions they have posed and are genuinely interested in answering. Students share their learning at the end of the unit, as Mrs. Zumwalt's students did in the vignette at the beginning of the chapter, and are assessed on what they have learned as well as on the processes they used in learning and working in the classroom.

How to Develop a Thematic Unit

To begin planning a thematic unit, teachers choose the general topic and determine the instructional focus using literacy and content-area standards. Next, teachers identify the resources they have available for the unit and develop their teaching plan, integrating content-area study with reading and writing activities. Here's an overview of the important considerations in developing a thematic unit:

1. **Determine the focus for the unit.** Teachers identify three or four big ideas to emphasize in the unit because the goal isn't to teach a collection of facts but to help students grapple with several big understandings. Teachers also choose which literacy and content-area standards to teach during the unit.

2. **Collect a text set of books.** Teachers collect stories, informational books, and poems on topics related to the unit for the text set and place them in a special area in the classroom library. Teachers will read aloud some books, and students will read others independently or in small groups. Other books are used for minilessons or as models or patterns for writing projects.

3. **Coordinate content-area textbook readings.** Teachers review the content-area textbook chapters related to the unit and decide how to use them most effectively. For example, they might use one as an introduction, have students read others during the unit, or read the chapters to review the big ideas. They also think about how to make the textbook more comprehensible, especially for English learners and struggling readers.

4. **Locate Internet and other multimedia materials.** Teachers locate websites, DVDs, maps, models, artifacts, and other materials for the unit. Some materials are used to build students' background knowledge and others to teach the big ideas. Also, students create multimedia materials to display in the classroom.

5. **Plan instructional activities.** Teachers think about ways to teach the unit using reading and writing as learning tools, brainstorm possible activities, and then develop a planning cluster with possible activities. They also make decisions about coordinating the thematic unit with a literature focus unit using one book related to the unit, literature circles featuring books from the text set, or reading and writing workshop.

6. **Identify topics for minilessons.** Teachers plan minilessons to teach strategies and skills related to reading and writing nonfiction as well as content-area topics related to the unit based on state standards as well as needs teachers have identified from students' work.

7. **Consider ways to differentiate instruction.** Teachers devise ways to use flexible grouping to adjust instruction to meet students' developmental levels and language proficiency levels, provide appropriate books and other instructional materials for all students, and scaffold struggling students and challenge high achievers with tiered activities and projects.

8. **Brainstorm possible projects.** Teachers think about projects students can develop to apply and personalize their learning at the end of the unit. This planning makes it possible for teachers to collect needed supplies and have suggestions ready for students who need assistance in choosing a project. Students usually work independently or in small groups, but sometimes the whole class works together on a project.

9. **Plan for assessment.** Teachers consider how they'll monitor students' learning and evaluate learning at the end of the unit. In this way, they can explain to students at the beginning of the unit how they will be evaluated and check to see that their assessment emphasizes students' learning of the big ideas.

After considering unit goals, standards to teach, the available resources, and possible activities, teachers are prepared to develop a time schedule, write lesson plans, and create rubrics and other assessment tools.

urturing English Learners

Teachers have two goals in mind as they consider how to accommodate English learners' instructional needs when they develop thematic units: They want to maximize students' opportunities to learn English and develop content-area knowledge, and they have to consider the instructional challenges facing their students and how to adjust instruction and assessment to meet their needs (Peregoy & Boyle, 2008).

Challenges in Learning Content-Area Information. English learners often have more difficulty learning during thematic units than during literacy instruction because of the additional language demands of unfamiliar topics, vocabulary words, and informational books (Rothenberg & Fisher, 2007). Here are the most important challenges facing many of these students:

English Language Proficiency. Students' ability to understand and communicate in English has an obvious effect on their learning. Teachers address this challenge by teaching English and content-area information together. They use realia and visual materials to support students' understanding of the topics they're teaching and simplify the language, when necessary, in their explanations of the big ideas. They consider the reading levels of the informational books and content-area textbooks they're using, and when students can't read these books themselves, they read them aloud. But if the books are still too difficult, they find others to use instead. Teachers also provide frequent opportunities for ELs to use the new vocabulary as they talk informally about the topics they're learning.

Background Knowledge. English learners often lack the necessary background knowledge about content-area topics, especially about American history, so teachers need to take time to expand students' knowledge base using artifacts, photos, models, picture books, videos, and field trips, and they need to make clear links between the topics and students' past experiences and previous thematic units; otherwise, the instruction won't be meaningful. Finding time to preteach this information isn't easy, but without it, English learners aren't likely to learn much during the unit. Teachers also involve all students, including ELs, in making **K-W-L charts**, doing **exclusion brainstorming**, and marking **anticipation guides** to activate their background knowledge.

Vocabulary. English learners are often unfamiliar with content-area vocabulary because these words aren't used in everyday conversation; they're technical terms, such as *prairie schooner, democracy, scavenger,* and *photosynthesis.* Because some words, such as *democracy,* are cognates, students who speak Spanish or another Latin-based language at home may be familiar with them, but other technical terms have entered English from other languages. Teachers address this challenge by preteaching key vocabulary words, posting words (with picture clues, if needed) on **word walls**, and using realia, photos, and picture books to introduce the words. They also involve students in a variety of vocabulary activities, including doing **word sorts**, making a **semantic feature analysis**, and drawing diagrams and posters about the words.

Reading. Informational books and content-area textbooks are different than stories: Authors organize information differently, incorporate special features, and use more-sophisticated sentence structures. In addition, nonfiction text is dense, packed with facts and technical vocabulary. Teachers address the challenge of an unfamiliar genre in three ways. First, they teach students about nonfiction books, including the expository text structures and the distinctive text features of this genre. Next, they teach the strategies that readers use to comprehend nonfiction books, including determining the big ideas and summarizing. Third, they teach ELs to make graphic organizers and take notes to highlight the big ideas and the relationships among them. Through this instruction, English learners are equipped with the necessary tools to read informational books and textbooks more effectively.

Writing. Writing is difficult for English learners because it reflects their English proficiency, but it also supports their learning of content knowledge and English. All students should use writing as a tool for learning during thematic units. As they **quickwrite**, draw graphic organizers, make charts and diagrams, take notes, and write in **learning logs**, they're grappling with the big ideas and the vocabulary they're learning. Students also use writing to demonstrate learning. This more-formal type of writing is much more difficult for English learners because of increased language demands. Teachers address this challenge by choosing a project that requires less writing or by having students work with partners or in small groups.

These challenges are primarily the result of the students' limited knowledge of English, and when teachers address them, ELs are more likely to be successful in learning content-area information and developing English language proficiency.

Adjusting Instruction. Teachers address the challenges facing English learners as they adjust instruction to maximize students' learning. They also find ways to maximize students' participation in instructional activities because many ELs avoid interacting with mainstream classmates or fear asking questions in class (Peregoy & Boyle, 2008; Rothenberg & Fisher, 2007). Here are some suggestions to guide teachers in adjusting their instruction:

◆ Use visuals and manipulatives, including artifacts, videos, photographs, and models
◆ Preteach big ideas and key vocabulary
◆ Teach students about expository text structures
◆ Practice taking notes with students
◆ Use graphic organizers and other diagrams to highlight relationships among big ideas
◆ Organize students to work in small collaborative groups and with partners
◆ Include frequent opportunities for students to talk informally about big ideas
◆ Provide opportunities for students to use oral language, reading, and writing
◆ Collect text sets, including picture books and online resources
◆ Use a textbook as only one resource
◆ Review big ideas and key vocabulary

These suggestions take into account students' level of English development, their limited background knowledge and vocabulary about many unit topics, and their reading and writing levels.

Choosing Alternative Assessments. Teachers monitor English learners' progress using a combination of observing them and asking questions. Too often, teachers ask ELs if they understand, but that usually isn't effective because they tend respond positively, even when they're confused. It's more productive to interact with students, talking with them about the activity they're involved in or asking questions about the book they're reading.

Teachers also devise alternative assessments to learn more about English learners' achievement when they have difficulty on regular evaluations (Rothenberg & Fisher, 2007). For example, instead of writing an essay, students can draw pictures or graphic organizers about the big ideas and add words from the word wall to label them to demonstrate their learning, or they can talk about what they've learned in a conference with the teacher. Instead of giving written tests, teachers can simplify the wording of the test questions and have ELs answer them orally. When it's important to have English learners create written projects, they'll be more successful if they work collaboratively in small groups. Portfolios are especially useful in documenting ELs' achievement. Students also place work samples in their portfolios to show what they've learned about content-area topics and how their English proficiency has developed.

A First-Grade Unit on Trees

During this 4-week unit, first graders learn about trees and their importance to people and animals. Students observe trees in their community and learn to identify the parts of a tree and types of trees. Teachers use the interactive read-aloud procedure to share books from the text set and list important words on the word wall. A collection of leaves, photos of trees, pictures of animals that live in trees, and products that come from trees is displayed in the classroom, and students learn about categorizing as they sort types of leaves, shapes of trees, foods that grow on trees and those that don't, and animals that live in trees and those that don't. Students learn how to use writing as a tool for learning as they make entries in learning logs, and teachers use interactive writing to make charts about the big ideas. They also view information on book-marked websites to learn more about trees. As a culminating activity, students plant a tree at their school or participate in a community tree-planting campaign. Figure 12–9 shows the planning cluster for this unit.

A Fourth-Grade Unit on Desert Ecosystems

During this 3-week unit, students investigate the plants, animals, and people that live in the desert and learn how they support each other. They keep learning logs in which they take notes and write reactions to books they're reading. Students divide into book clubs during the first week to read books about the desert. During the second week of the unit, students participate in an author study of Byrd Baylor, a woman who lives in the desert and writes about desert life, and they read many of her books. During the third week, students participate in reading workshop to read other desert books and reread favorites. To extend their learning, students create projects, including writing desert riddles, making a chart of a desert ecosystem, and drawing a desert mural. Together as a class, students write a desert alphabet book. A planning cluster for a unit on desert life is presented in Figure 12–10.

A Sixth-Grade Unit on Ancient Egypt

Students learn about this great ancient civilization during a monthlong unit. Key concepts include the influence of the Nile River on Egyptian life, the contributions of this civilization to contemporary America, a comparison of ancient to modern Egypt, and the techniques Egyptologists use to locate tombs of the ancient rulers and decipher Egyptian hieroglyphics. Students read books in literature circles and read other books from the text set independently. They also consult online resources and complete a webquest about ancient Egypt. Teachers teach minilessons on map-reading skills, taking notes from content-area textbooks, Egyptian gods, and writing poems. At the end of the unit, students create projects and share them on Egypt day, when they assume the roles of ancient Egyptians, dressing as ancient people did and eating foods of the period. Figure 12–11 presents a planning cluster for the unit.

Figure 12–9 ◆ A Planning Cluster for a First-Grade Unit on Trees

Graphic Organizers

- Venn diagram comparing ways people and animals use trees.
- Circle diagram with the life cycle of a tree.
- Data chart about the shapes of trees or features of leaves.

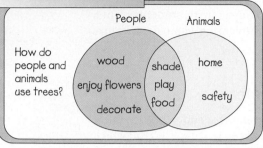

How do people and animals use trees?

People — Animals

wood
enjoy flowers
decorate

shade
play
food

home
safety

Learning Logs

- Bark rubbings.
- Parts of a tree.
- Shapes of trees.
- Leaf collection.
- Trunk cross-section.

Field Trips

- Walking field trip of neighborhood.
- Visit to a forest.
- Visit to a plant nursery.

Projects

- Plant a tree.
- Write "All About Trees" books.
- Create books of tree riddles.
- Develop multigenre projects.

Text Set

Brown, R. (2007). *The old tree.* Cambridge, MA: Candlewick.

Cherry, L. (2000). The *great kapok tree.* San Diego: Harcourt Brace.

Ehlert, L. (1999). *Red leaf, yellow leaf.* San Diego: Harcourt Brace.

Ganeri, A. (2006). *From seed to apple.* Portsmouth, NH: Heinemann.

Gibbons, G. (2002). *Tell me, tree: All about trees for kids.* Boston: Little, Brown.

Hiscock, B. (1999). *The big tree.* Honesdale, PA: Boyds Mills Press.

Iverson, D. (1999). *My favorite tree: Terrific trees of North America.* Nevada City, CA: Dawn.

Miller, D. S. (2002). *Are trees alive?* New York: Walker.

Pfeffer, E. W. (2007). *A log's life.* New York: Simon & Schuster.

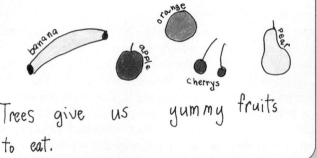

What Trees Need

Trees need 3 things to live. They need sunlight to shine on them. They need water because they get thirsty. They need good soil to grow strong. With these 3 things trees will be healthy.

Interactive Writing

- Parts of a tree.
- Shapes of trees.
- How we use trees.
- What trees need to live.
- How to take care of trees.
- Trees in our community.

TREES

Language Experience Approach

- Make a scrapbook of tree photos and dictate a sentence to describe each photo.
- Compile a class collaboration book with each student drawing a picture and dictating a sentence on one page.
- Paint picture of trees in each season, display them on a poster, and dictate a sentence to describe each painting.

vein

vein

Food gos in the vein to the leaf.

Object and Word Sorts

- Types of leaves.
- Shapes of trees.
- Foods from trees.
- Animals that live in trees.
- Ways people and animals use trees.

Tree Shapes

1
2
3

Vocabulary

- Make word posters.
- Collect pictures and objects to represent words.
- Do word and object sorts.

Websites

- Trees Are Terrific
  www.urbanext.uiuc.edu/trees1
- Exploring the Secret Life of Trees
  www.urbanext.uiuc.edu/trees2

Literacy Strategies and Skills

- Summarize information.
- Locate words on word wall.
- Sort objects and word cards.
- Make word posters.
- Write learning log entries.
- Write "All About . . . " books.

Word Wall

ABCD	EFGHI	JKLM	NO
bark	fruit	leaf	needle
branch	flower	leaves	nuts
birds	evergreen	jagged	nest
acorn		maple syrup	owl
chocolate			oak
beaver			oxygen
PQR	ST	UVW	XYZ
root	trunk	wood	
paper	shade	wide	
rough	smooth	vein	
palm tree	seed		
pine	squirrel		

Content-Area Textbook

- Teach students about unique conventions of content-area textbooks.
- Have students listen to teacher read the chapter aloud before reading it independently or with partners.
- Use modeling to teach students how to take notes.

Literacy Strategies and Skills

- Read informational books to locate information.
- Identify big ideas.
- Write information on a data chart.
- Use an index.
- Draw a life cycle chart.
- Create riddles.
- Recognize problem-and-solution structure.
- Compare ecosystems.

Learning Logs

- Take notes.
- Write quickwrites.
- Draw a food chain.
- List vocabulary words.

Vocabulary Activities

- Make word posters and word maps.
- Do a word sort.
- Create a semantic feature analysis about how plants and animals survive in a desert habitat.

Word Wall

ABC	DEFGH	IJKL
cactus	desert	kangaroo rat
coral snake	Death Valley	king snake
camouflage	dunes	jackrabbit
camels	Gobi Desert	Joshua tree
coyote	exoskeleton	lizard
cacti	hawk	javelina

MNOP	QRST	UVWXYZ
Mojave Desert	Sahara Desert	yucca
oasis	scorpion	
owl	spines	
	saguaro	
	tortoise	
	sidewinder	

Centers

- Add information about desert plants and animals to a data chart.
- Listen to a book at the listening center.
- Draw the life cycle of a desert animal.
- Write a class alphabet book about deserts.
- Read Byrd Baylor's books and others from the text set.
- Write letters to author Byrd Baylor.
- Sort words from the word wall.
- Compare hot and cold deserts.
- Participate in making a tabletop desert diorama.

Maps and Diagrams

- Read landform maps.
- Draw a map of the desert.
- Draw the life cycle of a desert animal.
- Make a problem-solution chart on desert adaptations.
- Identify deserts on a world map.
- Compare deserts and forests.

Technology

- View websites about the desert and the plants, animals, and people living there, including *www.desertusa.com* and *www.inthedesertchildrensproject.org*
- Complete a webquest about desert life.
- Develop a multimodal presentation about the desert.
- Create a website about the desert.

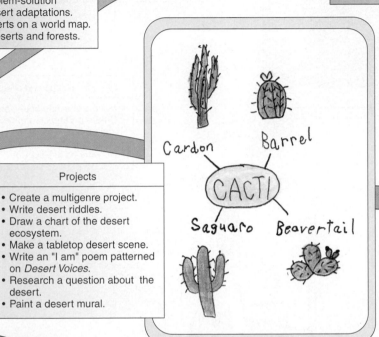

Projects

- Create a multigenre project.
- Write desert riddles.
- Draw a chart of the desert ecosystem.
- Make a tabletop desert scene.
- Write an "I am" poem patterned on *Desert Voices*.
- Research a question about the desert.
- Paint a desert mural.

K-W-L Chart

- Use to introduce the theme.
- Identify research questions.
- Use to conclude unit.

Author Study

- Share information about Byrd Baylor.
- Read her books set in the desert.
- Write letters to the author.

Text Set

Bash, B. (2002). *Desert giant.* Boston: Little, Brown.

Baylor, B. (1993). *Desert voices.* New York: Scribner.

Fowler, A. (1997). *It could still be a desert.* Chicago: Children's Press.

George, J. C. (1996). *One day in the desert.* New York: HarperTrophy.

Gibbons, G. (1999). *Deserts.* New York: Holiday House.

Guiberson, B. Z. (2007). *Cactus hotel.* New York: Holt.

Johnson, R. L. (2000). *A walk in the desert.* Minneapolis: Carolrhoda.

Mora, P. (2008). *The desert is my mother.* Houston: Piñata Books.

Siebert, D. (1992). *Mojave.* New York: HarperTrophy.

Simon, S. (1990). *Deserts.* New York: Morrow.

Taylor, B. (1998). *Desert life.* New York: Dorling Kindersley.

Wallace, M. D. (1996). *America's deserts.* Golden, CO: Fulcrum Kids.

Figure 12–11 ◆ A Planning Cluster for a Sixth-Grade Unit on Ancient Egypt

K-W-L Chart

- Introduce K-W-L chart at the beginning of the unit.
- Identify research questions for collaborative or individual reports.
- Use to conclude the unit.

Maps and Diagrams

- Make a time line of ancient Egypt.
- Create a Venn diagram comparing ancient and modern Egypt.
- Read maps of ancient and modern Egypt.
- Draw maps of Egypt.

Projects

- Keep a simulated journal as an ancient Egyptian.
- Make a time line of the ancient civilization.
- Make a poster about a god or goddess.
- Present an oral report about how to mummify someone.
- Create a website about ancient Egypt.
- Write a collection of poems about ancient Egypt using *Voices of Ancient Egypt* as a model.
- Complete a webquest.
- Present an "interview" of several ancient Egyptians.
- Write a book about the ways the Egyptian civilization has influenced ours.
- Research the Rosetta stone.
- Make a chart comparing ancient and modern Egypt.
- Create a multigenre project.

Literacy Strategies and Skills

- Use anticipation guides.
- Learn to take notes.
- Analyze expository text structures.
- Make a time line.
- Analyze Greek root words.
- Examine QARs in content-area textbooks.

Text Set

Aliki. (1985). *Mummies made in Egypt.* New York: HarperCollins.

Der Manueliàn, P. (1996). *Hieroglyphs from A to Z.* New York: Scholastic.

Giblin, J. C. (1993). *The riddle of the Rosetta stone.* New York: HarperCollins.

Gregory, K. (1999). *Cleopatra VII, daughter of the Nile.* New York: Scholastic.

Harris, G. (1993). *Gods and pharaohs from Egyptian mythology.* New York: Peter Bedrick.

Hart, G. (2004). *Ancient Egypt.* New York: DK Publishing.

Hinshaw, K. C. (2007). *Ancient Egypt.* San Francisco: Chronicle Books.

Honan, L. (1999). *Spend the day in ancient Egypt.* New York: Wiley.

Lattimore, D. N. (1995). *The winged cat: A tale of ancient Egypt.* New York: HarperCollins.

Macaulay, D. (1982). *Pyramid.* Boston: Houghton Mifflin.

Milton, J. (2000). *Hieroglyphs.* New York: Grosset & Dunlap.

Perl, L. (1990). *Mummies, tombs, and treasure: Secrets of ancient Egypt.* New York: Clarion Books.

Rubalcaba, J. (2007). *Ancient Egypt: Archaeology unlocks the secrets of Egypt's past.* Washington, DC: National Geographic Children's Books.

Stanley, D., & Vennema, P. (1997). *Cleopatra.* New York: HarperTrophy.

Winters, K. (2003). *Voices of ancient Egypt.* Washington, DC: National Geographic Children's Books.

Word-Study Activities

- Make word maps.
- Do a word sort.
- Create a semantic feature analysis.
- Make a word chain.
- Write an alphabet book on Egypt.

Word Wall

ABCD	EFGH	IJKLM
canopic jars	Egypt	irrigation
Africa	Hatshepsut	lotus
Champollion	embalming	Imhotep
Amun-Ra	hieroglyphs	Luxor
dynasty	Egyptologist	Memphis
Cleopatra		mummification
		Middle Kingdom
NOPQ	RST	UVWXYZ
pharaohs	Ramses the Great	Valley of the Kings
Nile River	Tutankhamun	vizier
Nefertiti	senet	
natron	scribes	
pyramid	Rosetta stone	
Old Kingdom		
New Kingdom		
obelisk		
papyrus		

Literature Circles

Have students read and discuss a book about ancient Egypt in small groups.

Content-Area Textbook

- Preview chapter with students before reading.
- Divide chapter into sections and have a small group read each section and report to the class.
- Have students complete study guides.
- Use QAR procedure to answer end-of-chapter questions.

Technology

- View websites about ancient Egypt, including the British Museum's website, *www.ancientegypt.co.uk*
- Conduct a webquest at *www.iwebquest.com/egypt/ancientegypt* and other quest sites.
- Create a multigenre project on life in ancient Egypt that includes a digital component.

Centers

- Draw a map of Egypt.
- Make a mummy.
- Write hieroglyphics.
- Make a god or goddess poster.
- Sort words from the word wall.
- Write in learning logs.
- Read text set books.
- Research ancient Egypt online.

Chapter 12 Review

How Effective Teachers Use Reading and Writing in the Content Areas

▶ Teachers have students use reading and writing as learning tools.

▶ Teachers teach students about the features of content-area textbooks.

▶ Teachers use a variety of activities to make content-area textbooks more comprehensible.

▶ Teachers teach students how to take notes and study effectively.

▶ Teachers focus on big ideas in content-area units.

myeducationlab
Where the Classroom Comes to Life

Go to MyEducationLab at www.myeducationlab.com to deepen your understanding of the concepts presented in this chapter:

▶ Check your understanding of chapter concepts with the multiple-choice and essay quizzes in the Study Plan.
▶ Apply some of the main ideas discussed in the chapter in the Activities and Applications section of the website.
▶ Practice what you've learned in this chapter in Building Teaching Skills and Dispositions before applying the ideas in your own classroom.

PROFESSIONAL REFERENCES

Allen, C. A. (2001). *The multigenre research paper: Voice, passion, and discovery in grades 4–6*. Portsmouth, NH: Heinemann.

Armbruster, B. B., McCarthey, S. J., & Cummins, S. (2005). Writing to learn in elementary classrooms. In R. Indrisano & J. R. Paratore (Eds.), *Learning to write, writing to learn: Theory and research in practice* (pp. 71–96). Newark, DE: International Reading Association.

Daniels, H., & Zemelman, S. (2004). *Subjects matter: Every teacher's guide to content-area reading*. Portsmouth, NH: Heinemann.

Dorfman, L. R., & Cappelli, R. (2007). *Mentor texts: Teaching writing through children's literature, K–6*. Portland, ME: Stenhouse.

Harvey, S. (1998). *Nonfiction matters: Reading, writing, and research in grades 3–8*. York, ME: Stenhouse.

Harvey, S., & Goudvis, A. (2000). *Strategies that work: Teaching comprehension to enhance understanding*. York, ME: Stenhouse.

Ikpeze, C. H., & Boyd, F. B. (2007). Web-based inquiry learning: Facilitating thoughtful literacy with webquests. *The Reading Teacher, 60,* 644–654.

Leu, D. J., Leu, D. D., & Coiro, J. (2004). *Teaching with the Internet K–12: New literacies for new times* (4th ed.). Norwood, MA: Christopher-Gordon.

Moline, S. (1995). *I see what you mean: Children at work with visual information*. York, ME: Stenhouse.

Opitz, M. F., & Ford, M. P. (2008). *Do-able differentiation: Varying groups, texts, and supports to reach readers*. Portsmouth, NH: Heinemann.

Peregoy, S. F., & Boyle, O. F. (2008). *Reading, writing, and learning in ESL: A resource book for teaching K–12 English learners*. Boston: Allyn & Bacon/Pearson.

Pryle, M. (2007). *Teaching students to write effective essays.* New York: Scholastic.

Raphael, T. E. (1986). Teaching question-answer-relationships, revisited. *The Reading Teacher, 39,* 516–523.

Readence, J. E., Moore, D. W., & Rickelman, R. J. (2000). *Prereading activities for content area reading and learning* (3rd ed.). Newark, DE: International Reading Association.

Robb, L. (2002). Multiple texts: Multiple opportunities for teaching and learning. *Voices From the Middle, 9*(4), 28–32.

Robb, L. (2003). *Teaching reading in social studies, science, and math.* New York: Scholastic.

Robb, L. (2004). *Nonfiction writing: From the inside out.* New York: Scholastic.

Romano, T. (2000). *Blending genre, alternating style: Writing multiple genre papers.* Portsmouth, NH: Heinemann/Boynton/Cook.

Rothenberg, C., & Fisher, D. (2007). *Teaching English language learners: A differentiated approach.* Upper Saddle River, NJ: Merrill/Prentice Hall.

Stead, T. (2002). *Is that a fact? Teaching nonfiction writing K–3.* Portland, ME: Stenhouse.

Tierney, R. J., & Shanahan, T. (1996). Research on the reading-writing relationship: Interactions, transactions, and outcomes. In R. Barr, M. L. Kamil, P. Mosenthal, & P. D. Pearson (Eds.), *Handbook of reading research* (Vol. 2, pp. 246–280). Mahwah, NJ: Erlbaum.

Tompkins, G. E. (2008). *Teaching writing: Balancing process and product* (5th ed.). Upper Saddle River, NJ: Merrill/Prentice Hall.

Topping, D., & McManus, R. (2002). *Real reading, real writing: Content-area strategies.* Portsmouth, NH: Heinemann.

CHILDREN'S BOOK REFERENCES

Aquatic life of the world. (2001). New York: Marshall Cavendish.

Avi. (1993). *Nothing but the truth.* New York: Avon.

Bausum, A. (2006). *Freedom riders: John Lewis and Jim Zwerg on the front lines of the civil rights movement.* Washington, DC: National Geographic Children's Books.

Bing, C. (2000). *Ernest L. Thayer's Casey at the bat: A ballad of the republic sung in the year 1888.* Brooklyn, NY: Handprint Books.

Bruchac, J. (2001). *The journal of Jesse Smoke: A Cherokee boy, Trail of Tears, 1838.* New York: Scholastic.

Cole, J. (1996). *The magic school bus inside a beehive.* New York: Scholastic.

Cole, J. (1999). *The magic school bus and the electric field trip.* New York: Scholastic.

Cushman, K. (1994). *Catherine, called Birdy.* New York: HarperTrophy.

Denenberg, B. (1999). *The journal of Ben Uchida: Citizen 13559, Mirror Lake Internment Camp.* New York: Scholastic.

Fleischman, P. (1999). *Whirligig.* New York: Laurel Leaf.

Fleischman, P. (2004). *Joyful noise: Poems for two voices.* New York: HarperCollins.

Fraustino, L. R. (2004). *I walk in dread: The diary of Deliverance Trembly, witness to the Salem witch trials.* New York: Scholastic.

Guiberson, B. Z. (2007). *Cactus hotel.* New York: Henry Holt.

Hinton, S. E. (2007). *The outsiders.* New York: Viking.

Holms, J. L. (2007). *Middle school is worse than meatloaf.* New York: Atheneum.

Janke, K. (2002). *Survival in the storm: The dust bowl diary of Grace Edwards.* New York: Scholastic.

Judge, L. (2007). *One thousand tracings: Healing the wounds of World War II.* New York: Hyperion Books.

Lester, J. (2005). *To be a slave.* New York: Puffin Books.

Mannis, C. D. (2003). *The queen's progress: An Elizabethan alphabet.* New York: Viking.

Marrin, A. (2006). *Oh, rats! The story of rats and people.* New York: Dutton.

McKissack, P. C. (1997). *A picture of freedom: The diary of Clotee, a slave girl.* New York: Scholastic.

McLimans, D. (2006). *Gone wild: An endangered animal alphabet.* New York: Walker.

Napier, M. (2002). *Z is for Zamboni: A hockey alphabet.* Chelsea, MI: Sleeping Bear Press.

Paulsen, G. (2006). *Hatchet.* New York: Aladdin Books.

Schlitz, L. A. (2007). *Good masters! Sweet ladies! Voices from a medieval village.* Cambridge, MA: Candlewick Press.

Snicket, L. (2003). *Lemony Snicket: The unauthorized autobiography.* New York: HarperCollins.

Thimmesh, C. (2006). *Team moon: How 400,000 people landed Apollo 11 on the moon.* Boston: Houghton Mifflin.

White, E. E. (2002). *The journal of Patrick Seamus Flaherty: United States Marine Corps.* New York: Scholastic.

PART 4

Compendium of Instructional Procedures

Forty instructional procedures that effective teachers use to teach reading and writing are presented in this Compendium, with step-by-step directions. You've read about minilessons, hot seat, guided reading, K-W-L charts, interactive writing, word walls, and other procedures in this text; they were highlighted in orange to cue you to consult the Compendium for more detailed information. Teachers use these procedures in a variety of ways in their instructional programs. Here are three of the most important uses:

▶ Explicit instruction
▶ Authentic application activities
▶ Learning across the curriculum

To see some of these instructional procedures—making words and shared reading, for example—being used in real classrooms, go to the MyEducationLab website (www.myeducationlab.com).

Explicit Instruction

Teachers use some instructional procedures such as these to provide explicit instruction and guide practice activities:

▶ Guided reading
▶ Interactive writing
▶ Making words
▶ Minilessons
▶ Think-alouds
▶ Word ladders

Authentic Application Activities

Teachers use other instructional procedures for authentic application activities where students participate in real-life reading and writing projects. Here are some examples:

▶ Book talks
▶ Double-entry journals
▶ Grand conversations
▶ Hot seat
▶ Sustained Silent Reading
▶ Writing groups

Learning Across the Curriculum

Teachers use additional instructional procedures such as these to support students' learning across the curriculum and during thematic units:

▶ Anticipation guides
▶ K-W-L charts
▶ Learning logs
▶ Question-Answer-Relationships
▶ Tea party
▶ Word walls

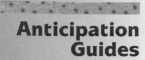

Anticipation Guides

Teachers use anticipation guides (Head & Readence, 1986) to activate students' background knowledge before they read content-area textbooks and informational books. Teachers prepare a list of statements about the topic for students to discuss. Some of the statements are true, and others are incorrect or based on common misconceptions. Students discuss each statement and decide whether they agree with it. Then after reading the selection, students discuss the statements again and decide whether they agree with them. Usually students change some of their opinions, and they realize that they've refined their understanding of the subject through the activity.

An anticipation guide about immigration that eighth graders considered before reading a chapter in their social studies textbook included these statements:

> *There are more people immigrating to the United States today than ever before in history.*
>
> *The government sets a quota for the number of people allowed to enter the United States each year.*
>
> *Most people immigrate to the United States because they want to find better jobs and earn more money.*
>
> *Aliens are people who are in the United States illegally.*
>
> *Refugees are people who are forced to flee from their homeland because of war or other disasters.*
>
> *Many immigrants have difficulty adjusting to the new ways of life in America.*

You probably agree with some of these statements and disagree with others; perhaps you're unsure about a couple of them. Having these questions in mind when you begin reading gives you a purpose for reading and directs your attention to the big ideas. And, as you read, you might find that your initial assessment of one or two statements wasn't accurate, and when you repeat the assessment afterward, you'll make some changes.

Teachers follow these steps to develop and use anticipation guides:

1. *Identify several major concepts related to the reading assignment.* Teachers keep in mind students' knowledge about the topic and any misconceptions they might have about it.

2. *Develop a list of four to six statements.* Teachers compose statements that are general enough to stimulate discussion and are useful in clarifying misconceptions and make copies for students. The guide has space for students to mark whether they agree with each statement before and again after reading.

3. *Discuss the anticipation guide.* Teachers introduce the anticipation guide and have students respond to the statements. Working in small groups, in pairs, or individually, students decide whether they agree with each one. Then, as a class, students discuss their responses to each statement and defend their positions.

4. *Read the text.* Students read the text and compare their responses to what's stated in the reading material.

5. *Discuss each statement again.* Students talk about the statements again, citing information in the text that supports or refutes each one. Or, students can again respond to each of the statements and compare their answers before and after reading. When students use the anticipation guide, have them fold back their first set of responses on the left side of the paper and then respond to each item again on the right side of the paper.

Anticipation Guide on Gangs

Before Reading		Gangs	After Reading	
Agree	Disagree		Agree	Disagree
		1. Gangs are bad.		
		2. Gangs are exciting.		
		3. It is safe to be a gang member.		
		4. Gangs make a difference in a gang member's life.		
		5. Gangs fill a need.		
		6. Once you join a gang, it is very difficult to get out.		

Although anticipation guides are more commonly used before reading informational books and content-area textbooks, they can also be used to explore complex issues in novels, including homelessness, crime and punishment, and immigration. An eighth-grade class, for example, studied gangs in preparation for reading S. E. Hinton's *The Outsiders* (1997), and they completed the anticipation guide shown in the box above before and after reading the novel. The statements about gangs in the anticipation guide probe important points and lead to lively discussion and thoughtful responses.

Book Talks

Book talks are brief teasers that teachers give to introduce students to particular books and interest them in reading the books. Teachers show the book, summarize it without giving away the ending, and read a short excerpt aloud to hook students' interest. Then they pass the book off to an interested reader or place it in the classroom library for students to read.

Students use the same steps when they give book talks to share the books they've read during reading workshop. Here's a transcript of a third grader's book talk about Paula Danziger's *Amber Brown Is Not a Crayon* (2006):

> This is my book: Amber Brown Is Not a Crayon. It's about these two kids—Amber Brown, who is a girl, and Justin Daniels, who is a boy. See? Here is their picture. They are in third grade, too, and their teacher—his name is Mr. Cohen—pretends to take them on airplane trips to the places they study. They move their chairs so that it is like they are on an airplane and Amber and Justin always put their chairs side by side. I'm going to read you the very beginning of the book. [She reads the first three pages aloud to the class.] This story is really funny and when you are reading you think the author is telling you the story instead of you reading it. And there are more stories about Amber Brown. This is the one I'm reading now — You Can't Eat Your Chicken Pox, Amber Brown [1995].

There are several reasons why this student and others in her class are so successful in giving book talks. The teacher has modeled how to give a book talk, and students are reading books that they've chosen—books they really like. In addition, these students are experienced in talking with their classmates about books.

Here are the steps in conducting a book talk:

1. *Select a book to share.* Teachers choose a new book to introduce to students or a book that students haven't shown much interest in. They familiarize themselves with the book by reading or rereading it.

2. *Plan a brief presentation.* Teachers plan how they will present the book to interest students in reading it. They usually begin with the title and author of the book, and they mention the genre or topic and briefly summarize the plot without giving away the ending. Teachers also decide why they liked the book and think about why students might be interested in it. Sometimes they choose a short excerpt to read and an illustration to show.

3. *Show the book and present the planned book talk.* Teachers present the book talk and show the book. Their comments are usually enough so that at least one student will ask to borrow the book to read.

Teachers use book talks to introduce students to books in the classroom library. At the beginning of the school year, teachers take time to introduce students to many of the books in the library, and during the year, they introduce new books that they add to the library. They also introduce the books for a literature circle, or a text set of books for a thematic unit (Gambrell & Almasi, 1996). During a seventh-grade unit on the Underground Railroad, for example, teachers might introduce five books about Harriet Tubman and the Underground Railroad and then have students form book groups to read one of them.

Choral Reading

Students use choral reading to orally share poems and other brief texts. This group reading activity provides students, especially struggling readers, with valuable oral reading practice. They learn to read more expressively and increase their reading fluency (Rasinski & Padak, 2004). In addition, it's a great activity for English learners because they practice reading aloud with classmates in a nonthreatening group setting (McCauley & McCauley, 1992). As they read with English-speaking classmates, they hear and practice English pronunciation of words, phrasing of words in a sentence, and intonation patterns.

Many arrangements for choral reading are possible: Students read the text together as a class or divide it and read sections in small groups. Or, individual students may read particular lines or stanzas while the class reads the rest of the text. Here are four arrangements:

- ◆ **Echo Reading.** A leader reads each line and the group repeats it.
- ◆ **Leader and Chorus Reading.** A leader reads the main part, and the group reads the refrain in unison.
- ◆ **Small-Group Reading.** The class divides into two or more groups, and each group reads part of the poem.
- ◆ **Cumulative Reading.** One student reads the first line or stanza, and another student joins in as each line or stanza is read to create a cumulative effect.

Students read the text aloud several times, experimenting with different arrangements until they decide which one conveys meaning most effectively.

Here are the steps in this instructional procedure:

1. *Select a poem to use for choral reading.* Teachers choose a poem or other text and copy it onto a chart or make multiple copies for students to read.

2. *Arrange the text for choral reading.* Teachers work with students to decide how to arrange the text. They add marks to the chart, or they have students mark individual copies so that they can follow the arrangement.

3. *Rehearse the poem.* Teachers read the poem with students several times at a natural speed, pronouncing words carefully.

4. *Have students read the poem aloud.* Teachers emphasize that students pronounce words clearly and read with expression. They can tape-record students' reading so that they can hear themselves, and sometimes students want to rearrange the choral reading after hearing an audiotape of their reading.

Choral reading makes students active participants in the poetry experience, and it helps them learn to appreciate the sounds, feelings, and magic of poetry. Many poems can be used for choral reading, and poems with repetitions, echoes, refrains, or questions and answers work well. Try these poems, for example:

"My Parents Think I'm Sleeping," by Jack Prelutsky (2007)

"I Woke Up This Morning," by Karla Kuskin (2003)

"Every Time I Climb a Tree," by David McCord (Paschen, 2005)

"Ode to La Tortilla," by Gary Soto (2005)

"The New Kid on the Block," by Jack Prelutsky (2008)

"Mother to Son," by Langston Hughes (2007)

"A Circle of Sun," by Rebecca Kai Dotlich (Yolen & Peters, 2007)

Poems written specifically for two readers are very effective, including Donald Hall's book-length poem *I Am the Dog/I Am the Cat* (1994), and Paul Fleischman's collection of insect poems, *Joyful Noise: Poems for Two Voices* (2004). Teachers can also use speeches, songs, and longer poems for choral reading. Try, for example, *Brother Eagle, Sister Sky: A Message From Chief Seattle* (Jeffers, 1993) and Woody Guthrie's *This Land Is Your Land* (2002).

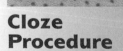

Cloze Procedure

The cloze procedure is an informal diagnostic assessment that teachers use to gather information about readers' abilities to deal with the content and structure of texts they're reading (Taylor, 1953). Teachers construct a cloze passage by selecting an excerpt from a book—a story, an informational book, or a content-area textbook—that students have read and deleting every fifth word in the passage. The deleted words are replaced with blanks. Then students read the passage and add the missing words, using their knowledge of syntax (the order of words in English) and semantics (the meaning of words within sentences) to successfully predict the missing words in the text passage. Only the exact word is considered a correct answer.

Here's a cloze passage about wolves:

> *The leaders of a wolf pack are called the alpha wolves. There is an _____ male and an alpha _____. They are usually the _____ and the strongest wolves _____ the pack. An alpha _____ fight any wolf that _____ to take over the _____. When the alpha looks _____ other wolf in the _____, the other wolf crouches _____ and tucks its tail _____ its hind legs. Sometimes _____ rolls over and licks _____ alpha wolf's face as _____ to say, "You are _____ boss."*

The missing words are *alpha, female, largest, in, will, tries, pack, the, eye, down, between, it, the, if,* and *the.*

The cloze procedure assesses sentence-level comprehension (Tierney & Readence, 2005). It's a useful classroom tool for determining which texts are at students' instructional levels and for monitoring students' understanding of novels they're reading. A caution, however: Cloze doesn't measure comprehension globally; it only assesses students' ability to use syntax and semantics within individual sentences and paragraphs.

Teachers follow these steps to use the cloze procedure:

1. *Select a passage from a textbook or trade book.* Teachers select a passage and retype it. The first sentence is typed exactly as it appears in the original text, but beginning with the second sentence, one of the first five words is deleted and replaced with a blank. Then every fifth word in the remainder of the passage is deleted and replaced with a blank.

2. *Complete the cloze activity.* Students read the passage all the way through once silently and then reread it and predict or "guess" the word that goes in each blank. They write the deleted words in the blanks.

3. *Score students' work.* Teachers award one point each time the missing word is identified. A percentage of correct answers is determined by dividing the number of points by the number of blanks. Compare the percentage of correct word placements with this scale:

61% or more correct replacements: independent reading level

41–60% correct replacements: instructional level

less than 40% correct replacements: frustration level

The cloze procedure can be used to judge students' reading level in unfamiliar books, or to assess students' comprehension after reading a book. When teachers use the cloze procedure to check students' comprehension, specific words, such as character names, facts related to the setting or key events, are deleted, rather than every fifth word. This assessment procedure can also be used to judge whether a particular book is appropriate for classroom instruction. Teachers prepare a cloze passage and have students follow the steps described here to predict the missing words (Jacobson, 1990). Then teachers score students' predictions and use a one-third to one-half formula to determine the text's appropriateness: If students correctly predict more than 50% of the deleted words, the passage is easy reading, but if they predict less than 30% of the missing words, the passage is too difficult for classroom instruction. The instructional range is 30–50% correct predictions (Reutzel & Cooter, 2008).

Students work together in small groups to make collaborative books. They each contribute one page or work with a classmate to write a page or a section of the book, using the writing process as they draft, revise, and edit their pages. Teachers often make class collaborations with students as a first bookmaking project and to introduce the stages of the writing process. Students write collaborative books to retell a favorite story, illustrate a poem with one line or a stanza on each page, or write an informational book or biography. The benefit of collaborative books is that students share the work so that the books are completed much more quickly and easily than individual books. Because students write only one page or section, it takes less time for teachers to conference with students and assist them with time-consuming revising and editing.

Teachers follow these steps in making a collaborative book:

1. *Choose a topic.* Teachers choose a topic related to a literature focus unit or thematic unit. Then students choose specific topics or pages to prepare.

2. *Introduce the page or section design for the book.* If students are each contributing one page for a class informational book on penguins, for example, they choose a fact or other piece of information about penguins to write. They might draw a picture related to the fact at the top of the page and write the fact underneath the picture. Teachers often model the procedure and write one page of the book together as a class before students begin working on their pages.

3. *Have students make rough drafts of their pages.* Students write rough drafts and share the pages in writing groups. They revise their pictures and text after getting feedback from classmates. Then they correct mechanical errors and make the final copy of their pages.

4. *Compile the pages to complete the book.* Students add a title page and covers. Older students might also prepare a table of contents, an introduction, and a conclusion, and add a bibliography at the end. To make the book sturdier, teachers often laminate the covers (or all pages in the book) and have the book bound.

5. *Make copies of the book for students.* Teachers often make copies of the book for each student. The specially bound copy is then placed in the class or school library.

As part of literature focus units, students often retell a story or create an innovation or new version of a story in a collaborative book. They can also retell a novel by having each student retell one chapter. Students also can illustrate a poem or song by writing one line or stanza on each page and then drawing or painting an illustration. *The Lady With the Alligator Purse* (Hoberman, 2003), *There Was an Old Lady Who Swallowed a Fly* (Taback, 1997), and *America the Beautiful* (Bates, 2003) are picture-book examples of song and poem retellings that students can examine before they write their own collaborative retellings.

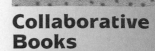

Collaborative Books

A double-entry journal is a special type of reading log in which the pages are divided into two columns; students write different types of information in each column (Berthoff, 1981). In the left column, students write quotes from the story or informational book they're reading, and in the right column, they reflect on each quote. They may relate a quote to their own lives, react to it, write a question, or make some other connection. Excerpts from a fifth grader's double-entry journal about *The Lion, the Witch and the Wardrobe* (Lewis, 2005) are shown in the box on page 434. Teachers use double-entry journals to help students structure their thinking about a text (Tovani, 2000). The quotes that students select indicate what they think is important, and the responses they make in the right column reveal their understanding of what they've read.

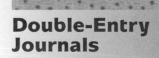

Double-Entry Journals

Excerpts From a Fifth Grader's Double-Entry Journal About *The Lion, the Witch and the Wardrobe*	
Quotes	Reflections
Chapter 1 I will tell you this is the sort of house where no one is going to mind what we do.	I remember the time that I went to Beaumont, Texas to stay with my aunt. My aunt's house was very large. She had a piano and she let us play it. She told us that we could do whatever we wanted to.
Chapter 5 "How do you know?" he asked, "that your sister's story is not true?"	It reminds me of when I was little and I had an imaginary place. I would go there in my mind. I made up all kinds of make-believe stories about myself in this imaginary place. One time I told my big brother about my imaginary place. He laughed at me and told me I was silly. But it didn't bother me because nobody can stop me from thinking what I want.
Chapter 15 Still they could see the shape of the great lion lying dead in his bonds. They're nibbling at the cords.	When Aslan died I thought about when my Uncle Carl died. This reminds me of the story where the lion lets the mouse go and the mouse helps the lion.

Students usually write double-entry journals independently after reading each chapter or two of a novel or informational book, and they follow these steps:

1. *Design journal pages.* Students divide the pages in their reading logs into two columns. They may label the left column "Quotes" and the right column "Comments" or "Reflections."

2. *Write quotes in journals.* As students read or immediately after reading, they copy one or more important or interesting quotes in the left column.

3. *Reflect on the quotes.* Students reread the quotes and make notes in the right column about their reasons for choosing each quote or what the quote means to them. Sometimes it's easier if students share the quotes with a reading buddy or in a grand conversation before they write comments or reflections in the right column.

Sometimes teachers change the headings for the two columns. Students can write "Reading Notes" in the left column and add "Reactions" in the right one. Young children can use the double-entry format in their journals (Macon, Bewell, & Vogt, 1991), labeling the left column "Predictions" and the right one "What Happened." In the left column, they write or draw what they think will happen before they begin to read, and afterward, they draw or write what actually happened in the right column.

Teachers use exclusion brainstorming to activate students' background knowledge and expand their understanding about a social studies or science topic before reading (Blachowicz, 1986). Teachers present a list of words, and students identify the ones that don't relate to the topic. Then after reading, students review the list of words and decide whether they chose correctly. Exclusion brainstorming is a useful prereading activity because as students talk about the words on the list to decide which ones aren't related, they refine their knowledge, think about some key vocabulary words, and develop a purpose for reading.

Exclusion Brainstorming

Here are the steps in exclusion brainstorming:

1. *Prepare a word list.* Teachers identify words related to an informational book or content-area textbook chapter that students will read and include a few words that don't fit with the topic. They write the list on the chalkboard or make copies for students.

2. *Read the list of words.* Teachers read the list, and then, in small groups or together as a class, students decide which words they think aren't related to the text and draw circles around those words.

3. *Learn about the topic.* Students read the text, noticing whether the words in the exclusion brainstorming exercise are mentioned in the text.

4. *Review the list.* Students check their exclusion brainstorming list and make corrections based on their reading. They put checkmarks by related words and cross out unrelated words, whether they circled them earlier or not.

Teachers use exclusion brainstorming as a prereading activity to familiarize students with key concepts and vocabulary before reading informational books and articles. An eighth-grade teacher prepared the list of words shown below before his students read an article on the Arctic Ocean; all of the words except *penguins*, *South Pole*, and *precipitation* are related to the Arctic Ocean. Students circled seven words as possibly unrelated, and after reading, they crossed out the three words that their teacher expected them to eliminate.

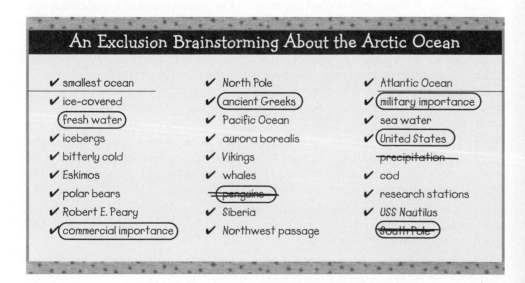

An Exclusion Brainstorming About the Arctic Ocean

✔ smallest ocean
✔ ice-covered
(fresh water)
✔ icebergs
✔ bitterly cold
✔ Eskimos
✔ polar bears
✔ Robert E. Peary
✔(commercial importance)

✔ North Pole
✔(ancient Greeks)
✔ Pacific Ocean
✔ aurora borealis
✔ Vikings
✔ whales
(penguins)
✔ Siberia
✔ Northwest passage

✔ Atlantic Ocean
✔(military importance)
✔ sea water
✔(United States)
~~precipitation~~
✔ cod
✔ research stations
✔ USS Nautilus
(South Pole)

Grand Conversations

Grand conversations are discussions about stories in which students explore the big ideas and reflect on their feelings (Peterson & Eeds, 2007). They're different than traditional discussions because they're student centered. Students do most of the talking as they voice their opinions and support their views with examples from the story. They talk about what puzzles them, what they find interesting, their personal connections to the story, connections to the world, and connections they see between this story and others they've read. Students usually don't raise their hands to be called on by the teacher; instead, they take turns and speak when no one else is speaking, much as adults do when they talk with friends. Students also encourage their classmates to contribute to the conversation. Even though teachers participate, the talk is primarily among the students.

Grand conversations have two parts. The first part is open ended: Students talk about their reactions to the book, and their comments determine the direction of the conversation; teachers share their responses, ask questions, and provide information. Later, teachers focus students' attention on one or two topics that they didn't talk about in the first part of the conversation. In order for English learners to participate successfully in grand conversations, they need to feel comfortable and safe in the group (Graves & Fitzgerald, 2003).

Teachers follow these steps in using this instructional procedure:

1. *Read the book.* Students read a story or part of story, or they listen to the teacher read it aloud.

2. *Prepare for the grand conversation.* Students think about the story by drawing pictures or writing in **reading logs**. This step is especially important when students don't talk much because with this preparation, they're more likely to have ideas to share with classmates.

3. *Have small-group conversations.* Students form small groups to talk about the story before getting together as a class. This step is optional and is generally used when students are uncomfortable about sharing with the whole class or when they need more time to talk about the story.

4. *Begin the grand conversation.* Students form a circle for the class conversation so that everyone can see each other. Teachers begin by asking, "Who would like to begin?" or "What are you thinking about?" One student makes a comment, and classmates take turns talking about the idea the first student introduced.

5. *Continue the conversation.* A student introduces a new idea, and classmates talk about it, sharing ideas, asking questions, and reading excerpts to make a point. Students limit their comments to the idea being discussed, and after students finish discussing this idea, a new one is introduced. To ensure that everyone participates, teachers often ask students to make no more than three comments until everyone has spoken at least once.

6. *Ask questions.* Teachers ask questions to direct students to aspects of the story that have been missed; for example, they might focus on an element of story structure or the author's craft. Or they may ask students to compare the book to the film version of the story or to other books by the same author.

7. *Conclude the conversation.* After all of the big ideas have been explored, teachers end the conversation by summarizing and drawing conclusions about the story or the chapter of the novel.

8. *Reflect on the conversation.* Students write (or write again) in reading logs to reflect on the ideas discussed in the grand conversation.

When students get together for a whole-class conversation during literature focus units, a feeling of community is established. Young children usually meet as a class; older students get together as a class when they're participating in a literature focus unit or listening to the teacher read a book aloud, but during literature circles, students meet in small groups because they're reading different books. When the entire class meets, students have only a few opportunities to talk, but when they meet in small groups, they have many more opportunities to share their ideas.

Guided reading is a small-group instructional procedure that teachers use to read a book with a small group of students who read at approximately the same level. They select a book that students can read at their instructional level, that is, with approximately 90% accuracy, and they support students' reading and their use of reading strategies (Fountas & Pinnell, 1996). Students do the actual reading themselves, and they usually read silently at their own pace through the entire book. Emergent readers often mumble the words softly as they read, which helps the teacher keep track of students' reading and the strategies they're using.

Teachers use guided reading with young English learners just as they do with their native English-speaking classmates, and this instructional procedure can also be used with older ELs, especially if they aren't fluent readers and don't know how to use word-identification and comprehension strategies. It's important to choose the right books for older students—ones that are appropriate for their interests and their reading levels. Peregoy and Boyle (2008) point out that guided reading is effective because ELs experience success as they read interesting books in small, comfortable groups with teacher guidance.

Teachers adapt the procedure for guided reading to meet their students' needs, but they generally follow these steps:

1. *Choose an appropriate book.* Teachers choose a book that students in the small group can read with 90% accuracy. They collect copies of the book for each student.

2. *Introduce the book.* Teachers set the purpose for reading and show the book's cover, reading the title and the author's name. Next, they activate students' background knowledge on a topic related to the book, often introducing key vocabulary as they talk. Students "picture walk" through the book, looking at the illustrations, talking about them, and making predictions. And finally, teachers review one or more of the reading strategies they've already taught and remind these students to use them as they read.

3. *Have students read the book.* Teachers provide support to students with decoding and reading strategies as needed. Students either "mumble" read softly or read silently, depending on their reading level. Teachers observe students as they read and assess their use of word-identification and comprehension strategies. They help individual students decode unfamiliar words, deal with unfamiliar sentence structures, and comprehend ideas presented in the text whenever assistance is required. They offer prompts, such as "Look at how that word ends" or "Does that make sense?"

4. *Encourage students to respond.* Students talk about the book, ask questions, and relate it to others they've read, as in a grand conversation. Teachers also compliment students on the strategies they used while they were reading.

5. *Have students revisit the text.* Teachers use the text that students have just read to demonstrate a comprehension strategy, teach a phonics concept or word-identification skill, or review new vocabulary words.

6. *Provide opportunities for independent reading.* Teachers place the book in a book basket or in the classroom library so that students can reread it.

Guided Reading

Teachers teach guided reading lessons to small groups of students using leveled books while their classmates are involved in other literacy activities; classmates are often reading independently, writing books, and doing phonics and spelling activities at centers. Teachers rotate the groups every 20–30 minutes so that students participate in a variety of teacher-directed and independent activities each day.

Hot Seat

Hot seat is a role-playing activity that builds students' comprehension. Students assume the persona of a character from a story, the featured person from a biography they're reading, or an author whose books they've read, and they sit in a chair designated as the "hot seat" to be interviewed by classmates. It's called *hot seat* because students have to think quickly and respond to their classmates' questions and comments. Wilhelm (2002) explains that through the hot seat activity, students explore the characters, analyze story events, draw inferences, and try out different interpretations. Students aren't intimidated by performing for classmates; in fact, in most classrooms, the activity is very popular. Students are usually eager for their turn to sit in the hot seat. They often wear a costume they've created when they assume the character's persona and share objects they've collected and artifacts they've made.

Here are the steps in the hot seat activity:

1. *Learn about the character.* Students prepare for the hot seat activity by reading a story or a biography to learn about the character they will impersonate.

2. *Create a costume.* Students design a costume appropriate for their character. In addition, they often collect objects or create artifacts to use in their presentations.

3. *Prepare opening remarks.* Students think about the most important things they'd like to share about the character and plan what they'll say at the beginning of the activity.

4. *Introduce the character.* One student sits in front of classmates in a chair designated as the "hot seat," tells a little about the character he or she is role-playing using a first-person viewpoint (e.g., "I was the first person to step onto the moon's surface"), and shares artifacts.

5. *Ask questions and make comments.* Classmates ask thoughtful questions to learn more about the character and offer advice, and the student remains in the role to respond to them.

6. *Summarize the ideas.* The student doing the role-play selects a classmate to summarize the important ideas that were presented about the character. The student in the hot seat clarifies any misunderstandings and adds any big ideas that classmates don't mention.

During literature focus units, students take turns role-playing characters and being interviewed. Students representing different characters can also come together for a conversation—a group hot seat activity. For example, during a literature focus unit on *The View From Saturday* (Kongisburg, 1998), the story of a championship sixth-grade Academic Bowl team that's told from the perspectives of the team members, students representing Noah, Nadia, Ethan, Julian, and their teacher, Mrs. Olinski, take turns sitting on the hot seat, or they come together to talk about the story. Similarly, when students are participating in literature circles, they can take turns role-playing characters from the story they're reading, or each student in the group can assume the persona of a different character at the same time for a group hot seat activity.

Teachers use interactive read-alouds to share books with students. The focus is on enhancing students' comprehension by engaging them in the reading process before, during, and after reading. Teachers introduce the book and activate students' background knowledge before beginning to read. Next, they engage students during reading through conversation and other activities. Afterward, they involve students in responding to the book. What's most important is how teachers engage students while they're reading aloud (Fisher, Flood, Lapp, & Frey, 2004).

Teachers often engage students by pausing periodically to talk about what's just been read. The timing is crucial: When reading stories, it's more effective to stop where students can make predictions and connections, after episodes that students might find confusing, and just before the ending becomes clear. When reading nonfiction, teachers stop to talk about big ideas as they're presented, briefly explain technical terms, and emphasize connections among the ideas. Teachers often read a poem from beginning to end once, and then stop as they're rereading it for students to play with words, notice poetic devices, and repeat favorite words and lines. The box below lists interactive techniques that teachers use. Deciding how often to pause for an activity and knowing when to continue reading develop through practice and vary from one group of students to another.

Teachers follow these steps to conduct interactive read-alouds:

1. *Pick a book.* Teachers choose award-winning and other high-quality books that are appropriate for students and that fit into their instructional programs.

2. *Prepare to share the book.* Teachers practice reading the book to ensure that they can read it fluently and to decide where to pause and engage students with the text; they write prompts on self-stick notes to mark these pages. Teachers also think about how they'll introduce the book and highlight difficult vocabulary words.

3. *Introduce the book.* Teachers activate students' background knowledge, set a clear purpose for listening, and preview the text.

4. *Read the book interactively.* Teachers read the book aloud, modeling fluent reading. They stop periodically to ask questions to focus students on specific points in the text and involve them in other activities.

5. *Involve students in after-reading activities.* Students participate in discussions and other response activities.

Interactive Techniques

Stories	• Make and revise predictions at pivotal points. • Share personal, world, and literary connections. • Draw a picture of a character or an event. • Assume the persona of a character and share the character's thoughts. • Reenact a scene from the story.
Nonfiction	• Ask questions or share information. • Raise hands when specific information is read. • Restate the headings as questions. • Take notes. • Complete graphic organizers.
Poetry	• Add sound effects. • Mumble read along with the teacher. • Repeat lines after the teacher. • Clap when rhyming words, alliteration, or other poetic devices are heard.

Teachers use this instructional procedure whenever they're reading aloud, no matter whether it's an after-lunch read-aloud period or during a literature focus unit, reading workshop, or a thematic unit. Reading aloud has always been an important activity in kindergarten and first-grade classrooms. Sometimes teachers think they should read to children only until they learn to read, but reading aloud to share the excitement of books, especially those that students can't read themselves, should remain an important part of the literacy program at all grade levels. Older students report that when they listen to the teacher read aloud, they get more interested in the book and understand it better, and the experience often makes them want to read it themselves (Ivey, 2003).

Interactive Writing

Teachers use interactive writing to create a message with students and write it on chart paper (Button, Johnson, & Furgerson, 1996). The text is composed by the group, and the teacher guides students as they write it word by word. Students take turns writing known letters and familiar words, adding punctuation marks, and marking spaces between words. As students participate in creating and writing the text on chart paper, they also write it on small dry-erase boards. Afterward, students read and reread the text using shared reading at first, and then read it independently.

Interactive writing is used to demonstrate how writing works and show students how to construct words using their knowledge of sound-symbol correspondences and spelling patterns, and it's a powerful instructional procedure to use with English learners, no matter whether they're first graders or eighth graders (Tompkins & Collom, 2004). It was developed by the well-known English educator Moira McKenzie, who based it on Don Holdaway's work in shared reading (Fountas & Pinnell, 1996).

Teachers follow these steps to do interactive writing with small groups of students or the entire class:

1. Collect materials for interactive writing. Teachers collect chart paper, colored marking pens, white correction tape, an alphabet chart, magnetic letters or letter cards, and a pointer. They also collect these materials for individual students' writing: small dry-erase boards, pens, and erasers.

2. Set a purpose. Teachers present a stimulus activity or set a purpose for interactive writing. Often they read or reread a trade book as a stimulus, but students also share daily news summarize or information they're learning in social studies or science.

3. Choose a sentence to write. Teachers negotiate the text—often a sentence or two—with students. Students repeat the sentence several times and segment it into words. The teacher also helps the students remember the sentence as it is written.

4. Pass out writing supplies. Teachers distribute individual dry-erase boards, pens, and erasers for students to use to write the text individually as it is written together as a class on chart paper. They periodically ask students to hold their boards up so they can see what the students are writing.

5. Write the first sentence. The teacher and students slowly pronounce the first word, "stretching" it out, and students identify the sounds and the letters that represent them and write the letters on chart paper. The teacher chooses students to write letters and words, depending on their knowledge of phonics and spelling. They use one color pen, and the teacher uses another color to write words students can't spell to keep track of how much writing students are able to do. Teachers have an alphabet poster with upper- and lowercase letters available for students to refer to when they're unsure how to form a letter, and white correction tape (sometimes called "boo-boo" tape) to correct poorly formed letters and misspellings. After writing each word, one student serves as the "spacer" and uses his or her hand to mark the space between words. This procedure is repeated to write each word in the sentence, and students reread the sentence from the beginning after each new word is completed. When appropriate, teachers point out capital letters, punctuation marks, and other conventions of print.

6. *Write additional sentences.* Teachers follow the procedure described in the fifth step to write the remaining sentences to finish the text.

7. *Display the completed text.* After completing the message, teachers post the chart in the classroom and have students reread it using shared reading or independent reading. Students often reread interactive charts when they "read the room," and teachers use the charts in teaching high-frequency words and phonics concepts.

Interactive writing can be used as part of literature focus units, in social studies and science thematic units, and for many other purposes, too. Here are some uses:

Write predictions before reading   Write responses after reading
Write letters and other messages   Write information or facts
Make K-W-L charts   Create new versions of a familiar text
Write class poems   Make posters

When students begin interactive writing in kindergarten, they use letters to represent the beginning sounds in words and write familiar words such as *the*, *a*, and *is*. As they learn more about sound-symbol correspondences and spelling patterns, they do more of the writing. Once they're writing words fluently, students do interactive writing in small groups. Each group member uses a different color pen and takes turns writing words. They also sign their names in color on the page so that the teacher can track which words each student wrote.

K-W-L Charts

Teachers use K-W-L charts during thematic units to activate students' background knowledge about a topic and to scaffold them as they ask questions and organize the information they're learning (Ogle, 1986). Teachers create a K-W-L chart by hanging up three sheets of butcher paper on a classroom wall and labeling them *K*, *W*, and *L*; the letters stand for "What We **K**now," "What We **W**onder," and "What We **L**earned." A K-W-L chart developed by a kindergarten class as they were hatching chicks is shown on page 442. The teacher did the actual writing on the K-W-L chart, but the children generated the ideas and questions. It often takes several weeks to complete this activity because teachers introduce the K-W-L chart at the beginning of a unit and use it to identify what students already know and what they wonder about the topic. Toward the end of the unit, students complete the last section of the chart, listing what they've learned.

This procedure helps students activate background knowledge, combine new information with prior knowledge, and learn technical vocabulary related to a thematic unit. Students become curious and more engaged in the learning process, and teachers can introduce complex ideas and technical vocabulary in a nonthreatening way. Teachers direct, scribe, and monitor the development of the K-W-L chart, but it's the students' talk that makes this such a powerful instructional procedure. Students use talk to explore ideas as they create the K and W columns and to share new knowledge as they complete the L column.

Teachers follow these steps:

1. ***Post a K-W-L chart.*** Teachers post a large chart on the classroom wall, divide it into three columns, and label them *K* (What We **K**now), *W* (What We **W**onder), and *L* (What We **L**earned).

2. ***Complete the K column.*** At the beginning of a thematic unit, teachers ask students to brainstorm what they know about the topic and write this information in the K column. Sometimes students suggest information that isn't correct; these statements should be turned into questions and added to the W column.

3. ***Complete the W column.*** Teachers write the questions that students suggest in the W column. They continue to add questions to the W column during the unit.

4. ***Complete the L column.*** At the end of the unit, students reflect on what they've learned, and teachers record this information in the L column of the chart.

Sometimes teachers organize the information on the K-W-L chart into categories to highlight the big ideas and to help students remember more of what they're learning; this procedure is called K-W-L Plus (Carr & Ogle, 1987). Teachers either provide three to six big-idea categories when they introduce the chart, or they ask students to decide on categories after they brainstorm information about the topic for the K column. Students then focus on these categories as they complete the L column, classify-

A Kindergarten Class's K-W-L Chart on Baby Chicks

K	W	L
What We Know	**What We Want to Learn**	**What We Learned**
They hatch from eggs.	Are their feet called wabbly?	Chickens' bodies are covered with feathers.
They sleep.	Do they live in the woods?	Chickens have 4 claws.
They can be yellow or other colors.	What are their bodies covered with?	Yes, they do have stomachs.
They have 2 legs.		
They have 2 wings.	How many toes do they have?	Chickens like to play in the sun.
They eat food.	Do they have a stomach?	
They have a tail.		They like to stay warm.
They live on a farm.	What noises do they make?	They live on farms.
They are little.		
They have beaks.	Do they like the sun?	
They are covered with fluff.		

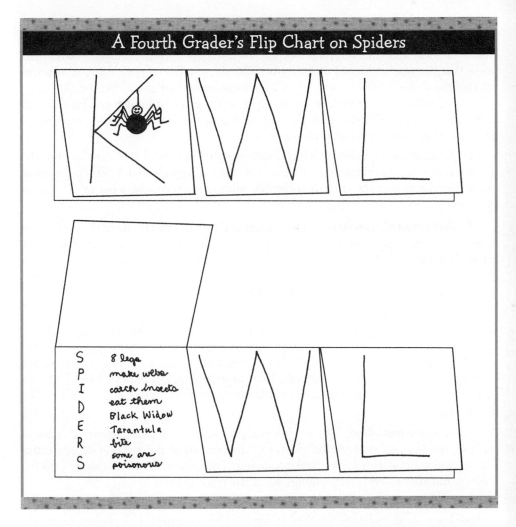

A Fourth Grader's Flip Chart on Spiders

ing each piece of information according to one of the categories. When categories are used, it's easier to make sure students learn about each of the big ideas being presented.

Students also make individual K-W-L charts. As with class K-W-L charts, they brainstorm what they know about a topic, identify questions, and list what they've learned. They can make their charts in **learning logs** or construct flip books with K, W, and L columns. Students make individual flip charts by folding a legal-size sheet of paper in half, lengthwise, cutting the top flap into thirds, and labeling the flaps *K*, *W*, and *L*. Then students lift the flaps to write in each column, as shown here. Checking how students complete their L columns is a good way to monitor their learning.

Language Experience Approach

The Language Experience Approach (LEA) is a reading and writing procedure that's based on students' language and experiences (Ashton-Warner, 1965). A student dictates words and sentences about an experience, and the teacher writes the dictation. As the words and sentences are written, the teacher models how written language works. The text becomes the student's reading material. Because the language comes from the student and because the content is based on his or her experiences, the student is usually able to read the text. It's an effective way to help children begin reading; even those who haven't been successful with other types of reading activities can read what they've dictated.

Teachers use LEA to create reading materials that English learners can read. The EL cuts pictures out of magazines and glues them in a book. Then the teacher and the student identify and label several important words in a picture and create a related sentence that the teacher writes underneath it for the student to read. LEA is effective because the texts students create and read are meaningful to them (Crawford, 2003).

This flexible procedure can be used with the entire class, with small groups, and with individual students, depending on the teacher's purpose. Teachers follow these steps when working with individual students:

1. *Provide an experience.* The experience that serves as the stimulus for the writing can be an experience shared in school, a book read aloud, a field trip, or some other experience that the student is familiar with, such as having a pet or playing in the snow.

2. *Talk about the experience.* The teacher and the student talk about the experience to generate words and review the experience so that the student's dictation will be more interesting and complete. Teachers often begin with an open-ended question, such as "What are we going to write about?" The student talks about the experience to clarify and organize ideas and use more-specific vocabulary.

3. *Record the student's dictation.* The teacher takes the student's dictation. If the student hesitates, the teacher rereads what has been written and encourages him or her to continue. Teachers print neatly and spell words correctly, but they preserve students' language as much as possible. It's a great temptation to change the student's language to their own, in either word choice or grammar, but editing should be kept to a minimum so that students don't get the impression that their language is inferior or inadequate.

4. *Read the text aloud.* The teacher reads the text aloud, pointing at each word as it's read; this reading reminds the student of the content of the text and demonstrates how to read it aloud with appropriate intonation. Then the student reads along with the teacher, and after several joint readings, he or she reads the text alone.

5. *Make sentence strips.* The teacher rewrites the text on sentence strips that the student keeps in an envelope attached to the back of the paper. The student reads and sequences the sentence strips, and once he or she can read them smoothly, the student cuts the strips into individual words. He or she arranges the words into the familiar sentence and then creates new sentences with the word cards.

6. *Add word cards to word bank.* The student adds the word cards to his or her word bank (a small box that holds the word cards) after working with this text. They use these word cards for a variety of activities, including word sorts.

LEA is often used to create texts students can read and use as a resource for writing. For example, during a thematic unit on insects, first graders learned about ladybugs and created a big book with this dictated text:

Part 1: What Ladybugs Do

Ladybugs are helper insects. They help people because they eat aphids. They make the earth pretty. They are red and they have 7 black spots. Ladybugs keep their wings under the red wing cases. Their wings are transparent and they fly with these wings. Ladybugs love to eat aphids. They love them so much that they can eat 50 aphids in one day!

Part 2: How Ladybugs Grow

Ladybugs live on leaves in bushes and in tree trunks. They lay eggs that are sticky and yellow on a leaf. The eggs hatch and out come tiny and black larvae. They like to eat aphids, too. Next the larva becomes a pupa and then it changes into a ladybug. When the ladybugs first come out of the pupa, they are yellow but they change into red and their spots appear. Then they can fly.

Part 3: Ladybugs Are Smart

Ladybugs have a good trick so that the birds won't eat them. If a bird starts to attack, the ladybug turns over on her back and squeezes a stinky liquid from her legs. It smells terrible and makes the bird fly away.

Each part was written on a large sheet of paper, and the pages were bound into a book. After reading and rereading the book, the children each chose a sentence to be written on a sentence strip. Some children wrote their own sentences, and the teacher wrote them for others. They practiced reading their sentences, next they cut the sentences apart and rearranged them, and finally they used the sentences in writing their own "All About Ladybugs" books.

Learning Logs

Students write in learning logs as part of thematic units. Learning logs, like other journals, are booklets of paper in which students record information they're learning, write questions, summarize big ideas, draw diagrams, and reflect on their learning. Their writing is impromptu, and the emphasis is on using writing as a learning tool rather than creating polished products. Even so, students should be encouraged to work carefully and to spell content-related words posted on the **word wall** correctly. Teachers monitor students' logs, and they can quickly see how well students understand the big ideas they're learning.

Students each construct learning logs at the beginning of a thematic unit and then make entries in them during the unit. Here are the steps in this instructional procedure:

1. *Prepare learning logs.* At the beginning of a thematic unit, students construct learning logs using a combination of lined and unlined paper that's stapled into booklets with tagboard or laminated construction-paper covers.

2. *Have students use their learning logs.* Students take notes, draw diagrams, list vocabulary words, do **quickwrites**, and write summaries.

3. *Monitor students' entries.* Teachers read students' learning logs and answer their questions and clarify confusions.

4. *Have students write reflections.* Teachers often have students review their entries at the end of the thematic unit and write a reflection about what they've learned during the unit.

Students use learning logs during social studies units to make notes and respond to information they're learning as they read informational books and content-area textbooks. During a thematic unit on pioneers, for example, students do these activities in learning logs:

◆ Write questions to investigate during the unit
◆ Draw and label pictures of covered wagons
◆ List items the pioneers carried west

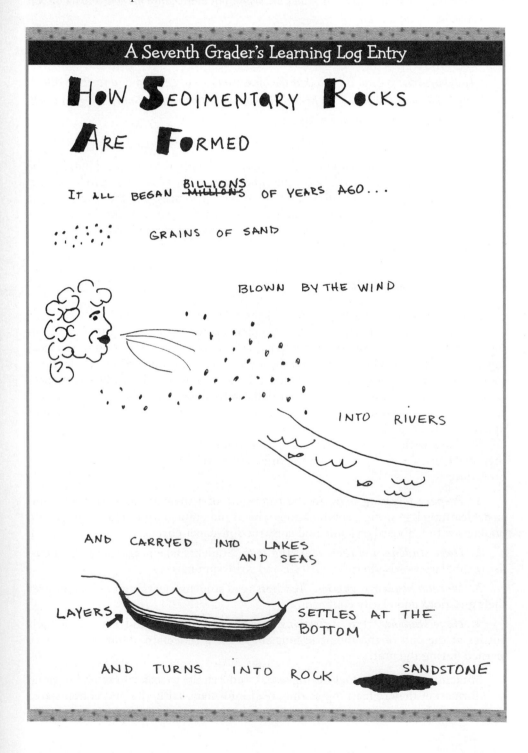

A Seventh Grader's Learning Log Entry

HOW SEDIMENTARY ROCKS ARE FORMED

IT ALL BEGAN ~~MILLIONS~~ BILLIONS OF YEARS AGO...

GRAINS OF SAND

BLOWN BY THE WIND

INTO RIVERS

AND CARRYED INTO LAKES AND SEAS

LAYERS → SETTLES AT THE BOTTOM

AND TURNS INTO ROCK   SANDSTONE

◆ Mark the Oregon Trail on a map of the United States
◆ Write responses to videos about pioneers
◆ Write a rough draft of a poem about life on the Oregon Trail
◆ Write a letter to the teacher at the end of the unit listing five things they learned

Learning logs are used for similar purposes in science units. During a unit on rocks and minerals, for example, seventh graders drew graphic organizers that they completed as they read a chapter in the science textbook, compiled lab reports as they did experiments, did **quickwrites** after watching videos, and drew diagrams and charts about scientific information. One student drew a series of illustrations to explain how sedimentary rocks form in the entry shown on the preceding page.

Making Words

Making words is a teacher-directed spelling activity in which students arrange letter cards to spell words (Cunningham & Cunningham, 1992). Teachers choose key words from books students are reading that exemplify particular phonics or spelling patterns for students to practice. Then they prepare a set of letter cards that small groups of students or individual students can use to spell words. The teacher leads students as they create a variety of words using the letters. For example, after reading *Diary of a Spider* (Cronin, 2005), a group of first graders built these short-*i* and long-*i* words using the letters in the word *spider*: *is, sip, rip, dip, drip, side, ride,* and *ripe.* After spelling these words, students used all of the letters to spell the key word—*spider.* As students make words, they're practicing what they know about sound-symbol correspondences and spelling patterns, and teachers get feedback on what students understand, correct confusions, and review phonics and spelling concepts when necessary.

Teachers often use this activity with small groups of English learners to practice spelling strategies and skills. It's effective because ELs collaborate with classmates, and the activity is both nonthreatening and hands-on. Sometimes teachers bring together a group of ELs to do a making words activity as a preview before doing it with the whole class (or afterward as a review), and sometimes a different word is used to reinforce a spelling pattern that they're learning.

Here are the steps in making words:

1. Make letter cards. Teachers prepare a set of small letter cards with multiple copies of each letter, especially common letters such as *a, e, i, r, s,* and *t,* printing the lowercase letterform on one side and the uppercase form on the reverse. They package the cards letter by letter in small plastic bags or partitioned plastic boxes.

2. Choose a word. Teachers choose a word to use in the word-making activity, and without disclosing it, have a student distribute the needed letter cards to classmates.

3. Name the letter cards. Teachers ask students to name the letter cards and arrange them on their desks with consonants in one group and vowels in another.

4. Make words. Students use the letter cards to spell words containing two, three, four, five, six, or more letters, and they list the words they can spell on a chart. Teachers monitor students' work and encourage them to fix any misspelled words.

5. Share words. Teachers have students identify two-letter words they made with the letter cards and continue to report longer and longer words until they identify the chosen word made using every letter card. After students share all of the words, teachers suggest any words they missed and point out recently taught spelling patterns.

A Sixth-Grade Making Words Activity Using the Word *Hieroglyphics*

h i e r o g l y p h i c s

2	3	4	5	6	7
go	her	hope	cries	prices	crisply
he	she	high	horse	highly	spicier
or	yes	hero	chose	chores	hospice
so	ice	rose	girls	psycho	
is	pig	rice	chili	higher	
hi	hop	chip	Chile	Crispy	
	cry	iris	crisp		
	shy	pigs	shore		
	lie	girl	spice		
	pie	core	spire		
	ore	rosy	choir		
		goes	price		
		pier			

Teachers choose words for word-making lessons from books they are reading with students. For example, for Eric Carle's *A House for Hermit Crab* (2005), *hermit crabs* offers many word-making possibilities; and for *Number the Stars* (Lowry, 1998), *resistance fighters* can be used. Teachers also choose words for making words activities from thematic units. While a sixth-grade class was studying ancient Egypt, they completed the making words activity shown here using the word *hieroglyphics*. Teachers can get additional ideas for word-making activities using books that Patricia Cunningham and Dorothy Hall have compiled (1994a, 1994b).

Minilessons

Teachers teach short, focused lessons called *minilessons* on literacy strategies and skills (Atwell, 1998; Hoyt, 2000). Topics include how to write an entry in a reading log, use commas in a series, draw inferences, and use sentence combining. In these lessons, teachers introduce a topic and connect it to the reading or writing students are involved in, provide information, and supervise as students practice the topic. Minilessons usually last 15 to 30 minutes, and sometimes teachers extend the lesson over several days as students apply the topic in reading and writing activities. The best time to teach a minilesson is when students will have immediate opportunities to apply what they're learning.

It's not enough to simply explain strategies and skills or remind students to use them. Minilessons are an effective way to teach strategies and skills so that students actually do learn to use them. Teachers must actively engage students, encourage and scaffold them while they're learning, and then gradually withdraw their support (Dorn & Soffos, 2001).

Teachers follow these steps to present minilessons to small groups and to the whole class:

1. *Introduce the topic.* Teachers introduce the strategy or skill by naming it and making a connection between the topic and activities going on in the classroom.

2. *Share examples.* Teachers show how to use the topic with examples from students' own writing or from books students are reading.

3. *Provide information.* Teachers provide information, explaining and demonstrating the strategy or skill.

4. *Supervise practice.* Students practice using the strategy or skill with teacher supervision.

5. *Assess learning.* Teachers monitor students' progress and evaluate their use of newly learned strategies or skills.

Teachers teach minilessons on literacy strategies and skills as a part of literature focus units, reading and writing workshop, and other instructional approaches. Other minilessons focus on instructional procedures, such as how to use a dictionary or share writing from the author's chair, and concepts, such as homophones or adjectives.

Students draw open-mind portraits to help them think more deeply about a character, reflect on story events from the character's viewpoint, and analyze the theme (McLaughlin & Allen, 2001). The portraits have two parts: the character's face on the top, "portrait" page, and several "thinking" pages revealing the character's thoughts at pivotal points in the story. The two pages of a fourth grader's open-mind portrait on Sarah, the mail-order bride in *Sarah, Plain and Tall* (MacLachlan, 2004), is shown on page 450. The words and pictures on the "thinking" page represent her thoughts at the end of the story.

Students follow these steps to make open-mind portraits while they're reading a story or immediately afterward:

Open-Mind Portraits

1. *Make a portrait of a character.* Students draw and color a large portrait of the head and neck of a character in a story they're reading.

2. *Cut out the "portrait" and "thinking" pages.* Students cut out the portrait and attach it with a brad or staple on top of several more sheets of drawing paper. It's important that students place the brad or staple at the top of the portrait so that there's space available to draw and write on the "thinking" pages.

3. *Design the "thinking" pages.* Students lift the portrait page and draw and write about the character's thoughts at key points in the story.

4. *Share the completed open-mind portraits.* Students share their portraits with classmates and talk about the words and pictures they chose to include on the "thinking" pages.

Students create open-mind portraits to think more deeply about a character in a story they're reading in literature focus units and literature circles. They often reread parts of the story to recall specific details about the character's appearance before they draw the portrait, and they write several entries in a simulated journal to start thinking from that character's viewpoint before making the "thinking" pages. In addition to making open-mind portraits of characters in stories they're reading, students can make open-mind portraits of historical figures as part of social studies units, and of well-known personalities after reading biographies.

An Open-Mind Portrait of Sarah From *Sarah, Plain and Tall*

Prereading Plan

Teachers use the prereading plan (PReP) to diagnose and build necessary background knowledge before students read informational books and content-area textbooks (Langer, 1981; Vacca & Vacca, 2008). Teachers introduce a key concept discussed in the reading assignment and ask students to brainstorm related words and ideas. Teachers and students talk about the concept, and afterward students quickwrite to reflect on it. This activity is especially important for English learners who have limited background knowledge about a topic and technical vocabulary so that they'll be prepared to read informational books or content-area textbooks. An added benefit is that students' interest in the topic often increases as they participate in this activity.

Teachers follow these steps when they use this instructional procedure:

1. *Discuss a key concept.* Teachers introduce a key concept using a word, phrase, object, or picture to initiate a discussion.

2. *Brainstorm.* Teachers ask students to brainstorm words about the topic and record their ideas on a chart. They also help students make connections among the brainstormed ideas.

3. *Introduce vocabulary.* Teachers present additional vocabulary words that students need to read the assignment and clarify any misconceptions.

4. *Quickwrite about the topic.* Teachers have students quickwrite about the topic using words from the brainstormed list.

5. *Share the quickwrites.* Students share their quickwrites with the class, and teachers ask questions to help classmates clarify and elaborate their thinking.

6. *Read the assignment.* Students read the assignment and relate what they're reading to what they learned before reading.

Teachers use this instructional procedure during thematic units. Before reading a social studies textbook chapter about the Bill of Rights, for example, an eighth-grade teacher used PReP to introduce the concept that citizens have freedoms and responsibilities. Students brainstormed this list during a discussion about the Bill of Rights:

guaranteed in the Constitution	*James Madison*
1791	*10 amendments*
citizens	*freedom of speech*
freedom of religion	*owning guns and pistols*
homes can't be searched without a search warrant	*act responsibly*
limits on these freedoms for everyone's good	*serve on juries*
"life, liberty, and the pursuit of happiness"	*right to a jury trial*
no cruel or unusual punishments	*vote intelligently*

Then before reading the chapter, students wrote quickwrites to make personal connections to the ideas they'd brainstormed. Here is one student's quickwrite:

> *I always knew America was a free country but I thought it was because of the Declaration of Independence. Now I know that the Bill of Rights is a list of our freedoms. There are 10 freedoms in the Bill of Rights. I have the freedom to go to any church I want, to own guns, to speak my mind, and to read newspapers. I never thought of serving on a jury as a freedom and my Mom didn't either. She was on a jury about a year ago and she didn't want to do it. It took a whole week. Her boss didn't like her missing work. The trial was about someone who robbed a store and shot a man but he didn't die. I'm going to tell her that it is important to do jury duty. When I am an adult, I hope I get to be on a jury of a murder trial. I want to protect my freedoms and I know it is a citizen's responsibility, too.*

When the teacher read this student's quickwrite, she noticed that the student confused the number of amendments with the number of freedoms listed in the amendments, so she clarified the misunderstandings individually with her.

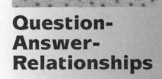

Question-Answer-Relationships

Taffy Raphael's Question-Answer-Relationships (QARs) procedure teaches students to be consciously aware of whether they are likely to find the answer to a comprehension question "right there" on the page, between the lines, or beyond the information provided in the text so that they're better able to answer it (Raphael, Highfield, & Au, 2006). Students use the QAR procedure when they're reading both narrative and expository texts and answering comprehension questions independently.

This procedure differentiates among the types of questions and the kinds of thinking required to answer them: Some questions require only literal thinking whereas others demand higher levels of thinking. Here are Raphael's four types of questions:

◆ **Right There Questions.** Readers find the answer "right there" in the text, usually in the same sentence as words from the question. These are literal-level questions.

◆ **Think and Search Questions.** The answer is in the text, but readers must search for it in different parts of the text and put the ideas together. These are inferential-level questions.

◆ **Author and Me Questions.** Readers use a combination of the author's ideas and their own to answer the question. These questions combine inferential and application levels.

◆ **On My Own Questions.** Readers use their own ideas to answer the question; sometimes they don't need to read the text to answer it. These are application- and evaluation-level questions.

The first two types of questions are known as "in the book" questions because the answers can be found in the book, and the last two types are "in the head" questions because they require information and ideas not presented in the book. An eighth grader's chart describing these types of questions is shown below.

Here are the steps in the QAR procedure:

1. *Read the questions first.* Students read the questions as a preview before reading the text to give them an idea of what to think about as they read.

2. *Predict how to answer the questions.* Students consider which of the four types each question represents and the level of thinking required to answer it.

3. *Read the text.* Students read the text while thinking about the questions they will answer afterward.

4. *Answer the questions.* Students reread the questions, determine where to find the answers, locate the answers, and write them.

5. *Share answers.* Students read their answers aloud and explain how they answered the questions. Students should again refer to the type of question and whether the answer was "in the book" or "in the head."

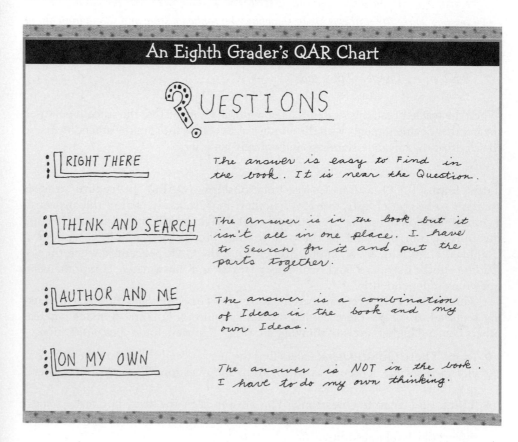

An Eighth Grader's QAR Chart

QUESTIONS

RIGHT THERE — The answer is easy to find in the book. It is near the question.

THINK AND SEARCH — The answer is in the book but it isn't all in one place. I have to search for it and put the parts together.

AUTHOR AND ME — The answer is a combination of ideas in the book and my own ideas.

ON MY OWN — The answer is NOT in the book. I have to do my own thinking.

Students use the QAR procedure whenever they're expected to answer questions after reading a story, informational book, or content-area textbook. They can also write their own "in the book" and "in the head" questions. An eighth-grade teacher, for instance, asked his students to write questions representing the four levels in their reading logs as they were reading *The Giver* (Lowry, 2006). Here are some of their questions:

Right There Questions

What was the first color Jonas could see?

What does a Receiver do?

Think and Search Questions

How is Jonas different than the other people?

Why did Rosemary ask to be released?

Author and Me Questions

What happened to Jonas and Gabe at the end of the book?

Was the Giver an honorable person?

On My Own Questions

What would you have done if you were Jonas?

Could this happen in the United States?

Students also write questions when reading informational books and content-area textbooks.

Questioning the Author

Questioning the Author (QtA) teaches students how to construct meaning from a text. Isabel Beck and Margaret McKeown (2006) developed this instructional procedure to encourage students to question texts, particularly content-area textbooks, that they read. Students learn to view texts as fallible products written by authors who make errors and sometimes don't write as clearly as they should. Once students understand this tenet of fallibility, they read differently than they have before. Too often, students assume that if they don't understand something, it's because they aren't smart or don't read well enough.

Teachers teach students to ask questions, called *queries*, and talk about the text with classmates while they're reading to make sense of it. Queries support students as they develop comprehension. Sometimes the focus is on a single sentence, and at other times, it's on a paragraph or longer chunk of text in these whole-class discussions. Teachers and students ask queries such as these:

What is the author trying to tell us here?
What is the author talking about here?
How does this fit with what the author told us before?
Why is the author telling us this?

As students respond to questions like these, they share ideas and work together to construct meaning.

Teachers use six discussion moves as they orchestrate the discussion:

◆ **Marking.** Teachers draw attention to particular ideas students have expressed.
◆ **Turning-Back.** Teachers return responsibility for exploring the text to students and turn students' attention back to the text.
◆ **Revoicing.** Teachers interpret and rephrase students' ideas that they're struggling to express.
◆ **Recapping.** Teachers summarize the big ideas.

♦ **Modeling.** Teachers make their thinking public as they talk about a point students may have missed.

♦ **Annotating.** Teachers provide information during a discussion. (Beck & McKeown, 2006)

Although teachers prompt students to think more deeply, they should do less talking than the students do.

They follow these steps as they teach QtA to the whole class:

1. *Analyze the text.* Teachers identify the big ideas that they want students to focus on and decide how to segment the text to facilitate students' comprehension.

2. *Develop queries.* Teachers brainstorm a list of queries to ask about the big ideas in each segment. For example: "What's the author trying to tell us?" and "Why did the author say _____?" These queries are used to encourage students to probe the ideas, facilitate their discussion, and extend their understanding. Teachers often jot them on self-stick notes that they place in their copy of the book students are reading.

3. *Have students read.* Students read the first segment of text, stopping at a predetermined point to talk about what they've read.

4. *Ask queries.* Teachers present a query to begin the discussion. Students respond by sharing their interpretations, reading excerpts from the text, questioning ideas, clarifying confusions, and talking together to deepen their understanding. Teachers orchestrate the discussion using marking, revoicing, modeling, and the other discussion moves, and they ask additional questions based on the students' comments, including "Do you agree with what _____ said?" and "How does this information connect with what you already know?"

5. *Repeat reading and asking queries.* Teachers repeat steps 3 and 4 as students read and discuss each segment of text.

6. *Discuss the text.* Teachers lead a discussion based on students' responses to the queries to bring closure to the reading experience. They raise issues of accuracy and viewpoint; invite students to make personal, world, and textual connections; and compare this text to other books on the same topic or to other books by the same author.

Teachers explain the central tenet of QtA, that authors and their texts are fallible, at the beginning of the school year to give students more confidence in their abilities to read and understand books. They also teach students how to ask questions and talk about a text so that they're ready to use QtA whenever they're reading difficult texts. Teachers can use this procedure during literature focus units or literature circles whenever students have difficulty understanding a particular passage, and they use it during thematic units when they're reading chapters in content-area textbooks and other informational books.

Quickwriting

Quickwriting is an impromptu writing activity in which students explore a topic or respond to a question (Brozo & Simpson, 2007). They write for five to 10 minutes, letting their thoughts flow without stopping to make revisions or correct misspelled words; the focus is on generating ideas and developing writing fluency. Students think about ideas, reflect on what they know about a topic, ramble on paper, and make connections among ideas. Here's a series of quickwrites that a fifth grader wrote as she listened to her teacher read aloud *The Higher Power of Lucky* (Patron, 2006), an award-winning story of a plucky 10-year-old girl named Lucky who tries to surmount her problems and bring stability to her life:

Prompt: Why do you think the main character is named Lucky?

I don't know. At this point I don't think Lucky is lucky at all. Her mom died and her dad doesn't want her. She seems pretty unlucky. All that I can think is that Lucky is going to get more lucky at the end of the book. I hope something really good happens to her because she deserves it.

Prompt: Do you think Brigitte will abandon Lucky?

Lucky is really afraid that Brigitte will go back home to Paris. I don't think Brigitte is going to leave. It would be a really mean thing to do and Brigitte is sort of a mom and moms don't do that. I also think it's bad for a girl to have to worry about being abandoned. That's really sad. I predict that Lucky will have a real family at the end of the book.

Prompt: What happened when Lucky hit bottom?

It happened when she ran away from home. There was a bad dust storm and Miles was lost and it was her fault that Miles was lost. She was wearing Brigitte's beautiful red dress and she probably ruined it. I thought she'd get in big trouble and maybe she'd even die and so would Miles and her dog but it didn't happen that way. Everybody in town drove their cars out to the caves to find her and they were so happy to see her and Miles that they didn't even get mad. Lots of good things happened. Best of all, she found out that Brigitte was going to adopt her and would always be her mom. I love this book.

Students wrote their quickwrites after the teacher finished reading each chapter or two, and the quickwrites helped them reflect on what was happening in the story and prepare for the grand conversations.

Here are the steps in this instructional procedure:

1. *Choose a topic.* Students choose a topic or question (or the teacher assigns one) for the quickwrite, and they write it at the top of their papers.

2. *Write about the topic.* Students write sentences and paragraphs to explore the topic for 5 to 10 minutes. They focus on interesting ideas, make connections between the topic and their own lives, and reflect on their reading or learning. They rarely, if ever, stop writing to reread or correct errors in what they've written.

3. *Read quickwrites.* Students meet in small groups to read their quickwrites, and then one student in each group is chosen to share with the class. That student rereads his or her quickwrite in preparation for sharing with the whole class and adds any missing words and completes any unfinished thoughts.

4. *Share chosen quickwrites.* Students in each group who have been chosen to share their quickwrites with the whole class take turns reading them aloud.

5. *Write a second time.* Sometimes students write a second time on the same topic or on a new topic that emerged through writing and sharing; this second quickwrite is usually more focused than the first. Or students can expand their first quickwrite after listening to classmates share theirs or after learning more about the topic.

Teachers use quickwriting to promote thinking during literature focus units and thematic units. They're used as a warm-up at the beginning of a lesson or to promote reflection at the end of a lesson. Sometimes students identify the topics or questions for the quickwrite, and at other times, the teacher provides them. Quickwrites are also an effective prewriting procedure (Routman, 2004). Students often do several quick-writes to explore what they know about a topic before beginning to write; they brainstorm ideas and vocabulary, play with language, and identify ideas they need to learn more about before moving on to the drafting stage.

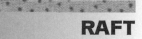

RAFT

Teachers use RAFT to create projects and other assignments to enhance students' comprehension of novels they're reading and information they're learning in thematic units (Holston & Santa, 1985). RAFT is an acronym for *role, audience, format,* and *topic,* and teachers consider these four dimensions as they design projects:

◆ **Role.** The role is the person or people the student becomes for this project. Sometimes students take on the role of a book character, historical figure, or contemporary personality, such as Oprah, and at other times, they are themselves.

◆ **Audience.** The audience is the person or people who will read or view this project. They may include students, teachers, parents, or community members, as well as simulated audiences, such as book characters and historical personalities.

◆ **Format.** The format is the genre or activity that students create. It might be a letter, brochure, cartoon, journal, poster, essay, newspaper article, speech, or digital scrapbook.

◆ **Topic.** The topic is the subject of the project. It may be an issue related to the text, an essential question, or something of personal interest.

When students develop projects, they process ideas and information in different ways as they assume varied viewpoints and complete projects directed to specific audiences. Their thinking is imaginative and interpretive; in contrast, students' comprehension tends to be more literal when they do more-traditional assignments, such as writing answers to questions.

RAFT is an effective way to differentiate instruction by providing tiered activities: Projects on the same text or topic can be adjusted according to students' achievement levels, English proficiency, and interests. For example, a seventh-grade teacher developed the chart of RAFT ideas on the next page for the Newbery Honor Book *The Wednesday Wars* (Schmidt, 2007); this coming-of-age novel chronicles the everyday trials of Holling Hoodhood, who is at odds with his seventh-grade English teacher, Mrs. Baker.

Teachers follow these steps to use RAFT after reading a book or studying a topic during a thematic unit:

1. ***Establish the purpose.*** Teachers reflect on what they want students to learn through this activity and consider how it can enhance students' comprehension of a book they're reading or a social studies or science topic they're learning.

2. ***Prepare a RAFT chart.*** Teachers prepare a RAFT chart of possible projects by brainstorming roles, choosing audiences, identifying genres and other formats for projects, and listing topics.

3. ***Read the book or study the topic.*** Students read and discuss a book or learn about a topic before they create RAFT projects.

RAFT Ideas for *The Wednesday Wars*

Role	Audience	Format	Topic
Holling and William Shakespeare	Our class	Interview	Explain "To thine own self be true" and other life lessons.
Mrs. Baker	Her son, a U.S. soldier in Vietnam	Letter	Tell why you took such an interest in Holling.
You	Our class	Poster	Describe the cultural and political uproar of the 1960s.
You	Newbery Award committee	Persuasive essay	Present reasons why this book should win the Newbery Award.
Bullies	Students at Camillo Jr. High	Speech	Research bullying, and explain how to deal with bullies.
Mai Thi (Holling's classmate)	Our class	Digital scrapbook	Share information about Vietnam and the war's effect on you and your home country.
Holling	Mrs. Baker	Letter, written when Holling is 30 years old	Explain how you've followed Mrs. Baker's advice: "Learn everything you can—everything. And then use all that you have learned to be a wise and good man."

   4. *Choose projects.* Sometimes teachers assign the same project for all students, but at other times, they vary the assignment for small groups or let students choose a project from the RAFT chart.

   5. *Create projects.* Students create their projects using the writing process and get feedback from the teacher as they work.

   6. *Shared completed projects.* Students share their projects with small groups or the whole class and other appropriate audiences.

   RAFT is usually an applying-stage activity because students develop these projects after reading and discussing a novel or after studying a social studies or science topic, but it can also be used in preparation for grand conversations or literature circle discussions. In addition, many teachers use RAFT as a prewriting activity to help students understand the relationships among topics, formats or genres, authors, and readers.

Readers theatre is a dramatic performance of a script by a group of readers (Black & Stave, 2007). Students each assume a part, rehearse by reading and rereading their characters' lines in the script, and then do a performance for their classmates. Students can read scripts in trade books and textbooks, or they can create their own scripts. The box on page 458 lists 10 books of narrative and informational scripts. What's valuable about readers theatre is that students interpret the story with their

Readers Theatre

voices, without using much action. They may stand or sit, but they must carry the whole communication of the plot, characterization, mood, and theme by using their voices, gestures, and facial expressions. In addition, readers theatre avoids many of the problems inherent in theatrical productions: Students don't memorize their parts; elaborate props, costumes, and backdrops aren't needed; and long, tedious hours aren't spent rehearsing.

There are many reasons to recommend readers theatre. Students have opportunities to read good literature, and through this procedure they engage with text, interpret characters, and bring the text to life (Keehn, Martinez, & Roser, 2005; Worthy & Prater, 2002). Moreover, English learners and other students who are not yet fluent readers gain valuable oral reading practice in a relaxed small-group setting. They practice reading high-frequency words, increase their reading speed, learn how to phrase and chunk words in sentences, and read with more expression.

Teachers follow these steps as they work with a small group or the whole class:

1. *Select a script.* Students select a script and then read and discuss it as they would any story. Afterward, they volunteer to read each part.

2. *Rehearse the reading.* Students decide how to use their voice, gestures, and facial expressions to interpret the characters they're reading. They read the script several times, striving for accurate pronunciation, voice projection, and appropriate inflections. Less rehearsal is needed for an informal, in-class presentation than for a more formal production; nevertheless, interpretations should always be developed as fully as possible.

3. *Stage the reading.* Readers theatre can be presented on a stage or in a corner of the classroom. Students stand or sit in a row and read their lines. They stay in position through the production or enter and leave according to the characters' appearances "onstage." If readers are sitting, they stand to read their lines; if they're standing, they step forward to read. The emphasis isn't on production quality; rather, it's on the interpretive quality of readers' voices and expressions. Costumes and props aren't necessary; however, adding a few small props enhances interest as long as they don't interfere with the interpretive quality of the reading.

Students create their own readers theatre scripts from stories they've read and about topics related to thematic units (Flynn, 2007). When students are creating a script, it's important to choose a story with lots of conversation; any parts that don't

Readers Theatre Scripts

Barchers, S. I. (1997). *50 fabulous fables: Beginning readers theatre*. Portsmouth, NH: Teacher Ideas Press.

Barchers, S. I., & Pfeffinger, C. R. (2006). *More readers theatre for beginning readers*. Portsmouth, NH: Teacher Ideas Press.

Fredericks, A. D. (2007). *Nonfiction readers theatre for beginning readers*. Portsmouth, NH: Teacher Ideas Press.

Laughlin, M. K., Black, P. T., & Loberg, M. K. (1991). *Social studies readers theatre for children: Scripts and script development*. Portsmouth, NH: Teacher Ideas Press.

Martin, J. M. (2002). *12 fabulously funny fairy tale plays*. New York: Scholastic.

Pugliano-Martin, C. (1999). *25 just-right plays for emergent readers*. New York: Scholastic.

Shepard, A. (2005). *Stories on stage: Children's plays for reader's theater with 15 play scripts from 15 authors*. Olympia, WA: Shepard.

Wolf, J. M. (2002). *Cinderella outgrows the glass slipper and other zany fractured fairy tale plays*. New York: Scholastic.

Wolfman, J. (2004). *How and why stories for readers theatre*. Portsmouth, NH: Teacher Ideas Press.

Worthy, J. (2005). *Readers theatre for building fluency: Strategies and scripts for making the most of this highly effective, motivating, and research-based approach to oral reading*. New York: Scholastic.

include dialogue can become narrator parts. Depending on the number of narrator parts, one to four students can share the narrator duties. Teachers often make photocopies of the story for students to mark up or highlight as they develop the script. Sometimes students simply use their marked-up copies as the finished script, and at other times, they retype the finished script, omitting the unnecessary parts.

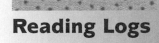

Reading Logs

Reading logs are journals in which students write their reactions and opinions about books they're reading or listening to the teacher read aloud. Through their reading log entries, students clarify misunderstandings, explore ideas, and deepen their comprehension (Barone, 1990; Hancock, 2008). They also add lists of words from the word wall, diagrams about story elements, and information about authors and genres (Tompkins, 2008). For a chapter book, students write after reading every chapter or two, and they often write single entries after reading picture books or short stories. Often students write a series of entries about a collection of books written by the same author, such as books by Eric Carle or Chris Van Allsburg, or about versions of the same folktale or fairy tale.

Sometimes students choose what they'll write about in reading log entries, and at other times, they respond to questions or prompts that teachers have prepared. Both student-choice and teacher-directed entries are useful: When students choose their own topics, they delve into their own ideas and questions, sharing what's important to them, and when teachers prepare prompts, they direct students' thinking to topics and questions that students might otherwise miss. When teachers know their students well and are familiar with the books students are reading, they choose the best mix of student-choice and teacher-directed entries.

Students follow these steps as they write independently in reading logs:

1. *Prepare reading logs.* Students make reading logs by stapling paper into booklets, and they write the title of the book on the cover.

2. *Write entries.* Students write their reactions and reflections about the book or chapter. Sometimes they choose their own topics, and at other times, teachers pose topics and questions. Students often summarize events and make connections to the book. They also list interesting or unfamiliar words, jot down memorable quotes, and take notes about characters, plot, or other story elements.

3. *Share entries.* Students share their reading logs with teachers so they can monitor students' work. Teacher also write comments back to students about their interpretations and reflections.

Students at all grade levels can write and draw reading log entries to help them understand stories they're reading and listening to read aloud during literature focus units and literature circles (Daniels, 2001). As a sixth-grade class read *The Giver* (Lowry, 2006), a Newbery Award–winning story of a not-so-perfect society, students discussed each chapter and brainstormed several possible titles for the chapter. Then they wrote entries in their reading logs and labeled each chapter with the number and the title they felt was most appropriate. The following three reading log entries show how a sixth grader grappled with the idea of "release":

Chapter 18: "Release"

I think release is very rude. People have a right to live where they want to. Just because they're different they have to go somewhere else. I think release is when you have to go and live elsewhere. If you're released you can't come back to the community.

Chapter 19: "Release—The Truth"

It is so mean to kill people that didn't do anything bad. They kill perfectly innocent people. Everyone has a right to live. The shot is even worse to give them. They should be able to die on their own. If I were Jonas I would probably go insane. The people who kill the people that are to be released don't know what they're doing.

Chapter 20: "Mortified"

I don't think that Jonas is going to be able to go home and face his father. What can he do? Now that he knows what release is he will probably stay with The Giver for the rest of his life until he is released.

After reading and discussing Chapter 18, this student doesn't understand that "release" means "killing," but he grasps the awful meaning of the word as he reads Chapter 19.

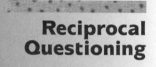

Reciprocal Questioning

Teachers use reciprocal questioning to involve students more actively in reading and understanding informational texts (Ciardello, 1998). In this instructional procedure, teachers segment content-area textbook chapters and informational books and articles into sentences or paragraphs, and teachers and students read a segment and ask each other questions about the text they've read. Students and teachers ask these types of questions during reciprocal questioning:

◆ Questions about the meaning of particular words
◆ Questions that are answered directly in the text
◆ Questions that can be answered using common knowledge about the world
◆ Questions that relate the text to students' own lives
◆ "I wonder why" questions that go beyond the information provided in the text
◆ Questions that require students to locate information not contained in the text

This procedure is effective because students read more purposefully when they read to create questions and to prepare to answer questions than when they're reading independently to finish an assignment.

Teachers follow these steps as they implement reciprocal questioning:

1. *Prepare for the reciprocal questioning activity.* Teachers read the text and chunk it into segments. They choose the length of a segment—from a sentence to a paragraph or two—depending on the complexity of the material being presented and students' reading levels.

2. *Introduce the assignment.* Teachers introduce the reading assignment and have students silently read a small segment of the text.

3. *Ask questions.* Students ask several questions about the text they've just read; the teacher closes the book and answers the questions as fully as possible.

4. *Reverse roles.* This time, the teacher questions the students after they've read a segment of text and closed their books. Teachers model asking a range of questions, from factual to interpretive questions. Or students and the teacher can alternate asking and answering questions after reading each segment of text.

5. *Repeat steps 2, 3, and 4 to read and discuss more of the text.* At an appropriate point, the teacher asks students to predict what information they expect to read and learn in the rest of the text, and then students continue reading the rest of the assignment independently.

Questions About *The Real McCoy: The Life of an African-American Inventor*

Page 1	What does "the real McCoy" mean?	S
	Who was Elijah McCoy?	S
	What did he invent?	S
Page 2	Was Elijah McCoy born in the United States?	T
	Do you think Elijah's parents ever knew Harriet Tubman?	T
	Was Elijah McCoy free or a slave?	T
Page 3	Did Elijah McCoy learn to read and write?	S
	What did Elijah McCoy like to do?	S
	Do you think he was a smart boy?	T
Page 4	Why did Elijah McCoy go to Scotland?	T
	What did he study in college?	T
Page 5	When did Elijah come to the United States?	S
	Why was it hard for him to get a job?	S
	What was the only job he could find?	S
Page 6	What does a fireman do on a train?	T
	Was it a good job?	S
Page 7	What was Elijah's other job?	S
	What does an oilman do?	S
Page 8	What was Elijah's invention?	T
	What does <u>lubrication</u> mean?	T
Page 9	What does <u>skeptical</u> mean?	S
	What does the saying "the real McCoy" mean?	T

Teachers use reciprocal questioning to support students' reading of difficult nonfiction texts. For example, a fifth-grade teacher used reciprocal questioning to read *The Real McCoy: The Life of an African-American Inventor* (Towle, 1993), an informational book about Elijah McCoy, whose name became an eponym. Because there is only a paragraph or two of text on each page of this picture book, it works well for reciprocal questioning. The teacher began by talking about words and phrases that came from people's names, such as *Levi's*. A list of the questions that students and the teacher asked is presented above; questions that students asked are marked with *S*, and questions asked by the teacher are marked with *T*. After the class read the first nine pages together, the teacher asked students to predict what the rest of the book was about, and the students read the rest of the book independently. After reading, students made a lifeline of the events in this African American inventor's life.

Rubrics are scoring guides that teachers use to assess students' writing (Spandel, 2005). These guides usually have 4, 5, or 6 levels, ranging from high to low, and assessment criteria are described at each level. Students receive a copy of the rubric as they begin writing so that they understand what's expected and how they'll be assessed. Depending on the rubric's intricacy, teachers mark the assessment criteria either while they're reading students' writing or immediately afterward and then determine the overall score for the piece of writing.

Rubrics

The assessment criteria on some rubrics describe general qualities of effective writing, such as ideas, organization, word choice, and mechanics, but in others, they focus on genre characteristics. Teachers often use genre-specific rubrics to assess stories, reports, letters, and autobiographies. No matter which assessment criteria are used, the same criteria are addressed at each level. If a criterion addresses sentence fluency, for example, descriptors about sentence fluency are included at each level; the statement "contains short, choppy sentences" might be used at the lowest level and "uses sentences that vary in length and style" at the highest level. Each level represents a one-step improvement in students' application of that criterion.

Rubrics can be constructed with any number of levels, but it's easier to show growth in students' writing when the rubric has more levels. Much more improvement is needed for students to move from one level to another if the rubric has 4 levels than if it has 6 levels. A rubric with 10 levels would be even more sensitive to student growth, but rubrics with many levels are harder to construct and more time-consuming to use. Researchers usually recommend that teachers use rubrics with either 4 or 6 levels so that there is no middle score—each level is either above or below the middle—because teachers are inclined to score students at the middle level, when there is one.

Rubrics are often used for determining proficiency levels and assigning grades. The level that is above the midpoint is usually designated as "proficient," "competent," or "passing"—that's a 3 on a 4-point rubric and a 4 on a 5- or 6-point rubric. The levels on a 6-point rubric can be described this way:

1 = minimal level	4 = proficient level
2 = beginning or limited level	5 = excellent level
3 = developing level	6 = superior level

Teachers also equate levels to letter grades.

These scoring guides help students become better writers because they lay out the qualities that constitute excellence and clarify teachers' expectations so students understand how the assignment will be assessed. Students, too, can use rubrics to improve their writing: Based on the rubric's criteria, they can examine their rough drafts and decide how to revise their writing to make it more effective. In addition, Vicki Spandel (2005) claims that rubrics are time savers: She says that rubrics drastically reduce the time it takes to read and respond to students' writing because the criteria on the rubric guide the assessment and reduce the need to write lengthy comments back to students.

Teachers follow these steps:

1. *Choose a rubric.* Teachers choose a rubric that's appropriate to the writing project or create one that reflects the assignment.

2. *Introduce the rubric.* Teachers distribute copies of the rubric to students and talk about the criteria used at each level, focusing on the requirements at the proficient level.

3. *Have students self-assess their writing.* Students use the rubric to self-assess their writing as part of the revising stage. They highlight phrases in the rubric or check off items that best describe their writing. Then they determine which level has the most highlighted words or checkmarks; that level is the overall score, and students circle it.

4. *Assess students' writing.* Teachers assess students' writing by highlighting phrases in the rubric or checking off items that best describe the composition. Then they assign the overall score by determining which level has the most highlighted words or checkmarks and circle it.

5. *Conference with students.* Teachers talk with students about the assessment, identifying strengths and weaknesses. Then students set goals for the next writing assignment.

Students use rubrics during writing workshop or whenever they're using the writing process to draft and refine a piece of writing. Many commercially prepared rubrics are currently available: State departments of education post rubrics for mandated writing tests on their websites, and school districts hire teams of teachers or consultants to develop writing rubrics for each grade level. Spandel (2005) provides rubrics that assess the six traits of writing. Other rubrics are provided with basal reading programs, in professional books for teachers, and on the Internet.

Even though commercially prepared rubrics are convenient, they may not be appropriate for some groups of students or for specific writing assignments. The rubrics may have only 4 levels when 6 would be better, or they may have been designed for a different grade level. They also may not address a specific genre, or they may have been written for teachers, not in kid-friendly language. Because of these limitations, teachers often decide to develop their own rubrics or adapt commercial rubrics to meet their own needs.

In this reading-stage activity, teachers observe individual students as they read aloud and record information to analyze their reading fluency (Clay, 2000). They calculate the percentage of words the student reads correctly and then analyze the miscues or errors. Teachers make a checkmark on a copy of the text as the student reads each word correctly and use other marks to indicate words that the student doesn't know or mispronounces.

Running Records

Teachers conduct running records with individual students using these steps:

1. *Choose a book.* Teachers have the student choose an excerpt at least 100 words in length from a book he or she is reading for the assessment. For beginning readers, the text can be shorter.

2. *Take the running record.* As the student reads the excerpt aloud, the teacher records information about the words read correctly as well as those misread. The teacher makes checkmarks on a copy of the text for each word read correctly and uses other marks for miscues. The box on page 464 shows how to mark miscues.

3. *Calculate the percentage of miscues.* Teachers calculate the percentage of miscues by dividing the number of miscues by the total number of words read. When the student makes 5% or fewer errors, the book is considered to be at the student's independent level. When there are 6–10% errors, the book is at the student's instructional level, and when there are more than 10% errors, the book is too difficult—the student's frustration level.

4. *Analyze the miscues.* Teachers look for patterns in the miscues in order to determine how the student is growing as a reader and what strategies and skills should be taught next.

Many teachers conduct running records on all their students at the beginning of the school year and at the end of grading periods. In addition, teachers do running records more often during guided reading groups and with students who aren't making expected progress in reading to diagnose their reading problems and make instructional decisions.

How to Mark Miscues

Miscue	Explanation	Marking
Incorrect word	If the student reads a word incorrectly, the teacher writes the incorrect word and the correct word under it.	take / taken
Self-correction	If the student self-corrects an error, the teacher writes SC (for "self-correction") following the incorrect word.	for SC / from
Unsuccessful attempt	If the student attempts to pronounce a word, the teacher records each attempt and adds the correct text underneath.	be-bēf-before / before
Skipped word	If the student skips a word, the teacher marks the error with a dash.	— / the
Inserted word	If the student says words that are not in the text, the teacher writes an insertion symbol (caret) and records the inserted words.	not / ^
Supplied word	If the student can't identify a word, the teacher supplies it and writes T above the word.	T / which
Repetition	If the student repeats a word or phrase, it isn't scored as a miscue, but the teacher notes it by making a checkmark for each repetition.	✓✓✓ / so

Semantic Feature Analysis

Teachers create a semantic feature analysis to help students examine the characteristics of vocabulary words or content-area concepts (Pittelman, Heimlich, Berglund, & French, 1991). They draw a grid for the analysis with words or concepts listed on one axis and the characteristics or components listed on the other. Students reading a novel, for example, can do a semantic feature analysis with vocabulary words listed on one axis and the characters' names on the other; they decide which words relate to which characters and use pluses and minuses to mark the relationships on the grid. Teachers often do a semantic feature analysis with the whole class, but students can work in small groups or individually to complete the grid. The examination should be done as a whole-class activity, however, so that students can share their insights.

Here are the steps in doing a semantic feature analysis:

1. *Create a grid.* Teachers create a grid with vocabulary or concepts listed on the vertical axis and characteristics or categories on the horizontal axis.

2. *Complete the grid.* Students complete the grid, cell by cell, by considering the relationship between each item on the vertical axis and the items on the horizontal axis. Then they mark the cell with a plus to indicate a relationship, a minus to indicate no relationship, and a question mark when they're unsure.

3. *Examine the grid.* Students and the teacher examine the grid for patterns and then draw conclusions based on the patterns.

Teachers have students do a semantic feature analysis as part of a literature focus unit or a thematic unit. In a thematic unit on immigration, for example, fifth-grade class did a semantic feature analysis, shown on the next page, to review what they were learning about America as a culturally pluralistic society. They listed the groups of peo-

Fifth Graders' Semantic Feature Analysis on Immigration

	Arrived in the 1600s	Arrived in the 1700s	Arrived in the 1800s	Arrived in the 1900s	Came to to Ellis Island	Came for religious freedom	Came for safety	Came for opportunity	Were refugees	Experienced prejudice
English	+	+	–	–	–	+	–	+	–	–
Africans	+	+	+	–	–	–	–	–	–	+
Irish	–	–	+	–	–	–	+	+	+	+
Other Europeans	–	+	+	+	+	–	+	+	+	+
Jews	–	–	+	+	+	+	+	–	+	+
Chinese	–	–	+	–	–	–	–	–	–	+
Latinos	–	–	–	+	–	–	–	+	–	+
Southeast Asians	–	–	–	+	–	–	+	+	+	+

Code: + = yes
     – = no
     ? = don't know

ple who immigrated to the United States on one axis and historical features on the other. Next, they completed the grid by marking each cell. Afterward, the students examined it for patterns and identified these big ideas:

> *Different peoples immigrated to America at different times.*
>
> *The Africans who came as slaves were the only people who were brought to America against their will.*
>
> *The English were the only immigrants who didn't suffer prejudice.*

Teachers use shared reading to read authentic literature—stories, informational books, and poems—with students who couldn't read those books independently (Holdaway, 1979). Teachers read the book aloud, modeling fluent reading, and then they read the book again and again for several days. The focus for the first reading is students' enjoyment. Teachers draw students' attention to concepts about print, comprehension, and interesting words and sentences during the next couple of readings. Finally, students focus on decoding particular words during the last reading or two.

Shared Reading

Students are actively involved in shared reading. Teachers encourage them to make predictions and to chime in on reading repeated words and phrases. Individual students or small groups take turns reading brief parts once they begin to recognize words and phrases. Students examine interesting features that they notice in the book—punctuation marks, illustrations, tables of contents, for example—and teachers point out others. They also talk about the book, both while they're reading and afterward. Shared reading builds on students' experience listening to their parents read bedtime stories (Fisher & Medvic, 2000).

Teachers follow these steps to use shared reading with the whole class or small groups of students:

1. *Introduce the text.* Teachers talk about the book or other text by activating or building background knowledge on topics related to the book and by reading the title and the author's name aloud.

2. *Read the text aloud.* Teachers read the story aloud to students, using a pointer (a dowel rod with a pencil eraser on the end) to track as they read. They invite students to be actively involved by making predictions and by joining in the reading, if the story is repetitive.

3. *Have a* grand conversation. Students talk about the story, ask questions, and share their responses.

4. *Reread the story.* Students take turns using the pointer to track the reading and turning pages. Teachers invite students to join in reading familiar and predictable words. Also, they take opportunities to teach and use graphophonic cues and reading strategies while reading. Teachers vary the support that they provide, depending on students' reading expertise.

5. *Continue the process.* Teachers continue to reread the story with students over a period of several days, again having students turn pages and take turns using the pointer to track the text while reading. They encourage students who can read the text to read along with them.

6. *Have students read independently.* After students become familiar with the text, teachers distribute individual copies of the book or other text for students to read independently and use for a variety of activities.

Teachers use shared reading during literature focus units, literature circles, and thematic units. When doing shared reading with young children, teachers use enlarged texts, including big books, poems written on charts, Language Experience stories, and interactive writing charts, so that students can see the text and read along. Teachers also use shared reading techniques to read books that older students can't read themselves (Allen, 2002). Students each have a copy of the novel, content-area textbook, or other book, and the teacher and students read together. The teacher or another fluent reader reads aloud while students follow along in the text, reading to themselves.

Sketch-to-Stretch

Sketch-to-stretch is a tool for helping students deepen their comprehension of stories they've read (Short & Harste, 1996). Students work in small groups to draw pictures or diagrams that represent what the story means to them, not pictures of their favorite character or episode. In particular, they focus on theme and on symbols to represent the theme as they make sketch-to-stretch drawings (Dooley & Maloch, 2005). An added benefit is that students learn that stories rarely have only one interpretation and that by reflecting on the characters and events, they usually discover one or more themes.

Students need many opportunities to experiment with this activity before they move beyond drawing pictures of the story events or characters to be able to think symbolically. It's helpful to introduce this instructional procedure through a **minilesson** and to draw several sketches together as a class before students do their own. With practice, students learn that there isn't a single correct interpretation, and teachers help students focus on the interpretation rather than on their artistic talents. The box below shows a fourth grader's sketch-to-stretch made after reading *The Ballad of Lucy Whipple* (Cushman, 1996), a story set during the California gold rush. The sketch-to-stretch emphasizes two themes of the book—you make your own happiness, and home is where you are.

Teachers follow these steps as they implement this instructional procedure:

1. *Read and respond to a story.* Students read a story or several chapters of a longer book, and they respond to the story in a **grand conversation** or in **reading logs**.

2. *Discuss the themes.* Students and the teacher talk about the themes in the story and ways to symbolize meanings. Teachers remind students that there are many ways to represent the meaning of an experience, and they explain that students can use lines, colors, shapes, symbols, and words to visually represent what a story means to them. They talk about possible meanings and ways they might visually represent these meanings.

3. *Draw the sketches.* Students work in small groups to draw sketches that reflect what the story means to them. Teachers emphasize that students should focus on their thinking about the meaning of the story, not on their favorite part, and that there's no single correct interpretation of the story. They also remind students that the artistic quality of their drawings is less important than their interpretation.

A Fourth Grader's Sketch-to-Stretch About *The Ballad of Lucy Whipple*

4. *Share the sketches.* Students meet in small groups to share their sketches and talk about the symbols they used. Teachers encourage classmates to study each student's sketch and tell what they think the student is trying to convey.

5. *Share some sketches with the class.* Each group chooses one sketch from their group to share with the class.

6. *Revise sketches and make final copies.* Students add to their sketches based on feedback they received and ideas from classmates, and then they make a final copy of their sketches.

Students can use sketch-to-stretch whenever they're reading stories. In literature circles, for example, students create sketch-to-stretch drawings about themes and symbols that they share during group meetings (Whitin, 2002). Through this sharing, students gain insights about their classmates' thinking and clarify their own understanding. The same is true when students create and share sketch-to-stretch drawings during literature focus units.

Story Boards

Story boards are cards on which the illustrations and text from a picture book have been attached. Teachers make story boards by cutting apart two copies of a picture book and gluing the pages on pieces of tagboard. The most important use of story boards is to sequence the events of a story by lining the cards up on a chalkboard tray or hanging them on a clothesline. Once the pages of the picture book have been laid out, students visualize the story and its structure in new ways and examine the illustrations more closely. For example, students arrange story boards from *How I Became a Pirate* (Long, 2003) to retell the story and pick out the beginning, middle, and end. They use story boards to identify the dream sequences in the middle of *Abuela* (Dorros, 1997) and compare versions of folktales, such as *The Mitten* (Brett, 1989; Tresselt, 1989) and *The Woodcutter's Mitten* (Koopmans, 1995).

Teachers use this instructional procedure because it allows students to manipulate and sequence stories and examine illustrations more carefully. Story boards are especially useful tools for English learners who use them to preview a story before reading or to review the events in a story after reading. ELs also draw story boards because they can often share their understanding better through art than through language. In addition, story boards present many opportunities for teaching comprehension when only one copy of a picture book is available.

Teachers generally use story boards with a small group of students or with the whole class, but individual students can reexamine them as part of center activities. Here are the steps:

1. *Collect two copies of a book.* Teachers use two copies of a picture book for the story boards. Paperback copies are preferable because they're less expensive. In a few picture books, all the illustrations are on right-hand or left-hand pages, so only one copy is needed.

2. *Cut the books apart.* Teachers remove the covers and separate the pages, evening out the cut edges.

3. *Attach the pages to pieces of cardboard.* Teachers glue each page or double-page spread to a piece of cardboard, making sure that pages from each book are alternated so that each illustration is included.

4. *Laminate the cards.* Teachers laminate the cards so that they can withstand use by students.

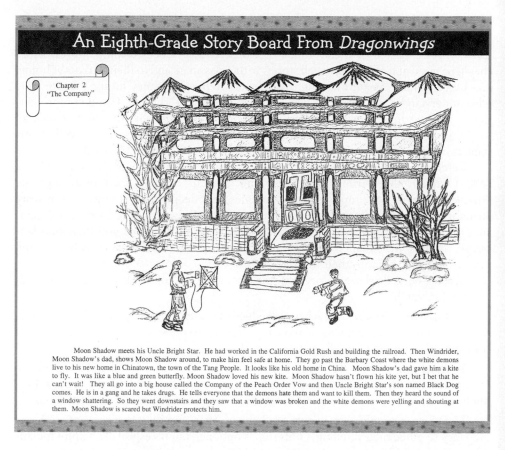

An Eighth-Grade Story Board From *Dragonwings*

Chapter 2
"The Company"

Moon Shadow meets his Uncle Bright Star. He had worked in the California Gold Rush and building the railroad. Then Windrider, Moon Shadow's dad, shows Moon Shadow around, to make him feel safe at home. They go past the Barbary Coast where the white demons live to his new home in Chinatown, the town of the Tang People. It looks like his old home in China. Moon Shadow's dad gave him a kite to fly. It was like a blue and green butterfly. Moon Shadow loved his new kite. Moon Shadow hasn't flown his kite yet, but I bet that he can't wait! They all go into a big house called the Company of the Peach Order Vow and then Uncle Bright Star's son named Black Dog comes. He is in a gang and he takes drugs. He tells everyone that the demons hate them and want to kill them. Then they heard the sound of a window shattering. So they went downstairs and they saw that a window was broken and the white demons were yelling and shouting at them. Moon Shadow is scared but Windrider protects him.

5. *Use the cards in sequencing activities.* Teachers use the story board cards for a number of activities, including sequencing, story structure, rereading, and word-study activities.

Students use story boards for a variety of activities during literature focus units. For a sequencing activity, teachers pass out the cards in a random order, and students line up around the classroom to sequence the story events. Story boards can also be used when only a few copies of a picture book are available so that students can identify words for the word wall, notice literary language, examine an element of story structure, or study the illustrations. When students read novels, they create their own story boards. Partners work together to create a story board for one chapter: They make a poster with a detailed drawing illustrating events in the chapter and write a paragraph-length summary of it. Two eighth graders' story board summarizing Chapter 2 of *Dragonwings* (Yep, 1975) is shown here.

Teachers use story retelling to monitor students' comprehension (Morrow, 1985). Teachers sit one-on-one with individual students in a quiet area of the classroom and ask them to retell a story they've just read or listened to read aloud. While the student is retelling, teachers use a teacher-made scoring sheet to mark the information that the student includes. If the student hesitates or doesn't finish retelling the story, teachers ask questions, such as "What happened next?" When they retell a story, students organize the information they remember to provide a personalized summary that reveals their level of comprehension (Hoyt, 1999).

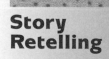

Story Retelling

Teachers can't assume that students already know how to retell stories, even though many do. Through explanations and demonstrations of the retelling procedure, students learn what's expected of them. Students also need to practice retelling stories before they'll be good at it. They can retell stories with a classmate and to their parents at home.

Once teachers begin listening to students retell stories, they notice that students who understand a story retell it differently than those who don't. Good comprehenders' retellings make sense: They reflect the organization of the story and include all of the important story events. In contrast, weak comprehenders often recall events haphazardly or omit important events, especially those in the middle of the story.

Retelling is an instructional tool as well as an assessment tool. McKenna and Stahl (2003) explain that through story retelling, students expand their oral language, enhance their use of comprehension strategies, and deepen their knowledge of story structure. When students participate regularly in retelling activities, their comprehension improves as they learn to focus on the big ideas in the story, and their oral language abilities are enhanced as they incorporate sentence patterns, vocabulary, and phrases from stories into their own talk.

Teachers usually share a story with the class and then follow these steps as individual students retell it:

1. Introduce the story. Teachers introduce the story by reading the title, examining the cover of the book, or talking about a topic related to the story. They also explain that students will be asked to retell the story afterward.

2. Read and discuss the story. Students read the story or listen to it read aloud. When students are reading the story themselves, it's essential that the story is at their reading level. Afterward, they talk about the story, sharing ideas and clarifying confusions.

3. Create a graphic organizer. Students create a graphic organizer or a series of drawings to guide their retelling. (This step is optional, but it's especially helpful for students who have difficulty retelling stories.)

4. Have a student retell the story. Teachers ask students to individually retell the story in their own words, asking questions, if necessary, to elicit more information:

Who was the story about?

What happened next?

Where did the story take place?

What did the character do next?

How did the story end?

5. Mark the scoring guide. Teachers assess the retelling using a scoring guide that they mark as the student retells the story. The scoring guide lists important information about characters and events in the story, usually organized into beginning, middle, and end sections. As they listen to the student's retelling, teachers place checkmarks by each piece of information that the student recalls. If a student omits important information, teachers ask questions to prompt the student's recall, and they write P beside information that was recalled with prompting.

Teachers often use this instructional procedure during literature focus units and guided reading to monitor students' comprehension of stories they've read and listened to read aloud. Students can also retell informational books; in these retellings, the focus is on summarizing the big ideas and their relationships rather than on story events (Flynt & Cooter, 2005). Their retellings should address these questions:

What are the big ideas?

How are the big ideas structured?

What is the author's purpose?

What did students learn that they didn't already know?

For students to remember the big ideas they're learning, it's essential that they make personal, world, and textual connections to them. They need adequate background knowledge about a topic to make connections—and if they can't make any connections, it's unlikely they'll understand or remember the big ideas.

Sustained Silent Reading

Sustained Silent Reading (SSR) is an independent reading time set aside during the school day for students in one class or the entire school to silently read self-selected books (Gardiner, 2005). In some schools, everyone—students, teachers, principals, secretaries, and custodians—stops to read, usually for a 15- to 30-minute period. SSR is a popular reading activity that's known by a variety of names, including "drop everything and read" (DEAR), "sustained quiet reading time" (SQUIRT), and "our time to enjoy reading" (OTTER).

Teachers use SSR to increase the amount of reading students do every day and to develop their ability to read silently and without interruption (Hunt, 1967). SSR follows these guidelines:

- ◆ Students choose the books they read.
- ◆ Students read silently.
- ◆ The teacher serves as a model by reading.
- ◆ Students choose one book or other reading material for the entire reading time.
- ◆ The teacher sets a timer for a predetermined, uninterrupted time period, usually 15–30 minutes.
- ◆ Everyone participates.
- ◆ The teacher doesn't keep records or evaluate students on their performance. (Pilgreen, 2000)

Even though SSR was specifically developed without follow-up activities, many teachers use a few carefully selected and brief follow-up activities to sustain students' interest in reading books. For example, students often discuss their reading with a partner, or volunteers give **book talks** to tell the whole class about their books. As students listen to one another, they get ideas about books that they might like to read. In some classrooms, students develop a ritual of passing on the books they've finished reading to interested classmates.

Through numerous studies, SSR has been found to be beneficial in developing students' reading ability—fluency, vocabulary, and comprehension (Krashen, 1993; Marshall, 2002; Pilgreen, 2000). In addition, it promotes a positive attitude toward reading and encourages students to develop the habit of daily reading. Because students choose the books they'll read, they have the opportunity to develop their own tastes and preferences as readers.

Teachers follow these steps in implementing this instructional procedure:

1. *Set aside a time for SSR.* Teachers allow time every day for uninterrupted, independent reading; it may last for only 10 minutes in first-grade classrooms or 20 to 30 minutes or more in the upper grades. Teachers often begin with a 10-minute period and then extend the time as students build endurance and want to continue reading.

2. *Ensure that students have books to read.* Students read independently in books they keep at their desks. Beginning readers often reread three or four leveled readers that they've already read during SSR.

3. *Set a timer for a predetermined time.* Teachers set the timer for the SSR reading period. To ensure that students aren't disturbed during SSR, some teachers place a "do not disturb" sign on the door.

4. *Read along with students.* Teachers read a book, magazine, or newspaper for pleasure while students read to model what capable readers do and to show that reading is a pleasurable activity.

When all teachers in a school are working together to set up SSR, they meet to set a daily time for this special reading activity and lay the ground rules for the program. Many schools have SSR first thing in the morning or at some other convenient time during the day. What's most important is that SSR is held every day at the same time, and that all students and adults in the school stop what they're doing to read. If teachers use the time to grade papers or work with individual students, the program won't be effective. The principal and other staff members should also make a habit of visiting a different classroom each day to join in the reading activity.

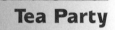

Tea Party

Students participate in a tea party to read or reread excerpts from a story, informational book, or content-area textbook. It's an active, participatory activity with students moving around the classroom and socializing with classmates as they read short excerpts aloud to each other and talk about them (Beers, 2003). Teachers choose and make copies of excerpts, back them with tagboard, and laminate them. Then they distribute the excerpts to students, provide some rehearsal time, and have students participate in the tea party activity.

Teachers often use tea party as a prereading activity to introduce a new chapter in a content-area textbook. They usually select the excerpts in order to introduce big ideas and related vocabulary, familiarize students with a new text, and build background knowledge. At other times, teachers invite students to reread favorite excerpts to celebrate a book they've finished reading. When tea party is used as a postreading activity, students review big ideas, summarize the events in a story, or focus on an element of story structure. Students can also create vocabulary cards, each featuring a word from the word wall, its definition, and an illustration. After making the cards, students participate in a tea party, sharing their word cards and explaining the words to their classmates.

This instructional procedure is especially valuable for English learners because students have opportunities to build background knowledge before reading and review texts after reading in a supportive, social classroom environment (Rea & Mercuri, 2006). It's important that teachers choose excerpts that are written at English learners' reading levels or adapt them so that these students will be able to read them fluently.

Teachers follow these steps as they implement tea party:

1. *Make the cards.* Teachers make cards with excerpts from a story, informational book, or content-area textbook that students are reading. They laminate the cards, or they use sentence strips with younger students.

2. *Practice reading.* Students practice reading the excerpts to themselves several times until they can read them fluently.

3. *Share excerpts.* Students move around the classroom, stopping to read their excerpts to classmates. When students pair up, they take turns reading their excerpts. After the first student reads, both students discuss the text; then the other student reads and both students comment on the second student's text. Then students move apart and find other classmates to read their cards to.

Tea Party Cards With Information About Ecology

Recycling means using materials over and over or making them into new things instead of throwing them away.	Acid rain happens when poisonous gases from factories and cars get into rain clouds. Then the gases mix with rain and fall back to earth. It is harmful to our environment and to the people and animals on earth.
Plastic bottles, plastic forks, and plastic bags last forever! A big problem with plastic is that it doesn't biodegrade. Instead of filling landfills with plastic, it should be recycled.	Many cities have air filled with pollution called smog. This pollution is so bad that the sky looks brown, not blue.
The ozone layer around the earth protects us from the harmful rays of the sun. This layer is being damaged by gases called chloro-fluorocarbons or CFCs. These gases are used in air conditioners, fire extinguishers, and styrofoam.	Americans cut down 850 million trees last year to make paper products. Sound like a lot of trees? Consider this: One tree can be made into approximately 700 grocery bags, and a large grocery store uses about that many bags in an hour!

4. Share excerpts with the class. Students return to their desks after 10 to 15 minutes, and teachers invite several students to read their excerpts to the class or talk about what they learned through the tea party activity.

Tea party is a good way to celebrate the conclusion of a literature focus unit or a thematic unit, and the activity reinforces the main ideas taught during the unit. Teachers also use tea party to introduce a thematic unit by choosing excerpts from informational books or content-area textbooks that present the main ideas and key vocabulary to be taught during the unit. The box above shows six tea party cards from a class set that a seventh-grade teacher used to introduce a unit on ecology. The teacher collected some of the sentences and paragraphs from informational books and a textbook chapter that students would read, and she wrote other selections herself. Students read and discussed the excerpts and began a **word wall** with the key words. These two activities activated students' background knowledge about ecology and began to build new concepts.

Think-Alouds

Teachers use the think-aloud procedure to teach students how to direct and monitor their thinking during reading (Wilhelm, 2001). By making their thinking explicit, they're demonstrating what capable readers do implicitly (Keene & Zimmerman, 2007). After they watch teachers think aloud, students practice the procedure by thinking aloud about the literacy strategies they're learning. As they think aloud, students respond to the text, identify big ideas, ask self-questions, make connections, figure out how to solve problems that arise, and reflect on their use of strategies. This procedure is valuable because students learn to be more active readers. They learn how to think metacognitively and to regulate their own cognitive processes (Baker, 2002).

Teachers use these steps to teach students to think aloud:

1. *Choose a book.* Teachers who work with younger children usually choose a big book, and those who teach older students often make copies of an excerpt from a book they're reading aloud to the class to demonstrate how to think aloud.

2. *Plan the think-aloud.* Teachers decide which strategies they want to demonstrate, where they'll pause, and the kinds of thinking they want to share.

3. *Demonstrate a think-aloud.* Teachers read the text, pausing to think aloud, explaining what they're thinking and how they're using a strategy or solving a reading problem. They often use these "I" sentence starters to talk about their thinking:

I wondered if . . .

This makes me think of . . .

I was confused by . . .

I didn't understand why . . .

I think the big idea is . . .

I reread this part because . . .

4. *Annotate the text.* Teachers write a small self-stick note about their thinking and attach it next to the text that prompted the think-aloud. They often use a word or phrase, such as *picture in my mind*, *context clues*, or *reread*, to quickly document their thinking.

5. *Continue thinking aloud.* Teachers continue reading the book, pausing to think aloud again and annotate the text with additional notes about their thinking.

6. *Reflect on the procedure.* Teachers review their annotations, talk about their strategy use, and reflect on the usefulness of think-alouds as a tool for comprehending what they're reading.

7. *Repeat the procedure.* Teachers read another book and have students take turns thinking aloud and annotating the text. Once students are familiar with the procedure, they practice doing think-alouds in small groups and with partners.

Once students know how to think aloud, teachers can use this procedure as an assessment tool. During student–teacher conferences, students reflect on their reading and evaluate how well they use particular strategies, and they think about what they could do differently to comprehend more effectively. Students can also refer to their annotations and write reflections about their use of particular strategies.

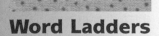

Word Ladders

Word ladders are games where students change one word into another through a series of steps, altering a single letter at each step. The goal is to use as few steps as possible to change the first word into the last word. This type of puzzle was invented by Lewis Carroll, author of *Alice in Wonderland*, in 1878. Typically, the first and last words are related in some way, such as *fall–down*, *slow–fast*, and *trick–treat*, and all the middle words must be real words. A well-known word ladder is *cat–dog*, which can be solved in three steps: *cat–cot–dot–dog*.

A Cat–Dog Word Ladder

The teacher says:	Students write:
Begin with the word *cat*.	cat
Change the vowel to form another word for *bed*, sometimes the kind of bed you use when you're camping.	cot
Change one letter to form a word that means "a tiny, round mark."	dot
Finally, change the final consonant to make a word that goes with the first word, *cat*.	dog

Teachers can create a variation of word ladders to practice phonics, spelling, and vocabulary skills with their students (Rasinski, 2006). They guide students to build a series of words as they provide graphophonemic and semantic clues about the words. Like traditional word ladder puzzles, each word comes from the previous word, but students may be asked to add, delete, or change one or more letters from the previous word to make a new word. Students write the words vertically in list form so they can see the words they've written. A *cat–dog* word ladder is shown above. Teachers make their own word ladders to reinforce the phonics concepts and spelling patterns their students are learning; in this case, it's not necessary to ensure that the first and last words are related as in traditional word ladders. A word ladder to practice words with the short and long sounds of /oo/ is shown on page 476.

Here's the procedure for using word ladders:

1. Create the word ladder. Teachers create a word ladder with 5 to 15 words, choosing words from spelling lists or phonics lessons, and they write clues for each word, trying to incorporate a combination of graphophonemic and semantic clues.

2. Pass out supplies. Teachers often have students use dry-erase boards and marking pens for this activity, but they can also use blank paper or paper with word ladders already drawn on them.

3. Do the word ladder. Teachers read the clues they've prepared and have students write the words. Students take turns identifying the words and spelling them correctly. When necessary, teachers provide additional clues and explain any unfamiliar words, phonics rules, or spelling patterns.

4. Review the word ladder. Once students complete the word ladder, they reread the words and talk about any words they had difficulty writing. They also volunteer other words they can write using these letters.

Word ladders are a fun way for students to practice the phonics skills they're learning and, at the same time, think about the meanings of words. The activity's gamelike format makes it engaging for students and teachers. To see more word ladders, check Rasinski's (2005a, 2005b) books of easy-to-use word ladder games for second through sixth graders; word ladder games are also available on the Internet.

An /oo/ Word Ladder

The teacher says:	Students write:
Write the word *good*. We're practicing words with *oo* today.	good
Change the beginning sound to write the past tense of *stand*. The word is *stood*.	stood
Change the ending sound to write a word that means "a seat without arms or a back."	stool
Change the beginning sound to write a word that means the opposite of *warm*.	cool
Add two letters—one before and one after the *c*—to spell where we are right now.	school
Change the beginning sound to spell *tool*.	tool
Drop a letter to make a word that means *also*.	too
Change the first letter to write a word that means "a place where people can go to see wild animals."	zoo
Add a letter to *zoo* to spell the sound a car makes.	zoom
Change the beginning sound—use two letters for this blend—to spell something we use for sweeping.	broom
Change one letter to spell a word that means *creek*.	brook
Change the beginning sound to make a word that means "a dishonest person."	crook

Word Sorts

Students use word sorts to examine and categorize words according to their meanings, sound-symbol correspondences, or spelling patterns (Bear, Invernizzi, Templeton, & Johnston, 2008). The purpose of word sorts is to help students focus on conceptual and phonological features of words and identify recurring patterns. For example, as students sort cards with words such as *stopping, eating, hugging, running*, and *raining*, they discover the rule for doubling the final consonant in short-vowel words before adding an inflectional ending.

Teachers choose categories for word sorts, depending on instructional goals or students' developmental levels:

◆ Rhyming words, such as words that rhyme with *ball, fat, car*, and *rake*
◆ Consonant sounds, such as pictures of words beginning with *r* or *l*
◆ Sound-symbol relationships, such as words in which the final *y* sounds like long *i* (*cry*) and others in which the final *y* sounds like long *e* (*baby*)
◆ Spelling patterns, such as long-*e* words with various spelling patterns (*sea, greet, be, Pete*)
◆ Number of syllables, such as *pig, happy, afternoon*, and *television*
◆ Root words and affixes
◆ Conceptual relationships, such as words related to different characters in a story or to big ideas in a thematic unit

Many of the words chosen for word sorts come from books students are reading or thematic units. The boxes on the next page show two word sorts using words from *Holes* (Sachar, 2003); the first is a conceptual sort and the second is a grammar sort.

A Concept Sort Using Words From *Holes*

Stanley	Zero	Camp Green Lake	Mr. Sir	The Warden	The Escape
unlucky	nobody	wasteland	grotesque	Ms. Walker	miracle
sneakers	Hector Zeroni	guards	cowboy hat	holes	sploosh
Caveman	confession	investigation	swollen	venom	thumbs-up sign
overweight	homeless	yellow-spotted lizard	tattoo	miserable	impossible
callused	Clyde Livingston's shoes	scorpions	sunflower seeds	fingernail polish	ledges
million dollars	digger	girl scout camp	guard	make-up kit	Big Thumb
suitcase	frail	temperature	tougher	freckles	happiness

A Grammar Sort Using Words From *Holes*

Adjectives	Nouns	Verbs	Adverbs
half-opened	wasteland	chewing	surely
scratchy	curiosity	waits	previously
tougher	fossil	howled	quickly
desolate	allergies	startled	well
throbbing	pitchfork	watches	intently
metallic	warden	gazes	supposedly
shriveled	sneakers	wiggled	always
callused	Caveman	scooped	angrily

Word sorts are effective for English learners because students build skills to understand how English differs from their native language, and they develop knowledge to help them predict meaning through spelling (Bear, Helman, Invernizzi, & Templeton, 2007). Because word sorts can be done in small groups, teachers can choose words for the sorts that are appropriate for students' developmental levels.

Here are the steps for conducting a word sort:

1. *Choose a topic.* Teachers choose a language skill or content-area topic for the word sort and decide whether it will be an open or closed sort. In an open sort, students determine the categories themselves based on the words they're sorting. In a closed sort, teachers present the categories as they introduce the sorting activity.

2. *Compile a list of words.* Teachers compile a list of 6 to 20 words, depending on grade level, that exemplify particular categories, and they write the words on small cards. Or, small picture cards can be used.

3. *Introduce the sorting activity.* If it's a closed sort, teachers present the categories and have students sort word cards into these categories. If it's an open sort, students identify the words and look for possible categories. Students arrange and rearrange the cards until they are satisfied with the sorting. Then they add category labels.

4. *Make a permanent record.* Students make a permanent record of their sort by gluing the word cards onto a large sheet of construction paper or poster board or by writing the words on a sheet of paper.

5. *Share word sorts.* Students share their word sorts with classmates, explaining the categories they used (for open sorts).

Teachers use word sorts to teach phonics, spelling, and vocabulary. During literature focus units, students sort vocabulary words according to the beginning, middle, or end of the story or according to character. During thematic units, students sort vocabulary words according to big ideas.

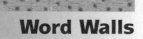

Word Walls

Word walls are collections of words posted in the classroom that students use for word-study activities and refer to when they're writing (Wagstaff, 1999). Teachers make word walls using construction-paper squares or sheets of butcher paper that have been divided into alphabetized sections. Students and the teacher write on the word wall interesting, confusing, or other important words from books they're reading and about big ideas they're learning during thematic units. Usually students choose the words to write on the word wall, and they may even do the writing themselves, but teachers add any important Tier 2 words that students haven't chosen.

A second type of word wall for high-frequency words is used in primary-grade classrooms: Teachers hang large sheets of construction paper, one for each letter of the alphabet, on a wall of the classroom, and then post high-frequency words such as *the*, *is*, *are*, *you*, *what*, and *to* as they're introduced (Cunningham, 2005; Lynch, 2005). This word wall remains on display, and additional words are added throughout the year. In kindergarten classrooms, teachers begin the school year by placing word cards with students' names on the wall chart and add common environmental print, such as *K-Mart* and *McDonald's*. Later in the year, they add words such as *I*, *love*, *the*, *you*, *Mom*, *Dad*, *good*, and other words that students want to be able to read and write.

Teachers usually create word walls with the whole class, and they follow these steps:

1. *Prepare the word wall.* Teachers prepare a blank word wall in the classroom from sheets of construction paper or butcher paper, dividing it into 12 to 24 boxes and labeling the boxes with letters of the alphabet.

2. *Introduce the word wall.* Teachers introduce the word wall and write several key words on it before beginning to read.

3. *Add words to the word wall.* Students suggest "important" words for the word wall as they are reading a book or participating in thematic-unit activities. Students and the teacher write the words in the alphabetized blocks, making sure to write large enough so that most students can see the words. If a word is misspelled, it's corrected because students will be using the words in various activities. Sometimes the teacher adds a small picture or writes a synonym for a difficult word, puts a box around the root word, or writes the plural form or other related words nearby.

4. *Use the word wall.* Teachers use the word wall for a variety of vocabulary activities, and students refer to the word wall when they're writing.

Teachers use word walls during literature focus units and thematic units, and primary-grade teachers also teach high-frequency words using word walls. They involve students in a variety of word-study activities. For example, students do quickwrites using words from the word wall and refer to the word wall when they're writing journal entries and books. Teachers also use words from the word wall for word sorts and tea party activities. In addition, primary-grade teachers use words from high-frequency word walls for phonics and other word-study activities. One example is a popular word hunt game: Teachers distribute small dry-erase boards and have students identify and write words from the word wall on their boards according to the clues they provide. For example, teachers say "Find the word that begins like _____," "Look for the word that rhymes with _____," "Find the word that alphabetically follows _____," or "Think of the word that means the opposite of _____," depending on what students are learning. Students read and reread the words, apply phonics and word-study concepts, and practice spelling high-frequency words as they play this game.

Writing Groups

During the revising stage of the writing process, students meet in writing groups to share their rough drafts and get feedback on how well they're communicating (Tompkins, 2008). Writing group members offer compliments about things writers have done well and make suggestions for improvement. Their comments reflect these topics and other aspects of the writer's craft:

leads	word choice	voice
dialogue	sentences	rhyme
endings	character development	sequence
description	point of view	flashbacks
ideas	organization	alliterations

These topics are used for both compliments and suggestions. When students are offering a compliment, they might say, "I liked your lead. It grabbed me and made me keep listening," and when they're making a suggestion, they say, "I wonder if you could start with a question to make your lead more interesting. Maybe you could say, 'Have you ever ridden in a police car? Well, that's what happened to me!'"

Teaching students how to share their rough drafts in a writing group and offer constructive feedback isn't easy. When teachers introduce revision, they model appropriate responses because students may not know how to offer specific and meaningful comments tactfully. Teachers and students can brainstorm a list of appropriate compliments and suggestions and post it in the classroom to refer to. Comments should usually begin with "I," not "you." Notice the difference in tone in these two sentence stems: "I wonder if . . ." versus "You need to . . ." Here are some ways to begin compliments:

I like the part where . . .

I learned how . . .

I like the way you described . . .

I like how you organized the information because . . .

Students also offer suggestions about how classmates can revise their writing. It's important that students phrase what they say in helpful ways. Here are some ways to begin suggestions:

I got confused in the part about . . .

I wonder if you need a closing . . .

I'd like you to add more about . . .

I wonder if these paragraphs are in the right order . . .

I think you might want to combine these sentences . . .

Student-writers also ask classmates for help with specific problems they've identified. Looking to classmates for feedback is a big step in learning to revise. Here are some questions writers can ask:

What do you want to know more about?

Is there a part that I should throw away?

What details can I add?

What do you think is the best part of my writing?

Are there some words I need to change?

Writing groups work effectively once students understand how to support and help their classmates by offering compliments, making suggestions, and asking questions.

Revising is the most difficult part of the writing process because it's hard for students to stand back and evaluate their writing objectively in order to make changes to communicate more effectively. As students participate in writing groups, they learn how to accept compliments and suggestions and to provide useful feedback to classmates.

Teachers teach students how to use this instructional procedure so that they can then work in small groups to get ideas for revising their writing. Here are the steps:

1. *Read drafts aloud.* Students take turns reading their rough drafts aloud to the group. Everyone listens politely, thinking about compliments and suggestions they will make after the writer finishes reading. Only the writer looks at the composition because when classmates look at it, they quickly notice and comment on mechanical errors, even though the emphasis during revising is on content. Listening to the writing read aloud keeps the focus on content.

2. *Offer compliments.* After listening to the rough draft read aloud, classmates in the writing group tell the writer what they liked about the composition. These positive comments should be specific, focusing on strengths, rather than the often-heard "I liked it" or "It was good"; even though these are positive comments, they don't provide effective feedback.

3. *Ask clarifying questions.* Writers ask for assistance with trouble spots they identified earlier when rereading their writing, or they may ask questions that reflect more general concerns about how well they're communicating.

4. *Offer other revision suggestions.* Members of the writing group ask questions about things that were unclear to them and make suggestions about how to revise the rough draft.

5. *Repeat the process.* Members of the writing group repeat the process so that all students can share their rough drafts. The first four steps are repeated for each student's composition.

6. *Make plans for revision.* Students each make a commitment to revise their writing based on the comments and suggestions of the group members. The final decision on what to revise always rests with the writers themselves, but with the understanding that their rough drafts aren't perfect comes the realization that some revision will be necessary. When students verbalize their planned revisions, they're more likely to complete the revision stage.

Students meet in writing groups whenever they're using the writing process. Once they've written a rough draft, students are ready to share their writing and get some feedback from classmates. They often meet with the same writing group throughout the school year, or students can form groups when they're ready to get feedback about their rough drafts. Many teachers have students sign up on the chalkboard; this way, whenever four students are ready, they form a group. Both established and spontaneously formed groups can be effective. What matters most is that students get feedback about their writing when they need it.

PROFESSIONAL REFERENCES

Allen, J. (2002). *On the same page: Shared reading beyond the primary grades.* York, ME: Stenhouse.

Ashton-Warner, S. (1965). *Teacher.* New York: Simon & Schuster.

Atwell, N. (1998). *In the middle: New understandings about writing, reading, and learning.* Portsmouth, NH: Heinemann/Boynton/Cook.

Baker, L. (2002). Metacognition in comprehension instruction. In C. C. Block & M. Pressley (Eds.), *Comprehension instruction: Research-based best practices* (pp. 77–95). New York: Guilford Press.

Barone, D. (1990). The written responses of young children: Beyond comprehension to story understanding. *The New Advocate, 3,* 49–56.

Bear, D. R., Helman, L., Invernizzi, M., & Templeton, S. R. (2007). *Words their way with English learners: Word study for spelling, phonics, and vocabulary instruction.* Upper Saddle River, NJ: Merrill/Prentice Hall.

Bear, D. R., Invernizzi, M., Templeton, S., & Johnston, F. (2008). *Words their way: Word study for phonics, vocabulary, and spelling instruction* (4th ed.). Upper Saddle River, NJ: Merrill/Prentice Hall.

Beck, I. L., & McKeown, M. G. (2006). *Improving comprehension with questioning the author: A fresh and expanded view of a powerful approach.* New York: Scholastic.

Beers, K. (2003). *When kids can't read, what teachers can do.* Portsmouth, NH: Heinemann.

Berthoff, A. E. (1981). *The making of meaning.* Montclair, NJ: Boynton/Cook.

Blachowicz, C. L. Z. (1986). Making connections: Alternatives to the vocabulary notebook. *Journal of Reading, 29,* 643–649.

Black, A., & Stave, A. M. (2007). *A comprehensive guide to readers theatre: Enhancing fluency and comprehension in middle school and beyond.* Newark, DE: International Reading Association.

Brozo, W. G., & Simpson, M. L. (2007). *Content literacy for today's adolescents: Honoring diversity and building competence* (5th ed.). Upper Saddle River, NJ: Prentice Hall.

Button, K., Johnson, M. J., & Furgerson, P. (1996). Interactive writing in a primary classroom. *The Reading Teacher, 49,* 446–454.

Carr, E., & Ogle, D. (1987). K-W-L Plus: A strategy for comprehension and summarization. *Journal of Reading, 31,* 626–631.

Ciardello, A. V. (1998). Did you ask a good question today? *Journal of Adolescent and Adult Literacy, 42,* 210–220.

Clay, M. M. (2000). *Running records for classroom teachers.* Portsmouth, NH: Heinemann.

Crawford, A. N. (2003). Communicative approaches to second-language acquisition: The bridge to second-language literacy. In G. G. Garcia (Ed.), *English learners: Reaching the highest level of English literacy* (pp. 152–181). Newark, DE: International Reading Association.

Cunningham, P. M. (2005). *Phonics they use: Words for reading and writing* (4th ed.). New York: HarperCollins.

Cunningham, P. M., & Cunningham, J. W. (1992). Making words: Enhancing the invented spelling-decoding connection. *The Reading Teacher, 46,* 106–115.

Cunningham, P. M., & Hall, D. P. (1994a). *Making big words.* Parsippany, NJ: Good Apple.

Cunningham, P. M., & Hall, D. P. (1994b). *Making words.* Parsippany, NJ: Good Apple.

Daniels, H. (2001). *Literature circles: Voice and choice in book clubs and reading groups.* York, ME: Stenhouse.

Dooley. C. M., & Maloch, B. (2005). Exploring characters through visual representations. In N. L. Roser & M. G. Martinez (Eds.), *What a character! Character study as a guide to literary meaning making in grades K–8* (pp. 111–123). Newark, DE: International Reading Association.

Dorn, L. J., & Soffos, C. (2001). *Shaping literate minds: Developing self-regulated learners.* York, ME: Stenhouse.

Farr, R., & Tone, B. (1994). *Portfolio and performance assessment: Helping students evaluate their progress as readers and writers.* Fort Worth, TX: Harcourt Brace.

Fisher, B., & Medvic, E. F. (2000). *Perspectives on shared reading: Planning and practice.* Portsmouth, NH: Heinemann.

Fisher, D., Flood, K., Lapp, D., & Frey, N. (2004). Interactive read-alouds: Is there a common set of implementation practices? *The Reading Teacher, 58,* 8–17.

Flynn, R. M. (2007). *Dramatizing the content with curriculum-based readers theatre, grades 6–12.* Newark, DE: International Reading Association.

Flynt, E. S., & Cooter, R. B., Jr. (2005). Improving middle-grades reading in urban schools: The Memphis Comprehension Framework. *The Reading Teacher, 58,* 774–780.

Fountas, I. C., & Pinnell, G. S. (1996). *Guided reading: Good first teaching for all children.* Portsmouth, NH: Heinemann.

Gambrell, L. B., & Almasi, J. F. (Eds.). (1996). *Lively discussions! Fostering engaged reading.* Newark, DE: International Reading Association.

Gardiner, S. (2005). *Building students' literacy through SSR.* Alexandria, VA: Association for Supervision and Curriculum Development.

Graves, M. F., & Fitzgerald, J. (2003). Scaffolding reading experiences for multilingual classrooms. In G. G. Garcia (Ed.), *English learners: Reaching the highest level of English literacy* (pp. 96–124). Newark, DE: International Reading Association.

Hancock, M. R. (2008). *A celebration of literature and response: Children, books, and teachers in K–8 classrooms* (3rd ed.). Upper Saddle River, NJ: Merrill/Prentice Hall.

Head, M. H., & Readence, J. E. (1986). Anticipation guides: Meaning through prediction. In E. K. Dishner, T. W. Bean, J. E. Readence, & D. W. Moore (Eds.), *Reading in the content areas* (2nd ed., pp. 229–234). Dubuque, IA: Kendall/Hunt.

Holdaway, D. (1979). *Foundations of literacy.* Auckland, NZ: Ashton Scholastic.

Holston, V., & Santa, C. (1985). RAFT: A method of writing across the curriculum that works. *Journal of Reading, 28,* 456–457.

Hoyt, L. (1999). *Revisit, reflect, retell: Strategies for improving reading comprehension.* Portsmouth, NH: Heinemann.

Hoyt, L. (2000). *Snapshots.* Portsmouth, NH: Heinemann.

Hunt, L. (1967). Evaluation through teacher-pupil conferences. In T. C. Barrett (Ed.), *The evaluation of children's reading achievement* (pp. 111–126). Newark, DE: International Reading Association.

Ivey, G. (2003). "The teacher makes it more explainable" and other reasons to read aloud in the intermediate grades. *The Reading Teacher, 56,* 812–814.

Jacobson, J. M. (1990). Group vs. individual completion of a cloze passage. *Journal of Reading, 33,* 244–250.

Keehn, S., Martinez, M. G., & Roser, N. L. (2005). Exploring character through readers theatre. In N. L. Roser & M. G. Martinez (Eds.), *What a character! Character study as a guide to literary meaning making in grades K–8* (pp. 96–110). Newark, DE: International Reading Association.

Keene, E. O., & Zimmerman, S. (2007). *Mosaic of thought: The power of comprehension strategy instruction* (2nd ed.). Portsmouth, NH: Heinemann.

Krashen, S. (1993). *The power of reading.* Englewood, CO: Libraries Unlimited.

Langer, J. A. (1981). From theory to practice: A prereading plan. *Journal of Reading, 25,* 152–157.

Lynch, J. (2005). *High frequency word walls.* New York: Scholastic.

Macon, J. M., Bewell, D., & Vogt, M. E. (1991). *Responses to literature: Grades K–8*. Newark, DE: International Reading Association.

Marshall, J. C. (2002). *Are they really reading? Expanding SSR in the middle grades*. Portland, ME: Stenhouse.

McCauley, J. K., & McCauley, D. S. (1992). Using choral reading to promote language learning for ESL students. *The Reading Teacher, 45*, 526–533.

McKenna, M. C., & Stahl, S. A. (2003). *Assessment for reading instruction*. New York: Guilford Press.

McLaughlin, M., & Allen, M. B. (2001). *Guided comprehension: A teaching model for grades 3–8*. Newark, DE: International Reading Association.

Morrow, L. M. (1985). Retelling stories: A strategy for improving children's comprehension, concept of story structure, and oral language complexity. *Elementary School Journal, 85*, 647–661.

Ogle, D. M. (1986). K-W-L: A teaching model that develops active reading of expository text. *The Reading Teacher, 39*, 564–570.

Peregoy, S. F., & Boyle, O. F. (2008). *Reading, writing, and learning in ESL: A resource book for K–12 teachers* (5th ed.). Boston: Allyn & Bacon/Pearson.

Peterson, R., & Eeds, M. (2007). *Grand conversations: Literature groups in action* (updated ed.). New York: Scholastic.

Pilgreen, J. L. (2000). *The SSR handbook: How to organize and manage a sustained silent reading program*. Portsmouth, NH: Boynton/Cook/Heinemann.

Pittelman, S. D., Heimlich, J. E., Berglund, R. L., & French, M. P. (1991). *Semantic feature analysis: Classroom applications*. Newark, DE: International Reading Association.

Raphael, T. E., Highfield, K., & Au, K. H. (2006). *QAR now: A powerful and practical framework that develops comprehension and higher-level thinking in all students*. New York: Scholastic.

Rasinski, T. (2005a). *Daily word ladders: Grades 2–3*. New York: Scholastic.

Rasinski, T. (2005b). *Daily word ladders: Grades 4–6*. New York: Scholastic.

Rasinski, T. (2006). Developing vocabulary through word building. In C. C. Block & J. N. Mangieri (Eds.), *The vocabulary-enriched classroom: Practices for improving the reading performance of all students in grades 3 and up* (pp. 36–53). New York: Scholastic.

Rasinski, T., & Padak, N. (2004). *Effective reading strategies: Teaching children who find reading difficult*. Upper Saddle River, NJ: Merrill/Prentice Hall.

Rea, D. M., & Mercuri, S. P. (2006). *Research-based strategies for English language learners: How to teach goals and meet standards, K–8*. Portsmouth, NH: Heinemann.

Reutzel, D. R., & Cooter, R. B., Jr. (2008). *Teaching children to read: From basals to books* (5th ed.). Upper Saddle River, NJ: Merrill/Prentice Hall.

Routman, R. (2004). *Writing essentials: Raising expectations and results while simplifying teaching*. Portsmouth, NH: Heinemann.

Short, K. G., & Harste, J. (1996). *Creating classrooms for authors and inquirers*. Portsmouth, NH: Heinemann.

Spandel, V. (2005). *Creating writers: Through 6-trait writing assessment and instruction* (4th ed.). Boston: Allyn & Bacon.

Taylor, W. L. (1953). "Cloze procedure": A new tool for measuring readability. *Journalism Quarterly, 30*, 415–433.

Tierney, R. J., & Readence, J. E. (2005). *Reading strategies and practices: A compendium* (6th ed.). Boston: Allyn & Bacon.

Tompkins, G. E. (2008). *Teaching writing: Balancing process and product* (5th ed.). Upper Saddle River, NJ: Merrill/Prentice Hall.

Tompkins, G. E., & Collom, S. (Eds.). (2004). *Sharing the pen: Interactive writing with young children*. Upper Saddle River, NJ: Merrill/Prentice Hall.

Tovani, C. (2000). *I read it, but I don't get it: Comprehension strategies for adolescent readers*. York, ME: Stenhouse.

Vacca, R. T., & Vacca, J. L. (2008). *Content area reading: Literacy and learning across the curriculum* (9th ed.). Boston: Allyn & Bacon/Pearson.

Wagstaff, J. (1999). *Teaching reading and writing with word walls*. New York: Scholastic.

Whitin, P. E. (2002). Leading into literature circles through the sketch-to-stetch strategy. *The Reading Teacher, 55*, 444–450.

Wilhelm, J. D. (2001). *Improving comprehension with think-aloud strategies*. New York: Scholastic.

Wilhelm, J. D. (2002). *Action strategies for deepening comprehension*. New York: Scholastic.

Worthy, J., & Prater, K. (2002). "I thought about it all night": Readers theatre for reading fluency and motivation. *The Reading Teacher, 56*, 294–297.

CHILDREN'S BOOK REFERENCES

Bates, K. L. (2003). *America the beautiful*. New York: Putnam.

Brett, J. (1989). *The mitten*. New York: Putnam.

Carle, E. (2005). *A house for hermit crab*. New York: Aladdin Books.

Cronin, D. (2005). *Diary of a spider*. New York: HarperCollins.

Cushman, K. (1996). *The ballad of Lucy Whipple*. New York: Clarion Books.

Danziger, P. (1995). *You can't eat your chicken pox, Amber Brown*. New York: Putnam.

Danziger, P. (2006). *Amber Brown is not a crayon*. New York: Scholastic.

Dorros, A. (1997). *Abuela*. New York: Puffin Books.

Fleischman, P. (2004). *Joyful noise: Poems for two voices*. New York: HarperTrophy.

Guthrie, W. (2002). *This land is your land*. Boston: Little, Brown.

Hall, D. (1994). *I am the dog/I am the cat*. New York: Dial Books.

Hinton, S. E. (1997). *The outsiders*. New York: Puffin Books.

Hoberman, M. A. (2003). *The lady with the alligator purse*. Boston: Little, Brown.

Hughes, L. (2007). *The dream keeper and other poems*. New York: Knopf.

Jeffers, S. (1993). *Brother eagle, sister sky: A message from Chief Seattle*. New York: Puffin Books.

Konigsburg, E. L. (1998). *The view from Saturday*. New York: Aladdin Books.

Koopmans, L. (1995). *The woodcutter's mitten*. New York: Crocodile Books.

Kuskin, K. (2003). *Moon, have you met my mother? The collected poems of Karla Kuskin*. New York: HarperCollins.

Lewis, C. S. (2005). *The lion, the witch and the wardrobe*. New York: HarperCollins.

Long, M. (2003). *How I became a pirate*. San Diego: Harcourt.

Lowry, L. (1998). *Number the stars*. New York: Laurel Leaf.

Lowry, L. (2006). *The giver*. New York: Delacorte.

MacLachlan, P. (2004). *Sarah, plain and tall*. New York: HarperTrophy.

Paschen, E. (Ed.). (2005). *Poetry speaks to children*. Naperville, IL: Sourcebooks/MediaFusion.

Patron, S. (2006). *The higher power of Lucky*. New York: Atheneum.

Prelutsky, J. (2007). *My parents think I'm sleeping*. New York: Greenwillow.

Prelutsky, J. (2008). *The Random House book of poetry*. New York: Greenwillow.

Sachar, L. (2003). *Holes*. New York: Yearling.

Schmidt, G. D. (2007). *The Wednesday wars*. New York: Clarion Books.

Soto, G. (2005). *Neighborhood odes*. San Diego: Harcourt.

Taback, S. (1997). *There was an old lady who swallowed a fly*. New York: Viking.

Towle, W. (1993). *The real McCoy: The life of an African-American inventor*. New York: Scholastic.

Tresselt, A. (1989). *The mitten*. New York: HarperTrophy.

Yolen, J., & Peters, A. F. (Eds.). (2007). *Here's a little poem*. Cambridge, MA: Candlewick Press.

Aesthetic reading   Reading for pleasure.

Affix   A syllable added to the beginning (prefix) or end (suffix) of a word to change the word's meaning (e.g., *il-* in *illiterate* and *-al* in *national*).

Alphabetic principle   The assumption underlying alphabetical language systems that each sound has a corresponding graphic representation (or letter).

Antonyms   Words with opposite meanings (e.g., *good–bad*).

Applying   The fifth stage of the reading process, in which readers go beyond the text to use what they have learned in another literacy experience, often by making a project or reading another book.

Authentic   Activities and materials related to real-world reading and writing.

Automaticity   Identifying words accurately and quickly.

Background knowledge   A student's knowledge or previous experiences about a topic.

Basal readers   Reading textbooks that are leveled according to grade.

Basal reading program   A collection of student textbooks, workbooks, teacher's manuals, and other materials and resources for reading instruction used in kindergarten through sixth grade.

Big books   Enlarged versions of picture books that teachers read with children, usually in the primary grades.

Blend   To combine the sounds represented by letters to pronounce a word.

Bound morpheme   A morpheme that is not a word and cannot stand alone (e.g., *-s*, *tri-*).

Closed syllable   A syllable ending in a consonant sound (e.g., *make*, *duck*).

Cloze   An activity in which students replace words that have been deleted from a text.

Cluster   A spiderlike diagram used to collect and organize ideas after reading or before writing; also called a *map* or a *web*.

Comprehension   The process of constructing meaning using both the author's text and the reader's background knowledge for a specific purpose.

Concepts about print   Basic understandings about the way print works, including the direction of print, spacing, punctuation, letters, and words.

Consonant   A speech sound characterized by friction or stoppage of the airflow as it passes through the vocal tract; usually any letter except *a*, *e*, *i*, *o*, and *u*.

Consonant digraph   Two adjacent consonants that represent a sound not represented by either consonant alone (e.g., *th–this*, *ch–chin*, *sh–wash*, *ph–telephone*).

Content-area reading   Reading in social studies, science, and other areas of the curriculum.

Context clue   Information from the words or sentences surrounding a word that helps to clarify the word's meaning.

Cueing systems   The phonological, semantic, syntactic, and pragmatic information that students rely on as they read.

Decoding   Using word-identification strategies to pronounce and attach meaning to an unfamiliar word.

Diagnosis   Determining specific problems readers are having, generally using a test.

Differentiated instruction   Procedures for assisting students in learning, providing options, challenging students, and matching books to students to maximize their learning.

Diphthong   A sound produced when the tongue glides from one sound to another; it is represented by two vowels (e.g., *oy–boy*, *ou–house*, *ow–how*).

Drafting   The second stage of the writing process, in which writers pour out ideas in a rough draft.

Echo reading   The teacher or other reader reads a sentence and a group of students reread or "echo" what was read.

Editing   The fourth stage of the writing process, in which writers proofread to identify and correct spelling, capitalization, punctuation, and grammar errors.

Efferent reading   Reading for information.

Elkonin boxes   A strategy for segmenting sounds in a word that involves drawing a box to represent each sound.

Emergent literacy   Children's early reading and writing development before conventional reading and writing.

Environmental print   Signs, labels, and other print found in the community.

Etymology   The origin and history of words; the etymological information is enclosed in brackets in dictionary entries.

Explicit instruction   Systematic instruction of concepts, strategies, and skills that builds from simple to complex.

Exploring   The fourth stage of the reading process, in which readers reread the text, study vocabulary words, and learn strategies and skills.

Expository text   Nonfiction.

Family literacy   Home–school partnerships to enhance students' literacy development.

Fluency   Reading smoothly, quickly, and with expression.

Free morpheme   A morpheme that can stand alone as a word (e.g., *book, cycle*).

Frustration level   The level of reading material that is too difficult for a student to read successfully.

Genre   A category of literature such as folklore, science fiction, biography, or historical fiction, or a writing form.

Goldilocks principle   A strategy for choosing "just right" books.

Grand conversation   A small-group or whole-class discussion about literature.

Grapheme   A written representation of a sound using one or more letters.

Graphic organizers   Diagrams that provide organized visual representations of information from texts.

Graphophonemic   Referring to sound-symbol relationships.

Guided reading   Students work in small groups to read as independently as possible a text selected and introduced by the teacher.

High-frequency word   A common English word, usually a word among the 100 or 300 most common words.

Homographic homophones   Words that sound alike and are spelled alike but have different meanings (e.g., baseball *bat* and the animal *bat*).

Homographs   Words that are spelled alike but are pronounced differently (e.g., a *present* and to *present*).

Homonyms   Words that sound alike but are spelled differently (e.g., *sea–see, there–their–they're*); also called *homophones*.

Hyperbole   A stylistic device involving obvious exaggerations.

Imagery   The use of words and figurative language to create an impression.

Independent reading level   The level of reading material that a student can read independently with high comprehension and an accuracy level of 95–100%.

Inflectional endings   Suffixes that express plurality or possession when added to a noun (e.g., *girls, girl's*), tense when added to a verb (e.g., *walked, walking*), or comparison when added to an adjective (e.g., *happier, happiest*).

Informal reading inventory (IRI)   An individually administered reading test composed of word lists and graded passages that are used to determine students' independent, instructional, and frustration levels and listening capacity levels.

Instructional reading level   The level of reading material that a student can read with teacher support and instruction with 90–94% accuracy.

Interactive writing   A writing activity in which students and the teacher write a text together, with the students taking turns to do most of the writing themselves.

Intervention   Intense, individualized instruction for struggling readers to solve reading problems and accelerate their growth.

Invented spelling   Students' attempts to spell words that reflect their developing knowledge about the spelling system.

K-W-L   An activity to activate background knowledge and set purposes for reading an informational text and to bring closure after reading. The letters stand for What I (We) Know, What I (We) Wonder, and What I (We) Learned.

Language Experience Approach (LEA)   A student's dictated composition is written by the teacher and used as a text for reading instruction; it is generally used with beginning readers.

Leveling books   A method of estimating the difficulty level of a text.

Lexile scores   A method of estimating the difficulty level of a text.

Listening capacity level   The highest level of graded passage that can be comprehended well when read aloud to the student.

Literacy   The ability to read and write.

Literal comprehension   The understanding of what is explicitly stated in a text.

Literature circle   An instructional approach in which students meet in small groups to read and respond to a book.

Literature focus unit   An approach to reading instruction in which the whole class reads and responds to a piece of literature.

Long vowels   The vowel sounds that are also names of the alphabet letters: /ā/ as in *make*, /ē/ as in *feet*, /ī/ as in *ice*, /ō/ as in *coat*, and /ū/ as in *rule*.

Lowercase letters   The letters that are smaller and usually different from uppercase letters.

Metacognition   Students' awareness of their own thought and learning processes.

Metaphor   A comparison expressed directly, without using *like* or *as*.

Minilesson   Explicit instruction about literacy procedures, concepts, strategies, and skills that are taught to individual students, small groups, or the whole class, depending on students' needs.

Miscue analysis   A strategy for categorizing and analyzing a student's oral reading errors.

Mood   The tone of a story or poem.

Morpheme   The smallest meaningful part of a word; sometimes it is a word (e.g., *cup, hope*), and sometimes it is not a whole word (e.g., *-ly, bi-*).

Narrative   A story.

New literacies   The ability to use digital and multimodal technologies to communicate and learn effectively.

Onset The part of a syllable (or one-syllable word) that comes before the vowel (e.g., *str* in *string*).

Open syllable A syllable ending in a vowel sound (e.g., *sea*).

Orthography The spelling system.

Personification Figurative language in which objects and animals are represented as having human qualities.

Phoneme A sound; it is represented in print with slashes (e.g., /s/ and /th/).

Phoneme-grapheme correspondence The relationship between a sound and the letter that represents it.

Phonemic awareness The ability to manipulate the sounds in words orally.

Phonics Predictable relationships between phonemes and graphemes.

Phonics instruction Teaching the relationships between letters and sounds and how to use them to read and spell words.

Phonological awareness The ability to identify and manipulate phonemes, onsets and rimes, and syllables; it includes phonemic awareness.

Phonology The sound system of language.

Polysyllabic Containing more than one syllable.

Pragmatics The social use system of language.

Prediction A strategy in which students predict what will happen in a story and then read to verify their guesses.

Prefix A syllable added to the beginning of a word to change the word's meaning (e.g., *re-* in *reread*).

Prereading The first stage of the reading process, in which readers activate background knowledge, set purposes, and make plans for reading.

Prevention Identifying potentially struggling readers and providing appropriate instruction so that failure is avoided.

Prewriting The first stage of the writing process, in which writers gather and organize ideas for writing.

Proofreading Reading a composition to identify and correct spelling and other mechanical errors.

Prosody The ability to orally read sentences expressively, with appropriate phrasing and intonation.

Publishing The fifth stage of the writing process, in which writers make the final copy of their writing and share it with an audience.

Quickwrite An activity in which students explore a topic through writing.

Readability formula A method of estimating the difficulty level of a text.

Reading The second stage of the reading process, in which readers read the text for the first time using independent reading, shared reading, or guided reading, or by listening to it read aloud.

Reading rate Reading speed, usually reported as the average number of words read correctly in 1 minute.

Reading workshop An approach in which students read self-selected texts independently.

Reciprocal teaching An activity in which the teacher and students take turns modeling the use of strategies.

Responding The third stage of the reading process, in which readers respond to the text, often through grand conversations and by writing in reading logs.

Revising The third stage of the writing process, in which writers clarify meaning in the writing.

Rhyming Words with the same rime sound (e.g., *white, bright*).

Rime The part of a syllable (or one-syllable word) that begins with the vowel (e.g., *ing* in *string*).

Scaffolding The support a teacher provides to students as they read and write.

Segment To pronounce a word slowly, saying each sound distinctly.

Semantics The meaning system of language.

Shared reading The teacher reads a book aloud with a group of children as they follow along in the text, often using a big book.

Short vowels The vowel sounds represented by /ă/ as in *cat*, /ĕ/ as in *bed*, /ĭ/ as in *big*, /ŏ/ as in *hop*, and /ŭ/ as in *cut*.

Simile A comparison expressed using *like* or *as*.

Skill An automatic processing behavior that students use in reading and writing, such as sounding out words, recognizing antonyms, and capitalizing proper nouns.

Strategy A problem-solving behavior that students use in reading and writing, such as predicting, monitoring, visualizing, and summarizing.

Struggling reader or writer A student who isn't meeting grade-level expectations in reading or writing.

Suffix A syllable added to the end of a word to change the word's meaning (e.g., *-y* in *hairy*, *-ful* in *careful*).

Sustained Silent Reading (SSR) Independent reading practice in which all adults and students in the class or in the school stop what they are doing and spend time (20–30 minutes) reading a self-selected book.

Syllable An uninterrupted segment of speech that includes a vowel sound (e.g., *get, a-bout, but-ter-fly, con-sti-tu-tion*).

Symbol The author's use of an object to represent something else.

Synonyms Words that mean nearly the same thing (e.g., *road–street*).

Syntax The structural system of language or grammar.

Text Words appearing in print.

Trade book A published book that is not a textbook; the type of books in bookstores and libraries.

Uppercase letters The letters that are larger and are used as first letters in a name or at the beginning of a sentence; also called "capital letters."

Vowel A voiced speech sound made without friction or stoppage of the airflow as it passes through the vocal tract; the letters *a, e, i, o, u*, and sometimes *w* and *y*.

Vowel digraph Two or more adjacent vowels in a syllable that represent a single sound (e.g., *bread, eight, pain, saw*).

Word families Groups of words that rhyme (e.g., *ball, call, fall, hall, mall, tall*, and *wall*).

Word identification Strategies that students use to decode words, such as phonic analysis, analogies, syllabic analysis, and morphemic analysis.

Word sort A word-study activity in which students group words into categories.

Word wall An alphabetized chart posted in the classroom listing words students are learning.

Writing genres Forms of writing, such as stories, friendly letters, essays, and poems.

Writing process The process in which students use prewriting, drafting, revising, editing, and publishing to develop and refine a composition.

Writing workshop An approach in which students use the writing process to write books and other compositions on self-selected topics.

Zone of proximal development The distance between a child's actual developmental level and his or her potential developmental level that can be reached with scaffolding by the teacher or classmates.

Author and Title INDEX

Subject INDEX

monitoring progress, 81–86
Reading fluency, 126–127
    accuracy and, 208, 209
    assessment, 215–216
    characteristics of, 126–127
    components of, 188, 207–208
    comprehension and, 260
    defining, 206
    developing reading stamina, 212–213
    development of, 118
    practice in reading and, 211
    promoting, 209–214
    prosody and, 208, 210–211
    qualities of dysfluent readers, 208–209
    reading speed and, 124, 208, 210, 211
    struggling readers and, 209
    see also Comprehension
Reading level, 2
    determining students', 28, 81, 86
    see also Instructional reading level
Reading logs, 365, 459–460
    for assessment, 275
    journals as, 433
    making connection charts in, 262
    in portfolios, 91
    responding to stories, 467
    sample, 138
    steps for writing independently in, 459–460
    writing in, 47, 344, 346, 347–348, 358, 378
    see also Journals
Reading materials, text sets of, 366
Reading process, 42–52, 328, 331
    applying stage, 49
    comprehension strategies for, 269
    engaging students in, 439
    exploring stage, 48
    overview of, 43
    prereading stage, 42–44
    reading stage, 44–47
    responding stage, 47–48
    stages in, 331, 342, 349
Reading programs
    commercial, 24–25, 328
    computer-based, 364
    traditional, 344
    literature-based, 330 - 349
Reading projects, 49
Reading rate, 124, 208, 210, 211
Reading Recovery, 382
Reading skills, 50. *See* Reading
    strategies
Reading speed, 208, 210, 211

Reading stage, in reading process, 44–47
Reading stages. *See* Reading process
Reading stamina, 212–213
Reading strategies, 12, 50–52
    appropriate use of, 50
    guidelines for instruction, 51
    for Internet reading, 6
    minilessons on, 40, 51–52
    types of, 50
    in young children, 124
Reading While Listening, 210
Reading workshops
    components of, 344–349
    overview of, 3, 25, 26, 109, 279, 343, 351
    schedules for, 345
    types of response patterns in, 346–347
    vocabulary development and, 226
Realistic fiction, 292, 295, 365
Reciprocal questioning, 408, 460–461
    questions to ask, 460
Reciprocal teaching, 271
Repairing, 12
    online, 265
Repairing strategy, 267
Repetend, 404
Repetition, 133, 310
    in books, 134
Reports
    individual, 400
    types of, 398–400
Rereading, 48, 55
Responding, 348
    in classroom community, 17
    in literature circles, 342
    purposes in, 408–410
    to reading, 333
    in reading workshop, 347, 349
    response patterns, 347–348
    teacher's role in, 347
    writing for, 410
Responding stage, in reading process, 47–48, 331
Responding stage, in writing process, 47–48, 311
Response to Intervention (RTI), 382–383
Responsibility, in classroom community, 16, 17
Retelling. *See* Story retelling
Retelling center, 187
Revising centers, 56–57
Revising conferences, 83
Revising stage, in writing process, 12, 55, 56, 322, 352, 479, 480

Revision, 60, 480
Rewards, 278
Rhyme, 133, 134, 310
Rhymed verse, 309
Rhyming, 150, 174
Rhythm, 133, 134, 309
Riddles, homograph, 224
Rime, 158–159
Risk taking, in classroom community, 16, 17
Role-playing. *See* Hot seat
Root words, 224, 360
    Latin and Greek, . . . 202–204
    morphemic analysis and, 201
    sources of, 234–235
    spelling and, 170
    whole words and word parts, 202, 245, 246
Rough drafts, 54–55
    rereading, 55
    revising, 56
Round-robin reading, 213
Rubrics, 29, 84, 90, 461–462
    for assessment, 29, 90, 289, 461–462
    to determine proficiency levels, 462
    developing, 65
    museum, 319
    oral-presentation, 249
    as a scoring guide, 462–463
    for stories, 64
Running records, 29, 71, 463–464
    for assessment, 86–89, 275
    calculating miscues, 463–464
    determining knowledge of high-frequency words, 73
    determining reading levels, 70
    of leveled books, 216
    for monitoring, 329
    of oral reading, 29, 86
    steps in conducting, 463
    for word identification, 207
Running Record Scoring Sheet, 72

Scaffolding, 8–9
    with ELs, 26–28
    in reading, 20–23
    in writing, 20–23
Schema theory, 7–8
Scholastic Reading Inventory (SRI), 81
Science center, 187
Science fiction, 292, 293–294
Scott Foresman basal reading program, 325
Scripts, readers theatre, 211, 458–459